The Original Pets Welcome!

Summer 2010

- Guide to Pet Friendly Pubs
- Holidays with Horses
- Preparing your cat or dog for travelling abroad
- Holidays in France for you and your Pets
- Readers' Offer Vouchers
- 55th Edition

Photo: David Guiterman

© FHG Guides Ltd, 2010
ISBN 978-1-85055-429-5

Maps: ©MAPS IN MINUTES™ / Collins Bartholomew 2007

Typeset by FHG Guides Ltd, Paisley.
Printed and bound in China by Imago.

Distribution. Book Trade: ORCA Book Services, Stanley House,
3 Fleets Lane, Poole, Dorset BH15 3AJ
(Tel: 01202 665432; Fax: 01202 666219)
e-mail: mail@orcabookservices.co.uk
Published by FHG Guides Ltd., Abbey Mill Business Centre,
Seedhill, Paisley PA1 ITJ (Tel: 0141-887 0428 Fax: 0141-889 7204).
e-mail: admin@fhguides.co.uk

Pets Welcome! is published by FHG Guides Ltd,
part of Kuperard Group.

Cover design: FHG Guides
Cover Picture: with thanks to David Guiterman for "Fauna"

All the advertisers in **PETS WELCOME!** have an entry in the appropriate classified section and each classified entry may carry one or more of the following symbols:

- 🐕 This symbol indicates that pets are welcome free of charge.
- £ The £ indicates that a charge is made for pets. We quote the amount where possible, either per night or per week.
- pw! This symbol shows that the establishment has some special provision for pets; perhaps an exercise facility or some special feeding or accommodation arrangements.
- ⌂ Indicates separate pets' accommodation.

PLEASE NOTE that all the advertisers in **PETS WELCOME!** extend a welcome to pets and their owners but they may attach conditions. The interests of other guests have to be considered and it is usually assumed that pets will be well trained, obedient and under the control of their owner.

Contents

Editorial Section	2-64
Foreword	4
Holidays in France	15
Donate £1 to Pets' Charity	37
Readers' Pet Pictures	43
Dog Walks	52

SOUTH WEST ENGLAND — 68
Cornwall, Devon, Dorset, Gloucestershire, Somerset, Wiltshire

SOUTH EAST ENGLAND — 192
Berkshire, Buckinghamshire, Hampshire, Isle of Wight, Kent, Oxfordshire, Surrey, East Sussex, West Sussex

EAST OF ENGLAND — 214
Cambridgeshire, Essex, Norfolk, Suffolk

MIDLANDS — 238
Derbyshire, Herefordshire, Leicestershire & Rutland, Lincolnshire, Nottinghamshire, Shropshire, Staffordshire, Warwickshire, Worcestershire

YORKSHIRE — 262
East Yorkshire, North Yorkshire, West Yorkshire

NORTH EAST ENGLAND — 282
Durham, Northumberland

NORTH WEST ENGLAND — 292
Cheshire, Cumbria, Lancashire

SCOTLAND

Aberdeen, Banff & Moray	331
Angus & Dundee	332
Argyll & Bute	333
Ayrshire & Arran	343
Borders	345
Dumfries & Galloway	350
Edinburgh & Lothians	358
Fife	359
Highlands	361
Lanarkshire	374
Perth & Kinross	375
Stirling & The Trossachs	380
Scottish Islands	381

WALES

Anglesey & Gwynedd	387
North Wales	396
Carmarthenshire	406
Ceredigion	408
Pembrokeshire	410
Powys	421
South Wales	427

IRELAND — 430

Narrowboat Holidays	431
Holidays with Horses	432
Guide to Pet-Friendly Pubs	438
Readers' Offer Vouchers	445
Index of Towns & Counties	455

Foreword

We are delighted to introduce this 55th edition of **Pets Welcome!** with its varied selection of holidays for pets and their owners. The choice of accommodation includes not only self-catering properties and caravans as one might expect, but also many hotels, guest houses and B&B establishments, and if you are considering taking your dog on holiday to France you will find a selection of holiday choices on **pages 15-34.**

As in previous issues, we urge owners to behave responsibly and to ensure their pet does not jump on furniture or beds, and they should not be left unattended for long periods. In this climate of environmental awareness and concern about pollution on our beaches and elsewhere, pet owners should abide by the relevant local authority rules regarding 'doggy' access to beaches and other areas. But for many of us enjoying a country holiday means taking the dog on scenic walks and you'll find a useful selection of especially recommended walks on **pages 52-63.**

Most of our entries are of long standing and are tried and tested favourites with animal lovers. However as publishers we do not inspect the accommodation advertised in Pets Welcome! and an entry does not imply our recommendation. Some proprietors offer fuller facilities for pets than others, and in the classified entry which we give each advertiser we try to indicate by symbols whether or not there are any special facilities and if additional charges are involved. However, we suggest that you raise any queries or particular requirements when you make enquiries and bookings.

If you have any problems or complaints, please raise them on the spot with the owner or his representative in the first place. We will follow up complaints if necessary, but we regret that we cannot act as intermediaries nor can we accept responsibility for details of accommodation and/or services described here. Happily, serious complaints are few. Finally, if you have to cancel or postpone a holiday booking, please give as much notice as possible. This courtesy will be appreciated and it could save later difficulties.

Preparing your Dogs and Cats for Travel Abroad (Page 12), Holidays with Horses (Page 432), and The Guide to Pet Friendly Pubs (Page 438) are now regular features. Our latest selection of Pets Pictures starts on page 43.

We would be happy to receive readers' suggestions on any other useful features. Please also let us know if you have had any unusual or humorous experiences with your pet on holiday. This always makes interesting reading! And we hope that you will mention **Pets Welcome!** when you make your holiday inquiries or bookings.

Around the magnificent coast of Wales
Pembrokeshire, Cardigan Bay, Snowdonia, Anglesey, Lleyn Peninsula, Borders

Choose from over 300 Quality Cottages

Pets Welcome Free

A small specialist agency with over 40 years experience letting quality cottages.

Enjoy unashamed luxury in traditional Welsh Cottages. Situated near safe sandy beaches and in the heart of Wales — famed for scenery, walks, wild flowers, birds, badgers and foxes.

Pets welcome FREE at most of our properties

Leonard Rees, Quality Cottages, Cerbid, Solva, Haverfordwest, Pembrokeshire.
SA62 6YE

**Telephone: (01348) 837871
for our FREE Colour Brochure**

www.qualitycottages.co.uk

100s of pictures of quality cottages and beautiful Wales

Pets stay free!

We know your pet is one of the family, so they should come with you too...

That's why 1 or more pets can stay **FREE** at a great selection of UK, Ireland and France properties. Discover the perfect holiday cottage **EVERYONE** can enjoy - pond dipping, stick finding and beach bounding. Relax and enjoy being together.

For a brochure, call **0845 268 6982**
www.welcomecottages.co.uk

Terms and conditions apply see brochure or website for details

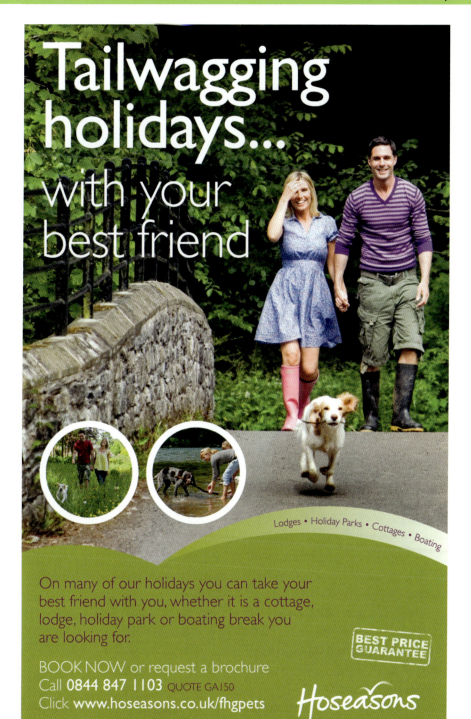

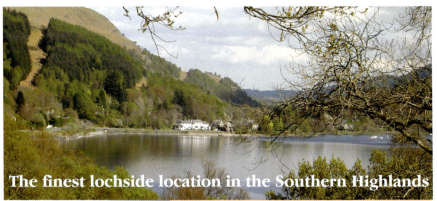

The finest lochside location in the Southern Highlands

The Four Seasons Hotel
St Fillans, Perthshire PH6 2NF
Tel: 01764 685 333
e-mail: sham@thefourseasonshotel.co.uk

See Advertisement under
Perthshire, St. Fillans

THE INDEPENDENT TRAVELLER

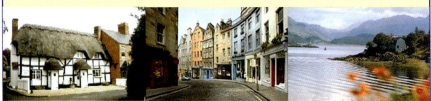

for a wide choice of quality cottages & apartments throughout

★ Heart of England ★ Scotland
★ City apartments in London, Edinburgh and many UK cities
★ Family Vacations ★ Walking Holidays ★ Business Travel
★ Pets welcome in many country cottages
★ Minimum stay from 3 nights in some properties

Contact: Mary & Simon Ette,
Orchard Cottage, Thorverton, Exeter EX5 5NG
Tel: 01392 860807
e-mail: help@gowithit.co.uk
www.gowithit.co.uk

www.classic.co.uk

classic cottages

Featuring 700 hand selected coastal and country holiday homes throughout the West Country

01326 565 555

Over 4000 places to camp... pets on leads welcome

- Visit one of our award-winning UK Club Sites
- Our sites have dog walking areas for you and your dog to explore
- A friendly welcome will be given to you and your pet on our sites, joining is great value for money at only £37*

It's never been easier to join, CLICK ON:

 www.**campingandcaravanningclub**.co.uk

Please quote reference number 0716

* Cost is £37, plus a £10 joining fee which is waived if paid by Direct Debit. To join call **0845 130 7632**.

MISTY, the nature lover.
Mrs M. Bryan, Paisley

Special offer to all **Pets Welcome!** Readers

  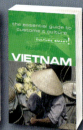 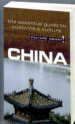 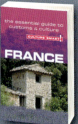 

Order Culture Smart! and receive 50% off the RRP (£6.95)

For full range of titles visit our website
www.culturesmart.co.uk
or telephone 020 8446 2440 and use code **PETSOFFER**

The Essential Guide to Customs and Culture

CULTURE SMART! are the essential guides to customs and cultural understanding in over 75 countries.

Providing you with practical and invaluable information, **CULTURE SMART!** guides offer rare insights into what really makes a country tick!

From day to day life, customs, traditions and historical perspectives, these pocket sized guides promote and encourage a depth of well-informed and responsible travel.

'Full of fascinating tips to help you avoid embarrassing faux pas' ....The Observer
'These cultural guides offer glimpses into the psyche of a faraway world' ....The New York Times
'This series is different ...a valuable tool' ....Weekly Telegraph

Offer expires 31/12/10

Published by
·K·U·P·E·R·A·R·D·

If you've got a small dog, then you'll already know how special they can be.

Winalot® Specials is specially formulated for small dogs. It comes in 150g servings and two ranges:

- **Casseroles:** carefully selected meat combined with vegetables and delicious gravy for an irresistible taste experience.

- **Roasts:** carefully selected meat cooked to give that extra special roasted taste, then smothered in a meaty gravy to give that extra taste sensation.

Perfect for little appetites!

IN STORE NOW!

Trademark owned by Société des Produits Nestlé S.A., Vevey, Switzerland

Preparing your Dogs and Cats for travel abroad

How can my pet travel? Because of stringent requirements, dogs and cats travelling under the so-called pet passport scheme cannot make last minute reservations; in general, six-month advance planning is required. Veterinarians must implant a microchip in the animal, inoculate it against rabies, have a laboratory recognized by the Department for Environment, Food and Rural Affairs (DEFRA) confirm by blood sample that the vaccine is active, and issue a PETS certificate. Certificates are valid from six months after obtaining the blood sample results until the date of the animal's next rabies booster shot. (Dogs and cats resident in Britain whose blood sample was drawn before Feb 29, 2000 are exempt from this six month rule). Dogs and cats must also be treated against ticks and tapeworms no less than 24 nor more than 48 hours before check-in (when the animal enters carrier's custody). Animals travelling by air are placed in containers bearing an official seal (the number of which is also inscribed on the PETS certificate) to ensure animals are not exposed to disease en route. Sealing requirements do not apply to Cyprus or Malta. Owners must also sign a certificate attesting that the animal has not been outside participating territories in the last six months. Travellers are cautioned that Britain will enforce its rules rigorously.

Your pet must be injected with a harmless identification ISO (International Standards Organisation) approved microchip. This chip will be read by a handheld scanning device.

From and back to the UK

Ask your vet to implant an ISO (International Standards Organisation) approved microchip - then to vaccinate against rabies recording the batch number of the vaccine on a veterinary certificate together with the microchip number.

Approximately 30 days later your vet should take a blood sample and send it to one of the DEFRA approved laboratories to check that the vaccine has provided the correct level of protection.

Your vet will then issue you with a certificate confirming all the above – in the UK this is called The Pet Travel Scheme Re-Entry Certificate. It is valid for the life of the rabies vaccine, so keep your rabies vaccine up to date and a new certificate will be issued without the need for further blood tests.

TAKING YOUR PET ABROAD

Six months from the taking of a successful blood test you will be able to enter or re-enter the UK from Western Europe and 28 other countries including Australia, Japan and Singapore.

Pets must be treated for ticks and for the echinococcus parasite by a qualified vet who will record this on an official UK certificate not less than 24 hours and not more than 48 hours before entry into the UK. We are trying to secure changes in this very awkward timetable, which is being rigidly enforced.

On entering the UK you must therefore have two official certificates; one for the microchip, rabies vaccine and blood test; the second for treatment against ticks and parasites. You will also have to sign a residence declaration form - provided by the travel operator who is carrying out the checking. It simply confirms that the pet has not been outside the approved countries in the previous six months.

From Europe to the UK

As above, you must microchip your pet, vaccinate against rabies and approximately 30 days later your vet will take a blood test sending it to one of the laboratories from the list of those approved by MAFF. SIX MONTHS after a successful blood test your pet will be allowed to travel to the UK providing it has been treated against ticks and worms.

Costs:

- Microchip: Should be in the region of £25.00
- Vaccine: Varies according to vet but again approximately £30.00
- Blood test: We know that the blood testing laboratory at Weybridge (VLA) charge £49.50 per test.

Therefore anything in addition is that levied by the vet. Providing the rabies vaccination is kept up to date the blood test will not have to be repeated. Should there be a break between rabies vaccines a further blood test would have to be taken and then a period of 6 months allowed before re-entry to the UK would be permitted.

Therefore: Microchip and blood-test are one-off costs but the rabies vaccination is a yearly or 3 yearly cost depending on the vaccine used.

More information can be obtained from

Department of Environment, Food and Rural Affairs PETS
website: www.defra.gov.uk/animalh/quarantine/index.htm

Scottish Executive Environment and Rural Affairs Department
website: www.scotland.gov.uk/AHWP

PETS Helpline:
0870 241 1710 (Monday to Friday – 08.30 to 17.00 UK time)
E-mail:
pets.helpline@defra.gsi.gov.uk (enclose your postal address and daytime telephone number)

Who benefits from your Will – the taxman, or the ones you love?

This year over £2 <u>billion</u> from Wills went to pay inheritance tax in the UK. Those Wills could easily have been made more tax efficient by leaving something to a charity such as the RSPCA.

Nobody does more for animals than the RSPCA and its branches.

And for every £10 we need to spend, £6 comes from people's Wills.

Our simple guide in plain English could help <u>your</u> Will be more tax efficient.

For a free copy, simply phone the number below,
(quoting reference 08NL010140).

0300 123 0239
or e-mail jcurtis@rspca.org.uk

Registered charity no: 219099

Holidays in France

For you and your pets

Since the advent of the pet's passport scheme more and more owners are opting to take their 'best friend' on holiday to other countries.

With that in mind, we have included in this edition of **Pets Welcome!** a small selection of holiday properties in France.

You will find details of each property, plus some very useful practical information and a brief description of the regions.

Enjoy your stay!

AQUITAINE

This region of wide open spaces includes Europe's largest forest and offers a long list of outdoor activities. There are many quality golf courses which makes this France's leading region for golfers. For those interested in the past, there are a number of prehistoric sites and a fascinating variety of artefacts. Visitors should make a point of seeing the many cave paintings and engravings found in the Dordogne Valley. Enjoy the bustling towns, peaceful countryside and villages, and sample the fine wines of Bordeaux and the gastronomic specialties of the region, which include Foie Gras and truffles.

The Farmhouse

Gurs • Pyrénées Atlantique 64190 • Tel: 01622 747840
e-mail: sam@mountains-2-coast.co.uk

Delightful Bearnaise farmhouse, recently renovated to a very high standard with all modern conveniences, yet retaining many original features. The accommodation sleeps up to 8 people, plus 2 cots, and full baby facilities are available. There is a newly fitted kitchen with plenty of workspace, sitting/diningroom with wood burning fire, comfortable seating, TV and DVD. Two double and one twin bedrooms, plus sleeping area for 2 on mezzanine floor. The half-acre grounds have outdoor table and chairs and a barbecue area. Plenty of holiday attractions within an hour, including golf, fishing, tennis, paragliding and sightseeing.

Gurs (Pyrenees Atlantique)

Village near the town of Oloron-Ste-Marie with town lovely Romanesque churches.

THE FARMHOUSE, GURS, PYRENEES ATLANTIQUE 64190 (01622 747840). Farmhouse, recently renovated to a very high standard, sleeping up to 8, plus 2 cots. Newly fitted kitchen. Two double and one twin bedrooms, plus sleeping area for 2 on mezzanine. Half-acre grounds.
e-mail: sam@mountains-2-coast.co.uk

Family outings in Dordogne

Bergerac Aquapark – four swimming pools with water chutes and other activities.

Prehisto Parc, Les Eyzies – cavemen, mammoths and everything prehistoric.

Jacqou Park, Le Bugue – three parks on one site, an animal park, and aqua park and an amusement park.

Le village du Bournat, Le Bugue – a reconstructed village showing life in 1900. With animals on a working organic farm, crafts, and a working windmill.

Airparc Perigord, St-Vincent-de-Cosse – a treetop adventure park on the river, one of the most exciting parks for children.

Aquitaine

HOLIDAYS IN FRANCE 17

Three period cottages with fenced pool in South Dordogne, set in 65 acre private estate with fishing lake.

- **Kiwi** sleeps 2/3. One double bedroom. Separate shower room.
- **Wren** sleeps 4/6 Two double bedrooms. Separate shower room.
- **Honeysuckle** sleeps 6. Two separate shower rooms.

Great countryside for walking. 10 minutes to the nearest shops/restaurants and convenient for Sarlat and Bergerac.

Local English-speaking vet to assist with formalities for pets' return to UK.

Please visit our website for details/photos - www.lessarrazinies.com - or telephone Mike/Lindy Crowcroft on 0033 (0) 553 03 23 20 (summer) • 020 8340 2027 (winter)
e-mail: mikecrowcroft@onetel.com

Le Bugue (Dordogne)

The pretty town of Le Bugue provides an excellent range of shops, including supermarkets, banks, chemists, post office and English-speaking doctor. There is a colourful and busy market every Tuesday, offering a wide selection of local produce, poultry, meats, pates and cheeses. Further afield you can visit prehistoric caves, some with world-famous cave drawings.

SOUTH DORDOGNE. Three period cottages with fenced pool on 65-acre estate with fishing lake. Sleep 2/6. Great countryside for walking. Local English-speaking vet. Contact Mike/Lindy Crowcroft 0033 (0) 553 03 23 20 (summer); 020 8340 2027 (winter). [🐾]
e-mail: mikecrowcroft@onetel.com   website: www.lessarrazinies.com

Sleeping up to six people, La Blottière is ideal for couples, yet it is also suitable for families and small groups of friends. There is a well-equipped kitchen/diningroom with wood-burning stove (logs provided). Comfortable sitting room with French doors to private terrace with table and chairs. Laundry room with washing machine etc. One double bedroom, and one room with four single beds. Shower room with shower, washbasin WC and bidet. Cot available. Swimming pool. Non-smoking. Pets welcome.

La Blottière

St Crèpin d'Auberoche 24330 Dordogne • Tel 0033 553 048619
www.holiday-cottage-in france.co.uk

St Crèpin d' Auberoche (Dordogne)

Town with shops and all facilities, approximately 10 miles east of Périgueux, the centre of the Perigord region. Around an hour's drive from the airports at Bergerac and Limoges, and less than 2 hours drive from Bordeaux and Angoulême airports.

LA BLOTTIERE. St CREPIN D' AUBEROCHE, 24330 DORDOGNE (0033 553 048619). Sleeps up to six in one double and one room with 4 single beds. Well-equipped kitchen/diningroom with wood burning stove. Comfortable sitting room. Private terrace. Laundry room. Swimming pool. Non-smoking.
website: www.holiday-cottage-in-france.co.uk

Symbols

🐾	Indicates that pets are welcome free of charge.
£	Indicates that a charge is made for pets: nightly or weekly.
pw!	Shows some special provision for pets; exercise facility, feeding or accommodation arrangement.
⌂	Indicates separate pets accommodation.

AUVERGNE

Lying in the heart of France only an hour from Lyon or three hours from Paris the Auvergne region has a volcanic terrain with a natural beauty and dramatic landscapes. The area is ideal for sporting activities, including skiing, golfing, hiking and hang-gliding, and for the watersports enthusiast, there are excellent opportunities for canoeing, fishing, swimming and sailing.

Gîtes du Château de Coisse ❖ Auvergne

Situated in a small hamlet in the heart of the Livradois Forez Regional Park, get away from the stress and grind of daily life in this tranquil, beautiful part of France.
★★ **2 person gîte** is on the ground floor of this recently converted 18th century barn.
★★★ **6 person gîte** forms the first and second floors and has its own south-facing terrace.
Both have been carefully restored to keep many original features but are also modern, fully equipped and child/pet friendly.

Fiona & Graham Sheldon, Gîtes du Château de Coisse,
63220 Arlanc, France • Tel: 04 73 95 00 45
e-mail: gitereservation@chateaudecoisse.com • www.chateaudecoisse.com

Coisse (Puy-de-Dôme)

Tiny village in the rolling hills of Monts du Livradois, an area of outstanding natural beauty. Town of Arlanc, 2km away, has all amenities.

FIONA & GRAHAM SHELDON, GITES DU CHATEAU DE COISSE, 63220 ARLANC (04 73 95 00 45)
Two restored gîtes in this tranquil, beautiful part of France. 2 star/2 person gîte on ground floor of 18th century barn. 3 star/ 6 person gîte on first and second floors with its own south-facing terrace. Child/pet friendly.[🐕]
e-mail: gitereservation@chateaudecoisse.com   website: www.chateaudecoisse.com

Things to do and see in Puy-de-Dome

Parc Naturel Régional du Livradois-Forez – an area of outstanding beauty with a volcanic region to the north west and many mountains. A rambler's paradise.

Rock climbing and paragliding at Job – for the more adventurous.

The Plan D'Eau near Arlanc – for those who love being beside the water. There is also an open air swimming pool, and tennis courts. Nearby is the Jardin pour la Terre, which is a large map of the world planted with trees and flowers from their native countries.

Chantagrele, Auvergne

Two beautifully restored stone Gites, in a stunning location within the Livradois Forez National Park, with undisturbed valley views.

Light and spacious, these pretty stone cottages are bright, clean and comfortable, and tastefully decorated, with exposed beams, stone walls and wooden floors. Fully equipped, with three bedrooms, sleeping 4/5; log burners; central heating.

Secluded spacious garden with plunge pool, summer house and BBQ area.

Sauxillanges, 6km away, has all amenities, including convenience shopping and quality restaurants.

Mountain biking, walking, horse riding and fishing are all popular in the area, and skiing is available a short drive away. Open all year.

Contact:

Richard and Elaine Clements
Chantagrele
63490 Condat les Montboissier
Auvergne, France
Tel: 0033 (0) 4 73 72 18 95
e-mail: elaine-clements@hotmail.co.uk

Sauxillanges (Puy-de-Dôme)

Small village with all amenities, including convenience shopping, 2 highly acclaimed restaurants, 4 bars and a weekly market. Ambert and Issoire, two historic towns, and Clermont Ferrand are within easy reach.

RICHARD & ELAINE CLEMENTS, CHANTAGRELE 63490, CONDAT LES MONTBOISSIER, AUVERGNE (0033 (0) 4 73 72 18 95). Two beautifully restored stone Gites, in a stunning location within the Livardois Forez National Park, with undisturbed valley views. Light and spacious. Fully equipped. 3 bedrooms, sleep 4/5. Plunge pool, summer house and BBQ area. Mountain biking, walking, horse riding and fishing in the area, and skiing a short drive away. Open all year.
e-mail: elaine-clements@hotmail.co.uk

Things to do and see in High Auvergne

Vulcania – a science oriented Theme Park dedicated to volcanoes.

Haras National d'Aurillac – one of the world's largest studs of heavy breed stallions.

Ecomusée de la Margeride near St Flour - several sites, telling the past and present story of the people of the area, includes houses, gardens, objects, sounds and smells.

Lioran Aventure at Le Lioran – an adventure playground claiming to be a cross between Tarzan and Indiana Jones.

Le Train Touristique running from Bort Les Orgues to Lugarde – a relaxing way to explore the countryside.

BRITTANY

This is a region steeped in tradition, and has maintained its Celtic traditions throughout the centuries. Mont Saint-Michel is reputed to be Brittany's best-known attraction. The beautiful bay of the Gulf of Morbihan is dotted with dozens of little islands, and you can visit fairy tale woods in the Ille aux Moines. Inland is the medieval forest of Merlin the Magician, where it is said that the Knights of the Round Table searched for the Holy Grail. The coast is a great attraction for tourists, who enjoy such activities as wind surfing, water skiing and underwater diving and, as you would expect, there is a wonderful variety of seafood available, including lobsters, oysters salmon and trout.

Les Cheminées
Gite Accommodation in Baud, Brittany

Beautiful 300 year old Farmhouse and Longeres set in 2 acres in a quiet location. Easy walking distance to the town of Baud. The Morbihan beaches are easily accessible together with many other activities including horse riding and golf tours.

Farmhouse 1 Sleeps 4/6 2 bedrooms with en suite facilities, one double and one twin with a third single bed, with large landing for 2 single beds. Lounge/dining room with open fireplace, fitted kitchen including washing machine.

Longere 1 Sleeps 4, up to 6 with sofa bed. Very spacious accommodation, one double and one twin bedroom. Bathroom with shower over. Large open- plan lounge, diningroom and fitted kitchen

The Stable Sleeps 2/4 comfortably. Very pretty house with one double bedroom, and bunk bed plus cot on the large landing. Open plan ground floor accommodation includes lounge/dining area and fitted kitchen.

Longere 2 Sleeps 6 (or 8 with sofa bed). Very spacious house with one double en suite and two twin bedrooms. Family bathroom. Spacious ground floor open-plan with lounge, dining area and fitted kitchen

All accommodation includes:
- Swimming pool • All linen provided • BBQ & Patio furniture.
- Kitchens include fridge, washing machine, microwave.
- Games area with swings, slide and table tennis.

Open all year including Christmas.

Bed & Breakfast available from October to May.

Please contact: Jackie or David Giles
Les Cheminées, Baud 56150 France
Tel: 00 33 2 97 39 14 61
E-mail: info@baud-gites.com • www.baud-gites.com

Baud (Morbihan)

Small town overlooking the picturesque Eivel Valley, located within easy reach of the major towns of Vannes amd Lorient. Well supplied with shopping facilities, including two supermarkets, four boulangeries and eight restaurants to suit all tastes.

JACKIE & DAVID GILES, LES CHEMINEES, BAUD 56150 (00 33 2 97 39 14 61). Beautiful 300 year old Farmhouse and Longeres set in 2 acres in a quiet location on the edge of Baud. Sleep 2-8. Morbihan beaches easily accessible; horse riding and golf tours. All linen provided. Swimming pool, BBQ, patio and games area.
e-mail: info@baud-gites.com   website: www.baud-gites.com

Brittany

Blavet River Cottage
La Couarde
Bieuzy les Eaux
Morbihan 56310

Cottage situated in one the most beautiful areas of Brittany, 10 minutes from the towns of Pontivy and Baud. Ideal for exploring the region, or for visiting the numerous sandy beaches along the Morbihan coast. Boat trips, horse riding, walking and cycling are available locally The cottage sleeps six, plus cot and there is a pool and summerhouse, large decked terrace with patio table and chairs, a barbecue and a large barn with table tennis, pool table and darts. The garden area has swings and football goal. The ground floor has lounge/diner with log fire, Satellite TV and DVD; fully equipped kitchen; shower room. Upstairs there are three bedrooms and a bathroom.

Tel: 0033 (0) 297 518974

Bieuzy Les Eaux (Morbihan)

Village with restaurants and bars. Golf 3 miles away.

BLAVET RIVER COTTAGE, BIEUZY LES EAUX, MORBIHAN 56310 (0033 (0)297 518974).Cottage sleeping six, plus cot. Pool and summerhouse. Large decked terrace. Ground floor has lounge/diner with log fire. Fully equipped kitchen; shower room. Three bedrooms and a bathroom upstairs.

Auberge du Bon Cidre

37 rue de Cornouaille 29170 FOUESNANT
Tél: 02.98.56.00.16 • Fax : 02.98.51.60.15
www.aubergeduboncidre.com
E-mail: contact@aubergeduboncidre.com

Small family-run hotel in a charming small town famous for its production of Brittany's finest cider. The dining room in the main house serves excellent local cuisine and the comfortable, simply furnished bedrooms are in a modern, quiet annexe overlooking the pleasant garden. The town of Quimper is within easy reach, as are the beautiful sandy beaches of Bénodet and Pont l'Abbé for sailing, diving and sea angling, or take a relaxing boat trip along the river Odet. Leisure centre nearby with tennis courts and an indoor pool; golf courses 8 kilometres.

Fouesnant (Finistere)

Town with grocers, restaurant and Leisure Centre.

AUBERGE DU BON CIDRE, 37 RUE DE CORNOUAILLE (02.98.56.00.16; Fax: 02.98.51.60.15) Small family-run hotel serving excellent local cuisine. Comfortable, simply furnished bedrooms in a modern, quiet annexe overlooking the pleasant garden.
e-mail: contact@aubergeduboncidre.com   website: www.aubergeduboncidre.com

Publisher's note

While every effort is made to ensure accuracy, we regret that FHG Guides cannot accept responsibility for errors, misrepresentations or omissions in our entries or any consequences thereof. Prices in particular should be checked.
We will follow up complaints but cannot act as arbiters or agents for either party.

22 HOLIDAYS IN FRANCE   **Brittany**

La Ferme de la Baie
1 La Rue, 35610 Roz-Sur-Couesnon
Tel: 0033 (0)2 99 80 23 90 • Ruth George & Henry Maisey
e-mail: welcome@fermedelabaie.com

Perfect location for a relaxing holiday, with easy access to coast, historic towns and many tourist attractions and sporting facilities. There are three self-catering properties available, each with its own small garden and outdoor furniture.
The cottages are comfortable and fully equipped, and a cot and other baby equipment is available. Bed and Breakfast accommodation is available in the main farmhouse, and we can provide Evening Meals with 24 hours notice, or provide a home-cooked 'takeaway' to be eaten in your own cottage.

La Rue (Ille et Villaine)

Quiet hamlet near the village of Roz-sur-Couesnon. Good choice of shops in nearby town of Pontorson.

RUTH GEORGE AND HENRY MAISEY, LA FERME DE LA BAIE, 1 LA RUE, 35610 ROZ-SUR-COUESNON (0033 (0)2 99 80 23 90). Three self-catering properties available, each with its own small garden and outdoor furniture. Comfortable and fully equipped. Bed and Breakfast accommodation is available in the main farmhouse.
e-mail: welcome@fermedelabaie.com

Clair de Lune
Le Hazay • Caulnes • Côte d'Armor 22350
Tel: 0033 (0) 296 838284

Set in rolling countryside, this gite has been fully refurbished to provide a cosy and welcoming interior. There is an attractive garden with comfortable garden furniture and barbecue. Swings and see-saw for children and plenty of parking adjacent. The property sleeps up to five in two bedrooms, and all essentials are provided. Just 30 minutes from the glorious beaches of Rennes, and the Port of St Malo is just 45 minutes.

Great diversity of rural pursuits, lovely beaches with many leisure activities in Côte d'Armor as well as stunning coastlines and dramatic inland landscapes.

Le Hazay (Côte de Armor)

Small hamlet two minutes' drive from the towns of Caulnes and Broons, perfect for your every day needs. Dinan 20 minutes north.

CLAIR DE LUNE, LE HAZAY, CAULNES, COTE D'ARMOR 22350 (0033 (0) 296 838284) Refurbished Gite in rolling countryside. Attractive garden. Sleeps up to five in two bedrooms, and all essentials are provided.

FHG Guides
publish a large range of well-known accommodation guides.
We will be happy to send you details or you can use the order form
at the back of this book.

Brittany

HOLIDAYS IN FRANCE 23

Riverside Cottage
17 Rue de l'Ecluse, Malon, Ille et Vilaine 35480

This spacious detached riverside cottage has stunning views of the river from every room. There is a large mature garden with garden furniture. Ideal for barbecues. Accommodation consists of two double bedrooms and there is a double bed-settee in the lounge. Fully equipped kitchen/diner; lounge with inglenook fireplace and woodburner, plus TV/video/DVD player and radio/CD player. Separate laundry room. This is an ideal area for a relaxing holiday, or for exploring Brittany. Local activities include cycling, walking, fishing, riding, golf, swimming, tennis and boating, and safe beaches are within easy driving distance. The towns of Rennes and Nantes offer sightseeing opportunities, shopping and eating places and there is something of interest for all ages.

Pets Welcome • **Tel: 01707 694173** • **Short Breaks available** **No Smoking**

Malon (Ille et Vilaine)

A quiet, rural hamlet 25 kilometres SW of Rennes. Local villages of Guipry and Messac, 2 kilometres, have bars, restaurants, supermarkets and chemists. Market day Thursday.

RIVERSIDE COTTAGE, 17 RUE DE L'ECLUSE, MALON, ILLE ET VILAINE 35480 (01707 694173). Spacious detached riverside cottage with stunning views. Large mature garden. Two double bedrooms and fully equipped kitchen/diner; lounge with inglenook fireplace and woodburner. Short Breaks available. Non-smoking.

Hôtel de l'Europe
1 Rue d'Aiguillon, 29600 Morlaix

Tel. 33 (0)2 98 62 11 99 • Fax 33 (0)2 98 88 83 38
e-mail: reservations@hotel-europe-com.fr

Close to the imposing viaduct in the centre of this sheltered yacht haven, the stylish yet homely Hôtel de l'Europe offers good value for money. Guests will find warm welcome and comfortably furnished bedrooms offering old fashioned elegance; internet access available. Good, modern restaurant next door. There are charming villages in the countryside around Morlaix and 31 challenging golf courses within easy driving distance; tee times can be arranged. Other activities nearby include horse riding, hiking tours, tennis, swimming, fishing, bowling, and deep-sea diving. There is also a casino, cinema, discotheque and amusement park.

Morlaix (Finistere)

Breton city and port with cobbled streets and medieval buildings. There are lots of good shops and a wonderful Saturday morning market selling everything from meat, vegetables, fish and cheeses to clothing, books and bric-a-brac.

HOTEL DE L'EUROPE, 1 RUE D'AIGUILLON, 29600 MORLAIX (33 (0)2 98 62 11 99; Fax: 33 (0)2 98 88 83 38). Stylish yet homely hotel offers good value for money. Warm welcome and comfortably furnished bedrooms. Good, modern restaurant next door.
e-mail: reservations@hotel-europe-com.fr

Please mention Pets Welcome!
when making enquiries about accommodation featured in these pages

24 HOLIDAYS IN FRANCE   Languedoc-Roussillon

LANGUEDOC-ROUSSILLON

The region has a widely varying landscape from mountains and plateaux, to moorlands and coastal plains. The coast is a blend of resorts such as Cap d'Agde and Port Camargue, and old villages and fishing ports. Good beaches offer a variety of watersports and there are many golf courses throughout the region. There are health spas and nature reserves as well as good fishing, cycling and riding, and the area is ideal for walkers. In winter there are good cross-country ski routes and excellent skiing. Markets can be found in towns and villages from early spring until late autumn, and festivals, fetes and concerts can all be enjoyed.

The area is noted for its seafood, including oysters and anchovies, and Sete, the largest Mediterranean fishing port on the coast of France has many excellent fish restaurants. Strong Mediterranean flavours dominate the local dishes, with rich game or beef stews, and, of course, the famed Cassoulet. Other regional specialities include olives, fruit, honey, full fruity red wines and delicious dessert wines.

This old winery lies at the end of a quiet cul-de-sac and has a private garden, safe for children and pets. The house has recently been redecorated to a high standard and sleeps four persons in one double room, and one room with bunk beds. The newly fitted kitchen is fully equipped with all amenities. There is a large terrace opening out from the living room and the garden offers a natural shelter from the sun. The house is situated beside a river which is ideal for swimming. There are also swimming pools locally and the surrounding area is great for trekking and climbing. Pets welcome. Short breaks available.

STONE HOUSE
**23 Rue Charles Nel • Camplong
Herault 34260 • Tel: 0033 624772546**

Camplong (Hérault)

Small, pretty village in the heart of the Languedoc National Park. Four miles from the village of Medieval which has a good restaurant and a market selling local produce, and the nearest town is 7 kilometres away.

STONE HOUSE, 23 RUE CHARLES NEL, CAMPLONG, HERAULT 34260 (0033 624772546). Old winery with safe private garden. Sleeps four in one double room, and one room with bunk beds. Fully equipped kitchen, large terrace. Pets welcome. Short breaks available.

Please note

All the information in this book is given in good faith in the belief that it is correct. However, the publishers cannot guarantee the facts given in these pages, neither are they responsible for changes in policy, ownership or terms that may take place after the date of going to press. Readers should always satisfy themselves that the facilities they require are available and that the terms, if quoted, still apply.

Près de la Tour Adelard

Tel 00 32 (0)656 31394
Fax 0032 (0)656 31394

Haut du Village • La Capelle Masmolène • Gard 30700

Villa in quiet, residential area on the edge of a picturesque village and close to an ancient chapel. Ideal for enjoying the sports and activities in the village itself, including tennis, climbing, hiking, cycling, fishing, petanque and walking, or for touring the many towns and villages in the area. The accommodation sleeps up to six in three bedrooms, and there is a lounge, kitchen, hall, conservatory, bathroom and separate toilet. Terrace has barbecue with garden furniture and offers a breathtaking view of the surrounding countryside. Ideal for holidays all year round.

La Capelle Masmolène (Gard)

Typical French village near Uzes, Pont du Gard, Nîmes and Avignon.

PRES DE LA TOUR ADELARD, HAUT DU VILLAGE, LA CAPELLE MASMOLENE, GARD 30700 (Tel & Fax: 00 32 (0)656 31394). Villa in quiet, residential area on the edge of a picturesque village. Sleeps up to six in three bedrooms. Terrace with barbecue. Pets welcome.

La Vieille Grange

10 Rue des Astres
Les Angles, Pyrenees Orientales 66210

Two recently renovated barn apartments with exposed beams. Sleep up to six in two bedrooms and mezzanine floor, cot available. Fully fitted kitchen; lounge with sofas, satellite TV, video and DVD player; shower room/WC. Prices include all linen and towels, electricity and welcome pack of essential groceries.
As well as being a good ski area, the village is just 30 minutes from the Spanish border and 90 minutes from the Mediterranean, making it ideal for touring.

Tel 0033 (0)468043728
e-mail: info@pyrenean-trails.com

Les Angles (Pyrenees Orientales)

A Pyrenees mountain village, considered to be one of France's premier ski locations. Ski lifts, shops and a good selection of restaurants locally.

LA VIEILLE GRANGE, 10 RUE DES ASTRES, LES ANGLES, PYRENEES ORIENTALES 66210 (0033 (0)468043728). Two recently renovated barn apartments, sleeping up to six in two bedrooms and mezzanine floor, cot available. Fully fitted kitchen; lounge; shower room/WC. Pets welcome. Short breaks available.
e-mail: info@pyrenean-trails.com

Please mention **Pets Welcome!**
when making enquiries about accommodation featured in these pages

LIMOUSIN

The Limousin region, situated in the centre of France, offers visitors a peaceful and traditional way of life. This is a charming and historic land of hills and valleys, forests and plains, rivers and picturesque ancient cities. The region takes its name from the Capital Limoges, which is renowned for its exquisite enamel and porcelain. This pleasant town has many parks and gardens, and the old quarter with its narrow medieval streets and houses is worth a visit. There are many opportunities to enjoy swimming, sailing, canoeing and water skiing on the numerous rivers and lakes, and there are several golf courses throughout the region. There is good riding country in the south and many riding establishments catering for all standards of rider. Here you will find the National Stud and racecourse at Arnac-Pompadour. There are many fairs and markets in towns and villages on various days of the week, and you can enjoy pates and foie gras, and perhaps even sample the local speciality, an excellent potato pie made with smoked ham and herbs.

Upper Dordogne Valley • Limousine • Corrèze • Near Argentat

Character Cottage, sleeps 2

On the edge of a picturesque village. One bedroom with en suite shower room.

Low Season £140
Mid Season £160
High Season £190
15% off second week booked

Kitchen/diner. Sitting room. Terrace and sun deck.
Walk from cottage into amazing countryside.

See other cottages and B&B on www.argentat.co.uk. Contact Jim Mallows e-mail: au-pont@wanadoo.fr

---

Argentat (Corréze)

This delightful market town is an ideal holiday destination offering peace and quiet, and beautiful scenery. Excellent food and wine can be enjoyed in attractive riverside restaurants and other good eating places. There is a wide variety of cultural and sporting activities to enjoy, and many shows and exhibitions take place during the summer.

UPPER DORDOGNE VALLEY. Character Cottage, sleeps two. On the edge of a picturesque village. One bedroom with en suite shower room. Kitchen/diner. Sitting room. Terrace and sun deck. Walk from cottage into amazing countryside. Contact JIM MALLOWS for details
e-mail: au-pont@wanadoo.fr   website: www.argentat.co.uk

FHG Guides

publish a large range of well-known accommodation guides.
We will be happy to send you details or you can use the order form
at the back of this book.

NORMANDY

The region of Normandy, with its lush countryside and a coastline warmed by the Gulf Stream, has long been a favourite destination with holidaymakers. There are many resorts and seaside towns and, inland, magnificent forests, tranquil streams and the many orchards which are indicative of this fruit producing region. There are many delights to discover such as the picturesque harbour of Honfleur, the Bayeux Tapestry and William the Conqueror's birthplace. Normandy promises many gastronomic delights, from seafood and duck, to cream, cheeses and the famous Calvados. Why not explore the 'Cider Road' and the 'Cheese Road', or simply relax on a horse drawn carriage ride.

Country cottage in Normandy
L'Etre Bidault, near Bagnoles de l'Orne
www.propertiesinnormandy.com

L'Etre Bidault is a beautiful detached stone cottage set in its own grounds on the edge of the Forêt des Andaines, which stretches for over ten miles and is full of wildlife including red squirrels and red deer. Medieval towns, chateaux, local markets are close by, as well as opportunities for many outdoor activities.

Sleeps 4 + cot. 2 bedrooms, one double, one twin, large, well equipped kitchen/diner with woodburner, spacious lounge with exposed stonework and beams, open fireplace. Bathroom and separate toilet. Central heating, satellite TV and ADSL, internet. Large, enclosed private garden with furniture and BBQ provided. Mountain bikes for hire. Golf and horse riding nearby. No smoking. Pets welcome. The perfect location for holidays with pets, as forest walks can be enjoyed directly from the cottage.

If you would like to request more information or wish to make a booking, please contact Dave and Lyn on
00 33 6 77 31 80 35 or 07914 190925 • e-mail: info@propertiesinnormandy.com

Bagnoles de l'Orne (Orne)

The spa town and local area offer a diverse selection of activities of interest to all age groups. These include visiting castles, museums or the casino, to more active pursuits such as canoeing, fishing or horse riding.

DAVE & LYN NEWNHAM (00 33 6 77 31 80 35 OR 07914 190925). Pretty detached stone cottage set in its own grounds on the edge of the Forêt des Andaines. Sleeps 4 plus cot. Pets welcome. No smoking. [🐕]
e-mail: info@propertiesinnormandy.com   website: www.propertiesinnormandy.com

Normandy Thatched Cottages

Situated in the village of Berville sur mer, La Ferme du Chalet is a charming group of four person and six person thatched cottages converted from a 17th Century stable.

Set in 2 hectares these gites offer a wonderful tranquil holiday destination, only 500 metres from the River Seine.

The beautiful historic port of Honfleur with its picturesque Saturday market is 10 minutes away by car or you can walk along the riverbank which offers spectacular views of the Pont de Normandie. On days out you are well placed to explore the sights of Normandy and Brittany. You can visit the landing beaches after a visit to the museum at Arromanches, or explore the many beautiful beaches of the area.

Berville sur Mer is part of the Natural Park of Brotonne and there are many cycle paths, picnic areas and hiking paths on both sides of the River Seine.

Channel Ports: Le Havre 25 minutes. Caen 1 hour. Calais 2.5 hours. Boulogne 2.15 hours.

Tel: 01463 717874 • E-mail: info@topsun.co.uk
www.topsun.co.uk
Reservations: Top Sun Ltd.
17 Springfield Gardens, Inverness IV3 5SJ

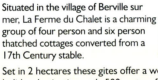

Berville sur Mer (Eure)

A small Normandy village on the banks of the Seine, about five miles from Honfleur, where there are many shops and restaurants. There is also good shopping at Beuzville, and at the out of town Supermarket on the way to Honfleur.

LA FERME DU CHALET, BERVILLE SUR MER. Charming group of thatched cottages converted from a 17th Century stable, only 500 metres from the River Seine. The beautiful historic port of Honfleur with its picturesque Saturday market is 10 minutes away by car. Le Havre 25 minutes, Caen 1 hour. **TOP SUN LTD, 17 SPRINGFIELD GARDENS, INVERNESS IV3 5SJ. (01463 717874).** [Pets 20 euros per stay].
e-mail: info@topsun.co.uk   website: www.topsun.co.uk

Visit the FHG website
www.holidayguides.com
for details of the wide choice of accommodation featured in the full range of FHG titles

MIDI-PYRENEES

The largest region in France, the Midi Pyrenees lies midway between the Mediterranean and the Atlantic and subsequently enjoys a particularly pleasant climate. The varied landscape and wide open spaces offer all kinds of holiday opportunities such as rafting, canoeing and skiing, as well as hiking, horse riding and cycling. There is also a choice of spas for the health and fitness enthusiast. The fascinating sites of Rocamadour and Padirac in Lot and the medieval village of Cordes-sur-Ciel in Tarn are certainly worth a visit, and don't overlook the must-see museum of Toulouse-Lautrec's work in Albi. On the other hand, whether religious or not, a visit to Lourdes can be inspiring.

Wherever you travel in the region you will be overwhelmed by the friendliness of the people. There is usually some sort of festival being held, and countless local markets will give you the opportunity to sample such culinary delights as Roquefort cheese, cassoulet and foie gras, or to enjoy the wines of Cahors and Armagnac.

32160 Beaumarches • Tel 0033 0562 691734
e-mail: frances.nustedt@gmail.com

Early 19th century farmhouse amidst some of the most beautiful countryside of this region offers a newly converted, light and spacious apartment with its own entrance; shared swimming pool and south-facing terrace. There are double and twin en suite bedrooms, and a large living area with new kitchenette, and a boiler room that houses washing machine, ironing facilities and freezer. Motoring, cycling and walking is really enjoyable on the deserted country lanes and quiet countryside of the region. There are numerous medieval villages within a few miles, with traditional French fruit and vegetable markets, and the food served in the local restaurants is very good, and very affordable.

Beaumarches (Gers)

Village just 10 minutes from the small medieval town of Marciac, famous for its annual Jazz Festival.

A BERTIN, QUARTIER RICAU, 32160 BEAUMARCHES (0033 0562 691734). Newly converted, light and spacious apartment with its own entrance in early 19th Century farmhouse. Shared swimming pool and south-facing terrace. Double and twin en suite bedrooms, and a large living area with new kitchenette.
e-mail: frances.nustedt@gmail.com

Visit the FHG website
www.holidayguides.com
for details of the wide choice of accommodation featured in the full range of FHG titles

Bellegarde Adoulins (Gers)

Village with beautiful views of The Pyrenees, 4km from the old market town of Masseube which offers all amenities.

AUX MEMES, 32140 BELLEGARDE, GERS (Tel & Fax: +33 (0)5 62 66 91 45; Mobile: +33 (0)6 83 63 02 22). Gite with two bedrooms, sleeping up to five. Large shower room, living/diningroom with wood burning stove. Attached kitchen. Private gardens with garden furniture, barbecue. Swimming pool.
e-mail: enquiries@auxmemes.com

Castelau de Montmiral (Tarn)

Historic village with good amenities including grocers, bakers, post office and two hotels. Tuesday is market day.

LA GREZE, CASTELNAU DE MONTMIRAL, TARN 81140 (0033 (0)563 332875). Luxury gites in meadowland with beautiful views. Open-plan livingroom/kitchen. Comfortable lounge with double sofa bed; one double bedroom; luxury bathroom. Private terrace for outdoor eating.

Please mention **Pets Welcome!** when making enquiries about accommodation featured in these pages

POITOU-CHARENTES

Poitou-Charentes is a very unspoilt region with pleasant countryside, bustling ports and harbours, long sandy beaches, islands and marinas. Enjoy 300 miles of Atlantic coast for sunbathing, sailing or windsurfing, take a cruise on the Charente River or discover the secrets of Cognac by visiting its cellars and distilleries. There are numerous vineyards, castles and Romanesque churches to visit, or experience the futuristic universe at Futuroscope Theme Park outside Poitiers. If walking or cycling is your thing the mainly flat agricultural land away from the coastline is ideal. The cuisine of this abundant region includes the famous Marennes Oleron oysters, melons, goat cheeses such as chabichou and Pineau, a mixture of grape juice and cognac.

Fourwinds

**Beauregard
Juillac Le Coq
Charente 16130**

Self-catering accommodation is offered in this delightful holiday home in the heart of Charente countryside, a very peaceful area with plenty to do and see. The many outdoor activities include tennis, swimming, guided walks and a superb 18 hole golf course. Cruises, canoeing and kayaking are available on the Charente river. The accommodaton sleeps up to 5 in one double and one twin bedroom, plus extra single bed. Travel cot available. There is a fully fitted kitchen, diningroom/lounge, shower room and laundry facilities. Two patio areas, BBQ and swimming pool are all available. B&B can be provided if preferred.

Tel: 0033 545 800259

Beauregard (Charente)

Hamlet on the outskirts of the town of Juillac Le Coq, 12km from Cognac.

FOURWINDS, BEAUREGARD, JUILLAC LE COQ, CHARENTE 16130 (0033 545 800259). Self-catering accommodation in the heart of Charente countryside. Sleeps up to 5. Fully fitted kitchen, diningroom/lounge, shower room and laundry facilities. Two patio areas, BBQ and swimming pool. B&B available.

FHG Guides

publish a large range of well-known accommodation guides.
We will be happy to send you details or you can use the order form
at the back of this book.

Salles Lavalette (Charente)

Lovely village with bar, restaurant, shops and post office. Many towns nearby provide a wide range of shops, restaurants and tourist attractions.

LYMERAC, SALLES LAVALETTE, CHARENTE 16190 (0033 (0)545 647341). Spacious farmhouses with swimming pool, horse riding facilities, children's play area and panoramic views. Fully equipped. Sleeps 2-8. Large lounge, dining area. Wet room, separate toilet. Modern fitted kitchen.

La Remigeasse
4 Rue de Chez Mesnard, Fleac Sur Seugne
Ile d'Oleron, Charente Maritime 17800
Tel: 0033 546905460

The house is situated on a small site of 38 holiday homes, within five minutes' walk of the beach. Ample car parking. Open-plan lounge/kitchen/dining area and separate bathroom on ground floor. Mezzanine floor bedroom sleeps two people, and there are bunk beds in a small outbuilding, ideal for teenagers or older children. Small back garden. Sleeps 2-4. Disabled access.

Seugne (Charente Maritime)

Small town on Ile d'Oleron, an island with beautiful sandy beaches connected to the mainland by a viaduct.

LA REMIGEASSE, 4 RUE DE CHEZ MESARD, FLEAC SUR SEUGNE, ILE D'OLERON, CHARENTE MARITIME 17800 (0033 546 905 460). Holiday home five minutes from beach. Ample car parking. Open-plan lounge/kitchen/dining area, separate bathroom on ground floor. Mezzanine bedroom sleeps two, small outbuilding with bunk beds. Small back garden. Disabled access.

www.holidayguides.com

Western Loire

HOLIDAYS IN FRANCE 33

WESTERN LOIRE

This region, with its pleasing warm climate, has long been a favourite holiday destination. The visitor is spoilt for choice as lush countryside, vineyards, long sandy beaches and salt marshes vie for attention with fascinating cities, sleepy villages, ancient buildings and castles with stunning artwork, and cultural festivals galore. The famous 24-hour race is held at Le Mans-Laval, and there are facilities throughout the region for a huge variety of sporting activities, both land and water based. The countryside is easily explored by bicycle or on foot, or you may prefer to spend a day cruising on the tranquil waterways. Explore the Loire Valley vineyards, and enjoy the delicious and famous wines of the area with fresh fruit and vegetables, game, wild mushrooms and generous platters of seafood from the region's rivers and the sea.

Private house in Vienne area, Southern Loire valley, Roiffe, FRANCE

B&B accommodation to let daily, weekly or longer
Set evening meals also available.
Managed by family members.
Great location near to Saumur with the stunning Loire River running alongside. Especially ideal for visiting local award winning vineyards, an array of different historic chateaux, mushroom and troglodyte caves. Beautiful lush countryside for walking, cycling and watching birds.
Dogs welcome.

**Please contact Angela Jackson for bookings & details
01732 863437 or angelaandmartyn@aol.com**

Saumur (Maine-et Lóire)

Town on the Loire overlooked by graceful Château. Local caves are popular tourist attraction with their troglodyte drawings.

B&B ACCOMMODATION in family managed house. In great location near to Saumur with River Loire running alongside. Ideal for visiting local chateaux, vineyards and caves. Beautiful; lush countryside for walking, cycling and watching birds. Dogs welcome. For bookings ad details contact ANGELA JACKSON (01732 863437).
e-mail: angelaandmartyn@aol.com

FHG Guides

publish a large range of well-known accommodation guides. We will be happy to send you details or you can use the order form at the back of this book.

Symbols

- ❀   Indicates that pets are welcome free of charge.
- £   Indicates that a charge is made for pets: nightly or weekly.
- pw!   Shows some special provision for pets; exercise facility, feeding or accommodation arrangement.
- ⌂   Indicates separate pets accommodation.

Western Loire

Les Augerelles
Vendée/Charentes Border
3 bed house (7/9) and 1 bed gite (2/4)

- Well equipped and recently refurbished • secure garden with sun and shade • part-covered barbeque area with furniture
- 4.5m raised pool with removable steps • heating for off-season, thick stone walls • quiet hamlet but with market town nearby
- 200 hectares of common land opposite, good walks
- ideal location for Atlantic coast, Marais and Bocage
- managed by family members resident in the region
- available together for main holiday season or separately for longer lets and off-season by negotiation.

For more details contact:
Janet & John Nuthall • 01249 443458
e-mail: jnuthall2@toucansurf.com for brochure
or visit www.vendee-gites.co.uk/lesaugerelles.htm for much more information and pictures

Fonteney le Comte (Vendée)

A town of art and history with elegant squares and gardens. Nôtre Dame church and the Vendée museum are worth a visit. Numerous festivals and events take place throughout the year..

LES AUGERELLES, VENDEE/CHARENTES BORDER. 3 Bed house (sleeps 7/9) and 1 bed gite (sleeps 2/4). Well equipped and recently refurbished. Swimming pool. Heating for off season. Quiet hamlet with market town nearby. Managed by family members resident in the region. Contact: JANET & JOHN NUTHALL (01249 443458) [🐕]
e-mail: jnuthall2 @toucansurf.com   website: www.vendee-gites.co.uk/lesaugerelles.htm

La Belle Maison
5 Rue du Moutier
Marsais Ste Radegonde Vendée 85570
Tel 0033 (0)251876353 or 00 0251 876353
E-mail: alfred.stradling@wanadoo.fr

Apartment sleeping from 2-6 people, can be rented out for self-catering, or on a bed and breakfast basis with a minimum of two nights' stay.
There are beautiful rooms and a comfortable sitting area, and guests are free to relax in the tranquil garden and make use of the Jacuzzi under the trees. The house is in an ideal position for visiting many attractions in the surrounding area including beaches and historic sites. There is a large swimming pool a few minutes away, open in summer months, and an Adventure Park and zoo are just 10 minutes away.

Marsais Ste Radegronde (Vendée)

Peaceful village near Fontenay Le Comte and the medieval town of Vouvant.

LA BELLE MAISON, 5 RUE DU MOUTIER, MARSAIS STE RADEGONDE, VENDEE 8557 (0033 (0)251876353 or 00 0251 876353). Apartment sleeping from 2-6 people, self-catering or B&B (min. two nights stay). Beautiful rooms and a comfortable sitting area, tranquil garden. In an ideal position for visiting many attractions in the surrounding area.
e-mail:alfred.stradling@wanadoo.fr

Symbols

🐕	Indicates that pets are welcome free of charge.
£	Indicates that a charge is made for pets: nightly or weekly.
pw	Shows some special provision for pets; exercise facility, feeding or accommodation arrangement.
⌂	Indicates separate pets accommodation.

DogsTrust : A Dog is For Life

Are you thinking of going on holiday in the UK with your dog?

If so, the Dogs Trust has a free factsheet which will be of particular interest.

"Safe travel and happy holidays with your hound in the UK"

For this and any other of our free Dogs Trust factsheets please contact us at:

**Dogs Trust,
17 Wakley St. London EC1V 7RQ.
Tel: 020 7837 0006**

Website: www.dogstrust.org.uk
or e-mail us, info@dogstrust.org.uk

Last year Dogs Trust cared for over 16,000 stray and abandoned dogs at our network of 18 Rehoming Centres. So if you are looking for a companion for your dog or you have a friend who might like a dog, just contact your nearest Dogs Trust Rehoming Centre.

We care for around 1,600 dogs on any given day, so we are sure we will be able to find your perfect partner. The Dogs Trust never destroys a healthy dog.

For details of our Sponsor-a-Dog scheme please call **020 7837 0006**
or visit **www.sponsoradog.org.uk**

Dogs Trust Rehoming Centres

LONDON
Dogs Trust Harefield
0845 076 3647

ENGLAND
Dogs Trust Canterbury
01227 792 505

Dogs Trust Darlington
01325 333 114

Dogs Trust Evesham
01386 830 613

Dogs Trust Ilfracombe
01271 812 709

Dogs Trust Kenilworth
01926 484 398

Dogs Trust Leeds
01132 613 194

Dogs Trust Merseyside
0151 480 0660

Dogs Trust Newbury
01488 658 391

Dogs Trust Roden
01952 770 225

Dogs Trust Salisbury
01980 629 634

Dogs Trust Shoreham
01273 452 576

Dogs Trust Snetterton
01953 498 377

WALES
Dogs Trust Bridgend
01656 725 219

SCOTLAND
Dogs Trust Glasgow
0141 773 5130

Dogs Trust West Calder
01506 873 459

NORTHERN IRELAND
Dogs Trust Ballymena
028 2565 2977

IRELAND
Dogs trust Dublin
enquiries@dogstrust.ie

Registered Charity No. 227523

Donate £1 to your favourite Pets Charity

FHG has agreed to donate £1 from the price of this
Pets Welcome! Guide to EITHER
The Royal Society For The Prevention of Cruelty to Animals,
Dogs Trust,
The Kennel Club,
or the Scottish Society for the Prevention of Cruelty to Animals

To allow the Charity of your choice to receive this donation simply complete the slip below and return to FHG at

**FHG Guides Ltd, Abbey Mill Business Centre
Seedhill, Paisley PA1 1TJ
Closing date end October 2010**

Note: Original forms only please, do not send photocopies.

Please donate £1 from the price of this **Pets Welcome!** guide to:

RSPCA ☐   DOGS TRUST ☐   KENNEL CLUB ☐   SSPCA ☐

Name..

Address..

....

Postcode ....Date ....

FHG Guides may send readers details of discount offers for our holiday guides.
If you do not wish to receive this information please tick here ☐
Your details will not be passed on to any other organisation.

Dogs and the Kennel Club

Founded well over a hundred years ago, in 1873, the Kennel Club registers around 275,000 dogs a year. It is the governing body of dogs in the United Kingdom, and its main objective is to promote in every way, the general improvement of dogs, and encourage responsible dog ownership.

From running the largest dog show in the world, Crufts, to giving critical advice to owners, the media and politicians alike, as well as providing educational schemes, such as teaching safety around dogs. It covers both the fun and the serious side of dogs, and dog ownership, and is central to all dogs and dog owners.

The number of breeds recognised by the Kennel Club is ever increasing, with 208 breeds currently eligible for registration. The KC has three registers - the Breed, the Activity and the Companion Dog register – one for every kind of dog and activity, as both the Activity register and Companion Dog register are open for crossbreeds.

The small cost to register dogs ensures that money is being put back into dogs, enabling the Kennel Club to run its schemes, and also to be the voice for dogs in Government on behalf of all their owners. The variety of schemes run by the KC, reflect its diverse role with dogs and their place in society as a whole.

For those wanting to buy a pedigree dog there is access to, and information on, the best breeders through the Accredited Breeder Scheme and the Puppy Sales Register, all easily accessible on the Kennel Club website, as well as breed specific health research. And for those who want a pedigree dog but would prefer an adult dog, there are many breed specific rescue centres. They also offer the support of expert knowledge and advice on specific breeds.

The Kennel Club Charitable Trust raises and disburses funds to a variety of deserving causes, such as canine health research projects, specialist studies and canine charities. Every penny that is raised goes directly to the Trust, ensuring that our dog friends and people within the canine field enjoy the maximum benefit.

The Kennel Club has a role to play for lost dogs through Petlog, the UK's largest national pet identification scheme. The details on Petlog (www.petlog.org.uk) are available to local authorities, police and established welfare and rescue organisations. This ensures that lost or stray animals are speedily reunited with their owners when found and scanned for details on a previously inserted microchip, even when abroad.

Safety for children around dogs is another priority for the Kennel Club, which has led to the development of its fun and informative popular online game called 'Safe and Sound' (www.safeandsound.org.uk), which is free to play. Children's lives are enriched by living with dogs, as they learn responsibility and empathy while interaction with a dog can increase their self-esteem.

THE KENNEL CLUB 39

Ensuring dogs are well behaved means also teaching the owners how to achieve this, which is where the Good Citizen Dog Scheme (GCDS) comes into focus. It is the largest dog training programme in the UK and has four levels of assessment, from Puppy Foundation through to Gold. 190,000 dogs have successfully passed through the scheme, with more than 1,800 training clubs across the UK running the programme. Training your dog helps to create a better bond between a dog and its owner, and it is a responsible dog owner's job to ensure that you have a well behaved and lovable dog.

The Accredited Instructors scheme for dog training and canine behaviour is for anyone training dogs or teaching people to train dogs. It provides a network of instructors, trainers and advisors to help, and is a voluntary scheme, which aims to give a worthwhile qualification, in which scheme members and the public can have confidence.

The Young Kennel Club (YKC) is a vital part of the Kennel Club, ensuring that youngsters have an opening into the world of dogs. The Young Kennel Club is for young members from 6 – 24 years (**www.ykc.org.uk**)

If you are a dog-friendly business then you can benefit by getting on board with the Kennel Club's Open for Dogs sticker campaign. Hundreds of businesses – from hotels and pubs to castles and cafes – are already displaying the stickers to alert the nation's many millions of dog owners that their canine companions are welcome.

To request your free sticker or if you already display one and would like to get your website added to the list of dog-friendly places located at **www.openfordogs.org.uk,** then email **press.office@thekennelclub.org.uk**

For more information about this or any of the Kennel Club's activities visit www.thekennelclub.org.uk or make an appointment at the Kennel Club's headquarters, which also hold the UK's definitive canine library and art gallery, in Piccadilly, London. The press office is available to comment on all canine issues.

Telephone 020 7518 1008
press.office@thekennelclub.org.uk
www.thekennelclub.org.uk

www.winalot-dog.co.uk

For many of us enjoying a country holiday also means taking our dogs on scenic walks, or for a journey in the car - often in warm weather, and at these times they may need a little extra care and attention. The following tips could make your pet's life on hot days considerably more comfortable:

WATER!
A normal 20kg dog will drink about one and a half pints of water a day. In the heat this can increase by 200 to 300%. Water should always be available. Make sure you take plenty for your pet, as well for yourself when out walking and in the car. Stabilising non-spill water bowls are great for travel, while handy inflatable bowls are ideal for stowing in your knapsack. You can even buy water bottles that your dog can carry.

SHADE
Encourage your dog to favour shady, cool spots when you stop for a rest - rather than sunbathe with the rest of the family!

CAR
NEVER leave your dog in the car unattended. Placing a dog in the back of any car even with an open rear window is undesirable and may be fatal. Remember - even a car parked in shade in the morning when it's cool could reach over 100 degrees very quickly as the sun moves. Heat stroke can occur within minutes.

EXERCISE
Plan your walk so you avoid strenuous exercise during the hottest part of the day. Some dogs like to paddle or swim - if there is no water around and your dog seems uncomfortably hot, seek a shady spot and provide water.

HEALTH
A dog's heat loss system is dependent on overall health. If your dog is fit, supple and active then walking will be a pleasurable experience, however, if there is any indication of heart or respiratory problems arising, controlled exercise in the cool is recommended. Veterinary advice should be sought if problems persist during heat stressful times.

HEAT STROKE
This is an emergency and potentially life threatening situation. If in doubt take the following action, then seek advice. A chilled dog is better than an overheated one.

- Cease any form of exercise.
- Move the dog into a cool place.
- Sponge the dog with cold water - all over, avoiding water round the mouth or nose.
- Do not offer food or fluids until evident recovery.
- Seek veterinary advice if in doubt.

Winalot Roasts – Mealtimes never tasted so good!

Tender pieces of meat, gently cooked to give that special roasted taste, then smothered in a thick meaty gravy to give your dog that extra taste sensation he deserves!

Available in Chicken, Beef and Lamb varieties.

Trademark owned by Société des Produits Nestlé S.A., Vevey, Switzerland

Each portion of Meaty Duos has a mix of roasted flavoured meaty pieces and a generous serving of tender meaty chunks. It's packed full of flavours and textures to give your dog a delicious, wholesome meal.

An irresistible taste experience!

Meaty Duos is available in:

Chicken & Liver in Gravy

Chicken & Lamb in Jelly

Beef & Kidney in Gravy

Beef & Turkey in Jelly

Duck & Rabbit in Gravy

Lamb & Duck in Jelly

In store NOW!

Trademark owned by Société des Produits Nestlé S.A., Vevey, Switzerland

READERS' PET PICTURES 43

Readers' Pets Pictures

Send us your favourite Pet Photo!

On the following pages are a selection of Pets photos sent in by readers of **Pets Welcome!** If you would like to have a photo of your pet included in the next edition (published in October 2010), send it along with a brief note of the pet's name and any interesting anecdotes about them. Please remember to include your own name and address and let us know if you would like the pictures returned. FHG will give a FREE copy of the relevant guide in which the picture appears, PLUS our sponsors Winalot will provide a free packet of treats.

We will be happy to receive prints, or pictures by e-mail to
editorial@fhguides.co.uk

ISLA is looking forward to a day out,
Miss E. Gorman, Paisley, Renfrewshire

All pictures should be forwarded by the middle of July 2010.
Thanks to everyone who sent in pictures of their pets and regret that we were unable to include all of them, pictures not included in this edition will be considered for use in the future.

See the following pages for this year's selection.
**Send your Pet photo to:
FHG Guides, Abbey Mill Business Centre, Seedhill, Paisley PA1 1TJ**

READERS' PET PICTURES 45

BOUSTEAD enjoys a night on the tiles.
Muriel Jones, St Annes, Lancashire

CHLOE
is looking for a game of football.
Miss G. Caldwell, Paisley, Renfrewshire

YASSKO & CERYS
are ready for some fun.
Mrs Wendy Halling, Madrid

BUDDY & POPPY wonder if the rain will
stop so they can go out to play.
Ivor & Jo Gilbert, Louth, Lincolnshire

READERS' PET PICTURES 49

MILLIE
The most important thing about a holiday is a swim in the sea.
Paul & Liz Chandler, Nuneaton

HARLEY enjoys a run on the beach,
Lisa Waterman,
Letchworth, Hertfordshire

...m just too comfortable to move, says **HARVEY**.
...are Mansfield-Smith, Horbury, West Yorkshire

SALLY says, it's a dog's life.
Jennifer & Victor Gibbons,
High Peak, Derbyshire

One day we'll be as big as **HARVEE** the cat, say the pups.
Jackie Whitaker

IF YOU LOVE DOGS YOU'LL LOVE YOUR DOG

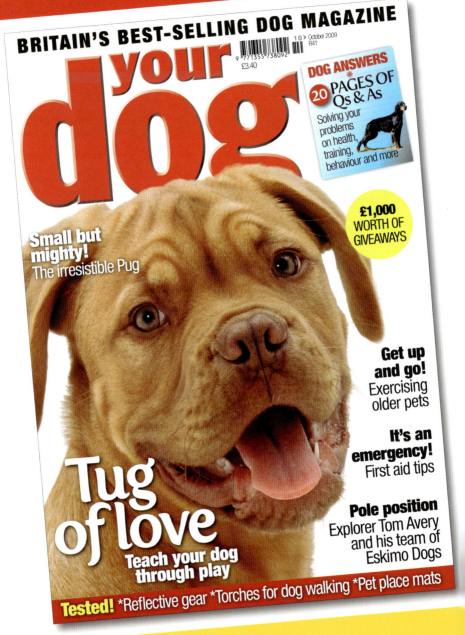

MAGAZINE your dog

Your Dog is Britain's **best-selling dog magazine,** a monthly read that's packed with tips and advice on how to get the best out of life with your pet.

Every issue contains in-depth features on your dog's health, behaviour and training, and looks at subjects such as how to pick the perfect puppy for your lifestyle.

Breeds
Facts, figures and practical advice on all your favourite breeds of dog.

Dog Answers
Twenty pages of your problems solved by our panel of experts — everything from training, health, behaviour, feeding, breeds, grooming, legal and homeopathy.

Tested!
Long and short-term testing of a range of dog-related products — everything from tough toys to wellies.

And lots, lots more...

Your Dog Magazine is available from your newsagent, price £3.40. Alternatively, why not take out a subscription? To find out more, contact the subscriptions hotline on 01858 438854 and quote ref PW09.

A dog-friendly walk in...
Loch Lomond and The Trossachs

The first beauty spot we are stopping off at on our dog-friendly tour of the UK is Loch Lomond and The Trossachs.

Balquhidder

This walk, which begins in Balquhidder, takes you along pine-scented forest paths where you will be able to enjoy fine views of Kirkton Glen and the surrounding scenery.
By Mary Welsh.

The lovely view of Loch Voil.

Majestic Loch Lomond is not far from Balquhidder.

Pic: Loch Lomond and the Trossachs National Park Authority.

Fact file

Distance: 9km/ 5½ miles.
Time: 3 hours.
Map: Explorer 365.
Start/parking: In Balquhidder; grid reference 536209.
Terrain: Good tracks throughout, may be muddy after rain.
Nearest town: Callander.
Refreshments: Kings House Hotel, Balquhidder; Monachyle Mhor, Balquhidder.
Public toilets: None en route.
Public transport: Contact Traveline on 0871 200 2233.
Stiles: One.
Suitable for: All the family. Dogs should be on leads if there is livestock about.

These walks have been reproduced from Your Dog Magazine, Britain's best-selling dog magazine, available from all good newsagents from the seventh of every month. Your Dog is priced at £3.40 and is packed with practical advice on every aspect of caring for and enjoying your pet. For more information, contact the editorial department on 01780 766199; for subscription details contact 01858 438854 or visit www.yourdog.co.uk

1 Wind left of the new church (built in 1853) to take a tree-lined gravelled track, directing you towards a waterfall. Beside you hurries the Kirkton Burn. Ignore the path to the right, which is your onward route, to walk to a footbridge from where you have a fine view of the delectable fall. Return to the path you ignored earlier, now on your left, and signposted 'Creag an Tuirc and Kirkton Glen'. The pleasing path climbs uphill, through trees, to go over an easy stile, and then winds steadily through tall conifers. Watch out for the sign on the right directing you to Creag an Tuirc. After 0.5km go through a hurdle gate on the right, descend steps to cross a stream and climb up the other side. Ascend to a cairn and a seat on the top of a crag, with a lovely view of Loch Voil below.

2 Return from the crag and on through the hurdle. Continue, left, down the path to the main track, where you turn right along a way that leads through Kirkton Glen. Go past a track coming in on the left and then another on the right. Go ahead into the glen to walk through an area where young conifers have been planted. Stride on through a fine stand of Scots pine and carry on. Now that much of the forest has been felled it is possible to see the shape of the glen.

3 Follow the track to the head of the glen to reach a signpost. Bear right, still on the forestry track, and return down the glen. Because the track is at a higher altitude you are able to see the glen stretching down below you. About a mile along you have another fine view of Loch Voil. Follow the track as it winds right and joins your outward route. Turn left and follow back to Balquhidder church and the parking area.

A dog-friendly walk in... The Brecon Beacons

The Brecon Beacons stretch from Llandeilo in the west to Hay-on-Wye in the east, and is one of three national parks in Wales. This stunning area is a popular destination for visitors who enjoy the freedom and remoteness of the Welsh countryside.

Enjoy the views at Blaen Llia.

Blaen Llia & Sarn Helen

The main sandstone mass of the Brecon Beacons meets a narrow strip of limestone just north of Ystradfellte, on the southern edge of Fforest Fawr (the Great Forest). This open-country walk cuts across these contrasting landscapes on moorland tracks, past a small Iron Age hill fort, and finally along a section of Roman road. **By Evelyne Sansot.**

Along the Roman road with Fan Llia in the background.

A derelict limekiln on the route.

Your Dog Magazine is available from all good newsagents. For more information, contact the editorial department on 01780 766199 or visit www.yourdog.co.uk

Fact file

Distance: 8km (5 miles).
Time: Allow 3 hours.
Map: Explorer OL12 Brecon Beacons National Park, West and Central.
Start/parking: Blaen Llia car park; grid reference SN927166.
Terrain: Mainly good tracks and footpaths across pastures with gentle ascents and descents.
Nearest towns: Glyn-Neath, Merthyr Tydfil, Brecon.
Refreshments: None.
Public toilets: None.
Public transport: None.
Stiles: None.
Suitable for: All.

1 As you leave the car park, turn left on to the road and follow it for 0.8km (half a mile). At a sharp bend to the left, continue straight on to a walled track. After a gate, take the right fork as waymarked.

2 After the next gate take the left fork across the pasture, heading for the right of a limestone crag. Pass a derelict limekiln just below the crag and continue along the same path as it makes a curve to the left between the limestone escarpments of Carnau Gwynion. About 200m into the next field keep along this main track, ignoring another one shooting off to the right.

3 Make an elbow turn to the right in front of the gate in the bottom corner (at an angle between the wall and the track you have just followed). The path is not clearly defined at this point as it cuts across the rough pasture. Keep heading towards some scraggy hawthorn trees in the distance then, as you reach the brink of the field, aim for a small circular wire fence enclosure around a swallow-hole, cross a track and continue straight up the slope to a gate in the wall.

4 Bear left past the remains of an Iron Age hill fort on the crest on your right, suddenly emerging above the valley of Nedd Fechan, with views to the north over some of Fforest Fawr's sandstone summits (from right to left, Fan Nedd and Fan Gyhirych). Go through a gate and walk down several fields along the clearly waymarked footpath to the bottom of the valley.

5 Turn right on to the narrow road and enter Blaen-nedd-Isaf Farm. Walk past the farmhouse then turn immediately left across the farmyard to walk round the left-hand side of the barn. Cross the river over a footbridge and walk straight up a small wooded area, then a pasture.

6 Turn right at the top, on to Sarn Helen, the Roman road, thereby joining the Beacons Way. Cross the river again over a footbridge and continue straight up the other bank, later to pass the Maen Madoc standing stone.

7 Turn right on to the road to rejoin the car park on your left.

A dog-friendly walk on... Dartmoor

Dartmoor has wild dramatic vistas and a colourful history steeped in folklore.

Lustleigh Cleave

This exploration of Lustleigh Cleave combines a fine ridge walk with a woodland and riverside ramble through a deep and sequestered valley, with a lovely boulder-strewn waterfall. The views over eastern Dartmoor, including Hound Tor and Haytor Rocks, are superb and there is a good deal of off-lead walking. We start and end at Lustleigh, one of Dartmoor's prettiest villages. **By Robert Hesketh.**

A Dartmoor mare and foal on Hunter's Tor.

There is plenty to see from Hunter's Tor.

Your Dog Magazine is available from all good newsagents. For more information, contact the editorial department on 01780 766199 or visit www.yourdog.co.uk

Fact file

Distance: 8.5km (5 miles).
Time: Allow 3 hours.
Maps: Landranger 191, Explorer OL 28 or Harvey's Dartmoor.
Start/parking: Roadside parking in Lustleigh; grid reference SX785813.
Terrain: Footpaths, bridlepaths and lanes well-signed; some short but steep ascents and descents.
Nearest towns: Moretonhampstead and Bovey Tracey.
Refreshments: Both Primrose Cottage Tearooms (home-made cakes) and the Cleave Hotel (real ales and a good menu) in Lustleigh welcome dogs.
Public toilets: Lustleigh.
Public transport: Bus no. 178 from Newton Abbot to Moretonhampstead via Bovey Tracey (Monday to Saturday).
Stiles: None.
Suitable for: Anyone who is fairly fit.

1 From Lustleigh's church, turn left. Follow the lane signed for Rudge. Cross the bridge and keep right when the lane forks. Turn first right at the chapel and walk uphill before turning left by Oakehurst on to the signed path. Follow this uphill past houses and gardens to a group of three stone and thatched houses. Turn left and then turn right at the T-junction. About 50m ahead, turn left on to the bridlepath for Lustleigh Cleave.

2 Continue ahead through Heaven's Gate. At the junction of paths, follow the bridlepath ahead signed Manaton via Water. Bear right and uphill when the path forks. Continue uphill for Hammerslake at the next fingerpost. Turn left at the following fingerpost, signed Bridge (originally Foxworthy Bridge but the fingerpost has been damaged). Ignore the side turnings and then about 1.5km (1 mile) ahead divert left for 200m on the path for Horsham to see Horsham Steps, a beautiful boulder-strewn waterfall. Be careful of slippery moss, which grows thickly on trees and boulders in the clean, moist air of the Cleave. Return to the main path and turn left for Foxworthy. Pass behind the house and through a gate. Just beyond the converted barn take the path right signed Peck Farm.

3 When the path meets a concrete track turn right. Bypass Peck Farm, taking the signed public bridlepath through the gate to the right. Carry on to the top of the ridge. Hunter's Tor, a superb viewpoint, includes the eroded ramparts of an Iron Age fort — easily missed unless you look for them.

4 Follow the fine and clearly defined ridge path on to Harton Chest, a massive granite boulder, which can be climbed with care. Looking down nearly 500ft to the floor of the Cleave gives a dramatic impression of its size and steepness.

5 Entering woodland, littered with boulders, the path descends gently at first and then sharply. At the fingerpost, ignore the sign for Heaven's Gate and go straight ahead through the gate in front of you.

6 Turn right on to the metalled lane and first left after 250m. Follow the lane down past Ellimore Farm. At the bottom of the hill, take the signed public footpath left. Walk down through the woods, ignoring the first gated path on the left. Leave the wood by a gate and cross the brook via a wooden bridge. The large boulder in the centre of Lustleigh Orchard is surmounted by a stone seat, the May Queen's throne. Walk straight on through the orchard back to the start of the route at Lustleigh's church.

A dog-friendly walk in... The North York Moors National Park

The North York Moors National Park, with its wild and wonderful dales and hills, is a fantastic place to visit.

The White Horse above the village of Kilburn.

Kilburn White Horse

High on the edge of the Hambleton Hills a giant white horse keeps watch over the village of Kilburn. Standing below it all you can see is a mass of white. From the village the rather oddly shaped large horse with a small head, stubby legs and a long tail, stands out stark against the deciduous woodland all about it.
By Mary Welsh.

The church in Kilburn village.

The cottage of carpenter Robert Thompson — otherwise known as the Mouseman of Kilburn.

Your Dog Magazine is available from all good newsagents. For more information, contact the editorial department on 01780 766199 or visit www.yourdog.co.uk

1 From the car park at Sutton Bank visitor centre, with dogs on the lead, cross the main road, the A170, with care. Turn left along the signposted level footpath to walk along the edge of the escarpment. From here you can see the Vale of York with the Pennines as a backdrop, considered by James Herriot as the 'best view in Yorkshire'. To your left is Kilburn Moor Plantation. Carry on ahead along the delightful way, ignoring the path descending right.

2 Stroll on, now with the Yorkshire Gliding Club's airfield to your left.

Watch out for falling tow lines as you go and keep to the path — gliders approach from any direction and are silent, so you will have no warning to get out of the way. Follow the path as it continues above the White Horse. When you reach the top of the tail, take the railed steps down the steep hillside to arrive in a small car park.

3 Here you have a choice. If you wish to visit Kilburn village on foot, join the narrow road (known locally as the Mare's Tail) and turn right to walk for a mile. In summer this can be quite busy but there are several verges you can walk on. Remember that you will have to return up the road (for a mile). To continue with the walk, if you decide not to visit Kilburn, turn right at the bottom of the steps (left through the car park if you have walked from Kilburn), go through the car park and then a gate on to a track into the forest. Where the track divides take the signposted right fork and follow the path below the limestone cliffs of Roulston Scar.

4 When the way forks again, take the right branch, known as the Thief's Highway, and strike steeply uphill through the fine woodland. At the top of the slope, join the path along the escarpment, turning left to walk your outward route.

Fact file

Distance: 5km/3 miles or 8km/5 miles.
Time: 2 hours or 4 hours.
Map: Explorer OL26.
Start/parking: Sutton Bank National Park centre; grid reference 516831.
Terrain: Mostly on level paths and tracks with a steepish descent of many steps and steepish return ascent to the scarp edge.
Nearest towns: Thirsk and Helmsley.
Refreshments: Sutton Bank National Park centre cafe and Kilburn village.
Public toilets: Sutton Bank centre.
Public transport: Moors Bus network. For information contact 01845 597000.
Suitable for: All the family. Dogs on leads on road to Kilburn.

A dog-friendly walk on... The South Downs

Stop off at the South Downs, with its chalk hills that afford beautiful views of the coast and nearby beaches. Designated as an Area of Outstanding Natural Beauty, the South Downs extends through the counties of East Sussex, West Sussex and part of Hampshire.

The view over the downs from Chanctonbury.

Chanctonbury Ring

Take the opportunity to explore one of the most mysterious and magical sites on the South Downs. The ring is a fascinating place at any time of year and in any weather. Don't be deterred if the top is shrouded in low cloud as this only adds to the atmosphere. On a clear day the views are second to none and a camera can't do them justice. **By Sylvie Dobson.**

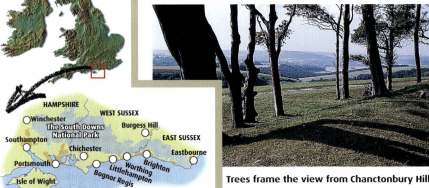

Trees frame the view from Chanctonbury Hill.

1 Leave the car park and continue ahead along the rough ascending track. Soon you will be in the shelter of the trees covering the flanks of the hill. Bear left at an apparent fork and then just keep climbing on the main track. From the bottom the climb looks daunting but once you get started you will quickly get into a rhythm and before long will emerge from the trees to join a wide crossing track. This is the renowned South Downs Way.

2 From here the views are limited, so walk along to the right for a short while before turning and looking back. In the distance you will see Cissbury Ring and beyond that the sea. Ahead the imposing sight of the Chanctonbury Ring comes into view. Pass through a gate and on to access land where you can roam freely.

3 By all means explore the ring but then keep over to the right and aim for the trig point from where you can get an all-round view of the surrounding area. On a clear day you can see the Isle of Wight away to the south-west and far away to the north beyond the Weald you should be able to make out the North Downs. Return to the main track, spending a few minutes by the nearby dew pond, and continue the walk. You may be tempted to use an alternative route through the adjoining access land but be aware that there are likely to be sheep grazing. The track is a safer proposition and just as enjoyable.

4 Keep right at a fork and start a steady descent.

You will pass another gate leading on to the access land and over to your left you will see a short, grassy runway used for the occasional light aircraft. You should look for the track that leads to this airstrip; immediately beyond this take the narrow path on the right following it down the hillside to a stile and on to a road.

5 Turn right and just beyond the turning to St Mary's Church you will see a stile on the right. Pass over the stile and then a short footbridge before climbing some strategically placed steps up the hillside. Continue through open pasture where sheep may be grazing. Keep walking with the hedge to your left but be alert for a fingerpost that may at times be partly hidden by foliage. You are directed diagonally right across open fields and on to a gate at the foot of Chanctonbury Hill — you don't have to climb it again! Turn left along a wide track which contours the lower slopes of the scarp before eventually joining the path you followed from the car park.

Your Dog Magazine is available from all good newsagents. For more information, contact the editorial department on 01780 766199 or visit www.yourdog.co.uk

Fact file

Distance: 2.5km to 3km (4½ miles).
Time: 2 – 3 hours.
Map: Explorer 121, Arundel and Pulborough.
Start/parking: Chanctonbury Ring car park and picnic area signed from the A283 between Washington and Steyning; grid reference 146123.
Terrain: An initial climb on to the ridge of the downs followed by a less noticeable descent. Paths are well used and clearly defined.
Nearest town: Worthing.
Refreshments: The Frankland Arms in Washington village.
Public toilets: None.
Public transport: Full details from Traveline, contact 0871 200 2233. Compass Travel operates a local service that passes the track to the car park, contact tel. 01903 690025.
Stiles: Six.
Suitable for: Dogs and owners used to exercise. Lots of off-lead opportunities.

A dog-friendly walk in...
The Lake District

The Lake District has high mountains, sweeping views, wonderful woodlands and a myriad of becks and fine lakes.

Broughton-in-Furness

In 1859 Coniston village was linked by rail to the main west coast line. This line enabled slate quarried in the fells to be transported. The trains also carried goods, tourists and schoolchildren. In the late 1960s the nine-mile line was closed. In 2003, the national park resurfaced and refurbished the track, and the new trail was officially opened and is a very popular route with walkers. **By Mary Welsh.**

The second lake beside the railway track.

The Lake District offers fantastic views.

Your Dog Magazine is available from all good newsagents. For more information, contact the editorial department on 01780 766199 or visit www.yourdog.co.uk

1 Leave Broughton's village square in the direction of the signed public toilets. Follow the track as it bends right to join the trackbed of the railway. Here, wind left, go round the barrier and dogs can start their 1¼ miles of freedom. Walk left, through the deep cutting. Just before the old bridge over the line, on the left, is the first of the two lakes. Go on under the bridge and up the short sloping path, on the left, to a seat overlooking the beautiful second lake.

2 Stroll the lovely way to cross a fine wooden bridge spanning a farm track. Carry on, soon to pass through another cutting shaded by tall forest trees, until you reach a fence supporting a 'no path' sign. Here bear right to descend through two gates on to Five Arches Road, named after a demolished bridge that carried the old railway line. Walk right to pass Mireside Farm and wind on along the narrow quiet road, through pastures and mixed woodland to come to a signposted bridleway on your right.

3 Pass between small plantations of firs, where dogs can have more freedom and then ascend the continuing steepish track that climbs through deciduous woodland to where it divides. Take the short right fork to the side of the access lane to Wall End Farm, which you cross.

4 Climb the stile, ascend a little slope and then descend the ongoing path over rough pasture, where there might be sheep or deer. This path keeps parallel with the wall on your right but keeping a short distance away from it. Press on until you can take the easy to miss gap stile in the wall, a 'fat man's agony'— two stone slabs that you have to squeeze between and which stout dogs may find difficult. Walk ahead beside another wall, also on your right, and go through the next gap stile or use the gate to its left, which is usually open. Walk ahead to the fenced edge of the railway cutting, high above where you walked earlier. Turn left and walk on through a gateless gap and on again to a step stile in the right corner on to the railway track. Cross and walk up the track ahead. Wind left to return to the village square.

Fact file

Distance: 6.5km (4 miles).
Time: 2 – 3 hours.
Map: Explorer OL6.
Start/parking: Broughton-in-Furness square, just off the A595.
Terrain: Level, easy walking along railway track; a little quiet road walking; the track from Five Arches Road to the access track at the top of slope can be muddy in the dip.
Nearest towns: Ulverston, Millom.
Refreshments: In Broughton there is a good choice of inns and cafes, and one restaurant, all offering excellent food.
Public toilets: Just off the village square.
Public transport: Stagecoach bus service from Millom and Ulverston. For details, contact Traveline on 0871 200 2233.
Stiles: Several.
Suitable for: All the family.

People-friendly Cottages for Pets!

Lovely locations with superb walks in some of England's most picturesque countryside. From Windsor to the Welsh Borders, with lots to choose from in the Cotswolds and Shakespeare's Country.

Small, friendly company with personal knowledge of the area, – why not tell US what your pet likes and we'll do our best for him ... and you!

enquiries@cottageinthecountry.co.uk
www.cottageinthecountry.co.uk
Tel: 01608 646833 • Fax: 01608 646844
Tukes Cottage, 66 West Street,
Chipping Norton, Oxon OX7 5ER

COTTAGE IN THE COUNTRY COTTAGE HOLIDAYS (01608 646833; Fax: 01608 646844). Lovely locations with superb walks in some of England's most picturesque countryside. Small friendly company with personal knowledge of the area.
e-mail: enquiries@cottageinthecountry.co.uk   website: www.cottageinthecountry.co.uk

HOSEASONS. Over 200 pet-friendly countryside and seaside locations in the best areas of Britain. Peaceful, stylish lodges and lively holiday parks, some with pools, bars and restaurants. Lowest price guaranteed. Call 0844 847 1103 Quote GA150 or book on-line.
website: www.hoseasons.co.uk

CLAYMOORE NARROWBOATS. Canal Holidays from base in Cheshire. Boats sleep 2-10. Fully equipped. Fuel included in hire. Full instruction. Day and Short Break hire. Car parking. Pets welcome.
website: www.claymoore.co.uk

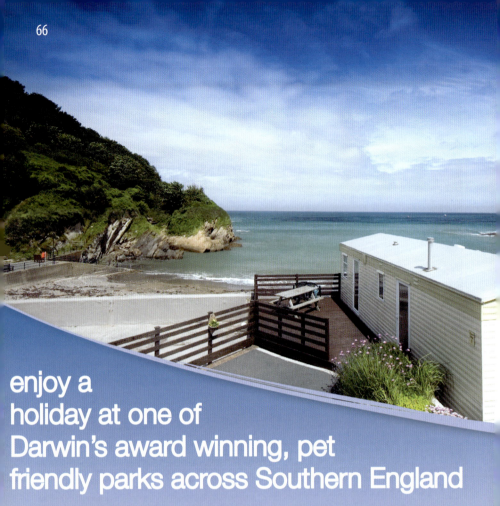

enjoy a holiday at one of Darwin's award winning, pet friendly parks across Southern England

Darwin Holiday Parks bring you a choice of unique destinations across southern Engla[nd] each offering top-class facilities and pet-friendly accommodation in stunning setti[ngs] across Devon, Dorset, Somerset and Surrey.

All of our parks lie within easy reach of an array of breathtaking sites and attractions, f[rom] the spectacular rugged Jurassic Coastline, to historical cities such as Bath, Dorches[ter,] Guildford and Salisbury.

The range of amenities on offer across our portfolio include restaura[nts] and bars, swimming pools, children's playgrounds, crazy golf [and] even a BMX track.

In contrast, a number of the parks offer low-key holidays with a fo[cus] on relaxation, tranquillity and sublime views.

So, whether you are looking for a fun-packed family holiday [or] a peaceful break on which to unwind, Darwin Holiday Park[s are] guaranteed to have an option to suit your needs – and all [at] outstanding value for money.

range of facilities include:*
- Fully Serviced Caravan Pitches
- Grass Camping Pitches
- Motor Home Facilities
- Lodges & Holiday Homes
- Seasonal Pitches
- Children's Activities & Playgrounds
- Shops, Bars & Restaurants
- Family Entertainment
- Swimming Pools
- Olympic BMX Track
- Dedicated Rally & Festival Areas
- Modern Toilet & Wash Facilities
- Transport Links

www.darwinholidays.co.uk
enquiries@darwinholidays.co.uk

special offers & discounts online

Pet Friendly

website for individual park site facilities. Darwin Holiday Parks are managed by Darwin Contract Management Ltd. Terms & Conditions apply.

BLUE CHIP VACATIONS. Choose from the largest selection of pet-friendly holiday homes in Devon, Cornwall, Dorset and Somerset with outstanding views the whole family can enjoy. (0844 561 2001). website: www.bluechipvacations.com

DARWIN HOLIDAY PARKS. Award-winning pet friendly parks in the beautiful South West. A choice of six unique destinations each offering top-class facilities and pet friendly accommodation set within stunning surroundings. Special offers and discounts online.
e-mail: enquiries@darwinsholidays.co.uk   website: www.darwinholidays.co.uk

CLASSIC COTTAGES (01326 565 555). Featuring 700 hand selected coastal and country holiday homes throughout the West Country.
website: www.classic.co.uk

THE INDEPENDENT TRAVELLER, ORCHARD COTTAGE, THORVERTON, EXETER EX5 5NG (01392 860807). For a wide choice of cottages and apartments throughout England, Scotland & the Isles. Pets welcome in many properties. Quality Cottages in coastal, country and mountain location. Property finding service.
e-mail: help@gowithit.co.uk   website: www.gowithit.co.uk

CAMPING & CARAVANNING CLUB (0845 130 7632). Visit one of our award-winning UK Club Sites. Most of our sites have dog walking areas for you and your dog to explore. A friendly welcome will be given to you and your pet on our sites, joining is great value for money. [🐾] QUOTE REF NO 0716
website: www.campingandcaravanningclub.co.uk

Free or reduced rate entry to
Holiday Visits and Attractions - see our
READERS' OFFER VOUCHERS on pages 445-454

Cottage Holidays for laid back dogs.
300 quality waterside & rural properties in beautiful locations.
People welcome too!
For our fabulous fully detailed brochure

telephone 01548 853089 (24 hours)
www.toadhallcottages.co.uk

A fine selection of holiday cottages throughout Cornwall. Pets welcome in many.
01208 821666 | corncott.com

Cornish Seaview Cottages

18 gorgeous holiday properties on the North Cornish coast. Sleeping from 2 – 20.

All our properties are in fantastic locations with great views. They are ideal for walking the coastal paths and accessing the local beaches. Pets are welcome at most and we pride ourselves on our personal service and welcome.

The houses are tastefully furnished and are equipped to a high standard with all the comforts required for a relaxing holiday. All have central heating, dishwashers and washing machines.

For full information with photographs and virtual tours please visit our own website
www.cornishseaviewcottages.co.uk
Tel: 01428 723819 • e-mail: enquiries@cornishseaviewcottages.co.uk

We look forward to welcoming you

West Cornwall Cottage Holidays

Choose from a large selection of dog-friendly cottages with beaches and walks just a ball's throw away.

www.westcornwallcottageholidays.com
Tel: 01736 368575

Looking for Holiday Accommodation?

for details of hundreds of properties throughout the UK, visit our website

www.holidayguides.com

Cornwall
Bodmin, Bodmin Moor

Penrose Burden Holiday Cottages
St Breward, Bodmin, Cornwall PL30 4LZ
Tel: 01208 850277/850617 • Fax: 01208 850915
www.penroseburden.co.uk

Situated within easy reach of both coasts and Bodmin Moor on a large farm overlooking a wooded valley with own salmon and trout fishing. These stone cottages with exposed beams and quarry tiled floors have been featured on TV and are award-winners.
All are suitable for wheelchair users and dogs are welcomed.
Our cottages sleep from two to seven and are open all year.
Please write or telephone for a colour brochure.   Nancy Hall

Close to The Eden Project

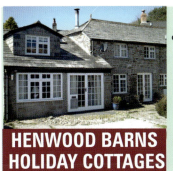

HENWOOD BARNS HOLIDAY COTTAGES

Three stone barns set around original courtyard on the edge of Bodmin Moor, with stunning views. Tranquil, village location, horse riding two minutes' walk. Woodburning stoves; sleep 2/5; within easy reach of North Cornwall and Devon.

HENWOOD, LISKEARD PL14 5BP
01579 363576/07956 864263
e-mail: henwoodbarns@tiscali.co.uk
www.henwoodbarns.co.uk

Publisher's note
While every effort is made to ensure accuracy, we regret that FHG Guides cannot accept responsibility for errors, misrepresentations or omissions in our entries or any consequences thereof. Prices in particular should be checked.
We will follow up complaints but cannot act as arbiters or agents for either party.

Please mention *Pets Welcome!*
when making enquiries about accommodation featured in these pages

72 SOUTH WEST ENGLAND — Cornwall

Bodmin Moor, Botallack, Bude, Crackington Haven

DARRYNANE COTTAGES

3 fabulous detached cottages all with private, gated gardens. Situated in a unique moorland valley, with oak woods, waterfalls and the river. The cottages provide a homely base for walking, relaxing or touring Cornwall. Eden Project and Camel Trail close by. Woodburning stoves, four-poster beds. Fishing and Trails. Open all year.

Darrynane, St Breward, Bodmin Moor PL30 4LZ • Tel/Fax: 01208 850885
enquiries@darrynane.co.uk • www.darrynane.co.uk

Trevaylor Caravan & Camping Park Botallack TR19 7PU

A sheltered grassy site located off the beaten track in a peaceful location at the western tip of Cornwall. The dramatic coastline and the pretty villages nearby are truly unspoilt. Clean, well maintained facilities and a good shop are offered, along with a bar serving bar meals. 6-acre site with 50 touring pitches. *AA 3 Pennants*.
01736 787016 • www.cornishcamping.co.uk • trevaylor@cornishcamping.co.uk

Hedley Wood Caravan & Camping Park
Bridgerule (Near Bude), Holsworthy, Devon EX22 7ED
Tel: 01288 381404 • Fax: 01288 382011

16 acre woodland family-run site with outstanding views, where you can enjoy a totally relaxing holiday with a laid-back atmosphere, sheltered and open camping areas. Just 10 minutes' drive from the beaches, golf courses, riding stables and shops.

On site facilities include: Children's Adventure Areas, Bar, Clubroom, Shop, Laundry, Meals and all amenities. Free Hot Showers/Water. **Nice dogs/pets are very welcome. Daily kennelling facility. Dog walks/nature trail**.

Static caravans for hire. Caravan storage available. **Open all year.**
Visit our website: www.hedleywood.co.uk or write or phone for comprehensive brochure

HENTERVENE HOLIDAY PARK
Crackington Haven, Near Bude EX23 0LF   Tel: 01840 230365

Two miles from unspoilt sandy beach in an Area of Outstanding Natural Beauty. Luxury caravans and pine lodges to let with first class facilities for families and pets. Open all year. Short breaks available. Caravan and Lodge Sales.
e-mail: contact@hentervene.co.uk   website: www.hentervene.co.uk

Visit the FHG website
www.holidayguides.com
for details of the wide choice of accommodation
featured in the full range of FHG titles

Cornwall
SOUTH WEST ENGLAND 73
Crackington Haven, Crantock

Five 18th Century converted barns, beamed ceilings, log fires and secluded rural setting. Ideal touring base. Five miles to coast at Crackington Haven. Sleep 2/6. Pets welcome. Open all year. From £100 short breaks, £195 per week.

Lorraine Harrison, Trenannick Cottages, Warbstow, Launceston, Cornwall PL15 8RP • Tel: 01566 781443
e-mail: trenannick–1@tiscali.co.uk • www.trenannickcottages.co.uk

Give your pet the holiday it deserves

Crackington Haven, Bude, Cornwall

Quality Cornish Cottages sleeping from 1 to 8, at a price you can afford.
Situated in peaceful wooded valley leading to the beach.
Perfect location for walking, touring or just relaxing.
14 acres of fields/woodlands to exercise your dog.

website: www.mineshop.co.uk
or phone Charlie or Jane on **01840 230338**

We are proud that all our properties are inspected by, and featured in,

The Good Holiday Cottage Guide

CRANTOCK BAY HOTEL
a very special place all year round

Crantock Bay Hotel is superbly located for a holiday with your dogs. Our gardens lead direct to the Cornish coastal path and within 10 minutes walk of the 'dogs welcome' beaches of Polly Joke and Crantock Bay. Facilities include: comfortable bedrooms - many with sea views, a quality restaurant, indoor pool, spa bath, gym and tennis court. Beauty Spa. Well known for our friendly and helpful service, The Crantock Bay Hotel appeals to family members of all ages and has been welcoming families for over fifty years. There is a great choice of Special Interest Breaks.

Crantock Bay Hotel
West Pentire, Crantock, Cornwall TR8 5SE
Tel: 01637 830229 Fax: 01637 831111
E-mail: stay@crantockbayhotel.co.uk • www.crantockbayhotel.co.uk

FHG Guides
publish a large range of well-known accommodation guides.
We will be happy to send you details or you can use the order form
at the back of this book.

Cornwall
Falmouth

Creekside Cottages • Cornwall
31 Exclusive Holiday Cottages in South Cornwall

A fine selection of individual water's edge, village and rural cottages, sleeping from 2-10, situated around the creeks of the Carrick Roads, near Falmouth, South Cornwall. Set in enchanting and picturesque positions, with many of the cottages offering panoramic creek views. Perfect locations for family holidays, all close to superb beaches, extensive sailing and boating facilities, Cornish gardens and excellent walks. The majority of the cottages are available throughout the year, and all offer peaceful, comfortable and fully equipped accommodation; most have open fires. Dogs welcome.

Just come and relax

For a colour brochure please phone **01326 375972**
www.creeksidecottages.co.uk

CREEKSIDE HOLIDAY HOUSES

Spacious houses sleep 2/4/6/8. Peaceful, picturesque water's edge hamlet. Boating facilities. Use of boat. Own quay, beach. Secluded gardens. Near Pandora Inn. Friday bookings. Dogs welcome.
PETER WATSON, CREEKSIDE HOLIDAY HOUSES, RESTRONGUET, FALMOUTH TR11 5ST • 01326 372722   www.creeksideholidayhouses.co.uk

for a FREE brochure call 01326 250339
www.CornishHolidayCottages.net
Quality, self-catering accommodation in Falmouth & Helford River

Pet-Friendly
Pubs, Inns & Hotels
on pages 438-443
Please note that these establishments may not feature in the main section of this book

Cornwall

Falmouth, Fowey

Tudor Court

55 McIvill Road, Falmouth TR11 4DF

Strikingly stylish, mock-Tudor family-run guest house, in award-winning gardens. Comfortable, friendly, non-smoking accommodation, a short walk from town and beaches. Sea view rooms.

Business or pleasure, short or long stay, a warm welcome awaits you.

Sue & Dick Barrett • 01326 312807
enquiries@tudorcourthotel.com
www.tudorcourtguesthouse.co.uk

Open all year incl. Christmas
£32- £40ppn

AA ★★★ Guest House

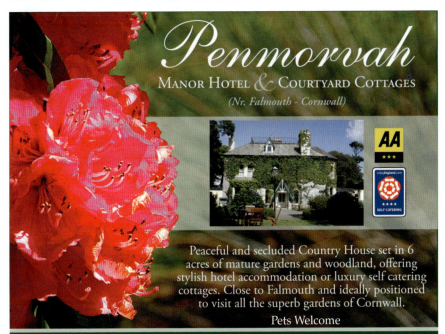

Penmorvah
Manor Hotel & Courtyard Cottages
(Nr. Falmouth - Cornwall)

Peaceful and secluded Country House set in 6 acres of mature gardens and woodland, offering stylish hotel accommodation or luxury self catering cottages. Close to Falmouth and ideally positioned to visit all the superb gardens of Cornwall.

Pets Welcome

tel: 01326 250277 • www.penmorvah.co.uk

LANCROW BARN
NEAR FOWEY

www.rentahouseincornwall.com
tel: 01726 814263
sarahfurniss@aol.com

Quality barn conversion close to sea with spectacular coastal and countryside views. Furnished to a high standard with Amdega Conservatory and large open plan sitting room. Well equipped kitchen. 3 en suite bedrooms. Central heating. Sky+ and flat screen TVs. Large enclosed garden with BBQ. Pets welcome. Good walks from property. Close to harbour town of Fowey and few minutes' drive from The Eden Project.

Prices from £650 to £1000.

The Old Ferry Inn

Why not bring your dog for its well deserved holiday to the family-run Old Ferry Inn, close to the edge of the beautiful River Fowey. There are many varied walks from country and riverside to breathtaking views along the Cornwall Coastal Path. The 400-year-old hotel has an excellent à la carte restaurant for evening meals and a comprehensive bar menu for lunch and evening. The Inn has 12 letting rooms with tea and coffee making facilities, colour TV and telephone, all rooms en suite or with private bathroom, most with views of the Fowey river.

Prices are from £90-£130 per night for two people sharing.

Bodinnick-by-Fowey PL23 1LX
Tel: (01726) 870237 • Fax: (01726) 870116
www.oldferryinn.com • e-mail: royce972@aol.com

Looking for Holiday Accommodation?

for details of hundreds of properties throughout the UK, visit our website

www.holidayguides.com

Cornwall

SOUTH WEST ENGLAND

Fowey, Helford, Helston, Launceston, Liskeard

Driftwood, Polruan-by-Fowey. Dogs Encouraged!!
Spacious and well presented holiday cottage sleeping 2 - 8 in 4 bedrooms/3 bathrooms.
Great views & fabulous walks on doorstep. Garden/ch/woodburner/ broadband. Parking.
Lovely village with shops, quay (ferry to Fowey) and two pubs.
£400 - £1500 pw. Off-peak discounts for smaller parties.
Our dogs love it here - we are sure yours will too!!
www.seasidecottageholiday.co.uk • 01608 674601

St Anthony – Helford River
www.StAnthony.co.uk

Enchanting creekside cottages in a timeless and tranquil hamlet. Springtime bluebell woods and hedgerows banked with primroses, reflections of multi-coloured sails off sandy beaches, the solitary blue flash of a Kingfisher in autumn, smoke grey herons and shining white egrets standing patiently by the shoreline all evoke the atmosphere of this truly beautiful corner of Cornwall.

- Stunning coastal and riverside walks
- Great country inns and local food
- Warm and comfortable with cosy log fires
- Our own sailing dinghies and fishing boats
- Moorings and easy launching
- National Trust and private gardens nearby
- Short breaks, open all year including Christmas

St Anthony Holidays, Manaccan, Helston, Cornwall TR12 6JW
Tel: 01326 231 357 • e-mail: info@stanthony.co.uk

BOSCREGE Caravan & Camping Park
Ashton, Nr Helston, Cornwall

- Static caravans available for holidays
- Touring caravans, tents & motor homes
- Child's play area
- Pets welcome

from **£59** pppw

01736 762231
caravanparkcornwall.com AA

SILVER SANDS HOLIDAY PARK, Gwendreath, near Kennack Sands, Ruan Minor, Helston TR12 7LZ • Tel/Fax: 01326 290631
Quiet, family-run park. Pets welcome with well-trained owners. Short walk through woodland path to award-winning dog beach. Ideal for families - no clubhouse or bar to disturb the peace. Choice of holiday homes, touring and camping in mature parkland setting.
ETC ★★★★ • AA 3 Pennants. www.silversandsholidaypark.co.uk

Lower Dutson Farm, Launceston PL15 9SP • Tel: 01566 776456

Swallows & Meadow Cottage

Wander down across the fields with your dog to the River Tamar and lakeside walks. Five minutes to breathtaking views across to Dartmoor. Ideal cottage for touring Devon and Cornwall. Salmon, trout, carp etc fishing.
e-mail: holidays@farm-cottage.co.uk • www.farm-cottage.co.uk

Boturnell Barns Cornwall

Really dog friendly self catering accommodation
Set in 25 acres,
no limit on number of pets,
Dog crèche

Tel 01579 320880 website: www.dogs-holiday.co.uk e-mail sue@dogs-holiday.co.uk

---

Butterdon Mill Holiday Homes

Detached 2-bedroom bungalows, accommodate up to 4, 5 or 6 persons, in a delightfully sheltered wooded valley 3 miles from Liskeard (8 miles from Looe). Pets welcome. Games barn. Outdoor play area. Phone **01579 342636**, e-mail **butterdonmill@btconnect.com** for brochure and availability or see our website: **www.bmhh.co.uk**
Butterdon Mill Holiday Homes, Merrymeet, Liskeard, Cornwall PL14 3LS

CUTKIVE WOOD HOLIDAY LODGES

Nestling in the heart of a peaceful family-owned country estate are six well-equipped comfortable cedar-clad lodges.
Set on the edge of ancient bluebell woods with lovely rural views, you can relax and enjoy yourself in this tranquil and idyllic setting.
Help with the animals, explore the woods and fields, fun play area.
So much for everyone to see and do – memorable beaches, wonderful coasts, walk the moors, inspiring gardens and Eden, theme attractions, historic gems.
Dogs welcome. Ideally situated to enjoy coast and country holidays whatever the time of year.

St Ive, Liskeard, Cornwall PL14 3ND
Tel: 01579 362216
www.cutkivewood.co.uk
e-mail: holidays@cutkivewood.co.uk

Cornwall
Liskeard, Lizard

Caradon Country Cottages

in magnificent countryside between Bodmin Moor and Looe. Ideal for exploring Devon and Cornwall, Eden Project, coast and countryside. Central heating and log burners for cosy Winter Breaks. 5-acre grounds. Every comfort for you and your pets.

www.caradoncottages.co.uk
Telephone & Fax: 01579 320355
e-mail: celia@caradoncottages.co.uk
East Taphouse, Liskeard, Cornwall PL14 4NH

Moorland location

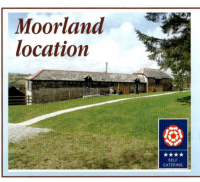

Hopsland Cottages
Commonmoor, Liskeard PL14 6EJ
Tel & Fax: 01579 344480

A beautiful barn on our farm which has been converted into 3 well-equipped self-catering cottages (all with DVD), which sleep between 4 and 6 persons. Beautiful views and very peaceful. Own exercise fields for dogs, or just 150 yards from Bodmin Moor, with miles of open space. Many ancient monuments to visit.

www.hopslandholidays.co.uk
e-mail: hopslandholidays@btinternet.com

Redgate Smithy B&B
Redgate, St Cleer, Liskeard, Cornwall PL14 6RU

Redgate Smithy is a 200-year-old converted smithy, situated just above the beautiful Golitha Falls on the southern edge of Bodmin Moor. We provide an extensive and tasty breakfast menu, served in the conservatory. A friendly dog is our Special Guest! Excellent pubs and restaurants locally for your evening meals.
Tel: 01579 321578 • e-mail: enquiries@redgatesmithy.com
Visit our B&B website at: www.redgatesmithy.co.uk

Gallen-Treath GUEST HOUSE

PORTHALLOW, HELSTON, CORNWALL TR12 6PL
Tel & Fax: 01326 280400
Friendly guesthouse with spectacular coastal views, comfortable en suite rooms, hearty meals and a warm welcome. Close to coastal path, diving, gardens and more. Traditional breakfasts.
e-mail: gallentreath@btclick.com • www.gallen-treath.com

Dogs stay for **FREE** during Low Season at Mullion Cove Hotel

MULLION COVE HOTEL

...located on the Cornwall Coast Path in a spectacular position on the Lizard Peninsula. Stunning country and coastal walks. Hotel facilities include a dog-friendly lounge, dog welcome pack, comfortable bedrooms and excellent food. **Tel: 01326 240328**

Email: enquiries@mullion-cove.co.uk
www.mullion-cove.co.uk

SOUTH WEST ENGLAND — Cornwall
Lizard, Longrock, Looe

POLURRIAN HOTEL

e-mail: relax@polurrianhotel.com • www.polurrianhotel.com

Set in 12 acres with stunning views across Mount's Bay. The hotel has two pools, gym, snooker room, tennis court, sun terraces and secluded gardens. Most of the recently refurbished bedrooms have sea views. Our restaurant offers excellent food in stylish surroundings. Whether it is a more casual atmosphere in the Lounge Bar or a formal dinner in the main Dining Room, we have something for everyone.

Mullion, Lizard Peninsula, Cornwall TR12 7EN • Tel: 01326 240421 • Fax: 01326 240083

• Mount View Hotel •

A family-run pub with comfortable accommodation, situated 100 yards from Mount's Bay in Longrock village. Three en suite rooms and two with shared bathroom. Breakfast in dining room, lunch and dinner available. Dogs welcome by arrangement. Prices from £20 pppn.

Longrock, Penzance, Cornwall TR20 8JJ • Tel: 01736 710416

Badham Farm, St Keyne, Liskeard PL14 4RW • 01579 343572
www.badhamfarm.co.uk • e-mail: badhamfarm@yahoo.co.uk

Farmhouse and farm buildings converted to a high standard. Sleep 2-10. All well furnished/equipped; prices include electricity, bed linen and towels. Most have a garden. Tennis, putting, children's play area, fishing lake, animal paddock, games room with pool and table tennis. Separate bar. Laundry. Barbecue.
Well behaved dogs welcome (not in high season). Prices from £120 per week.

Fox Valley Cottages
Lanlawren, Trenewan, Looe PL13 2PZ

Set in beautiful countryside
For a peaceful and relaxing holiday

A warm welcome from Andy & Linda, who are two of the partners who live on site.
• Indoor heated pool, spa and sauna • Cleaned to a high standard, warm, comfortable and well equipped
• Log fires for those cosy winter nights
• Dedicated field for dog owners to let their dog off the lead and let them have a good run around
• Country and Coastal walks nearby. Polperro and Looe just a short drive away. • We are open all year round, including Christmas and New Year. • Short breaks, long weekends or midweek breaks out of season.

Tel: 01726 870115 • e-mail: info@foxvalleycottages.co.uk • www.foxvalleycottages.co.uk

Cornwall

SOUTH WEST ENGLAND

Looe

COLDRINNICK COTTAGES

Duloe, Near Looe PL14 4QF

Coldrinnick Cottages are attractively converted barns, set in their own large secure, secluded gardens on a working dairy farm. Outstanding views, woodland walks to west Looe valley, close to moors and coast. Excellent locality for walking and relaxing.

Well Meadow *sleeps 2 people,* **Wagon** *sleeps 2/4 and* **Rose** *2/6*.

Heating, electricity, bed linen etc all inclusive. An ideal place for families and dogs alike. For a brochure or any information please contact:

Bill and Kaye Chapman on 01503 220251 * www.cornishcottage.net

Cornish Dream

Idyllic 18th Century 5 Star Country Cottages for romantics and animal lovers, near the sea. Your own delightful private garden with breathtaking views. Crackling log fires, candlelit meals, four-posters. On-farm riding, heated pool, tennis, wonderful walks.
Sea and golf nearby. Always open. Pets are welcome.

Tel: 01503 262730 • www.cornishdreamcottages.co.uk

Cornwall

Looe

Talehay Holiday Cottages
Pelynt, Near Looe PL13 2LT

A Quiet Haven in the Countryside near the Sea

Beautiful, traditional cottages with many original features retained provide superb holiday accommodation on 17C non-working farmstead. Set in 4 acres of unspoilt countryside offering peace and tranquillity with breathtaking coastal and country walks on your doorstep. This is an ideal location for dogs and their owners alike. Close to the Eden Project.

Tel: Mr & Mrs Dennett • 01503 220252
e-mail: infobookings@talehay.co.uk • www.talehay.co.uk

Contact us on 01503 272 667

AA 3 Star Award   AA Rosette Award

Talland Bay Hotel is situated in a unique position overlooking the bay on Cornwall's South Coast. Recently refurbished to enhance its stunning position with sea views from most bedrooms and of course the all important Terrace Restaurant where you can have lunch or an evening meal just gazing at those great sea views. Our commitment to ensuring every meal we serve is exceptional has been rewarded with two AA Rosettes. Our incredible location enables you to escape the hustle and bustle of everyday life and enjoy the peace and quiet that makes this hotel so very special.

THE TALLAND BAY HOTEL
PORTHALLOW, CORNWALL PL13 2JB
T: 01503 272667   E: info@tallandbayhotel.co.uk
www.tallandbayhotel.co.uk

Cottages for Romantics

Old world charm, log fires, antiques, beautifully furnished with the comforts of home. Private gardens, spectacular views, peace ~ for families, friends and couples to enjoy. Nestling on a south-facing hillside, near coast ~ heated pool, tennis, badminton, lake, shire horses, etc. Enchanting 70-acre estate with bluebell wood, walking and wildlife. Delicious fare also available by candlelight 'at home' or in our tiny inn.

O. Slaughter, Trefanny Hill, Duloe, Near Liskeard PL14 4QF
Tel: 01503 220 622
e-mail: enq@trefanny.co.uk
www.trefanny.co.uk

'relax in a little bit of heaven'

A Country Lover's Paradise with an abundance of country walks from your garden gate and coastal walks only 4 miles away.

THE COTTAGES AT *Trefanny Hill* Nr. LOOE

Discover the magic of Trefanny Hill

Cornwall

Looe

TREMAINE GREEN
for MEMORABLE HOLIDAYS

"A beautiful private hamlet" of 11 traditional cosy Cornish craftsmen's cottages between **Looe** and **Polperro.** Clean, comfortable and well equipped, with a warm friendly atmosphere, for pets with 2 to 8 people. Set in award-winning grounds, only 12 miles from the **Eden Project** with country and coastal walks nearby. Pets £18 pw; owners from only £126**.**

• Towels, Linen, Electric & Hot Water included • Dishwashers in larger cottages • Launderette • Kid's Play Area • Games Room • Tennis Court • TV/DVDs • Cots & Highchairs • Pubs & Restaurants in easy walking distance • Activities Area

Mr & Mrs J Spreckley, Tremaine Green Country Cottages, Pelynt, Near Looe, Cornwall PL13 2LT
www.tremainegreen.co.uk • e-mail: stay@tremainegreen.co.uk • **Tel: (01503) 220333**

Trenant Park Cottages

e-mail: Liz@holiday-cottage.com

Secluded traditional cottages set in the grounds of a country estate minutes from Looe and the coast.
- Private gardens and grounds
- Log fires and generous heating
- Delicious optional home-cooked food delivery
- Coastal path, woodland and moor walking nearby
- Well-behaved dogs welcome
- Open all year, winter short breaks

www.trenantcottages.com
www.trenantcottage.co.uk
Tel: 01503 263639

TREWITH HOLIDAY COTTAGES
Self Catering Accommodation Open All Year

**Paul & Barbie Higgins
Trewith, Duloe,
Near Liskeard
Cornwall
PL14 4PR**

enjoyEngland.com
★★★★
SELF CATERING

Tel: 01503 262184
mobile: 07968 262184

Situated in a superb elevated position of outstanding natural beauty. Just 1½ miles from Looe. Choice of 4 refurbished cottages with 1-3 bedrooms. Fully-equipped and tastefully furnished with full central heating. Use of laundry room. Peaceful location with delightful walks. Many beaches, coves, fishing, shopping close by in Looe. Because of ponds young children need supervision. Well behaved dogs welcome.

e-mail: info@trewith.co.uk • www.trewith.co.uk

Cornwall

Looe, Lostwithiel

- All accommodation dog friendly - 2 dogs maximum
- Individual fenced gardens
- Dog walk and off-lead paddock on site
- Many dog friendly beaches
- Dog friendly local pubs
- Day kennelling nearby
- Open all year
- Short breaks available

Valleybrook

Villas & Cottages

Nestling in a tranquil country valley in the heart of Cornish farmlands, bordered by a sparkling stream, the 6 superb villas and 2 delightful cottages are located between Fowey, Polperro and Looe and just 2½ miles from the SW Coastal Path. At Valleybrook you can enjoy the space and freedom of luxury self-catering accommodation with all of life's little luxuries and everyday conveniences at your fingertips. To make your stay even more special, pre-ordered chef selected local food can be delivered to your accommodation prior to your arrival.

Valleybrook Peakswater Lansallos
Looe Cornwall PL13 2QE

Tel: 01503 220493
www.valleybrookholidays.com

WRINGWORTHY COTTAGES
LOOE

Our 8 traditional stone cottages are set amongst unspoilt Cornish hills in 4 acres of space. Wringworthy is minutes from Looe with its stunning coastal path and sandy beaches. Walks from our door; dog-friendly beaches within a short drive. The perfect base to explore the delights of Cornwall and Devon – hidden gardens, Eden, Bodmin Moor, NT and more.

Sleeping 2-8, each cottage layout is unique but all are fully equipped with fridges, washing machines, DVD/video, microwaves, linen, towels etc. You can't help but relax at Wringworthy – outdoor heated pool, games barn, BBQ areas, lawns, outdoor games and friendly farm animals. Safe fun for children and wide open spaces for everyone.

Whether you take a short break or longer our heated cottages and warm welcome await you all year round.

Green Acorn Award holders for sustainable tourism and commitment to the environment.

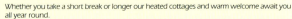

Tel: 01503 240685   www.wringworthy.co.uk   pets@wringworthy.co.uk

PENROSE
Bed & Breakfast

Elegant Victorian house with a homely atmosphere in the picturesque and historic town of Lostwithiel. Many local amenities.

Penrose Bed and Breakfast,
1 The Terrace, Lostwithiel,
Cornwall PL22 0DT
T : 01208 871417 M: 07766 900179
E: enquiries@penrosebb.co.uk
www.penrosebb.co.uk

Please mention **Pets Welcome!**
when making enquiries about accommodation featured in these pages

Cornwall

SOUTH WEST ENGLAND 85

Marazion, Mawgan Porth, Mevagissey, Mousehole

THE GODOLPHIN ARMS
West End, Marazion, Cornwall TR17 0EN

Perched on the edge of the sand, directly opposite St Michael's Mount. The Godolphin Arms has 10 en suite bedrooms, most with breathtaking sea views. Relaxing, comfortable bars and terraced beer garden. Perfect for exploring coast and coves.

01736 710202
e-mail: enquiries@godolphinarms.co.uk
www.godolphinarms.co.uk

Highly Commended in Cornwall Tourism Awards
"Pub of the Year"

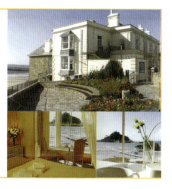

a secret shared.....

Hotel, Restaurant and Lodges in fantastic location between Padstow and Newquay overlooking Mawgan Porth beach

Hotel prices from £33 pppn
Lodge prices from £50 per lodge per night. Sleeps 4-8
01637 860324
visit our website at:
www.bluebaycornwall.co.uk

Kilbol Country House Hotel & Cottages
'Perfect Peace in Hidden Cornwall'

Polmassick, Mevagissey PL26 6HA

A small, cottage-style country hotel set in 5-acre grounds. Dating back to the 16th century, it has been fully refurbished and offers 8 rooms, as well as two self-catering cottages. Two miles from the Lost Gardens of Heligan and Mevagissey, and close to the Eden Project. Outdoor swimming pool, riverside walk, wooded area. No children under 12 years in the hotel. Pets welcome. **Winter & Christmas Breaks available.**

Tel: 01726 842481 • e-mail: Hotel@kilbol-hotel.co.uk • www.kilbol-hotel.co.uk

Traditional cottage, sleeps two to five. Linen, towels, electricity supplied. Beach one mile. Large garden. Central for touring/walking. Near Heligan Gardens and Eden Project. Pets welcome.
**MRS M.R. BULLED, MENAGWINS, GORRAN PL26 6HP
MEVAGISSEY 01726 843517**

POLVELLAN FLATS
Mousehole

In Mousehole, a quaint and unspoilt fishing village, is a personally supervised and fully equipped self-catering flat, with full sea views. It has a microwave, cooker, fridge, and TV; all bedding and towels provided. Pets welcome. Open all year.

Contact Mr A.G. Wright, Leafields Farm, Uttoxeter Road, Abbots Bromley, Staffs WS15 3EH
Tel & Fax: 01283 840651 • e-mail: alang23@hotmail.com

Quarryfield Holiday Park

CAMPING AND TOURING • CARAVANS

Bar • Pool Children's Play Area

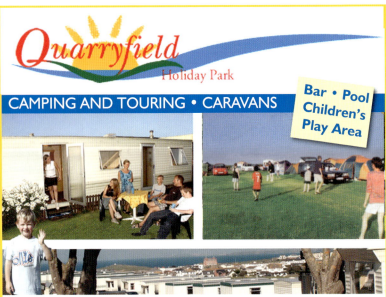

Welcome to Quarryfield Holiday Park

Quarryfield Holiday Park, situated in Crantock near Newquay, is the perfect location for your camping or touring holiday.

Situated overlooking the beautiful Crantock Beach, and next to the estuary of the River Gannel, you have plenty of choices on how to spend your time. You can relax on the beach, swim, surf or just play with the children, or you can walk up alongside the river, which is particularly beautiful. Newquay is just on the other side of the estuary and is within walking distance. If the tide is in then just take the row boat ferry to get across the river.

Quarryfield is a well established Holiday Park wtih 150 pitches, 50 hook up points, 42 Static Caravans and 2 chalets. With all this space and variety we are bound to have something to suit your needs!

The site itself is large enough to enjoy plenty of room for playing and for the family to spread out and enjoy their holiday. Outdoor swimming pool. Small shop on site.

The on-site Inn allows the family to enjoy some drinks and food as well as the shop which has plenty of supplies. And an amusement arcade with pool table and other facilities is available also to help keep the children busy and entertained.

Contact: MRS WINN, TRETHERRAS, NEWQUAY, CORNWALL TR7 2RE
Tel & Fax: 01637 872792
e-mail: quarryfield@crantockcaravans.orangehome.co.uk
www.quarryfield.co.uk

Cornwall
Newquay, Padstow

SOUTH WEST ENGLAND

A park for all seasons

Trethiggey Touring Park

Quintrell Downs, Newquay TR8 4QR

Our friendly, family-run park is just minutes by car from Newquay's famous surf beaches and 15 miles from the amazing Eden Project. Beautifully landscaped, the park has panoramic countryside views and is ideal for touring caravans, tents and campervans.

We also have luxury holiday homes for hire. Facilities include shop, off-licence, free showers, electric hook-ups, laundry, children's play area, TV/games room, fishing, cafe, licensed bar, Bistro, take-away food in summer.

Open from March 1st to January 1st including Christmas and New Year. Short Breaks available. Off season rallies welcome.

For more information phone 01637 877672 or see our website: www.Trethiggey.co.uk e-mail: enquiries@trethiggey.co.uk

Retorrick Mill • *Self-catering accommodation*

offers two cottages, six chalets, traditional camping and licensed bar. Set in 27 acres and nestled within the tranquil Lanherne Valley, perfectly located for Cornwall's finest beaches, attractions and activities. Pets, including horses, are very welcome.

For a brochure or further assistance please contact Chris Williams.

The Granary, Retorrick Mill, St Mawgan, Newquay TR8 4BH
Tel: 01637 860460
www.retorrickmill.co.uk • e-mail: wilf@retorrickmill.co.uk

On the outskirts of picturesque St Mawgan village between Newquay and Padstow

Cornwall's best kept secret

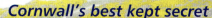

Dewolf Guest House 100 Henver Road, Newquay TR7 3BL

The amenities of Newquay are close at hand. Porth Beach only a short walk from the Guest House. Single, Double and Family rooms, all en suite, plus two chalet-style rooms. From £30 per person. Licensed. Off-road parking. Open all year. Suitable for M1 disabled. Non-smoking.

Dogs welcome AA ★★★★

Tel: 01637 874746 • e-mail: holidays@dewolfguesthouse.com • www.dewolfguesthouse.com

"Yes, you can bring your dog!"

Here at The Metropole we welcome dogs and their owners. This is an ideal base for lots of walks on the coast path and some of the beaches.
See our website for more details of the hotel and best available rates.
www.the-metropole.co.uk or give us a call on **0800 2300 365**
The Metropole Hotel, Padstow, Cornwall PL28 8DB

Cornwall

Padstow, Penzance, Perranporth

The best family houses to let at Padstow's beaches around Trevose Head in North Cornwall

- Yards from the best beaches, the best walking, the best golf and the best restaurants in Cornwall.
- Enjoy holidays with family, friends, and your dogs.

Email enquiries@raintreehouseholidays.co.uk
or ring 01841 520228
www.raintreehouseholidays.co.uk

The most dog friendly houses and beaches

A warm welcome awaits pets and owners alike at Penmorvah. We are ideally situated for long coastal walks and exploring, and shops and restaurants are in easy walking distance.
Penmorvah Guest Accommodation, 61 Alexandra Road, Penzance TR18 4LZ • 01736 363711
www.penmorvah.net • e-mail: penmorvah_penzance@talktalk.net

TORWOOD HOUSE HOTEL
ALEXANDRA ROAD, PENZANCE TR18 4LZ
01736 360063

Torwood is a small, family-run Victorian hotel, situated in a beautiful tree-lined avenue 500 metres from the seafront and town centre. All rooms en suite, with TV/DVD, tea/coffee makers, central heating and radios. Comfortable dining area where a generous full English breakfast is served - other options available on request. Dinner available on request. Well behaved pets by arrangement. B&B from £25-£29pppn, evening meal £18.

For further details telephone LYNDA SOWERBY

e-mail: Lyndasowerby@aol.com • ww.torwoodhousehotel.co.uk

Near Perranporth

Greenmeadow Cottages

Highly praised luxury cottages. Sleep 6.
Superbly clean, comfortable and spacious.
Open all year. Short Breaks out of season.
Pets welcome in two of the cottages.
Non-smoking. Ample off-road parking.
For brochure and bookings
Tel: 01872 540483
www.greenmeadow-cottages.co.uk

FHG Guides

publish a large range of well-known accommodation guides.
We will be happy to send you details or you can use the order form
at the back of this book.

• POLPERRO •
near LOOE, CORNWALL

VIEW FROM THE PROPERTIES

Affectionately let for 30 years for good old-fashioned family holidays, as well as for friends and couples to enjoy, where pets and children are most welcome.

Comfortable holiday cottages, built around 250 years ago, full of character and charm, sleeping from 2 -14, with sunny terraced gardens, giving a Mediterranean-type setting.

Definitely located in one of the best positions in the village, directly overlooking picturesque harbour, of 16th century origins with smuggling connections, now a conservation area. 14 miles breathtaking panoramic sea views, stretching to Eddystone Lighthouse, with naval shipping, ocean-going yachts, local fishing boats and pleasure craft often forming part of the seascape.

The cottages are only 2 minutes from shops, excellent selection of quality restaurants, tearooms, olde-worlde pubs and the availability of Cornish pasties, ice cream and fish and chips. Close by, there is a small, sandy beach with rock pools, quay, pier and rock fishing and the beginning of miles of unspoilt National Trust cliff walks along stunning coastal paths of outstanding natural beauty, leading to outlying hamlets, with rocky inlets, beaches, coves and 13th century churches.
Between Looe and Fowey, on South Cornish coast, 25 miles city of Plymouth, 12 miles A38 and 15 miles Eden Project.

Prices from £175-£595 per cottage, per week
• PETS COME FREE • PRIVATE PARKING FREE

For brochure, please telephone GRAHAM WRIGHTS OFFICES

01579 344080

Cornwall
Polperro, Port Gaverne

Classy Cottages

2 cottages just feet from beach in Polperro + 3 other coastal cottages. Out of season all cottages priced for 2 people. Cottages sleep 2-16.

Access to INDOOR POOL, well equipped GYM and TENNIS COURTS

Very high quality cottages with open log fires. Pets very welcome.

Please contact FIONA and MARTIN NICOLLE on 01720 423000
e-mail: nicolle@classycottages.co.uk • www.classycottages.co.uk

Step onto The Coastal Path...

Escape the pressures of life. Relax! explore the Cornish Coast from Green Door Cottages in Port Gaverne.

8 comfortable, restored 18th Century cottages set around a sheltered courtyard, plus 2 prestigious apartments with panoramic sea views beside a picturesque cove, directly on the Coastal path, less than half a mile from Port Isaac.

An ideal location for your holiday and short breaks. Well behaved dogs are very welcome.

Call now for a brochure on:
01208 880293

Green Door Cottages
PORT GAVERNE
email: enquiries@greendoorcottages.co.uk
web: www.greendoorcottages.co.uk

★★★★ SELF CATERING

Cornwall

SOUTH WEST ENGLAND

Polruan, Porthleven, Port Isaac

POLRUAN-BY-FOWEY
Lovely property near quay.
Superb views. Parking (for 2 cars). Garden,
Sleeps 6/8. Pets.
Woodburning stove.
Enjoy sailing, fishing, walking or just watching!
Pubs and shops.

People say "Good Morning!"

Brochure & Bookings: 01726 870582
www.polruancottages.co.uk

PORTHLEVEN *"Kernow agas dynargh" - "Cornwall welcomes you"*
Fishermen's cottages. Harbour, bay or country views.
3 minutes to beach, coast path, harbourside eating places.
Open fires. Pets welcome. **Tel: 01209 860410**

The Garden House   near Port Isaac, Cornwall

Secure garden for dogs (1 large or 2 small maximum). Doggy shower. Lovely far-reaching view across open countryside. Very warm and cosy for all year round. Full central heating, electricity, bed linen and towels included. One bedroom with twin or double. Lounge/kitchen/dining and shower room all fully equipped to very high standards.
Central location in small quiet hamlet near Michaelstow and within 8 miles of Port Isaac, Boscastle, Tintagel, Polzeath, Rock, Wadebridge, Bodmin Moor and Camel Trail. From £188 pw.
Contact David & Jenny Oldham • 01208 850529
Trevella, Treveighan, St Teath, Cornwall PL30 3JN
email: david.trevella@btconnect.com   www.trevellacornwall.co.uk

This renowned 17th century inn is situated in an unspoilt fishing cove on the rugged North Coast of Cornwall. The beach is just 50 yards from the front door and the Coastal Path offers miles of breathtaking scenery. For a relaxing break with a friendly atmosphere you need look no further. Golf, fishing, sailing and riding are all nearby.
Pets welcome in the Inn and Self-catering accommodation available.

Port Gaverne Hotel Near Port Isaac, Cornwall PL29 3SQ Tel: 01208 880244 Fax: 01208 880151

LONGCROSS HOTEL & VICTORIAN GARDENS
TRELIGHTS, PORT ISAAC PL29 3TF

Lovely Victorian country house hotel with four acres of restored gardens set in beautiful tranquil location overlooking the coast. Close to the area's best beaches, golf courses and other attractions. Spacious, comfortable interior, with newly refurbished en suite bedrooms and suites.

Tel: 01208 880243
www.longcrosshotel.co.uk

SOUTH WEST ENGLAND

Cornwall
Port Isaac, Portreath, St Agnes

GULLROCK COTTAGES
Port Gaverne Port Isaac North Cornwall

Personal attention from resident owner ensures your home from home comfort in a tranquil setting just yards from the sea at bygone Port Gaverne.
Tel: Malcolm Lee (01208) 880106 • www.gullrock-port-gaverne.co.uk

Friesian Valley Cottages

Six luxury cottages in the peaceful rural hamlet of Mawla, one mile from the beaches of Portreath and Porthtowan, on Atlantic coast. Near to the National Trust coastal paths, between St Ives and Newquay. Swimming, surfing, horse riding, boat trips, cycle hire, golf, lake and sea fishing. We are central for Eden, National Trust gardens and many other attractions. Games room, laundrette and ample parking. Sleep two to six. Open all year.

£180 to £635 per week. For brochure please ring 01209 890901

- Caravan Holiday Homes
- Touring & Camping
- Families & Couples
- Pets Welcome
- Exclusive leisure facility:
- Gym, Sauna & Steamroom
- Shop • Free Wifi
- Laundry room • Games room
- Children's play area
- Multi-service hook-ups
- Satellite TV in all units
- No club, bar or disco

Chiverton Park

Set in the heart of Cornish countryside, yet only a short distance from superb beaches, this spacious, well-run park offers peace and relaxation in a delightful rural setting. Holiday homes are fully equipped (except linen, which may be hired)

Chiverton Park, Blackwater, Truro TR4 8HS • 01872 560667
info@chivertonpark.co.uk • www.chivertonpark.co.uk

Blue Hills TOURING PARK
Cross Coombe, Trevellas, St Agnes, Cornwall TR5 0XP

Set in a beautiful rural position close to a coastal footpath, a small site with good toilets. A pleasant location for exploring nearby coves, beaches and villages.
2-acre site with 30 touring pitches
01872 552999 • loo@zoom.co.uk
www.bluehillscamping.co.uk

Cornwall
Portwrinkle

Whitsand Bay
SELF CATERING HOLIDAYS

www.whitsandbayselfcatering.co.uk

Children and pet-friendly

Whitsand Bay Self Catering Holidays have Holiday Houses, Cottages and Villas, sleeping 4-10, to rent in Portwrinkle in Cornwall. Portwrinkle itself is located directly on the UK's heritage coastline in a designated Area of Outstanding Natural Beauty. All our accommodation has sea views and is priced to suit all pockets.

Whatever your holiday requirements, we're sure you'll find something to your liking, be it an active holiday with golf, swimming, walking or fishing, or just relaxing on our local beaches. For those more culturally minded there are historic fishing villages, historic homes and gardens as well as the Eden Project and Lost Gardens of Heligan, both only 40 minutes away.

Tel: 01579 345688
e-mail: ehwbsc@hotmail.com

SOUTH WEST ENGLAND — Cornwall
St Agnes, St Austell

Driftwood Spars   St. Agnes

Dining Bars Music Rooms Brewery *"Priding ourselves on serving the best of local produce"*

Built in 1650 with Enormous Beams. Serving Breakfast, Morning Coffees

Brunch, Light Lunches, Cakes, Desserts, Evening Meals

& The Best Roast on the North Coast. Live Music every Weekend

En Suite Rooms Available With Sea or Garden View. Pets Welcome

CAMRA Kernow Pub of The Year 2009

www.driftwoodspars.co.uk   (01872) 552428

PENKERRIS — Penwinnick Road, St Agnes TR5 0PA
Tel & Fax: 01872 552262
Dorothy Gill-Carey
B&B/Guest House/Hotel with lawned garden, picnic tables, barbeque, ample parking. Comfortable rooms, "real" food. Country/cliff walks, beaches (dog-friendly). B&B £20-£35pppn. Open all year. ETC ★★ *Guest House.*
e-mail: info@penkerris.co.uk • www.penkerris.co.uk

BOSINVER FARM COTTAGES

Best Self-catering Establishment 2005, 2006 & 2007 • Cornwall Tourism Awards

Bosinver's individual farm cottages are so nice our guests often don't want to leave. Here you can relax in real comfort, with 30 acres of wildflower meadows to walk your dog, and a short stroll to the village pub. Located near St Austell and the sea, Bosinver is a great base for glorious walks, Heligan Gardens and the Eden Project. Ideal all year round, particularly spring, autumn and winter when the crowds are gone, the colours are changing and the cottages are as warm as the welcome.

Brochure from: Mrs Pat Smith, Bosinver Farm, Trelowth, St Austell, Cornwall PL26 7DT
01726 72128 • e-mail: reception@bosinver.co.uk
www.bosinver.co.uk

www.holidayguides.com

Cornwall
St Ives, St Mawes

The Links Holiday Flats
Lelant, St Ives
Cornwall
TR26 3HY

If it's views you want, this is the place for you!

- Magnificent location alongside and overlooking West Cornwall Golf Course, Hayle Estuary and St Ives Bay.
- Both flats have lovely views. Wonderful spot for walking.
- Five minutes from the beach and dogs are allowed there all year round.
- Two well-equipped flats which are open all year.

Your hosts are Bob and Jacky Pontefract
Phone 01736 753326
e-mail: bobandjacky@btinternet.com

SANDBANK HOLIDAYS
St Ives Bay, Hayle,
Cornwall TR27 5BL
www.sandbank-holidays.co.uk

High quality Apartments and Bungalows for 2-6 persons. Peaceful garden setting close to miles of sandy beach, acres of grassy dunes and SW Fully equipped for your self-catering holiday. Heated, Colour TV, Microwave etc. Spotlessly clean. Coastal Path. **Dogs Welcome.**

All major debit and credit cards accepted.

Tel: 01736 752594

Sea Pink
Near St Mawes, South Cornwall

Nestling in a picturesque setting overlooking the little bay of St Just-in-Roseland, Sea Pink is ideally located for exploring the coast and attractions. Recently refurbished, there is a spacious lounge, dining area opening on to sun terrace and lawned garden; three bedrooms. Brochure available.

Contact Judy Juniper • Tel: 01872 863553
e-mail: cottageinfo@btconnect.com • www.luxury-holiday-cottages.com

Dalswinton House

St. Mawgan-in-Pydar, Cornwall TR8 4EZ. Tel: 01637 860385
www.dalswinton.com • dalswintonhouse@tiscali.co.uk

HOLIDAYS FOR DOGS AND THEIR OWNERS

Overlooking the village of St Mawgan, Dalswinton House stands in 10 acres of gardens and meadowland midway between Padstow and Newquay with distant views to the sea at dog-friendly Mawgan Porth.

- Dogs free of charge and allowed everywhere except the restaurant
- 8 acre meadow for dog exercise. Nearby local walks. Beach 1.5 miles
- Heated outdoor pool (May-Sep). Off street car parking
- All rooms en suite with tea/coffee fac., digital TV and clock radios
- Wifi access in public rooms and some bedrooms
- Residents' bar and restaurant serving breakfast and dinner
- Bed and breakfast from £44 per person per night
- Weekly rates available and special offers in Mar/Apr/May/Oct
- Self-catering lodge sleeps 3 adults
- Easy access to Padstow, Eden Project, Newquay Airport & Coastal Path
- New from 2009: dog-friendly self-catering near Falmouth

Regret no children under 16
Maximum 3 dogs per room at proprietor's discretion

Cornwall

SOUTH WEST ENGLAND

St Tudy, St Wenn, Tintagel, Tregarne, Truro

Comfortable end of terrace cottage in picturesque and friendly village. Enclosed garden and parking. Ideal location for exploring all Cornwall. Short Breaks and brochure available. Contact:
MRS R. REEVES, POLSTRAUL, TREWALDER, DELABOLE PL33 9ET
Tel & Fax: 01840 213100 • e-mail: ruth.reeves@hotmail.co.uk
www.maymear.co.uk

TREWITHIAN FARM — St Wenn, Bodmin PL30 5PH

Comfortable, well equipped wing of farmhouse, edge of Bodmin Moor, central location in Cornwall. Beautiful countryside, very secluded position. Sleeps 2, satellite TV, central heating. Dog welcome, use of kennels and exercise field. Good walking and dog-friendly beaches nearby. Excellent winter rates.

Tel: 01208 895181 www.cornwall-online.co.uk/trewithianfarm

Comfortable, well-equipped, centrally heated cottages sleeping two. Ideal for touring, walking and relaxing. Close to Coastal Path and village amenities. Private parking. Ring for brochure. Pets free.
MR & MRS N. CAREY, SALUTATIONS, ATLANTIC ROAD, TINTAGEL PL34 0DE • 01840 770287
e-mail: salutations@talktalk.net • www.salutationstintagel.co.uk

The Hen House • Tregarne, Near Helford TR12 6EW, B&B or Self-Catering
Idyllic peaceful country setting a mile from the sea. Superb walks in all directions with year-round dog-friendly beaches. Delightful spacious barns each opening onto the courtyard garden. Wild flower meadow, bird song and complete relaxation. Complimentary tai-chi. Hearty local breakfast platters. Award winners for green ethos and quality.

Phone 01326 280316 • e-mail: henhouseuk@aol.com • www.thehenhouse-cornwall.co.uk

TRENONA FARM
Ruan High Lanes, Truro, Cornwall TR2 5JS

Enjoy a relaxing stay on this mixed farm, on the unspoilt Roseland Peninsula midway between Truro and the Eden Project at St Austell.
B&B in the Victorian farmhouse in double/family rooms, either en suite or with private bathroom.
Self-catering in three renovated barns, two sleeping 6, the other sleeping 4, all well equipped and furnished. Ample parking with room for boats and trailers.
Pets welcome by arrangement. Wheelchair access.

Tel: 01872 501339 • e-mail: info@trenonafarmholidays.co.uk • www.trenonafarmholidays.co.uk

Cornwall

Truro, Wadebridge

King Harry Cottages
CORNWALL

High Quality Cottages to let near Truro & Falmouth

Two cosy cottages nestled in woodland above the River Fal in Cornwall, both with views over the river. Free use of boat. Dogs welcome. Near Truro.

t: 01872 861917
e: beverley@kingharry.net
www.kingharrycottages.co.uk

King Harry Cottages,
2 Ferry Cottages, Feock, Truro,
Cornwall TR3 6QJ

Higher Trewithen is the ideal centre for your pet and your family. We are surrounded by public footpaths and have 3½ acres of fields.

www.trewithen.com • trewithen@talk21.com

Higher Trewithen, Stithians, Truro, Cornwall TR3 7DR • Tel: 01209 860863

Our three luxury cottages are converted from original farm buildings and feature mellow stone elevations under slate roofs. Sleeping between 2 and 7 and surrounded by open Cornish farmland, Colesent is ideally situated between the coast (Padstow, Wadebridge, Rock & Polzeath) and Bodmin Moor. The inland start of the famous "Camel Trail" is at the end of our drive and provides a traffic free walking and cycling path to Bodmin, Wadebridge and Padstow. Two dogs welcome per cottage.

CORNWALL TOURISM AWARDS 2002 - Self Catering Establishment of the Year - Highly Commended.

GARY & MAUREEN NEWMAN, COLESENT COTTAGES, ST TUDY, WADEBRIDGE PL30 4QX
Tel & Fax: 01208 850112 • e-mail: relax@colesent.co.uk • www.colesent.co.uk

Please mention **Pets Welcome!**
when making enquiries about accommodation featured in these pages

Free or reduced rate entry to
Holiday Visits and Attractions - see our
READERS' OFFER VOUCHERS on pages 445-454

Cornwall

SOUTH WEST ENGLAND

TOAD HALL COTTAGES (01548 853089 24 hrs). 300 outstanding waterside and rural properties in truly beautiful locations in Devon, Cornwall and Exmoor. Call for our highly acclaimed brochure. Pets welcome.
e-mail: thc@toadhallcottages.co.uk website: www.toadhallcottages.co.uk

FARM & COTTAGE HOLIDAYS (01237 459897). An inspiring collection of holiday cottages throughout Cornwall, Devon, Somerset and Dorset in stunning rural and coastal locations. [Pets £20 per week]
website: www.holidaycottages.co.uk

CORNISH TRADITIONAL COTTAGES. A fine selection of self-catering cottages on both coasts of Cornwall and on Scilly. Pets welcome in many cottages. Free colour brochure: 01208 821666 or visit our website. [Pets £16 per week]
website: www.corncott.com

CORNISH SEAVIEW COTTAGES (01428 723819). Ideal for walking coastal paths and accessing beaches. Pets welcome at most. Furnished and equipped to high standard; all have central heating, dishwashers etc. Visit our website for photos and virtual tours. [Pets £20 per week].
e-mail: enquiries@cornishseaviewcottages.co.uk   website: www.cornishseaviewcottages.co.uk

WEST CORNWALL COTTAGE HOLIDAYS, 4 ALBERT STREET, PENZANCE TR18 2LR (01736 368575). Coastal and country cottages, town houses and apartments. Pets with well behaved owners welcome in many of our properties. [Charge for pets.]
website: www.westcornwallcottageholidays.com

Bodmin

Quaint county town of Cornwall, standing steeply on the edge of Bodmin Moor. Pretty market town and touring centre. Plymouth 31 miles, Newquay 20, Wadebridge 7.

PENROSE BURDEN, ST BREWARD, BODMIN PL30 4LZ (01208 850277 & 850617; Fax: 01208 850915). Holiday Care Award Winning Cottages featured on TV. Open all year. Outstanding views over wooded valley. Free Salmon and Trout fishing. Superb walking area. Dogs welcome, wheelchair accessible. [Pets £15 per week]
website: www.penroseburden.co.uk

Bodmin Moor

Superb walking area attaining a height of 1375 feet at Brown Willy, the highest point in Cornwall.

HENWOOD BARNS HOLIDAY COTTAGES, HENWOOD, LISKEARD PL14 5BP (01579 363576/07956 864263). Three stone barns set around original courtyard on the edge of Bodmin Moor, with stunning views. Tranquil, village location, horse riding two minutes' walk. Woodburning stoves; sleep 2/5; within easy reach of North Cornwall and Devon. [Pets £15 per week]
e-mail: henwoodbarns@tiscali.co.uk   website: www.henwoodbarns.co.uk

DARRYNANE COTTAGES, DARRYNANE, ST BREWARD, BODMIN MOOR PL30 4LZ (Tel & Fax: 01208 850885). Absolutely fabulous detached cottages. Set in private gated gardens. Unique moorland valley setting. Waterfalls, woods, river. Woodburning stoves, four-poster beds, Eden Project and Camel Trail close by. [Pets £15 per week, £7 per short break]
e-mail: enquiries@darrynane.co.uk   website:www.darrynane.co.uk

Botallack

Village 2 miles North of St Just.

TREVAYLOR CARAVAN & CAMPING PARK, BOTALLACK TR19 7PU (01736 787016). Sheltered grassy site in a peaceful location at the western tip of Cornwall. The dramatic coastline and the pretty villages nearby are truly unspoilt. Clean, well maintained facilities and a good shop are offered, along with a bar serving bar meals. 6-acre site with 50 touring pitches. AA 3 Pennants. [🐾]
e-mail: trevaylor@cornishcamping.co.uk   website: www.cornishcamping.co.uk

SOUTH WEST ENGLAND — Cornwall

Bude

Popular seaside resort overlooking a wide bay of golden sand and flanked by spectacular cliffs. Ideal for surfing; sea water swimming pool for safe bathing.

IVYLEAF BARTON HOLIDAY COTTAGES, NEAR BUDE EX23 9LD. Five cottages sleeping 2-8 in converted stone barns, well equipped with all modern conveniences. Laundry. Tennis court. Certain cottages welcome pets. ★★★★/★★★★★ Contact: ROBERT B. BARRETT (01288 321237 or 07525 251773). [Pets £20 per week].
e-mail: info@ivyleafbarton.co.uk   website: www.ivyleafbarton.co.uk

HEDLEY WOOD CARAVAN & CAMPING PARK, BRIDGERULE, (NR BUDE), HOLSWORTHY EX22 7ED (01288 381404). 16 acre woodland family-run site; children's adventure areas, bar, clubroom, shop, laundry, meals & all amenities. Static caravans for hire, Caravan Storage available. Dog walk nature trail. See main advertisement under Bude. [pw! 🐕]
website: www.hedleywood.co.uk

Crackington Haven

Small coastal village in North Cornwall set amidst fine cliff scenery. Small sandy beach, Launceston 18 miles, Bude 10, Camelford 10.

HENTERVENE HOLIDAY PARK, CRACKINGTON HAVEN, NEAR BUDE EX23 0LF (01840 230365). Luxury caravans to let. First-class facilities for families and pets. Open all year. Short breaks. Caravan and Lodge Sales. [Pets £20 per week].
e-mail: contact@hentervene.co.uk   website: www.hentervene.co.uk

Five 18th century converted barns, beamed ceilings, log fires and secluded rural setting. Ideal touring base. Five miles to coast at Crackington Haven. Sleep 2/6. Pets welcome. Open all year. From £100 short breaks, £195 per week. ETC ★★★/★★★★. GOLD AWARD. APPLY: LORRAINE HARRISON, TRENANNICK COTTAGES, WARBSTOW, LAUNCESTON PL15 8RP (01566 781443). [pw! Pets £10 per stay]
e-mail: trenannick–1@tiscali.co.uk   website: www.trenannickcottages.co.uk

MINESHOP, CRACKINGTON HAVEN, BUDE EX23 0NR. Cornish Character Cottages, sleep 1 to 8, in tranquil location. Footpath leads through fields/woods to beach/pub. Excellent walking, breathtaking scenery. Open all year. Proud to be inspected and featured in The Good Holiday Cottage Guide. For more details phone CHARLIE or JANE (01840 230338). [£17 per pet per week.]
e-mail: info@mineshop.co.uk   website: www.mineshop.co.uk

Crantock

Village near the coast 2 miles/3 km SW of Newquay across the River Gannel.

CRANTOCK BAY HOTEL, WEST PENTIRE, CRANTOCK TR8 5SE (01637 830229; Fax: 01637 831111). Superbly located for a holiday with your dogs; beach 10 minutes' walk. Comfortable bedrooms, quality restaurant, indoor pool, tennis etc. AA ★★★ [Pets £5 per night]
e-mail: stay@crantockbayhotel.co.uk   website: www.crantockbayhotel.co.uk

Falmouth

Well-known port and resort on Fal estuary, ideal for boating, sailing and fishing; safe bathing from sandy beaches. Of interest is Pendennis Castle (18th century). Newquay 26, Penzance 26, Truro 11.

SELF-CATERING BUNGALOW. Sleeps 6. Walking distance of harbour and town. Dogs welcome. For prices and availability contact MRS J.A. SIMMONS (01277 654425) or see our website. ETC ★★★. [Pets £10 per week]
website: www.parklandsbungalow.co.uk

PETER WATSON, CREEKSIDE HOLIDAY HOUSES, RESTRONGUET, FALMOUTH TR11 5ST (01326 372722). Spacious houses sleep 2/4/6/8. Peaceful, picturesque water's edge hamlet. Boating facilities. Use of boat. Own quay, beach. Secluded gardens. Near Pandora Inn. Friday bookings. Dogs welcome. [Pets £15 per week]
website: www.creeksideholidayhouses.co.uk

Cornwall

CREEKSIDE COTTAGES offer a fine selection of individual water's edge, village and rural cottages, sleeping from 2-10. All offer peaceful, comfortable and fully equipped accommodation. Just come and relax. For a colour brochure phone 01326 375972. [Pets £20 per week]
website: www.creeksidecottages.co.uk

PENMORVAH MANOR HOTEL & COURTYARD COTTAGES, BUDOCK WATER, NEAR FALMOUTH TR11 5ED (01326 250277; Fax: 01326 250509). Situated in 6 acres of mature gardens and woodland. Ideal for visiting Cornwall's superb gardens.Close to Falmouth and Coastal Paths. Well behaved dogs welcome. AA ★★★ Hotel, ETC ★★★★ Self-catering. [Pets £7.50 per night.]
e-mail: reception@penmorvah.co.uk   website: www.penmorvah.co.uk

CORNISH HOLIDAY COTTAGES (01326 250339). Quality, self-catering accommodation in Falmouth and Helford River. Call for a FREE brochure.
website: www.CornishHolidayCottages.net

SUE & DICK BARRETT, TUDOR COURT, 55 MELVILL ROAD, FALMOUTH TR11 4DF (01326 312807) Strikingly stylish, mock-Tudor family-run guest house, in award-winning gardens. Comfortable, friendly, non-smoking accommodation, a short walk from town and beaches. Open all year incl. Christmas.
e-mail: enquiries@tudorcourthotel.com   website: www.tudorcourtguesthouse.co.uk

Fowey

Historic town, now a busy harbour, Regatta and Carnival Week in August.

LANCROW BARN, NEAR FOWEY (01726 814263). Quality barn conversion close to sea with spectacular views. Amdega Conservatory, open plan sitting room. Well equipped kitchen. 3 en suite bedrooms.Large enclosed garden with BBQ. Pets welcome. [Pets £20 per week]
e-mail: sarahfurniss@aol.com   website: www.rentahouseincornwall.com

OLD FERRY INN, BODINNICK-BY-FOWEY PL23 1LX (01726 870237; Fax: 01726 870116). Family-run Inn, ideal for many varied walks. Excellent à la carte restaurant; bar meals available. Comfortable bedrooms with colour TV and tea/coffee. Rate £90-£130 per night for two people sharing. ETC ★★★★ Inn [Pets £3.50 per night per pet]
e-mail: royce972@aol.com   website: www.oldferryinn.com

DRIFTWOOD, POLRUAN-BY-FOWEY. Dogs encouraged!! Spacious and well presented holiday cottage sleeping 2-8. Great views and fabulous walks on doorstep. Garden/ch/woodburner/broadband. Lovely village with shops, quay (ferry to Fowey) and 2 pubs. £400 - £1500 pw. Contact: MRS S. COKER (01608 674601).
website: www.seasidecottageholiday.co.uk

Helford

Village on Helford River 6 miles East of Helston.

Enchanting creekside cottages in a timeless and tranquil hamlet. Stunning coastal and riverside walks, country inns, local food, warm and comfortable with cosy log fires. Boat hire, moorings. Short breaks. Open all year. ST ANTHONY HOLIDAYS, MANACCAN, HELFORD TR12 6JW (01326 231 357). [Pets £3 per night, £21 per week].
e-mail: info@stanthony.co.uk   website: www.StAnthony.co.uk

Helston

Ancient Stannary town and excellent touring centre, noted for the annual "Furry Dance". Nearby is Looe Pool, separated from the sea by a bar. Truro 17 miles, St Ives 15, Redruth 11, Falmouth & Penzance 12.

BOSCREGE CARAVAN & CAMPING PARK, ASHTON, HELSTON TR13 9TG (01736 762231) Award-winning, quiet, family park close to beaches and attractions. No bar or clubs. Laundry. Static vans available. Pets welcome. AA Three Pennants. [🐾]
e-mail: enquiries@caravanparkcornwall.com   website: www.caravanparkcornwall.com

SILVER SANDS HOLIDAY PARK, GWENDREATH, KENNACK SANDS, RUAN MINOR, HELSTON TR12 7LZ (Tel/Fax: 01326 290631). Quiet, family-run park. Pets welcome with well-trained owners. Short walk through woodland path to award-winning dog beach. Choice of holiday homes, touring and camping. ETC ★★★★, AA 3 Pennants.
website: www.silversandsholidaypark.co.uk

Launceston

Town on hill above River Kensey, 20 miles NW of Plymouth.

SWALLOWS & MEADOW COTTAGE. Well equipped cottages with field to the rear. Riverside walks. TV lounge and kitchen. Centrally located for visiting NT houses and gardens, Dartmoor, Bodmin Moor, beaches and harbours. Pets welcome by arrangement. ETC ★★★ Contact: LOWER DUTSON FARM, LAUNCESTON PL15 9SP (01566 776456).
e-mail: holidays@farm-cottage.co.uk　　　website: www.farm-cottage.co.uk

Liskeard

Pleasant market town and good centre for exploring East Cornwall. Bodmin Moor and the quaint fishing villages of Looe and Polperro are near at hand. Plymouth 19 miles, St Austell 19 miles, Launceston 16, Fowey (via ferry) 15, Bodmin 13, Looe 9.

SUE JEWELL, BOTURNELL FARM COTTAGES, ST PINNOCK, LISKEARD PL14 4QS (01579 320880). Cosy character cottages set in 25 acres of fields and woodland between Looe and Bodmin. Linen, electricity included. Well equipped. Dog creche. Pets welcome free. [🐾]
e-mail: sue@dogs-holiday.co.uk　　　website: www.dogs-holiday.co.uk

BUTTERDON MILL HOLIDAY HOMES, MERRYMEET, LISKEARD PL14 3LS (01579 342636) Two-bedroom detached bungalows on idyllic rural site. Sleep up to six. Games barn; children's play areas. Ideal for touring coasts & moors. Discounts for Senior Citizens/couples Sept to June. Brochure available. [🐾]
e-mail: butterdonmill@btconnect.com　　　website: www.bmhh.co.uk

CUTKIVE WOOD HOLIDAY LODGES, ST IVE, LISKEARD PL14 3ND (01579 362216). Six well-equipped comfortable cedar-clad lodges on country estate with wonderful views. Great for children, dogs welcome. Ideal for coasts, beaches, moors etc. Short breaks. Open all year. [pw! Pets £10 per week]
e-mail: holidays@cutkivewood.co.uk　　　website: www.cutkivewood.co.uk

CELIA HUTCHINSON, CARADON COUNTRY COTTAGES, EAST TAPHOUSE, NEAR LISKEARD PL14 4NH (Tel & Fax: 01579 320355). Luxury cottages in the heart of the Cornish countryside. Ideal centre for exploring Devon and Cornwall, coast and moor and Eden Project. Meadow and paddock (enclosed). Central heating and log burners for cosy off-season breaks. [pw! Pets £15 per week.]
e-mail: celia@caradoncottages.co.uk　　　website: www.caradoncottages.co.uk

LINDA & NEIL HOSKEN, HOPSLAND HOLIDAYS, HOPSLAND COMMONMOOR, LISKEARD, CORNWALL PL14 6EJ (Tel & Fax: 01579 344480). Hi, I'm Ki, an adorable border collie. Come and stay with your pets at my converted barn cottages. Fully equipped, all with DVD. Own field to exercise in or 150 yards from open moorland. ETC ★★★★ [pw! 🐾]
e-mail: hopslandholidays@btinternet.com　　　website: www.hopslandholidays.co.uk

CLIVE & JULIE FFITCH, REDGATE SMITHY B&B, REDGATE, ST CLEER, LISKEARD PL14 6RU (01579 321578). 200-year-old converted smithy, situated on the southern edge of Bodmin Moor. Extensive and tasty breakfast menu. Excellent pubs and restaurants locally. AA ★★★★
e-mail: enquiries@redgatesmithy.co.uk　　　website: www.redgatesmithy.co.uk

Lizard

The most southerly point in England, with fine coastal scenery and secluded coves. Sandy beach at Housel Bay. Truro 28 miles, Helston 11.

GALLEN-TREATH GUEST HOUSE, PORTHALLOW TR12 6PL (Tel & Fax: 01326 280400). Spectacular coastal views, comfortable en suite rooms, hearty meals and a warm welcome await. Close to coastal path, diving, gardens and more. AA ★★★ [pw! Pets £2 per night]
e-mail: gallentreath@btclick.com　　　website: www.gallen-treath.com

MULLION COVE HOTEL, MULLION COVE, THE LIZARD TR12 7EP (01326 240328). Located on the Cornish Coastal Path in a spectacular position on the Lizard Peninsula. Stunning country and coastal walks. Dog-friendly lounge, comfortable bedrooms, excellent food. AA ★★★ [pw! Pets £7 per night – free in low season]
e-mail: enquiries@mullion-cove.co.uk　　　website: www.mullion-cove.co.uk

POLURRIAN HOTEL, MULLION, LIZARD PENINSULA TR12 7EN (01326 240421; Fax: 01326 240083). Set in 12 acres with stunning views across Mount's Bay. Two pools, gym, snooker room, tennis court, sun terraces and secluded gardens. Most bedrooms have sea views. VisitBritain/AA ★★★ Hotel [Pets £8 per night.]
e-mail: relax@polurrianhotel.com　　　website: www.polurrianhotel.com

Cornwall

SOUTH WEST ENGLAND 103

Longrock

Hamlet to the east of Penzance. Submerged forest to the east.

MRS DOREEN CAPPER, MOUNT VIEW HOTEL, LONGROCK, PENZANCE TR20 8JJ (01736 710416) A family-run pub with comfortable accommodation, situated 100 yards from Mount's Bay in Longrock village. Three en suite rooms and two with shared bathroom. Breakfast in dining room, lunch and dinner available. Dogs welcome by arrangement. Prices from £20 pppn. [🐾]

Looe

Twin towns linked by a bridge over the River Looe. Capital of the shark fishing industry; nearby Monkey Sanctuary is well worth a visit.

BADHAM FARM, ST KEYNE, LISKEARD PL14 4RW (01579 343572). Farmhouse and farm buildings converted to a high standard. Sleep 2-10. All well furnished/equipped; prices include electricity, bed linen and towels. Well behaved dogs welcome (not in high season). Prices from £120 per week. ETC ★★★★. [Pets £4 per night, £20 per week].
e-mail: badhamfarm@yahoo.co.uk   website: www.badhamfarm.co.uk

FOX VALLEY COTTAGES, LANLAWREN, TRENEWAN, LOOE PL13 2PZ (01726 870115). Set in beautiful countryside, just three miles from Polperro. Indoor heated pool and spa. Open all year round. Field for dogs to run around. Contact Andy & Linda for details. [pw! Pets £15 per week]
e-mail: info@foxvalleycottages.co.uk   website: www.foxvalleycottages.co.uk

COLDRINNICK COTTAGES, DULOE, NEAR LOOE. Attractively converted barns set in large secluded gardens. Excellent locality for walking and relaxing. Sleep 2/6 people. Ideal place for families and dogs alike. For a brochure contact BILL AND KAYE CHAPMAN, COLDRINNICK FARM, DULOE, LISKEARD PL14 4QF (01503 220251). [Pets £15 per week, per dog].
website: www.cornishcottage.net

Idyllic 18th century country cottages for romantics and animal lovers. Looe three miles. Wonderful walks from your gate. Cottages warm and cosy in winter. Personal attention and colour brochure from: B. WRIGHT, TREWORGEY COTTAGES, DULOE, LISKEARD PL14 4PP (01503 262730). VisitBritain ★★★★★ Quality Assurance Scheme. [Pets £20.50 per week.]
website: www.cornishdreamcottages.co.uk

NEIL AND THERESA DENNETT, TALEHAY HOLIDAY COTTAGES, PELYNT, NEAR LOOE PL13 2LT (Tel & Fax: 01503 220252). Beautiful, traditional cottages set in four acres of unspoilt countryside offering peace and tranquillity. Breathtaking coastal and country walks. An ideal location for dogs and their owners. Non-smoking. Close to the Eden Project. ETC ★★★★ [Pets £3 per night, £20 per week]
e-mail: infobookings@talehay.co.uk   website: www.talehay.co.uk

THE TALLAND BAY HOTEL, PORTHALLOW PL13 2JB (01503 272667). At Talland Bay, you'll know you're somewhere special as soon as you arrive. Elegant surroundings, efficient yet discreet service and friendly atmosphere. We are happy to accommodate your four-legged friends too. AA★★★.Two Rosettes.
e-mail: info@tallandbayhotel.co.uk   website: www.tallandbayhotel.co.uk

O. SLAUGHTER, TREFANNY HILL, DULOE, NEAR LISKEARD PL14 4QF (01503 220622). Nestling on a south-facing hillside, near coast. Delicious food. Heated pool, tennis, badminton, lake, shire horses. Enchanting 70 acre estate with bluebell wood, walking and wildlife.
e-mail: enq@trefanny.co.uk   website: www.trefanny.co.uk

TREMAINE GREEN COUNTRY COTTAGES, PELYNT, NEAR LOOE PL13 2LT (01503 220333). A beautiful hamlet of 11 award-winning traditional cosy craftsmen's cottages. Clean, comfortable and well equipped. Set in award-winning grounds with country/coastal walks and The Eden Project nearby. [pw! Pets £18 per week]
e-mail: stay@tremainegreen.co.uk   website: www.tremainegreen.co.uk

🐾 Indicates that pets are welcome free of charge.

£ Indicates that a charge is made for pets: nightly or weekly.

pw! Shows some special provision for pets; exercise facility, feeding or accommodation arrangement.

⌂ Indicates separate pets accommodation.

TRENANT PARK COTTAGES (01503 263639). Secluded traditional cottages in grounds of country estate. Private gardens and grounds. Open log fires. Open all year, winter short breaks. Well behaved dogs welcome. [Pets £20 per week].
e-mail: Liz@holiday-cottage.com   websites: www.trenantcottages.com
                                                   www.trenantcottage.co.uk

NEAR LOOE. In the picturesque Cornish fishing village of Polperro, comfortable, charming holiday cottages, sleeping 2-14, with terraced gardens and private parking, affectionately let for 30 years for family holidays, as well as for friends and couples to enjoy. Definitely located in one of the best positions in the village, directly overlooking 16th century harbour, with 14 miles breathtaking panoramic sea views. 2 minutes shops, excellent selection quality restaurants, tearooms, olde worlde pubs. Close by sandy beaches, quay, pier and rock fishing, miles of unspoilt National Trust cliff walks, along stunning coastal paths. Located between Looe and Fowey, on the South Cornish coast, 25 miles city of Plymouth, 12 miles main A38 and about 15 miles Eden Project and Lost Gardens of Heligan. Prices from £175-£595 per cottage, per week. Pets come free. For brochure, please telephone Graham Wrights offices (01579 344080). [🐾]

MRS BARBIE HIGGINS, TREWITH HOLIDAY COTTAGES, TREWITH, DULOE PL14 4PR (01503 262184; mobile: 07968 262184). Four refurbished cottages in peaceful location with panoramic views near Looe. Fully equipped, 1-3 bedrooms, tastefully furnished. Full central heating. Well behaved dogs welcome. VisitBritain ★★★★ Self-catering. [Pets from £17 per week]
e-mail: info@trewith.co.uk   website: www.trewith.co.uk

VALLEYBROOK, PEAKSWATER, LANSALLOS, LOOE PL13 2QE. Peaceful nine acre site with six superb villas and two delightful cottages, all dog friendly. Individual fenced gardens, dog walks, dog friendly beaches nearby. Short breaks. Open all year. 2 dogs max. ETC ★★★/★★★★. Contact DENISE, KEITH or BRIAN HOLDER (01503 220493). [pw! Pets £3 per night]
website: www.valleybrookholidays.com

WRINGWORTHY COTTAGES, LOOE (01503 240685). 8 traditional stone cottages set in 4 peaceful acres offer you and your pet space for the perfect break. A friendly welcome awaits in our fully equipped, centrally heated cottages, sleeping 2-8. Linen included, walks from our door and more! ETC ★★★★, Green Acorn Award. [Pets £18 per week, pw!]
e-mail: pets@wringworthy.co.uk   website: www.wringworthy.co.uk

Lostwithiel

Town on River Fowey 5 miles SE of Bodmin.

PENROSE BED AND BREAKFAST, 1 THE TERRACE, LOSTWITHIEL PL22 0DT (01208 871417; Mobile: 07766 900179). Elegant Victorian house with a homely atmosphere in the picturesque and historic town of Lostwithiel. Many local amenities. AA ★★★★.[🐾]
e-mail: enquiries@penrosebb.co.uk   website: www.penrosebb.co.uk

Marazion

Quaint little village, the oldest town in Britain. Good beach and splendid fishing, sailing waters.

THE GODOLPHIN ARMS, WEST END, MARAZION TR17 0EN (01736 710202) Perched on the edge of the sand, facing St Michael's Mount. Ten en suite bedrooms, most with breathtaking sea views. Relaxing bars. Perfect for exploring coast and coves. AA ★★ [🐾]
e-mail: enquiries@godolphinarms.co.uk   website: www.godolphinarms.co.uk

Mawgan Porth

Modern village on small sandy bay. Good surfing. Inland stretches the beautiful Vale of Lanherne. Rock formation of Bedruthan Steps is nearby. Newquay 6 miles west..

BLUE BAY HOTEL, TRENANCE, MAWGAN PORTH TR8 4DA (01637 860324). Hotel, restaurant and lodges in fantastic location between Padstow and Newquay, overlooking Mawgan Porth beach. ETC ★★ Hotel, ★★★ Self-catering. [pw! Pets £5 per night, max. £20 per visit].
e-mail: hotel@bluebaycornwall.co.uk   website: www.bluebaycornwall.co.uk

Cornwall　　　　　　　　　　　　　　SOUTH WEST ENGLAND

Mevagissey

Central for touring and walking. Eden project nearby.

KILBOL COUNTRY HOUSE HOTEL & COTTAGES, POLMASSICK, MEVAGISSEY PL26 6HA (01726 842481). 'Perfect Peace in Hidden Cornwall'. Small country hotel set in 5-acre grounds, two miles from the coast. Eight rooms, and two self-catering cottages. Outdoor swimming pool, riverside walk. No children under 12 years in hotel. [pw! Pets £10 per week].
e-mail: Hotel@kilbol-hotel.co.uk　　　　　website: www.kilbol-hotel.co.uk

MRS M.R. BULLED, MENAGWINS, GORRAN PL26 6HP (MEVAGISSEY 01726 843517). Traditional cottage, sleeps two to five. Linen, towels, electricity supplied. Beach one mile. Large garden. Central for touring/walking. Near Eden Project and Heligan Gardens. Pets welcome. [🐕]

Mousehole

Picturesque fishing village with sand and shingle beach. Penzance 3 miles.

POLVELLAN HOLIDAY FLAT. In Mousehole, a quaint and unspoilt fishing village, a fully equipped self-catering flat with full sea views. Sleeps two. Microwave, cooker, fridge, TV, all bedding and towels provided. Open all year. Apply: MR A.G. WRIGHT, LEAFIELDS FARM, UTTOXETER ROAD, ABBOTS BROMLEY, STAFFS WS15 3EH (01283 840651)[🐕]
e-mail: alang23@hotmail.com

Newquay

Popular family holiday resort surrounded by miles of golden beaches. Semi-tropical gardens, zoo and museum. Ideal for exploring all of Cornwall.

QUARRYFIELD CARAVAN & CAMPING PARK, CRANTOCK, NEWQUAY. Fully equipped modern caravans overlooking beautiful Crantock Bay. Separate camping field. Bar, pool, children's play area. Contact: MRS WINN, TRETHERRAS, NEWQUAY TR7 2RE (Tel & Fax: 01637 872792). [Pets £1.50 to £3.50 per night (camping only); £10 to £20 per week in caravan]
e-mail: quarryfield@crantockcaravans.orangehome.co.uk　　website: www.quarryfield.co.uk

TRETHIGGEY TOURING PARK, QUINTRELL DOWNS, NEWQUAY TR8 4QR (01637 877672). Friendly, family-run park minutes from surfing beaches. Touring caravans, tent and campervans welcome. Luxury holiday homes for hire. Shop, off-licence, free showers, electric hook-ups, laundry, children's play area, TV/games room, fishing, licensed bar, Bistro, take-away food in summer. ETC ★★★★
e-mail: enquiries@trethiggey.co.uk　　　　website: www.Trethiggey.co.uk

THE GRANARY, RETORRICK MILL, ST MAWGAN, NEWQUAY TR8 4BH (01637 860460). Set in 27 acres, self-catering Retorrick Mill offers two cottages, six chalets, traditional camping and licensed bar. Pets including horses very welcome. For a brochure or further assistance contact Chris Williams.
website: www.retorrickmill.co.uk

MRS DEWOLFREYS, DEWOLF GUEST HOUSE, 100 HENVER ROAD, NEWQUAY TR7 3BL (01637 874746). Single, double or family rooms, two chalets in rear garden. All rooms non-smoking with en suite facilities, colour TV and tea/coffee making facilities. AA ★★★★ [🐕]
e-mail: holidays@dewolfguesthouse.com　　website: www.dewolfguesthouse.com

Padstow

Bright little resort with pretty harbour on Camel estuary. Extensive sands. Nearby is Elizabethan Prideaux Place. Newquay 15 miles, Wadebridge 8.

THE METROPOLE HOTEL, STATION ROAD, PADSTOW PL28 8DB (0800 2300365) Here at The Metropole we welcome dogs and their owners. This is an ideal base for lots of walks on the coast path and some of the beaches. See our website for more details of the hotel and best available rates. [Pets £10 per night]
website: www.the-metropole.co.uk

RAINTREE HOUSE HOLIDAYS (01841 520228). The best family houses to let at Padstow's beaches in North Cornwall. Yards from the best beaches, the best walking, the best golf and the best restaurants in Cornwall. [🐕]
e-mail: enquiries@raintreeholidays.co.uk　　website: www.raintreehouseholidays.co.uk

Penzance

Well-known resort and port for Scilly Isles, with sand and shingle beaches. Truro 27 miles, Helston 13, Land's End 10, St Ives 8.

PENMORVAH GUEST ACCOMMODATION, 61 ALEXANDRA ROAD, PENZANCE TR18 4LZ (01736 363711). A warm welcome awaits pets and owners alike at Penmorvah. We are ideally situated for long coastal walks and exploring, and shops and restaurants are in easy walking distance.
e-mail: penmorvah_penzance@talktalk.net   website: www.penmorvah.net

TORWOOD HOUSE HOTEL, ALEXANDRA ROAD, PENZANCE TR18 4LZ. Torwood is a small, family-run hotel, situated in a beautiful tree-lined avenue 500 metres from the seafront. All rooms en suite, with TV/DVD, tea/coffee makers and radios. Dinner available on request. For further details telephone LYNDA SOWERBY on 01736 360063. [🐾]
e-mail: Lyndasowerby@aol.com   website: www.torwoodhousehotel.co.uk

Perranporth

North Coast resort 6 miles SW of Newquay.

GREENMEADOW COTTAGES, NEAR PERRANPORTH. Spacious, clean luxury cottages. Sleep six. Open all year. Short breaks out of season. Non-smoking. Ample off road parking. Pets welcome in two of the cottages. ETC ★★★ For brochure and bookings: 01872 540483. [Pets £25 per week].
website: www.greenmeadow-cottages.co.uk

Polperro

Picturesque and quaint little fishing village and harbour. Of interest is the "House of the Props". Fowey 9 miles, Looe 5...

POLPERRO. In the picturesque Cornish fishing village of Polperro, comfortable, charming holiday cottages, sleeping 2-14, with terraced gardens and private parking, affectionately let for 30 years for family holidays, as well as for friends and couples to enjoy. Definitely located in one of the best positions in the village, directly overlooking 16th century harbour, with 14 miles breathtaking panoramic sea views. 2 minutes shops, excellent selection quality restaurants, tearooms, olde worlde pubs. Close by sandy beaches, quay, pier and rock fishing, miles of unspoilt National Trust cliff walks, along stunning coastal paths. Located between Looe and Fowey, on the South Cornish coast, 25 miles city of Plymouth, 12 miles main A38 and about 15 miles Eden Project and Lost Gardens of Heligan. Prices from £175-£595 per cottage, per week. Pets come free. For brochure, please telephone Graham Wrights offices (01579 344080). [🐾]

CLASSY COTTAGES – Spectacular cottages feet from beach. Isolated residences on coast, isolated garden cottage. Open log fires. Dog-friendly beaches. Access to indoor swimming pool, gym and tennis courts. Local pubs serving good food and allowing dogs. Contact FIONA & MARTIN NICOLLE (01720 423000). [pw/ Pets £12 per week]
e-mail: nicolle@classycottages.co.uk   website: www.classycottages.co.uk

Polruan

Village at mouth of River Fowey, opposite the town of Fowey.

POLRUAN-BY-FOWEY, Lovely property near quay. Superb views. Parking (for 2 cars). Garden, Sleeps 6/8. Pets. Woodburning stove. Enjoy sailing, fishing, walking or just watching! Pubs and shops. MR T. NEWPORT, POLRUAN HOLIDAY SERVICES LTD, 1 FOWEY VIEW, POLRUAN PL23 1PA (01726 870582)
website: www.polruancottages.co.uk

Port Gaverne

Hamlet on east side of Port Isaac, near Camel Estuary.

GREEN DOOR COTTAGES. PORT GAVERNE. A delightful collection of 18C Cornish buildings built around a sunny enclosed courtyard, and 2 lovely apartments with stunning sea views. Situated in a picturesque, tranquil cove ideal for children. Dogs allowed on the beach year round. Half a mile from Port Isaac, on the Cornish Coastal Path. Traditional pub directly opposite. ETC ★★★★. For brochure: (01208 880293) [🐾]
e-mail: enquiries@greendoorcottages.co.uk   website: www.greendoorcottages.co.uk

Cornwall

SOUTH WEST ENGLAND 107

Porthleven

Small town with surprisingly big harbour. Grand woodland walks. 2 miles SW of Helston.

PORTHLEVEN. "Kernow agas dynargh" - "Cornwall welcomes you". Fishermen's cottages. Harbour, bay or country views. 3 minutes to beach, coast path, harbourside eating places. Open fires. Pets welcome. Please contact: MRS KERNO (01209 860410). [Pets welcome at a charge]

Port Isaac

Attractive fishing village with harbour. Much of the attractive coastline is protected by the National Trust. Camelford 9 miles. Wadebridge 9.

DAVID AND JENNY OLDHAM, THE GARDEN HOUSE, MICHAELSTOW (01208 850529). Secure garden for dogs. Doggy shower. Lovely far reaching views. Full central heating and electric inc. Bed linen and towels inc. One bedroom with twin or double. Central location in small quiet hamlet. From £188 pw. e-mail: david.trevella@btconnect.com   website: www.trevellacornwall.co.uk

PORT GAVERNE HOTEL, NEAR PORT ISAAC PL29 3SQ (01208 880244; Fax: 01208 880151). Renowned 17th century inn in an unspoilt fishing cove on the rugged North Coast of Cornwall. Beach just 50 yards away. Pets welcome. Self-catering accommodation available. [Pets £3.50 per night].

Homes from home around our peaceful courtyard garden 100 yards from sea in bygone fishing hamlet. Each sleeps six and has full CH, fridge/freezer, washer/dryer, dishwasher, microwave, DVD, video, computer and broadband. £200 (February), £760 (August) weekly. Resident owner. APPLY:- MALCOLM LEE, GULLROCK, PORT GAVERNE, PORT ISAAC PL29 3SQ (01208 880106). [🐾]
e-mail: gullrock@ukonline.co.uk   website: www.gullrock-port-gaverne.co.uk

LONGCROSS HOTEL & VICTORIAN GARDENS, TRELIGHTS, PORT ISAAC PL29 3TF (01208 880243). Lovely Victorian country house hotel with four acres of restored gardens. Close to the area's best beaches, golf courses and other attractions. Newly refurbished en suite bedrooms and suites. [Pets £5.00 per night.]
website: www.longcrosshotel.co.uk

Portreath

Coastal village 4 miles north west of Redruth.

Charming, elegantly furnished, self-catering cottages between Newquay and St Ives. Sleep 2 to 6. Fully equipped including linen. Beautiful beaches. Laundry and games room. Ample parking. Colour brochure – FRIESIAN VALLEY COTTAGES, MAWLA, CORNWALL TR16 5DW (01209 890901) [🐾]

Portwrinkle

Village on Whitsand Bay, 6 miles west of Torpoint.

WHITSAND BAY SELF-CATERING (01579 345688). Twelve cottages sleeping 4-10, all with sea views and situated by an 18-hole clifftop golf course. Children and pet-friendly. [Pets £20 per week].
e-mail: ehwbsc@hotmail.com   website: www.whitsandbayselfcatering.co.uk

St Agnes

Patchwork of fields dotted with remains of local mining industry. Watch for grey seals swimming off St Agnes Head.

CHIVERTON PARK, BLACKWATER, TRURO TR4 8HS (01872 560667). Caravan and touring holidays only a short drive from magnificent beaches. Quiet, spacious; exclusive gym, sauna, steamroom; laundry, shop, play area and games room. All amenities. No club, bar or disco. [Dogs £15 per week]
e-mail: info@chivertonpark.co.uk   website: www.chivertonpark.co.uk

BLUE HILLS TOURING PARK, CROSS COOMBE, TREVELLAS, ST AGNES TR5 0XP (01872 552999). In a beautiful rural position close to a coastal footpath, a small site with good toilets. Pleasant location for exploring nearby coves, beaches and villages. Two-acre site with 30 touring pitches. [🐾]
e-mail: loo@zoom.co.uk   website: www.bluehillscamping.co.uk

DRIFTWOOD SPARS, TREVAUNANCE COVE, ST AGNES TR5 0RT (01872 552428). Take a deep breath of Cornish fresh air at this comfortable B&B ideally situated for a perfect seaside holiday. Dogs allowed on beach. Miles of footpaths for 'walkies'. Children and pets welcome. AA ★★★★ [Pets £3 per night]. website: www.driftwoodspars.co.uk

PENKERRIS, PENWINNICK ROAD, ST AGNES TR5 0PA (01872 552262). B&B/Guest House/Hotel with lawned garden, picnic tables, barbeque, ample parking. Comfortable rooms, "real" food. Country/cliff walks, beaches (dog-friendly). B&B £20-£35pppn. Open all year. ETC ★★ [Pets £3 per night.]
e-mail: info@penkerris.co.uk   website: www.penkerris.co.uk

St Austell

Old Cornish town and china clay centre with small port at Charlestown (1½ miles). Excellent touring centre. Newquay 16 miles, Truro 14, Bodmin 12, Fowey 9, Mevagissey 6.

BOSINVER HOLIDAY COTTAGES, ST MEWAN, ST AUSTELL PL26 7DT (01726 72128). Award-winning individual cottages in peaceful garden surroundings. Close to major holiday attractions. Short walk to shop and pub. Phone for brochure. No pets during Summer School holidays. ETC ★★★★ [pw!, Pets £30 per week].
e-mail: reception@bosinver.co.uk   website: www.bosinver.co.uk

St Ives

Picturesque resort, popular with artists, with cobbled streets and intriguing little shops. Wide stretches of sand.

SPACIOUS COTTAGE. Sleeps 7. Near beaches, harbour, shops, Tate Gallery. Terms £390 to £835 per week. Dogs welcome. Available all year. Telephone: CAROL HOLLAND (01736 793015). [Pets £10 per week]

BOB & JACKY PONTEFRACT, THE LINKS HOLIDAY FLATS, LELANT, ST IVES TR26 3HY (01736 753326). Magnificent location overlooking golf course and beach. Wonderful spot for walking. Five minutes from beach where dogs allowed all year. Two well-equipped flats open all year. [🐕]
e-mail: bobandjacky@btinternet.com

SANDBANK HOLIDAYS, ST IVES BAY, HAYLE (01736 752594). High quality Apartments and Bungalows for 2-6 persons. Heated, Colour TV, Microwave etc. Dogs welcome. [Pets £14 to £21 per week]
website: www.sandbank-holidays.co.uk

St Mawes

Village with harbour and two good beaches, excellent for swimming.

SEA PINK, NEAR ST MAWES, SOUTH CORNWALL. In a picturesque setting overlooking the little bay of St Just in Roseland, Sea Pink is ideally located for exploring the coast and attractions. Spacious lounge, dining area opening on to sun terrace and lawned garden, three bedrooms. Brochure available. Contact JUDY JUNIPER (01872 863553). [Pets £15 per week].
e-mail: cottageinfo@btconnect.com   website: www.luxury-holiday-cottages.com

St Mawgan

Delightful village in wooded river valley. Ancient church has fine carvings.

DALSWINTON HOUSE, ST MAWGAN, CORNWALL TR8 4EZ (01637 860385). Old Cornish house standing in ten acres of secluded grounds. All rooms en suite, colour TV, tea/coffee facilities. Solar heated outdoor swimming pool. Restaurant and bar. Out-of-season breaks. No children under 16. ETC ★★★★ [🐕 pw!]
e-mail: dalswintonhouse@tiscali.co.uk   website: www.dalswinton.com

www.holidayguides.com

Cornwall

St Tudy

Village 5 miles north east of Wadebridge.

Comfortable end of terrace cottage in picturesque and friendly village. Enclosed garden and parking. Ideal location for exploring all Cornwall. Short Breaks and brochure available. Contact: MRS R REEVES, POLSTRAUL, TREWALDER, DELABOLE PL33 9ET (Tel & Fax: 01840 213120). [🐕]
e-mail: ruth.reeves@hotmail.co.uk   website: www.maymear.co.uk

St Wenn

Village 4 miles East of St Columb Major.

TREWITHIAN FARM, ST WENN PL30 5PH (01208 895181). Comfortable, well equipped wing of farmhouse, edge of Bodmin Moor. Very secluded position. Dog welcome, use of kennels, exercise field. Good walking and dog-friendly beaches nearby. VisitBritain ★★★★ [pw! Pets £25 per week.]
website: www.cornwall-online.co.uk/trewithianfarm

Tintagel

Attractively situated amidst fine cliff scenery; small rocky beach. Famous for associations with King Arthur, whose ruined castle on Tintagel Head is of interest. Bude 19 miles, Camelford 6.

MR & MRS N. CAREY, SALUTATIONS, ATLANTIC ROAD, TINTAGEL PL34 0DE (01840 770287). Comfortable, well-equipped, centrally heated cottages sleeping two. Ideal for touring, walking and relaxing. Close to Coastal Path and village amenities. Private parking. Ring for brochure. Pets Free. [🐕]
e-mail: salutations@talktalk.net   website: www.salutationstintagel.co.uk

Tregarne

On the Lizard peninsula, 8 miles east of Helston.

THE HEN HOUSE, TREGARNE, NEAR HELFORD TR12 6EW (01326 280236). Idyllic peaceful country setting a mile from the sea. Superb walks in all directions with year-round dog-friendly beaches Delightful spacious barns each open onto courtyard garden. Wild flower meadow, bird song and complete relaxation. Complimentary Tai-chi. Award Winners for Green Ethos and Quality. AA ★★★★. [pw! Pets £5 per night]
e-mail: henhouseuk@aol.com   website: www.thehenhouse-cornwall.co.uk

Truro

Bustling Cathedral City with something for everyone. Museum and Art Gallery with interesting shop and cafe is well worth a visit.

MRS PAMELA CARBIS, TRENONA FARM, RUAN HIGH LANES, TRURO TR2 5JS (01872 501339). Enjoy a relaxing stay on the unspoilt Roseland Peninsula between Truro and St Austell. Self-catering in three renovated barns, B&B in Victorian farmhouse. Children and pets welcome. Brochure available. [Pets £10 per stay, ⌂]
e-mail: info@trenonafarmholidays.co.uk   website: www.trenonafarmholidays.co.uk

KING HARRY COTTAGES, FEOCK, TRURO TR3 6QJ (01872 861917). Two comfortable, well equipped cottages in own charming gardens. Dogs welcome. Beautiful woodland walks. Perfect for fishing and bird watching. Free use of boat. [🐕]
e-mail: beverley@kingharry.net   website: www.kingharrycottages.co.uk

HIGHER TREWITHEN, STITHIANS, TRURO TR3 7DR (01209 860863) The ideal centre for your pet and your family. We are surrounded by public footpaths and have 3½ acres of fields. [🐕]
e-mail: trewithen@talk21.com   website: www.trewithen.com

Please mention Pets Welcome!
when making enquiries about accommodation featured in these pages

Wadebridge

Town on River Camel, 6 miles north-west of Bodmin

Three barn converted luxury cottage-style self catering homes near Wadebridge. Found along a leafy drive, with wonderful views, beside the lazy twisting Camel River with its "Trail" for walking and cycling. CORNWALL TOURISM AWARDS 2002 - Self Catering Establishment of the Year - "Highly Commended". Sleep 2-7 plus cot. Two dogs per cottage welcome. GARY NEWMAN, COLESENT COTTAGES, ST TUDY, WADEBRIDGE, CORNWALL PL30 4QX (Tel & Fax: 01208 850112). [pw! 🐾]
e-mail: relax@colesent.co.uk   website: www.colesent.co.uk

Isles of Scilly
St Mary's, Tresco

SALLAKEE COTTAGE. Self-catering farm cottage, available all year round. Lounge area with TV/DVD, well equipped kitchen, two large bedrooms, modern bathroom. Woodburner. Groceries can be delivered for your arrival. Near beach and coastal paths. Pets welcome. Write or phone for details.
MRS PAMELA MUMFORD, SALLAKEE FARM, ST MARY'S, ISLES OF SCILLY TR21 0NZ • TEL: 01720 422391

Welcome to Hell Bay...
HELL BAY BRYHER ISLAND

Hell Bay – the ultimate gourmet escape and a perfect place to relax and re-charge your batteries. It provides immeasurable peace and tranquillity. It offers privacy and seclusion. An informal and relaxed hideaway in extensive private grounds, with beautifully furnished rooms. New England and the Caribbean meet Cornwall.

Hell Bay, Bryher,
Isles of Scilly,
Cornwall TR23 0PR
Tel: 01720 422947 • Fax: 01720 423004
Email: contactus@hellbay.co.uk
www.hellbay.co.uk

St Mary's

Largest of group of granite islands and islets off Cornish Coast. Terminus for air and sea services from mainland. Main income from flower-growing. Seabirds, dolphins and seals abound.

MRS PAMELA MUMFORD, SALLAKEE FARM, ST MARY'S TR21 0NZ (01720 422391). Self-catering farm cottage, available all year round. Two large bedrooms. Woodburner. Near beach and coastal paths. Pets welcome. Write or phone for details. ETC ★★★

Tresco

Second largest of Isles of Scilly, 28 miles from Cornish coast. Can be reached by helicopter, boat or ferry.

HELL BAY, BRYHER, ISLES OF SCILLY TR23 0PR. (01720 422947; Fax: 01720 423004). The ultimate gourmet escape and a perfect place to relax and re-charge your batteries. An informal and relaxed hideaway in extensive private grounds, with beautifully furnished rooms.
e-mail: contactus@hellbay.co.uk   website: www.hellbay.co.uk

...and Bertie came too!

Helpful Holidays have a wonderful variety of cottages, houses, apartments all over the **West Country** - seaside, moorland, farmland and villages. Many of our properties welcome pets and are in ideal locations for countryside rambles!
All properties are inspected, star rated & frankly described by us in our full colour brochure.

01647 433535

Helpful Holidays

www.helpfulholidays.co.uk

Want the best of Devon & Cornwall self-catering?

All our properties are VisitBritain approved

Many of our 250 properties welcome pets. Please contact us to find the best property for your whole family.

www.marsdens.co.uk

✉ holidays@marsdens.co.uk ✆ 01271 813777

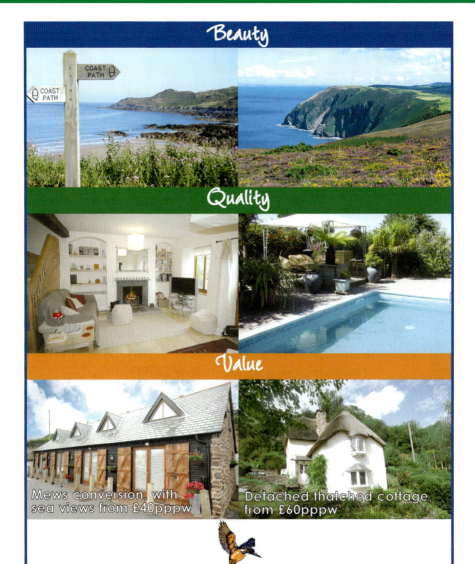

PORT LIGHT
Hotel, Restaurant & Inn

As featured in Times, Guardian, Mail, Telegraph, Express, Dogs Today, Your Dog and many pet-friendly internet sites

- Luxury en suite rooms, easy access onto the gardens
- Close to secluded sandy cove (dogs permitted) 20 minutes' walk
- No charge for pets which are most welcome throughout the hotel
- Recognised for outstanding food and service with a great reputation for superb home-cooked fayre
- Set alongside the famous National Trust Salcombe to Hope Cove coastal walk
- Fully licensed bar - log burner - real ale
- Winner 2004 "Dogs Trust" Best Pet Hotel in England
- Large free car park ◆ Open Christmas & New Year ◆ Self-catering cottages nearby

A totally unique location, set amidst acres of National Trust coastal countryside with panoramic views towards Cornwall, Dartmoor and France.

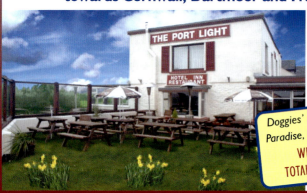

Important advice: always check to ensure other so-called 'pet-friendly' hotels really are! Talk to us to find out more.

Doggies' Heaven, Walkers' Paradise, Romantics' Dream
WE ARE REALLY, TOTALLY PET-FRIENDLY

Bolberry Down, Malborough, Near Salcombe, South Devon TQ7 3DY
e-mail: info@portlight.co.uk • www.portlight.co.uk
Tel: (01548) 561384 or (07970) 859992 • Sean & Hazel Hassall

❖ Bolberry Farm Cottages ❖
Bolberry, Near Salcombe, Devon TQ7 3DY

Luxury two and three bedroom barn conversion cottages
• Private enclosed gardens • Shared orchard • Views across valley • Gas, coal, open fires • Parking • Finished to a very high standard • Linen and towels included • Central heating • Close to coastal path and pet-friendly beaches
• Dog wash • Superb meals available at our nearby Port Light Inn & Hotel • Credit/Debit cards accepted

Tel: 01548 561384 • e-mail: info@bolberryfarmcottages.co.uk • www.bolberryfarmcottages.co.uk

Hazel & Sean Hassall • *The Pet Holiday Specialist* •

Appledore, Ashburton

CROSS HOUSE
Fore Street, Northam,
Bideford EX39 1AN
Tel: 01237 472042
info@crosshouseandcottages.co.uk
www.crosshouseandcottages.co.uk

'Come as a guest leave as a friend'. We can offer you three 'Home from Home' cottages, all with 'Olde Worlde' charm and up-to-date amenities. We are ideally situated for touring with Exmoor, Clovelly, Lynton, Lynmouth, Tarka Trail within easy reach. Relax on one of the many beaches, the nearest one mile away. Well-behaved owners welcome!

Parkers Farm Holiday Park
STATIC CARAVANS • TOURING SITE

Friendly, family-run touring site and static caravans situated in unspoilt countryside. Spectacular views to Dartmoor. Two modern shower blocks; electric hook-ups. Bar and restaurant with area for dogs. Large dog-walking fields. Shop, launderette and indoor/outdoor play areas. 12 miles to coast. Short Breaks available.

HIGHER MEAD FARM, ASHBURTON, DEVON TQ13 7IJ
Tel: 01364 654869 • Fax: 01364 654004
e-mail: parkersfarm@btconnect.com
www.parkersfarm.co.uk

PETS WELCOME

www.holidayguides.com

SOUTH WEST ENGLAND

Devon
Ashburton, Ashwater

ETC ★★★ - ★★★★

Mrs Angela Bell
Wooder Manor, Widecombe in the Moor,
Near Ashburton TQ13 7TR
Tel & Fax: (01364) 621391
www.woodermanor.com
e-mail: angela@woodermanor.com

Cottages and converted coach house nestled in the picturesque valley of Widecombe, surrounded by unspoilt woodland moors and granite tors. Half-a-mile from village with post office, general stores, two good pubs (dogs welcome) and National Trust Information Centre. Excellent centre for touring Devon with a variety of places to visit and exploring Dartmoor by foot or on horseback. Accommodation is clean and well-equipped with colour TV, central heating, laundry room. Children welcome. Large gardens and courtyard for easy parking. Open all year, so take advantage of off-season reduced rates. Short Breaks available. Two properties suitable for disabled visitors. Colour Brochure.

PARKERS FARM COTTAGES
Come and stay on a real 400-acre farm in South Devon
FARM COTTAGES • STATIC CARAVANS

Friendly, family-run self-catering complex with cottages and static caravans surrounded by beautiful countryside. 12 miles from the sea and close to Dartmoor National Park. Perfect for children and pets, with farm animals and plenty of space to roam. Large area to walk your dogs. Laundry, bar and restaurant. Good discounts for couples. A warm welcome awaits you. British Farm Tourist Award • ETC ★★★★ (CARAVAN PARK) • ETC ★★★ (SELF CATERING).

PETS WELCOME

DOGS' PARADISE
MEAD, ALSTON CROSS, ASHBURTON, DEVON TQ13 7IJ • Tel: 01364 653008
e-mail: parkerscottages@btconnect.com • www.parkersfarm.co.uk

---

Blagdon Manor
Ashwater, Near Beaworthy, N. Devon EX21 5DF
Tel: 01409 211224 • Fax: 01409 211634

AA ★★★

Liz and Steve, along with our three Chocolate Labradors, Nutmeg, Cassia and Mace, look forward to welcoming you to Blagdon Manor.

Restaurant: Enjoy excellent cuisine using locally sourced produce. Dinner available Wednesday - Sunday.
Accommodation: 7 en suite bedrooms
Panoramic views of the Devon countryside and Dartmoor. Beautifully restored Grade II Listed building. Enjoy a peaceful location halfway between Dartmoor and Exmoor and only 20 minutes from the North Cornish coast at Bude.

3 acres of gardens and 17 acres of fields.
Children over the age of 12 and dogs are welcome.
Double/twin rooms £145-£195 per night, based on two sharing. Single occupancy £85. Dogs £8 per night.
Closed Monday and Tuesday nights.

e-mail: stay@blagdon.com
www.blagdon.com

Devon
Axminster

Fairwater Head Hotel
3 Star Accommodation at Sensible Prices

75% ★★★

Located in the tranquil Devon countryside and close to Lyme Regis, this beautiful Edwardian Country House Hotel has all you and your dog need for a peaceful and relaxing holiday.

Dogs Most Welcome and Free of Charge
Countryside location with panoramic views • AA Rosette Restaurant

The Fairwater Head Hotel
Hawkchurch, Near Axminster, Devon EX13 5TX
Tel: 01297 678349 • Fax: 01297 678459
e-mail: stay@fairwaterheadhotel.co.uk
www.fairwaterheadhotel.co.uk

Devon

Axminster, Bantham, Barnstaple

Lea Hill
MEMBURY, AXMINSTER EX13 7AQ
Tranquil location • Wonderful scenery • Close to World Heritage Coast • Eight acres of grounds and gardens • Walks, footpaths, dog exercise field • Hot tub and barbecue. Comfortable, well equipped self-catering cottages with en suite bedrooms and own gardens

e-mail: reception@leahill.co.uk • 01404 881881
www.leahill.co.uk

Lilac Cottage

Smallridge • Axminster

Detached cottage, carefully renovated, retaining the inglenook fireplace, oak beams, floors and doors. Oil-fired central heating, colour TV, fully-equipped all-electric kitchen. Furnished to a high standard, sleeps six plus cot. Children and pets are welcome. Walled garden and garage. The villages and surrounding countryside are beautiful on the borders of Devon, Dorset, and Somerset. Many seaside towns within 10 miles – Lyme Regis, Charmouth and Seaton.

Contact: Mrs J.M. Stuart, 2 Sandford House, Kingsclere RG20 4PA
Tel & Fax: 01635 291942 • Mobile: 07624 101285 • e-mail: joanna.sb@free.fr

Sloop Holiday Cottages
Bantham South Devon

The Sloop Holiday Cottages offer comfortable, modern, self catering accommodation, with a high standard of furnishings and wonderful views looking over Bigbury Bay and Burgh Island. Beach and Coastal Path nearby.
Each cottage is luxuriously fitted, carpeted and equipped. Cottages 1,2 & 3, can sleep a maximum of 6 people. Cottage no. 4 is a ground floor flat sleeping a maximum of 4 people. All our accommodation is Non Smoking.

Mrs Libby Simmons, 2 The Watch, Bantham, Kingsbridge, South Devon TQ7 3AJ
Tel: Bookings & Enquiries: 01548 560810 • E-mail: info@sloopholidayapartments.co.uk
www.sloopholidaycottages.co.uk

Lower Yelland Farm Guest House

Situated half way between Barnstaple and Bideford, this delightfully modernised 17th Century farmhouse accommodation is part of a working farm. The farm is centrally located for easy access to the many attractions of North Devon, its beautiful beaches, varied walks and sports facilities including golf, surfing, fishing, riding etc. Its proximity to both Exmoor and Dartmoor makes this location perfect for those who wish to explore. Instow with its sandy beach, pubs and restaurants is a just mile away. It lies adjacent to the Tarka Trail, part of the South West Coastal Footpath, and RSPB bird sanctuary. The bed and breakfast accommodation comprises 3 twin/super king-size and 2 rooms with four-poster beds, 1 double room and 2 single rooms; all rooms en suite, with TV and tea/coffee making facilities. Breakfast includes eggs from our free-range chickens, home-made bread, jams and marmalade. The delightful sitting room has a large selection of books for those who want to relax and browse.
Please visit our website for further details   www.loweryellandfarm.co.uk

Winner Golden Achievement Award of Excellence for Devon Retreat of the Year

Lower Yelland Farm Guest House, Fremington, Barnstaple EX31 3EN
Tel: 01271 860101 • e-mail: peterday@loweryellandfarm.co.uk

Martinhoe Cleave Cottages
Martinhoe, Parracombe, Barnstaple, Devon EX31 4PZ

Overlooking the beautiful Heddon valley and close to the dramatic coast of the Exmoor National Park, these delightful cottages, equipped to a very high standard throughout, offer perfect rural tranquillity. Open all year. Sleep 1-2. • **Tel: 01598 763313**
e-mail: info@exmoorhideaway.co.uk • www.exmoorhideaway.co.uk

Devon
Barnstaple, Bideford

Welcome to North Hill
deep in the rolling hills of Devon, a truly pastoral retreat

Carol Ann and Adrian Black, North Hill, Shirwell, Barnstaple EX31 4LG
Tel: 01271 850611
Mobile: 07834 806434
www.north-hill.co.uk

17th century farm buildings, sympathetically converted into cottages sleeping 2-6, with exposed beams, wood stoves and central heating. Set in 9 acres of pastures and gardens with a children's play area. Facilities include: indoor heated swimming pool, jacuzzi, sauna, all-weather tennis court and games room.

This area of North Devon offers some of the finest beaches in the country and the National Park of Exmoor offers thousands of acres of moorland to explore.

Terms from £195 to £935

Mead Barn Cottages
Welcombe, North Devon EX39 6HQ

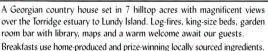

ETC ★★★-★★★★ Graded Quality Self-Catering Cottages sleeping 2 - 26 people. Set in 1½ acres.
- Games Room • Tennis court • Play Area
- Swings • Trampoline
- Gardens with Barbecue Area

Proprietors: Robert & Lisa Ireton. **Tel: 01288 331 721**
e-mail: holidays@meadbarns.com
Visit: www.meadbarns.com

A Georgian country house set in 7 hilltop acres with magnificent views over the Torridge estuary to Lundy Island. Log-fires, king-size beds, garden room bar with library, maps and a warm welcome await our guests.

Breakfasts use home-produced and prize-winning locally sourced ingredients.

There are ground floor rooms set around the courtyard garden with easy access. All rooms are en suite and have teletext television, well-stocked hospitality tray with tea and coffee making facilities, telephones and hairdryers.

Selected by the AA as "One of Britain's Best in 2010."

Bed & Breakfast from £30pp.
No Smoking.

The Pines at Eastleigh

Fully Serviced Rooms & Cottages

Eastleigh, Near Bideford, North Devon EX39 4PA
Tel: 01271 860561

AA ★★★★

www.thepinesateastleigh.co.uk
e-mail: pirrie@thepinesateastleigh.co.uk

YOUR PET STAYS FREE

ETC ★★★

Sandy Cove Hotel stands in 20 acres of cliff, coast and garden. The Hotel Restaurant overlooks the sea and cliffs with spectacular views of the bay. Mini-breaks are available as well as special weekly rates, all of which offer a five-course meal including seafood platters with lobster, smoked salmon and steak. Every Saturday there is a Swedish Smorgasbord and Carvery followed by dancing till late. All bedrooms have colour TV, telephone, teamaking and are en suite. There is an unique indoor swimming pool with rolling back sides to enjoy the sun, as well as a whirlpool, sauna, steam-room and fitness area with gym equipment.

Please return this advertisement to qualify for "Pets Stay Free" offer.
Children have free accommodation sharing parents' room.
Children under 5 years completely free, including meals.

You'll love the special atmosphere of Sandy Cove, why not find us on our website at www.sandycove-hotel.co.uk or ring to request a brochure

Combe Martin Bay,
Devon EX34 9SR
Tel: 01271 882243
      01271 882888

Devon — **SOUTH WEST ENGLAND**

Bideford, Bigbury-on-Sea, Bradworthy, Braunton

THE HOOPS INN & COUNTRY HOTEL Horns Cross,
Near Clovelly, Bideford, Devon EX39 5DL Tel: 01237 451222 Fax: 01237 451247

Thatched country inn with open log fires. All bedrooms en suite. Splendid base for touring and outdoor pursuits. Dartmoor and Exmoor within easy reach.

sales@hoopsinn.co.uk www.hoopsinn.co.uk

MOUNT FOLLY FARM
Cliff top position, with outstanding views of Bigbury Bay. Spacious, self catering wing of farmhouse, attractively furnished. Farm adjoins golf course and River Avon. Lovely coastal walks, ideal centre for South Hams and Dartmoor. No smoking.

Always a warm welcome, pets too!

MRS J. TUCKER, BIGBURY-ON-SEA, KINGSBRIDGE TQ7 4AR (01548 810267).
e-mail: info@bigburyholidays.co.uk • www.bigburyholidays.co.uk

Lake House Cottages and B&B
Lake Villa, Bradworthy, Devon EX22 7SQ *North Devon/Cornwall Border*

Four cosy, well equipped, character cottages sleeping 2 to 5/6 in peaceful countryside. Large gardens and tennis court. Half-a-mile from village shops and pub. Near dog-friendly beaches, coast path and moors. Also two en suite B&B rooms with balcony.

Brochure: Peter & Lesley Lewin on 01409 241962 • e-mail: lesley@lakevilla.co.uk • www.lakevilla.co.uk

A HAVEN OF PEACE AND TRANQUILLITY
at Little Comfort Farm, Braunton,
North Devon EX33 2NJ ETC★★★

Five spacious self-catering cottages with secluded gardens on organic family farm. Just minutes from golden sandy beaches where dogs are allowed. Well stocked coarse fishing lake. Private 1½km walk. Wood fires for cosy winter breaks. Pets very welcome.

Tel: 01271 812 414 • info@littlecomfortfarm.co.uk

www.littlecomfortfarm.co.uk

Other specialised holiday guides from FHG

PUBS & INNS OF BRITAIN • **COUNTRY HOTELS** OF BRITAIN
WEEKEND & SHORT BREAK HOLIDAYS IN BRITAIN
THE GOLF GUIDE WHERE TO PLAY, WHERE TO STAY
500 GREAT PLACES TO STAY • **SELF-CATERING HOLIDAYS** IN BRITAIN
BED & BREAKFAST STOPS • **CARAVAN & CAMPING HOLIDAYS**
FAMILY BREAKS IN BRITAIN

Published annually: available in all good bookshops or direct from the publisher:
FHG Guides, Abbey Mill Business Centre, Seedhill, Paisley PA1 1TJ
Tel: 0141 887 0428 • Fax: 0141 889 7204
e-mail: admin@fhguides.co.uk • www.holidayguides.com

DEVONCOURT HOLIDAY FLATS

BERRYHEAD ROAD, BRIXHAM, DEVON TQ5 9AB

Devoncourt is a development of 24 self-contained flats, occupying one of the finest positions in Torbay, with unsurpassed views. At night the lights of Torbay are like a fairyland to be enjoyed from your very own balcony.

MasterCard VISA

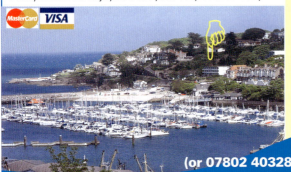

EACH FLAT HAS:
Heating
Sea Views over Torbay
Private balcony
Own front door
Separate bathroom and toilet
Separate bedroom
Bed-settee in lounge
Lounge sea views over Marina
Kitchenette - all electric
Private car park
Opposite beach
Colour television
Overlooks lifeboat
Short walk to town centre
Double glazing
Open all year
Mini Breaks October to April

Tel: 01803 853748
(or 07802 403289 after office hours)
website: www.devoncourt.info

Brixham HOLIDAY PARK

Friendly, comfortable, family-run park offering all you could want from a holiday. Relax under the palm trees, laze by the superb indoor swimming pool, enjoy a drink or meal at the club.

Choose from apartments, chalets in a lawned setting, all fully furnished and equipped – pets welcome in many.

150 yards from beach • 10 minutes' walk from Brixham Harbour • Free Club membership with entertainment • Comfortable bar with meals and takeaway service • Shop and Launderette • Special off-season breaks

BROCHURE HOTLINE
01803 853324
www.brixhamholidaypark.co.uk
enquiries@brixhamholpk.fsnet.co.uk

Fishcombe Cove,
Brixham,
South Devon TQ5 8RB

Devon SOUTH WEST ENGLAND 123

Broadwoodwidger, Chittlehamholt, Chulmleigh, Colebrook, Combe Martin

West Banbury Farm Cottages...where relaxation is a way of life

Come to West Banbury and you'll discover a rural haven where you can unwind and relax. We are near Broadwoodwidger, West Devon, ideally located for exploring Devon and Cornwall, including the north and south coasts. Plenty of family attractions are within easy reach. We have ten charming cottages, each spacious and very comfortable, set around two courtyards with stunning views to Dartmoor. The cottages sleep 2 to 8. Large indoor heated pool, sauna, games room, children's play area, fun pitch and putt, and a grass tennis court. Open all year. Dogs welcome. Short breaks available.

For more information call Anna-Rose on 01566 780423

www.westbanbury.co.uk

Enchanted woods & meadows...easy reach of both sea and moors

In glorious North Devon countryside down our private tree lined ½ mile lane, you'll find just 6 holiday caravans on our well spread out leafy site – with space for children to run and have a wonderful time. Groom and pet our lovely rescue goats, spot wildlife, and enjoy a walk through 100 acres of fields, meadows and bluebell woods.

From £128-£335 per week for up to 6 people inc gas & elec. **Ideal for families, couples and well behaved pets!**

Snapdown Farm, Chittlehamholt, Umberleigh, N. Devon. EX37 9PF   Tel: 01769 540366   www.snapdown.co.uk

Northcott Barton Farm Cottage

Beautifully equipped, spotlessly clean three bedroom cottage with large enclosed garden. A walker's and country lover's ideal: for a couple seeking peace and quiet or a family holiday. Very special rates for low season holidays, couples and short breaks. Near golf, riding, Tarka trail and R.H.S. Rosemoor. Character, comfort, beams, log fire, *"Perfick"*. Pets Welcome, no charge.

For availability please contact Sandra Gay,
Northcott Barton, Ashreigney, Chulmleigh, Devon EX18 7PR
Tel/Fax: 01769 520259
e-mail: sandra@northcottbarton.co.uk
www.northcottbarton.co.uk

The Oyster is a modern bungalow in the pretty, peaceful village of Colebrooke in the heart of Mid Devon. There is a spacious garden for children to play around or sit on the patio. Comfortable accommodation with tea/coffee making facilities, with TV in bedroom and lounge. Bedrooms en suite or with private bathroom - two double and one twin. Walking distance to the New Inn, Coleford, a lovely 13th century free house. Dartmoor and Exmoor are only a short drive away. Central heating. Open all year. Ample parking. Terms from £25 per person for Bed and Breakfast. Children and pets welcome. Smoking accepted.

The Oyster 01363 84576

To find us take the Barnstaple road (A377) out of Crediton, turn left after one-and-a-half miles at sign for Colebrooke and Coleford. In Coleford village turn left at the crossroads, then in Colebrooke village take the left hand turning before the church, the Oyster is the second on the right.

Pearl Hockridge, The Oyster, Colebrooke, Crediton EX17 5JQ

Watermouth Cove Cottages
Nr Combe Martin, Ilfracombe EX34 9SJ
Tel: 0845 029 1958 • or 01271 883931

8 beautiful cottages, most with four-poster and log fire, set beside grounds of Watermouth Castle, 200 yards from the harbour/coastal path. Pets welcome. Open all year.

e-mail: watermouthcove@googlemail.com • www.watermouth-cove-cottages.co.uk

SOUTH WEST ENGLAND — Devon

Combe Martin, Cullompton

Yetland Farm Cottages

Yetland Farm Cottages are six well equipped cottages formed from the old 18thC farm barns, surrounding a pretty paved courtyard. Situated within an Area of Outstanding Natural Beauty, they are ideally situated for North Devon beaches, Exmoor, the South West Coastal Path and many tourist and leisure attractions. Linen and towels supplied. Sleep 3-6 plus cot.

- Two games rooms - one with a pool table, one with table tennis and table football.
- A small DVD library (all cottages have a DVD player).
- FREESAT digital TV in all cottages
- Plenty of off-road parking
- Children's playfield and tennis court.

We welcome well behaved pets and have lots of room to exercise them in our fields (one of which has stunning views across the sea to South Wales).

- Within easy reach of local shops and a short drive from Ilfracombe.
- 15 minute drive from Woolacombe with its three-mile long sandy/surfing beach
- Short Breaks welcome

Yetland Farm Cottages, Berry Down
Combe Martin, North Devon EX34 0NT
Tel: 01271 883655
enquiries@yetlandfarmcottages.co.uk
www.yetlandfarmcottages.co.uk

Northcote Manor Farm Holiday Cottages
Near Combe Martin, North Devon EX31 4NB
e-mail: info@northcotemanorfarm.co.uk
www.northcotemanorfarm.co.uk

Five 4★ self-catering holiday cottages grouped around the courtyard of an historic and beautiful North Devon farm. Dogs are warmly welcomed in all of the cottages, three of which have enclosed gardens. 34 acres of fields, woods and rivers to explore. Extremely peaceful setting with no roads or noise. Information in the cottages on dog-friendly places to visit/eat. Very sociable resident dog. Indoor heated pool, games room and playground.

Full details on our website or please contact Linda on 01271 882376.

Caravan & Camping Park

A small country estate surrounded by forest in which deer roam. Situated in an Area of Outstanding Natural Beauty.

Large, flat, sheltered camping/touring pitches
Central facilities building, 6-berth full service holiday homes, also self contained flat for 2 persons. Forest walks with dog.

**CULLOMPTON
DEVON
EX15 2DT**

COLOUR BROCHURE ON REQUEST
Tel: (01404) 841381

FREE Indoor Heated Pool

Fax: (01404) 841593 • www.forest-glade.co.uk • email: enquiries@forest-glade.co.uk

Devon
Dartmoor

TWO BRIDGES HOTEL
Two Bridges, Princetown, Dartmoor PL20 6SW • ETC/AA ★★

To enter the Two Bridges is like stepping back in time. Sink back into the leather chairs around the blazing log fires, with the gleam of copper and brass. The Tors Restaurant serves the very finest West Country cuisine. Premier bedrooms with four-poster bed and jacuzzi bath. A warm welcome awaits all our guests.

Tel: 01822 890581

www.warm-welcome-hotels.co.uk • e-mail: enquiries@warm-welcome-hotels.co.uk

DEVONSHIRE INN
STICKLEPATH, OKEHAMPTON EX20 2NW • Tel: 01837 840626

A real country pub! Out the back door, past the water wheels, cross the river and up through the woods onto the north edge of Dartmoor proper. Dogs and horses always welcome, fed and watered.

The Rosemont
Dartmoor National Park

4 star quality B&B in village. Short walk to pubs. Open access moorland all around. Excellent walking country. Modern, spacious rooms, all en suite.

Rooms: Single £40 • Double £60-£70

For details and pictures www.therosemont.co.uk
e-mail: office@therosemont.co.uk • Tel. 01822 852175

Chris and Julie Eastaugh, The Rosemont, Yelverton, Devon PL20 6DR

Where else would your dog rather walk?

Walk straight from the hotel... for miles, then relax with our traditional country house hospitality, where dogs are genuinely welcomed. Indulge in our AA Rosetted restaurant with local produce and hearty breakfasts. Country pursuits such as fishing and riding, or golf, and garden or historic house visits are all within easy reach. Tranquillity abounds. No charge for well-behaved dogs.

01822 890403

AA/VisitBritain ★★
Silver SILVER AWARD

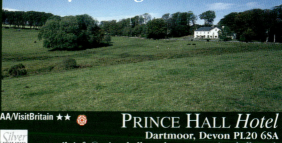

PRINCE HALL *Hotel*
Dartmoor, Devon PL20 6SA

e-mail: info@princehall.co.uk • www.princehall.co.uk

Walkies on DARTMOOR is FANTASTIC!

The Cherrybrook

Stay at The Cherrybrook with your owners and you can step straight from the hotel onto the high moor and walk with them for miles. In the evenings, they can enjoy a drink in our cosy bar followed by our delicious home-made meals.

They must deserve a treat – go on, get them to call!

The Cherrybrook, Two Bridges, Devon PL20 6SP
Call **01822 880260** for details

e-mail: info@thecherrybrook.co.uk • www.thecherrybrook.co.uk

Devon
Dartmoor

Peaceful woodland setting next to the River Walkham in the Dartmoor National Park. Ideally placed to explore the beauty of Devon. Purpose - built lodges available all year round, sleeping 2-7, tastefully blending into the surroundings. Interior specification and furnishings to a high standard - including fully-fitted kitchen with oven, microwave and dishwasher.

- 3 golf courses a short drive away • Easy walk to village and shops
- Scenic walks • Fishing • Dogs accepted • Horse riding nearby
- Small, select touring area for caravans, tents and motor caravans
- Launderette • On A386 Plymouth-Tavistock road.

For Free Brochure:
Dept PW, Dartmoor Country Holidays,
Magpie Leisure Park, Horrabridge,
Yelverton, Devon PL20 7RY.
Tel:01822 852651   or visit our website:
www.dartmoorcountryholidays.co.uk

The Edgemoor
Country House Hotel
Haytor Road, Lowerdown Cross,
Bovey Tracey, Devon TQ13 9LE
Tel: 01626 832466

Charming Country House Hotel in peaceful wooded setting adjacent Dartmoor National Park.
Many lovely walks close by.
All rooms en suite. Excellent food.
Dogs (with well-behaved owners) welcome.

For more information, photographs, current menus and general information about the area see our website.

www.edgemoor.co.uk or e-mail: reservations@edgemoor.co.uk

Devon
Dartmouth, Dunsford, Exeter

SOUTH WEST ENGLAND 127

Watermill Cottages
We really welcome pets! Close to dog-friendly beaches and pubs, the Coastal Path and the National Nature Reserve at Slapton Ley. Five comfy old stone cottages in 13 acres of unspoilt valley round a historic former watermill and stream. Walks from your cottage door, wood-burning stoves, private enclosed gardens, no traffic. A brook to play in, beautiful views and peace and tranquillity.

Higher North Mill, Hansel, Dartmouth, Devon TQ6 0LN
Tel: 01803 770219

e-mail: christine@watermillcottages.co.uk • www.watermillcottages.co.uk

THE OLD BAKEHOUSE
7 Broadstone, Dartmouth TQ6 9NR
Tel & Fax: 01803 834585 • mobile: 07909 680884
oldbakehousecottages@yahoo.com • www.oldbakehousedartmouth.co.uk

Four character cottages with free parking, one with garage. Cottages are in the centre of Dartmouth, two minutes' walk from River Dart, Royal Avenue Gardens, Coronation Park, shops and restaurants. The beautiful Blackpool Sands is a 15 minute drive away. The historic town of Dartmouth is a good centre for boating, fishing, sailing and swimming. National Trust, coastal and inland walks. Four cottages with beams and old stone fireplaces, one with four-poster bed. Open all year. Central heating. Specialising in Autumn, Winter and Spring Breaks. Pets welcome free. Non-smoking. Terms from £290 to £750.

THE ROYAL OAK INN
Dunsford, Near Exeter EX6 7DA
Tel: 01647 252256

Enjoy a friendly welcome in our traditional Country Pub in the picturesque thatched village of Dunsford. Quiet en suite bedrooms are available in the tastefully converted cob barn. Ideal base for touring Dartmoor, Exeter and the coast, and the beautiful Teign Valley. Real Ale and home-made meals are served.

Well-behaved children and dogs are welcome

Regular dog Kizzy • Resident dog Connie   *Please ring Mark or Judy Harrison for further details.*

Bussells Farm, Huxham, Exeter EX5 4EN
Lucy & Andy Hines • Tel 01392 841238
Set in the picturesque Exe Valley, seven luxury barn conversion cottages with access to thirty acres of farmland. Sleep 6/7. Excellent coarse fishing lakes (securely fenced). Outdoor heated swimming pool (May to September), adventure playground and indoor games room. Sandy beaches, Dartmoor and Exmoor within easy reach. 4 miles Exeter. Open all year.

BUSSELLS FARM COTTAGES

e-mail: bussellsfarm@aol.com • www.bussellsfarm.co.uk

128 SOUTH WEST ENGLAND — Devon
Exeter, Exmoor

The perfect venue for a quiet get-away break with your beloved pet. Acres of private grounds, mile of driveway for exercise and animals are welcome in guests' bedrooms by arrangement. The hotel stands in its own grounds, four miles south west of Exeter. AA Rosette Restaurant, also intimate Lounge Bar which serves bar food. Free hotel brochure on request, or visit our website: **www.lordhaldonhotel.co.uk**

Best Western Lord Haldon Hotel, Dunchideock, Near Exeter EX6 7YF
Tel: 01392 832483 • Fax: 01392 833765 • e-mail: enquiries@lordhaldonhotel.co.uk

---

THORVERTON ARMS Thorverton EX5 5NS
Traditional coaching inn just 7 miles north of Exeter. Small, well behaved dogs welcome. 6 en suite bedrooms. Award-winning restaurant. Excellent choice of real ales. Ideal touring base for Dartmoor, Exmoor and Devon's beaches.
Tel: 01392 860205 • www.thethorvertonarms.co.uk

Station Lodge, Doddiscombsleigh, Exeter, Devon

Comfortably furnished apartment In the beautiful Teign River valley. Excellent location for exploring Devon's moors, coasts and villages. Kitchen, lounge/diner, en suite bedroom with double bed. Private garden, extensive grounds. Pubs, shops and walks nearby, golf, fishing, horseriding, tennis and swimming pools within 10 miles. Central heating. Colour TV. All linen provided. Parking. Non-smokers only. Well behaved dogs welcome. From £220 per week.

Short Breaks welcome Oct-April. For further details contact:
Ian West, Station House, Doddiscombsleigh, Exeter EX6 7PW • Tel: 01647 253104
e-mail: enquiries@station-lodge.co.uk • www.station-lodge.co.uk

---

RYDON FARM
WOODBURY, EXETER EX5 1LB   Tel: 01395 232341
www.rydonfarmwoodbury.co.uk
16th Century Devon Longhouse on working dairy farm.
Open all year. 4 Star Silver Award. From £37 to £60pppn.

Staghunters Inn/Hotel • Brendon, Exmoor EX35 6PS
A friendly, family-run Exmoor village inn with frontage to the East Lyn River. Beautiful landscaped garden to the rear; 12 en suite rooms. Varied menu of home-made food using fresh local produce. Log fires, fine wines and local cask ales. A walkers' paradise in the Doone Valley, close to Watersmeet, Lynton and Lynmouth. Ample off-road parking. B&B from £30. *New owners: The Wyburn Family.*
e-mail: stay@staghunters.com • www.staghunters.com • Tel: 01598 741222 • Fax: 01598 741352

Comfort for country lovers in Exmoor National Park.
High quality en suite rooms. Breakfast prepared with local and organic produce. Farm walk through fields to village pub.
One dog free, two dogs £6. • B&B £26–£36. • ETC ★★★★
Jaye Jones & Helen Asher, Twitchen Farm, Challacombe, Barnstaple EX31 4TT
Telephone 01598 763568 • e-mail: holidays@twitchen.co.uk • www.twitchen.co.uk

---

FHG Guides
publish a large range of well-known accommodation guides.
We will be happy to send you details or you can use the order form
at the back of this book.

Devon

SOUTH WEST ENGLAND

Hexworthy (Dartmoor), Holsworthy, Honiton, Ilfracombe

THE FOREST INN
Hexworthy, Dartmoor PL20 6SD

A haven for walkers, riders, fishermen, canoeists or anyone just looking for an opportunity to enjoy the natural beauty of Dartmoor. We specialise in homemade food using local produce wherever possible. With the emphasis on Devon beers and ciders, you have the opportunity to quench your thirst after the efforts of the day with a drink at the bar or relaxing on the chesterfields in the lounge area, complete with log fire for winter evenings.

Tel: 01364 631211 • Fax: 01364 631515 • e-mail: info@theforestinn.co.uk

Tinney Waters

Coarse Fishing Holidays
Self Catering • Bed & Breakfast
No closed Season

Beautiful setting where you will be able to enjoy peace and tranquillity in the heart of rural Devon. Lots of non-fishing activities.

Telephone: 01409 271362
www.tinneywaters.co.uk

Combe House
Gittisham, Honiton, Nr Exeter, Devon EX14 3AD tel: 01404 540 400

somewhere different, somewhere special
A Worldwide Top 100 Hotel
Sunday Times Travel Magazine

Visitors always most welcome for coffee, lunch, tea or dinner

www.combehousedevon.com

Strathmore 57 St Brannocks Road, Ilfracombe EX34 8EQ • Tel: 01271 862248
e-mail: info@the-strathmore.co.uk
www.the-strathmore.co.uk

A delightful and friendly Victorian Licensed guest house, situated just a 10-minute stroll to both seafront and town centre. 8 individually designed bedrooms, with either en suite shower or bath. Cosy lounge bar and secluded terraced garden. Children and pets are always welcome. High chairs and cots available.

AA Pet-Friendly Accommodation of the Year 2006.
Contact Pete and Heather Small

AA ★★★★
Highly Commended

HOPE BARTON BARNS

Nestling in its own valley close to the sandy cove, Hope Barton Barns is an exclusive group of 17 stone barns in two courtyards and 3 luxury apartments in the converted farmhouse. Superbly furnished and fully equipped, each cottage is unique, and vary from a studio to four bedrooms, sleeping 2 to 10.

Farmhouse meals • Ample parking • Golf, sailing and coastal walking nearby
• A perfect setting for family summer holidays, walking in Spring/Autumn or just a "get away from it all" break.
• Free-range children and well behaved dogs welcome • Open all year.
• Heated indoor pool, sauna, gym, lounge bar, tennis court, trout lake and a children's play barn. We have 35 acres of pastures and streams with sheep, goats, pigs, chickens, ducks and rabbits.

For full colour brochure please contact:

Mr & Mrs M. Pope, Hope Cove, Near Salcombe, South Devon TQ7 3HT • Tel: 01548 561393
e-mail: info@hopebarton.co.uk • www.hopebarton.co.uk

Widmouth Farm

Widmouth Farm has 35 acres of gardens, woodland, pastures and a private beach on National Heritage Coastline. There are 11 one, two, three and four bedroom cottages, some early Victorian, some conversions from farm buildings. All are comfortable and well equipped. From £250-£1560 per week. We have alpacas, sheep, goats, chickens, ducks, rabbits, guinea pigs and much wildlife (seals sometimes play off our coast). The surroundings are tranquil, the views superb and access easy (on the A399 between Ilfracombe and Combe Martin). Ideal for walking (the coastal footpath runs around the property), bird watching, painting and sea fishing. Ilfracombe Golf Club quarter of a mile. Pets welcome.

Watermouth, Near Ilfracombe. Devon EX34 9RX • Tel: 01271 863743
e-mail: holiday@widmouthfarmcottages.co.uk • www.widmouthfarmcottages.co.uk

The Foxhunters Inn

West Down, Near Ilfracombe EX34 8NU

• *300 year-old coaching Inn conveniently situated for beaches and country walks.*
• *Serving good local food.*
• *En suite accommodation.*
• *Pets allowed in bar areas and beer garden, may stay in accommodation by prior arrangement. Water bowls provided.*

Tel: 01271 863757 • Fax: 01271 879313
www.foxhuntersinn.co.uk

Devon
Kingsbridge

SOUTH WEST ENGLAND 131

beachdown

Relax in a setting so peaceful, you can actually hear the silence! Comfortable and unpretentious. Your pets more than welcome.

Comfortable, fully-equipped, detached cedarwood chalets, most with small enclosed garden for your pet. Car parking alongside. Just 150 yards away from the beach and the South West Coastal Path. We are situated within the beautiful South Hams area of South Devon. Just a 10 minute walk from Burgh Island. Open all year round.

• **SHORT BREAKS AVAILABLE** •

Call for a brochure on 01548 811277 or visit our website for more details.
Mobile: 07725 053439
Challaborough Bay, Kingsbridge, South Devon TQ7 4JB • Tel: 01548 811277
e-mail: kimm@beachdown.co.uk • www.beachdown.co.uk

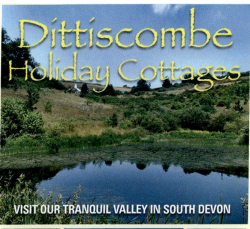

"Dog heaven" says Moses.
We humans loved it too!

Perfect location for dogs and their owners.

Six stone cottages with country views.

Wildlife nature trail for 'walkies' on site.

Dog-friendly beaches and pubs nearby.

Woodburners and private gardens.

• Short Breaks off season
• Open all year

Dittiscombe Holiday Cottages,
Slapton. Near Kingsbridge,
South Devon TQ7 2QF

For more information, prices and availability, please visit our website:

Tel: 01548 521272   www.dittiscombe.co.uk

BLACKWELL PARK
LODDISWELL • KINGSBRIDGE

Bed, Breakfast and Evening Meal is offered in Blackwell Park, a 17th century farmhouse situated 5 miles from Kingsbridge.
Six bedrooms, some en suite, and all with washbasins and tea-making facilities.
Large garden, also adjoining 54 acres of woodland/Nature Reserve.
Ample food with choice of menu.
Pets welcome FREE of charge.
Dogsitting available.

Dartmoor, Plymouth, Torbay, Dartmouth and many beaches lie within easy reach.
Same family ownership since 1971.
Bed and Breakfast • Evening Meal optional
Proprietress: Mrs B. Kelly • Tel: 01548 821230
Blackwell Park, Loddiswell, Devon TQ7 4EA

Mounts Farm Touring Park

The Mounts, Near East Allington, Kingsbridge TQ9 7QJ

MOUNTS FARM is a family-run site in the heart of South Devon. On-site facilities include FREE hot showers, flush toilets, FREE hot water in washing-up room, razor points, laundry and information room, electric hook-ups and site shop. We welcome tents, touring caravans and motor caravans. No charges for awnings. Children and pets welcome. Ideal base for exploring Dartmouth, Salcombe, Totnes, Dartmoor and the many safe, sandy beaches nearby.

www.mountsfarm.co.uk • **01548 521591**

COLLACOTT FARM
Quality Country Cottages

Eight delightful country cottages sleeping 2-12 set around a large cobbled courtyard, amidst twenty acres of tranquil Devon countryside. All are well equipped with wood-burning stove, dishwashers, heating, bed linen, and their own individual patio and garden. A tennis court, heated swimming pool, games room, children's play area, trampoline room and BHS approved riding centre makes Collacott an ideal holiday for the whole family.

Collacott Farm, King's Nympton,
Umberleigh, North Devon EX37 9TP
Telephone: South Molton 01769 572491
www.collacott.co.uk
e-mail: info@collacott.co.uk

Devon
Lapford, Lydford, Lynton/Lynmouth

SOUTH WEST ENGLAND 133

House built in the 14th Century. Listed as of special historical and architectural interest. Set in beautiful grounds with pond, orchard and woods. Trout fishing and almost 200 acres to wander in. Much wildlife and perfect for watching buzzards and badgers. House very tastefully furnished and fully equipped. Will sleep up to 8. No charge for dogs, linen or fuel. David and Marion Mills look forward to meeting you. **Send for our brochure.**
LAPFORD • CREDITON • DEVON • EX17 6NG
TEL: 01363 83268

Set in 8 acres of beautiful grounds within the Dartmoor National Park, this 5 star establishment offers well appointed en suite bedrooms, log fires in the guest lounge and genuine Italian cuisine in "La Cascata" restaurant. Stables allow the horses of guests to stay at small extra cost and dog baskets are provided for canine companions. Private access onto the "Granite Way" off-road cycle path, combined with on-site cycle hire, can make for an alternative safe way to view the spectacular countryside. The South Devon coast, North Cornish coast, Eden Project, Exeter and Plymouth are all less than an hour's drive away.

Lydford Country House
Lydford, Okehampton
Devon EX20 4AU
Tel: 01822 820347
Fax: 01822 820654
info@lydfordcountryhouse.co.uk
www.lydfordcountryhouse.co.uk

LYNTON AND LYNMOUTH RAILWAY STATION
Self-contained holiday accommodation. Ideal for four in two bedrooms (cot available). Sitting room. Bathroom and separate WC. Kitchen/dining room. Children and pets welcome.
W. PRYOR, STATION HOUSE, LYNTON, DEVON EX35 6LB
Tel: 01598 752275 or 752381 • Fax: 01598 752475 • e-mail: advertise@lyntonadvertiser.com

NEED A WORK OUT? Get your owner to take you to England's "Little Switzerland" — Exmoor National Park. Run on most beaches, splash in the rivers and waterfalls. Miles of spectacular walks on or off the lead - you don't need a car. The sea, countryside and village facilities are all within walking distance. Our quality assured cottages sleeping 2,4,6 are comfy and cosy with no petty restrictions. Open all year. Short breaks from just £99. Thinking of NOW? Late specials possible!
Get your owner to ring for details or brochure.

PRIME SPOT COTTAGES
Lynmouth • Lynton
Combe Martin
★★★ & ★★★★
Martin & Margaret Wolverson
01271 882449

Lynhurst, Lynton, Devon
•self-catering • sleeps up to 22•

Elegant late Victorian country house, retaining many original features, totally hidden in gardens and natural woodland, yet just a short stroll from all Lynton's attractions.
- 10 well appointed, spacious bedrooms
- Two comfortable lounges
- Dining room • Large, farmhouse-style kitchen
- Laundry room • Large garden with BBQ area
- Terrace and conservatory • Dogs welcome
- Short Breaks available

For bookings: ring Jane on
01598 753757 or 07807 183814
www.thelynhurst.com

Clooneavin Holiday Apartments • Where Exmoor meets the Sea

Eight well equipped self contained apartments and chalet. Numerous coastal and river walks through idyllic countryside.
Clooneavin Holiday Apartments, Clooneavin Path,
Lynmouth, Devon EX35 6EE • Tel: 01598 753334
e-mail: relax@clooneavinholidays.co.uk • www.clooneavinholidays.co.uk

**Woody Bay, Parracombe
Devon EX31 4RA
01598 763224**

Moorlands, formerly the Woody Bay Station Hotel, is a family-run Guesthouse in a most beautiful part of North Devon, surrounded by Exmoor countryside and within two miles of the spectacular coastline.

Within the building are two self-contained apartments sleeping 2/3 persons. Our ground floor apartment comprises double bedroom, lounge, kitchen and bathroom; own entrance through a private courtyard garden. The second apartment, on the first floor, is larger with two bedrooms, shower room, lounge with screened kitchen and dining area and has views over the gardens and surrounding Exmoor countryside. Set within the National Park, the spectacular Southwest Coastal Path and Lynton and Lynmouth are within easy reach, all offering excellent walks for you and your dogs.

Evening meals and breakfasts are both available in our licensed dining room by arrangement.

*Where countryside and comfort combine
Further information and online booking is available on our website.*

www.moorlandshotel.co.uk

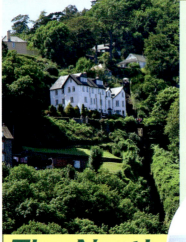

Situated on the South West Coastal Path with wonderful views, and delicious home cooking, the North Cliff is an ideal base for discovering Exmoor and the North Devon Coast.
We welcome pets, children and groups.

*Tel: 01598 752357
e-mail: holidays@northcliffhotel.co.uk
www.northcliffhotel.co.uk*

The North Cliff Hotel
North Walk, Lynton,
North Devon EX35 6HJ

Devon
Lynton / Lynmouth

Blue Ball Inn
formerly The Exmoor Sandpiper Inn

is a romantic Coaching Inn dating in part back to the 13th century, with low ceilings, blackened beams, stone fireplaces and a timeless atmosphere of unspoilt old world charm. Offering visitors great food and drink, a warm welcome and a high standard of accommodation.

The inn is set in an imposing position on a hilltop on Exmoor in North Devon, a few hundred yards from the sea, and high above the twin villages of Lynmouth and Lynton, in an area of oustanding beauty.

The spectacular scenery and endless views attract visitors and hikers from all over the world.

We have 16 en suite bedrooms, comfortable sofas in the bar and lounge areas, and five fireplaces, including a 13th century inglenook. Our extensive menus include local produce wherever possible, such as locally reared meat, amd locally caught game and fish, like Lynmouth Bay lobster; specials are featured daily. We also have a great choice of good wines, available by the bottle or the glass, and a selection of locally brewed beers, some produced specially for us.

Stay with us to relax, or to follow one of the seven circular walks through stunning countryside that start from the Inn. Horse riding for experienced riders or complete novices can be arranged. Plenty of parking. Dogs (no charge), children and walkers are very welcome!

Blue Ball Inn formerly The Exmoor Sandpiper Inn
Countisbury, Lynmouth, Devon EX35 6NE
01598 741263
www.BlueBallinn.com • www.exmoorsandpiper.com

Lynmouth, Exmoor

Bath & Tors

Bath Hotel AA ★★ — Prices from £35.00 pppn

Tors Hotel AA ★★★ — Prices from £40.00 pppn

Off Season discounts available. Great views of harbour.
Quality rooms and service. Ideal for moors. Pets Welcome.

01598 752238 info@bathhotellynmouth.co.uk
www.bathhotellynmouth.co.uk **01598 753236**

Brendon House is a licensed country guesthouse with five well appointed en suite bedrooms with colour TV and tea/coffee making facilities. There is a residents' lounge with log fire in the winter months, and an award-winning restaurant serving local food and game and home grown seasonal vegetables from the garden.

Sitting in almost an acre of mature gardens, Brendon House provides the ideal location to just relax and unwind or as a base from which to explore the beautiful countryside, walks and views of the Exmoor National Park and the rugged North Devon coast.

BRENDON HOUSE
Brendon, Lynton, Devon EX35 6PS
Tel: 01598 741206 • e-mail: brendonhouse4u@aol.com
www.brendonhouse4u.com

Jim and Susan Bingham,
New Mill Farm, Barbrook,
Lynton, North Devon EX35 6JR
Tel: (01598) 753341
e-mail: info@outovercott.co.uk

EXMOOR VALLEY

Two delightful genuine modernised XVII Century Cottages by a stream on a 100-acre farm with "ABRS Approved" Riding Stables. Also a Bungalow with fenced garden and panoramic views of Exmoor. All have modernised kitchens, central heating, colour television and video, washing machine, tumble dryers, dishwasher and microwave. Linen provided. Thoroughly inspected before arrival. Pets welcome at £15 each weekly. Safe for children and pets to play. Horse riding over Exmoor from our own A.B.R.S. Approved stables. Free fishing.

We offer weekend and midweek breaks throughout the year.

Please ask for a brochure.

www.outovercott.co.uk

Devon

Mortehoe, Noss Mayo, Okehampton

DOGS WELCOME
Relax and unwind @ the hotel by the sea!
Set directly on the North Devon coastline, the Lundy House Hotel is a small family-run hotel where we aim to give our guests a comfortable, relaxing and truly memorable holiday in idyllic surroundings. Stunning sea views. Terraced gardens lead onto the South West Coastal Path. *Dogs and dirty boots welcome!*

Lundy House Hotel
Mortehoe, North Devon EX34 7DZ
• Tel: 01271 870372 •
e-mail: info@lundyhousehotel.co.uk • www.lundyhousehotel.co.uk

---

THE SMUGGLERS

Situated in the pretty village of Mortehoe, The Smugglers offers luxury accommodation from twin rooms to family suites. Treat yourselves and your pets to beautiful coastal walks and golden beaches, before you sample our delicious home-cooked meals, real ales and warm, year round hospitality.

The Smugglers Rest Inn, North Morte Road, Mortehoe, North Devon EX34 7DR • Tel/Fax: 01271 870891
info@smugglersmortehoe.co.uk
www.smugglersmortehoe.co.uk

CRAB COTTAGE NOSS MAYO SOUTH DEVON
www.crab-cottage.co.uk

• Charming fisherman's cottage, 50 yards from the quay on the River Yealm
• Watch the boats on the river from the cottage gardens and window seats • Delightful, quiet village in an area of outstanding natural beauty • Fantastic walks, beaches and dog-friendly pubs on the doorstep • Walk across to village shops in Newton Ferrers at low tide
• Close to the South Devon Coastal Path • Sleeps 5

Phone 01425 471372 for a brochure • e-mail: 07enquiries@crab-cottage.co.uk

---

Northlake Bed & Breakfast
STOCKLEY, OKEHAMPTON EX20 1QH
Tel: 01837 53100

Homemade cake and a warm welcome await at this friendly B&B with views across Dartmoor. We are well sited for walking, cycling, riding, touring and golf. You are welcome to picnic or BBQ in the gardens, coracle on the pond, or play croquet to while away the summer evenings. Doggie day-care available.

e-mail: pam@northlakedevon.co.uk • www.northlakedevon.co.uk

Ottery St Mary, Paignton

AA ★★

Cat lovers' paradise in charming 16th century farmhouse set in lovely Otter Valley. Two acres of beautiful gardens with pond and stream. All rooms en suite, TV and Teasmaids. Pets welcome free of charge. Plenty of dog walking space. Brochure available.
Terms from: B&B £27.50pppn.

FLUXTON FARM
Ottery St Mary, Devon EX11 1RJ
Tel: 01404 812818
www.fluxtonfarm.co.uk

The Commodore
AA Tel. 01803 553107 **AA**

The diverse walk options available will keep your dog fit and healthy. Dog friendly beaches, The South West Coast Path, Cockington Country Park, The Occombe Valley, River Dart, River Teign, Dartmoor National Park and Haldon Forest, to name but a few.

www.commodorepaignton.com
**14 Esplanade Road
Paignton
Devon
TQ4 6EB
Free Parking, Clean, Friendly, Relaxing, Great British Breakfast.**

Goodrington North Beach
Doggy Heaven all year.

AMBER HOUSE
6 Roundham Road, Paignton, Devon TQ4 6EZ • Tel: 01803 558372

Silver SILVER AWARD

- ❋ Overlooks Goodrington Sands. ❋ Ground floor rooms.
- ❋ All en suite, some with bath and shower. ❋ Non-smoking.
- ❋ Satellite digital TV or Freeview TV and DVD player in all rooms.
- ❋ Computer room, wi-fi access in some rooms.
- ❋ Good food; special diets catered for. ❋ Large car park.
- ❋ English Riviera climate ideal for Spring/Autumn breaks.
- ❋ Park and beach 5 minutes' walk. ❋ Walkers welcome.
- ❋ We pride ourselves on our high standards.

e-mail: enquiries@amberhousehotel.co.uk
www.amberhousehotel.co.uk
Contact: Christine Clark & Lloyd Hastie.

Devon
Plymouth, Salcombe

Give your pets a holiday at
Churchwood Valley

**Fourteen times David Bellamy Gold Award Winner
Gold in Green Tourism Business Scheme**

Relax in one of our comfortable log cabins, set in a peaceful wooded valley near the beach. Wonderful walks in woods and along the coast. Abundance of birds and wildlife. Up to two pets per cabin.

Open Mid-March to Mid-January including special Christmas and New Year Breaks.

Wembury Bay, Near Plymouth
churchwoodvalley@btconnect.com
www.churchwoodvalley.com
Tel: 01752 862382

The Cranbourne
278/282 Citadel Road,
The Hoe, Plymouth PL1 2PZ
Tel: 01752 263858/661400/224646
Fax: 01752 263858

- Equidistant City Centre and Hoe Promenade • All bedrooms beautifully decorated, heated, with colour TV, tea/coffee facilities • ¼ mile Ferry Terminal • Keys for access at all times
- Licensed Bar • Pets by prior arrangement (no charge) • Large secure car park • Free wifi

Under the personal supervision of The Williams Family

AA ★★★ Guest Accommodation

e-mail: cran.hotel@virgin.net • www.cranbournehotel.co.uk

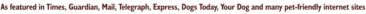

PORT LIGHT Hotel, Restaurant & Inn

As featured in Times, Guardian, Mail, Telegraph, Express, Dogs Today, Your Dog and many pet-friendly internet sites

- Luxury en suite rooms, easy access onto the gardens • Close to secluded sandy cove (dogs permitted) 20 minutes' walk • No charge for pets which are most welcome throughout the hotel. • Outstanding reputation for superb home-cooked fayre specialising in fresh sea food • Set alongside the famous National Trust Salcombe to Hope Cove coastal walk • Fully licensed bar – log burner – real ale
- Winner 2004 "Dogs Trust" Best Pet Hotel in England • Large free car park
- Open Christmas & New Year • Self-catering cottages nearby.

Doggies' Heaven, Walkers' Paradise, Romantics' Dream
Important advice: always try to ensure both other so-called 'pet-friendly' hotels really are! Talk to us to find out more.
WE ARE REALLY, TOTALLY PET-FRIENDLY

Bolberry Down, Malborough, Near Salcombe, South Devon TQ7 3DY
e-mail: info@portlight.co.uk • www.portlight.co.uk
Tel: (01548) 561384 or (07970) 859992 • Sean & Hazel Hassall

A totally unique location, set amidst acres of National Trust coastal countryside with panoramic views towards Cornwall, Dartmoor and France.

MILKBERE
Cottage Holidays

Devon/Dorset Border
Seaton, Beer and Sidmouth
3 Fore Street • Seaton • EX12 2LE
Phone: 01297 22925 (brochure)
01297 20729 (bookings)
Look and book online
www.milkberehols.com

Cottages
Bungalows
Houses
Apartments
Caravans

All VisitBritain inspected

Regional Tourist Board
southwesttourism MEMBER

Axevale Caravan Park
Colyford Road, Seaton EX12 2DF • Tel: 0800 0688816

A quiet, family-run park with 68 modern and luxury caravans for hire. The park overlooks the delightful River Axe Valley, and is just a 10 minute walk from the town with its wonderfully long, award-winning beach. Children will love our extensive play area, with its sand pit, paddling pool, swings and slide. Laundry facilities are provided and there is a wide selection of goods on sale in the park shop which is open every day. All of our caravans have a shower, toilet, fridge and TV with digital channels. Also, with no clubhouse, a relaxing atmosphere is ensured. Prices from £80 per week; reductions for three or fewer persons early/late season.

www.axevale.co.uk

THE WOODLANDS HOTEL

20-bedroom hotel just a few minutes' easy walk from both Sidmouth town centre and seafront; spacious bar and lounge. Well behaved pets welcome.

Woodlands Hotel, Station Road, Sidmouth, Devon EX10 8HG
Tel: 01395 513120 • Fax: 01395 513348
e-mail: info@woodlands-hotel.com • www.woodlands-hotel.com

LEIGH COTTAGES
WESTON, SIDMOUTH, DEVON EX10 0PH

Cottages for couples and families close to SW Coast Path, Weston Combe and Donkey Sanctuary. Dog-friendly beaches and pubs nearby. Peaceful location.
Contact: Alison Clarke • Tel: 01395 516065/514764 • Fax: 01395 512563
e-mail: Alison@leighcottages.co.uk • www.leighcottages.co.uk

ETC ★★★★

Oakdown

SIDMOUTH'S MULTI AWARD-WINNING HOLIDAY PARK
Weston - Sidmouth - Devon - EX10 0PT
Telephone: Park/Reservations 01297 680387 • Fax: 01297 680541
e-mail: enquiries@oakdown.co.uk • www.oakdown.co.uk

Welcome to Oakdown, set near the "Jurassic Coast" World Heritage Site, and a winner of "Caravan Holiday Park of The Year" – Sidmouth's multi-award-winning Park. Oakdown is level, sheltered and landscaped into groves to give privacy. Our luxurious amenities include aids for the disabled. Enjoy our Field Trail to the famous Donkey Sanctuary.
Free colour brochure with pleasure.

Devon

SOUTH WEST ENGLAND 141

Sidmouth, Tavistock

SWEETCOMBE
Cottage Holidays

ATTRACTIVE, CAREFULLY SELECTED COASTAL COTTAGES, FARMHOUSES AND FLATS IN SIDMOUTH & EAST DEVON

All very well equipped.
Gardens, Pets welcome

SWEETCOMBE COTTAGE HOLIDAYS,
ROSEMARY COTTAGE, WESTON, NEAR SIDMOUTH, DEVON EX10 0PH
Tel: 01395 512130
e-mail: enquiries@sweetcombe-ch.co.uk • www.sweetcombe-ch.co.uk

Heaven in Devon and a Paradise for your Pet

Luxury cottages and lodges in 120 acres, three coarse fishing lakes, indoor heated pool, sauna, tennis court, 9-hole pitch and putt course, indoor games rooms and a friendly Bar/Bistro for relaxing drinks or an evening meal.

Wonderful doggy walks including off-lead areas. Heritage Coast beaches at Sidmouth, Seaton, Branscombe and Lyme Regis a short drive away.

Otterfalls
Holiday Cottages & Lodges

For Reservations and Brochures call free 0808 145 2700
www.otterfalls.co.uk • e-mail: hols@otterfalls.co.uk

**New Road, Upottery
Honiton, Devon EX14 9QD**

LANGSTONE MANOR HOLIDAY PARK

Peaceful Holiday Park, offering camping, apartment, cottages, static caravans. Ideal location outside Tavistock with direct access onto Dartmoor. Bar and evening meals. Walks straight onto moor. Excellent location.

Moortown, Tavistock PL19 9JZ

Tel & Fax: 01822 613371
jane@langstone-manor.co.uk
www.langstone-manor.co.uk

TAVISTOCK • EDGE OF DARTMOOR

Comfortably furnished studio cottage five miles from the market town of Tavistock. Ideal for two. Private walled garden. Pets welcome. Private parking, free coal for open fire. All linen provided. Wonderful walking, riding, fishing country with excellent local pubs. Terms £225 per week.

Higher Quither
Milton Abbot, Tavistock, Devon PL19 0PZ
Contact: Mrs P.G.C. Quinton
Tel: 01822 860284 • www.higherquither.2day.ws/

Cutaway Cottage • Thurlestone, Kingsbridge TQ7 3NF
Self-catering cottage within fenced garden in the middle of the village, on private road. • 5 minutes to pub and shop. • 20 minutes' walk to beaches and sea • Ideal for children, dog walkers and bird watchers.
Pets free of charge ° Phone Pat on 01548 560688

NEWHOUSE FARM COTTAGES

Superior Quality
Self-catering Accommodation

Nine beautifully converted, well equipped, Grade II Listed stone barns, with a choice of accommodation ranging from a one-bedroom cottage with four-poster bed through to our spacious five-bedroom barn sleeping 10. Take a stroll through 23 acres of flower-filled meadows and woodland, or simply relax in our heated indoor swimming pool and games room.

**For long or short breaks and more information, please call us on
01884 860266 or visit our website at www.newhousecottages.com
Newhouse Farm, Witheridge, Tiverton, Devon EX16 8QB**

Free or reduced rate entry to
Holiday Visits and Attractions - see our
READERS' OFFER VOUCHERS on pages 445-454

Devon   **SOUTH WEST ENGLAND** 143

Torbay, Torquay

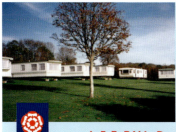

SOUTH DEVON • NEAR TORBAY

6 and 8 berth caravans new in 2007 and other 4 and 6 berths to let. All with toilets and showers. All with electricity, colour TV and fridges. Dogs on lead welcome.

Launderette, shop and payphone.
Also separate area for tourers, motor caravans and tents with modern toilet/ shower block with family rooms. Electric hook-ups and hard standings.

J. & E. BALL, Dept PW, HIGHER WELL FARM HOLIDAY PARK
Stoke Gabriel, Totnes, South Devon TQ9 6RN • Tel: 01803 782289
www.higherwellfarmholidaypark.co.uk

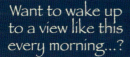

Want to wake up to a view like this every morning...?

The Downs Babbacombe

Room with a View ...?

41-43 Babbacombe Downs Road
Babbacombe - Torquay TQ1 3LN
Tel: 01803 328543 / 0845 051 0989
www.downshotel.co.uk

Situated directly above Babbacombe & Oddicombe beaches, we are a fully licensed family run establishment with 12 en-suite guest rooms, 8 have private balconies which enjoy fabulous unobstructed views over Babbacombe Downs and out over Lyme Bay all the way to Portland Bill.

We welcome young and old, couples and singles alike. We can accommodate families in our 4 family rooms, with reduced rates for under 12's, and are Dog friendly.

We do, so why not join us

If you are looking for a guest house or hotel in Torquay, try The Norwood first. Just a stroll from the seafront, town centre, Riviera Conference Centre and all local attractions. We provide a quality holiday experience focussing on old-fashioned hospitality, clean comfortable rooms and beautifully presented, home-cooked food.

The Norwood
60 Belgrave Road, Torquay TQ2 5HY • Tel: 01803 294236, Fax: 01803 294224
E-mail: enquiries@norwoodhoteltorquay.co.uk
www.norwoodhoteltorquay.co.uk

 **Avron House** *Babbacombe, Torquay*

An elegant family-run guesthouse in a quiet residential location. Many local attractions, free on-road parking, a quiet retreat for a relaxing break.
Clive Mason and Diane Shelton, 70 Windsor Road, Torquay, Devon TQ1 1SZ
Tel: 01803 294182 • email: avronhouse@blueyonder.co.uk
www.avronhouse.co.uk

Visit the FHG website
www.holidayguides.com

for details of the wide choice of accommodation

featured in the full range of FHG titles

SOUTH WEST ENGLAND — Devon

Torrington, Woolacombe

Cloister Park Cottages

Frithelstock, Torrington North Devon
EX38 8JH • Tel: 01805 622518
www.cloisterpark.co.uk

Three recently converted cottages (sleep 6/4/2), all fully equipped, with own patio areas. The attractive market town of Great Torrington is just 2 miles away. Tarka Trail and North Devon beaches close by.

STOWFORD LODGE
LANGTREE, GREAT TORRINGTON EX38 8NU

Picturesque and peaceful. Four delightful cottages and log cabin set within 6 acres of private land with heated indoor pool. Magnificent countryside. Convenient North Devon coast and moors. Sleep 4/6. Phone for brochure. **01805 601549**

e-mail: enq@stowfordlodge.co.uk • www.stowfordlodge.co.uk

Sunnymeade • Tel: 01271 863668

- Friendly, comfortable Country Hotel • Lovely countryside views
- Centrally placed close to Woolacombe's dog-friendly beach, Ilfracombe and Exmoor • Off-season special breaks & Christmas
- 12 en suite bedrooms, 4 on ground floor
- Deaf accessible BSL signed • Award-winning home-cooked food
- Pets welcome • Lots of lovely walks from the front door

www.sunnymeade.co.uk • Fax: 01271 866061

**SUNNYMEADE COUNTRY HOTEL
DEAN CROSS, WEST DOWN, DEVON EX34 8NT**

EUROPA
www.europapark.co.uk

**BOOKINGS & ENQUIRIES
01271 871425**

- CLUBHOUSE
- RESTAURANT
- HAPPY HOUR
- SAUNA
- SPAR SHOP
- INDOOR POOL
- GAMES ROOM
- LAUNDERETTE

CAMPING FROM £7.50 PPPN

LOG CABINS FROM £12.50 PPPN

WOOLACOMBE DEVON

CHICHESTER HOUSE HOLIDAY APARTMENTS

Quiet, relaxing, fully furnished apartments. Opposite Barricane Shell Beach – central seafront position with outstanding sea and coastal views.

Watch the sun go down into the sea from your own balcony.

• Open all year • Free parking • Pets by arrangement.

SAE to resident proprietor, Joyce Bagnall.

Off-peak reductions. Short Break details on request.

The Esplanade, Woolacombe EX34 7DJ
Tel: 01271 870761

Sampford Manor — Bed & Breakfast in the wilds of Dartmoor

Double or Twin Bedded rooms with private bathroom or shower.
£24.00–£35.00 per person per night. Dogs welcome. Stabling or grazing for horses.
Sampford Manor, Sampford Spiney, Yelverton, Devon PL20 6LH
Tel: 01822 853442 • Fax: 01822 855691 • e-mail: manor@sampford-spiney.fsnet.co.uk
www.sampford-spiney.fsnet.co.uk

COAST & COUNTRY COTTAGES. Over 425 self-catering properties in and around Salcombe, Dartmouth and Hope Cove and throughout the beautiful South Devon coast and countryside, the ideal destination for a holiday or short break with your dog all year round. Free brochure. [Pets £20 per week].
website: www.coastandcountry.co.uk

TOAD HALL COTTAGES (01548 853089 24 hrs). 300 outstanding waterside and rural properties in truly beautiful locations in Devon, Cornwall and Exmoor. Call for our highly acclaimed brochure. Pets welcome.
e-mail: thc@toadhallcottages.co.uk   website: www.toadhallcottages.co.uk

HELPFUL HOLIDAYS (01647 433535). Wonderful variety of cottages all over the West Country. Ideal for countryside rambles. Many welcome pets.
website: www.helpfulholidays.co.uk

MARSDENS COTTAGE HOLIDAYS, 2 THE SQUARE, BRAUNTON EX33 2JB (01271 813777; Fax: 01271 813664). Want the best of Devon and Cornwall self-catering? All our properties are VisitBritain approved and with many welcoming pets. Contact us and we can help you find the best property for your whole family.
e-mail: holidays@marsdens.co.uk   website: www.marsdens.co.uk

NORTH DEVON HOLIDAY HOMES, 19 CROSS STREET, BARNSTAPLE EX31 1BD (01271 376322). Free colour guide to the best value pet friendly cottages around Exmoor and Devon's National Trust Coast. [Pets £12 per week.]
e-mail: info@northdevonholidays.co.uk   website: www.devonandexmoor.co.uk

PORT LIGHT, BOLBERRY DOWN, MALBOROUGH, NEAR SALCOMBE TQ7 3DY (01548 561384 or 07970 859992). A totally unique location set amidst acres of National Trust coastline. Luxury en suite rooms. Superb home-cooked fare, specialising in local seafood. Licensed bar. Pets welcome throughout the hotel. Short Breaks throughout the year. Self-catering cottages also available. Contact: Sean and Hazel Hassall. [🐾]
e-mail: info@portlight.co.uk   website: www.portlight.co.uk

FARM & COTTAGE HOLIDAYS (01237 459897). An inspiring collection of holiday cottages throughout Cornwall, Devon, Somerset and Dorset in stunning rural and coastal locations. [Pets £20 per week]
website: www.holidaycottages.co.uk

Appledore

Delightful quayside village, ideal base to explore North Devon.

MRS CYMA CASSAR, CROSS HOUSE, FORE STREET, NORTHAM, BIDEFORD EX39 1AN (01237 472042). Three cottages, all with 'Olde Worlde' charm and up-to-date amenities. Exmoor, Clovelly, Lynton, Lynmouth, Tarka Trail within easy reach. Many beaches, the nearest one mile away. [🐾]
e-mail: info@crosshouseandcottages.co.uk   www.crosshouseandcottages.co.uk

Ashburton

Delightful little town on southern fringe of Dartmoor. Centrally placed for touring and the Torbay resorts. Plymouth 24 miles, Exeter 20, Kingsbridge 20, Tavistock 20, Teignmouth 14, Torquay 14, Totnes 8, Newton Abbot 7.

PARKERS FARM HOLIDAY PARK, HIGHER MEAD FARM, ASHBURTON TQ13 7LJ (01364 654869; Fax: 01364 654004). Static caravans to let, also level touring site with two toilet/shower blocks and electric hook-ups. Central for touring; 12 miles Torquay. ETC ★★★★, AA Four Pennants. [pw! Pets £1.50 per night touring, £17 per week static caravans]

MRS A. BELL, WOODER MANOR, WIDECOMBE IN THE MOOR, NEAR ASHBURTON TQ13 7TR (Tel & Fax: 01364 621391). Cottages nestled in picturesque valley. Surrounded by unspoilt woodland and moors. Clean and well equipped, colour TV, central heating, laundry room. Two properties suitable for disabled visitors. Colour brochure available. ETC ★★★ to ★★★★ [pw! £15–£20 per week].
e-mail: angela@woodermanor.com   website: www.woodermanor.com

PARKERS FARM COTTAGES & CARAVANS, MEAD, ALSTON CROSS, ASHBURTON TQ13 7LJ (01364 653008). Farm Cottages and Static Caravans to let surrounded by beautiful countryside. Perfect for children and pets. Central for touring; 12 miles Torquay. ETC ★★★/★★★★ [pw! Pets £17 per week]
e-mail: parkerscottages@btconnect.com   website: www.parkersfarm.co.uk

Ashwater

Village 6 miles south-east of Holsworthy.

BLAGDON MANOR RESTAURANT WITH ROOMS, ASHWATER, NORTH DEVON EX21 5DF (01409 211224; Fax: 01409 211634). Beautifully restored Grade II Listed building in peaceful location 20 minutes from Bude. 7 en suite bedrooms, three-acre gardens. No children under 12 years. AA Three Red Stars, 2 Rosettes. [pw! Dogs £8 per night]
email: stay@blagdon.com   website: www.blagdon.com

Axminster

Small friendly market town, full of old world charm, set in the beautiful Axe Valley. Excellent centre for touring Devon, Somerset and Dorset. 5 miles from coast.

THE FAIRWATER HEAD HOTEL, HAWKCHURCH, NEAR AXMINSTER EX13 5TX (01297 678349; Fax: 01297 678459). Located in the tranquil Devon countryside and close to Lyme Regis, this beautiful Edwardian Country House Hotel has all you and your dog need for a peaceful and relaxing holiday. Dogs most welcome. Countryside location with panoramic views. AA ★★★, Rosette. [🐾]
e-mail: e-mail: stay@fairwaterheadhotel.co.uk   website: www.fairwaterheadhotel.co.uk

LEA HILL, MEMBURY, AXMINSTER EX13 7AQ (01404 881881). Tranquil location. Wonderful scenery. Close to World Heritage Coast. Eight acres of grounds and gardens. Walks, footpaths and exercise fields. Hot tub and barbecue. Comfortable, well equipped self-catering cottages with en suite bedrooms and own gardens. Green Tourism Silver Award, VB ★★★★. [pw! Pets £15 per week]
e-mail: reception@leahill.co.uk   website: www.leahill.co.uk

LILAC COTTAGE. Detached cottage, furnished to a high standard, sleeps six plus cot. Children and pets are welcome. Walled garden and garage. On borders of Devon, Dorset, and Somerset; many seaside towns within 10 miles. Contact: MRS J.M. STUART, 2 SANDFORD HOUSE, KINGSCLERE RG20 4PA (Tel & Fax: 01635 291942; Mobile: 07624 101285).
e-mail: joanna.sb@free.fr

Bantham

Unspoilt village near market town of Kingsbridge in the South Hams area.

MRS LIBBY SIMMONS, SLOOP HOLIDAY APRTMENTS, 2 THE WATCH, BANTHAM, KINGSBRIDGE TQ7 3AJ (01548 560810). Comfortable, modern, self catering accommodation, with a high standard of furnishings and wonderful views. Cottages 1,2 & 3, sleep 6. No. 4 is ground floor flat sleeping 4. Non Smoking. EnjoyEngland ★★★★.[🐕]
e-mail: info@sloopholidayapartments.co.uk   website: www.sloopholidaycottages.co.uk

Barnstaple

Market town at head of River Taw estuary, 34 miles north west of Exeter.

LOWER YELLAND FARM GUEST HOUSE, FREMINGTON, BARNSTAPLE EX31 3EN (01271 860101). Delightfully modernised farmhouse accommodation on working farm. Central for North Devon attractions. All rooms en suite, with TV and tea/coffee making. Breakfast includes free-range eggs and home-made bread etc. [Pets £2.50 per night, £15 per week]
e-mail: peterday@loweryellandfarm.co.uk   website: www.loweryellandfarm.co.uk

MARTINHOE CLEAVE COTTAGES, MARTINHOE, PARRACOMBE, BARNSTAPLE EX31 4PZ (01598 763313). Perfect rural tranquillity overlooking the beautiful Heddon valley and close to the Exmoor National Park. Delightful cottages, equipped to a very high standard throughout. Open all year. Sleep 1-2. [🐕].
e-mail: info@exmoorhideaway.co.uk   website:www.exmoorhideaway.co.uk

NORTH HILL COTTAGES, NORTH HILL, SHIRWELL, BARNSTAPLE EX31 4LG (01271 850611; mobile: 07834 806434). Sleep 2-6. 17th century farm buildings, sympathetically converted into cottages. Indoor heated swimming pool, jacuzzi, sauna, all-weather tennis court and games room. [Pets £25 per week]
website: www.north-hill.co.uk

Berrynarbor

This peaceful village overlooking the beautiful Sterridge valley has a 17th century pub and even older church, and is half-a-mile from the coast road between Combe Martin and Ilfracombe.

SANDY COVE HOTEL, BERRYNARBOR EX34 9SR (01271 882243 or 882888). Hotel set amidst acres of gardens and woods. Heated swimming pool. Children and pets welcome. A la carte restaurant. All rooms en suite with colour TV, tea-making. Free colour brochure on application. ETC ★★★ [🐕 one dog]
website: www.sandycove-hotel.co.uk

Bideford

Neat port village overlooking the beautiful Sterridge Valley has a 17th century pub and even older church, and is half-a-mile from the coast road between Combe Martin and Ilfracombe.

ROBERT & LISA IRETON, MEAD BARN COTTAGES, WELCOMBE, NEAR BIDEFORD EX39 (01288 331721). 3/4 Star Graded quality, self-catering cottages sleeping 2-26 people. Set in one and a half acres. Games room, tennis court, play area, swings, trampoline and gardens with barbecue area. [Pets £20 per week] ETC ★★★/★★★★
e-mail: holidays@meadbarns.com   website: www.meadbarns.com

THE PINES AT EASTLEIGH, NEAR BIDEFORD EX39 4PA (01271 860561). Luxury B&B and cottages. Log-fires, king-size beds, garden room bar with library, maps and a warm welcome await our guests. B&B from £30pp. No smoking. AA ★★★★ [pw! 🐕]
e-mail: pirrie@thepinesateastleigh.co.uk   website: www.thepinesateastleigh.co.uk

THE HOOPS INN & COUNTRY HOTEL, HORNS CROSS, NEAR CLOVELLY, BIDEFORD EX39 5DL (01237 451222; Fax: 01237 451247). Thatched country inn with open log fires. All bedrooms en suite. Splendid base for touring and outdoor pursuits. Dartmoor and Exmoor within easy reach. AA★★★ and Rosette
e-mail: sales@hoopsinn.co.uk   website: www.hoopsinn.co.uk

SOUTH WEST ENGLAND 149

Bigbury-on-Sea

A scattered village overlooking superb coastal scenery and wide expanses of sand.

MR SCARTERFIELD, HENLEY HOTEL, FOLLY HILL, BIGBURY-ON-SEA TQ7 4AR (01548 810240). Edwardian cottage-style hotel, spectacular sea views. Overlooking beach, dog walking. En suite rooms with telephone, tea making, TV etc. No smoking establishment. Licensed. ETC ★★ HOTEL and SILVER AWARD. AA ★★, GOOD HOTEL GUIDE, CESAR AWARD WINNER 2003, "WHICH?" GUIDE, COASTAL CORKER 2003. [Pets £5.00 per night.]

MRS J. TUCKER, MOUNT FOLLY FARM, BIGBURY-ON-SEA, KINGSBRIDGE TQ7 4AR (01548 810267). Cliff top position, with outstanding views of Bigbury Bay. Spacious, self-catering wing of farmhouse, attractively furnished. Farm adjoins golf course and River Avon. Lovely coastal walks, ideal centre for South Hams and Dartmoor. No smoking. Always a warm welcome, pets too! ETC ★★★ [pw! Pets £15 per week]
e-mail: info@bigburyholidays.co.uk   website: www.bigburyholidays.co.uk

Bradworthy

Village to the north of Holsworthy. Well placed for North Devon and North Cornish coasts.

PETER & LESLEY LEWIN, LAKE HOUSE COTTAGES AND B&B, LAKE VILLA, BRADWORTHY DEVON EX22 7SQ (01409 241962). Four well equipped cottages sleeping two to five/six. Quiet rural position; one acre gardens and tennis court. Half-a-mile from village shops and pub. Dog-friendly beaches eight miles. Also two lovely en suite B&B rooms with balcony, all facilities, from £30. [🐾]
e-mail: lesley@lakevilla.co.uk   website: www.lakevilla.co.uk

Braunton

5 miles north west of Barnstaple. To the south west are Braunton Burrows nature reserve, a lunar landscape of sand dunes noted for rare plants, and the 3 mile stretch of Saunton Sands.

LITTLE COMFORT FARM, BRAUNTON, NORTH DEVON EX33 2NJ (01271 812 414). Five spacious self-catering cottages sleeping 2-10 on organic family farm, just minutes from golden sandy beaches where dogs are allowed. Well stocked coarse fishing lake. Private 1½km farm trail. Wood fires for cosy winter breaks. PETS VERY WELCOME [pw! Pets £20 per week].
e-mail: info@littlecomfortfarm.co.uk   website: www.littlecomfortfarm.co.uk

Brixham

Lively resort and fishing port, with quaint houses and narrow winding streets. Ample opportunities for fishing and boat trips.

DEVONCOURT HOLIDAY FLATS, BERRYHEAD ROAD, BRIXHAM TQ5 9AB (01803 853748 or 07802 403289 after office hours). 24 self-contained flats with private balcony, colour television, heating, private car park, all-electric kitchenette, separate bathroom and toilet. Open all year. Pets welcome.
website: www.devoncourt.info

BRIXHAM HOLIDAY PARK, FISHCOMBE COVE, BRIXHAM TQ5 8RB (01803 853324). Situated on coastal path. Choice of one and two-bedroomed chalets. Indoor heated pool, free club membership, comfortable bar offering meals and takeaway service, launderette. 150 yards from beach with lovely walks through woods beyond. ETC ★★★★. [Pets £30 per week]
e-mail: enquiries@brixhamholpk.fsnet.co.uk   website: www.brixhamholidaypark.co.uk

Broadwoodwidger

Village 6 miles north-east of Launceston.

WEST BANBURY FARM COTTAGES, BROADWOODWIDGER (01566 780423). 10 charming cottages, set around two courtyards. Sleep 2-8 (dogs welcome in all). Large indoor pool, sauna, games room etc. Ideal for exploring Devon and Cornwall. Contact ANNA-ROSE for details. [Pets £20 per week].
website: www.westbanbury.co.uk

SOUTH WEST ENGLAND

Chittlehamholt

Standing in beautiful countryside in Taw Valley. Barnstaple 9 miles, South Molton 5.

SNAPDOWN FARM, CHITTLEHAMHOLT, UMBERLEIGH EX37 9PF (01769 540366). Set amidst glorious North Devon countryside, six holiday caravans on a well spread out leafy site with space for children to run and have a wonderful time. Ideal for families, couples and well behaved pets. From £128 - £335 per week for up to 6 people inc. gas and elec. [Charge for pets].
Website: www.snapdown.co.uk

Chulmleigh

Mid-Devon village set in lovely countryside, just off A377 Exeter to Barnstaple road. Exeter 23 miles, Tiverton 19, Barnstaple 18.

SANDRA GAY, NORTHCOTT BARTON FARM COTTAGE, NORTHCOTT BARTON, ASHREIGNEY, CHULMLEIGH EX18 7PR (Tel & Fax: 01769 520259). Three bedroom character cottage, large enclosed garden, log fire. Special rates low season, couples and short breaks. Near golf, riding, Tarka Trail and RHS Rosemoor. ETC ★★★★ [🐾]
e-mail: sandra@northcottbarton.co.uk   website: www.northcottbarton.co.uk

Colebrooke

Village 4 miles west of Crediton.

PEARL HOCKRIDGE, THE OYSTER, COLEBROOKE, CREDITON EX17 5JQ (01363 84576). Modern bungalow in pretty, peaceful village. Bedrooms en suite or with private bathroom. Dartmoor and Exmoor a short drive. Children and pets welcome. Open all year. Smoking accepted. [🐾]

Combe Martin

Coastal village with harbour set in sandy bay. Good cliff and rock scenery. Of interest is the Church and "Pack of Cards" Inn. Barnstaple 14 miles, Lynton 12, Ilfracombe 6.

WATERMOUTH COVE COTTAGES, WATERMOUTH, NEAR COMBE MARTIN EX34 9SJ (0845 029 1958 or 01271 883931). 8 beautiful cottages, most with four-poster and log fire, set beside grounds of Watermouth Castle, 200 yards from harbour/coastal path. Pets welcome. Open all year. [Pets £25 per week]
e-mail: watermouthcove@googlemail.com   website: www.watermouth-cove-cottages.co.uk

YETLAND FARM COTTAGES, BERRY DOWN, COMBE MARTIN EX34 0NT (01271 883655). 6 well equipped cottages surrounding a pretty paved courtyard. Ideally situated for North Devon beaches, Exmoor, the South West Coastal Path and many tourist and leisure attractions. Linen and towels supplied. Sleep 3-6 plus cot. Well behaved pets welcome. ETC ★★★★ [Pets £15 per week]
e-mail: enquiries@yetlandfarmcottages.co.uk   www.yetlandfarmcottages.co.uk

NORTHCOTE MANOR FARM HOLIDAY COTTAGES, NEAR COMBE MARTIN EX31 4NB (01271 882376). Five self-catering holiday cottages grouped around a courtyard. Dogs are warmly welcomed in all of the cottages, three of which have enclosed gardens. 34 acres of fields, woods and rivers to explore. Indoor heated pool, games room and playground. [Pets £25 per week]
e-mail: info@northcotemanorfarm.co.uk   website: www.northcotemanorfarm.co.uk

Cullompton

Small market town off the main A38 Taunton - Exeter road. Good touring centre. Noted for apple orchards which supply the local cider industry. Taunton 19 miles, Exeter 13, Honiton 11, Tiverton 9.

FOREST GLADE HOLIDAY PARK (PW), KENTISBEARE, CULLOMPTON EX15 2DT (01404 841381; Fax: 01404 841593). Country estate surrounded by forest with modern 6-berth holiday caravans, all well-equipped. Free indoor heated swimming pool. Tents, touring caravans and motor homes welcome. ETC ★★★★, AA 4 Pennants, David Bellamy Gold Award. [Pets £2 per night, pw!]
e-mail: enquiries@forest-glade.co.uk   website: www.forest-glade.co.uk

Devon
SOUTH WEST ENGLAND 151

Dartmoor

365 square miles of National Park with spectacular unspoiled scenery, fringed by picturesque villages.

TWO BRIDGES HOTEL, TWO BRIDGES, DARTMOOR PL20 6SW (01822 890581; Fax: 01822 892306). Famous Olde World riverside Inn. Centre Dartmoor. Log fires, very comfortable, friendly, excellent food. Ideal walking, touring, fishing, riding, golf. Warning – Addictive. ETC/AA ★★[🐾]
e-mail: enquiries@warm-welcome-hotels.co.uk   website: www.warm-welcome-hotels.co.uk

DEVONSHIRE INN, STICKLEPATH, OKEHAMPTON EX20 2NW (01837 840626) A real country pub! Out the back door onto the north edge of Dartmoor proper. Dogs and horses always welcome, fed and watered.

CHRIS & JULIE EASTAUGH, THE ROSEMONT, YELVERTON PL20 6DR (01822 852175). Four star quality B&B in village. Open access to moorland. Excellent walking country. Modern, spacious en suite rooms. B&B per room per night: Single £40, Double £60-70.
e-mail: office@therosemont.co.uk   website: www.therosemont.co.uk

PRINCE HALL HOTEL, DARTMOOR PL20 6SA (01822 890403). Small, friendly, relaxed country house hotel with glorious views onto open moorland. Walks in all directions. Nine en suite bedrooms. Log fires. Gourmet cooking. Excellent wine list. Fishing, riding, golf nearby. Three-Day Break from £100pppn. AA/VisitBritain ★★, AA Rosette for food. [🐾]
e-mail: info@princehall.co.uk   website: www.princehall.co.uk

THE CHERRYBROOK, TWO BRIDGES PL20 6SP (01822 880260). In the middle of Dartmoor National Park with seven comfortable en suite bedrooms. Excellent quality home-made meals. See our website for details, tariff and sample menu. [🐾]
e-mail: info@thecherrybrook.co.uk   website: www.thecherrybrook.co.uk

DARTMOOR COUNTRY HOLIDAYS, MAGPIE LEISURE PARK, DEPT PW, BEDFORD BRIDGE, HORRABRIDGE, YELVERTON PL20 7RY (01822 852651). Purpose-built pine lodges in peaceful woodland setting. Sleep 2-7. Furnished to very high standard (microwave, dishwasher etc). Easy walk to village and shops. Launderette. Dogs permitted. [Pets £2.50 per night].
website: www.dartmoorcountryholidays.co.uk

THE EDGEMOOR COUNTRY HOUSE HOTEL, HAYTOR ROAD, LOWERDOWN CROSS, BOVEY TRACEY TQ13 9LE (01626 832466; Fax: 01626 834760). Country House Hotel in peaceful wooded setting adjacent Dartmoor National Park. Many lovely walks close by. All rooms en suite. Dogs welcome. See our website for further details. ETC ★★★ Silver Award [pw! 🐾]
e-mail: reservations@edgemoor.co.uk   website: www.edgemoor.co.uk

Dartmouth

Historic port and resort on the estuary of the River Dart, with sandy coves and pleasure boat trips up the river. Car ferry to Kingswear.

WATERMILL COTTAGES, HIGHER NORTH MILL, HANSEL, DARTMOUTH TQ6 0LN (01803 770219). Five comfy old stone cottages in 13 acres of unspoilt valley close to dog-friendly beaches and coastal path. Walks from your cottage door, enclosed gardens, log burners. We really welcome pets! [Pets £25 per week]
e-mail: christine@watermillcottages.co.uk   website: www.watermillcottages.co.uk

MRS S.R. RIDALLS, THE OLD BAKEHOUSE, 7 BROADSTONE, DARTMOUTH TQ6 9NR (Tel & Fax: 01803 834585). Four cottages (one with four-poster bed). Sleep 2–6. Near river, shops, restaurants. Blackpool Sands 15 minutes' drive. TV, DVD, linen free. Open all year. Free parking. Non-smoking. ETC ★★★ [🐾]
e-mail: oldbakehousecottages@yahoo.com   website: www.oldbakehousedartmouth.co.uk

Dunsford

Attractive village in upper Teign valley with Dartmoor to the west. Plymouth 35 miles, Okehampton 16, Newton Abbot 13, Crediton 9, Exeter 8.

ROYAL OAK INN, DUNSFORD, NEAR EXETER EX6 7DA (01647 252256). Welcome to our Victorian country inn with real ales and home-made food. All en suite rooms are in a 300-year-old converted barn. Well behaved children and dogs welcome. [🐾]

Exeter

Chief city of the South-West with a cathedral and university. Ample shopping, sports and leisure facilities.

LUCY & ANDY HINES, BUSSELLS FARM COTTAGES, BUSSELLS FARM, HUXHAM, EXETER EX5 4EN (01392 841238). Seven luxury barn conversion cottages, sleep 6/7. Coarse fishing lakes (securely fenced). Outdoor heated swimming pool (May to September), adventure playground and indoor games room. Open all year. ETC ★★★★ [🐾]
e-mail: bussellsfarm@aol.com   website: www.bussellsfarm.co.uk

BEST WESTERN LORD HALDON HOTEL, DUNCHIDEOCK, NEAR EXETER EX6 7YF (01392 832483, Fax: 01392 833765). Extensive gardens amid miles of rolling Devon countryside. ETC ★★★, AA ★★★ and Rosette. [Pets £5 per night.]
e-mail: enquiries@lordhaldonhotel.co.uk   website: www.lordhaldonhotel.co.uk

THORVERTON ARMS, THORVERTON EX5 5NS (01392 860205). Traditional coaching inn just 7 miles north of Exeter. Small, well behaved dogs welcome. 6 en suite bedrooms. Award-winning restaurant. Excellent choice of real ales. Ideal touring base for Dartmoor, Exmoor and Devon's beaches. [Pets £5 per night, pw!]
website: www.thethorvertonarms.co.uk

STATION LODGE, DODDISCOMBSLEIGH, EXETER (01647 253104). Comfortably furnished apartment for two people in beautiful Teign River valley. Excellent location for exploring Dartmoor. From £220 per week. For further details contact: IAN WEST, STATION HOUSE, DODDISCOMBSLEIGH, EXETER EX6 7PW. [pw! 🐾]
e-mail: enquiries@station-lodge.co.uk   website: www.station-lodge.co.uk

MRS SALLY GLANVILL, RYDON FARM, WOODBURY, EXETER EX5 1LB (01395 232341). 16th Century Devon Longhouse on working dairy farm. Open all year. 4 Star Silver Award. From £37 to £60pppn. ETC/AA ★★★★ [🐾]
website: www.rydonfarmwoodbury.co.uk

Exmoor

265 square miles of unspoiled heather moorland with deep wooded valleys and rivers, ideal for a walking, pony trekking or fishing holiday

THE STAGHUNTERS INN/HOTEL, BRENDON, EXMOOR EX35 6PS (01598 741222; Fax: 01598 741352). Family-run village inn with river frontage. Beautiful gardens. 12 en suite rooms. Varied menu, log fires, fine wines and cask ales. A walkers' paradise. [Pets £2.50 per night]
e-mail: stay@staghunters.com   website: www.staghunters.com

JAYE JONES AND HELEN ASHER, TWITCHEN FARM, CHALLACOMBE, BARNSTAPLE EX31 4TT (01598 763568). Comfort for country lovers in Exmoor National Park. High quality en suite rooms. Breakfast prepared with local and organic produce. Farm walk through fields to village pub. B&B £26–£36. ETC ★★★★ [One dog free, two dogs £6]
e-mail: holidays@twitchen.co.uk   website: www.twitchen.co.uk

Hexworthy (Dartmoor)

Hamlet on Dartmoor 7 miles west of Ashburton.

THE FOREST INN, HEXWORTHY, DARTMOOR PL20 6SD (01364 631211; Fax: 01364 631515). A haven for walkers, riders, fishermen, canoeists or anyone just looking for an opportunity to enjoy the natural beauty of Dartmoor. Restaurant using local produce wherever possible; extensive range of snacks; Devon beers and ciders. ETC ★★★ [🐾]
e-mail: info@theforestinn.co.uk

Holsworthy

Town 9 miles east of Bude.

TINNEY WATERS, PYWORTHY. Self-catering. Three beautiful lakes - carp, tench, bream. No day tickets, no close season. Ideal for birdwatching. Contact: J. MASON (01409 271362).
e-mail: jeffmason@freenetname.co.uk   website: www.tinneywaters.co.uk

Devon

SOUTH WEST ENGLAND 153

Honiton

Town on River Otter 16 miles East of Exeter.

COMBE HOUSE DEVON, GITTISHAM, HONITON, NEAR EXETER EX14 3AD (01404 540400). Magical Elizabethan Manor in 3,500 acres of idyllic countryside. Fabulous food, 15 rooms, one cottage with secure walled garden. Dogs Monthly Petometer 09 "Excellent". Warm welcoming hospitality for owners and their friends. [Pets £9 per night, pw!]
e-mail: stay@combehousedevon.com website: www.combehousedevon.com

Hope Cove

Attractive fishing village, flat sandy beach and safe bathing. Fine views towards Rame Head; cliffs. Kingsbridge 6 miles.

HOPE BARTON BARNS, HOPE COVE, NEAR SALCOMBE TQ7 3HT (01548 561393). 17 stone barns in two courtyards and three luxury apartments in farmhouse. Farmhouse meals. Free range children and well behaved dogs welcome. For full colour brochure please contact: MR & MRS M. POPE. [pw! Pets £20 per week]
e-mail: info@hopebarton.co.uk website: www.hopebarton.co.uk

Ilfracombe

This popular seaside resort clusters round a busy harbour. The surrounding area is ideal for coastal walks.

STRATHMORE, 57 ST BRANNOCKS ROAD, ILFRACOMBE EX34 8EQ (01271 862248) Delightful and friendly Victorian Licensed guest house, 10-minute stroll to both seafront and town centre. 8 individually designed en suite bedrooms. Cosy lounge bar, secluded terraced garden. Children and pets always welcome. AA ★★★★ [Pets £6.50 per night]. Please contact PETE OR HEATHER for more details.
e-mail: info@the-strathmore.co.uk www.the-strathmore.co.uk

WIDMOUTH FARM, NEAR ILFRACOMBE EX34 9RX (01271 863743). Comfortable, well equipped cottages in 35 acres of gardens, pasture, woodland and private beach. Wonderful scenery. Ideal for birdwatching, painting, sea fishing & golf. Dogs welcome. VisitBritain ★★★/★★★★. [pw! Pets £25 per week each].
e-mail: holiday@widmouthfarmcottages.co.uk website: www.widmouthfarmcottages.co.uk

THE FOXHUNTERS INN, WEST DOWN, NEAR ILFRACOMBE EX34 8NU (01271 863757; Fax: 01271 879313). 300 year-old coaching Inn conveniently situated for beaches and country walks. En suite accommodation. Pets welcome by prior arrangement.[🐾]
website: www.foxhuntersinn.co.uk

Kingsbridge

Pleasant town at head of picturesque Kingsbridge estuary. Centre for South Hams district with its lush scenery and quiet coves.

BEACHDOWN, CHALLABOROUGH BAY, KINGSBRIDGE TQ7 4JB (01548 811277; mobile: 07725 053439). Comfortable, fully-equipped chalets on private, level and secluded site in beautiful South Hams. 150 yards from beach and South West Coastal Path. [pw! Pets £15.00 per week].
e-mail: kimm@beachdown.co.uk website: www.beachdown.co.uk

DITTISCOMBE HOLIDAY COTTAGES, SLAPTON, NEAR KINGSBRIDGE, SOUTH DEVON TQ7 2QF (01548 521272). Nature trail and 20 acres of open space. Perfect holiday location for dogs and owners. All cottages have gardens and views of surrounding valley. ETC ★★★★. [Pets £20 per week]
e-mail: info@dittiscombe.co.uk website: www.dittiscombe.co.uk

MRS B. KELLY, BLACKWELL PARK, LODDISWELL, KINGSBRIDGE TQ7 4EA (01548 821230). 17th century Farmhouse, five miles from Kingsbridge. Ideal centre for Dartmoor, Plymouth, Torbay, Dartmouth and many beaches. Some bedrooms en suite. Bed and Breakfast. Evening meal optional. Dogsitting. Pets welcome free of charge. [🐾]

MOUNTS FARM TOURING PARK, THE MOUNTS, NEAR EAST ALLINGTON, KINGSBRIDGE TQ9 7QJ (01548 521591). Family-run site in the heart of South Devon. We welcome tents, touring caravans and motor caravans. Children and pets welcome. Many safe, sandy beaches nearby.
website: www.mountsfarm.co.uk

King's Nympton

3 miles north of Chulmleigh. Winner of CPRE Award for Devon Village of the year 1999.

COLLACOTT FARM, KING'S NYMPTON, UMBERLEIGH, NORTH DEVON EX37 9TP (01769 572491). Eight Country Cottages sleeping from 2 to 12 in rural area; lovely views, private patios and gardens. Well furnished and equipped. Heated pool, tennis court, BHS approved riding school. Laundry room. Open all year. [pw!, Pets £20 per week]
e-mail: info@collacott.co.uk   website: www.collacott.co.uk

Lapford

Village 5 miles south-east of Chulmleigh.

DAVID & MARION MILLS, RUDGE FARM, LAPFORD, CREDITON EX17 6NG (01363 83268). Set in beautiful grounds with pond, orchard and woods. Trout fishing and almost 200 acres to wander in. House very tastefully furnished and fully equipped (sleeps 8). No charge for dogs, linen or fuel. Send for brochure. [🐕]

Lydford

A Dartmoor village of national historical importance, 12 km south of Okehampton and 9km north of Tavistock.

LYDFORD COUNTRY HOUSE, LYDFORD, OKEHAMPTON EX20 4AU (01822 820347; Fax: 01822 820654). Set in 8 acres of beautiful grounds. En suite bedrooms, Italian restaurant. Stables for guests' horses; dog baskets available. Ideal for exploring coastline, Eden Project etc. ETC ★★★★★, Silver Award. [Pets £5 per night].
e-mail: info@lydfordcountryhouse.co.uk   website: www.lydfordcountryhouse.co.uk

Lynton/Lynmouth

Picturesque twin villages joined by a unique cliff railway (vertical height 500 ft). Lynmouth has a quaint harbour and Lynton enjoys superb views over the rugged coastline.

MRS W. PRYOR, STATION HOUSE, LYNTON EX35 6LB (01598 752275/752381; Fax: 01598 752475). Holiday accommodation situated in the former narrow gauge railway station closed in 1935, overlooking the West Lyn Valley. Centrally placed for Doone Valley and Exmoor. Parking available. [🐕]
e-mail: advertise@lyntonadvertiser.com

PRIME SPOT CHARACTER COTTAGES. Spectacular area for dog walking and mountain biking. Riverbank cottage for 1-6 at Lynmouth harbour. Romantic thatched cottage for two at Lynton. Seaside cottage for 1-4 at Combe Martin harbour. Available all year. Cosy winter breaks. ★★★/★★★★. Details/ brochures from MRS WOLVERSON (01271 882449).[one pet 🐕]

LYNHURST, LYNTON. Elegant late Victorian country house, retaining many original features, sleeps up to 22 for self-catering. Fully equipped kitchen, 10 bedrooms; linen, towels incl. Dogs welcome. For bookings ring Jane on 01598 753757 or 07807 183814. [🐕, pw!]
website: www.thelynhurst.com

CLOONEAVIN HOLIDAY APARTMENTS, CLOONEAVIN PATH, LYNMOUTH EX35 6EE (01598 753334). Eight well equipped self contained apartments and chalet. A short walk to the harbour. Numerous coastal and river walks through idyllic countryside. [Pets £15 per week].
e-mail: relax@clooneavinholidays.co.uk   website: www.clooneavinholidays.co.uk

---

Symbols

🐕   Indicates that pets are welcome free of charge.

£   Indicates that a charge is made for pets: nightly or weekly.

pw!   Shows some special provision for pets; exercise facility, feeding or accommodation arrangement.

⌂   Indicates separate pets accommodation.

Devon

SOUTH WEST ENGLAND 155

MOORLANDS. Where countryside and comfort combine. Two self-contained apartments within a family-run guesthouse, within the Exmoor National Park. Hotel amenities available for guests' use. Contact: MR I. CORDEROY, MOORLANDS, WOODY BAY, PARRACOMBE, NEAR LYNTON EX31 4RA (01598 763224). ETC ★★★★ [🐾]
website: www.moorlandshotel.co.uk

THE NORTH CLIFF HOTEL, NORTH WALK, LYNTON EX35 6HJ (01598 752357). On the South West Coastal Path, the North Cliff is an ideal base for discovering Exmoor and the North Devon Coast. Delicious home cooking. We welcome pets, children and groups. [Pets £4 per night, £20 per week].
e-mail: holidays@northcliffhotel.co.uk   website: www.northcliffhotel.co.uk

BLUE BALL INN (formerly The Exmoor Sandpiper Inn), COUNTISBURY, LYNMOUTH EX35 6NE (01598 741263). Romantic coaching inn on Exmoor. 16 en suite bedrooms, extensive menus with daily specials, good wines. Horse riding, walking. No charge for dogs. [🐾]
website: www.BlueBallinn.com or www.exmoorsandpiper.com

BATH HOTEL, TORS HOTEL, LYNMOUTH, EXMOOR, NORTH DEVON EX35 6EL (01598 752238). Great views of harbour. Quality rooms and service. Ideal for moors. Pets welcome. Off-season discounts available. [🐾]
e-mail: info@bathhotellynmouth.co.uk   website: www.bathhotellynmouth.co.uk

MR AND MRS I. RIGBY, BRENDON HOUSE, BRENDON, LYNTON EX35 6PS (01598 741206). Licensed country guesthouse in beautiful Lyn Valley. Ideal walking, fishing, riding. Award winning restaurant serving local food. Weekly discounts and short breaks. VisitBritain ★★★★ [🐾]
email: brendonhouse4u@aol.com   website: www.brendonhouse4u.com

JIM AND SUSAN BINGHAM, NEW MILL FARM, BARBROOK, LYNTON EX35 6JR (01598 753341). Exmoor Valley. Two delightful genuine modernised XVII century cottages by stream on 100-acre farm with A.B.R.S. Approved riding stables. Free fishing. ETC ★★★★. [pw! Pets £15 per week.]
e-mail: info@outovercott.co.uk   website: www.outovercott.co.uk

Mortehoe

Adjoining Woolacombe with cliffs and wide sands. Interesting rock scenery beyond Morte Point. Barnstaple 15 miles.

LUNDY HOUSE HOTEL, MORTEHOE, NORTH DEVON EX34 7DZ (01271 870372). Quality en suite accommodation in small, friendly hotel. TV & tea-making facilities in all rooms. Stunning views. Write or phone for full details. [Dogs £2.50 per night]
e-mail: info@lundyhousehotel.co.uk   website: www.lundyhousehotel.co.uk

THE SMUGGLERS REST INN, NORTH MORTE ROAD, MORTEHOE EX34 7DR (Tel & Fax: 01271 870891). In the pretty village of Mortehoe. The Smugglers offers luxury accommodation from twin rooms to family suites. En suite rooms, TV, full English breakfast, licensed bar, beer garden, home-cooked meals. Well trained pets welcome. [Pets £5 per week].
e-mail: info@smugglersmortehoe.co.uk   website: www.smugglersmortehoe.co.uk

Noss Mayo

Village 3 miles south west of Yealmpton, on south side of creek running into River Yealm estuary, opposite Newton Ferrers.

CRAB COTTAGE, NOSS MAYO. Charming fisherman's cottage, 50 yards from the quay. Fantastic walks, beaches and dog-friendly pubs on the doorstep. Close to the South Devon Coastal Path. Sleeps 5. Phone 01425 471372 for a brochure. [£25 per pet, per week]
e-mail: 07enquiries@crab-cottage.co.uk   website: www.crab-cottage.co.uk

Okehampton

Historic town, centrally located with easy access to Dartmoor and A30.

NORTHLAKE BED & BREAKFAST, STOCKLEY, OKEHAMPTON EX20 1QH (01837 53100). Homemade cake and a warm welcome await at this friendly B&B, well sited for walking, cycling, riding, touring and golf. You are welcome to picnic or BBQ in the gardens, coracle on the pond, or play croquet. Doggie day-care available. [🐾]
e-mail: pam@northlakedevon.co.uk   website: www.northlakedevon.co.uk

Ottery St Mary

Pleasant little town in East Devon, within easy reach of the sea. Many interesting little buildings including 11th century parish church. Birthplace of poet Coleridge.

MRS A. FORTH, FLUXTON FARM, OTTERY ST MARY EX11 1RJ (01404 812818). Charming 16th Century farmhouse. B&B from £27.50. Peace and quiet. Cat lovers' paradise. Masses of dog walks. AA ★★ [🐶 pw!]
website: www.fluxtonfarm.co.uk

Paignton

Popular family resort on Torbay with long, safe sandy beaches and small harbour. Exeter 25 miles, Newton Abbott 9, Torquay 3.

THE COMMODORE, 14 ESPLANADE ROAD, PAIGNTON TQ4 6EB (01803 553107). Ideally situated on Paignton sea front, sea view rooms. Luxury en suites, refreshments, sea view guest lounge, bar, gift shop. Excellent breakfast. Close to harbour, bus and rail stations. AA ★★★★ [Pets £5 per night].
e-mail: info@commodorepaignton.com   website: www.commodorepaignton.com

CHRISTINE CLARK & LLOYD HASTIE, AMBER HOUSE, 6 ROUNDHAM ROAD, PAIGNTON TQ4 6EZ (01803 558372). All en suite; ground floor rooms. Good food. Highly recommended. Non-smoking. A warm welcome assured to pets and their families. ETC ★★★★ Silver Award.
e-mail: enquiries@amberhousehotel.co.uk   website: www.amberhousehotel.co.uk

Plymouth

Historic port and resort, impressively rebuilt after severe war damage. Large naval docks at Devonport. Beach of pebble and sand.

CHURCHWOOD VALLEY, WEMBURY BAY, NEAR PLYMOUTH PL9 0DZ (01752 862382). Relax in one of our comfortable log cabins, set in a peaceful wooded valley near the beach. Enjoy wonderful walks in woods and along the coast. Abundance of birds and wildlife. Up to two pets per cabin. [Pets £5 per week each]
e-mail: churchwoodvalley@btconnect.com   website: www.churchwoodvalley.com

THE CRANBOURNE, 278/282 CITADEL ROAD, THE HOE, PLYMOUTH PL1 2PZ (01752 263858/ 661400/224646; Fax: 01752 263858). Convenient for Ferry Terminal and City Centre. All bedrooms with colour TV and tea/coffee. Licensed bar. Keys provided for access at all times. Free wifi. Under personal supervision. Pets by arrangement. AA ★★★ [🐶]
e-mail: cran.hotel@virgin.net   website: www.cranbournehotel.co.uk

Salcombe

Fishing and sailing centre in sheltered position. Fine beaches and coastal walks nearby.

PORT LIGHT, BOLBERRY DOWN, MALBOROUGH, NEAR SALCOMBE TQ7 3DY (01548 561384 or 07970 859992). A totally unique location set amidst acres of National Trust coastline. Luxury en suite rooms. Superb home cooked fare, specialising in local seafood. Licensed bar. Pets welcome throughout the hotel. Short Breaks throughout the year. Contact: Sean and Hazel Hassall. [🐶]
e-mail: info@portlight.co.uk   website: www.portlight.co.uk

Seaton

Bright East Devon resort near Axe estuary. Shingle beach and chalk cliffs; good bathing, many lovely walks in vicinity. Exeter 23 miles, Sidmouth 11.

MILKBERE COTTAGE HOLIDAYS, 3 FORE STREET, SEATON EX12 2LE (Brochure: 01297 22925 / Bookings: 01297 20729). Specialising in coast/country holidays on the Devon/Dorset border. Cottages, bungalows, houses, apartments and caravans, ideally situated for walking and exploring the Jurassic Coast. [Pets £20 per week.] VisitBritain ★★★/★★★★★★.
e-mail: info@milkberehols.com   website: www.milkberehols.com

AXEVALE CARAVAN PARK, COLYFORD ROAD, SEATON EX12 2DF (0800 0688816). A quiet, family-run park with 68 modern and luxury caravans for hire. Laundry facilities, park shop. All caravans have a shower, toilet, fridge and TV. Relaxing atmosphere. ETC ★★★★ [Pets £10 per week]
website: www.axevale.co.uk

Sidmouth

Sheltered resort, winner of many awards for its floral displays. Good sands at Jacob's Ladder beach.

WOODLANDS HOTEL, STATION ROAD, SIDMOUTH EX10 8HG 01395 513120; Fax: 01395 513348). 20-bedroom hotel just a few minutes' easy walk from both Sidmouth town centre and seafront; spacious bar and lounge. Well behaved pets welcome. AA ★★.
e-mail: info@woodlands-hotel.com   website: www.woodlands-hotel.com

LEIGH COTTAGES, WESTON, SIDMOUTH EX10 0PH. Cottages for couples and families close to SW Coast path, Weston Combe and Donkey Sanctuary. Dog friendly beaches and pubs nearby. Peaceful location. ETC ★★★★ Contact: ALISON CLARKE (01395 516065/514764; Fax: 01395 512563). [pw! Pets £18 per week]
e-mail: Alison@leighcottages.co.uk   website: www.leighcottages.co.uk

OAKDOWN HOLIDAY PARK, WESTON, SIDMOUTH EX10 0PT (01297 680387; Fax: 01297 680541). Sidmouth's multi-award-winning holiday park. Welcome to Oakdown, set near the "Jurassic Coast" World Heritage Site, and a winner of "Caravan Holiday Park of The Year". Oakdown is level, sheltered and landscaped into groves to give privacy. Our luxurious amenities include aids for the disabled. Enjoy our Field Trail to the famous Donkey Sanctuary. Free colour brochure with pleasure. ETC ★★★★★, David Bellamy Gold Award, Loo of the Year Award, Best of British, Excellence in England 2007.
e-mail: enquiries@oakdown.co.uk   website: www.oakdown.co.uk

SWEETCOMBE COTTAGE HOLIDAYS, ROSEMARY COTTAGE, WESTON, NEAR SIDMOUTH EX10 0PH (01395 512130). Selection of Cottages, Farmhouses and Flats in Sidmouth and East Devon, all personally selected and very well-equipped. Gardens. Pets welcome. Please ask for our colour brochure.
e-mail: enquiries@sweetcombe-ch.co.uk   website: www.sweetcombe-ch.co.uk

OTTERFALLS HOLIDAY COTTAGES & LODGES, NEW ROAD, UPOTTERY, HONITON EX14 9QD (FREECALL 0808 145 2700; Fax: 01404 861706). Luxurious fully equipped self-catering cottages and lodges set in 120 acres. Fishing lakes, heated indoor pool. Wonderful walking, including special pet "off-lead" walkways. [pw! Pets £30 per week]
e-mail: hols@otterfalls.co.uk   website: www.otterfalls.co.uk

Tavistock

Birthplace of Sir Francis Drake and site of a fine ruined Benedictine Abbey. On edge of Dartmoor, 13 miles north of Plymouth

LANGSTONE MANOR HOLIDAY PARK, MOORTOWN, TAVISTOCK PL19 9JZ (Tel & Fax 01822 613371). Peaceful Holiday Park, offering camping, cottages, apartment, static caravans. Ideal location outside Tavistock with direct access onto Dartmoor. Bar and evening meals. Excellent location. ETC ★★★★, AA ★★★ [Pets £20 per week.]
e-mail: jane@langstone-manor.co.uk   website: www.langstone-manor.co.uk

MRS P.G.C. QUINTON, HIGHER QUITHER, MILTON ABBOT, TAVISTOCK PL19 0PZ (01822 860284). Modern self-contained barn conversion. Own private garden. Terms from £225 inc. linen, coal and logs. Electricity metered. [pw! 🐾]
website: www.higherquither.2day.ws/

Thurlestone

Village resort above the cliffs to the north of Bolt Tail, 4 miles west of Kingsbridge.

CUTAWAY COTTAGE, THURLESTONE, KINGSBRIDGE TQ7 3NF. Self-catering cottage within a fenced garden in the middle of the village. Private road, 5 minutes to pub and shop, 20 minutes' walk to beaches & sea. Ideal for children, dog walkers and bird watchers. Phone Pat on 01548 560688 [🐾]

Please mention Pets Welcome! when making enquiries about accommodation featured in these pages

Tiverton

Busy market town situated north of Exeter on the A396.

NEWHOUSE FARM COTTAGES, WITHERIDGE, TIVERTON EX16 8QB (01884 860266). Nine well equipped Grade II Listed stone barns, with accommodation ranging from a one bedroom cottage to a 5- bedroom barn. 23 acre grounds, heated indoor pool and games room. [Pets £20 per week, pw!].
website: www.newhousecottages.com

Torbay

An east-facing bay and natural harbour at the western end of Lyme Bay, midway between the cities of Exeter and Plymouth.

J. AND E. BALL, DEPARTMENT P.W., HIGHER WELL FARM HOLIDAY PARK, STOKE GABRIEL, TOTNES TQ9 6RN (01803 782289). Within 4 miles Torbay beaches and one mile of River Dart. Central for touring. Dogs on leads. Tourist Board Graded Park ★★★★. [pw! Pets £2 per night, £15 per week in statics, free in tents and tourers]
website: www.higherwellfarmholidaypark.co.uk

Torquay

Popular resort on the English Riviera with a wide range of attractions and entertainments. Yachting and watersports centre with 10 superb beaches and coves.

THE DOWNS HOTEL, 41-43 BABBACOMBE DOWNS ROAD, TORQUAY TQ1 3LN (01803 328543/ 0845 051 0989). Fully licensed family-run establishment with 12 en suite rooms, eight with private balconies and superb views. Family rooms, reduced rates for under 12s. Dog-friendly. [Pets £5 per night].
website: www.downshotel.co.uk

THE NORWOOD, 60 BELGRAVE ROAD, TORQUAY TQ2 5HY (01803 294236, Fax: 01803 294224). Just a stroll from the seafront, town centre and all local attractions. A quality holiday experience focussing on old-fashioned hospitality, clean comfortable rooms and beautifully presented, home-cooked food. VisitBritain ★★★★.
e-mail: enquiries@norwoodhoteltorquay.co.uk   website: www.norwoodhoteltorquay.co.uk

CLIVE MASON AND DIANE SHELTON, AVRON HOUSE, 70 WINDSOR ROAD, TORQUAY TQ1 1SZ (01803 294182). An elegant family-run guesthouse in a quiet residentional location. Many local attractions, free on-road parking, a quiet retreat for a relaxing break. EnjoyEngland ★★★★.[🐾]
e-mail: avronhouse@blueyonder.co.uk   website: www.avronhouse.co.uk

Torrington

Pleasant market town on River Torridge. Good centre for moors and sea. Exeter 36 miles, Okehampton 20, Barnstaple 12, Bideford 7.

CLOISTER PARK COTTAGES, FRITHELSTOCK, TORRINGTON EX38 8JH (01805 622518). Three recently converted cottages (sleep 6/4/2), all fully equipped, with own patio areas. The attractive market town of Great Torrington is just 2 miles away. Tarka Trail and North Devon beaches close by. ETC ★★★★. [First pet free, additional pets £15 per week]
website: www.cloisterpark.co.uk

RICH AND DIANA JONES, STOWFORD LODGE, LANGTREE, GREAT TORRINGTON EX38 8NU (01805 601540). Sleep 4/6. Picturesque and peaceful. Four delightful cottages and log cabin set within 6 acres of private land with heated indoor pool. Magnificent countryside. Convenient North Devon coast and moors. Phone for brochure. VisitBritain ★★★ [Pets £15 per week, pw!]
e-mail: enq@stowfordlodge.co.uk   website: www.stowfordlodge.co.uk

**Free or reduced rate entry to
Holiday Visits and Attractions - see our
READERS' OFFER VOUCHERS on pages 445-454**

Devon   **SOUTH WEST ENGLAND** 159

Woolacombe

Favourite resort with long, wide stretches of sand. Barnstaple 15 miles, Ilfracombe 6.

SUNNYMEADE COUNTRY HOTEL, WEST DOWN, NEAR WOOLACOMBE EX34 8NT (01271 863668; Fax: 01271 866061). Small country hotel set in beautiful countryside. A few minutes away from Ilfracombe, Exmoor and Woolacombe's Blue Flag Beach. 12 en suite rooms, 4 on the ground floor. Deaf accessible. Pets welcome. [pw!]
e-mail: holidays@sunnymeade.co.uk   website: www.sunnymeade.co.uk

EUROPA PARK, BEACH ROAD, WOOLACOMBE (01271 871425). Static caravans, chalets, camping, surf lodges and surf cabins. Full facilities. Pets welcome. Indoor heated swimming pool, sauna, site shop. [Pets £3 per night]
e-mail: holidays@europapark.co.uk   website: www.europapark.co.uk

WOOLACOMBE BAY HOLIDAY PARKS (0844 770 0384). Four award-winning Holiday Parks set in delightful surroundings, all beside three miles of golden Blue Flag sandy beach in Devon. Pet-friendly holiday homes with pet pack and "Woof" Guide to Woolacombe.
website: www.woolacombe.com/fpw

MRS JOYCE BAGNALL, CHICHESTER HOUSE, THE ESPLANADE, WOOLACOMBE EX34 7DJ (01271 870761). Holiday apartments on sea front. Fully furnished, sea and coastal views. Watch the sun go down from your balcony. Open all year. SAE Resident Proprietor. [Pets £12 per week, pw!]

Yelverton

Large village on edge of Dartmoor. Nearby attractions include Buckland Abbey.

SAMPFORD MANOR, SAMPFORD SPINEY, YELVERTON PL20 6LH (01822 853442; Fax 01822 855691). Bed and Breakfast in the wilds of Dartmoor. Double or twin bedded rooms with private bathroom or shower. Dogs welcome. Stabling or grazing for horses.
e-mail: manor@sampford-spiney.fsnet.co.uk   website: www.sampford-spiney.fsnet.co.uk

Dorset

DORSET COTTAGE HOLIDAYS
PETS GO FREE.
Self-catering cottages, town houses, bungalows and apartments. All within 10 miles of Heritage Coastline and sandy beaches. Excellent walking in idyllic countryside. Short breaks from £95, weekly from £170 (per cottage). Open all year.
Free brochure tel: 01929 553443
e-mail: enq@dhcottages.co.uk
www.dhcottages.co.uk

Dorset Coastal Cottages

www.dorsetcoastalcottages.com
Tel: 0800 9804070

Carefully selected, traditional cottages in or near villages within ten miles of Dorset's spectacular World Heritage Coast. Many are thatched and have open fires or logburners.

Over half of our cottages welcome dogs.
Full weeks or Short Breaks all year round.
Rents include linen/towels and electricity/gas etc.

Abbotsbury, Bere Regis

The Old Coastguards • Holiday Cottages • Abbotsbury
17 miles of Chesil Beach at the end of the garden. Outstanding coastal views. Excellent walking. C.H. See our website for availability and details.
www.oldcoastguards.com • Tel: 01305 871335

Situated in an Area of Outstanding Natural Beauty. A good base for touring; direct access onto heathland and woodland walks. Ideal for nature lovers, bird watching and quiet family holidays. Park facilities include shop, launderette, gas exchange, children's play area, games room, clean, modern facilities, grassy pitches. Tents also welcome. Dogs welcome.
Mr & Mrs R. Cargill, Rye Hill, Bere Regis, Dorset BH20 7LP

Rowlands Wait Touring Park
Tel: 01929 472727

www.rowlandswait.co.uk

FHG Guides
publish a large range of well-known accommodation guides.
We will be happy to send you details or you can use the order form at the back of this book.

Dorset   **SOUTH WEST ENGLAND** 161

Blandford, Bournemouth

ANVIL INN

Salisbury Road, Pimperne,
Blandford, Dorset DT11 8UQ
Tel: 01258 453431
Fax: 01258 480182

A long, low thatched building set in a tiny village deep in the Dorset countryside – what could be more English? This typical Old English hostelry offering good old-fashioned English hospitality, a full à la carte menu with mouthwatering desserts in the charming beamed restaurant with log fire, together with specials of the day and light bites menu in the two bars.
All bedrooms with private facilities; wi-fi available in all rooms.
All bathrooms newly refurbished. Ample parking.
From £80 single, £105 double/twin.
e-mail: theanvil.inn@btconnect.com
www.anvilinn.co.uk

Stourcliffe Court Holiday Apartments • Bournemouth

Two fully furnished self-contained apartments in a quiet position, three minutes' walk to the beach. Forecourt parking. Sleep 2-5. Children welcome. Dogs welcome. From £200 per week.
Carol & Bob Hammond, 56 Stourcliffe Avenue, Southbourne, Bournemouth BH6 3PX
01202 420698 • e-mail: rjhammond1@hotmail.co.uk • www.stourcliffecourt.co.uk

Iona Holiday Flat, 71 Sea Road, Bournemouth

Ground floor studio apartment sleeping 2. Fully fitted kitchen. Shower room. Short distance to Blue Flag beaches. Small house-trained dogs welcome.
Contact Mr Andrew Hooper: 01202 460517 • Mob: 07967 027025
e-mail: reservemyholiday@yahoo.co.uk • www.ionaholidayflat.co.uk

Langtry Manor

"Best Hotel in Bournemouth"
- The Guardian

The Country House Hotel in Bournemouth

Derby road, East Cliff, Bournemouth BH1 3QB
0844 371 3705 (Local Rate)   www.langtrymanor.co.uk

White topps

THE *REALLY* DOG-FRIENDLY PLACE
WHITE TOPPS

Guests enjoying the lounge

Small, friendly and catering only for guests with dogs. In a nice quiet position close to lovely walks on the beach (dogs allowed) and Hengistbury Head. Plus the New Forest isn't far away. There's no charge for pets, of course and the proprietor, MARJORIE TITCHEN, just loves dogs.

We're 100% dog orientated, all our guests bring at least one dog and you're equally welcome whether you have one Yorkie or six Alsatians. Dogs are allowed anywhere - in bedrooms, lounges, even in the dining room should they be unhappy being left alone in the bedroom. Bring your own dog food, we are happy to cook it, free of charge, if required.

We have five bedrooms on the first floor with bathroom and toilets opposite and one room on the ground floor, suitable for elderly or disabled dogs. We do not have any en suite rooms but all have washbasins and tea/coffee making facilities.

- DOG(S) ESSENTIAL - ANY SIZE, ANY NUMBER, ANYWHERE
- GROUND FLOOR ROOM FOR ELDERLY DOGS
- ADULTS ONLY (14yrs +)
- GENEROUS HOME COOKING
- VEGETARIANS WELCOME
- NOT SUITABLE FOR DISABLED
- CAR PARKING

WRITE (SAE APPRECIATED) OR PHONE FOR FACT SHEET.

WHITE TOPPS, 45 CHURCH ROAD, SOUTHBOURNE, BOURNEMOUTH, DORSET BH6 4BB
TEL: 01202 428868

No Credit Cards - Cheque or Cash only

e-mail: thedoghotel@aol.com • www.whitetopps.co.uk
IF YOU DON'T LOVE DOGS YOU WON'T LIKE WHITE TOPPS

Dorset

SOUTH WEST ENGLAND 163

Bournemouth, Bridport

Alum Dene Hotel
2 Burnaby Road, Alum Chine, Bournemouth BH4 8JF Tel: 01202 764011

Renowned for good old fashioned hospitality and friendly service. Come and be spoilt at our licensed hotel. All rooms en suite, colour TV. Some have sea views. 200 metres sea. Parking. Christmas House party. No charge for pets. www.alumdenehotel.com • e-mail: alumdenehotel@hotmail.co.uk

Friendly, family-run hotel with beautiful garden and ample parking. Close to beach and shops. Ideal for exploring Bournemouth, Christchurch and the New Forest. Excellent food. En suite rooms, four-poster suite, ground floor rooms (one suitable for partially disabled) and large family bedrooms. Dogs welcome free. No smoking. **B&B from £24pn, from £140 per week.**
www.bournemouth.co.uk/southbournegrovehotel
SOUTHBOURNE GROVE HOTEL • 96 Southbourne Road, Southbourne, Bournemouth BH6 3QQ
Tel: 01202 420503 • Fax: 01202 421953 • e-mail: neil@pack1462.freeserve.co.uk

HOLIDAY FLATS AND FLATLETS 07788 952394

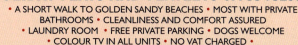

- A SHORT WALK TO GOLDEN SANDY BEACHES • MOST WITH PRIVATE BATHROOMS • CLEANLINESS AND COMFORT ASSURED
- LAUNDRY ROOM • FREE PRIVATE PARKING • DOGS WELCOME
- COLOUR TV IN ALL UNITS • NO VAT CHARGED

CONTACT: M. DE KMENT, 4 CECIL ROAD, BOURNEMOUTH BH5 1DU

BOURNEMOUTH HOLIDAY APARTMENTS
16 Florence Road, Bournemouth BH5 1HF
Tel: 01202 304925

Modern self-contained holiday apartments situated in a pleasant residential area of Boscombe offer accommodation for 1-10 persons in clean self-catering studios, one, two and four bedroom flats close to a superb sandy beach, shops and entertainments. Bournemouth town centre is a few minutes away by car or there is a frequent bus service. Car parking space provided. Free WiFi access.
An ideal base for touring many places of interest in the Dorset and Hampshire countryside.

e-mail: mikelyn_lambert@btinternet.com
www.selfcateringbournemouth.co.uk

Cogden Cottages · Near Bridport · Dorset

Seven beautifully presented and equipped beachfront sea view cottages, all with private sea-facing decks or patios. Pets can take advantage of the South West Coastal Path which runs through the property or use our private beach. £290-£650

**Kim Connelly, Old Coastguard Holiday Park, Burton Bradstock,
Near Bridport, Dorset DT6 4RL • Tel 01308 897223**
www.cogdencottages.co.uk

'Exclusively for Discerning Adults'

Quiet, peaceful park a few minutes drive to coastline.
Dogs welcome. Comfortable lounge bar and restaurant.

Binghams Farm, Melplash, Bridport, Dorset DT6 3TT • www.binghamgrange.co.uk • Tel: 01308 488234

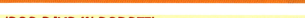

'DOG DAYS IN DORSET' Wonderful tail-wagging walks from a peaceful, privately run bungalow park. Just a short stroll from the beach on the beautiful Jurassic Coast. Our guests may bring more than one dog! For our brochure on SHORT BREAKS and WEEKLY HOLIDAYS please telephone **01308 421 521**

Golden Acre, Eype, Bridport, Dorset DT6 6AL
www.golden-acre.com

SOUTH WEST ENGLAND — Dorset

Bridport, Burton Bradstock

Lancombes House ~ Holiday Cottages

Three individually designed cottages and Farmhouse, arranged around a courtyard and set in 9 acres. Each has its own sitting out area, with garden furniture. Two with enclosed south-facing gardens. Central heating and wood burners/fires. In an Area of Outstanding Natural Beauty and surrounded by the beautiful hills and valleys of this unspoiled part of West Dorset, ideal for walking, riding and outdoor pursuits. Children and dogs welcome. Open all year.

Lancombes House, West Milton, Bridport DT6 3TN
Tel: 01308 485375 • www.lancombes-house.co.uk

17th Century FROGMORE FARM

Enjoy Bed and Breakfast or our delightful Self Catering cottage.

Frogmore is a 90-acre grazing farm situated tranquilly in beautiful West Dorset, overlooking the Jurassic Coast of Lyme Bay, and away from the crowds. En suite shower rooms available.

Ideal for walking, our land is adjacent to National Trust land to the cliffs, (Seatown 1½ miles) and the South West Coastal Path.

Well behaved dogs very welcome • Open all year
Car essential • Brochure and terms free on request.

Contact Mrs Sue Norman • Tel: 01308 456159
Frogmore Farm, Chideock, Bridport DT6 6HT
www.frogmorefarm.com
e-mail: bookings@frogmorefarm.com

Tamarisk Farm

Beach Road, West Bexington, Dorchester DT2 9DF
Tel: 01308 897784   Mrs Josephine Pearse

On slope overlooking Chesil beach between Abbotsbury and Burton Bradstock.
Three large (Mimosa is wheelchair disabled M3(i), Granary Lodge is disabled-friendly (M1) and The Moat) and two small cottages (VB 3/4 Stars). Each one stands in own fenced garden.
Glorious views along West Dorset and Devon coasts. Lovely walks by sea and inland. Part of mixed organic farm with arable, sheep, cattle, horses and market garden (organic vegetables, meat and wholemeal flour available). Sea fishing, riding in Portesham and Burton Bradstock, lots of tourist attractions and good markets. Good centre for touring Thomas Hardy's Wessex. Safe for children and excellent for dogs. Very quiet. Terms from £260 to £980.

e-mail: holidays@tamariskfarm.com • • www.tamariskfarm.com/holidays

Dorset   **SOUTH WEST ENGLAND**

Charmouth, Dorchester, Evershot, Lulworth, Lulworth Cove

MANOR FARM HOLIDAY CENTRE
Charmouth, Bridport, Dorset DT6 6QL (01297) 560226

Two and three bedroomed houses, Luxury caravans. All units for four to six people. Children and pets welcome. Swimming pool and children's pool. Licensed bar with family room. Shop. Launderette. Children's play area. Ten minutes' walk to safe sand and shingle beach. Many fine walks locally. Golf, riding, tennis, fishing and boating all nearby. **SAE TO MR. F. LOOSMORE FOR COLOUR BROCHURE.**

The Brewers Arms
Martinstown, Dorchester, Dorset DT2 9LB • 01305 889361
e-mail: jackie_smith54@hotmail.com • www.thebrewersarms.com

Country pub with a lovely garden. Pub food. Skittle alley and large car park. Area in the pub where customers can eat and sit with their dogs.

GREYGLES Melcombe Bingham, Near Dorchester. Enjoy rural peace in this spacious, well-equipped stone house on the edge of a friendly village, just 10 miles from Dorchester. It comfortably sleeps up to seven in four bedrooms (one on the ground floor). • Sitting room with open fire • Dining room • Kitchen with Aga, dishwasher etc • Garden with patio and Wendy house • Heating, electricity, linen and towels incl. • Short breaks available • No smoking • Ideal for exploring Dorset and the Jurassic Coast
Booking: Tel: 020 8969 4830 • Fax: 020 8960 0069 • e-mail: enquiry@greygles.co.uk
P. SOMMERFELD, 22 TIVERTON ROAD, LONDON NW10 3HL

THE STABLES, Hyde Crook, Frampton DT2 9NW • 01300 320075

Comfortable country house developed around a 1935 cottage overlooking the valley of Frampton. Set in the heart of Thomas Hardy country, we enjoy uninterrupted views of open countryside. Off-road parking and 20 acres of ground with wild life, ducks, sheep and horses. Guest accommodation is contained in a separate wing of the house. All rooms double glazed with central heating. Twin en suite from £55, Double from £52, Single from £30. We specialise in pet-friendly facilities for dogs (must have own beds and be kept under control).
e-mail: coba.stables@tiscali.co.uk • www.framptondorset.com

Summer Lodge Country House Hotel is a secluded escape from the pressures of everyday life. This is a tranquil haven full of Courtesy, Charm, Character, Calm and Cuisine.
Each of our rooms and luxury suites are individually designed.
Superb food and wines in the award-winning restaurant.
A luxury break with little extras that make all the difference.
We make you feel special from the moment you arrive.

Summer Lodge is a pet-friendly hotel, for an additional charge of £20 per night we will help to make your dog feel at home.
• Dog towels • Dog biscuits • Water Bowl • Dog basket

Fore Street, Evershot, Dorset DT2 0JR
Telephone: 01935 48 2000
e-mail: summer@relaischateaux.com
www.summerlodgehotel.co.uk

Luckford Wood Farmhouse • Church Street, East Stoke, Wareham, Dorset BH20 6AW

B&B classic farmhouse with style. Peaceful surroundings, delightful scenery. Breakfast served in conservatory, dining room or garden. Our camping and caravanning site nearby. Caravan and boat storage available. Near Lulworth Cove, Tank Museum, Monkey World. Open all year. B&B from £30pp per night.
Tel: 01929 463098 • Mobile: 07888 719002 • luckfordleisure@hotmail.com • www.luckfordleisure.co.uk

The Castle Inn • Lulworth Cove BH20 5RN
Family-run, dog-friendly inn with good food, local real ales and B&B accommodation in a wonderful dog walking area. Half a mile from the coast in the heart of the Purbecks. Pets free of charge
Tel: 01929 400311 • www.lulworthinn.com

166 SOUTH WEST ENGLAND — Dorset

Lyme Regis, North Perrott, Poole, Portland, Sherborne

Over 200 VisitBritain 3, 4, or 5 Star self-catering holiday properties in beautiful country and coastal locations in and around Lyme Regis, many of which welcome pets

visit our website www.lymebayholidays.co.uk or email email@lymebayholidays.co.uk

WESTOVER FARM COTTAGES

In an Area Of Outstanding Natural Beauty, Wootton Fitzpaine epitomizes picturesque West Dorset. Within walking distance of sea. 3 beautiful cottages sleep 6/8 with large secluded gardens. Car parking. Logs available, Linen supplied, 3 bedrooms. £240-£865. Pets welcome.

Wootton Fitzpaine, Near Lyme Regis, Dorset DT6 6NE
Brochure: Jon Snook & Debby Snook • 01297 560451/561395
e-mail: wfcottages@aol.com   www.westoverfarmcottages.co.uk   ETC ★★★/★★★★

WOOD DAIRY
WOOD LANE, NORTH PERROTT TA18 7TA

Three well-appointed stone holiday cottages set around courtyard in two and a half acres of Somerset/ Dorset countryside. Area of Outstanding Natural Beauty, close to Lyme Bay and Jurassic Coast. Excellent base for walking, trails and historic properties.

- Pets welcome by arrangement.
- Wheelchair friendly.
- All bookings will receive half price green fees.
- Direct access to Chedington Court Golf Club on the 8th and 9th greens.

Tel & Fax: 01935 891532
e-mail: liz@acountryretreat.co.uk
www.acountryretreat.co.uk

Poole • Harbour Holidays • Quay Cottage and Wychcott

Quay Cottage in quiet area with sea views. Sky TV and DVD. Dogs welcome.
Wychcott - detached bungalow 6 minutes' drive from beaches at Sandbanks. Fenced rear garden. Barbecue. Safe for young children and dogs. Sky TV/DVD.
Mrs Saunders, 15 White Cliff Road, Poole BH14 8DU (01202 741637)

Tranquil family-owned park set on clifftops of the Jurassic Coastline offering spectacular sea views.
• Holiday Homes to let or for sale • Short Breaks
• Shop, games room and launderette on site
• Pets Welcome • Open 46 weeks per year

'Holidays of quality for the discerning'

Cove Holiday Park, Pennsylvania Road, Portland, Dorset DT5 1HU
01305 821286 enquiries@coveholidaypark.co.uk www.coveholidaypark.co.uk

White Horse Farm   ETC ★★★/★★★★

Set in beautiful Hardy countryside, we have six cottages furnished to high standards and surrounded by two acres of paddock and garden with a duck pond. We lie between the historic towns of Sherborne, Dorchester and Cerne Abbas. Within easy reach of many tourist attractions. Next door to an Inn serving good food. Pets welcome. All cottages have central heating, colour digital TV and VCR with free video (500+) film rental. Electricity, bed linen, towels inclusive. Ample parking. Good value.

Self-Catering Cottages

The Willows sleeps 4/6; Otters Holt sleeps 6/8; Toad Hall sleeps 4; Badger's and Moley's sleep 2; Ratty's sleeps 2/4
White Horse Farm, Middlemarsh, Sherborne, Dorset DT9 5QN • 01963 210222

Visit our website: www.whitehorsefarm.co.uk   e-mail: enquiries@whitehorsefarm.co.uk

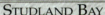

Established 1931

A peaceful and relaxing holiday for all ages
An independent country-house hotel, in an unrivalled position above three miles of golden beach. Dogs are especially welcome and may sleep in your room. Special diets arranged. Our 100 acre grounds offer nice walks; squirrels and rabbits!
~
Good food and a sensible wine list
Tennis courts; nine acre golf course and outdoor heated pool
Health spa with Jacuzzi, sauna, Turkish room, plunge pool and gym
Many ground-floor and single rooms for older guests
~
Family suites of connecting rooms with bathroom
Separate young children's dining room
Playrooms and fabulous adventure playground
~
Open Easter - end November

STUDLAND BAY
DORSET
BH19 3AH
01929 · 450450
info@knollhouse.co.uk
www.knollhouse.co.uk

ONLY 2 HOURS FROM HEATHROW

"Welcome to one of the most beautiful places in England. I can't take credit for the glorious views and the beaches. But I am proud to provide a comfortable and relaxing hotel with good food and attentive but informal service, to give you the break you deserve."

Andrew Purkis

Manor House Hotel, Studland, Dorset, BH19 3AU • T - 01929 450288
• W - www.themanorhousehotel.com • E - info@themanorhousehotel.com

---

★★★

THE LIMES

A warm welcome awaits all dogs – and their owners – at the Limes, only a few hundred yards from wonderful coastal walks and beach, surrounded by the unspoilt Purbeck Hills. En suite rooms with colour TV and hospitality trays. Pets come free!

• Car Park • Families Welcome •
• Open all Year for Bed and Breakfast •

48 Park Road, Swanage, Dorset BH19 2AE
Tel: 01929 422664
info@limeshotel.net • www.limeshotel.net

SWANAGE BAY VIEW HOLIDAY PARK

4/5/6 BERTH FULL MAINS CARAVANS
COMFORTABLE AND WELL EQUIPPED
*Colour TV * Launderette * Sea Views * Parking space * Pets welcome*
* Fully licensed club with entertainment. * Indoor swimming pool*
EASTER – OCTOBER, REDUCED TERMS EARLY/LATE HOLIDAYS
SAE: M. Stockley, 17 Moor Road, Swanage, Dorset BH19 1RG • Tel: 01929 424154

The Silent Woman Inn
Bere Road, Coldharbour, Wareham, Dorset BH20 7PA
Tel: 01929 552909 • www.thesilentwoman.co.uk
Traditional country inn nestling in the heart of Wareham Forest.
All fresh ingredients, wonderful food. Adults-only inside. Dogs allowed in bar areas and all outside areas except children's play areas.

Dorset
Wareham, West Bexington

••Lulworth Cove••
Cromwell House Hotel

Catriona and Alistair Miller welcome guests to their comfortable family-run hotel, set in secluded gardens with spectacular sea views. Situated 200 yards from Lulworth Cove, with direct access to the Jurassic Coast. Accommodation is in 20 en suite bedrooms, with TV, direct-dial telephone, wi-fi, and tea/coffee making facilities; most have spectacular sea views. There is disabled access and a room suitable for disabled guests.

- Self-catering flat and cottage available. • Restaurant, bar wine list.
- A heated swimming pool is available from May to October.

**Cromwell House Hotel,
Lulworth Cove BH20 5RJ**
Tel: 01929 400253/400332 • Fax: 01929 400566

www.lulworthcove.co.uk

Peace and Tranquillity

West Bexington-on-Sea,
Near Bridport, Dorset DT2 9DJ

★Small select park with stunning views over Jurassic Coastline

★Excellent beach fishing

★Pets Welcome

★Caravans & Apartments

★ Camping nearby mid July-August

★Shop & Launderette

★Village Pub 100 yards

★Beach & Car Park 1 mile

Tel: 01308 897232 Fax: 01308 897239
www.gorselands.co.uk
e-mail: info@gorselands.co.uk

DORSET COTTAGE HOLIDAYS. Self-catering cottages, town houses, bungalows and apartments. All within 10 miles of Heritage Coastline and sandy beaches. Excellent walking in idyllic countryside. Short breaks from £95, weekly from £170 (per cottage). Open all year. Free brochure tel: 01929 553443. [🐾]
e-mail: enq@dhcottages.co.uk   website: www.dhcottages.co.uk

DORSET COASTAL COTTAGES (0800 9804070). Carefully selected, traditional cottages in or near villages within ten miles of World Heritage Coast. Many are thatched; open fires or logburners; over half welcome dogs. Available all year. [Pets £15 per week]
website: www.dorsetcoastalcottages.com

FARM & COTTAGE HOLIDAYS (01237 459897). An inspiring collection of holiday cottages throughout Cornwall, Devon, Somerset and Dorset in stunning rural and coastal locations. [Pets £20 per week]
website: www.holidaycottages.co.uk

Abbotsbury

Village 8 miles NW of Weymouth.

THE OLD COASTGUARDS HOLIDAY COTTAGES, ABBOTSBURY. 17 miles of Chesil Beach at the end of the garden. Outstanding coastal views. Excellent walking. C.H. See our website for availability and details. Tel: 01305 871335. ETC ★★★★. [🐾]
website: www.oldcoastguards.com

Bere Regis

Village 7 miles north west of Wareham.

MR & MRS R. CARGILL, ROWLANDS WAIT TOURING PARK, RYE HILL, BERE REGIS BH20 7LP (01929 472727). Situated in an Area of Outstanding Natural Beauty. A good base for touring; direct access onto heathland and woodland walks. Ideal for nature lovers, bird watching and quiet family holidays. Tents also welcome. Dogs welcome. David Bellamy Gold Award. ETC ★★★.
website: www.rowlandswait.co.uk

Blandford

Handsome Georgian town that rose from the ashes of the 1731 fire; rebuilt with chequered brick and stone. Also known as Blandford Forum.

ANVIL INN & RESTAURANT, PIMPERNE, BLANDFORD DT11 8UQ (01258 453431; Fax: 01258 480182). A typical Old English hostelry offering good old-fashioned English hospitality. Full à la carte menu with mouthwatering desserts in the charming restaurant with log fire, delicious desserts, bar meals, specials board. All bedrooms with private facilities. Ample parking. ETC/AA ★★★★ [Pets £10 per night]
e-mail: theanvil.inn@btconnect.com   website: www.anvilinn.co.uk

Bournemouth

One of Britain's premier holiday resorts with miles of golden sand, excellent shopping and leisure facilities.

STOURCLIFFE COURT HOLIDAY APARTMENTS. Two fully furnished apartments, sleep 2/5. Three minutes' walk to beach. Linen provided free. Forecourt parking. Terms from £200. MRS HAMMOND, STOURCLIFFE COURT, 56 STOURCLIFFE AVENUE, SOUTHBOURNE, BOURNEMOUTH BH6 3PX (01202 420698). [Pets £10 weekly]
e-mail: rjhammond@hotmail.co.uk   website: www.stourcliffecourt.co.uk

IONA HOLIDAY FLAT, 71 SEA ROAD, BOURNEMOUTH (01202 460517; Mobile 07967 027025) Ground floor studio apartment sleeping 2. Situated within art deco marine building. Fully fitted kitchen. Shower room. Short distance to Blue Flag beaches. Small house-trained dogs welcome. [Pets £20 per week]
e-mail: reservemyholiday@yahoo.co.uk   website: www.ionaholidayflat.co.uk

LANGTRY MANOR, DERBY ROAD, EAST CLIFF, BOURNEMOUTH BH1 3QB (0844 371 3705 - local rate). A rare gem of a hotel where the building, food, service and history blend to form something quite exceptional. Midweek and weekend breaks. Pets welcome by arrangement. Bournemouth Tourism 'Best Small Hotel'. [🐾]
website: www.langtrymanor.co.uk

Dorset
SOUTH WEST ENGLAND 171

BILL AND MARJORIE TITCHEN, WHITE TOPPS HOTEL, 45 CHURCH ROAD, SOUTHBOURNE, BOURNEMOUTH BH6 4BB (01202 428868). Situated in quiet position close to lovely walks and beach. Dogs essential. Free parking. [🐾 pw!]
e-mail: thedoghotel@aol.com　　　　　　　website: www.whitetopps.co.uk

ALUM DENE HOTEL, 2 BURNABY ROAD, ALUM CHINE, BOURNEMOUTH BH4 8JF (01202 764011). Renowned for good old fashioned hospitality and friendly service. Come and be spoilt at our licensed hotel. All rooms en suite, colour TV. Some have sea views. 200 metres sea. Parking. Christmas House party. No charge for pets. [🐾]
e-mail: alumdenehotel@hotmail.co.uk　　　website: alumdenehotel.com

SOUTHBOURNE GROVE HOTEL, 96 SOUTHBOURNE ROAD, SOUTHBOURNE, BOURNEMOUTH BH6 3QQ (01202 420503; Fax: 01202 421953). Friendly, family-run hotel with beautiful garden and ample guest parking. Close to beach and shops. Excellent breakfast served in spacious restaurant. En suite, four-poster suite, ground floor and large family rooms available, all with colour TV and tea/coffee facilities. B&B from £24 per night, £140 per week. This is a no-smoking hotel. [🐾]
website: www.bournemouth.co.uk/southbournegrovehotel

HOLIDAY FLATS AND FLATLETS a short walk to golden, sandy beaches. Most with private bathrooms. Cleanliness and comfort assured. Dogs welcome. Contact: M DE KMENT, 4 CECIL ROAD, BOURNEMOUTH BH5 1DU (07788 952394). [Pets £30 per week]

MIKE AND LYN LAMBERT, 16 FLORENCE ROAD, BOURNEMOUTH BH5 1HF (01202 304925). Modern Holiday Apartments sleeping up to ten persons, close to sea and shops. Clean, well-equipped flats. Car park. Phone or e-mail for brochure. [Pets from £55 per week]
e-mail: mikelyn_lambert@btinternet.com　　website: www.selfcateringbournemouth.co.uk

Bridport

Market town of Saxon origin noted for rope and net making. Harbour at West Bay has sheer cliffs rising from the beach

COGDEN COTTAGES, NEAR BRIDPORT, DORSET. Seven beautifully presented and equipped beachfront sea view cottages all with private sea facing decks or patios. Pets can take advantage of the South West Coastal Path which runs through the property or our private beach. £290-£650. Contact: KIM CONNELLY, OLD COASTGUARD HOLIDAY PARK, BURTON BRADSTOCK, NEAR BRIDPORT DT6 4RL (01308 897223).
website: www.cogdencottages.co.uk

BINGHAM GRANGE TOURING AND CARAVAN PARK, BINGHAMS FARM, MELPLASH, BRIDPORT DT6 3TT (01308 488284). Quiet, peaceful park, exclusively for adults. a few minutes drive to coastline. Dogs welcome. Comfortable lounge bar and restaurant. Enjoy England ★★★★. AA 4 Pennants.
e-mail: enquiries@binghamgrange.co.uk　　website: www.binghamgrange.co.uk

GOLDEN ACRE, EYPE, NEAR BRIDPORT DT6 6AL (01308 421521). Private peaceful park. Close to beach. Chalet bungalows (1 or 2 bedrooms), sleep 2-4. Wonderful walks, on the Jurassic Coast. [Pets £49 per week]
website: www.golden-acre.com

LANCOMBES HOUSE, WEST MILTON, BRIDPORT DT6 3TN (01308 485375). Three cottages and farmhouse, two with enclosed gardens. Set in 9 acres in an area ideal for walking, riding and outdoor pursuits. Children and dogs welcome. Open all year. ETC ★★★★ [Pets £5 per night, £15 per week].
website: www.lancombes-house.co.uk

MRS S. NORMAN, FROGMORE FARM, CHIDEOCK, BRIDPORT DT6 6HT (01308 456159). The choice is yours - Bed and Breakfast in charming farmhouse, OR self-catering Cottage equipped for five, pets welcome. Brochure and terms free on request. [1st dog free, 2nd dog £3 per night, £15 per week]
e-mail: bookings@frogmorefarm.com　　website: www.frogmorefarm.com

Please mention **Pets Welcome!**
when making enquiries about accommodation featured in these pages

SOUTH WEST ENGLAND — Dorset

Burton Bradstock

Village near coast, 3 miles SE of Bridport.

MRS JOSEPHINE PEARSE, TAMARISK FARM, BEACH ROAD, WEST BEXINGTON, DORCHESTER DT2 9DF (01308 897784). Self Catering properties sleep 4/7. Overlooking Chesil Beach: three large (MIMOSA FOR WHEELCHAIR DISABLED M3 (1); GRANARY LODGE DISABLED-FRIENDLY M1 and THE MOAT), plus two small Cottages (ETC 3/4 Stars). Part of organic farm with arable, sheep, cattle, horses and market garden with organic vegetables, meat and wholemeal flour available. Good centre for touring, sightseeing, walking. Glorious sea views, very quiet. Lovely place for dogs. Terms from £260 to £980. Please telephone for details. [🐾]
e-mail: holidays@tamariskfarm.com   website: www.tamariskfarm.com/holidays

Charmouth

Small resort on Lyme Bay, 3 miles from Lyme Regis.

MR F. LOOSMORE, MANOR FARM HOLIDAY CENTRE, CHARMOUTH, BRIDPORT DT6 6QL (01297 560226). All units for four to six people. Ten minutes' level walk to beach, many fine local walks. Swimming pools, licensed bar with family room, shop, launderette. Sporting facilities nearby. Children and pets welcome. SAE for colour brochure. [Pets £30 per week]

Dorchester

Busy market town steeped in history. Roman remains include Amphitheatre and villa.

THE BREWERS ARMS, MARTINSTOWN, DORCHESTER DT2 9LB (01305 889761). Country pub with lovely garden. Pub food. Large car park and a large grassed area (which may be suitable for tents). Area in the pub where customers can eat and sit with their dogs.
e-mail: jackie_smith54@hotmail.com   website: www.thebrewersarms.com

GREYGLES, MELCOMBE BINGHAM, NEAR DORCHESTER. Spacious, well-equipped house just 10 miles from Dorchester. Sleep 7. Heating, electricity, linen and towels incl. No smoking. ETC ★★★★ Booking: P. SOMMERFELD, 22 TIVERTON ROAD, LONDON NW10 3HL (020 8969 4830; Fax: 020 8960 0069). [Pets £10 per week]
e-mail: enquiry@greygles.co.uk   website: www.greygles.co.uk

MRS JACOBINA LANGLEY, THE STABLES B&B, HYDE CROOK (OFF A37), FRAMPTON DT2 9NW (01300 320075; Fax: 01300 321718). Comfortable country house in 20 acres with uninterrupted country views. Guest accommodation in separate wing, fully double-glazed, with central heating. Dogs most welcome (must have own beds and be kept under control). [Pets £4 per night]
e-mail: coba.stables@tiscali.co.uk   website: www.framptondorset.com

Evershot

Village 5 miles North of Maiden Newton.

SUMMER LODGE COUNTRY HOUSE HOTEL, RESTAURANT & SPA, FORE STREET, EVERSHOT DT2 0JR (01935 48 2000). Tranquil haven full of Courtesy, Charm, Character, Calm and Cuisine. Individually designed rooms, superb food and wine. Dogs feel at home with towels, dog biscuits, water bowl and basket. AA ★★★★ [Pets £20 per night].
e-mail: summer@relaischateaux.com   website: www.summerlodgehotel.co.uk

---

Publisher's note

While every effort is made to ensure accuracy, we regret that FHG Guides cannot accept responsibility for errors, misrepresentations or omissions in our entries or any consequences thereof. Prices in particular should be checked.
We will follow up complaints but cannot act as arbiters or agents for either party.

Dorset

SOUTH WEST ENGLAND 173

Lulworth (near Wareham)

Village on coast 4 miles from Wool.

MRS L. S. BARNES, LUCKFORD WOOD FARMHOUSE, EAST STOKE, WAREHAM, NEAR LULWORTH BH20 6AW (01929 463098; Mobile: 07888719002). Peaceful surroundings, delightful scenery. B&B classic farmhouse with style. Breakfast served in conservatory, dining room or garden. Also our camping and caravanning site nearby includes showers, toilets. Caravan and boat storage available. Near Lulworth Cove, Studland, Tank Museum and Monkey World. Open all year. B&B from £30pp per night. Please phone for details. [Pets £5 per night, £30 per week]
e-mail: luckfordleisure@hotmail.com   website: www.luckfordleisure.co.uk

Lulworth Cove

Village and Cove on the World heritage Jurassic Coastline. Good beaches and numerous guided boat trips leaving from the cove showing the highlights of the area.

THE CASTLE INN, LULWORTH COVE BH20 5RN (01929 400311). Family-run, dog-friendly inn with good food, local real ales and B&B accommodation in a wonderful dog walking area. Half a mile from the coast in the heart of the Purbecks. [🐾]
website: www.lulworthinn.com

Lyme Regis

Picturesque little resort with harbour, once the haunt of smugglers. Shingle beach with sand at low tide. Fishing, sailing and water ski-ing in Lyme Bay. Taunton 28 miles, Dorchester 24, Seaton 8.

LYME BAY HOLIDAYS. Over 200 VisitBritain 3, 4, or 5 Star self catering holiday properties in beautiful country and coastal locations in and around Lyme Regis, many of which welcome pets.
e-mail: email@lymebayholidays.co.uk   website: www.lymebayholidays.co.uk

JON SNOOK AND DEBBY SNOOK, WESTOVER FARM COTTAGES, WOOTTON FITZPAINE, NEAR LYME REGIS DT6 6NE (01297 560451/561395). Within walking distance of the sea. Three beautiful cottages, sleep 6/8, with large secluded gardens. Car parking. Logs available, linen supplied. 3 bedrooms. Well behaved pets welcome. ETC ★★★/★★★★ [Pets £22 per week]
e-mail: wfcottages@aol.com   website: www.westoverfarmcottages.co.uk

North Perrott

Village 2 miles east of Crewkerne.

MRS E NEVILLE, WOOD DAIRY, WOOD LANE, NORTH PERROTT TA18 7TA (Tel & Fax: 01935 891532). Three well-appointed stone holiday cottages set around courtyard in two and a half acres of Somerset/Dorset countryside. Adjacent golf course. Close to Lyme Bay and Jurassic Coast, excellent base for walking, trails and historic properties. Wheelchair friendly. Pets welcome by arrangement. [🐾]
e-mail: liz@acountryretreat.co.uk   website: www.acountryretreat.co.uk

Poole

Flourishing port and market town. Three museums with interesting collections and lively displays.

HARBOUR HOLIDAYS. QUAY COTTAGE in quiet area with sea views. Sky TV and DVD. Dogs welcome. WYCHCOTT - detached bungalow 6 minutes' drive from beaches at Sandbanks. Fenced rear garden. Barbecue. Safe for young children and dogs. Sky TV/DVD. MRS SAUNDERS, 15 WHITE CLIFF ROAD, POOLE BH14 8DU (01202 741637). [🐾]

Portland

Connected to the Dorset mainland by a road bridge. Spectacular cliff views of the World Heritage coastline.

COVE HOLIDAY PARK, PENNSYLVANIA ROAD, PORTLAND DT5 1HU (01305 821286) Tranquil family-owned park offering spectacular sea views. Holiday Homes to let or for sale. Short Breaks Shop, games room and launderette on site. Pets Welcome Enjoy England ★★★★★.
e-mail: enquiries@coveholidaypark.co.uk   website: www.coveholidaypark.co.uk

Sherborne

Town with abbey and two castles, one of which was built by Sir Walter Raleigh with lakes and gardens by Capability Brown.

WHITE HORSE FARM, MIDDLEMARSH, SHERBORNE DT9 5QN. The Willows sleeps 4/6; Otters Holt sleeps 6/8; Toad Hall sleeps 4; Badger's & Moley's sleep 2; Ratty's sleeps 2/4. Character self-catering holiday cottages in rural location. Well equipped and comfortable. Digital TV. video, free films. 2 acres of paddock, garden and duck pond. Inn 100 yards. ETC ★★★/★★★★. AUDREY & STUART WINTERBOTTOM (01963 210222) [pw!]
e-mail: enquiries@whitehorsefarm.co.uk   website: www.whitehorsefarm.co.uk

Studland Bay

Unspoilt seaside village at south western end of Poole Bay, 3 miles north of Swanage.

THE KNOLL HOUSE, STUDLAND BH19 3AH (01929 450450). Country house hotel within National Trust reserve. Golden beach. 100 acre grounds. Family suites of connecting rooms. Tennis, golf, swimming, games rooms, health spa. See our Full Page Advertisement under Studland Bay. [Pets £5 per night, including food]
e-mail: info@knollhouse.co.uk   website: www.knollhouse.co.uk

THE MANOR HOUSE HOTEL, STUDLAND BAY BH19 3AU (01929 450288; Fax: 01929 452255). National Trust hotel set in 20 acres on cliffs overlooking Studland Bay. Superb food and accommodation. Log fires and four-posters. Tennis, horse-riding, golf and walking. [Pets £5 per night]
e-mail: info@themanorhousehotel.com   website: www.themanorhousehotel.com

Swanage

Traditional family holiday resort set in a sheltered bay ideal for water sports. Good base for a walking holiday.

THE LIMES, 48 PARK ROAD, SWANAGE BH19 2AE (01929 422664). Informal and friendly, with en suite rooms, TV, tea/coffee making facilities. Children and pets welcome. Credit cards accepted. ETC ★★★ [🐾]
e-mail: info@limeshotel.net   website: www.limeshotel.net

MRS M. STOCKLEY, SWANAGE BAY VIEW HOLIDAY PARK, 17 MOOR ROAD, SWANAGE BH19 1RG (01929 424154). 4/5/6-berth Caravans. Pets welcome. Easter to October. Colour TV. Shop. Parking space. Rose Award Park [🐾]

Wareham

Picturesque riverside town almost surrounded by earthworks, considered pre-Roman. Nature reserves of great beauty nearby. Weymouth 19 miles, Bournemouth 14, Swanage 10, Poole 6.

THE SILENT WOMAN INN, BERE ROAD, COLDHARBOUR, WAREHAM BH20 7PA (01929 552909). Traditional country inn nestling in the heart of Wareham Forest. All fresh ingredients, wonderful food. Adults-only inside. Dogs allowed in bar areas and all outside areas except children's play areas.
website: www.thesilentwoman.co.uk

CATRIONA AND ALISTAIR MILLER, CROMWELL HOUSE HOTEL, LULWORTH COVE BH20 5RJ (01929 400253/400332; Fax: 01929 400566). Comfortable family-run hotel, set in secluded gardens with spectacular sea views. Heated swimming pool, 20 en suite bedrooms. Restaurant, bar wine list. Self-catering. Disabled access. ETC/AA ★★ [Pets £2 per night]
website: www.lulworthcove.co.uk

West Bexington

Seaside village with pebble beach. Chesil beach stretches eastwards. Nearby is Abbotsbury with its Benedictine Abbey and famous Swannery. Dorchester 13 miles, Weymouth 13, Bridport 6.

GORSELANDS CARAVAN PARK, DEPT PW, WEST BEXINGTON-ON-SEA DT2 9DJ (01308 897232; Fax: 01308 897239). Holiday Park. Fully serviced and equipped 4/6 berth caravans. Shop and launderette on site. Glorious sea views. Good country and seaside walks. One mile to beach. Holiday apartments with sea views and private garden. Pets most welcome. Colour brochure on request. ETC ★★★★, David Bellamy Silver Award. [🐾]
e-mail: info@gorselands.co.uk   website: www.gorselands.co.uk

Gloucestershire
SOUTH WEST ENGLAND

Bibury, Bourton-on-the-Water, Chalford, Cheltenham

HARTWELL FARM COTTAGES Ready Token, Near Bibury, Cirencester GL7 5SY
Two traditionally built cottages with far reaching views, on the southern edge of the Cotswolds. Both are fully equipped to a high standard, with heating and woodburning stoves; large private enclosed gardens. Stabling for horses; tennis court. Ideal for touring and horse riding. Glorious walks, excellent pubs. Non-smoking. Children and well-behaved dogs welcome. Sleep 3-4 . • **Contact: Caroline Mann: Tel: 01285 740210**
e-mail: ec.mann@btinternet.com • www.selfcateringcotswolds.com

THE CHESTER HOUSE HOTEL
VICTORIA STREET,
BOURTON-ON-THE-WATER,
GLOUCESTERSHIRE GL54 2BU
TEL: 01451 820286 • FAX 01451 820471
e-mail: info@chesterhousehotel.com
www.chesterhousehotel.com

Chester House Hotel AND BAR

Bourton-on-the-Water – The Venice of the Cotswolds. A haven of peace and comfort tucked away in a quiet backwater of this famous village.

STRATHSPEY   AA ★★★
Lansdowne, Bourton-on-the-Water GL54 2AR
Tastefully furnished bedrooms with TV, refreshment tray, hairdryer, clock radio. Pleasant tranquil garden. Five minutes' walk from centre of village. Open all year.
Terms from £27.50pppn. Pets welcome by prior arrangement.
Tel: 01451 810321 • mobile: 07889 491993
e-mail: bookings@strathspey.org.uk   www.strathspey.org.uk

THE OLD COACH HOUSE • Toadsmoor Valley

Pretty 18th century cottage in the heart of the COTSWOLD HILLS and close to 600 acres of NT common. Sleeps 2 couples +1 child in two bedrooms. Beams, woodburner, outdoor heated swimming pool and bubbling hot tub. Enclosed hillside garden and 20 acres of woods. Free private kennel facilities (optional). Breaks £170-£850.

Ros Smith, Edgecombe House, Toadsmoor, Gloucestershire GL5 2UE
Tel: 01453 883147 • e-mail: ros@doggybreaks.co.uk
www.doggybreaks.co.uk

Ideally located for Cheltenham and the Cotswolds. Close to Cotswold Way. Friendly resident owners. No charge for dogs.
London Road, Cheltenham GL52 6UU
Tel: 01242 231061
www.charltonkingshotel.co.uk
enquiries@charltonkingshotel.co.uk

CHARLTON KINGS *hotel* and restaurant

FHG Guides
publish a large range of well-known accommodation guides.
We will be happy to send you details or you can use the order form at the back of this book.

Clearwell (Forest of Dean), Fairford, Forest of Dean

A historic country hotel whose heritage dates from the 13th Century, situated in the heart of the Forest of Dean, close to the Wye Valley. The hotel retains many of its original features, including beams, timber panelling and oak spiral staircases. 20 en suite bedrooms are located throughout the hotel grounds, including Four-Poster rooms and a Cottage Suite. All bedrooms are en suite and have colour TV, direct-dial telephones and tea and coffee making facilities. Our Two Red Rosette candlelit restaurant is renowned for its quality cuisine and friendliness of service. Tudor Farmhouse is the ideal retreat to relax and unwind.
Please contact us to discuss the availability of our pet-friendly rooms.

Tudor Farmhouse Hotel & Restaurant
Clearwell, Near Coleford, Gloucestershire GL16 8JS
Tel: 01594 833046 • Fax: 01594 837093
e-mail: info@tudorfarmhousehotel.co.uk • www.tudorfarmhousehotel.co.uk

The Bull Hotel
The Market Place, Fairford, Gloucs GL7 4AA
Tel: 01285 712535/712217 • Fax: 01285 713782
e-mail: info@thebullhotelfairford.co.uk
www.thebullhotelfairford.co.uk

15th century family-run coaching inn, situated in the South Cotswolds, ideal for touring. The hotel has a choice of 27 fully equipped bedrooms with sloping roofs and oak beams; four-poster beds available.
A la carte restaurant. Ideal for conferences and weddings. There are good golf courses, squash and tennis courts, sailing facilities within easy reach of the hotel. 1½ miles of private fishing on River Coln. *Tariff: £49.50 - £89.50*

Farmhouse B&B in The Royal Forest of Dean • *www.drysladefarm.co.uk*

Daphne Gwilliam **DRYSLADE FARM** *English Bicknor, Coleford, Gloucs GL16 7PA*
daphne@drysladefarm.co.uk • *Tel: 01594 860259* • *mobile: 07766 631888*

Daphne & Phil ensure a warm welcome for yourself and your dog. A relaxed, friendly atmosphere awaits you at their farmhouse, which dates back to 1780, on their 184-acre beef farm. It is situated in the small village of English Bicknor in the Royal Forest of Dean, with Symonds Yat only 2 miles.

Wharton Lodge Cottages

Two 5* beautifully furnished and fully equipped, self-catering retreats overlooking Herefordshire countryside, sleeping 2,3 or 4 guests.
Just 3 miles from Ross-on-Wye and adjacent to the Royal Forest of Dean, this is an ideal base for exploring this fabulous area designated as an Area of Outstanding Natural Beauty. In addition to the safe, walled, cottage courtyard gardens and the Italianate Garden, guests may also use the 14 acres of parkland. Dog paradise.
GROSVENOR - King-size double and single bedroom.
HAREWOOD - 2 double bedroooms (master with king-size bed).
e-mail: ncross@whartonlodge.co.uk • www.whartonlodge.co.uk
Weston-under-Penyard, Near Ross-on-Wye HR9 7JX • Tel/ Fax: 01989 750140

www.holidayguides.com

Gloucestershire SOUTH WEST ENGLAND 177

Nailsworth, South Cerney, Stow-on-the-Wold, Stroud

The Laurels at Inchbrook

Cow Lane, Inchbrook, Nailsworth GL5 5HA
Tel/Fax: 01453 834021 • e-mail: laurelsinchbrook@tiscali.co.uk
www.laurelsinchbrook.co.uk

A comfortable, rambling house, cottage and garden set beside the Inch Brook and adjoining fields. Lovely secluded garden, with badgers and bats: the stream is an otter route, and many birds come to visit us. Pets are most welcome, and there are dozens of splendid walks and the National Trust's Woodchester Park on our doorstep.

Nailsworth, a fashionable Cotswold town and a centre for excellence when it comes to eating out, is just under a mile away.

Ideally placed for exploring the West Country, Bath and Forest of Dean as well as the Cotswolds, our house is perfect for groups and family gatherings. Brochure on request. Self-catering facilities may be available at certain times of the year.

Rooms from £35 - £65 per night. Rooms: 4 double (one ground floor accessible), 2 twin, 2 family; all en suite. No smoking. Children and pets welcome. Open all year.

Orion Holidays
Cotswolds

A stunning collection of 4/5* lakeside homes. Perfect retreat with pets - Thames Footpath on the doorstep and idyllic countryside to explore.

Call 01285 861 839   Visit www.orionholidays.com

THE Old Stocks HOTEL, RESTAURANT & BAR
The Square, Stow-on-the-Wold GL54 1AF
Tel: 01451 830666 • Fax: 01451 870014

Ideal base for touring this beautiful area. Tasteful guest rooms including three 'garden' rooms located on the middle terrace of our patio garden. All rooms are in keeping with the hotel's old world character, yet with modern amenities. Mouth-watering menus offering a wide range of choices. Special bargain breaks are also available. *HETB/AA* ★★

e-mail: fhg@oldstockshotel.co.uk
www.oldstockshotel.co.uk

THE LIMES

Large Country House with attractive garden, overlooking fields. Four minutes to town centre. One four-poster bedroom; double, twin or family rooms, all en suite. Tea/coffee making facilities, colour TV in all rooms. TV lounge. Central heating. Children and pets welcome. Car park. Bed and Full English Breakfast from £27.00 to £35.00 pppn. Open all year except Christmas. *Established over 30 years*

Evesham Road, Stow-on-the-Wold, GL54 1EN • Tel: 01451 830034/831056
e-mail: gkeyte@sky.com • www.cotswold.info/webpage/thelimes-stow.htm

AA ★★★

Orchardene
Castle Street, Kings Stanley, Stonehouse, Gloucestershire GL10 3JA

Warm welcome at Cotswold Stone cottage. Ideal location to explore undiscovered Cotswolds and Severn Vale. Glorious walks. Evening Meal optional. Local and organic food. Pets welcome. Tom and Lesley Williams.

Tel: 01453 822684 • Fax: 01453 821554 • e-mail: toranda@btconnect.com

Gloucestershire

Stroud, Symonds Yat, Thornbury

Hyde Crest Beautiful country house with enclosed acre garden. All rooms on ground floor opening on to patios and lawns. 500 acres of commons, plus country walks nearby. **MRS A. RHOTON, HYDE CREST, CIRENCESTER ROAD, MINCHINHAMPTON GL6 8PE** 01453 731631 • e-mail: stay@hydecrest.co.uk • www.hydecrest.co.uk

The Withyholt Guest House
Paul Mead, Edge, near Stroud, Gloucestershire GL6 6PG

Modern guesthouse in Gloucestershire close to Gloucester Cathedral, Tetbury, Stroud. Many lovely country walks. Pets welcome. En suite bedrooms, large lounge. Large garden.

Telephone: 01452 813618
Fax: 01452 812375

SYMONDS YAT ROCK LODGE

4★ Apartments and B&B
Forest of Dean • Wye Valley

Pets very welcome. Walk straight into the forest. Stunning views. Guests' garden.

Claire & Darren Scales
Symonds Yat Rock Lodge, Hillersland, Coleford Glos GL16 7NY
01594 836191 • www.rocklodge.co.uk

THORNBURY CASTLE
Thornbury, Near Bristol South Gloucs BS35 1HH
Tel: 01454 281182 • Fax: 01454 416188
info@thornburycastle.co.uk • www.thornburycastle.co.uk

With a fascinating history, this 16th century building retains many features such as coats of arms, intricate oriel windows, arrow loops and ornate carved ceilings. Three dining rooms offer the finest à la carte menus, using only the finest and freshest ingredients, with a discerning choice of fine vintages and New World varieties from the well stocked cellar. The fabulously atmospheric bedchambers (most with real fires and four-poster beds) have all modern amenities, including opulent bathrooms. The unique surroundings and ambience of Thornbury Castle, together with the excellent and attentive service of the staff, make the Castle a superb venue for those seeking something special.

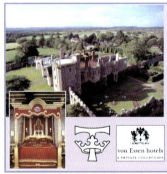

Symbols

🐾 Indicates that pets are welcome free of charge.
£ Indicates that a charge is made for pets: nightly or weekly.
pw! Shows some special provision for pets; exercise facility, feeding or accommodation arrangement.
⌂ Indicates separate pets accommodation.

Gloucestershire

Upper Hasfield

Rural Cottage B&B

Situated in pretty rural hamlet in gorgeous location close to Gloucester, Ledbury and Tewkesbury. Ideal walking country, Severn Way, and Malvern Hills. Double or twin en suite room in annex nearby, twin or double available in house. Horse riding and other leisure pursuits within easy reach. Excellent local pubs. Dogs welcome by arrangement
A warm welcome awaits you..

Mike and Liz Dawson, Rusts Meadow
Hasfield Road, Upper Hasfield,
Gloucestershire GL19 4LL
Tel: 01452 700814

Bibury

Village on the River Colne, 7 miles NE of Cirencester.

CAROLINE MANN, HARTWELL FARM COTTAGES, READY TOKEN, NEAR BIBURY, CIRENCESTER GL7 5SY (01285 740210). Two comfortable, fully equipped cottages with country views. Ideally located for touring. Stabling available. Glorious walks, excellent pubs. Non-smoking. Children and well-behaved dogs welcome. ETC ★★★★ [pw! Pets £15 per week]
e-mail: ec.mann@btinternet.com   website: www.selfcateringcotswolds.com

Bourton-on-the-Water

Delightfully situated on the River Windrush which is crossed by miniature stone bridges. Stow-on-the-Wold 4 miles.

CHESTER HOUSE HOTEL, VICTORIA STREET, BOURTON-ON-THE-WATER GL54 2BU (01451 820286). All rooms en suite, all with central heating, colour TV, phone, tea/coffee making facilities. Wheelchair friendly. Ideal for touring Cotswolds. [🐕]
e-mail: info@chesterhousehotel.com   website: www.chesterhousehotel.com

STRATHSPEY, LANSDOWNE, BOURTON-ON-THE-WATER GL54 2AR (01451 810321; mobile: 07889 491993). Tastefully furnished bedrooms with TV, refreshment tray, hairdryer, clock radio. Pleasant tranquil garden. Five minutes' walk from centre of village. Open all year. Terms from £27.50pppn. Pets welcome by prior arrangement. AA ★★★ [Pets £5 per week]
e-mail: bookings@strathspey.org.uk   website: www.strathspey.org.uk

Chalford

Village 4 miles south east of Stroud.

ROS SMITH, EDGECOMBE HOUSE, TOADSMOOR GL5 2UE (01453 883147). Pretty 18th century cottage in the heart of the Cotswold Hills. Sleeps 2 couples + 1 child in 2 bedrooms. Outdoor heated swimming pool and bubbling hot tub. Free private kennel facilities (optional). Breaks £170-£750. [[🐕 ⌂]
e-mail: ros@doggybreaks.co.uk   website: www.doggybreaks.co.uk

Cheltenham

Large residential town, formerly a spa, 8 miles East of Gloucester.

CHARLTON KINGS HOTEL & RESTAURANT, LONDON ROAD, CHELTENHAM GL52 6UU (01242 231061). Ideally located for Cheltenham and the Cotswolds. Close to Cotswold Way. Friendly resident owners. [🐕]
e-mail: enquiries@charltonkingshotel.co.uk   website: www.charltonkingshotel.co.uk

Clearwell (Forest of Dean)

Village 2 miles south of Coleford in the ancient Forest of Dean.

TUDOR FARMHOUSE HOTEL & RESTAURANT, CLEARWELL, NEAR COLEFORD GL16 8JS (01594 833046; Fax: 01594 837093). Charming 13th Century farmhouse hotel in extensive grounds, ideal for dog walking. 20 en suite bedrooms including Four Posters and Cottage Suite. Award-winning restaurant. AA ★★★ and Two Rosettes. [Pets £5 per night].
e-mail: info@tudorfarmhousehotel.co.uk   website: www.tudorfarmhousehotel.co.uk

Fairford

Small town 8 miles east of Cirencester.

THE BULL HOTEL, MARKET PLACE, FAIRFORD GL7 4AA (01285 712535/712217; Fax: 01285 713782). 15thC family-run coaching inn with 27 fully equipped bedrooms; four-poster beds available. A la carte restaurant. Ideal for touring; many leisure facilities within easy reach. ETC/AA ★★ [Pets £5 per night, £20 per week]
e-mail: info@thebullhotelfairford.co.uk   website: www.thebullhotelfairford.co.uk

Forest of Dean

Formerly a royal hunting ground, this scenic area lies between the rivers Severn and Wye.

DRYSLADE FARM, ENGLISH BICKNOR, COLEFORD GL16 7PA (01594 860259; Mobile: 07766 631988). Daphne & Phil ensure a warm welcome for yourself and your dog. A relaxed, friendly atmosphere awaits you at their farmhouse, which dates back to 1780, on their 184-acre beef farm. In the small village of English Bicknor in the Royal Forest of Dean, with Symonds Yat only 2 miles. AA ★★★★ Highly Commended. [🐾]
e-mail: daphne@drysladefarm.co.uk   website: www.drysladefarm.co.uk

WHARTON LODGE COTTAGES, WESTON-UNDER-PENYARD, NEAR ROSS-ON-WYE HR9 7JX (Tel & Fax: 01989 750140). Two elegantly furnished, fully equipped self-catering retreats overlooking Herefordshire countryside, sleeping 2, 3 or 4 guests. Fully inclusive rates. Dog paradise. Tourist Board ★★★★★ Gold Award. [pw! Pets £4 per night, £20 per week]
e-mail: ncross@whartonlodge.co.uk   website: www.whartonlodge.co.uk

Nailsworth

Hilly town 4 miles south of Stroud

THE LAURELS, INCHBROOK, NAILSWORTH GL5 5HA (01453 834021; Fax: 01453 835190). A lovely rambling house, cottage and secluded garden where dogs and their owners are encouraged to relax and enjoy. Ideally situated for touring all parts of the Cotswolds and West Country; splendid walks. Brochure. [🐾]
e-mail: laurelsinchbrook@tiscali.co.uk   website: www.laurelsinchbrook.co.uk

South Cerney

4 miles from Cirencester in the Cotswold Waterpark, an area of 40 square miles.

ORION HOLIDAYS, COTSWOLDS (01285 861839). A stunning collection of 4/5 ★ lakeside homes. Perfect retreat with pets - Thames Footpath on the doorstep and idyllic countryside to explore. [Pets £15 per week].
website: www.orionholidays.com

Please mention **Pets Welcome!** when making enquiries about accommodation featured in these pages

Gloucestershire

Stow-on-the-Wold

Charming Cotswold hill-top market town with several old inns and interesting buildings. Birmingham 45 miles, Gloucester 26, Stratford-upon-Avon 21, Cheltenham 18, Chipping Norton 9.

THE OLD STOCKS HOTEL, RESTAURANT & BAR, THE SQUARE, STOW-ON-THE-WOLD GL54 1AF (01451 830666; Fax: 01451 870014). Ideal base for touring this beautiful area. Tasteful guest rooms (including three 'garden' rooms) with modern amenities. Mouth-watering menus. Special bargain breaks also available. HETB/AA ★★ [Pets £5 per stay]
e-mail: fhg@oldstockshotel.co.uk   website: www.oldstockshotel.co.uk

THE LIMES, EVESHAM ROAD, STOW-ON-THE-WOLD GL54 1EN (01451 830034/831056). Large Country House. Attractive garden, overlooking fields, 4 minutes town centre. Television lounge. Central heating. Car park. Bed and Breakfast from £27 to £35pppn. Twin, double or family rooms, all en suite. Children and pets welcome. AA ★★★, Tourist Board Listed. [Pets £5 per visit]
e-mail: gkeyte@sky.com   website: www.cotswolds.info/webpage/thelimes-stow.htm

Stroud

Cotswold town on River Frome below picturesque Stroudwater Hills, formerly renowned for cloth making. Bristol 32 miles, Bath 29, Chippenham 25, Cheltenham 14, Gloucester 9.

TOM AND LESLEY WILLIAMS, ORCHARDENE, CASTLE STREET, KINGS STANLEY, STONEHOUSE GL10 3JA. (01453 822684; Fax: 01453 821554). Warm welcome at Cotswold Stone cottage. Ideal location to explore undiscovered Cotswolds and Severn Vale. Glorious walks. Evening Meal optional. Local and organic food. Pets welcome.
e-mail: toranda@btconnect.com

MRS A. RHOTON, HYDE CREST, CIRENCESTER ROAD, MINCHINHAMPTON GL6 8PE (01453 731631). Beautiful country house with enclosed acre garden. All rooms on ground floor opening on to patios and lawns. 500 acres of commons, plus country walks nearby. AA ★★★★ [pw! 🐾]
e-mail: stay@hydecrest.co.uk   website: www.hydecrest.co.uk

MRS UNA PEACEY, THE WITHYHOLT GUEST HOUSE, PAUL MEAD, EDGE, NEAR STROUD GL6 6PG (01452 813618: Fax: 01452 812375) Modern guesthouse in Gloucestershire close to Gloucester Cathedral, Tetbury, Stroud. Many lovely country walks. En suite bedrooms, large lounge. Large garden. ETC ★★★★ [🐾]

Symonds Yat

Well known beauty spot on River Wye, 4 miles from Monmouth.

SYMONDS YAT ROCK LODGE, HILLERSLAND, NEAR COLEFORD GL16 7NY (01594 836191). Family-run B&B and Self catering in Royal Forest of Dean near Wye Valley. All rooms en suite, colour TV. 4 poster and family rooms. Brochure available on request. Dogs welcome. [🐾]
e-mail: info@rocklodge.co.uk   website: www.rocklodge.co.uk

Thornbury

Market town 12 miles north of Bristol.

THORNBURY CASTLE, THORNBURY, NEAR BRISTOL BS35 1HH (01454 281182; Fax: 01454 416188).The unique surroundings and ambience of 16th Thornbury Castle, together with the excellent and attentive service of the staff, make the Castle a superb venue for those seeking something special.
e-mail: info@thornburycastle.co.uk   website: www.thornburycastle.co.uk

Upper Hasfield

Village 6 miles from Gloucester.

MIKE & LIZ DAWSON, RUSTS MEADOW, HASFIELD ROAD, UPPER HASFIELD GL19 4LL (01452 700814). Rural cottage B&B in pretty hamlet near Gloucester and Tewkesbury. Double or twin en suite in annexe, twin and double in house. Local walks, horse riding and golf nearby. Excellent local pubs. Dogs welcome by arrangement. [🐾]

Somerset

Bath, Blue Anchor, Brean, Bridgwater, Cheddar

BATH - TOGHILL HOUSE FARM Cottages and B&B

Luxury barn conversions on working farm just north of Bath. Each cottage is equipped to a very high standard with bed linen provided. You are welcome to roam amongst our many animals and enjoy the outstanding country views. We also provide Bed and Breakfast accommodation in our warm and cosy 17th century farmhouse where all rooms are en suite with TV and tea making facilities. Pets £2 per night, £8 per week.
Brochure - Tel: 01225 891261 • Fax: 01225 892128 • www.toghillhousefarm.co.uk
David and Jackie Bishop, Toghill House Farm, Freezing Hill, Wick, Near Bath BS30 5RT

Primrose Hill offers spacious, comfortable accommodation in a terrace of four bungalows. Private gardens with panoramic views over Blue Anchor Bay, Dunster Castle and Exmoor. A dog-friendly beach is a 10-minute walk away, with other lovely walks from your doorstep. Fully wheelchair accessible. *Winner Accessible Somerset Awards 2008 & 2009. Exmoor Excellence Awards Self-catering Holiday of the Year 2006/7.*
Primrose Hill Holidays, Wood Lane, Blue Anchor TA24 6LA (01643 821200)
info@primrosehillholidays.co.uk • www.primrosehillholidays.co.uk

WESTWARD RISE HOLIDAY PARK
Brean, Near Burnham-on-Sea TA8 2RD   Tel & Fax: 01278 751310

Highly Recommended Luxury 2/6 berth Chalet-Bungalows on a small quiet family-owned Park adjoining sandy beach. • 2 Double Bedrooms • Shower • Toilet • Colour TV • Fridge • Cooker • Duvets and Linen • Open all year • Centrally Heated during winter months • Laundry on Park • Caravan Sales Available • Shops • Clubs • Amusements & Restaurants Nearby • Dogs Welcome
Call now for a FREE BROCHURE   www.westwardrise.com

Beachside Holiday Park
Coast Road, Brean Sands, Somerset TA8 2QZ
Tel: 01278 751346 • Fax: 01278 751683

• 1,2 & 3 bedroom caravan holiday homes with sea views • Direct beach access • Digital TV •
• Children's Play Area • Sundowner Grill Bar • Pets welcome, £5 per night

e-mail: reception@beachsideholidaypark.co.uk • www.beachsideholidaypark.co.uk

The Hood Arms a famous 17th century coaching Inn. Situated on the A39 at the foot of the Quantock Hills, close to the spectacular fossil beach at Kilve, a paradise for walkers, mountain bikers, dogs, sporting parties or simply relaxing. The 12 recently refurbished en suite bedrooms include stylish four-posters. Stag Lodge in the courtyard garden has two luxury bedrooms and sitting room. The beamed restaurant offers a relaxed dining experience whilst providing delicious locally sourced food. A full à la carte menu, chef's specials and bar snacks are available 7 days a week. The bar is full of character and boasts an impressive array of real ales. A warm welcome awaits locals and traveller alike.
Please look at our website for more details and prices.
The Hood Arms, Kilve, Bridgwater, Somerset TA5 1EA • 01278 741210 • Fax: 01278 741477
e-mail: info@thehoodarms.com • www.thehoodarms.com

CHEDDAR - SUNGATE HOLIDAY APARTMENTS
Church Street, Cheddar, Somerset BS27 3RA

Delightful non-smoking apartments in Cheddar village, each fully equipped. Sleep one/four people. Laundry facilities. Private parking. Family, disabled, and pet friendly.

For full details contact: Mrs. M. M. Fieldhouse (proprietress)

Tel: 01934 842273/742264
enquiries@sungateholidayapartments.co.uk
www.sungateholidayapartments.co.uk

Somerset
SOUTH WEST ENGLAND
Clevedon, Dunster, Exford

Rose Cottage BED & BREAKFAST

Fancy a short break in Somerset or just a one night stop over? At the Rose Cottage Bed & Breakfast in Clevedon you are assured of a warm welcome. Private parking. Non-smoking. Well behaved dogs by arrangement

Proprietor: Mrs Jenny Hopkins
Rose Cottage, 36 Thackeray Ave, Clevedon, Somerset BS21 7JJ
Tel. 01275 879491 • e-mail: jenny.hopkins42@btopenworld.com • www.rosecottage-bandb.co.uk

The Yarn Market Hotel is a comfortable, family-run hotel which provides a friendly, relaxed atmosphere. Situated at the centre of a quaint English village it is an ideal location for walking and exploring Exmoor, the surrounding coastline and the many local attractions. All rooms are en suite, with tea and coffee making facilities and colour TV. Some have four-poster beds while others have spectacular views over the surrounding countryside. Family rooms are also available. The restaurant offers a mouth watering selection of dishes featuring local produce whenever possible. Packed lunches and drying facilities are also available. Non-smoking. Well behaved pets are welcome. Party bookings and midweek breaks a speciality. B&B from £40.

THE YARN MARKET HOTEL
High Street, Dunster TA24 6SF

Tel: 01643 821425   Fax: 01643 821475
e-mail: hotel@yarnmarkethotel.co.uk
www.yarnmarkethotel.co.uk

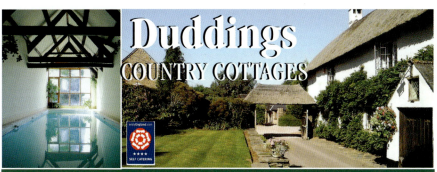

Duddings COUNTRY COTTAGES

Thatched longhouse and 12 cottages for 2-12 persons, beautifully converted from old stone barns and stables. Original beams and exposed stonework retain the character of the buildings. Two miles from the picturesque village of Dunster in the Exmoor National Park.

Luxury Cottages
Indoor Heated Pool • Tennis Court

Duddings Country Cottages
Timberscombe, Dunster, Somerset TA24 7TB
Tel: 01643 841123
e-mail: richard@duddings.co.uk
www.duddings.co.uk

As resident owners, we personally guarantee immaculate presentation of cottages on arrival. Each cottage has tasteful decor with matching, highest quality fabrics and is fully central heated. Amenities include comfortable lounges with colour TV/video/DVD, fully fitted modern kitchens with fridge-freezer, cooker and microwave. Our facilities include heated indoor pool, hard tennis court, putting green, pool and table tennis, trampoline, football net and play centre. Trout stream in 8.5 acres for fishing or picnics. Families and pets welcome, walking, riding, beaches nearby. Short breaks available off season, open all year.
Full details and plans of the cottages together with up to date prices and availablity can be found on our website, or please call for brochure.

Idyllic Scandinavian cottages in grass paddocks by stream, with views across river valley • Heart of Exmoor Woodburners • Four waymarked walks over 500-acre working farm • Disabled Category 2 • Separate campsite by river.

WESTERMILL, EXFORD, EXMOOR TA24 7NJ • Tel: 01643 831238
Fax: 01643 831216 • e-mail: pw@westermill.com • www.westermill.com

SOUTH WEST ENGLAND

Somerset
Exford, Exmoor

Exford, Exmoor National Park, Somerset TA24 7NA   ETC ★★★★

Charming, cosy, comfortable centrally heated detached bungalow with enclosed garden and superb views. A short walk from the village of Exford. Ideally located for walking, fishing, riding and exploring Exmoor, and the surrounding coastline. Bring your dog or horse for wonderful trips over the moor. Stabling available. B&B available at Edgcott, Exford, in 18thC cottage. • **Contact: Joan Atkins, 2 Edgcott Cottage, Exford, Somerset TA24 7QG**

e-mail: info@stilemoorexmoor.co.uk

Tel/Fax: 01643 831564 • mobile: 078914 37293 • www.stilemoorexmoor.co.uk

---

CHAPEL COTTAGE, EXFORD TA24 7PY • 01788 810275

Enjoy walking or riding on the moors, by the rivers or the beach. Return to our cosy cottage, log fire and beams. Two bedrooms (sleeps 4+2), two bathrooms. Excellent inns within 100 yards. Open all year.

e-mail: stay@chapelcottage-exmoor.co.uk
www.chapelcottage-exmoor.co.uk

Beside River Exe
Centre of Exmoor National Park

Close to coast. Four charming self-catering cottages.

Dogs and horses welcome. Stabling available.

Riscombe Farm Holiday Cottages
Exford, Somerset TA24 7NH
Tel: 01643 831480
www.riscombe.co.uk

Pyncombe Lane, Wiveliscombe, Taunton TA4 2BL Tel: 01984 623730

Traditional working farm set in 100 acres of natural beauty. All rooms tastefully furnished to high standard include en suite, TV, and tea/coffee facilities. Double, twin or single rooms available. Dining room and lounge with log fires; centrally heated and double glazed. Drying facilities. Dogs welcome. B&B £36pppn, 7 nights BB+EM £299pp. North Down Break: three nights BB+EM £145pp.

e-mail: jennycope@btinternet.com   www.north-down-farm.co.uk

Four-star lodges and cottages, sleeping from two in a cosy cottage up to 12 in our newly built Holly Lodge, all situated in 2½ acres of gardens overlooking the slopes of Exmoor. Superb walking; Minehead seafront within 1½ miles. Dogs permitted in some lodges. VisitBritain ★★★★

WOODCOMBE LODGES   Bratton, Near Minehead TA24 8SQ
Tel & Fax: 01643 702789 • nicola@woodcombelodge.co.uk

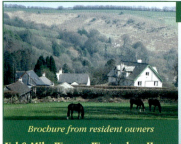

Holiday Cottages – Exmoor National Park

Quality cottages, including bungalows in the grounds of a former hunting lodge. Wonderful moorland location.
Totally peaceful with superb views. Beautiful coast and countryside. Shop and pub 300 metres. Excellent walking straight from your cottage. Log fires. Very well appointed. Dogs & horses welcome. Individual gardens. Sleep 2-6. Internet access. Open all year. Short breaks available.

ETC ★★★★

Brochure from resident owners
Val & Mike Warner, Westerclose House, Withypool, Somerset TA24 7QR
Tel/Fax: 01643 831302 • www.westerclose.co.uk

Somerset

SOUTH WEST ENGLAND

Exmoor, Minehead

Woolchamber Cottages set in the heart of Exmoor. A choice of self-catering cottages sleeping from two to six people adjoining **Simonsbath House Hotel**. Although the cottages are completely self contained the hotel restaurant and bar may be used by guests in the evening, and there is a village pub only 50 yards away. The cottages are all fully centrally heated and furnished to a very high standard. They feature comfortable living room, kitchen and additional gallery areas which give a feeling of extra space and offers additional sleeping accommodation if required. All the Cottages have fully fitted and equipped kitchen areas, fitted carpets throughout, satellite TV with remote control, and telephone. Dogs permitted by arrangement.
Local activities include walking, riding, water sports, fishing, mountain biking and hang-gliding

For details contact: Simonsbath House Hotel, Simonsbath, Exmoor, Somerset TA24 7SH
Tel: 01643 831259 • enquiries@simonsbathhousehotel.co.uk • www.simonsbathhouse.co.uk

---

West Withy Farm

UPTON,
NEAR WIVELISCOMBE,
TAUNTON, SOMERSET TA4 2JH
Tel: 01398 371 322
e-mail: laurencerye@byinternet.com
www.exmoor-cottages.com
ETC ★★★★ Self Catering

West Withy Farm offers you and your dog a haven of peace and tranquillity in the beautiful, undiscovered Brendon Hills on the edge of Exmoor. The glorious countryside of Exmoor, the Brendons and the Quantocks provides a walkers' paradise. Two well-equipped, detached character cottages, **Upton** and **Stable**, with full central heating and stoves, sleeping 2- 5.
• Private south-facing, enclosed, dog-proof gardens • Panoramic views • Excellent fly fishing locally
• Bed linen and towels provided • Colour TVs • Fully inclusive prices • From £180-£545 per week • Short breaks available

---

Exmoor •• The Pack Horse
Allerford, Near Porlock, Somerset TA24 8HW
Tel/Fax: 01643 862475
www.thepackhorse-exmoor.co.uk
e-mail: holidays@thepackhorse-exmoor.co.uk

Our self-catering apartments and cottage are situated in this unique location within a picturesque National Trust village which has local amenities. The Pack Horse sits alongside the shallow River Aller, overlooking the famous bridge. Enjoy immediate access from our doorstep to the beautiful surrounding countryside, pretty villages, spectacular coast, and Exmoor. *Terms from £310 to £555 per week*
OPEN ALL YEAR • PRIVATE PARKING • SHORT BREAKS
Very warm welcome assured

Occupying an unique location with breathtaking views within the National Park. A special place for you and man's best friends.
ETC ★★★★ Telephone or write for colour brochure:

Jane Styles, Wintershead Farm,
Simonsbath, Exmoor, Somerset TA24 7LF
Tel: 01643 831222 • www.wintershead.co.uk

Delightful family-run private guest house only a few minutes' level walking distance from sea front • Delicious home cooking • Full central heating
• 8 en suite bedrooms, all with courtesy tray, remote-control TV, hairdryer
• Children and well behaved pets welcome • Totally non-smoking
SUNFIELD, 83 Summerland Avenue, Minehead TA24 5BW
Tel: 01643 703565 • www.sunfieldminehead.co.uk

186 SOUTH WEST ENGLAND — Somerset

Minehead, Quantock Hills, Taunton, Watchet, Weston-super-Mare

MINEHEAD – 16th CENTURY THATCHED COTTAGES

ROSE-ASH – Sleeps 2 ♦ Prettily furnished ♦ All electric.

WILLOW – Sleeps 6 ♦ Inglenook ♦ one double and two twin bedrooms ♦ Oak panelling ♦ Electricity, Gas, CH.

LITTLE THATCH – Sleeps 5 ♦ Inglenook ♦ two double and a single bedroom ♦ Cosy location ♦ Electricity, Gas, CH.

All well equipped and attractively furnished, and situated within ten minutes' walk of shops, sea and moor. All have enclosed patio/garden and private parking. Electricity and gas are metered; bed linen can be provided at extra cost. Pets welcome.

SAE please to: Mr T. Stone, Troytes Farmstead, Tivington, Somerset TA24 8SU
Private car park – Enclosed gardens – Pets Welcome   **Tel: 01643 704531**

THE OLD CIDER HOUSE

4 ★ licensed guesthouse set in the picturesque and historic village of **Nether Stowey** at the foot of the beautiful **Quantock Hills**. The ideal place for walking, sightseeing or just relaxing.

2008 Winner: Kennel Club's 'Somewhere to Sleep' Award.

01278 732228 • info@theoldciderhouse.co.uk

25 Castle Street, Nether Stowey, Somerset TA5 1LN • www.theoldciderhouse.co.uk

FARTHINGS HOTEL & RESTAURANT
Hatch Beauchamp, Taunton TA3 6SG
Tel: 01823 480624 • Fax: 01823 481118
www.farthingshotel.co.uk
e-mail: info@farthingshotel.co.uk

Welcome to 'Farthings', an elegant Georgian hotel situated in the heart of the Somerset countryside in the historic village of Hatch Beauchamp. Set in three acres of peaceful gardens and overlooking the village green, it enjoys an enviable reputation for hospitality, comfort, pure relaxation and superb cuisine. All our bedrooms are individual, spacious and en suite, tastefully decorated and furnished, with the usual tea/coffee making facilities, including chilled fresh milk.

The hotel is an ideal base for visiting the many attractions just a short drive away. Within 30 minutes you can visit Wells Cathedral, Bath, Cheddar Gorge, Wookey Hole, the Mendips, Exmoor and both the North and South Devon coasts. Many National Trust and other heritage sites are also within easy reach.

20% discount if you mention FHG when booking.

Croft Holiday Cottages • The Croft, Anchor Street, Watchet TA23 0BY
Tel: 01984 631521 • ETC ★★★★

Courtyard of six cottages/bungalows situated in a quiet backwater of the small harbour town of Watchet. Parking, central heating, TV, DVD, washing machine, fridge/freezer, microwave. Use of heated indoor pool. Sleep 2-6 persons. £200-£750 per property per week. **Contact:** Mrs K. Musgrave • e-mail: croftcottages@talk21.com • www.cottagessomerset.com

Somerset Court Cottages
Wick St Lawrence, Near Weston-super-Mare BS22 7YR • Tel: 01934 521383
Converted stone cottages in mediaeval village. 1, 2 or 3 beds.
Some with four-posters, luxury whirlpool/spa baths. £210-£710 per week.
e-mail: peter@somersetcourtcottages.co.uk • www.somersetcottages.com

Braeside Hotel 2 Victoria Park, Weston-super-Mare BS23 2HZ
Delightful, family-run, 9-bedroom hotel only a two-minute walk from the seafront and sandy beach (dogs allowed all year). All bedrooms en suite.
Tel: 01934 626642 • ETC/AA ♦♦♦♦ (Awarded in 2005)
e-mail: enquiries@braesidehotel.com • www.braesidehotel.com

Somerset

SOUTH WEST ENGLAND 187

Williton

Arden Cottage • West Somerset B&B
A B&B offering quality, comfort and a 'home from home' atmosphere. Secure garden for dog(s) to play in. Beautiful countryside for walking and local dog walking guide available. Tea/coffee making and complimentary biscuits available in each room. Dogs go free on bookings of 3 nights and over.
Telephone: 01984 634090 • Mobile: 07794 656 484
e-mail: enquiries@ardencottagewilliton.co.uk • www.ardencottagewilliton.co.uk
Jane Snell and Paul Plumridge, Arden Cottage, 33 Long Street, Williton, Somerset TA4 4QU

FARM & COTTAGE HOLIDAYS (01237 459897). An inspiring collection of holiday cottages throughout Cornwall, Devon, Somerset and Dorset in stunning rural and coastal locations. [Pets £20 per week] website: www.holidaycottages.co.uk

Bath

The best-preserved Georgian city in Britain, Bath has been famous since Roman times for its mineral springs. It is a noted centre for music and the arts, with a wide range of leisure facilities.

DAVID & JACKIE BISHOP, TOGHILL HOUSE FARM, FREEZING HILL, WICK, NEAR BATH BS30 5RT (01225 891261; Fax: 01225 892128). Luxury barn conversions on working farm 3 miles north of Bath. Each equipped to very high standard, bed linen provided. Also en suite B&B accommodation in 17th century farmhouse. [pw! Pets £2 per night, £12 per week]
website: www.toghillhousefarm.co.uk

Blue Anchor

Hamlet two miles west of Watchet. Beautiful beaches, and rocks and cliffs of geological interest.

PRIMROSE HILL HOLIDAYS, WOOD LANE, BLUE ANCHOR TA24 6LA (01643 821200). Award-winning, spacious, comfortable accommodation in a terrace of four bungalows. Private gardens with panoramic views. A dog-friendly beach is a 10-minute walk away, with other lovely walks from your doorstep. Fully wheelchair accessible. ETC ★★★★ [Pets £15 per week].
e-mail: info@primrosehillholidays.co.uk   website: www.primrosehillholidays.co.uk

Brean

Coastal village with extensive sands. To north is the promontory of Brean Down. Weston-Super-Mare 9 miles.

WESTWARD RISE HOLIDAY PARK, SOUTH ROAD, BREAN, NEAR BURNHAM ON-SEA TA8 2RD (01278 751310). Highly Recommended Luxury 2/6 berth Chalet bungalows. 2 double bedrooms, shower, toilet, TV, fridge, cooker, duvets and linen. Open all year. Call for free brochure. [Pets £15 per week.]
website: www.westwardrise.com

BEACHSIDE HOLIDAY PARK, COAST ROAD, BREAN SANDS TA8 2QZ (01278 751346; Fax: 01278 751683). Caravan holiday homes on quiet park. Direct access to beach (dogs allowed). Full facilities. Digital TV. Cafe/bar. Golf courses nearby. [Pets £5 per night]
e-mail: reception@beachsideholidaypark.co.uk   website: www.beachsideholidaypark.co.uk

Bridgwater

An Area of Outstanding Natural Beauty at the foot of the Quantocks, a paradise for walkers.

THE HOOD ARMS, KILVE, BRIDGWATER TA5 1EA (01278 741210; Fax: 01278 741477). 17thC coaching inn on the A39 at the foot of the Quantock Hills. 12 en suite bedrooms, including four-posters. Beamed restaurant offering full à la carte menu; bar snacks and real ales available. Large garden. [🐕]
e-mail: info@thehoodarms.com   website: www.thehoodarms.com

SOUTH WEST ENGLAND
Somerset

Cheddar

Picturesque little town in the Mendips, famous for its Gorge and unique caves. Cheese-making is a speciality. Good touring centre. Bath 24 miles, Burnham-on-sea 13, Weston-Super-Mare 11.

SUNGATE HOLIDAY APARTMENTS, CHURCH STREET, CHEDDAR BS27 3RA. Ideally situated for walking, cycling and touring the Mendips and the West Country. Competitively priced for short or longer holidays. For full details contact MRS M. FIELDHOUSE (01934 842273/742264) ETC ★★ [Quote for Pets].
e-mail: enquiries@sungateholidayapartments.co.uk   web: www.sungateholidayapartments.co.uk

Clevedon

Small town on Bristol Channel with restored Victorian pier.

MRS JENNY HOPKINS, ROSE COTTAGE, 36 THACKERAY AVE, CLEVEDON BS21 7JJ (01275 879491) You are assured of a warm welcome at this pleasant semi-detached B&B. Private parking. Non smoking. Bristol 15 miles. Well behaved dogs by arrangement. [Pets £1 per night]
e-mail: jenny.hopkins42@btopenworld.com   website: www.rosecottage-bandb.co.uk

Dunster

Pretty village with interesting features, including Yarn Market, imposing 14th century Castle, Priory Church and old houses and cottages. Minehead 3 miles.

THE YARN MARKET HOTEL, HIGH STREET, DUNSTER TA24 6SF (01643 821425; Fax: 01643 821475). An ideal location for walking and exploring Exmoor. Family-run hotel with a friendly, relaxed atmosphere, home cooking, en suite rooms with colour TV and tea making facilities. Non-smoking. Mid-week breaks a speciality – Pets Welcome. ETC ★★★ Hotel [pw! 🐾]
e-mail: hotel@yarnmarkethotel.co.uk   website: www.yarnmarkethotel.co.uk

DUDDINGS COUNTRY COTTAGES, TIMBERSCOMBE DUNSTER TA24 7TB (01643 841123) Thatched longhouse and 12 cottages for 2-12 persons, beautifully converted from old stone barns and stables. Two miles from the village of Dunster in the Exmoor National Park. Pets and families welcome. Open all year. Visit Britain ★★★★ Self Catering. [pw!, Pets £20 per week].
e-mail: richard@duddings.co.uk   website: www.duddings.co.uk

Exford

Fine touring centre for Exmoor and North Devon, on River Exe. Dulverton 10 miles.

WESTERMILL, EXFORD, EXMOOR TA24 7NJ (01643 831238; Fax: 01643 831216). Idyllic Scandinavian cottages in grass paddocks by stream, with views across river valley. Heart of Exmoor. Woodburners. Four waymarked walks over 500 acre working farm. Disabled Category 2. Separate campsite by river. VisitBritain ★★★, David Bellamy Gold Award for Conservation. [Pets £2.50 per night, £15 per week.]
e-mail: pw@westermill.com   website: www.westermill.com

STILEMOOR, EXFORD, EXMOOR NATIONAL PARK TA24 7NA. Charming cosy centrally heated detached bungalow with enclosed garden, superb views, walking, fishing, riding. Sleeps 6. ETC ★★★★. JOAN ATKINS, 2 EDGCOTT COTTAGE, EXFORD, MINEHEAD TA24 7QG (Tel & Fax: 01643 831564; mobile: 078914 37293) [Pets £3 per night, £18 per week]
e-mail: info@stilemoorexmoor.co.uk   website: www.stilemoorexmoor.co.uk

CHAPEL COTTAGE, EXFORD TA24 7PY (01788 810275). Enjoy walking or riding on the moors, by the rivers or the beach. Return to our cosy cottage, log fire and beams. Two bedrooms (sleeps 4+2), two bathrooms. Excellent inns within 100 yards. Open all year. [🐾 Up to 2 dogs welcome, free of charge]
e-mail: stay@chapelcottage-exmoor.co.uk   website: www.chapelcottage-exmoor.co.uk

LEONE & BRIAN MARTIN, RISCOMBE FARM HOLIDAY COTTAGES, EXFORD, EXMOOR NATIONAL PARK TA24 7NH (01643 831480). Beside River Exe – centre of Exmoor National Park – close to coast. Four charming self-catering cottages. Dogs and horses welcome. Stabling available. VB ★★★★ [Pets £2.50 per night, £15 per week.]
website: www.riscombe.co.uk (with up-to-date vacancy info.)

Somerset

SOUTH WEST ENGLAND 189

Exmoor

265 square miles of unspoiled heather moorland with deep wooded valleys and rivers, ideal for a walking, pony trekking or fishing holiday.

JENNY COPE, NORTH DOWN FARM, PYNCOMBE LANE, WIVELISCOMBE, TAUNTON TA4 2BL (01984 623730). Traditional working farm. All rooms en suite, furnished to high standard. Log fires. Central heating. B&B £36pppn. BB&EM: 7 nights £299pp, 3-night B&B and evening meal £145pp. Dogs welcome. ETC ★★★★ Silver Award. [£10 per pet per visit].
e-mail: jennycope@btinternet.com   website: www.north-down-farm.co.uk

WOODCOMBE LODGES, BRATTON, NEAR MINEHEAD TA24 8SQ (Tel & Fax: 01643 702789). Four self-catering lodges in a tranquil rural setting on the edge of Exmoor National Park, standing in a beautiful 2½ acre garden with wonderful views. [Pets £10 per week]
e-mail: nicola@woodcombelodge.co.uk   website: www.woodcombelodge.co.uk

WESTERCLOSE HOUSE, WITHYPOOL, EXMOOR NATIONAL PARK TA24 7QR (01643 831302). Stunning views, complete peace, and wonderful moorland location. Five cosy cottages, including two bungalows, all with log fires and individual gardens. Pub/shop 300 metres. Dogs and horses welcome. ETC ★★★★ [pw! Dogs £12 per week]
website: www.westerclose.co.uk

WOOLCHAMBER COTTAGES. Set in the heart of Exmoor, a choice of self-catering cottages adjoining the Simonsbath House Hotel. Superbly equipped and completely self-contained. Guests have use of hotel restaurant and bar. Dogs permitted by arrangement. For details contact: SIMONSBATH HOUSE HOTEL, SIMONSBATH, EXMOOR TA24 7SH (01643 831259). [🐾 pw!]
e-mail: enquiries@simonsbathhousehotel.co.uk   website: www.simonsbathhouse.co.uk

LAURENCE & CATHERINE RYE, WEST WITHY FARM, UPTON, NEAR WIVELISCOMBE, TAUNTON TA4 2JH (01398 371258). Two cottages sleeping 2-5. Fully inclusive prices. Walkers' paradise in the Brendons and Quantocks. Enclosed, dog-proof gardens. Short breaks available. £180-£545 per week. ETC ★★★★ [Pets £12 per week]
e-mail: laurencerye@btinternet.com   website: www.exmoor-cottages.com

THE PACK HORSE, ALLERFORD, NEAR PORLOCK TA24 8HW (Tel & Fax: 01643 862475). Self-catering apartments and cottage within picturesque National Trust village. Immediate access to the beautiful surrounding countryside. Stabling available. Open all year. ETC ★★★/★★★★ [Pets £15 per week]
e-mail: holidays@thepackhorse-exmoor.co.uk   website: www.thepackhorse-exmoor.co.uk

JANE STYLES, WINTERSHEAD FARM, SIMONSBATH TA24 7LF (01643 831222). Five tastefully furnished and well-equipped cottages situated in the midst of beautiful Exmoor. Pets welcome, stabling and grazing, DIY livery. Colour brochure on request. ETC ★★★★ [Dogs £15 per week, Horses £20 per week.]
website: www.wintershead.co.uk

Minehead

Neat and stylish resort on Bristol Channel. Sandy bathing beach, attractive gardens, golf course and good facilities for tennis, bowls and horse riding. Within easy reach of the beauties of Exmoor.

SUNFIELD, 83 SUMMERLAND AVENUE, MINEHEAD TA24 5BW (01643 703565). Delightful family-run guest house only a few minutes' level walking distance from sea front. Delicious home cooking. 8 en suite bedrooms. Children and well behaved pets welcome. Totally non-smoking. ETC ★★★★ [🐾]
website: www.sunfieldminehead.co.uk

MINEHEAD 16TH CENTURY THATCHED COTTAGES. Rose Ash - Sleeps 2, prettily furnished, all electric. Willow - Inglenook, oak panelling, electricity, gas, CH, Sleeps 6. Little Thatch - Sleeps 5, Inglenook, Cosy location, Electricity. Gas, CH. Private car park. Enclosed gardens. Pets welcome. SAE: MR T. STONE, TROYTES FARMSTEAD, TIVINGTON, MINEHEAD TA24 8SU (01643 704531). [🐾]

Quantock Hills

Granite and limestone ridge running north-west and south-east from Quantoxhead and Kingston.

THE OLD CIDER HOUSE, 25 CASTLE STREET, NETHER STOWEY TA5 1LN (01278 732228). In picturesque, historic village at the foot of the Quantocks. All en suite; licensed dining. Own car parking, walled garden. B&B from £30pppn. Wonderful dog-walking country; only 4 miles from coast. EnjoyEngland ★★★★ Guest Accommodation. [Pets £3 per night].
e-mail: info@theoldciderhouse.co.uk   website: www.theoldciderhouse.co.uk

Taunton

County capital in Vale of Taunton Deane. Museum, Civic Centre, remains of Norman castle.

FARTHINGS HOTEL & RESTAURANT, HATCH BEAUCHAMP, TAUNTON TA3 6SG (01823 480664; Fax: 01823 481118). Nestled in the midst of the wild and fertile countryside of Somerset, just 3 miles from the M5 and Taunton. An elegant Georgian Hotel with beautiful grounds and gardens, orchards, roses, and our own poultry for your breakfast eggs. AA ★★★ Two Rosettes. [🛏]
e-mail: info@farthingshotel.co.uk   website: www.farthingshotel.co.uk

Watchet

Small port and resort with rocks and sands. Good centre for Exmoor and the Quantocks. Bathing, boating, fishing, rambling. Tiverton 24 miles, Bridgwater 19, Taunton 17, Dunster 6.

MRS K. MUSGRAVE, CROFT HOLIDAY COTTAGES, THE CROFT, ANCHOR STREET, WATCHET TA23 0BY (01984 631121) Courtyard of six cottages/bungalows situated in a quiet backwater of the small harbour town of Watchet. Parking, central heating. TV, DVD, washing machine, fridge/freezer, microwave. Use of heated indoor pool. Sleeps 2-6 persons. £200-£750 per property per week. ETC ★★★★ [Pets £15 per week]
e-mail: croftcottages@talk21.com   website: www.cottagessomerset.com

Wells

England's smallest city. West front of Cathedral built around 1230, shows superb collection of statuary.

INFIELD HOUSE, 36 PORTWAY, WELLS BA5 2BN (01749 670989; Fax: 01749 679093). Richard and Heather invite you and your dog (if older than one year) to visit England's smallest city. Wonderful walks on Mendip Hills. No smoking. Bountiful breakfasts, dinners by arrangement. AA ★★★★ [🛏]
website: www.infieldhouse.co.uk

Weston-Super-Mare

Popular resort on the Bristol Channel with a wide range of entertainments and leisure facilities. An ideal base for touring the West Country.

SOMERSET COURT COTTAGES, WICK ST LAWRENCE, NEAR WESTON-SUPER-MARE BS22 7YR (01934 521383). Converted stone cottages in mediaeval village. 1, 2 or 3 beds. Some with four-posters, luxury whirlpool/spa baths. Superb centre for touring West Country. Short Breaks available. £210-£710 per week. [Pets £2 per night]
e-mail: peter@somersetcourtcottages.co.uk   website: www.somersetcottages.com

MR C. G. THOMAS, ARDNAVE HOLIDAY PARK, KEWSTOKE, WESTON-SUPER-MARE BS22 9XJ (01934 622319). Caravans - De luxe. 2-3 bedrooms, shower, toilet, colour TVs, all bedding included. Parking. Dogs welcome. Graded ★★★. [🛏 pw!]

BRAESIDE HOTEL, 2 VICTORIA PARK, WESTON-SUPER-MARE BS23 2HZ (01934 626642). Delightful, family-run Hotel, close to shops, beach and park. Parking available. All rooms en suite, colour TV, tea/coffee making. November to March THIRD NIGHT FREE. ETC/AA ♦♦♦♦ (Awarded in 2005) [🛏]
e-mail: enquiries@braesidehotel.com   website: www.braesidehotel.com

Williton

Village 2 miles South of Watchet.

JANE SNELL AND PAUL PLUMRIDGE, ARDEN COTTAGE, 33 LONG STREET, WILLITON TA4 4QU (01984 634090; Mobile: 07794 656 484) A B&B offering quality, comfort and a 'home from home' atmosphere. Secure garden for dog(s) to play in. Beautiful countryside for walking. Dogs go free on bookings over 3 nights. EnjoyEngland ★★★★ Silver Award.
e-mail: enquiries@ardencottagewilliton.co.uk   website: www.ardencottagewilliton.co.uk

www.holidayguides.com

Wiltshire SOUTH WEST ENGLAND

Grittleton, Westbury

THE NEELD ARMS INN
THE STREET, GRITTLETON SN14 6AP
01249 782470 • Fax: 01249 782358 • e-mail: info@neeldarms.co.uk
17th century inn offering comfortable accommodation and home-cooked food; four-poster available. Children and pets welcome. Convenient for Bath, Stonehenge, Cotswolds.
www.neeldarms.co.uk

Spinney Farmhouse ~ Thoulstone, Chapmanslade, Westbury BA13 4AQ

Off A36, three miles west of Warminster; 16 miles from historic city of Bath. Close to Longleat, Cheddar and Stourhead. Reasonable driving distance to Bristol, Stonehenge, Glastonbury and the cathedral cities of Wells and Salisbury. Pony trekking and fishing available locally.

- Washbasins, tea/coffee-making facilities and shaver points in all rooms.
- Family room available. • Guests' lounge with colour TV.
- Central heating. • Children and pets welcome.
- Ample parking. • Open all year. • No smoking

*Enjoy farm fresh food in a warm, friendly family atmosphere.
Bed and Breakfast from £25 per night. Reduction after 2 nights.
Evening Meal £12.*
Telephone: 01373 832412 • e-mail: isabelandbob@btinternet.com

Grittleton

Village 6 miles north west of Chippenham.

THE NEELD ARMS INN, THE STREET, GRITTLETON SN14 6AP (01249 782470; Fax: 01249 782358). 17th century inn offering comfortable accommodation and home-cooked food; four-poster available. Children and pets welcome. Convenient for Bath, Stonehenge, Cotswolds. EnjoyEngland ★★★ Inn.
e-mail: info@neeldarms.co.uk   website: www.neeldarms.co.uk

Salisbury

13th century cathedral city, with England's highest spire at 404ft. Many fine buildings.

MR A. SHERING, SWAYNES FIRS FARM, GRIMSDYKE, COOMBE BISSETT, SALISBURY SP5 5RF (01725 519240). Small working farm with cattle, poultry, geese and duck ponds. Spacious rooms, all en suite with colour TV. Ideal for visiting the many historic sites in the area. ETC ★★★ [Pets £9 per night]
e-mail: swaynes.firs@virgin.net   website: www.swaynesfirs.co.uk

Westbury

Town at foot of Salisbury Plain, 4 miles south of Trowbridge.

SPINNEY FARMHOUSE, THOULSTONE, CHAPMANSLADE, WESTBURY BA13 4AQ (01373 832412). Enjoy farm fresh food in a warm, friendly, family atmosphere. Off A36, 16 miles from Bath. All rooms with washbasins, tea/coffee making. TV lounge. No smoking. Children and pets welcome. [✱]
e-mail: isabelandbob@btinternet.com

Publisher's note

While every effort is made to ensure accuracy, we regret that FHG Guides cannot accept responsibility for errors, misrepresentations or omissions in our entries or any consequences thereof. Prices in particular should be checked.
We will follow up complaints but cannot act as arbiters or agents for either party.

Berkshire

Reading Road, Streatley,
Reading, Berkshire RG8 9JJ

A warm welcome for visitors at this historic hostelry which dates back to the 15th Century. Situated on the main route between Oxford and Reading. Fine wines and beer. Wide range of excellent meals. Dogs welcome.
Tel: 01491 872392 • Fax: 01491 875231 • E-mail: bullatstreatley@hotmail.co.uk

Membury

Located close to Swindon, Newbury and Reading.

DAYS INN MEMBURY, WESTBOUND JUNCTION 14/15, M4 (Tel & Fax: 01488 72336). Modern, comfortable accommodation in peaceful setting. All rooms en suite, FREE SKY TV, Broadband WIFI, trouser press, hot drinks tray and free parking. Ideally located for visiting Swindon, Chippenham, Bristol, Bath, The Cotswolds, Gloucester and Oxford. AA Approved & Pet Friendly. [🐾]
e-mail: membury.hotel@welcomebreak.com   website: www.welcomebreak.com

Streatley

One of the twin riverside villages of Goring and Streatley, with many fine properties in the area, including NT Basildon Park.

THE BULL AT STREATLEY, READING ROAD, STREATLEY RG9 9JJ. (01491 872393; Fax: 01491 875231). A warm welcome for visitors at this historic hostelry which dates back to the 15th Century. Fine wines and beer. Wide range of excellent meals. Dogs welcome.
e-mail: bullatstreatley@hotmail.co.uk

Visit the FHG website
www.holidayguides.com
for details of the wide choice of accommodation featured in the full range of FHG titles

Buckinghamshire

SOUTH EAST ENGLAND

Chesham, Milton Keynes

Harvey welcomes you to...
49 LOWNDES AVENUE, CHESHAM HP5 2HH
B&B in detached house, 10 minutes from the Underground.
Private bathroom • Tea/coffee • TV.
Good walking country – Chiltern Hills 3 minutes.
GEORGE ORME • Tel: 01494 792647

★★★
BED & BREAKFAST

Church House Hotel
50 Rowsham Dell, Giffard Park, Milton Keynes, Buckinghamshire MK14 5SJ
Homely atmosphere. All rooms en suite. Restaurant/Bar. Ample car parking.
Tel: 01908 216030 • Fax: 01908 216332
info@churchhousehotel.co.uk • www.churchhousehotel.co.uk

DIFFERENT DRUMMER HOTEL
High Street, Stony Stratford, Milton Keynes, Bucks MK11 1AH
Tel: 01908 564733 • Fax: 01908 260646
Ancient inn transformed into a superbly furnished hotel.
En suite bedrooms • Restaurant serving Italian and seafood cuisine • Wine Bar
info@hoteldifferentdrummer.co.uk   www.hoteldifferentdrummer.co.uk

★★ SMALL HOTEL
AA
★★ SMALL HOTEL

Swan Revived Hotel
High Street, Newport Pagnell,
Milton Keynes MK16 8AR
Tel: 01908 610565 • Fax: 01908 210995

Delightful 15thC former coaching inn,
extensively modernised to provide 40 comfortable
guest rooms, two bars, à la carte restaurant,
meeting rooms and banqueting facilities.
Pets very welcome - no charge is made.

e-mail: info@swanrevived.co.uk • www.swanrevived.co.uk

Chesham

Town on south side of Chiltern Hills. Ideal walking area.

GEORGE ORME, 49 LOWNDES AVENUE, CHESHAM HP5 2HH (01494 792647). B&B in detached house, 10 minutes from the Underground. Private bathroom, tea/coffee, TV. Good walking country - Chiltern Hills three minutes. ETC ★★★ [🐕]

Milton Keynes

Purpose-built new city, home to the Open University. Midway between London, Birmingham, Leicester, Oxford and Cambridge.

CHURCH HOUSE HOTEL, 50 ROWSHAM DELL, GIFFARD PARK, MILTON KEYNES MK14 5SJ (01908 216030; Fax: 01908 216332). Homely atmosphere. All rooms en suite. Restaurant/Bar. Ample car parking.
e-mail: info@churchhousehotel.co.uk   website: www.churchhousehotel.co.uk

DIFFERENT DRUMMER HOTEL, HIGH STREET, STONY STRATFORD, MILTON KEYNES MK11 1AH (01908 564733; Fax: 01908 260646) Ancient inn transformed into a superbly furnished hotel. En suite bedrooms, restaurant, wine bar. EnjoyEngland/AA ★★.
e-mail: info@hoteldifferentdrummer.co.uk   website: www.hoteldifferentdrummer.co.uk

SWAN REVIVED HOTEL, HIGH STREET, NEWPORT PAGNELL, MILTON KEYNES MK16 8AR (01908 610565; Fax: 01908 210995). Delightful 15thC former coaching inn, extensively modernised to provide 40 comfortable guest rooms, two bars, à la carte restaurant, meeting rooms and banqueting facilities. Pets very welcome. [🐕]
e-mail: info@swanrevived.co.uk   website: www.swanrevived.co.uk

SOUTH EAST ENGLAND — Hampshire

Ashurst, Fordingbridge, Lymington

Woodlands Lodge — a new forest hotel ★★★

for somewhere to stay
A little piece of luxury in the heart of the New Forest
The traditional character of our country house offers the perfect opportunity to relax in comfort surrounded by the natural beauty of the New Forest. All of our rooms are en-suite with whirlpool baths. For that special occasion, why not book one of our four poster bedrooms. You deserve to be spoilt! Pets Welcome.

Bartley Road, Woodlands, New Forest, Southampton Hampshire SO40 7GN
Tel: +44 (23) 8029 2257 • Web: www.woodlands-lodge.co.uk • Email: reception@woodlands-lodge.co.uk • Fax: +44 (23) 8029 3090

Three Lions • Stuckton, near Fordingbridge, Hampshire SP6 2HF
Tel: 01425 652489 • Fax: 01425 656144

A place to relax in a beautiful setting and come and go as you please without the formality of a hotel. Hot tub and Sauna.
Three times Hampshire 'Restaurant of the Year', Good Food Guide.
www.thethreelionsrestaurant.co.uk

HONEYSUCKLE HOUSE
24 CLINTON ROAD, LYMINGTON SO41 9EA • Tel: 01590 676635
Lovely ground floor double room/single, en suite, non-smoking.
Woodland walk, park, quay and marinas nearby. B&B from £30.00 pppn.
e-mail: derekfarrell317@btinternet.com
http://explorethenewforest.co.uk/honeysuckle.htm

Efford Cottage

Everton, Lymington, Hampshire SO41 0JD

Tel: 01590 642315
Fax: 01590 641030

Guests receive a warm and friendly welcome to our home, which is a spacious Georgian cottage. All rooms are en suite with many extra luxury facilities. We offer a four-course, multi-choice breakfast with homemade bread and preserves. Patricia is a qualified chef and uses our home-grown produce. An excellent centre for exploring both the New Forest and the South Coast, with sports facilities, fishing, bird watching and horse riding in the near vicinity. Private parking. Dogs welcome. Sorry, no children. Bed and Breakfast from £25–£35 pppn. Mrs Patricia J. Ellis.

Winner of "England For Excellence 2000"
FHG Diploma 1997/1999/2000/2003 / Michelin / Welcome Host
Awards Achieved: Gold Award / RAC Sparkling Diamond & Warm Welcome
Nominated Landlady of Year & Best Breakfast Award.

e-mail: effordcottage@aol.com • www.effordcottage.co.uk

Hampshire
Lyndhurst, New Forest

Ormonde House Hotel

Southampton Road, Lyndhurst, Hampshire SO43 7BT
Tel: (023) 8028 2806 • Fax: (023) 8028 2004
e-mail: enquiries@ormondehouse.co.uk • www.ormondehouse.co.uk

A relaxed blend of professionalism and warm hospitality awaits you at our elegant, family-run, Two Star Hotel, situated opposite the open forest. Ideal for easy walking. 19 pretty, en suite rooms and four luxury self-contained suites, all with CTV, phone and beverage making. 'Superior' rooms have super king zip+link double/twin and sofa; some with whirlpool bath. Suites have super king zip+link double/twin, sofa (double sofa bed) and double whirlpool bath. Each has a full kitchen with washing/dryer machine and dishwasher. Dine with us - our Chefs have an excellent reputation amongst our regular guests for freshly prepared dishes, daily changing specials and wickedly tempting puddings. Close to Exbury Gardens and Beaulieu Motor Museum.

Special 4 night midweek breaks:
From £120pp B&B or from £171pp DB&B.

AA ★★★ The Crown Hotel, New Forest

Tired of the same old walks? Enjoy forest, heath and the beach whilst staying at The Crown Hotel.
38 en suite rooms, all individual and recently refurbished.
Our Chef of thirty years, Stephen Greenhalgh, delights us with his imaginative menus using local produce wherever possible, either in the informal bar or the Restaurant overlooking our water-featured garden.

Dogs are welcome to bring their well-behaved owners!

High Street, Lyndhurst, Hampshire SO43 7NF • Tel: 023 8028 2922 • Fax: 023 8028 2751
e-mail: reception@crownhotel-lyndhurst.co.uk • www.crownhotel-lyndhurst.co.uk

ST. URSULA
30 Hobart Road, New Milton, Hants. BH25 6EG

Between sea and New Forest, comfortable family home. Excellent facilities & warm welcome for well behaved pets and owners. Ground floor suite suitable for disabled guests, plus single and twin rooms.

Mrs Judith Pearce   B&B from £27.50   Tel: 01425 613515

In the heart of the New Forest - **THE WATERSPLASH HOTEL**
The Rise, Brockenhurst SO42 7ZP • Tel: 01590 622344

Prestigious family-run country house hotel set in large garden. Noted for fine personal service, accommodation and traditional English cuisine at its best. All rooms en suite. Luxury four-poster with double spa bath. Swimming pool. Short walk to open forest. AA ★★. Colour brochure available.

e-mail: bookings@watersplash.co.uk • www.watersplash.co.uk

SOUTH EAST ENGLAND — Hampshire
New Forest, Ringwood, Southsea

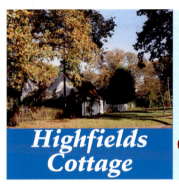

Highfields Cottage

New Forest
Charming, secluded cottage
Quiet country hamlet. Great walks
Pets welcome. Sleeps 2+2
Tel: 01425 471372
e-mail: 07enquiries@highfields-cottage.co.uk
www.highfields-cottage.co.uk

GORSE COTTAGE, BALMER LAWN ROAD, BROCKENHURST
Cottage/bungalow on open forest road close to the village in the New Forest. Beautifully decorated and appointed, sleeps 4 in 2 bedrooms. Conservatory, luxury bathroom, log fire, TV/Freeview/DVD, secluded sunny garden. Pets welcome.
Contact: MRS E. GILBERT (01727 850659) or website for details
e-mail: info@gorsecottage.co.uk   www.gorsecottage.co.uk
ETC ★★★★

LITTLE THATCH • 15 South Street, Pennington, New Forest
Beautiful Grade II Listed thatched cob cottage in village location. Sleeps 4 in 2 bedrooms. Superbly renovated to offer traditional cottage features, tastefully combined with luxury modern comforts, including washer/dryer, dishwasher, TV, freeview, video, DVD. Secluded secure garden. Pets welcome. **Contact: Mrs Suzannah Nash (01582 842831)**
e-mail: suzannah@littlethatchcottage.com • www.littlethatchcottage.com

Little Forest Lodge
Poulner Hill, Ringwood, Hampshire BH24 3HS

A warm welcome to you and your pets at this charming Edwardian house set in two acres of woodland. The six en suite bedrooms are pleasantly decorated and equipped with thoughtful extras. Both the attractive wood-panelled dining room and the delightful lounge, with bar and wood-burning fire, overlook the gardens. The Lodge is in an ideal location for exploring the ancient New Forest, historic Wessex, and the nearby sandy beaches. All well behaved dogs welcome.
Tel: 01425 478848 • Fax: 01425 473564

The High Corner Inn is set deep in the heart of The New Forest in seven beautiful acres of woodland, ideal for long forest walks. Seven en suite bedrooms; two oak-beamed bars with views across the patio and garden; outdoor adventure playground for children. Good choice of real ales, wines and spirits, quality home-cooked meals, Sunday carvery. Dogs and well behaved owners welcome throughout the inn and in the letting rooms, but horses must use our stables or paddocks.
Linwood, Ringwood, Hants BH24 3QY • Tel: 01425 473961 • Fax: 01425 483052

SEACREST Hotel
Quality Hotel accommodation with a superb sea front location. All rooms en suite, etc. Good Walking! Small charge for pets.
Mark and Jenny Brunning, The Seacrest Hotel,
11/12 South Parade, Southsea, Hampshire PO5 2JB
Tel: 02392 733192 • Fax: 02392 832523 •
e-mail: office@seacresthotel.co.uk • www.seacresthotel.co.uk

Hampshire

SOUTH EAST ENGLAND 197

Ashurst

Residential location 3 miles NE of Lyndhurst.

WOODLANDS LODGE HOTEL, BARTLEY ROAD, ASHURST, WOODLANDS SO40 7GN ((023) 80 292257; Fax: (023) 80 293090). Luxury Hotel offering peace and tranquillity. 16 bedrooms, all en suite with whirlpool bath, TV, hairdryer, telephone etc. Award winning Restaurant. Direct access to Forest. ETC ★★★ [Pets £5 per night].
e-mail: reception@woodlands-lodge.co.uk   website: www.woodlands-lodge.co.uk

Fordingbridge

Town on River Avon 6 miles North of Ringwood.

THREE LIONS, STUCKTON, NEAR FORDINGBRIDGE SP6 2HF (01425 652489; Fax: 01425 656144) Relax in a beautiful setting and come and go as you please without the formality of a hotel. Hot tub and sauna. Three times Hampshire 'Restaurant of the Year', Good Food Guide. [pw! Pets £10 per week]
website: www.thethreelionsrestaurant.co.uk

Lymington

Residential town and yachting centre 15 miles east of Bournemouth.

HONEYSUCKLE HOUSE, 24 CLINTON ROAD, LYMINGTON SO41 9EA (01590 676635). Ground floor double room/single, en suite, non-smoking. Woodland walk, park, quay and marinas nearby. B&B from £30.00 pppn. [🐾]
e-mail: derekfarrell317@btinternet.com   website: http://explorethenewforest.co.uk/honeysuckle.htm

MRS P. J. ELLIS, EFFORD COTTAGE, EVERTON, LYMINGTON SO41 0JD (01590 642315; Fax: 01590 641030). Outstanding B&B with old world charm in proprietor's own Georgian home. Excellent touring centre for New Forest and South Coast. All rooms en suite with luxury facilities. B&B from £25-£35pppn. No children. AA ★★★★, Michelin. [PW! Pets from £2 per night]
e-mail: effordcottage@aol.com   website: www.effordcottage.co.uk

Lyndhurst

Good base for enjoying the fascinating New Forest as well as the Hampshire coastal resorts. Bournemouth 20 miles, Southampton 9.

ORMONDE HOUSE HOTEL, SOUTHAMPTON ROAD, LYNDHURST SO43 7BT (023 8028 2806, Fax: 023 8028 2004). Opposite open forest, easy drive to Exbury Gardens and Beaulieu. Elegant, family-run Two Star Hotel with pretty, en suite rooms with CTV, phone and beverage making. Superior rooms and ground floor suites, all with kingsize bed and some with whirlpool bath. Bar, lounge and delicious dinners available. AA ★★. [Pets £3.50 per night, max. 2 per room]
e-mail: enquiries@ormondehouse.co.uk   website: www.ormondehouse.co.uk

THE CROWN HOTEL, LYNDHURST, NEW FOREST SO43 7NF (023 8028 2922; Fax: 023 8028 2751). A mellow, Listed building in the centre of the village, an ideal base for exploring the delights of the New Forest with your canine friend(s). Free parking, quiet garden, three star luxury and animal loving staff. AA ★★★ [Pets £7 per night].
e-mail: reception@crownhotel-lyndhurst.co.uk   website: www.crownhotel-lyndhurst.co.uk

Symbols

🐾   Indicates that pets are welcome free of charge.
£   Indicates that a charge is made for pets: nightly or weekly.
pw! Shows some special provision for pets; exercise facility, feeding or accommodation arrangement.
⌂   Indicates separate pets accommodation.

New Forest

Area of heath and woodland of nearly 150 square miles, formerly Royal hunting grounds.

MRS E.E. MATTHEWS, THE ACORNS, OGDENS, NEAR FORDINGBRIDGE SP6 2PY (01425 655552). Luxury two bedroom residential-type caravan. Sleeps 4/6. Maintained to high standard, kitchen, shower room, sitting/diningroom, outside laundry area, own garden. Lovely New Forest setting. Non-smoking, ample parking. Children over five years. Well-behaved dogs welcome (max. 2). Terms £195 - £375, Easter to mid-October. [pw! Pets £12 each per week].
e-mail: e_matthews@mypostoffice.co.uk   website: www.dogscome2.co.uk

MRS J. PEARCE, ST. URSULA, 30 HOBART ROAD, NEW MILTON BH25 6EG (01425 613515). Excellent facilities and warm welcome for well behaved pets and owners! Ground floor suite suitable for disabled guests, plus single and twin rooms. Bed & Breakfast from £27.50. [🐕]

THE WATERSPLASH HOTEL, THE RISE, BROCKENHURST SO42 7ZP (01590 622344). Prestigious New Forest family-run country house hotel set in large garden. Noted for fine personal service, accommodation and traditional English cuisine at its best. All rooms en suite. Luxury four-poster with double spa bath. Swimming pool. Short walk to open forest. AA ★★ Colour brochure available. [Pets from £5 per night.]
e-mail: bookings@watersplash.co.uk   website: www.watersplash.co.uk

NEW FOREST - HIGHFIELDS COTTAGE. Charming, secluded cottage. Quiet country hamlet. Great walks. Pets welcome. Sleeps 2+2. Tel: 01425 471372 . [Pets £25 per week]
e-mail: 07enquiries@highfields-cottage.co.uk   website: www.highfields-cottage.co.uk

GORSE COTTAGE, BALMER LAWN ROAD, BROCKENHURST. Cottage/bungalow on open forest road close to village in New Forest. Sleeps 4 in 2 bedrooms. Conservatory, luxury bathroom, log fire, TV/Freeview/DVD, secluded sunny garden. Pets welcome. Contact: MRS E. GILBERT (01727 850659). ETC ★★★★ [Pets £15 per week]
e-mail: info@gorsecottage.co.uk   website: www.gorsecottage.co.uk

LITTLE THATCH, 15 SOUTH STREET, PENNINGTON (01582 842831) Beautiful Grade II Listed thatched cob cottage, sleeps 4 in 2 bedrooms. Superbly renovated to offer traditional cottage features, tastefully combined with luxury modern comforts. Secluded secure garden.[🐕]
e-mail: suzannah@littlethatchcottage.com   website: www.littlethatchcottage.com

Ringwood

Busy market town, centre for trout fishing, trekking and rambling. Bournemouth 13 miles.

LITTLE FOREST LODGE, POULNER HILL, RINGWOOD BH24 3HS (01425 478848; Fax: 01425 473564). A warm welcome to you and your pets at this charming Edwardian house set in two acres of woodland. Six en suite bedrooms. All well behaved dogs welcome. AA ★★★★ Guest House. [Pets £5 per night].

DAVID SATCHELL, THE HIGH CORNER INN, LINWOOD, RINGWOOD, HANTS BH24 3QY (01425 473973, Fax: 01425 483052). Seven en suite bedrooms deep in the heart of The New Forest. Real ales, home-cooked food, Sunday carvery and log fires. Pets welcome. [🐕]

Southsea

Residential and holiday district of Portsmouth 2km South of the city centre.

Quality Hotel accommodation with a superb sea front location. Good walking! All rooms en suite, etc. Passenger lift, licensed bar/restaurant, car park. Small charge for pets. Contact: MARK & JENNY BRUNNING, THE SEACREST HOTEL, 12 SOUTH PARADE, SOUTHSEA, PORTSMOUTH PO5 2JB (02392 733192; Fax: 02392 832523). AA ★★ 75%.
e-mail: office@seacresthotel.co.uk   website: www.seacresthotel.co.uk

www.holidayguides.com

Island Cottage Holidays

More than 90 beautiful rural and seaside holiday cottages

Pets welcome at our cottages across the Isle of Wight

tel. 01929 481555
www.islandcottageholidays.com

Bonchurch, Cowes

THE LAKE Shore Road, Lower Bonchurch PO38 IRF
Tel: 01983 852613 • e-mail: fhg@lakehotel.co.uk
Lovely country house in a beautiful quiet two-acre garden on the seaward side of Bonchurch. The house offers first class food and service, all in a relaxed and friendly atmosphere. All rooms are en suite with complimentary tea/coffee facilities and TV. We can offer an Isle of Wight car ferry inclusive price of just £185 for four nights' B&B during March/April/May and October

www.lakehotel.co.uk

ACTUALLY ON THE BEACH

"The Waterfall", Shore Road, Bonchurch, Ventnor, I.O.W. PO38 1RN
Ground-floor self-contained flat. Sleeps 3 adults. Fully equipped. Parking.
Sun verandah and Garden.
Brochure from **Mrs A. Evans**   e-mail: benbrook.charioteer@virgin.net   Tel: 01983 852246

ASHCLIFF HOLIDAY APARTMENT

Bonchurch, Isle of Wight PO38 1NT • e-mail: linessidney@aol.com
Idyllic and secluded position in the picturesque seaside village of Bonchurch. Self-contained ground floor apartment (sleeps 2) adjoining Victorian house, set in large south-facing gardens with sea views and sheltered by a thickly wooded cliff. Large, private car park. ETC ★★★. Dogs very welcome. *For free brochure Tel: (01983) 853919*

SUNNYCOTT CARAVAN PARK
COWES • ISLE OF WIGHT

Small, quiet, family-run country park in rural surroundings close to Cowes.
All caravans have full cooker, microwave, fridge and colour TV. Shop and laundry room on site.
We welcome your pets. Short breaks can be arranged subject to availability.

Phone 01983 292859 for brochure • Proprietors: Jennifer Payne and Jim Payne
www.sunnycottcaravanpark.co.uk • e-mail: info@sunnycottcaravanpark.co.uk

Please mention **Pets Welcome!**
when making enquiries about accommodation featured in these pages

Isle of Wight
Freshwater, Totland Bay, Ventnor

A peaceful and beautiful 19th century rectory set in two-and-a-half acres of lovely gardens, just two minutes' drive from Freshwater Bay. Good area for walking, golfing, sailing, paragliding and bird watching. Close to National Trust areas. Double, family and twin rooms, all en suite. TV lounge, log fires. Children and pets welcome. B&B pppn: £33-£40 depending on season. Children ½ price.

Mr and Mrs B. Moscoff, Seahorses, Victoria Road, Freshwater, IOW PO40 9PP
Tel/Fax: 01983 752574 • seahorses-iow@tiscali.co.uk • www.seahorsesisleofwight.com

Littledene Lodge • Totland • Isle of Wight
A charming 7 bedroomed guesthouse, all rooms en suite with TV. Breakfast and meals available, friendly and personal service.
Littledene Lodge, Granville Road, Totland Bay, Isle of Wight PO39 0AX
Tel: 01983 752411 • E-mail: littledenehotel@aol.com
www.littledenehotel.co.uk

SENTRY MEAD HOTEL

Madeira Road, Totland Bay PO39 0BJ
Tel: 01983 753212 • Fax: 01983 754710
e-mail: info@sentrymead.co.uk • www.sentrymead.co.uk
"....a jewel in the crown of the West Wight"

The Country Garden Hotel

Church Hill, Totland Bay, Isle of Wight PO39 0ET
ANY DAY TO ANY DAY, B&B or HALF BOARD • ADULTS ONLY
Ferry inclusive rates
For brochure, sample menu, tariff, and testimonials from recent guests, please
Phone/Fax: 01983 754 521
e-mail: countrygardeniow@aol.com • www.thecountrygardenhotel.co.uk

Ventnor Holiday Villas
Apartments and Villas on a south-facing hillside leading down to a small rocky bay. Views are spectacular & the hillside sheltered but open to all the sunshine that is going. Apartments open all year; villas and caravans open April to October. Three night break per unit from £195. Pets welcome in villas. Write or phone for brochure. Wheelers Bay Road, Ventnor PO38 1HR • 01983 852973
e-mail: sales@ventnorholidayvillas.co.uk • www.ventnorholidayvillas.co.uk

Westfield Lodges & Apartments

Bonchurch, Isle of Wight PO38 1RH • www.westfieldlodges.co.uk
Situated in the peaceful and historic village of Bonchurch on the south west coast of the Island. On a quiet, private site five minutes from the beach. Open all year.
Tel: 01983 852268 • Fax: 01983 853992 • e-mail: mail@westfieldlodges.co.uk

Little Span Farm

Farmhouse B&B and Self-Catering Cottages

Rew Lane, Wroxall, Ventnor, Isle of Wight PO38 3AU
Arable and sheep farm in an Area of Outstanding Natural Beauty, close to footpaths and holiday attractions. Ideal for family holidays. B&B in farmhouse from £30 pppn or Self-Catering Cottages from £225-£725 per week. Dogs welcome – 2 private kennels with inside and outside runs.
Tel/Fax: 01983 852419 • e-mail: info@spanfarm.co.uk • www.spanfarm.co.uk • Freephone 0800 2985819

Isle of Wight

Yarmouth

ISLE OF WIGHT · Near YARMOUTH

- Indoor & Outdoor heated pools with poolside coffeeshop
- Luxury holiday caravans for hire
- Dog excercise areas
- 3/4 Day Mini Breaks
- Excellent facilities for caravanners and campers
- Special Ferry Deals
- Village location with wonderful views
- Excellent walking and cycling from the park
- New high quality Facilities Centre now open.

OPEN CHRISTMAS AND NEW YEAR

www.orchards-holiday-park.co.uk   t. 01983 531331

ISLAND COTTAGE HOLIDAYS (01929 481555). More than 90 beautiful rural and seaside holiday cotttages. Pets welcome at our cottages across the Isle of Wight.
website: www.islandcottageholidays.com

Bonchurch

One mile north-east of Ventnor.

THE LAKE, SHORE ROAD, LOWER BONCHURCH PO38 1RF (01983 852613). Lovely country house in a beautiful quiet two-acre garden. First class food and service, all in a relaxed and friendly atmosphere. All rooms en suite. Car ferry inclusive prices available. ETC ★★★★ [Pets £5 per night]
e-mail: fhg@lakehotel.co.uk   website: www.lakehotel.co.uk

A. EVANS, "THE WATERFALL", SHORE ROAD, BONCHURCH, VENTNOR PO38 1RN (01983 852246). Spacious, self-contained Flat. Sleeps 3 adults. Colour TV. Sun verandah and garden. The beach, the sea and the downs. [🐕]
e-mail: benbrook.charioteer@virgin.net

MRS J. LINES, ASHCLIFF HOLIDAY APARTMENT, BONCHURCH PO38 1NT (01983 853919). Self-contained ground floor apartment (sleeps 2) adjoining Victorian house. Large south-facing gardens. Sea views from garden. Large private car park. Pets welcome to use garden. ETC ★★★ [🐕]
e-mail: linessidney@aol.com

Cowes

Yachting centre with yearly regatta since 1814. Newport 4 miles.

SUNNYCOTT CARAVAN PARK, COWES PO31 8NN (01983 292859). Small, quiet, family-run park close to Cowes. All caravans have full cooker, microwave, fridge and colour TV. Shop and laundry room on site. We welcome pets. Short breaks arranged. ETC ★★★★ [Pets £20 per week]
e-mail: info@sunnycottcaravanpark.co.uk   website: www.sunnycottcaravanpark.co.uk

Freshwater

Two kilometres south of Totland. South-west of Farringford, formerly the home of Tennyson.

MR AND MRS B. MOSCOFF, SEAHORSES, VICTORIA ROAD, FRESHWATER PO40 9PP (Tel & Fax: 01983 752574). Peaceful 19th century rectory set in two-and-a-half acres of lovely gardens. Good area for walking, golfing, sailing, paragliding and bird watching. Double, family and twin rooms, all en suite. TV lounge, log fires. B&B pppn: £33-£40 depending on season. Children half price. [🐕 pw!]
e-mail: seahorses-iow@tiscali.co.uk   website: www.seahorsesisleofwight.com

Totland Bay

Small resort 3 miles south-west of Yarmouth Bay.

TREVOR & JUDY BARNES, LITTLEDENE LODGE GUEST HOUSE, GRANVILLE ROAD, TOTLAND BAY PO39 0AX (Tel & Fax: 01983 752411). Close to beach and scenic downland walking. Friendly and cosy with good fresh food. Small garden for use by all. Pets welcome; no charge. [🐾]
e-mail: littledenehotel@aol.com   website: www.littledenehotel.co.uk

SENTRY MEAD HOTEL, MADEIRA ROAD, TOTLAND BAY PO39 0BJ (01983 753212; Fax: 01983 754710). This beautiful Victorian villa is set in its own spacious gardens in the tranquil surroundings of West Wight. Just 150 yards from the beach, and with scenic downland walks on the doorstep, this is the perfect place to relax and unwind. All bedrooms en suite. ETC ★★★ Silver Award [Pets £3 per day, £15 per week]
e-mail: info@sentrymead.co.uk   website: www.sentrymead.co.uk

COUNTRY GARDEN HOTEL, CHURCH HILL, TOTLAND BAY PO39 0ET (Tel & Fax: 01983 754521). All en suite, garden and seaview rooms available; TV, phone, duvets, feather/down pillows, fridge, hairdryer etc. Special winter, spring, autumn rates. [pw! Pets £4 per day]
e-mail: countrygardeniow@aol.com   website: www.thecountrygardenhotel.co.uk

Ventnor

Well-known resort with good sands, downs, popular as a winter holiday resort. Nearby is St Boniface Down, the highest point on the island. Ryde 13 miles, Newport 12, Sandown 7, Shanklin 4.

VENTNOR HOLIDAY VILLAS, WHEELERS BAY ROAD, VENTNOR PO38 1HR (01983 852973). Apartments and Villas on south facing hillside leading down to a small rocky bay. Apartments open all year, villas and caravans April to October. Write or phone for a brochure. Pets welcome in villas. ETC ★★★ [Pets £20 per week]
e-mail: sales@ventnorholidayvillas.co.uk   website: www.ventnorholidayvillas.co.uk

WESTFIELD LODGES & APARTMENTS, BONCHURCH PO38 1RH (01983 852268; Fax: 01983 853992). Situated in the peaceful and historic village of Bonchurch on the south west coast of the Island. On a quiet, private site five minutes from the beach. Open all year. ETC ★★★/★★★★ Self-Catering. [Pets £35 per week]
e-mail: mail@westfieldlodges.co.uk   website: www.westfieldlodges.co.uk

MRS F. CORRY, LITTLE SPAN FARM, REW LANE, WROXALL, VENTNOR PO38 3AU (Tel & Fax: 01983 852419, Freephone 0800 2985819). Working farm in an Area of Outstanding Natural Beauty, close to footpaths and holiday attractions. Ideal for family holidays. B&B in farmhouse from £30 pppn or Self-Catering Cottages from £225-£725 per week. Dogs welcome. [pw! Pets £4 per night, £25 per week].
e-mail: info@spanfarm.co.uk   website: www.spanfarm.co.uk

Yarmouth

Coastal resort situated 9 miles west of Newport. Castle built by Henry VIII for coastal defence.

THE ORCHARDS HOLIDAY CARAVAN & CAMPING PARK, NEWBRIDGE, YARMOUTH PO41 0TS (Dial-a-brochure 01983 531331; Fax: 01983 531666). Luxury holiday caravans, most with central heating and double glazing. Excellent facilities including indoor pool with licensed coffeeshop. Dog exercise areas. Ideal walking and cycling. Open late February to New Year. Located in an Area of Outstanding Natural Beauty. Spectacular views. [Pets £1/£2.50 per night]
e-mail: info@orchards-holiday-park.co.uk   website:www.orchards-holiday-park.co.uk

Publisher's note

While every effort is made to ensure accuracy, we regret that FHG Guides cannot accept responsibility for errors, misrepresentations or omissions in our entries or any consequences thereof. Prices in particular should be checked.
We will follow up complaints but cannot act as arbiters or agents for either party.

Kent — SOUTH EAST ENGLAND

Garden of England Cottages
www.goec.co.uk
Accommodation for all seasons

BIG PAWS and LITTLE PAWS ARE WELCOME and GO FREE with every well-behaved owner.
ON-LINE BOOKING & AVAILABILITY Tel: +44 [0] 1892 510117
e-mail: holidays@gardenofenglandcottages.co.uk
All our properties are VisitBritain quality assured.

Ashford, Boughton Monchelsea, Broadstairs, Canterbury, Deal

Luxury pine lodges, superior self-catering accommodation overlooking two lakes in beautiful Kent countryside. Rough shooting and coarse fishing on our farms. Weeks or short breaks. Contact:
ASHBY FARMS LTD, PLACE FARM, KENARDINGTON, ASHFORD TN26 2LZ • Tel: 01233 733332 • Fax: 01233 733326
e-mail: info@ashbyfarms.com • www.ashbyfarms.com

COCK INN Boughton Monchelsea, Maidstone ME17 4JD
- Tel: 01622 743166 • http://cockinnboughtonmonchelsea.com
- e-mail: info@cockinnboughtonmonchelsea.com
- Glorious 16thC timbered black and white inn • Patio and outside eating area
- Inglenook fireplace and oak-beamed bar and restaurant.

Dogs are treated and watered, while their owners are cossetted and pampered!

THE HANSON (Lic.) 41 Belvedere Road, Broadstairs CT10 1PF
A small friendly Georgian hotel with relaxed atmosphere, centrally situated for beach, shops and transport. B&B only or, renowned for excellent food, we offer a 5-course Evening Dinner with choice of menu.
Children and pets welcome • Open all year • Spring and Winter Breaks
Tel: (01843) 868936   www.hansonhotel.co.uk
TREVOR & JEAN HAVE OVER 25 YEARS OF WELCOMING GUESTS

Within four acres of gardens in a delightful rural setting surrounded by orchards. Four converted two-bedroom cottages, sleeping four to five, one suitable for wheelchairs. Ideally situated for touring, cycling, walking, relaxing and exploring the Kent coastline. All bedlinen and towels provided. Children's play field and equipment. Ample parking. Pets welcome by arrangement. Contact **Doreen Ady**.
Hawthorn Farm Cottages • Ware, near Sandwich • ETC ★★★/★★★★
Tel: 01304 813560 • E-mail: hawthornfarmcottages@dsl.pipex.com • www.hawthornfarmcottages.co.uk

Hidden Gem 59 Gladstone Road, Deal, Kent CT14 7ET
A serene and luxuriously furnished and equipped one bedroom bungalow, with gas central heating, a secure private garden and off-street parking. Situated in a delightful side street next to Deal Castle, the beach, the lively and picturesque seaside town of Deal and endless beach and country walks. Sleeps 2 • No smoking • Pets welcome FREE
For details please tel Lucy on: 07590 756833 or email via the website www.selfcatering-deal.co.uk

---

www.holidayguides.com

SOUTH EAST ENGLAND — Kent

Margate, St Margaret's Bay

Smiths Court Hotel

Elegant, Victorian family-run premier hotel. 43 individually decorated rooms and suites, many with superb sea views. Pets welcome. Perfect for short breaks.
21-27 Eastern Esplanade, Cliftonville, Margate CT9 2HL
Tel: 01843 222210 • info@smithscourt.co.uk • www.smithscourt.co.uk

REACH COURT FARM COTTAGES
REACH COURT FARM, ST MARGARET'S BAY, DOVER CT15 6AQ
Tel & Fax: 01304 852159
Situated in the heart of the Mitchell family farm, surrounded by open countryside. Five luxury self-contained cottages set around the old farmyard, with open views of the rural valley both front and back.
e-mail: enquiries@reachcourtfarmcottages.co.uk
www.reachcourtfarmcottages.co.uk

GARDEN OF ENGLAND COTTAGES IN KENT & SUSSEX, CLAYFIELD HOUSE, 50 ST JOHNS ROAD, TUNBRIDGE WELLS, KENT TN4 9NY (01892 510117). Pets welcome in many of our holiday homes and go free. All properties VisitBritain quality assured. On-line booking and availability. [🐕]
e-mail: holidays@gardenofenglandcottages.co.uk   website: www.goec.co.uk

Ashford

Market town on Great Stour River, 13 miles south-west of Canterbury.

Luxury pine lodges, superior self-catering accommodation overlooking two lakes in beautiful Kent countryside. Rough shooting and coarse fishing on our farms. Weeks or short breaks. Contact: ASHBY FARMS LTD, PLACE FARM, KENARDINGTON, ASHFORD TN26 2LZ (01233 733332; Fax: 01233 733326). [Pets £10 per stay]
e-mail: info@ashbyfarms.com   website: www.ashbyfarms.com

Boughton Monchelsea

Village 3 miles south of Maidstone.

COCK INN, BOUGHTON MONCHELSEA, MAIDSTONE ME17 4JD (01622 743166) Glorious 16thC timbered black and white inn with inglenook fireplace and oak-beamed bar and restaurant. Patio and outside eating area.
e-mail: info@cockinnboughtonmonchelsea.com website: www.cockinnboughtonmonchelsea.com

Broadstairs

Quiet resort, once a favourite of Charles Dickens. Good sands and promenade.

THE HANSON, 41 BELVEDERE ROAD, BROADSTAIRS CT10 1PF (01843 868936). Small, friendly licensed Georgian Hotel. Home comforts; children and pets welcome. Attractive bar. SAE. [pw! Pets £1 per night, £5 per week]
website: www.hansonhotel.co.uk

Canterbury

Cathedral City on River Great Stour, 54 miles east of London.

DOREEN ADY, HAWTHORN FARM COTTAGES, WARE, NEAR SANDWICH (01304 813560). Four converted two-bedroom cottages, sleeping 4-5. Ideally situated for relaxing or exploring the Kent coastline. Children's play field. Ample parking. Pets welcome by arrangement. ETC ★★★/★★★★. [pw! Pets £20 per week]
e-mail: hawthornfarmcottages@dsl.pipex.com   website: www.hawthornfarmcottages.co.uk

Kent

SOUTH EAST ENGLAND 205

Deal

Cinque Port and resort on East coast 8 miles N.E. of Dover.

HIDDEN GEM, 59 GLADSTONE ROAD, DEAL CT14 7ET. Luxuriously furnished one bedroom bungalow, with gas central heating, secure private garden and off-street parking. Near Deal Castle, the beach, the town, and endless beach and country walks. No smoking. For details please tel Lucy on: 07590 756833 or e-mail via the website. ETC ★★★★ [🐾]
website: www.selfcatering-deal.co.uk

Margate

Traditional seaside resort, with a vibrant cultural quarter and several historic buildings.

SMITHS COURT HOTEL, 21-27 EASTERN ESPLANADE, CLIFTONVILLE, MARGATE CT9 2HL (01843 222310). Elegant, Victorian family-run premier hotel. 43 individually decorated rooms and suites, many with superb sea views. Perfect for short breaks. Pets welcome. EnjoyEngland ★★★. [Pets £10 per stay].
e-mail: info@smithscourt.co.uk   website: www.smithscourt.co.uk

St Margaret's Bay

4 miles north-east of Dover

DEREK AND JACQUI MITCHELL, REACH COURT FARM COTTAGES, REACH COURT FARM, ST MARGARET'S BAY, DOVER CT15 6AQ (Tel & Fax: 01304 852159). Situated in the heart of the Mitchell family farm, surrounded by open countryside, these five luxury self-contained cottages are very special. The cottages are set around the old farmyard, which has been attractively set to lawns and shrubs, with open views of the rural valley both front and back. [🐾]
e-mail: enquiries@reachcourtfarmcottages.co.uk   website: www.reachcourtfarmcottages.co.uk

Tower Fields

Tusmore Road, Near Souldern, Bicester OX27 7HY

Ground floor en suite rooms, all with own entrance and ample parking. Breakfast using local produce. Easy reach of Oxford, Stratford-upon-Avon, many National Trust houses. Silverstone, Towcester. *Dogs and horses welcome by arrangement.*
Contact: Toddy and Clive Hamilton-Gould 01869 346554
e-mail: toddyclive@towerfields.com • www.towerfields.com

The Inn for all Seasons

AA ★★★ AA ⊙

Dog owners themselves, Matthew and Heather Sharp extend a warm welcome to others who wish to bring their pets to visit the Cotswolds and stay in a genuinely dog-friendly Inn with dedicated ground floor rooms with direct access to gardens, exercise area and country walks. The Inn for all Seasons is a family-owned and run ★★★ Hotel based on a traditional 16th century English Coaching Inn. Character en suite bedrooms, inglenooks, log fires and a genuinely friendly inn atmosphere provide the perfect setting to enjoy a Rosetted menu prepared by Chef/Proprietor, Matthew, and his English-led kitchen team. An ideal base for touring, walking, garden visiting.
B&B from £45.00pppn • Dinner, B&B from £70.00pppn.

The Barringtons, Near Burford, Oxfordshire OX18 4TN
Tel: 01451 844324
e-mail: sharp@innforallseasons.com
www.innforallseasons.com

Nanford Guest House

Period guest house located five minutes on foot from the University of Oxford. Wide range and number of rooms, all with private shower and toilet.
MR B. CRONIN, NANFORD GUEST HOUSE, 137 IFFLEY ROAD, OXFORD OX4 1EJ
Tel: 01865 244743 • Fax: 01865 249596
e-mail: b.cronin@btinternet.com • www.nanfordguesthouse.com

Colliers B&B

www.colliersbnb.co.uk

Bed and Breakfast in Tackley. An ideal base for touring, walking, cycling and riding. Central for Oxford, The Cotswolds, Stratford-on-Avon, Blenheim Palace. Woodstock four miles. There is a regular train and bus service with local Hostelries serving excellent food.
JUNE AND GEORGE COLLIER, 55 NETHERCOTE ROAD, TACKLEY, KIDLINGTON, OXFORD OX5 3AT • 01869 331255 • Mobile: 07790 338225

Bicester

Town 11 miles NE of Oxford.

TODDY AND CLIVE HAMILTON-GOULD, TOWER FIELDS, TUSMORE ROAD, NEAR SOULDERN, BICESTER OX27 7HY (01869 346554). Ground floor en suite rooms, all with own entrance and ample parking. Breakfast using local produce. Easy reach of Oxford, Stratford-upon-Avon, many National Trust houses. Silverstone, Towcester. Dogs and horses welcome by arrangement. [🐕]
e-mail: toddyclive@towerfields.com   website: www.towerfields.com

Burford

Small Cotswold Town on River Windrush, 7 miles west of Witney.

THE INN FOR ALL SEASONS, THE BARRINGTONS, NEAR BURFORD OX18 4TN (01451 844324). Family-run and owned Hotel based on traditional 16th century English Coaching Inn. Ideal base for touring, walking and garden visiting. From £70.00pppn DB&B. [pw!]
e-mail: sharp@innforallseasons.com   website: www.innforallseasons.com

Oxfordshire / Surrey

SOUTH EAST ENGLAND 207

Oxford

City 52 miles from London. University dating from 13th century. Many notable buildings.

MR B. CRONIN, NANFORD GUEST HOUSE, 137 IFFLEY ROAD, OXFORD OX4 1EJ (01865 244743; Fax: 01865 249596). Period guest house located five minutes on foot from the University of Oxford. Wide range and number of rooms, all with private shower and toilet. [🐕]
e-mail: b.cronin@btinternet.com   website: www.nanfordguesthouse.com

Tackley/Kidlington

Village 3 miles north-east of Woodstock; approximately 5 miles north of Oxford.

JUNE AND GEORGE COLLIER, 55 NETHERCOTE ROAD, TACKLEY, KIDLINGTON, OXFORD OX5 3AT (01869 331255; mobile: 07790 338225). Bed and Breakfast in Tackley. An ideal base for touring, walking, cycling and riding. Central for Oxford, The Cotswolds, Stratford-on-Avon, Blenheim Palace. Woodstock four miles. There is a regular train and bus service with local Hostelries serving excellent food. [🐕 ⌂]
website: www.colliersbnb.co.uk

Thame

Town on River Thame 9 miles SW of Aylesbury.

MS. JULIA TANNER, LITTLE ACRE, TETSWORTH, NEAR THAME OX9 7AT (01844 281423; mobile: 07798 625252). Small country house retreat offering every comfort, set in several private acres. Most rooms en suite. Twin en suite £25pppn, king/double en suite £27.50pppn, family room (3 sharing) £75 per night. Full English breakfast. A perfect place to relax – your dog will love it. Three minutes Junction 6 M40. Also self-catering accommodation. [Pets £3 per night. Bring dog basket with you.]
website: www.little-acre.co.uk

Surrey

Kingston Upon Thames

Chase Lodge Hotel
An Award Winning Hotel
with style & elegance, set in tranquil surroundings at affordable prices.
10 Park Road Hampton Wick Kingston-Upon-Thames KT1 4AS Pets welcome
Tel: 020 8943 1862 . Fax: 020 8943 9363
E-mail: info@chaselodgehotel.com Web: www.chaselodgehotel.com

Quality en suite bedrooms
Close to Bushy Park
Buffet-style Full Continental Breakfast

Licensed bar
Wedding Receptions
Honeymoon suite
available with jacuzzi & steam area
20 minutes from Heathrow Airport
Close to Kingston town centre & all major transport links.

★★★

All Major Credit Cards Accepted

Kingston Upon Thames

Market town, Royal borough and administrative centre of Surrey. Kingston is ideally placed for London and environs.

CHASE LODGE HOTEL, 10 PARK ROAD, HAMPTON WICK, KINGSTON UPON THAMES KT1 4AS (020 8943 1862; Fax: 020 8943 9363). Award-winning hotel offering quality en suite bedrooms. Easy access to town centre and major transport links. Licensed bar. ★★★ [🐕]
e-mail: info@chaselodgehotel.com   website: www.chaselodgehotel.com

East Sussex

Alfriston, Brighton, Chiddingly, Fairlight

THE GEORGE INN
Relax • Indulge • Explore • Welcome

The emphasis at The George is on relaxation: with six sumptuous, relaxing and charming bedrooms, it's a very intimate and caring place to stay. Delicious food, refreshing ales, oak beams, open log fires, friendly atmosphere, quality service and a beautiful location.

High Street, Alfriston, East Sussex BN26 5SY
Telephone: 01323 870319 • Fax: 01323 871384
E-mail: info@thegeorge-alfriston.com
www.thegeorge-alfriston.com

BEST OF Brighton & Sussex COTTAGES
Quality Accredited Agency

+44 (0) 1273 308779
www.bestofbrighton.co.uk

- **Brighton & Hove**
- **Eastbourne**
- **Lewes**

A very good selection of houses, flats, apartments and cottages.

Town Centre, Seafront & Countryside locations – many taking pets (Pets £15/£30 per week)

CHIDDINGLY, EAST SUSSEX
Adorable, small, well-equipped cottage in grounds of Tudor Manor. Two bedrooms, sleeps 4-6. Full kitchen and laundry facilities. Telephone. Use of indoor heated swimming pool, sauna/jacuzzi, tennis and badminton court. Large safe garden. Pets and children welcome. From £420 – £798 per week incl. Short Breaks £258-£360. **Apply:** Eva Morris, "Pekes", 124 Elm Park Mansions, Park Walk, London SW10 0AR • Tel: 020-7352 8088 • ETC ★★★
Fax: 020-7352 8125 • e-mail: pekes.afa@virgin.net • www.pekesmanor.com

FAIRLIGHT COTTAGE

Warren Road (via Coastguard Lane), Fairlight, East Sussex TN35 4AG

Peace, tranquillity and a warm welcome await you at our comfortable country house, adjoining 650 acres of country park in an area of outstanding natural beauty – a paradise for dogs and owners. Panoramic sea views from large balcony. Centrally heated en suite bedrooms with beverage trays and colour TV. Comfortable guest lounge. Delicious breakfasts. No smoking. Ample parking. Pets stay with owners (free of charge). Badgers and foxes dine in the garden every evening.

B&B from £32.50pppn. • Single supplement
Janet & Ray Adams • 01424 812545
e-mail: fairlightcottage@supanet.com
www.fairlightcottage.co.uk

East Sussex
Rye, Seaford

BRANDY'S COTTAGE

Mrs Jane Apperly, Cadborough Farm, Rye, East Sussex TN31 6AA
Tel: 01797 225426 • www.cadborough.co.uk • apperly@cadborough.co.uk

Newly converted and sympathetically restored cottage provides luxurious and spacious accommodation for two people. Located one mile from Rye, close to 1066 Country walks. Facilities include TV/Video/Music Centre, full gas C/H, cooker/hob, microwave, washer/dryer, private courtyard with garden furniture and BBQ. Linen and towels incl. We accept one small well behaved dog and children over 12. Weekly rates from £285 low season to £425 high season. Short breaks available. Four other cottages also available. No Smoking.

"A little Gem of an Hotel"

RYE LODGE

This delightful award-winning Town House Hotel in the centre of Rye offers luxury, elegance and charm in a relaxed atmosphere. Take breakfast in the Terrace Room or enjoy breakfast in bed from Room Service – relax in the Venetian Leisure Centre with spa, pool and sauna and enjoy a glass of Champagne in the Champagne Bar – plus all the delights of the picturesque Ancient Cinque Port of Rye.

Short Break Package: 2 nights Room & Breakfast from £99.

★★★ AA & VB ★★★
GOLD AWARD
Recommended by Signpost and designated a
"Best Loved Hotel of the World"

RYE LODGE HOTEL
HILDER'S CLIFF, RYE, EAST SUSSEX
www.ryelodge.co.uk

JEAKE'S HOUSE
Mermaid Street, Rye, East Sussex TN31 7ET
Telephone: 01797 222828

e-mail: stay@jeakeshouse.com • www.jeakeshouse.com

Dating from 1689, this beautiful Listed Building stands in one of England's most famous streets. Oak-beamed and panelled bedrooms overlook the marsh to the sea. Brass, mahogany, half-tester and four-poster beds; honeymoon suite; TV, radio, telephone. Book-lined bar. Residential licence. Traditional and vegetarian breakfast served. £45–£63pp. Private car park. Visa and Mastercard accepted.

PREMIER SELECTED

Good Hotel Guide
César Award

AA Pet-Friendly Establishment of the Year 2005 ★★★★ *award winning guest house*

the silverdale
tel: 01323 491849

21 Sutton Park Road,
Seaford,
East Sussex,
BN25 1RH

www.silverdaleseaford.co.uk
info@silverdaleseaford.co.uk

We don't just accept dogs, we *welcome* them. Our guests are given a list of pubs and restaurants that welcome dogs in the town, as well as details of places where they can walk and exercise them. We are only a few minutes walk from the seafront and local parks. Our rooms are individually decorated with lots of extra touches.

BEACH COTTAGE • CLAREMONT ROAD, SEAFORD, EAST SUSSEX   BN25 2QQ

Well equipped, three-bedroomed terraced cottage on seafront. Sleeps 5. Central heating, open fire and woodburner. South-facing patio overlooking sea.
Downland walks (wonderful for dogs), fishing, golf, wind-surfing, etc.
Details from: Julia Lewis, 47 Wandle Bank, London SW19 1DW
Tel: 020 8542 5073   •   e-mail: cottage@beachcottages.info   •   www.beachcottages.info

Alfriston

Attractive village in heart of the South Downs, with old market square and village green.

THE GEORGE INN, HIGH STREET, ALFRISTON BN26 5SY (01323 870319; Fax: 01323 871384). Six relaxing and charming bedrooms. Delicious food, refreshing ales, oak beams, open log fires. Friendly atmosphere, quality service and a beautiful location.
e-mail: info@thegeorge-alfriston.com website: www.thegeorge-alfriston.com

Brighton

Famous resort with varied entertainment and night life, excellent shops and restaurants.

BEST OF BRIGHTON & SUSSEX COTTAGES has available a very good selection of houses, flats, apartments and cottages in Brighton and Hove, Eastbourne and Lewes. Town centre/seaside and countryside locations – many taking pets. (+44 (0)1273 308779). [Pets £15/£30 per week.]
website: www.bestofbrighton.co.uk

Chiddingly

Charming village, 4 miles north-west of Hailsham. Off the A22 London-Eastbourne road.

Adorable, small, well-equipped cottage in grounds of Tudor Manor. Two bedrooms, sleeps 4-6. Full central heating. Colour TV. Fridge/freezer, laundry facilities. Large safe garden. Use indoor heated swimming pool, sauna/jacuzzi and tennis. From £420 to £798 per week inclusive. ETC ★★★. Contact: EVA MORRIS, "PEKES", 124 ELM PARK MANSIONS, PARK WALK, LONDON SW10 0AR (020 7352 8088; Fax: 020 7352 8125). [pw! 2 dogs free, extra two £7 each].
e-mail: pekes.afa@virgin.net website: www.pekesmanor.com

Fairlight

Village 3 miles east of Hastings

JANET & RAY ADAMS, FAIRLIGHT COTTAGE, WARREN ROAD, FAIRLIGHT TN35 4AG (01424 812545). Country house in idyllic location with clifftop walks. Tasteful en suite rooms, comfortable guest lounge. Delicious breakfasts. No smoking. Dogs stay with owners. VB ★★★★ [🐾]
e-mail: fairlightcottage@supanet.com website: www.fairlightcottage.co.uk

Polegate

Quiet position, 5 miles from the popular seaside resort of Eastbourne. London 58 miles, Lewes 12.

MRS P. FIELD, 20 ST JOHN'S ROAD, POLEGATE BN26 5BP (01323 482691). Homely private house. Quiet location; large enclosed garden. Parking space. Ideally situated for walking on South Downs and Forestry Commission land. All rooms, washbasins and tea/coffee making facilities. Bed and Breakfast. Pets very welcome. [pw! 🐾]

Free or reduced rate entry to Holiday Visits and Attractions - see our READERS' OFFER VOUCHERS on pages 445-454

East Sussex

SOUTH EAST ENGLAND 211

Rye

Picturesque hill town with steep cobbled streets. Many fine buildings of historic interest. Hastings 12 miles, Tunbridge Wells 28.

RYE LODGE HOTEL, HILDER'S CLIFF, RYE TN31 7LD (01797 223838; Fax: 01797 223585). Luxury, elegance and charm in a relaxed atmosphere. Indoor swimming pool, spa and sauna. Delicious candlelit dinners in Terrace Restaurant. Ideal for exploring historic Rye. AA/VB ★★★ Gold Award. [Pets £8 per night, £50 per week]
website: www.ryelodge.co.uk

JEAKE'S HOUSE, MERMAID STREET, RYE TN31 7ET (01797 222828). Dating from 1689, this Listed building has oak-beamed and panelled bedrooms overlooking the marsh. TV, radio, telephone. Booklined bar. £45-£63pp. ETC/AA ★★★★★ [Pets £5 per night]
e-mail: stay@jeakeshouse.com   website: www.jeakeshouse.com

MRS JANE APPERLY, BRANDY'S COTTAGE, CADBOROUGH FARM, RYE TN31 6AA (01797 225426; Fax: 01797 224097).Newly converted cottage provides luxurious and spacious accommodation for two people. Private courtyard. One small well-behaved dog and children over 12 welcome. No-smoking. Short breaks available. ETC ★★★★ [🐾]
e-mail: apperly@cadborough.co.uk   website: www.cadborough.co.uk

Seaford

On the coast midway between Newhaven and Beachy Head.

THE SILVERDALE, 21 SUTTON PARK ROAD, SEAFORD BN25 IRH (01323 491849). We don't just accept dogs, we welcome them. Only a few minutes from seafront and parks. Delightful small dining room and bar. All rooms individually decorated. SEEDA award winner 2003, Clean Catering Award winner for 15 years. AA Pet Friendly Establishment of the Year 2005. ETC/AA ★★★★ [🐾].
e-mail: info@silverdaleseaford.co.uk   website: www.silverdaleseaford.co.uk

BEACH COTTAGE, CLAREMONT ROAD, SEAFORD BN25 2QQ. Well-equipped, three-bedroomed terraced cottage on seafront. CH, open fire and woodburner. South-facing patio overlooking sea. Downland walks (wonderful for dogs), fishing, golf, wind-surfing, etc. Details from JULIA LEWIS, 47 WANDLE BANK, LONDON SW19 1DW (020 8542 5073). [pw! 🐾]
e-mail: cottage@beachcottages.info   website: www.beachcottages.info

---

Other specialised holiday guides from FHG

PUBS & INNS OF BRITAIN • **COUNTRY HOTELS** OF BRITAIN
WEEKEND & SHORT BREAK HOLIDAYS IN BRITAIN
THE GOLF GUIDE WHERE TO PLAY, WHERE TO STAY
500 GREAT PLACES TO STAY • **SELF-CATERING HOLIDAYS** IN BRITAIN
BED & BREAKFAST STOPS • **CARAVAN & CAMPING HOLIDAYS**
FAMILY BREAKS IN BRITAIN

Published annually: available in all good bookshops or direct from the publisher:
FHG Guides, Abbey Mill Business Centre, Seedhill, Paisley PA1 1TJ
Tel: 0141 887 0428 • Fax: 0141 889 7204
e-mail: admin@fhguides.co.uk • www.holidayguides.com

SOUTH EAST ENGLAND — West Sussex

Arundel, Chichester, Eastgate, Pulborough, Selsey

Woodacre offers Bed and Breakfast in a traditional family home set in a beautiful garden surrounded by woodland. Well positioned for Chichester, Arundel, Goodwood and the seaside. Our rooms are clean and spacious; two on ground floor. Full English breakfast. Credit cards accepted. Pets welcome. B&B from £30.00pp. 3 nights for the price of 2 November to March. Contact: Mrs Vicki Richards Woodacre, Arundel Road, Fontwell, Arundel BN18 0QP • 01243 814301 e-mail: wacrebb@aol.com • www.woodacre.co.uk

ETC ★★★★

Spire Cottage

Built from the old spire of Chichester Cathedral that collapsed in 1861, is a Grade II Listed country cottage offering stylish bed and breakfast accommodation. Friendly, relaxed atmosphere, excellent facilities, village pub and two golf courses. Also available on a self-catering basis (sleeping 8). Please telephone for further details.

Jan & Andy, Spire Cottage, Church Lane,
Hunston, Chichester PO20 1AJ
Tel: 01243 778937
e-mail: jan@spirecottage.co.uk
www.spirecottage.co.uk

Wandleys Caravan Park

Eastergate, West Sussex PO20 3SE
Tel: 01243 543235 or 01243 543384
e-mail: amandagent@btinternet.com
www.wandleyscaravanpark.com

You will find peace, tranquillity and relaxation in one of our comfortable holiday caravans. All have internal WC and shower. Dogs welcome. The Sussex Downs, Chichester, Bognor Regis, Arundel, Littlehampton – all these historic and interesting places are only 15 minutes from our beautiful, small and quiet country park. Telephone for brochure. New and used holiday homes for sale when available.

Beacon Lodge Bed and Breakfast

Charming en suite B&B accommodation in self-contained annexe, in the heart of West Sussex, surrounded by beautiful countryside. Excellent for country walks. No charge for pets. B&B from £65 per night (family room).

London Road, Watersfield, Pulborough, West Sussex RH20 1NH
Tel & Fax: 01798 831026 • www: beaconlodge.co.uk

ST ANDREWS LODGE

Chichester Road, Selsey, West Sussex PO20 0LX
Tel: 01243 606899 • Fax: 01243 607826
e-mail: info@standrewslodge.co.uk
www.standrewslodge.co.uk

Welcome to St Andrews Lodge, the perfect place for a relaxing break. Situated in the small seaside town of Selsey and well located for Chichester and the South Downs; close to unspoilt beaches and 5 minutes from Pagham Harbour Nature Reserve. Enjoy our delicious breakfast and stay in one of our individually decorated rooms. All equipped with fridge, hospitality tray and ironing facilities. Rooms open on to our large garden to allow your dog to stretch his legs. No charge for dogs but donation to local nature reserve welcome. Licensed bar, wheelchair accessible room, large car park.

ETC ★★★★

Please apply for brochure and details of our special winter offer.

West Sussex

SOUTH EAST ENGLAND 213

Arundel

Arundel lies between Chichester and Brighton, 5 miles from Littlehampton on the south coast. Magnificent Arundel Castle with its impressive grounds overlooks the River Arun, and the town is also home to the Wildfowl and Wetlands Trust where thousands of rare and migratory birds can be seen.

MRS VICKI RICHARDS, WOODACRE, ARUNDEL ROAD, FONTWELL, ARUNDEL BN18 0QP (01243 814301). Bed & Breakfast in traditional family home. Ideal for Chichester, Goodwood and seaside. Clean, spacious rooms, two on ground floor. ETC ★★★★
e-mail: wacrebb@aol.com   website: www.woodacre.co.uk

Chichester

County town 9 miles east of Havant. Town has cathedral and 16th century market cross.

SPIRE COTTAGE, CHURCH LANE, HUNSTON, CHICHESTER PO20 1AJ (01243 778937). Stylish bed and breakfast accommodation in a friendly and relaxed atmosphere. Excellent facilities. Village pub and two golf courses. [Dogs £5 per night]
e-mail: jan@spirecottage.co.uk   website: www.spirecottage.co.uk

Eastergate

Village between the sea and South Downs. Fontwell Park nearby. Bognor Regis 5 miles south.

WANDLEYS CARAVAN PARK, EASTERGATE PO20 3SE (01243 543235 or 01243 543384). You will find peace, tranquillity and relaxation in one of our comfortable holiday caravans. All have internal WC and shower. Dogs welcome. Many historic and interesting places nearby. Telephone for brochure. [🐾]
e-mail: amandagent@btinternet.com   website: www.wandleyscaravanpark.com

Pulborough

Town on River Arun 12 miles NW of Worthing.

BEACON LODGE, LONDON ROAD, WATERSFIELD, PULBOROUGH RH20 1NH (Tel & Fax: 01798 831026). Charming self-contained annexe. B&B accommodation, en suite, TV, coffee/tea making facilities. Wonderful countryside views. B&B from £65 per night, family room. Excellent for country walks. No charge for your pets! Telephone for more details. [🐾]
e-mail: gbwingfield@yahoo.co.uk   website: www.beaconlodge.co.uk

Selsey

Seaside resort 8 miles south of Chichester. Selsey Bill is headland extending into the English Channel.

ST ANDREWS LODGE, CHICHESTER ROAD, SELSEY PO20 0LX (01243 606899; Fax: 01243 607826). 10 bedrooms, all en suite, with direct dial telephones and modem point, some on ground floor. Dining room overlooking garden; licensed bar for residents only. Wheelchair accessible room. Dogs welcome in rooms overlooking large garden. Apply for brochure and prices. ETC★★★★ [Pets £3 per stay (donation to local project)]
e-mail: info@standrewslodge.co.uk   website: www.standrewslodge.co.uk

---

Visit the FHG website
www.holidayguides.com
for details of the wide choice of accommodation featured in the full range of FHG titles

214 EAST OF ENGLAND

Cambridgeshire
Burwell, Ely, St Ives

THE MEADOW HOUSE
2a High Street, Burwell,
Cambridge CB5 0HB
Tel: 01638 741926 • Fax: 01638 741861

The Meadow House is a magnificent modern house set in two acres of wooded grounds offering superior Bed and Breakfast accommodation in spacious rooms, some with king-size beds. The variety of en suite accommodation endeavours to cater for all requirements; a suite of rooms sleeping six complete with south-facing balcony; a triple room on the ground floor with three single beds and the Coach House, a spacious annexe with one double and one single bed; also one double and two twins sharing a well equipped bathroom. All rooms have TV, central heating and tea/coffee facilities. Car parking. No smoking
Family rate available on request.

e-mail: hilary@themeadowhouse.co.uk   www.themeadowhouse.co.uk

The Old School B&B
Former village school set in an acre of gardens and horse paddocks, with splendid views across the Fens. Three ground floor bedrooms. Dogs very welcome.
The Old School, School Lane, Coveney, Ely, Cambridgeshire CB6 2DB
Tel : 01353 777087 • Mob: 07802 174541 • Fax : 01353 777091
e-mail: info@TheOldSchoolBandB.co.uk • www.TheOldSchoolBandB.co.uk

The St Ives Motel
London Road, St Ives,
Huntingdon, Cambridgeshire PE27 5EX

Family-run hotel with 15 spacious en suite rooms, all non smoking, each with its own patio leading to the garden or orchard. Large bar area, evening meal available.
Tel: 01480 463857 • Fax: 01480 492027
E-Mail: stivesmotel@btconnect.com • www.stivesmotel.co.uk

Burwell

One of the largest villages in Cambridgeshire, with over 60 listed buildings of interest, and the 15th century Church of St Mary's. Ideal area for walkers, fishing enthusiasts and nature lovers.

THE MEADOW HOUSE, 2A HIGH STREET, BURWELL, CAMBRIDGE CB5 0HB (01638 741926; Fax: 01638 741861). Modern house in two acres of wooded grounds offering superior Bed and Breakfast. Variety of en suite accommodation. All rooms have TV, central heating and tea/coffee facilities. No smoking. Family rate on request. ETC ★★★★ [🐾]
e-mail: hilary@themeadowhouse.co.uk   website: www.themeadowhouse.co.uk

Ely

Magnificent Norman Cathedral dating from 1083. Ideal base for touring the fen country of East Anglia.

MRS C. H. BENNETT, STOCKYARD FARM, WISBECH ROAD, WELNEY PE14 9RQ (01354 610433; Fax: 01354 610422). Comfortable converted farmhouse, rurally situated between Ely and Wisbech. Conservatory breakfast room, guests' lounge. Free-range produce. Miles of riverside walks. Vegetarians welcome. B&B from £25. [🐾 pw!]

THE OLD SCHOOL B&B, THE OLD SCHOOL, SCHOOL LANE, COVENEY, ELY CB6 2DB (01353 777087; Mob: 07802 174541; Fax : 01353 777091). Former village school set in an acre of gardens and horse paddocks, with splendid views across the Fens. Three ground floor bedrooms. Dogs very welcome. Twin kennels available if required. EnjoyEngland ★★★★. [pw! £3 per dog per night]
e-mail: info@TheOldSchoolBandB.co.uk   website: TheOldSchoolBandB.co.uk

St Ives

Ancient market town on the River Great Ouse 15 miles north west of Cambridge.

THE ST IVES MOTEL, LONDON ROAD, ST IVES, HUNTINGDON PE27 5EX (01480 463857; Fax: 01480 492027). Family-run hotel with 15 spacious en suite rooms, all non smoking, each with its own patio. Large bar area, evening meal available.
e-mail: stivesmotel@btconnect.com   website: www.stivesmotel.co.uk

Essex

Saffron Walden

With a history of hospitality dating back to its origins as one of the early coaching Inns on the original London to Newmarket road, The Crown House offers a different experience from the standard corporate hotel. With 22 individually designed en suite rooms, generous free on-site car parking and excellent food, The Crown House is a warm and welcoming venue set in tranquil landscaped gardens.
Relax in one of the comfy leather chairs in the lounge with a drink or a coffee, sit in the garden taking in the view or stroll round the historic village of Great Chesterford – whatever your choice – we are here to help you unwind. Privately owned and personally run, The Crown House is the ideal destination for either business or leisure.

The Crown House Hotel and Restaurant
Great Chesterford, Saffron Walden, Essex CB10 1NY
Phone: 01799 530515 or 530257 • Fax: 01799 530683
e-mail : reservations@crownhousehotel.com
www.crownhousehotel.com

Saffron Walden

Market town with many medieval buildings. Cambridge 15 miles, London 45 miles.

THE CROWN HOUSE HOTEL AND RESTAURANT, GREAT CHESTERFORD, SAFFRON WALDEN CB10 1NY (01799 530515 or 530257; Fax: 01799 530683). With 22 individually designed en suite rooms, generous free on site car parking and excellent food, The Crown House is a warm and welcoming venue set in tranquil landscaped gardens. [Pets £5 per night].
email : reservations@crownhousehotel.com   website: www.crownhousehotel.com

---

Visit the FHG website
www.holidayguides.com
for details of the wide choice of accommodation featured in the full range of FHG titles

Take a Blue Riband Holiday in beautiful Norfolk and take a pet free*

*One pet stays free when you book through this advert. Extra pet £10

Inexpensive Self Catering Holidays at ● Caister ● Hemsby ● Scratby ● Winterton ● California and ● Great Yarmouth **All year round**

Detached Bungalows at Parklands
Hemsby Village, Children's Playground, Digital Freeview TV, Miniature Railway.

Seafront Bungalows
Caister-on-Sea, with enclosed rear gardens leading to the beach.

Detached Chalets on Sea-Dell Park
Quiet location, Beach Road, Hemsby.

Belle Aire Park, Beach Rd, Hemsby
Premier Chalets. Free satellite TV. Clubhouse and safe children's playground.
Pets are allowed on local beaches.
All equipped to very high standard
★ Free car parking at all locations
Open Christmas & New Year

Quality, Value and Service from a family business, since 1955

● **Popular low season breaks, bungalows from only £90**

● **Bargain Spring & Autumn breaks, excellent value chalets from £75**

☎ **Direct Line for Bookings & Brochures**
01493 730445 – Call 8am to 9pm 7 days a week
Debit / Credit Cards Accepted

Or browse our full brochure on our website at: www.BlueRibandHolidays.co.uk

For your free colour brochure phone the above number or write to:
Don Witheridge, Blue Riband House, Parklands, North Road, Hemsby, Great Yarmouth, Norfolk NR29 4HA

Norfolk

EAST OF ENGLAND 217

We have more than 350 self catering cottages to choose from. Many accepting pets.

Sweeping beaches, pretty countryside and many rural footpaths make Norfolk the perfect destination for you and your discerning pets.

Norfolk Country Cottages

Reepham Office: Carlton House, Market Place, Reepham, Norfolk NR10 4JJ **T:** 01603 871872

Holt Office: The Old Crab Shop, 1 Cross Street, Holt, Norfolk NR25 6HZ **T:** 01263 715779

info@norfolkcottages.co.uk

www.norfolkcottages.co.uk

Burnham Market

the hoste arms

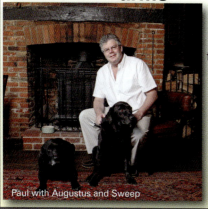

Paul with Augustus and Sweep

Situated on the Green in the pretty village of Burnham Market, this stylish hotel provides a relaxing friendly atmosphere, and owner Paul Whittome prides himself on everything being of the highest standard, from the individually designed bedrooms to the fabulous locally-sourced food. There is a cosy bar with log fire, popular with locals dogs and visitors alike, a pretty garden, terraced dining area, and comfortable conservatory perfect for coffee or a light lunch.

Amazing value Midweek Dinner, Bed and Breakfast Breaks

The Hoste Arms, The Green, Burnham Market, Norfolk PE31 8HD
Tel: 01328 738777 • Fax: 01328 730103
e-mail: reception@hostearms.co.uk • www.hostearms.co.uk

Castaways Holiday Park
BACTON-ON-SEA NORFOLK

For one of the best value holidays on the glorious North Norfolk Coast, welcome to Castaways Holiday Park

A small, family-run business situated in the quiet, peaceful village of Bacton, with direct access to fine sandy beach, and ideal for beach fishing and discovering Norfolk and The Broads.

Stunning sea views from most of our accommodation:
Fully equipped modern Caravans, comfortable three bedroom pine lodges and a choice of 2 ground floor and 2 first floor flats with all amenities. Licensed Club. Entertainment. Amusement Arcade. Children's Play Area.

PETS WELCOME

Enquiries and Bookings to:
Castaways Holiday Park,
Paston Road, Bacton-on-Sea,
Norfolk NR12 0JB •
BH & HPA approved

on-line booking facility available

Booking Hotline: 01692 650 436
www.castawaysholidaypark.net

Norfolk   **EAST OF ENGLAND**

Caister-on-Sea, Cromer

NOW OPEN MARCH TO JANUARY

Elm Beach is a small, select, 4-star Caravan Park with unique, uninterrupted views of the Sea and Caister's golden, sandy beaches. We offer a range of 4-6 berth, fully equipped Heated Caravans, many of which overlook the sea or have sea views. We are a quiet, privately-run park with no entertainment facilities, but enjoy, free of charge, entertainment supplied by neighbouring parks, both within easy walking distance. Pets very welcome.

Elm Beach Caravan Park Manor Road, Caister-on-Sea NR30 5HG
Freephone: 08000 199 360   www.elmbeachcaravanpark.com   e-mail: enquiries@elmbeachcaravanpark.com

Superior brick-built, tiled roof cottages • Newly fitted double glazing throughout
Adjacent golf course • Lovely walks on dunes and coast
2-4 night breaks early/late season • Terms from £69 to £355.
SAND DUNE COTTAGES, TAN LANE, CAISTER-ON-SEA,
GREAT YARMOUTH NR30 5DT (01493 720352; mobile: 07785 561363)
e-mail: sand.dune.cottages@amserve.net
www.eastcoastlive.co.uk/sites/sanddunecottages.php

30 en suite bedrooms, all with sea views
Executive Suites - A la carte Restaurant
Buttery and Bar - Bolton's Bistro specialising in
Fresh Fish Dishes - Cromer Crabs - Lobsters
Steaks - Pasta and Vegetarian Dishes
CLIFTONVILLE HOTEL — Indulge in Edwardian Elegance
AA ★★★ Grade II Listed   Pet-friendly staff - Dog meals available
www.cliftonvillehotel.co.uk   Tel: 01263 512483   e-mail: reservations@cliftonvillehotel.co.uk

KING'S CHALET PARK

Families Welcome & Pets Free of Charge

Well-equipped Chalets sleeping 2 to 6; shower/ bathroom, microwave, TV. Tourist Board and NNH/GHA Approved. One twin, one double bedroom, bed sofa in lounge. Well-equipped kitchenette.

Quiet site adjacent to woods, Golf Club and beach. Local shops nearby or pleasant 10 minutes' walk into town.

Telephone: 01263 511308

Enquiries to:
Mrs V. Bateman, 47 Norwich Road,
Cromer, Norfolk NR27 0EX

220 EAST OF ENGLAND — Norfolk
Cromer, Dereham

Pet welcome free of charge

Comfortable, well-equipped chalets situated on beautiful, landscaped, quiet site. Ideally placed for walks to adjacent woods, cliffs and sandy beaches. 10 minutes' walk to town. Golf course and local shops nearby. Plenty of local places of interest to visit. One twin, one double room, bathroom, colour TV, microwave, well-equipped kitchenette. Children welcome.

Short Breaks in Spring/Autumn 2 nights or more from £80
Spring/Autumn £150-£230 per week
June-September £250-£320 per week

DETAILS FROM: MRS I. SCOLTOCK, SHANGRI-LA, LITTLE CAMBRIDGE, DUTON HILL, DUNMOW, ESSEX CM6 3QU • TEL: 01371 870482

Kings Chalet Park Cromer, Norfolk
Sleep 2-4
Open March to October

CROMER — SELF CATERING COTTAGES

A terrace of four charming almshouses recently modernised and redecorated throughout. Providing either

2 & 3 bedroom accommodation for 4/6 persons plus a 4-Star detached bungalow on Forest Park.

Central heating is included in the letting fee during the low season.
Short breaks available.

Each cottage has its own enclosed garden, ideal for children and **pets always welcome!** Ample car parking in cottage grounds.

Enjoy a walk with your dog on the miles of open uncrowded beaches in North Norfolk. Cromer has a Cinema and Pier with first-rate live shows.

Also included is membership of Forest Park with its beautiful woodland walks, clubhouse and swimming pool open during the high season.
Detailed brochure and tariff (prices from £275 to £620 p.w.)

FOREST PARK
Outstanding Natural Beauty

**Broadgates Cottages, Northrepps,
Forest Park Caravan Site Ltd,
Northrepps Road, Cromer, Norfolk NR27 0JR
Tel: 01263 513290 • Fax: 01263 511992
e-mail: info@broadgates.co.uk • www.broadgates.co.uk**

Scarning Dale

Dale Road, Scarning, East Dereham NR19 2QN
Tel: 01362 687269

A warm welcome awaits you. Six self-catering cottages, sleeping 2 to 6 people, in the grounds of Scarning Dale, a 16th century house set in 25 acres of landscaped gardens, paddock and woodland. New log cabin, sleeps four. Indoor heated swimming pool. Good access Norfolk and Suffolk. Dogs welcome by arrangement. Grazing and stables available.

www.scarningdale.co.uk

Norfolk

Dereham, Diss, Foxley

EAST OF ENGLAND

Bed & Breakfast. En suite rooms in converted dairy.
Central heating, tea/coffee, freeview TV.
Village inn 100 yards for evening meal.
Bartles Lodge, Church Street, Elsing, Dereham NR20 3EA
Tel: 01362 637177
www.bartleslodge.co.uk • e-mail: bartleslodge@yahoo.co.uk

WAVENEY VALLEY HOLIDAY PARK

★ Touring Caravan and Camping Site ★ Licensed Bar ★ Electric Hook-ups ★ Restaurant, Shop, Laundry
★ Self-Catering Mobile Homes ★ Outdoor Swimming Pool ★ Horse Riding on Site ★ Good Fishing nearby

Airstation Lane, Rushall, Diss, Norfolk IP21 4QF • Tel: 01379 741228/741690
Fax: 01379 741228 • e-mail: waveneyvalleyhp@aol.com • www.caravanparksnorfolk.co.uk

4 B & B STRENNETH *Country Bed and Breakfast*

Airfield Road, Fersfield, Diss, Norfolk IP22 2BP

STRENNETH is well-established and family-run, situated in unspoiled countryside just a short drive from Bressingham Gardens and the picturesque market town of Diss. Offering first-class accommodation, the original 17th Century building has been carefully renovated to a high standard with a wealth of exposed oak beams, with a newer single storey courtyard wing and two converted cottages. There is ample off-road parking and plenty of nice walks nearby.

All seven bedrooms, including a Four-Poster and an Executive, are tastefully arranged with period furniture and distinctive beds. Each has remote-control colour television, hospitality tray, central heating and full en suite facilities. The establishment is smoke-free. Dinners are served by arrangement. There is an extensive breakfast menu using local produce. Ideal touring base. Pets most welcome. Outside kennels with runs if required. Bed and Breakfast from £25.00.

Telephone: 01379 688182 • Fax: 01379 688260
e-mail: pdavey@strenneth.co.uk • www.strenneth.co.uk

Located on a working farm, a courtyard of 2/3/4 bedroomed converted stables, 3 converted barns and 2 cottages, all fully equipped. Sleeps up to 10. Ideally situated for the beautiful North Norfolk coast, Sandringham, Norwich, and The Broads. 365 acres of mature woodland adjoining farm – private fishing in owners' lake. Indoor heated swimming Pool. Pets welcome at a charge of £10.

MOOR FARM STABLE COTTAGES
FOXLEY, NORFOLK NR20 4QP

Heated Indoor Swimming Pool, with Spa

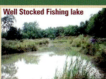
Well Stocked Fishing lake

Tel or Fax: 01362 688523
e-mail: mail@moorfarmstablecottages.co.uk
www.moorfarmstablecottages.co.uk

222 EAST OF ENGLAND — Norfolk

Great Yarmouth, Happisburgh, King's Lynn, Lowestoft

Sunwright Holiday Chalets

Sundowner Holiday Park, Newport, Hemsby, near Great Yarmouth. Fully furnished and equipped self-catering chalets, sleep up to 6. Two bedrooms, kitchen with all your cooking needs, lounge with TV, bathroom with shower over bath. Close to beach, Norfolk Broads and many attractions. Pets most welcome! Contact Mrs Michelle Browne, 50 Mariners Compass, Gorleston, Great Yarmouth, Norfolk NR31 6TS • 01493 304342 • e-mail: sunwrightholiday@aol.com • www.sunwrightholidays.com

---

A warm welcome for you and your pets. Inexpensive, 'live-as-you-please' self-catering holidays in beautiful Norfolk. Chalets, Bungalows, Caravans and Cottages near Great Yarmouth & Norfolk Broads.
SHORT BREAKS AVAILABLE ALL SEASON.

Colour Brochure : Carefree Holidays, Chapel Briers, Yarmouth Road, Hemsby, Norfolk NR29 4NJ.
Find us on the internet: www.carefree-holidays.co.uk   BOOKING HOTLINE 01493 732176

Ollands Farm Barn - Short Lane, Happisburgh NR12 0RR

Lovingly restored to a very high standard, this 18thC barn features a beamed cathedral ceiling, wood-burning stove, quaint paddle stairs, central heating, comfortable king-size bed in galleried bedroom, sofa-bed downstairs, fully fitted kitchen, shower room.
Well behaved dogs are welcome and receive a special treat when they come to stay. We are proud owners of two lurchers and two deerhounds, also two cats and small flock of chickens.
Tel: 01692 652280 • e-mail: mastuart@talk21.com • www.ollandsfarmbarn.co.uk

---

Pott Row

www.southsideholidayhome.co.uk

Detached 2 bedroom bungalow sleeps 4. In quiet rural Norfolk village close to Sandringham and beaches. Facilities include colour TV, video, microwave, fridge/freezer, washing machine, off road parking, dog run. All dogs welcome FREE. Open all year. Please telephone for brochure.
Mrs. J.E. Ford, 129 Leziate Drove, Pott Row, King's Lynn PE32 1DE Tel: 01553 630356

ETC ★★★

HOLMDENE FARM
BEESTON, KING'S LYNN PE32 2NJ

17th century farmhouse situated in central Norfolk within easy reach of the coast and Broads. Sporting activities available locally, village pub nearby. One double room, one twin and two singles. Pets welcome. Bed and Breakfast from £22.50 per person; Evening Meal from £15. Weekly terms available and child reductions. Two self-catering cottages. Sleeping 4/8. Terms on request.

MRS G. DAVIDSON • Tel: 01328 701284
e-mail: holmdenefarm@farmersweekly.net
www.holmdenefarm.co.uk

Broadland Holiday Village

Discover the delights of the Forgotten Norfolk Broad with your Faithful Friend
Stay in Cosy Brick Bungalows, **some with Private Outdoor Hot Tubs,** or Pine Lodges
Enjoy all the Countryside, Marsh and Beach Walks
And when you've worn him out, you can relax in our indoor heated pool
The perfect holiday for the whole family!
Oulton Broad, Lowestoft NR33 9JY • 01502 573003
www.broadlandvillage.co.uk

Norfolk
Mundesley-on-Sea

WHINCLIFF Bed & Breakfast
CROMER ROAD, MUNDESLEY NR11 8DU
Tel: 01263 721554

A warm welcome to all pets and their owners at "Whincliff" by the sea. Family/en suite, twin or single room available. Tea/coffee facilities, TV in all rooms, private parking, sea views, unspoilt beach and coastal walks to enjoy. **Anne & Alan Cutler.**

e-mail: cutler.a@sky.com

KILN CLIFFS CARAVAN PARK

Peaceful family-run site with NO clubhouse situated around an historic brick kiln. Luxury six-berth caravans for hire, standing on ten acres of grassy cliff top. Magnificent view out over the sea; private path leads down to extensive stretches of unspoilt sandy beach. All caravans fully equipped (except linen) and price includes all gas and electricity. Caravans always available for sale or for hire. Within easy reach are the Broads, Norwich, the Shire Horse Centre, local markets, nature reserves, bird sanctuaries; nearby golf, riding and fishing.

Facilities on site include general store and launderette. Responsible pet owners welcome.
Substantial discounts for off-peak bookings – phone for details.
Call for brochure.
**Mr R. Easton, Kiln Cliffs Caravan Park,
Cromer Road, Mundesley,
Norfolk NR11 8DF • Tel: 01263 720449**

47 SEAWARD CREST MUNDESLEY

West-facing brick built chalet on private site with lawns, flowers and parking. Large lounge/dining room, kitchenette, two bedrooms, bathroom. Beach and shops nearby. Pets most welcome. SAE please for further information.
Mrs Doar, 4 Denbury Road, Ravenshead, Notts. NG15 9FQ
Tel: 01623 798032

FHG Guides
publish a large range of well-known accommodation guides.
We will be happy to send you details or you can use the order form
at the back of this book.

Norfolk

North Walsham, Norwich, Old Hunstanton

DOLPHIN LODGE

Friendly B&B available in bungalow accommodation in a village setting just two-and-a-half miles from beaches. Many rural walks locally; within easy reach of all Norfolk's attractions including the Norfolk Broads. Golfing, horse riding and swimming nearby. All rooms en suite, with tea/coffee making facilities, TV, hairdryer. Enquiries by telephone only please.
Double room £35pppn; Single occupancy £45pppn; Weekly Single occupancy £40pppn

**Mrs G. Faulkner, Dolphin Lodge,
3 Knapton Road, Trunch, North Walsham
NR28 0QE • 01263 720961 • 07901 691084**

SOUTH NORFOLK'S GUEST HOUSE
Oakbrook House

Former village school with views over the quiet Tas Valley. Warm, comfortable en suite rooms of various sizes and prices. Ideal touring base for East Anglia. Long stay discounts.

**Oakbrook House, Frith Way, Great Moulton, Norwich NR15 2HE
Tel: 01379 677359 • Mobile: 07885 351212
oakbrookhouse@btinternet.com • www.oakbrookhouse.co.uk**

Self-catering accommodation seldom comes as well appointed as the cottages at White Lodge Farm. Set in the heart of the Norfolk countryside, but within walking distance of the beautiful village of Hingham, the cottages offer comfort and modern convenience all year round. Dogs very welcome.

White Lodge Farm, Hingham, Norfolk NR9 4LY

Call 01953 850435 or 07768 156680
e-mail: fhgp@whitelodgefarmcottages.co.uk
www.whitelodgefarmcottages.co.uk

ST CRISPINS SELF CATERING

OLD HUNSTANTON • Tel: 01485 534036
e-mail: st.crispins@btinternet.com

Quietly tucked away in Old Hunstanton village, near a sandy beach, golf course and long distance coastal footpath/Peddars Way, and the village P/O store. Situated a few miles from Norfolk Lavender, Royal Sandringham, and Titchwell/Snettisham RSPB.
Within a few hundred yards of three pubs/restaurants. Short notice bargain breaks usually available early and late season. Linen provided. Easy parking.
PETS WELCOME   Contact: *Ms L.D. Poore*

Publisher's note

While every effort is made to ensure accuracy, we regret that FHG Guides cannot accept responsibility for errors, misrepresentations or omissions in our entries or any consequences thereof. Prices in particular should be checked.
We will follow up complaints but cannot act as arbiters or agents for either party.

Norfolk

EAST OF ENGLAND

Thornham, Thorpe Market

The Lifeboat Inn
16th Century Smugglers' Ale House
Ship Lane, Thornham, Norfolk PE36 6LT
Tel: 01485 512236 • Fax: 01485 512323
e-mail: lifeboatinn@maypolehotels.com

THE LIFEBOAT INN has been a welcome sight for the weary traveller for centuries – roaring open fires, real ales and a hearty meal awaiting. The Summer brings its own charm – a cool beer, gazing over open meadows to the harbour, and rolling white horses gently breaking upon Thornham's sandy beach.

Dogs are welcome in all our bars and we provide the sort of breakfast that will enable you to keep up with your four-legged friend on the way to the beach!

Guests arriving at reception are greeted by our grand old fireplace in the lounge – ideal for toasting your feet after a day walking the coastal path – if you can coax your sleeping dog out of prime position! The restaurant (AA Rosette) opens every evening offering a varied selection of dishes to suit all tastes. Our extensive bar snack menu is also available if guests wish their pets to join them in the bar.

There are numerous and varied walks along miles of open beaches, across sweeping sand dunes, through pine woods or along chalk and sandstone cliff tops. It is truly a walker's paradise – especially if you're a dog.

We hope you will come and visit us. For our brochure and tariff which includes details of breaks please ring 01485 512236 or visit our website

www.maypolehotels.com

Green Farm Hotel & Restaurant
North Norfolk

For over 28 years Philip and Dee Dee Lomax have been extending a warm welcome to guests at the Green Farm, to enjoy the relaxed and friendly atmosphere and the highest standards of hospitality.

Enjoy this tranquil backwater of North Norfolk. Green Farm is the ideal base to discover and dip into the hidden delights of Norfolk. The Glorious Norfolk Broads, beautiful beaches, footpaths and bridleways and many National Trust houses.

The charming 16th Century flint-faced Farmhouse Inn offers 20 antique style bedrooms, all en suite, including four-posters. The converted dairy ground floor accommodation is ideal for guests who find stairs difficult. The food enjoys an enviable reputation for quality, presentation and service.

★★ **Please telephone for details of our special breaks available all year** ★★

Green Farm Hotel and Restaurant
Thorpe Market, North Walsham, North Norfolk NR11 8TH
Tel: 01263 833602 ❖ Fax: 01263 833163
e-mail: grfarmh@aol.com
www.greenfarmhotel.co.uk

The ideal holiday destination for your pet, be assured of a warm and friendly reception, sit back, close your eyes and soak up the history and atmosphere.

Norfolk

Thorpe Market, Thurne, Weybourne, Winterton-on-Sea

Poppyland Touring Park & Holiday Cottage

Poppyland is situated adjacent The Green in the middle of the picturesque village of Thorpe Market in North Norfolk just 4 miles from Cromer, 8 miles from Sheringham and 18 miles from the historic city of Norwich.

Poppyland is an ideal base from which to explore the North Norfolk coastline, the Norfolk Broads and the surrounding areas. Well behaved dogs (restrictions apply) are welcome both on the Touring Park and Holiday Cottage.
Puddleduck Cottage (sleeps 2) is a detached single storey cottage with a fully enclosed private garden. Short breaks available low season.
The Touring Park (adults only) is set in 1.5 acres and surrounded by high hedges and mature trees making it secluded and peaceful. Open Mar - Oct.
Excellent dog-friendly pubs nearby.

Tel: 01263 833219 • e-mail: poppylandpb@aol.co.uk • www.poppyland.com

HOLIDAY IN OUR ENGLISH COUNTRY GARDEN

Two acres in rural Norfolk. Ten spacious family-run bungalows and 7-bedroom farmhouse. Games room, heated pool, children's play area, fishing, boating, riding and golf nearby. Near River Staithe with access to Broads. Parking. For details/colour brochure contact:
F.G. Delf, Thurne Cottage, The Staithe, Thurne, Norfolk NR29 3BU
Tel: 01692 670242 or 01493 844568 • www.hederahouse.co.uk

Bolding Way Holidays
Weybourne, North Norfolk

BIDDLES COTTAGE (Self Catering), sleeps 2.
TACK ROOM (room only), sleeps 2.
Breakfast is NOT included in the price!
Well behaved pets are welcome in both. Open throughout the year. Weybourne is located in An Area of Outstanding Natural Beauty and on The Heritage Coast. Both have fenced gardens and excellent local walks. Use of owners' hot tub.

The Barn, Bolding Way, Weybourne, Holt, Norfolk NR25 7SW
Tel: 01263 588666 • e-mail: holidays@boldingway.co.uk • www.boldingway.co.uk

Winterton Holidays WINTERTON-ON-SEA • NORFOLK

For a peaceful, relaxing holiday.

1 and 2 bedroom self-catering chalets, furnished and equipped to a high standard

QUIET, PICTURESQUE PARK OVERLOOKING WINTERTON VALLEY WITH PANORAMIC SEA VIEWS

MILES OF WALKS ALONG THE VALLEY, DUNES AND BEACH.

MRS JUNE HUDSON, 42 LARK WAY, BRADWELL, GREAT YARMOUTH, NORFOLK NR31 8SB
01493 444700 • www.wintertonholidays.com

Free or reduced rate entry to
Holiday Visits and Attractions - see our
READERS' OFFER VOUCHERS on pages 445-454

Norfolk

Winterton-on-Sea

Winterton Valley Holidays
The Holiday Estate with a difference

A selection of modern superior fully appointed holiday chalets in a choice of locations near Great Yarmouth. Enjoy panoramic views of the sea from WINTERTON, a quiet and picturesque 35-acre estate minutes from the beach, while CALIFORNIA has all the usual amenities for the more adventurous holidaymaker, with free entry to the pool and clubhouse. Pets very welcome at both sites.

For colour brochure please ring
01493 377175 or write to
15 Kingston Avenue,
Caister-on-Sea, Norfolk NR30 5ET
www.wintertonvalleyholidays.co.uk

Fishermans Return

This 300-year-old brick and flint pub is situated in the unspoilt village of Winterton-on-Sea, just a few minutes' stroll from sandy beaches and beautiful walks. The Inn is popular with locals and visitors alike, serving excellent food, from simple bar snacks to more substantial fare, with a good choice of local real ales and fine wines. Accommodation is available on a B&B basis, in three tastefully furnished en suite double bedrooms.

The Lane, Winterton-on-Sea NR29 4BN
Tel: **01493 393305**
e-mail: fishermansreturn@yahoo.co.uk • www.fishermans-return.com

---

Pet-Friendly
Pubs, Inns & Hotels

on pages 438-443

Please note that these establishments may not feature in the main section of this book

EAST OF ENGLAND — Norfolk

NORFOLK COUNTRY COTTAGES (01603 871872/01263 715779). We have more than 350 self-catering cottages to choose from, many accepting pets. Sweeping beaches, pretty countryside and many rural footpaths make Norfolk the perfect destination for you and your discerning pets.
e-mail: info@norfolk.cottages.co.uk   website: www.norfolkcottages.co.uk

Go BLUE RIBAND for quality inexpensive self-catering holidays where your dog is welcome – choice of locations all in the borough of Great Yarmouth. Detached 3 bedroom bungalows, seafront bungalows, detached Sea-Dell chalets and modern sea front caravans. Free colour brochure: DON WITHERIDGE, BLUE RIBAND HOUSE, PARKLANDS, HEMSBY, GREAT YARMOUTH NR29 4HA (01493 730445). [pw! First pet free when booking through Pets Welcome!, 2nd pet £10 per week].
website: www.BlueRibandHolidays.co.uk

Bacton-on-Sea

Village on coast. 5 miles from North Walsham.

CASTAWAYS HOLIDAY PARK, PASTON ROAD, BACTON-ON-SEA NR12 0JB (01692 650436 and 650418). In peaceful village with direct access to sandy beach. Modern caravans, Pine Lodges and Flats, with all amenities. Licensed club, entertainment, children's play area. Ideal for discovering Norfolk. ETC ★★★. [Pets £20 per week]
website: www.castawaysholidaypark.co.uk

Burnham Market

Village 5 miles West of Wells.

THE HOSTE ARMS, THE GREEN, BURNHAM MARKET PE31 8HD (01328 738777; Fax: 01328 730103). Stylish hotel with relaxing friendly atmosphere and attentive service. Individually designed bedrooms. Cosy bar with log fire, terraced dining area, conservatory. Locally sourced food. Midweek breaks. AA 2 Rosettes for food. [Pets £7.50 per stay].
e-mail: reception@hostearms.co.uk   website: www.hostearms.co.uk

Caister-on-Sea

Historic site with Roman ruins and 15th century Caister Castle with 100 foot tower.

ELM BEACH CARAVAN PARK, MANOR ROAD, CAISTER-ON-SEA NR30 5HG (Freephone: 08000 199 360). Small, quiet park offering 4-6 berth, fully equipped caravans, most with sea views. Entertainment supplied free of charge by neighbouring park. Pets very welcome. [Pets £25 per week]
e-mail: enquiries@elmbeachcaravanpark.com   website: www.elmbeachcaravanpark.com

Superior brick-built, tiled roof cottages with double glazing throughout. Adjacent golf course. Lovely walks on dunes and coast. 2-4 night breaks early/late season. Terms from £69 to £355. SAND DUNE COTTAGES, TAN LANE, CAISTER-ON-SEA, GREAT YARMOUTH NR30 5DT (01493 720352; mobile: 07785 561363). ETC ★★ [Pets £15 per week]
e-mail: sand.dune.cottages@amserve.net
website: www.eastcoastlive.co.uk/sites/sanddunecottages.php

Symbols

- 🐾 Indicates that pets are welcome free of charge.
- £ Indicates that a charge is made for pets: nightly or weekly.
- pw! Shows some special provision for pets; exercise facility, feeding or accommodation arrangement.
- ⌂ Indicates separate pets accommodation.

Norfolk

EAST OF ENGLAND

Cromer

Attractive resort built round old fishing village. Norwich 21 miles.

CLIFTONVILLE HOTEL, SEAFRONT, CROMER NR27 9AS (01263 512543; Fax: 01263 515810). Ideally situated on the Norfolk coast. Beautifully restored Edwardian Hotel. 30 en suite bedrooms all with sea view. Executive suites. Seafood Bistro, à la carte Restaurant. AA ★★★ [pw! pets £4 per night)
e-mail: reservations@cliftonvillehotel.co.uk   website: www.cliftonvillehotel.co.uk

KINGS CHALET PARK, CROMER (01263 511308). Well-equipped chalets sleeping 2 to 6; shower/bathroom, microwave and TV. One twin, one double bedroom, bed sofa in lounge, well-equipped kitchenette. Quiet site adjacent to woods, golf club and beaches. Local shops nearby. Pleasant 10 minutes' walk to town. Families welcome. [🐾]

KINGS CHALET PARK, CROMER. Comfortable well-equipped chalets on quiet site; ideally placed for woodland and beach walks. 10 minutes' walk to town, shops nearby. Details from MRS I. SCOLTOCK, SHANGRI-LA, LITTLE CAMBRIDGE, DUTON HILL, DUNMOW, ESSEX (01371 870482). [one pet free]

All-electric two and three bedroom Holiday Cottages sleeping 4/6 in beautiful surroundings, also detached bungalow. Sandy beaches, sports facilities, Cinema and Pier (live shows). Parking. Children and pets welcome. ETC ★★-★★★ Brochure: **BROADGATES COTTAGES, NORTHREPPS, FOREST PARK CARAVAN SITE LTD, NORTHREPPS ROAD, CROMER, NORFOLK NR27 0JR (01263 513290; Fax: 01263 511992)** [Pets £10 weekly].
e-mail: info@broadgates.co.uk   website: www.broadgates.co.uk

Dereham

Situated 16 miles west of Norwich. St Nicholas Church has 16th century bell tower.

SCARNING DALE, SCARNING, EAST DEREHAM NR19 2QN (01362 687269). Self-catering cottages (not commercialised) in grounds of owner's house. On-site indoor heated swimming pool and full-size snooker table. B&B for six also available in house (sorry no pets in house). Grazing and Stables available.
website: www.scarningdale.co.uk

BARTLES LODGE, CHURCH STREET, ELSING, DEREHAM NR20 3EA (01362 637177). B&B in en suite rooms in converted dairy. Central heating, tea/coffee, freeview TV. Village inn 100 yards for evening meal [pw! Pets £2 per night, £10 per week]
e-mail: bartleslodge@yahoo.co.uk   website: www.bartleslodge.co.uk

Diss

Small market town on the River Waveney 19 miles SW of Norwich.

WAVENEY VALLEY HOLIDAY PARK, AIRSTATION LANE, RUSHALL, DISS IP21 4QF (01379 741228/741690; Fax: 01379 741228). Touring Caravan and Camping Site. Licensed bar, electric hook-ups, restaurant, shop, laundry. Self-catering mobile homes. Outdoor swimming pool, horse riding on site; good fishing nearby.
e-mail: waveneyvalleyhp@aol.com   website: www.caravanparksnorfolk.co.uk

PAUL AND YOLANDA DAVEY, STRENNETH, AIRFIELD ROAD, FERSFIELD, DISS IP22 2BP (01379 688182; Fax 01379 688260). Family-run, fully renovated period property with two cottages. All rooms en suite, colour TVs, hospitality trays. Ground floor rooms. Non-smoking. Extensive breakfast menu. Licensed. Bed and Breakfast from £25. ETC ★★★★ Silver Award. [🐾]
e-mail: pdavey@strenneth.co.uk   website: www.strenneth.co.uk

Foxley

Village 6 miles east of East Dereham.

Self-catering Cottages (2/3/4 bedrooms) on working farm. All fully equipped, with central heating. 20 miles from coast, 15 from Broads. Mature woodland nearby. Fishing in owner's lake. Indoor heated swimming pool. ETC ★★★/★★★★. **MOOR FARM STABLE COTTAGES, FOXLEY NR20 4QP (Tel & Fax: 01362 688523).** [Pets £10 per week]
e-mail: mail@moorfarmstablecottages.co.uk   website: www.moorfarmstablecottages.co.uk

Great Yarmouth

Traditional lively seaside resort with a wide range of amusements, including the Marina Centre and Sealife Centre.

MRS MICHELLE BROWNE, SUNWRIGHT HOLIDAYS, 50 MARINERS COMPASS, GORLESTON, GREAT YARMOUTH NR31 6TS (01493 304282) Sundowner Holiday Park, near Great Yarmouth. Fully furnished and equipped self catering chalets, sleep up to 6. Close to beach, Norfolk Broads and many attractions. [Pets £15 per week].
e-mail: sunwrightholiday@aol.com   website: www.sunwrightholidays.co.uk

CAREFREE HOLIDAYS, CHAPEL BRIERS, YARMOUTH ROAD, HEMSBY, GREAT YARMOUTH NR29 4NJ (01493 732176). A wide selection of superior chalets for live-as-you-please holidays near Great Yarmouth and Norfolk Broads. All amenities on site. Parking. Children and pets welcome. [Pets £25 per week.]
website: www.carefree-holidays.co.uk

Happisburgh

Coastal resort 6 miles East of North Walsham.

OLLANDS FARM BARN, SHORT LANE, HAPPISBURGH NR12 0RR (01692 652280). 18thC barn with beamed cathedral ceiling, wood-burning stove, quaint paddle stairs, central heating, comfortable king-size bed in galleried bedroom, sofa-bed downstairs, fully fitted kitchen, shower room. Well behaved dogs welcome.[Pets £10 per week].
e-mail: mastuart@talk21.com   website: www.ollandsfarmbarn.co.uk

King's Lynn

Ancient market town and port on the Wash with many beautiful medieval and Georgian buildings.

MRS J. E. FORD, 129 LEZIATE DROVE, POTT ROW, KING'S LYNN PE32 1DE (01553 630356). Detached bungalow sleeps 4. In quiet village close to Sandringham and beaches. Facilities include colour TV, video, microwave, fridge/freezer, washing machine, off road parking, dog run. [🐕]
website: www.southsideholidayhome.co.uk

MRS G. DAVIDSON, HOLMDENE FARM, BEESTON, KING'S LYNN PE32 2NJ (01328 701284). 17th century farmhouse situated in central Norfolk within easy reach of the coast and Broads. Sporting activities available locally, village pub nearby. One double room, one twin and one single. Pets welcome. Bed and Breakfast from £22.50pp; Evening Meal from £15. Weekly terms available and child reductions. Two self-catering cottages. Sleeping 4/8. Terms on request. ETC ★★★ [🐕]
e-mail: holmdenefarm@farmersweekly.net   website: www.holmdenefarm.co.uk

Lowestoft

Resort town on the North Sea coast, 38 miles north east of Ipswich.

BROADLAND HOLIDAY VILLAGE, OULTON BROAD, LOWESTOFT NR33 9JY (01502 573033). Discover the delights of the forgotten Norfolk Broad with your faithful friend. Stay in cosy brick bungalows, some with outdoor hot tubs, or pine lodges. Indoor heated pool. The perfect holiday for the whole family! [Pets £30 per week].
website: www.broadlandvillage.co.uk

Mundesley-on-Sea

Small resort backed by low cliffs. Good sands and bathing. Norwich 20 miles, Cromer 7.

ANNE & ALAN CUTLER, WHINCLIFF BED & BREAKFAST, CROMER ROAD, MUNDESLEY NR11 8DU (01263 721554). Clifftop house, sea views and sandy beaches. Rooms with colour TV and tea-making. Families and pets welcome. Open all year round. [🐕]
e-mail: cutler.a@sky.com

KILN CLIFFS CARAVAN PARK, CROMER ROAD, MUNDESLEY NR11 8DF (01263 720449). Peaceful family-run site situated around an historic brick kiln. Six-berth caravans for hire, standing on ten acres of grassy cliff top. All caravans fully equipped (except linen) and price includes all gas and electricity. [Pets £5 per week].

Norfolk

47 SEAWARD CREST, MUNDESLEY. West-facing brick built chalet on private site with lawns, flowers and parking. Large lounge/dining room, kitchenette, two bedrooms, bathroom. Beach and shops nearby. Pets most welcome. SAE please: MRS DOAR, 4 DENBURY ROAD, RAVENSHEAD, NOTTS. NG15 9FQ (01623 798032). [🐾]

North Walsham

Market town 14 miles north of Norwich, traditional centre of the Norfolk reed thatching industry.

MRS. G. FAULKNER, DOLPHIN LODGE, 3 KNAPTON ROAD, TRUNCH, NORTH WALSHAM NR28 0QE (01263 720961; Mobile: 07901 691084). Friendly B&B in village within easy reach of all Norfolk attractions including Norfolk Broads. All rooms en suite, tea/coffee facilities, TVs, hairdryers etc. Enquiries by telephone only. [🐾]
e-mail: dolphin_lodge@btopenworld.com   website: www.dolphinlodge.net

Norwich

Historic city with Cathedral, Castle, shops, restaurants and lots to see and do. Many medieval streets and lanes, with attractive timbered houses.

SOUTH NORFOLK'S GUEST HOUSE – OAKBROOK HOUSE, FRITH WAY, GREAT MOULTON, NORWICH NR15 2HE (01379 677359; Mobile: 07885 351212). Former village school with views over the quiet Tas Valley. Warm, comfortable en suite rooms of various sizes and prices. Ideal touring base for East Anglia. Long stay discounts. [Pets £5].
e-mail: oakbrookhouse@btinternet.com   website: www.oakbrookhouse.co.uk

WHITE LODGE FARM COTTAGES, HINGHAM NR9 4LY (01953 850435 or 07768 156680). Set in the heart of the Norfolk countryside, but within walking distance of the beautiful village of Hingham, the three cottages offer comfort and modern convenience all year round for weekend, midweek or longer stays. Dogs very welcome. EnjoyEngland ★★★★★ Gold Award.
e-mail: fhgp@whitelodgefarmcottages.co.uk   www.whitelodgefarmcottages.co.uk

Old Hunstanton

Coastal resort on the Wash 14 miles NE of King's Lynn.

ST CRISPINS, OLD HUNSTANTON (01485 534036). Near sandy beach, golf course; few miles from Norfolk attractions. Short notice bargain breaks early/late season. Linen provided. Pets welcome. [One or two dogs £15 per week]
e-mail: st.crispins@btinternet.com

Thornham

Village 4 miles east of Hunstanton. Site of Roman signal station.

THE LIFEBOAT INN, SHIP LANE, THORNHAM PE36 6LT (01485 512236; Fax: 01485 512323). A welcome sight for the weary traveller for centuries. Dogs welcome. Restaurant (one AA rosette). Bird watching and walking along miles of open beaches. Please ring for brochure and tariff. [Pets £8 per week.]
e-mail: lifeboatinn@maypolehotels.com   website: www.maypolehotels.com

---

Visit the FHG website
www.holidayguides.com
for details of the wide choice of accommodation featured in the full range of FHG titles

Thorpe Market

Village 4 miles south of Cromer.

GREEN FARM HOTEL AND RESTAURANT, THORPE MARKET, NORTH WALSHAM, NORTH NORFOLK NR11 8TH (01263 833602; Fax: 01263 833163). 16th Century flint-faced farmhouse inn. 20 antique style en suite bedrooms. Telephone for details of our special breaks available all year. [Pets £7.50 per night]
e-mail: grfarmh@aol.com website: www.greenfarmhotel.co.uk

POPPYLAND TOURING PARK & HOLIDAY COTTAGE, THE GREEN, THORPE MARKET NR11 8AJ (01263 833219). Ideal for guests who want to relax or explore local area. Puddleduck Cottage (sleeps 2) has private enclosed garden. Touring park (adults only) in landscaped gardens surrounded by trees. Excellent food nearby. [🐕]
e-mail: poppylandpb@aol.co.uk website: www.poppyland.com

Thurne

Idyllic Broadland village. Great Yarmouth 10 miles.

HEDERA HOUSE AND PLANTATION BUNGALOWS, THURNE NR29 3BU (01692 670242 or 01493 844568). Adjacent river, seven bedroomed farmhouse, 10 competitively priced bungalows in peaceful gardens. Outdoor heated pool. Enjoy boating, fishing, walking, touring, nearby golf, sandy beaches and popular resorts. [Pets £20 per week]
website: www.hederahouse.co.uk

Weybourne

Located in an Area of Outstanding Natural Beauty and part of the Heritage Coastline. Sheringham and Holt 4 miles.

BOLDING WAY HOLIDAYS, THE BARN, BOLDING WAY, WEYBOURNE, HOLT NR25 7SW (01263 588566). Biddles Cottage (SC), sleeps 2; Tack Room (room only), sleeps 2. In an Area of Outstanding Natural Beauty and on the Heritage Coast. Well behaved pets welcome. Both with fenced gardens. Use of owners' hot tub. Excellent local walks. [🐕]
e-mail: holidays@boldingway.co.uk website: www.boldingway.co.uk

Winterton-on-Sea

Good sands and bathing. Great Yarmouth 8 miles.

WINTERTON HOLIDAYS, WINTERTON-ON-SEA. Privately owned one and two-bedroom chalets, furnished and equipped to a high standard, on picturesque park few minutes' walk from sea. Dogs allowed on beach all year. Ideal for quiet, relaxing break and for exploring Broads, coast, Norwich. Village has pub, restaurant and shops. MRS JUNE HUDSON, 42 LARK WAY, BRADWELL, GREAT YARMOUTH NR31 8SB (01493 444370). [Pets £4 per night, £20 per week]
website: www.wintertonholidays.com

WINTERTON VALLEY HOLIDAYS. A selection of modern superior fully appointed holiday chalets in a choice of locations near Great Yarmouth. Enjoy panoramic views from WINTERTON, a quiet and picturesque 35-acre estate, while CALIFORNIA has all the usual amenities, with free entry to the pool and clubhouse. Pets are very welcome at both sites. For colour brochure: 15 KINGSTON AVENUE, CAISTER-ON-SEA NR30 5ET (01493 377175).
website: www.wintertonvalleyholidays.co.uk

FISHERMANS RETURN, THE LANE, WINTERTON-ON-SEA NR29 4BN (01493 393305). 300-year-old brick and flint pub, just a few minutes' stroll from sandy beaches and beautiful walks. Excellent food, simple bar snacks and good choice of real ales and fine wines. B&B available in 3 tastefully furnished en suite double bedrooms.
e-mail: fishermansreturn@yahoo.com website: www.fishermans-return.com

Suffolk

EAST OF ENGLAND 233

Aldeburgh, Bungay, Bury St Edmunds, Hadleigh

WENTWORTH HOTEL
WENTWORTH ROAD, ALDEBURGH, SUFFOLK IP15 5BD

Facing the sea, the Wentworth Hotel has the comfort and style of a country house. 35 bedrooms, many with sea views, two comfortable lounges with open fires and antique furniture, provide ample space to relax. The restaurant serves a variety of fresh produce, including local seafood, and a light lunch can be chosen from the bar menu and eaten "al fresco" in the terrace garden. There are many walks, some commencing from the Hotel. Aldeburgh is the perfect touring centre for East Anglia.

AA ★★★
Two Rosettes
87%

For a reservation, please Telephone 01728 452312 or Fax: 01728 454343
e-mail: stay@wentworth-aldeburgh.co.uk • www.wentworth-aldeburgh.com

ETC
Silver Award

The Old Rectory Flixton • Self-catering Holiday Cottages

4 one-bedroom self-catering holiday cottages in 7 acres on Suffolk/Norfolk border. Decorated and furnished to high standard. Well behaved dogs welcome. Contact: Jeannie and Keith Parker.
The Old Rectory, Abbey Road, Flixton, Suffolk NR35 1NL • Tel: 01986 893133
e-mail: enquiries@oldrectorycottagesflixton.co.uk • www.oldrectorycottagesflixton.co.uk

• Annie's Cottage • Suffolk •

The old wing of Hill Farm farmhouse. Peaceful, rural location in open countryside. 2 bedrooms, sleeps 4. Large lounge/dining room with woodburning stove. Central heating. Linen and towels provided. Electricity incl. Enclosed private garden.
e-mail: lynne@hillfarmholidays.com • www.hillfarmholidays.com
Contact Lynne Morton, Hill Farm Holidays, Ilketshall St John, Beccles, Suffolk NR34 8JE • Tel: 01986 781240

Earsham Park Farm   ETC/AA ★★★★ Gold Award

Superb Victorian property overlooking open countryside. Bedrooms attractively furnished; excellent breakfasts. Superb facilities for pets.
01986 892180 • www.earsham-parkfarm.co.uk
Old Railway Road, Earsham, Bungay NR35 2AQ

Rede Hall Farm Park

Rede Hall Farm, Rede, Bury St Edmunds IP29 4UG • Tel: 01284 850695 • Fax: 01284 850345
Two well equipped cottages with loads of Suffolk character and charm on moated mixed farm. Ideal for touring East Anglia and the Suffolk coast. Superb local pubs with good food. Open all year. Totally non-smoking. Hot Tub Spa available for exclusive use (incl). Oil-fired central heating • Electric cooker, microwave, washer/dryer, dishwasher • TV with DVD/VCR, hi-fi • Children's play area • BBQ with patio furniture • Well behaved dogs welcome
www.redehallfarmpark.co.uk • Livery for horses on request. ETC ★★★★ e-mail: chris@redehallfarmpark.co.uk

AA

16th century heavily beamed Tudor Hall set in 7 acres of perfect dog walks. Individually furnished en suite bedrooms; renowned restaurant; relaxing inglenook fires.

enquiries@ravenwoodhall.co.uk
www.ravenwoodhall.co.uk

Ravenwood Hall
Country Hotel and Restaurant

ROUGHAM, BURY ST EDMUNDS IP30 9JA
Tel: 01359 270345 • Fax: 01359 270788
Easy access from A14, Junction 45

Edge Hall   www.edgehall.co.uk
2 HIGH STREET, HADLEIGH IP7 5AP • 01473 822458

Truffles invites you to stay in her master's comfortable lodge house. Well behaved owners will enjoy the perfect walks and super breakfasts. Double/twin £85 per night, Single £57.50. Self-catering also available.   ETC/AA ★★★★★

234 EAST OF ENGLAND — Suffolk

Ipswich, Kessingland, Laxfield, Long Melford

DAMERONS FARM HOLIDAYS

Tel: 01473 832454 or 07881 824083

Five cottages, each sleeping 1-6, converted from an Old Granary and milking parlour into tasteful, modern accommodation. The owners, Wayne & Sue Leggett, guarantee a warm Suffolk welcome. Step out of your cottage and into beautiful countryside away from the hustle and bustle. The Old Dairy has a high level of accessibility for disabled visitors and three of the other cottages have ground floor bedrooms and bathrooms. Children (and the young at heart) will enjoy the 24' x 15' games room with table tennis, pool and table football and there is a large outdoor grass play area. Short breaks are offered out of high season. Less than 2 hours from London and 1 hour from Stansted Airport.

Henley, Ipswich IP6 0RU • www.dameronsfarmholidays.co.uk

Knights Holiday Homes at Kessingland

Kessingland is the most easterly village in the United Kingdom. *First to greet the sun.* Once known as the richest village in England because of its prolific fishing. Now known for its peaceful, pleasant surroundings, its spacious beach and a place where you can relax and watch the boats sail by. Or perhaps you would like to visit the Suffolk Wildlife Park or wine and dine at the local pubs and restaurants. There is a good local bus service.

Chalets and Holiday Homes: Accommodation for 1-6 persons
- Full size cooker • Colour Television • Parking
- Refrigerator • Video Recorder • Microwave
- Bed Linen Supplied • Electricity • Fully equipped Kitchen

Lots to see and do: • Horse Racing • Power Boat Racing
• Golf • Fishing • Bowls • Tennis • Coach Trips • Boating
• Art & Film Settings • Concert Hall & Art Centre • Theme Parks

22 Harrop Dale, Carlton Colville, Lowestoft, Suffolk NR33 8UY
FREEPHONE 0800 269067
e-mail : info@knightsholidays.co.uk • www.knightsholidays.co.uk

Lodge Cottage, Laxfield, Suffolk

Pretty 16C thatched cottage retaining some fine period features. Sleeps 4. Pets welcome. Fenced garden. One mile from village. 30 minutes to Southwold and coast. Rural, quiet and relaxing. For brochure phone Jane:
01986 798830 or 07788853884 or e-mail: janebrewer@ukonline.co.uk

THE BLACK LION HOTEL & RESTAURANT
The Green, Long Melford CO10 9DN • Tel:01787 312356
e-mail: enquiries@blacklionhotel.com • www.blacklionhotel.net

• The Georgian Black Lion Hotel overlooks the famous green and two of Suffolk's finest stately homes.
• Voted Suffolk's best restaurant • Lunches, Dinners, Teas.
• 10 en suite bedrooms refurbished to luxury status.
• Idyllic dog walks and lots of attention from dog-loving staff.

FHG Guides

publish a large range of well-known accommodation guides.
We will be happy to send you details or you can use the order form
at the back of this book.

Suffolk

EAST OF ENGLAND

Nayland, Orford, Saxmundham

Gladwins Farm — Cottages in Constable Country

Set in 22 acres of rolling Suffolk countryside, Gladwins Farm offers a selection of accommodation. Guests staying in any of our 4★ or 5★ self-catering cottages (sleeping 2-8) can enjoy our heated indoor pool, sauna, hot tub, the hard tennis court and playground. There is coarse fishing in our lake and farm animals to entertain the children. Pets welcome in most cottages and loads of dog walking! Riding, golf and beach within easy reach. *On-line booking through our website*,

If a quiet holiday in a charming area of Olde England is on your agenda, call Pauline or Robert Dossor on 01206 262261 and arrange a memorable stay. See us on the internet at www.gladwinsfarm.co.uk or call for our colour brochure and DVD. Winners, Suffolk Self-Catering Holiday of the Year 2007.

e-mail: gladwinsfarm@aol.com
Gladwins Farm, Harper's Hill, Nayland, Suffolk CO6 4NU

The Crown and Castle

Owned by Ruth Watson, presenter of Channel 4's Country House Rescue, the Crown and Castle is in the peaceful village of Orford on the Suffolk coast. It has 19 en suite bedrooms and a lively restaurant, the Trinity, which has been awarded 2 AA Rosettes and a Michelin bib gourmand for its good, honest food. It also has a doggie table where canine guests can join their owners. There are many woodland and coastal walks nearby, as well as Snape Maltings (home to the Aldeburgh Festival), Sutton Hoo, Minsmere and the delightful seaside town of Southwold to explore.

info@crownandcastle.co.uk
www.crownandcastle.co.uk
tel: 01394 450205

Set well back from the main road in a quiet location
- Always a warm welcome
- Ideal for walking/cycling and the Heritage Coast
- Vintage transport available free for longer stays
- Two double and one family room with en suite/ private bathrooms • Open all year.

SWEFFLING HALL FARM
Sweffling, Saxmundham IP17 2B
www.swefflinghallfarm.co.uk
Tel & Fax: 01728 663644 • e-mail: stephen.mann@unicombox.com

Aldeburgh

Coastal town 6 miles south-east of Saxmundham. Annual music festival at Snape Maltings.

WENTWORTH HOTEL, ALDEBURGH IP15 5BD (01728 452312). Country House Hotel overlooking the sea. Immediate access to the beach and walks. Two comfortable lounges with log fires and antique furniture. Refurbished bedrooms with all facilities and many with sea views. Restaurant specialises in fresh produce and sea food. ETC Silver Award. AA ★★★ Two Rosettes. [Pets £2 per day]
e-mail: stay@wentworth-aldeburgh.co.uk   website: www.wentworth-aldeburgh.com

Bungay

Attractive town in the Waveney Valley, with a wealth of historic sites. Town centre has a Roman well, a Saxon church, and the remains of a Norman castle and Benedictine priory. 14 miles south east of Norwich.

JEANNIE AND KEITH PARKER, THE OLD RECTORY, ABBEY ROAD, FLIXTON NR35 1NL (01986 893133). 4 one-bedroom self-catering holiday cottages in 7 acres on Suffolk/Norfolk border. Decorated and furnished to high standard. Well behaved dogs welcome. Enjoy England ★★★★. [🐾]
e-mail: enquiries@oldrectorycottagesflixton.co.uk website: www.oldrectorycottagesflixton.co.uk

ANNIE'S COTTAGE, SUFFOLK. Peaceful, rural location in open countryside. 2 bedrooms, sleeps 4. Large lounge/dining room, woodburning stove. Linen and towels provided. Electricity included. Enclosed private garden. Contact: LYNNE MORTON, HILL FARM HOLIDAYS, ILKETSHALL ST JOHN, BECCLES NR34 8JE (01986 781240). [🐾]
e-mail: lynne@hillfarmholidays.com   website: www.hillfarmholidays.com

EARSHAM PARK FARM, OLD RAILWAY ROAD, EARSHAM, BUNGAY NR35 2AQ (01986 892180). Superb Victorian property overlooking open countryside. Bedrooms attractively furnished; excellent breakfasts. All rooms en suite. ETC/AA ★★★★ Gold Award. [Pets £5 per night]
website: www.earsham-parkfarm.co.uk

Bury St Edmunds

This prosperous market town on the River Lark lies 28 miles east of Cambridge.

REDE HALL FARM PARK, REDE, BURY ST EDMUNDS IP29 4UG (01284 850695; Fax: 01284 850345). Two well equipped cottages, ideal for touring East Anglia and the coast. Totally non-smoking. Hot Tub Spa available for exclusive use (inclusive). Well behaved dogs welcome. ETC ★★★★ [🐾 ⌂]
e-mail: chris@redehallfarmpark.co.uk   website: www.redehallfarmpark.co.uk

RAVENWOOD HALL COUNTRY HOUSE HOTEL AND RESTAURANT, ROUGHAM, BURY ST EDMUNDS IP30 9JA (01359 270345; Fax: 01359 270788). 16th century heavily beamed Tudor Hall set in seven acres of perfect dog walks. Individually furnished en suite bedrooms; renowned restaurant; relaxing inglenook fires. AA ★★★, AA 2 Rosettes. [🐾 pw!]
e-mail: enquiries@ravenwoodhall.co.uk   website: www.ravenwoodhall.co.uk

Hadleigh

Historic town on River Brett with several buildings of interest including unusual 14th century church. Bury St Edmunds 20 miles, Colchester 14, Sudbury 11, Ipswich 10.

EDGE HALL, 2 HIGH STREET, HADLEIGH IP7 5AP (01473 822458). Truffles invites you to stay in her master's comfortable lodge house. Well behaved owners will enjoy the perfect walks and super breakfasts. Twin/double £85 per night, single £57.50. Self-catering also available. ETC/AA ★★★★★, ETC Silver Award. [Pets £5 per stay]
e-mail: r.rolfe@edgehall.co.uk   website: www.edgehall.co.uk

Ipswich

County town and port 66 miles NE of London.

WAYNE & SUE LEGGETT, DAMERONS FARM HOLIDAYS, HENLEY, IPSWICH IP6 0RU (01473 832454 or 07881 824083). Five cottages, each sleeping 1-6. The Old Dairy has a high level of accessibility for disabled visitors; three others have ground floor bedrooms and bathrooms. Games room with table tennis, pool and table football. Short Breaks out of season.
website: www.dameronsfarmholidays.co.uk

Suffolk

Kessingland

Little seaside place with expansive beach, safe bathing, wildlife park, lake fishing. To the south is Benacre Broad, a beauty spot. Norwich 26 miles, Adleburgh 23, Lowestoft 5.

Comfortable well-equipped bungalow on lawned site overlooking beach, next to Heritage Coast. Panoramic sea views. Easy beach access. Unspoiled walking area. ETC ★★ MRS L.G. SAUNDERS, 159 THE STREET, ROCKLAND ST MARY, NORWICH NR14 7HL (01508 538340). [Pets £10 per week].

Quality seaside bungalows in lawned surrounds overlooking the sea. Open all year, fully eqipped. Sleep 1/6. Direct access to award-winning beach. Parking Pets very welcome. APPLY– KNIGHTS HOLIDAY HOMES, 22 HARROP DALE, CARLTON COLVILLE, LOWESTOFT, SUFFOLK NR33 8UY (FREEPHONE 0800 269067). [🐕]
e-mail: info@knightsholidays.co.uk   website: www.knightsholidays.co.uk

Laxfield

Village 6 miles North of Framlingham.

LODGE COTTAGE, LAXFIELD. Pretty 16C thatched cottage retaining some fine period features. Sleeps 4. Pets welcome. Fenced garden. One mile from village. 30 minutes to Southwold and coast. Rural, quiet and relaxing. ETC ★★★★. For brochure phone: MRS JANE BREWER, LODGE COTTAGE, LAXFIELD ROAD, CRATFIELD, HALESWORTH IP19 0QG (01986 798830 or 07788853884). [Pets £10 per week].
e-mail: janebrewer@ukonline.co.uk

Long Melford

Village in the beautiful countryside of Suffolk, in the River Stour valley, just north of Sudbury, beside the A314 road to Bury St Edmunds.

THE BLACK LION HOTEL & RESTAURANT, THE GREEN, LONG MELFORD CO10 9DN (01787 312356). The Georgian Black Lion Hotel overlooks the famous green, and the cosy bar and restaurant offer a range of innovative dishes. 10 en suite bedrooms refurbished to luxury status. Idyllic dog walks. [🐕]
e-mail: enquiries@blacklionhotel.net   website: www.blacklionhotel.net

Nayland

Small town on River Stour, 6 miles north of Colchester.

GLADWINS FARM, HARPER'S HILL, NAYLAND CO6 4NU (01206 262261). Self-catering cottages (sleep 2-8) set in 22 acres of Suffolk countryside. Indoor heated pool, sauna, hot tub, tennis court and playground. Loads of dog walking. [Pets £20 per week] ETC ★★★★/★★★★★.
e-mail: gladwinsfarm@aol.com   website: www.gladwinsfarm.co.uk

Orford

Village on River Ore, 9 miles east of Woodbridge.

THE CROWN AND CASTLE, ORFORD, WOODBRIDGE IP12 2LJ (01394 450205). Comfortable and very dog-friendly hotel situated close to 12th century castle in historic and unspoilt village of Orford. Honest good food served in award-winning Trinity Restaurant. [Pets £5 per night]
e-mail: info@crownandcastle.co.uk   website: www.crownandcastle.co.uk

Saxmundham

Small town 18 miles NE of Ipswich.

SWEFFLING HALL FARM, SWEFFLING, SAXMUNDHAM IP17 2BT (Tel & Fax: 01728 663644). In a quiet location. One double and one family room with en suite/private bathrooms. Ideal for walking/cycling and Heritage Coast. Open all year. Always a warm welcome. [pw! 🐕 ⌂]
e-mail: stephen.mann@unicombox.com   website: www.swefflinghallfarm.co.uk

perfect cottage holidays

Enjoy the beauty of The Peak District and Derbyshire Dales in a luxurious, warm and comfortable cottage.

We have 250 quality, self-catering properties available, we surely have the perfect cottage to suit your holiday needs!

Brochure and bookings available online or by telephone

peakcottages.com
0844 770 8924

Peak Cottages

PEAK COTTAGES (0844 770 8924). Quality self-catering accommodation in the Derbyshire Dales and Peaks. Whether you are a walker, climber, potholer, antiquarian, historian, naturalist, gardener or sportsman – Derbyshire has it all. Pets welcome in many. Telephone for colour brochure. [Pets £12 per week.]
website: www.peakcottages.com

Derbyshire
Ashbourne, Belper

THROWLEY HALL FARM • ILAM, ASHBOURNE DE6 2BB (01538 308202/308243)
Self-catering accommodation in farmhouse for up to 12 and cottages for five and seven people (ETC ★★★★). Also Bed and Breakfast in farmhouse (ETC ★★★★). Central heating, en suite rooms. No Smoking. TV, tea/coffee facilities in rooms. Children and pets welcome. Near Alton Towers and stately homes.
www.throwleyhallfarm.co.uk • e-mail: throwleyhall@btinternet.com

DOG & PARTRIDGE
· COUNTRY INN ·

Mary and Martin Stelfox welcome you to a family-run 17th century Inn and Motel set in five acres, five miles from Alton Towers and close to Dovedale and Ashbourne. We specialise in family breaks, and special diets and vegetarians are catered for. All rooms have private bathrooms, colour TV, direct-dial telephone, tea-making facilities and baby listening service. Ideal for touring Stoke Potteries, Derbyshire Dales and Staffordshire Moorlands. Open Christmas and New Year. 'Staffs Good Food Winners 2003/2004'.

Restaurant open all day, non-residents welcome
e-mail: info@dogandpartridge.co.uk
Tel: 01335 343183 • www.dogandpartridge.co.uk
Swinscoe, Ashbourne DE6 2HS

Fleet Cottage • Belper, Derbyshire • enjoyEngland ★★★★
Renovated 18th century Grade II listed 2 bedroomed cottage, beamed throughout. Ideal base for the Peak District. Lovely walks and views.
Fleet Cottage, 66 The Fleet, Belper DE56 1NW Tel: 01773 823240
• Mobile: 0786 626 5446 • E-mail: info@thefleetcottage.co.uk
www.thefleetcottage.co.uk

Derbyshire

THE MIDLANDS 239

Burnaston, Buxton, Hope Valley, Matlock

Self contained in Derbyshire

Renovated Victorian stables with 7 self-contained en-suite apartments sleeping 4-5. Secure Dog-runs and optional Kennels
Grassy Lane, Burnaston, Derbyshire DE65 6LN Tel: 01332 510000

Stables Lodge

Overnight Accommodation · Holiday Accommodation · Weekend Breaks   www.stableslodge.co.uk

---

ALISON PARK HOTEL
3 Temple Road, Buxton SK17 9BA

Situated close to the Pavilion Gardens and within a few minutes' walk of the Opera House. • 17 bedrooms, all with either en suite or private bathroom. • Full English or Continental breakfast, full dinner menu and an extensive wine list; lunches, bar meals & dinner available daily. • Vegetarian and special diets catered for. • Lounge with colour TV. • All bedrooms have tea & coffee makers, colour TV etc. • Wheelchair ramp access. • Ground floor bedrooms. • Lift to all floors. • Conference facilities. • Licensed.

Tel: 01298 22473 • Fax: 01298 72709 • e-mail: reservations@alison-park-hotel.co.uk
www.alison-park-hotel.co.uk

The Devonshire Arms Peak Forest, Near Buxton, Derbyshire SK17 8EJ
Traditional inn in the heart of the Peak District. Close to all main attractions. Excellent walking country. All rooms refurbished to a high standard. En suite, TV, tea/coffee facilities. Excellent meals and traditional ales. Warm welcome to all. Dogs free. Prices from £32.50.

ETC ★★★   01298 23875 • lesleywoodward@tiscali.co.uk • www.devarms.com

---

PRIORY LEA HOLIDAY FLATS. Beautiful situation adjoining woodland walks and meadows. Cleanliness assured; comfortably furnished and well-equipped. Colour TV. Bed linen available. Full central heating. Sleep 2/6. Ample private parking. Close to Poole's Cavern Country Park. Brochure available from resident owner. Open all year. Terms from £115 to £295. Short Breaks available. ETC ★★/★★★.
Mrs Gill Taylor, 50 White Knowle Road, Buxton SK17 9NH • Tel: 01298 23737
e-mail: priorylea@hotmail.com • www.priorylea.co.uk

THE LITTLE JOHN HOTEL
Station Road, Hathersage
Hope Valley
Derbyshire S32 1DD
Tel: 01433 650225

This handsome stone building which dates from the 19th century is popular with locals and visitors alike. It has won awards for its ale and carries a good selection of refreshments. This is just the place for a relaxing drink or meal after a day walking on the high moors. Home-cooked food is served in the bar, and there are two plasma screen TVs. Accommodation is available in six en suite rooms and three charming cottages

Owner Stephanie Bushell offers all guests a warm welcome.

e-mail: littlejohnhotel@btconnect.com
www.littlejohnhotel.co.uk

AA **ALISON HOUSE HOTEL • Cromford, Derbyshire**
Georgian-style house set in the Derwent Valley World Heritage site. Beautiful gardens in a peaceful setting. 16 en suite rooms. Bar, lounge and restaurant.
Alison House, Intake Lane, Cromford, Matlock, Derbyshire DE4 3RH
Tel: 01629 822211 • Fax: 01629 822316 • e-mail: info@alison-house-hotel.co.uk
• www.alison-house-hotel.co.uk • *Pets Stay Free!*

THE MIDLANDS — Derbyshire

Peak District National Park

Welyarde ❖ Dogs – Bring your parents!

A delightful cottage with three bedrooms, with a beautiful landscaped garden. Sleeps 6, occasionally 8. We truly welcome dogs, and at the far end of the garden is **The Old Piggery** – an equally dog friendly establishment with fabulous views.
Paul Harrison and Carrie Warr, Devonshire House, High Street, Tideswell SK17 8LB
01298 872285 • e-mail: info@oldpiggery.co.uk • www.welyarde.co.uk

BIGGIN HALL

Tranquilly set 1000ft up in the White Peak District National Park, 17th century Grade II* Listed Biggin Hall – a country house hotel of immense character and charm where guests experience the full benefits of the legendary Biggin Air – has been sympathetically restored, keeping its character while giving house room to contemporary comforts. Rooms are centrally heated with bathrooms en suite, colour television, tea-making facilities, silent fridge and telephone. Those in the main house have stone arched mullioned windows, others are in converted 18th century outbuildings. Centrally situated for stately homes and for exploring the natural beauty of the area. Return at the end of the day to enjoy your freshly cooked dinner alongside log fires and personally selected wines.

Well behaved pets are welcome by prior arrangement

**Biggin-by-Hartington, Buxton, Derbyshire SK17 0DH
Tel: 01298 84451
www.bigginhall.co.uk**

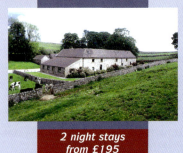

2 night stays from £195

Wheeldon Trees Farm
Earl Sterndale, Buxton SK17 0AA
Tel: 01298 83219

Relax and unwind in our unique award-winning barn conversion. Eight cosy, superbly equipped ★★★★ holiday cottages sleeping 2-5; sleeps 28 in total. Dogs and children welcome. Open all year.
stay@wheeldontreesfarm.co.uk
www.wheeldontreesfarm.co.uk

Please mention **Pets Welcome!** when making enquiries about accommodation featured in these pages

Derbyshire

THE MIDLANDS 241

Ashbourne

Market town on River Henmore, close to its junction with River Dove. Several interesting old buildings. Birmingham 42 miles, Nottingham 29, Derby 13.

MR & MRS LENNARD, WINDLEHILL FARM, SUTTON ON THE HILL, ASHBOURNE DE6 5JH (Tel & Fax: 01283 732377). Converted beamed barns on small organic farm - the Chop House sleeps 6 and has a fenced garden, the Hayloft sleeps 2 and is a first floor apartment. Well behaved pets welcome. ETC ★★★★ [pw! Pets £10 per week minimum]
e-mail: windlehill@btinternet.com   website: www.windlehill.btinternet.co.uk

MRS M.A. RICHARDSON, THROWLEY HALL FARM, ILAM, ASHBOURNE DE6 2BB (01538 308202/308243). Self-catering accommodation in farmhouse for up to 12 and cottages for five and seven people. Also Bed and Breakfast in farmhouse. Central heating, en suite rooms, TV, tea/coffee facilities in rooms. No smoking. Children and pets welcome. Near Alton Towers and stately homes. ETC ★★★★. [Pets £5 per week.]
e-mail: throwleyhall@btinternet.com   website: www.throwleyhallfarm.co.uk

MRS M.M. STELFOX, DOG AND PARTRIDGE COUNTRY INN, SWINSCOE, ASHBOURNE DE6 2HS (01335 343183). 17th century Inn offering ideal holiday accommodation. Many leisure activities available. All bedrooms with washbasins, colour TV, telephone and private facilities. ETC/AA ★★ [⛔, pw!]
e-mail: info@dogandpartridge.co.uk   website: www.dogandpartridge.co.uk

Belper

Town 7 miles North of Derby.

FLEET COTTAGE, 66 THE FLEET BELPER DE56 1NW (Tel: 01773 823240; Mobile: 0786 626 5446). Renovated 18th century Grade II listed 2 bedroomed cottage, beamed throughout. Ideal base for the Peak District. Lovely walks and views. ETC ★★★★ [⛔].
e-mail: info@thefleetcottage.co.uk   website: www.thefleetcottage.co.uk

Burnaston

Village 5 miles SW of Derby.

STABLES LODGE, GRASSY LANE, BURNASTON DE65 6LN (01332 510000). Renovated stables with seven self-contained en suite self-catering apartments, sleeping 4-5. Dog runs and optional kennels. Overnight accommodation and weekend breaks also available. [⛔ 🏠]
website: www.stableslodge.co.uk

Buxton

Well-known spa and centre for the Peak District. Beautiful scenery and good sporting amenities. Leeds 50 miles, Matlock 20, Macclesfield 12.

ALISON PARK HOTEL, 3 TEMPLE ROAD, BUXTON SK17 9BA (01298 22473; Fax: 01298 72709). Situated close to the Pavilion Gardens and Opera House. 17 bedrooms, all en suite or private bathroom. Lunches, bar meals and dinner available daily. Wheelchair ramp access; ground floor bedrooms. Licensed. ETC ★★ [⛔]
e-mail: reservations@alison-park-hotel.co.uk   website: www.alison-park-hotel.co.uk

THE DEVONSHIRE ARMS, PEAK FOREST, NEAR BUXTON SK17 8EJ (01298 23875) Situated in a village location in the heart of the Peak District. All rooms en suite with tea/coffee and colour TV. Meals served every day. Excellent walking area. ETC ★★★ [⛔]
e-mail: lesleywoodward@tiscali.co.uk   website: www.devarms.com

PRIORY LEA HOLIDAY FLATS. Close to Poole's Cavern Country Park. Fully equipped. Full central heating. Sleep 2/6. Cleanliness assured. Terms from £115-£295. Open all year. Short Breaks available. ETC ★★/★★★. MRS GILL TAYLOR, 50 WHITE KNOWLE ROAD, BUXTON SK17 9NH (01298 23737). [pw! Pets £2 per night.]
e-mail: priorylea@hotmail.co.uk   website: www.priorylea.co.uk

THE MIDLANDS — Derbyshire

Hope Valley

Large valley in Peak District, 4 miles from Hathersage.

THE LITTLE JOHN HOTEL, STATION ROAD, HATHERSAGE, HOPE VALLEY S32 1DD (01433 650225). Ideal for a relaxing drink or meal after walking the high moors. Popular local pub with award-winning ales and good selection of refreshments. Home cooked food. Six en suite rooms and three charming cottages [🐕].
e-mail: littlejohnhotel@btconnect.com   website: www.littlejohnhotel.co.uk

Matlock

County town of Derbyshire, situated on a bend of the River Derwent.

ALISON HOUSE, INTAKE LANE, CROMFORD, MATLOCK DE4 3RH (01629 822211; Fax: 01629 822316). Georgian-style house set in the Derwent Valley World Heritage site. Beautiful gardens in a peaceful setting. 16 en suite rooms. Bar, lounge and restaurant. AA ★★★★ [pw! 🐕].
e-mail: info@alison-house-hotel.co.uk   website: www.alison-house-hotel.co.uk

Peak District National Park

A green and unspoilt area at the southern end of the Pennines, covering 555 square miles.

WELYARDE. A delightful single cottage with three bedrooms, with a beautiful landscaped garden. Sleeps 6, occasionally 8. We truly welcome dogs. And THE OLD PIGGERY – an equally dog friendly establishment with fabulous views. For details contact: PAUL HARRISON AND CARRIE WARR, DEVONSHIRE HOUSE, HIGH STREET, TIDESWELL SK17 8LB (01298 872285).
e-mail: info@oldpiggery.co.uk   website: www.welyarde.co.uk

BIGGIN HALL, PEAK PARK (01298 84451). Close Dove Dale. 17th century hall sympathetically restored. Bathrooms en suite, log fires, C/H comfort, warmth and quiet. Fresh home cooking. Beautiful uncrowded footpaths and cycle trails. ETC ★★[🐕]
website: www.bigginhall.co.uk

WHEELDON TREES FARM, EARL STERNDALE, BUXTON SK17 0AA (01298 83219). Relax and unwind with your dog(s) in our unique award-winning barn conversion. Eight cosy, superbly equipped holiday cottages sleeping 2-5 (total 28). ETC ★★★★ [pw! 🐕]
e-mail: stay@wheeldontreesfarm.co.uk   website: www.wheeldontreesfarm.co.uk

---

Other specialised holiday guides from FHG

PUBS & INNS OF BRITAIN • **COUNTRY HOTELS** OF BRITAIN
WEEKEND & SHORT BREAK HOLIDAYS IN BRITAIN
THE GOLF GUIDE WHERE TO PLAY, WHERE TO STAY
500 GREAT PLACES TO STAY • **SELF-CATERING HOLIDAYS** IN BRITAIN
BED & BREAKFAST STOPS • **CARAVAN & CAMPING HOLIDAYS**
FAMILY BREAKS IN BRITAIN

Published annually: available in all good bookshops or direct from the publisher:
FHG Guides, Abbey Mill Business Centre, Seedhill, Paisley PA1 1TJ
Tel: 0141 887 0428 • Fax: 0141 889 7204
e-mail: admin@fhguides.co.uk • www.holidayguides.com

Herefordshire

THE MIDLANDS

Hereford, Kington, Ledbury, Much Cowarne, Ross-on-Wye

Sink Green Farm

Rotherwas, Hereford HR2 6LE
Tel: 01432 870223

16th century farmhouse overlooking picturesque Wye Valley. En suite rooms, one four-poster. Extensive garden with summer house and hot tub. Fishing. Prices from £32 per person • Children welcome • Pets by arrangement
e-mail: enquiries@sinkgreenfarm.co.uk • www.sinkgreenfarm.co.uk

The Rock Cottage — Huntington, Kington

Secluded, stone-built, character cottage overlooking picturesque farm and woodlands near Offa's Dyke footpath. Ideal for touring, birdwatching, golf and pony trekking. Hay-on-Wye and Black Mountains 20 minutes. Sleeps 4/6. Two bedrooms, fully equipped kitchen, lounge with wood-burner. Central Heating. Spacious garden with patio area. Children and pets welcome.
Details from Mrs C. Williams, Radnor's End, Huntington, Kington HR5 3NZ
Tel: 01544 370289   www.the-rock-cottage.co.uk

Church Farm Coddington, Ledbury HR8 1JJ
Tel: 01531 640271 • Mobile: 07861 358549

Relax and enjoy our lovely 16th century Listed timber framed farmhouse in the quiet hamlet of Coddington. The market town of Ledbury is 4 miles away, the Malvern Hills, with all their beautiful walks, 4 miles. Hereford, Worcester, Gloucester and Ross-on-Wye are all a half-hour drive, 3 Counties Showground 15 minutes. We are a working farm with a lovely garden and rural views. Immediate access to wonderful walks through peaceful country lanes and farmland. We offer a combination of en suite and shared bathroom accommodation. Comfortable lounge with TV and log fires on chilly evenings in the inglenook fireplace. Ample car parking space. Aga-cooked breakfast. Everything homemade where possible. Over 25 years' experience caring for guests, with a large number of repeat bookings. A warm welcome is assured in a quiet, relaxed atmosphere. B&B from £37pppn double.

www.dexta.co.uk

Relax, unwind and enjoy your holiday. Please phone Jane for further information.

Cowarne Hall Cottages

Much Cowarne, Herefordshire HR7 4JQ

Tel: 01432 820317 • E-mail: rm@cowarnehall.co.uk • www.cowarnehall.co.uk

Historic, comfortable cottages 'twixt the Malvern Hills and Wye Valley. In a quiet rural location with wonderful views of fields and hills. Large garden with access to lanes and footpaths. Private enclosed patios. Convenient for nearby towns and attractions. Free colour brochure and 'planner pack'. Richard and Margaret Bradbury.

LEA HOUSE BED & BREAKFAST
near the Forest of Dean and the Wye Valley.

Our 16th Century home is beautifully refurbished with antiques, an inglenook fireplace and loads of beams. Spacious bedrooms with kingsize or twin beds and en suite bathrooms with fluffy towels. AA award-winning breakfasts and dinners with all home-made and local produce. The area is a doggy paradise – walks galore.
Footpath and fields 20yds away for all your dog's needs.
Free Wi-Fi throughout.

Lea, Ross-on-Wye HR9 7JZ
Tel: 01989 750652
e-mail: enquiries@leahouse.co.uk
www.leahouse.co.uk

See guests' comments on www.tripadvisor.com
From £32.50pppn. Dogs welcome @ £7.50 per stay.

FHG Guides

publish a large range of well-known accommodation guides.
We will be happy to send you details or you can use the order form at the back of this book.

Great Malvern

The historical centre of the town of Malvern, famous for its large priory, dating from the 11thC.

WHITEWELLS FARM COTTAGES, RIDGEWAY CROSS, NEAR MALVERN WR13 5JR (01886 880607; Fax: 01886 880607). Charming converted Cottages, sleep 2–6. Fully equipped with colour TV, microwave, barbecue, fridge, iron, etc. Linen, towels also supplied. One cottage suitable for the disabled with full wheelchair access. Short breaks, long lets, large groups. ETC ★★★★ [pw! Pets £10 per week.] Also see Display Advert. Contact: DENIS KAVANAGH.
e-mail: info@whitewellsfarm.co.uk   website: www.whitewellsfarm.co.uk

Hereford

Cathedral town on River Wye 45 miles SW of Birmingham.

SINK GREEN FARM, ROTHERWAS, HEREFORD HR2 6LE (01432 870223). 16th century farmhouse overlooking picturesque Wye Valley. En suite rooms, one four-poster. Extensive garden with summer house and hot tub. Fishing. Prices from £32pp. Children welcome. Pets by arrangement. [🐕]
e-mail: enquiries@sinkgreenfarm.co.uk   website: www.sinkgreenfarm.co.uk

Kington

Town on River Arrow, close to Welsh border, 12 miles North of Leominster.

THE ROCK COTTAGE, HUNTINGTON, KINGTON. Secluded, stone-built cottage near Offa's Dyke footpath. Ideal for touring, birdwatching, golf and pony trekking. Sleeps 4/6. Fully equipped kitchen, lounge with wood-burner. Central Heating. Spacious garden. Children and pets welcome. Details from MRS C. WILLIAMS, RADNOR'S END, HUNTINGTON, KINGTON HR5 3NZ (01544 370289). [🐕]
website: www.the-rock-cottage.co.uk

Ledbury

Town 12 miles east of Hereford with many timbered houses.

CHURCH FARM, CODDINGTON, LEDBURY HR8 1JJ (01531 640271). Black and white 16th-century Farmhouse on a working farm close to the Malvern Hills — ideal for touring and walking. Two double and one twin bedrooms. Excellent home cooking. Warm welcome assured. Open all year. From £37. Single supplement. AA ★★★★ [🐕]
website: www.dexta.co.uk

Leominster

Known as "The Town in the Marches", this historic market town is located in the heart of the beautiful border countryside and possesses some fine examples of architecture throughout the ages, such as The Priory Church and Grange Court. Ludlow 9 ½ miles, Hereford 12 miles.

CLIVE & CYNTHIA PRIOR, MOCKTREE BARNS, LEINTWARDINE, LUDLOW SY7 0LY (01547 540441). Gold Award winning cottages around a sunny courtyard. Sleep 2-6. Comfortable, well-equipped. Friendly owners. Dogs and children welcome. Non-Smoking. Lovely country walks. Ludlow, seven miles. Brochure. NAS Level 1 Accessibility. VB ★★★ [🐕] See also colour advertisement page 252
e-mail: mocktreebarns@care4free.net   website: www.mocktreeholidays.co.uk

Much Cowarne

Village 5 miles SW of Bromyard.

RICHARD & MARGARET BRADBURY, COWARNE HALL COTTAGES, MUCH COWARNE HR7 4JQ (01432 820317) Historic, comfortable cottages 'twixt the Malvern Hills and Wye Valley. Large garden. Private enclosed patios. Convenient for nearby towns and attractions. Free brochure and 'planner pack'.
e-mail: rm@cowarnehall.co.uk   website: www.cowarnehall.co.uk

Ross-on-Wye

An attractive town standing on a hill rising from the left bank on the Wye. Cardiff 47 miles, Gloucester 17.

LEA HOUSE BED & BREAKFAST, LEA, ROSS-ON-WYE HR9 7JZ (01989 750652). Spacious bedrooms with kingsize or twin beds and en suite bathrooms; all individually styled, with TV and beverage tray. Secluded garden. Dogs very welcome. AA ★★★★ [Dogs £7.50 per stay]. See Display Advert.
e-mail: enquiries@leahouse.co.uk   website: www.leahouse.co.uk

Leicestershire & Rutland

THE MIDLANDS 245

Market Harborough, Melton Mowbray

BROOK MEADOW LAKESIDE HOLIDAYS

* 3 self-catering chalets
* Camping & Caravan site (electric hookups)
* Fully Stocked Carp Fishery

Brochure – Mary Hart, Welford Road, Sibbertoft,
Market Harborough, Leics LE16 9UJ
Tel: 01858 880886 • Fax: 01858 880485
e-mail: brookmeadow@farmline.com • www.brookmeadow.co.uk

SYSONBY KNOLL HOTEL Melton Mowbray, Leics LE13 0HP AA ★★★ ETC

Family-run hotel in rural setting on edge of market town. Grounds of five acres with river frontage. Superb food, individually styled rooms, and a genuine welcome for pets which is rarely found in a hotel of this standard. Prices from £42.50pppn. Please see website for special offers and further details.

Tel: 01664 563563 • www.sysonby.com

Market Harborough

Town on River Welland 14 miles south-east of Leicester.

BROOK MEADOW HOLIDAYS. Three self-catering chalets, Carp fishing, camping and caravan site with electric hookups. Phone for brochure. ETC ★★★. MRS MARY HART, WELFORD ROAD, SIBBERTOFT, MARKET HARBOROUGH LE16 9UJ (01858 880886). [🐾 camping, £12 Self-catering] e-mail: brookmeadow@farmline.com   website: www.brookmeadow.co.uk

Melton Mowbray

Old market town, centre of hunting country. Large cattle market. Church and Ann of Cleves' House are of interest. Kettering 29 miles, Market Harborough 22, Nottingham 18, Leicester 15.

SYSONBY KNOLL HOTEL, ASFORDBY ROAD, MELTON MOWBRAY LE13 0HP (01664 563563; Fax: 01664 410364.). Family-run hotel on edge of market town. Grounds of five acres with river frontage. Superb food, individually styled rooms, and a genuine welcome for pets. Please see website for special offers and further details. ETC/AA ★★★ [🐾]
website: www.sysonby.com

FHG Guides

publish a large range of well-known accommodation guides.
We will be happy to send you details or you can use the order form
at the back of this book.

Symbols

🐾 Indicates that pets are welcome free of charge.
£   Indicates that a charge is made for pets: nightly or weekly.
pw! Shows some special provision for pets; exercise facility, feeding or accommodation arrangement.
⌂   Indicates separate pets accommodation.

Lincolnshire

Barnoldby-le-Beck, Barton-upon-Humber, Gainsborough, Grantham, Horncastle

GRANGE FARM COTTAGES & RIDING SCHOOL

Three well appointed cottages and riding school situated in the heart of the Lincolnshire Wolds.

The tasteful conversion of a spacious, beamed Victorian barn provides stylish and roomy cottages, one sleeping 6, and two sleeping 4 in one double and one twin bedroom, comfy sittingroom and diningroom. Fully equipped kitchen. Bathroom with bath and shower.

You don't need to ride with us, but if you do....

The Equestrian Centre offers professional tuition, an all-weather riding surface, stabling for guests' own horses, and an extensive network of bridle paths.

GRANGE FARM COTTAGES & RIDING SCHOOL
Waltham Road, Barnoldby-le-Beck, N.E. Lincs DN37 0AR
For Cottage Reservations Tel: 01472 822216 • mobile: 07947 627663
www.grangefarmcottages.com

West Wold Farmhouse, Deepdale, Barton-upon-Humber DN18 6ED
Tel: 01652 633293 — NO SMOKING

Friendly farmhouse set in the hamlet of Deepdale. Rooms have en suite or private bathroom. We offer the 'Great British' breakfast, with fresh, locally sourced produce where possible; vegetarian and other diets as requested. Dogs and horses welcome by arrangement. We have plenty of off-road parking. Special breaks and long term discounts available
e-mail: pam@westwoldfarmhouse.co.uk   www.westwoldfarmhouse.co.uk

---

The Black Swan Guest House

21 High Street, Marton, Gainsborough, Lincs DN21 5AH • Tel: 01427 718878
info@blackswanguesthouse.co.uk • www.blackswanguesthouse.co.uk

We offer a warm welcome at our former 18th Century Coaching Inn. Fully refurbished to a high standard, the house and stable block now provide very comfortable accommodation. All rooms are en suite, and have digital TV and tea/coffee facilities. There is a guest lounge where our licence enables us to serve a good range of drinks, and you to relax. Our breakfasts are all freshly cooked to order using locally sourced best quality produce. The local area is steeped in history, and the city of Lincoln is only 12 miles away. Single from £45, Double/Twin from £68. We are a non-smoking establishment

---

WOODLAND WATERS Willoughby Road, Ancaster,
Grantham NG32 3RT • Tel & Fax: 01400 230888
e-mail: info@woodlandwaters.co.uk • www.woodlandwaters.co.uk
*Set in 72 acres of beautiful woodland walks. Luxury holiday lodges, overlooking the lakes and excellently equipped. Dogs welcome in some lodges. Bar/restaurant on site. Fishing. Golf nearby. Short Breaks available. Open all year.
From £425 per week. Caravan & camping also available.*

POACHERS HIDEAWAY HOLIDAY COTTAGES
FLINTWOOD FARM, BELCHFORD, HORNCASTLE LN9 5QN (01507 533555)

Gold award-winning self catering cottages set in 150 acres of wildflower meadows, fishing lakes and woodland. Sleep 2-24. 5 miles of private paths, direct access onto Viking Way.
Jacuzzi and Therapies available.
Linen and towels provided.
Kennels available.
Peaceful, relaxing with superb views.

e-mail: info@poachershideaway.com • www.poachershideaway.com

Lincolnshire — THE MIDLANDS

Horncastle, Langton-by-Wragby, Louth, Mablethorpe

Little London Cottages • Tetford • Horncastle

Very well-equipped property, standing in own garden, on our small estate. Lovely walks. 'Mansion Cottage', a 17th/18th century cottage with two bedrooms, low ceilings and doorways, and steep stairs. Special offers. Pets welcome free.

Contact: Mrs S. D. Sutcliffe, The Mansion House, Little London, Tetford, Horncastle LN9 6QL
Tel: 01507 533697 or 07767 321213 • debbie@sutcliffell.freeserve.co.uk •
www.littlelondoncottages.co.uk

ETC ★★★★

Ground floor accommodation in chalet-type house. Central for Wolds, coast, fens, historic Lincoln. Market towns, Louth, Horncastle, Boston, Spilsby, Alford, Woodhall Spa. Two double bedrooms. Washbasin, TV; bathroom, toilet adjoining; lounge with colour TV, separate dining room. Drinks provided. Children welcome reduced rates. Car almost essential, parking. Numerous eating places nearby. B&B from £25 per person (double/single let). Open all year. Tourist Board Listed. *** PETS WELCOME FREE ***
MISS JESSIE SKELLERN, LEA HOLME, LANGTON-BY-WRAGBY, LINCOLN LN8 5PZ (01673 858495)

Brackenborough Hall Coach House Holidays

3 self-catering apartments, 4/5 Star in a Listed 18th century Coach House in the beautiful county of Lincolnshire. Short Breaks available.
Winner 'Best Self-Catering Holiday in England 2009' Silver Award. Accommodates 1-24.
Paul & Flora Bennett, Brackenborough Hall, Louth, Lincolnshire LN11 0NS
Tel/Fax: 01507 603193 • e-mail: PaulandFlora@BrackenboroughHall.com
www.BrackenboroughHall.com

Grasswells Farm Holiday Cottages
South Cockerington, Louth • ETC ★★★★

Two single barn conversions - spacious, comfortable and well equipped. Set in three acres of grounds with private fishing lake. Pets welcome. Sleep 2-5. *Contact:* Ms J. Foster, Grasswells Holiday Cottages (Saddleback Leisure Ltd), Saddleback Road, Howdales, South Cockerington, Louth LN11 7DJ • 01507 338508 • www.grasswells.co.uk

Westfield Farm Self Catering Holiday Cottages

One, two and three bedroom converted cottages, sleeping 2, 4 or 6 people. Set in open countryside. just 2 miles from Louth.
Open all year, short breaks available.
Stewton, Louth, Lincolnshire LN11 8SD
Tel: 01507 354892 or 07885 280787
www.westfieldfarmcottages.co.uk

CAVENDISH LODGE • www.luxurycavendishlodge.co.uk
Kenwick Park Estate, Louth, Lincs LN11 8NR
Tel: 0115 984 7979 • e-mail: info@bunnyhall.co.uk

direct access to woodlands • 3 large bedrooms (one en suite) • ample facilities for cleaning muddy dogs! • nearby dog-friendly hotel with restaurant

Grange Farmhouse

MALTBY-LE-MARSH, ALFORD LN13 0JP
Tel: 01507 450267
e-mail: anngraves@btinternet.com

Farmhouse B&B, SELF-CATERING COTTAGES and CARAVANS set in 15 idyllic acres of Lincolnshire countryside. Peaceful base for leisure and sightseeing.

• Two private fishing lakes • Many farm animals
• Brochure available. Contact Mrs Graves.
••Pets welcome••

www.grange-farmhouse.co.uk

Lincolnshire

North Somercotes, Woodhall Spa

Three Luxury 4★ Cottages • North Somercotes • Two minutes to the sea
On a quiet lane leading to the sea, an ideal holiday home for people who want the best modern comforts, the calm of the Lincolnshire coast, and plenty to see and do nearby.
Each has 2 double bedrooms, sleeps 4/5. Disabled access M1.
Tel: 01507 358256/07724 764347
• e-mail: nurserycottage@hotmail.co.uk • www.mealsfarm.com

Stixwould Road, Woodhall Spa LN10 6QG • Tel: 01526 352411
Fax: 01526 353473 • reception@petwood.co.uk • www.petwood.co.uk
A country house hotel of unique charm, offering a high standard of comfort and hospitality in elegant surroundings. All bedrooms are fully equipped to meet the needs of today's discerning guests, and Tennysons Restaurant offers the very best of English and Continental cuisine. There are ample leisure opportunities available locally as well as tranquil villages and historic market towns to explore. **AA/ETC ★★★**

Barnoldby-le-Beck

Village 4 miles SW of Grimsby.

GRANGE FARM COTTAGES & RIDING SCHOOL, WALTHAM ROAD, BARNOLDBY-LE-BECK DN37 0AR (01472 822216; Fax: 01472 233550; mobile: 07947 627663). Three well appointed cottages and riding school situated in the heart of the Lincolnshire Wolds. Sleep 4/6. ETC ★★★★. Equestrian Centre offers tuition, all-weather riding, stabling. [Pets £10]
website: www.grangefarmcottages.com

Barton-Upon-Humber

Town on south bank of River Humber, 6 miles south west of Hull.

MRS PAM ATKIN, WEST WOLD FARMHOUSE, DEEPDALE, BARTON-UPON-HUMBER DN18 6ED (01652 633293). Friendly farmhouse. Rooms have en suite or private bathroom. We offer the 'Great British' breakfast, with fresh, locally sourced produce where possible; vegetarian and other diets as requested. Dogs and horses welcome by arrangement.
e-mail: pam@westwoldfarmhouse.co.uk   www.westwoldfarmhouse.co.uk

Gainsborough

Market town and River Port 15 miles NW of Lincoln.

THE BLACK SWAN GUEST HOUSE, 21 HIGH STREET, MARTON, GAINSBOROUGH DN21 5AH (01427 718878). Former 18th Century Coaching Inn, providing very comfortable accommodation. All rooms en suite, with digital TV and tea/coffee making facilities. Lincoln 12 miles away, many other attractions nearby. Non-smoking. AA ★★★★ [🐾]
e-mail: info@blackswanguesthouse.co.uk   website: www.blackswanguesthouse.co.uk

Grantham

Market town 24 miles south of Lincoln.

WOODLAND WATERS, WILLOUGHBY ROAD, ANCASTER, GRANTHAM NG32 3RT (Tel & Fax: 01400 230888). Set in 72 acres of beautiful woodland walks. Luxury holiday lodges, overlooking the lakes and excellently equipped. Dogs welcome in some lodges. Bar/restaurant on site. Fishing. Golf nearby. Short Breaks available. Open all year. [Pets £1 per night camping, £20 per week lodges.]
e-mail: info@woodlandwaters.co.uk   website: www.woodlandwaters.co.uk

www.holidayguides.com

Lincolnshire

Horncastle

Market town on banks of Rivers Waring and Bain noted for its many antique shops.

POACHERS HIDEAWAY HOLIDAY COTTAGES, FLINTWOOD FARM, BELCHFORD, HORNCASTLE LN9 5QN (01507 533555). Sleep 2-24. Gold award-winning self catering cottages set in 150 acres of wildflower meadows, fishing lakes and woodland. Jacuzzi and Therapies available. Linen and towels provided. Kennels available. ETC 4-5 Stars [Pets £10 per week]
e-mail: info@poachershideaway.com   website: www.poachershideaway.com

LITTLE LONDON COTTAGES, TETFORD, HORNCASTLE. Very well-equipped property standing in own garden, on our small estate. Lovely walks. Special offers. ETC ★★★★. Contact: MRS S.D. SUTCLIFFE, THE MANSION HOUSE, LITTLE LONDON, TETFORD, HORNCASTLE LN9 6QL (01507 533697; mobile: 07767 321213). [🐾]
e-mail: debbie@sutcliffell.freeserve.co.uk   website: www.littlelondoncottages.co.uk

Langton-by-Wragby

Village located south-east of Wragby.

MISS JESSIE SKELLERN, LEA HOLME, LANGTON-BY-WRAGBY, LINCOLN LN8 5PZ (01673 858339). Ground floor accommodation in chalet-type house. Central for Wolds, coast, fens, historic Lincoln. Market towns, Louth, Horncastle, Boston, Spilsby, Alford, Woodhall Spa. Two double bedrooms. Washbasin, TV; bathroom, toilet adjoining; lounge with colour TV, separate dining room. Drinks provided. Children welcome reduced rates. Car almost essential, parking. Numerous eating places nearby. B&B from £25 per person (double/single let). Open all year. Pets welcome free. Tourist Board Listed [🐾]

Louth

Quaint market town with old fashioned architecture. Knwn as the 'Capital of the Lincolnshire Wolds'. 26 miles from Lincoln.

BRACKENBOROUGH HALL COACH HOUSE HOLIDAYS. Winner: Best Self-Catering Holiday in England 2009, Silver Award. Three self-catering apartments in a listed 18thC Coach House in the beautiful county of Lincolnshire. Accommodates 1-24. Short Breaks available. PAUL & FLORA BENNETT, BRACKENBOROUGH HALL, LOUTH LN11 0NS. (Tel/Fax: 01507 603193). ★★★★/★★★★★ [Pets £10 per dog]
e-mail: PaulandFlora@BrackenboroughHall.com   website: www.BrackenboroughHall.com

GRASSWELLS FARM HOLIDAY COTTAGES SOUTH COCKERINGTON, LOUTH. Two single barn conversions - spacious, comfortable and well equipped. Set in three acres of grounds with private fishing lake. Pets welcome. Sleep 2-5. ETC ★★★★ Contact: MS J. FOSTER, GRASSWELLS HOLIDAY COTTAGES (SADDLEBACK LEISURE LTD), SADDLEBACK ROAD, HOWDALES, SOUTH COCKERINGTON, LOUTH LN11 7DJ (01507 338508). [🐾]
website: www.grasswells.co.uk

WESTFIELD FARM SELF-CATERING HOLIDAY COTTAGES, STEWTON, LOUTH LN11 8SD(01507 354892 or 07885 280787). One, two and three bedroom converted cottages, sleeping 2, 4 or 6 people. Set in open countryside, just 2 miles from Louth. Open all year, short breaks available. ETC★★★/★★★★.
website: www.westfieldfarmcottages.co.uk

CAVENDISH LODGE, KENWICK PARK ESTATE, LOUTH LN11 8NR (0115 984 7979). Direct access to woodlands. Three large bedrooms (one en suite). Ample facilities for cleaning muddy dogs! Nearby dog-friendly hotel with restaurant.
e-mail: info@bunnyhall.co.uk   www.luxurycavendishlodge.co.uk

Symbols

🐾   Indicates that pets are welcome free of charge.

£   Indicates that a charge is made for pets: nightly or weekly.

pw!   Shows some special provision for pets; exercise facility, feeding or accommodation arrangement.

⌂   Indicates separate pets accommodation.

THE MIDLANDS — Lincolnshire / Nottinghamshire

Mablethorpe

Coastal resort 11 miles from Louth.

MRS GRAVES, GRANGE FARM, MALTBY-LE-MARSH, ALFORD LN13 0JP (01507 450267). Farmhouse B&B and self-catering country cottages set in 15 idyllic acres of Lincolnshire countryside. 2 miles from beach. Peaceful base for leisure, walking and sightseeing. Two private fishing lakes. Many farm animals. Brochure available. [Pets £5 per night B&B, £30 per week in cottages, ⌂]
website: www.grange-farmhouse.co.uk

North Somercotes

Large coastal village in the Marshes area.

THREE LUXURY 4-STAR COTTAGES, LINCOLNSHIRE COAST. On a quiet lane leading to the sea, an ideal holiday home for people who want the best modern comforts, the calm of the Lincolnshire coast, and plenty to see and do nearby. Each has 2 double bedrooms, sleeps 4/5. (01507 358256/07724 76434) . EnjoyEngland ★★★★.
e-mail: nurserycottage@hotmail.co.uk   website: www.mealsfarm.com

Woodhall Spa

Edwardian Spa Town 6 miles SW of Horncastle.

PETWOOD HOTEL, STIXWOULD ROAD, WOODHALL SPA LN10 6QG (01526 352411 Fax: 01526 353473). A country house hotel of unique charm, offering a high standard of comfort and hospitality in elegant surroundings. Tennysons Restaurant offers the very best of English and Continental cuisine. Ample leisure opportunities locally. AA/ETC ★★★ [Pets £10 per night.]
e-mail: reception@petwood.co.uk   website: www.petwood.co.uk

Nottinghamshire

Burton Joyce

Residential area 4 miles north-east of Nottingham.

MRS V. BAKER, WILLOW HOUSE, BURTON JOYCE, NOTTINGHAM NG14 5FD (0115 931 2070 or 07816 347706). Large Victorian house, authentically furnished, in quiet village near beautiful stretch of River Trent. Four miles city. Close to station/bus stop. Bright, clean rooms. TV. En suite. Parking. From £26pppn. Good local eating. Please phone first for directions. [🐾]
website: www.willowhousebedandbreakfast.co.uk

Other specialised holiday guides from **FHG**

PUBS & INNS OF BRITAIN • **COUNTRY HOTELS** OF BRITAIN
WEEKEND & SHORT BREAK HOLIDAYS IN BRITAIN
THE GOLF GUIDE WHERE TO PLAY, WHERE TO STAY
500 GREAT PLACES TO STAY • **SELF-CATERING HOLIDAYS** IN BRITAIN
BED & BREAKFAST STOPS • **CARAVAN & CAMPING HOLIDAYS**
FAMILY BREAKS IN BRITAIN

Published annually: available in all good bookshops or direct from the publisher:
FHG Guides, Abbey Mill Business Centre, Seedhill, Paisley PA1 1TJ
Tel: 0141 887 0428 • Fax: 0141 889 7204
e-mail: admin@fhguides.co.uk • www.holidayguides.com

Shropshire

THE MIDLANDS

Bishop's Castle, Bridgnorth, Burford, Church Stretton

Broadway House

The 17th Century **Lodge** and 18th century **Coach House** are located in the grounds of a Regency gentleman's residence with picturesque views towards the South Shropshire hills and Clun Forest. Situated on the Wales/England border, steeped in a colourful history, with historic monuments, wonderful wildlife and country sports and pursuits nearby. Very well equipped. Linen and fuel included. Minimum price £230 per week. Sleep 5 and 2. Open all year.

Churchstoke, Powys SY15 6DU • Tel : 01588 620770
e-mail: enqs@bordercottages.co.uk • www.bordercottages.co.uk

Country House Holidays

The Granary

The Old Vicarage, Ditton Priors, Bridgnorth, Shropshire WV16 6SP
Tel: 01746 712272 • Fax: 01746 712288

Early 19th century Granary in hill country. Sleeps two/four with view over farmland. Antique furniture complements surroundings. Excellent walking, cycling. Pets welcome.
The combined sitting room and dining area has a good quality sprung sofa bed and the Gallery Style kitchen has everything you need for your stay. The library is something we are very proud of, especially if you like antiques, old houses and books on the countryside. The bedroom has two full-size twin beds. Laundry room. The village has a good pub, shops, post office, butcher and surgery. Contact Mrs S. Allen.

e-mail: allens@oldvicditton.freeserve.co.uk • www.stmem.com/thegranary

HARPFIELDS HOP-KILN, Burford • SELF CATERING
Unusual converted Victorian building in unspoilt countryside. Perfect for a rural self-catering holiday in a traditional farmyard setting. Sleeps 4.
Contact: Margaret Anderson, Old Harpfields Hop-Kiln, Harpfields, Burford, Tenbury Wells, Worcestershire, WR15 8HP
Tel: 01584 810099 or 01584 811298 • E-mail: janderson117@btinternet.com
www.harpfields-hopkiln.co.uk

COME TO THE SHROPSHIRE HILLS
A warm welcome awaits at our family-run cottages, maintained and equipped to a high standard. Beautiful location at Church Stretton in Shropshire, easy access to Ludlow, Shrewsbury, Ironbridge. Ideal for all the family. **Tel: 01694 722869** for a brochure or visit
www.botvylefarm.co.uk

North Hill Farm
Cardington, Church Stretton SY6 7LL • Tel: 01694 771532

B&B accommodation in the beautiful Shropshire hills, one mile from Cardington village. Quiet, rural setting with plenty of wildlife. Ideal walking and riding country. Rooms have wonderful views with TV and hot drinks tray. Great local pubs. Well behaved dogs and horses welcome. B&B from £27.50pp. En suite courtyard room £32pp. Dogs £2 per night. Non-smoking. *Mrs Chris Brandon-Lodge*
e-mail: cbrandon@btinternet.com • www.virtual-shropshire.co.uk/northhill/

BELVEDERE GUEST HOUSE
BURWAY ROAD, CHURCH STRETTON SY6 6DP
Pleasant family-run Guest House - attractive gardens. Parking.
All rooms en suite. Guest lounge with TV. Packed lunches available.
Don & Ewa Lovejoy • Tel: 01694 722232
e-mail: info@belvedereguesthouse.co.uk • www.belvedereguesthouse.co.uk

252 THE MIDLANDS — Shropshire

Craven Arms, Ludlow

Two well-equipped modern caravan holiday homes situated at the head of the Clun valley in South Shropshire's Area of Outstanding Natural Beauty. Perfect for walking, cycling, riding, or just unwinding! Each caravan has three bedrooms, TV, shower room with flush toilet, and kitchen with fridge and microwave. Further shower room and laundry/drying room on site. Well behaved pets and children welcome, horses also accommodated. Open April to September. From £160 per week incl. gas, electricity, bed linen and towels.

The Anchorage
www.adamsanchor.co.uk
nancynewcwm@btinternet.com
Anchor, Newcastle on Clun, Craven Arms, Shropshire SY7 8PR • 01686 670737

LUDLOW CASTLE

SIR HENRY SIDNEY APARTMENT • Superbly renovated apartment, full of charm and character – sitting/dining room, two twin bedrooms with en suite bathrooms and a car parking space in the heart of Ludlow – offers a unique opportunity to reside within the walls of Ludlow Castle. Open all year.

Please telephone 01584 874465 for full colour brochure
E-mail: info@ludlowcastle.com   www.castle-accommodation.com

Mocktree Barns Holiday Cottages

Gold Awards: 'Best Value for Money' 2006 • 'Sustainable Tourism' 2007

A small group of comfortable self-catering cottages around a sunny courtyard. Well-equipped. Sleeping 2-6. Two cottages with no stairs. Friendly owners. Open all year. Short breaks. Pets and children welcome. Lovely views. Excellent walks from the door through farmland and woods. Hereford, Cider Country, Black & White villages, Shropshire Hills, Shrewsbury, and Ironbridge all an easy drive. Beautiful Ludlow seven miles. Good food and drink nearby. Brochure available.

Clive and Cynthia Prior, Mocktree Barns, Leintwardine, Ludlow SY8 0LY
Tel: 01547 540441 • e-mail: mocktreebarns@care4free.net
www.mocktreeholidays.co.uk

THE MOOR HALL

Built in 1789, the Moor Hall is a splendid example of Georgian Palladian style and enjoys breathtaking views over miles of unspoilt countryside. The atmosphere is relaxed and friendly. The gardens, which extend to five acres, provide a perfect setting in which to idle away a few hours, whilst the hills beyond offer wonderful discoveries for the more energetic. B&B from £30 pppn.

Near Ludlow, Shropshire SY8 3EG • 01584 823209 • Fax: 01584 824216
e-mail: info@moorhall.co.uk • www.moorhall.co.uk

Warm, comfortable Georgian coach house, friendly informal atmosphere, good traditional English Breakfast; delightful en suite rooms. Easy walking distance from town centre and local inns. Lots of nice local walks. TV, tea/coffee making facilities in all rooms. One double, two twin, and one single room, all en suite. Bed and Breakfast from £28 pppn.

Henwick House, Gravel Hill, Ludlow SY8 1QU
ETC ★★★ B&B   Tel: 01584 873338 • Miss S.J. Cecil

TOP FARM HOUSE
Knockin, Near Oswestry SY10 8HN

Full of charm and character, this beautiful 16th century Grade 1 Listed black and white house is set in the delightful village of Knockin. Enjoy the relaxed atmosphere and elegant surroundings of this special house with its abundance of beams. Sit in the comfortable drawing room where you can read, listen to music, or just relax with a glass of wine (please feel free to bring your own tipple). Hearty breakfasts from our extensive menu are served in the lovely dining room which looks out over the garden. The large bedrooms are all en suite, attractively decorated and furnished. All have tea/coffee making facilities, colour TV, etc. Convenient for the Welsh Border, Shrewsbury, Chester and Oswestry. Friendly hosts and great atmosphere. *Bed and Breakfast from £30 to £35.*

Telephone: 01691 682582
e-mail: p.a.m@knockin.freeserve.co.uk
www.topfarmknockin.co.uk

"JOHANSEN" RECOMMENDED

GOOD HOTEL GUIDE

A WELSH RAREBIT HOTEL

MICHELIN RECOMMENDED

Food Award

Pen-y-Dyffryn COUNTRY HOTEL
RHYDYCROESAU, NEAR OSWESTRY, SHROPSHIRE SY10 7JD

This silver stone former Georgian Rectory, set almost a thousand feet up in the Shropshire/Welsh hills, is in a dream situation for both pets and their owners. Informal atmosphere, no traffic, just buzzards, badgers and beautiful country walks, yet Shrewsbury, Chester, Powis Castle & Lake Vyrnwy are all close by. The well-stocked bar and licensed restaurant are always welcoming at the end of another hard day's relaxing. All bedrooms en suite etc; four have private patios, ideal for pets; several have spa baths. Short breaks available from £85 pppd, Dinner, B&B. Pets free.

Tel: 01691 653700
e-mail: stay@peny.co.uk • www.peny.co.uk

THE MIDLANDS — Shropshire
Ludlow

Four delightful cottages thoughtfully converted and equipped to the highest standard. All with en suite facilities and garden or seating area. One cottage with disabled access. Situated in a secluded valley and ideally located to explore the beautiful South Shropshire countryside. Sleep 2-6.
SALLY AND TIM LOFT, GOOSEFOOT BARN, PINSTONES, DIDDLEBURY, CRAVEN ARMS SY7 9LB • 01584 861326   ETC ★★★★
info@goosefootbarn.co.uk • www.goosefootbarn.co.uk

Bishop's Castle

Small town in the hills on the Welsh Border, 8 miles from Craven Arms.

BROADWAY HOUSE, CHURCHSTOKE, POWYS SY15 6DU (01588 620770). 17th century Lodge and 18th century Coach House in the grounds of a Regency gentleman's residence on Wales/England border. Picturesque views. Linen and fuel included. Open all year. Sleep five and two. WTB ★★★★★ Self-Catering. [🐕]
e-mail: enqs@bordercottages.co.uk   website: www.bordercottages.co.uk

Bridgnorth

Town on cliff above River Severn.

THE GRANARY, THE OLD VICARAGE, DITTON PRIORS, BRIDGNORTH WV16 6SP (01746 712272; Fax: 01746 712288) Early 19th century Granary in hill country. Sleeps two/four with view over farmland. Antique furniture complements surroundings. Excellent walking, cycling. Pets welcome. Contact MRS S. ALLEN. VisitBritain ★★★. [🐕]
e-mail: allens@oldvicditton.freeserve.co.uk   website: www.stmem.com/thegranary

Burford

Small village to the north of the River Teme. Many NT properties in the area.

MARGARET ANDERSON, HARPFIELDS HOP-KILN, BURFORD, TENBURY WELLS WR15 8HP (01584 810099 or 01584 811298). Unusual converted Victorian building in unspoilt countryside. Perfect for a rural self-catering holiday in a traditional farmyard setting. Sleeps 4. EnjoyEngland ★★★★.[🐕]
e-mail: janderson117@btinternet.com   website: www.harpfields-hopkiln.co.uk

Church Stretton

Delightful little town in lee of Shropshire Hills. Walking and riding country. Facilities for tennis, bowls, gliding and golf. Knighton 22 miles, Bridgnorth 19, Ludlow 15, Shrewsbury 12.

BOTVYLE FARM, ALL STRETTON, CHURCH STRETTON SY6 7JN (01694 722869). A warm welcome awaits at our family-run cottages, maintained and equipped to a high standard. Beautiful location at Church Stretton, easy access to Ludlow, Shrewsbury, Ironbridge. Ideal for all the family. [Pets £15 per week]
website: www.botvylefarm.co.uk

MRS C.F. BRANDON-LODGE, NORTH HILL FARM, CARDINGTON, CHURCH STRETTON SY6 7LL (01694 771532). Rooms with a view! B&B in beautiful Shropshire hills. TV in rooms, tea etc. Ideal walking country. From £27.50 per person; en suite available. AA ★★★★ [pw! Pets £2 per night, 🏠]
e-mail: cbrandon@btinternet.com   website: www.virtual-shropshire.co.uk/northhill/

DON AND EWA LOVEJOY, BELVEDERE GUEST HOUSE, BURWAY ROAD, CHURCH STRETTON SY6 6DP (01694 722232). Pleasant family-run Guest House - attractive gardens. Parking. All rooms en suite. Guest lounge with TV. Packed lunches available. AA ★★★★ [🐕]
e-mail: info@belvedereguesthouse.co.uk   website: www.belvedereguesthouse.co.uk

Shropshire

THE MIDLANDS 255

Craven Arms

Surrounded by hills, Craven Arms is home to the Shropshire Hills Discovery Centre where you can experience virtual balloon rides and meet the "hairy mammoth". Beautiful Stokesey Castle lies just outside the town. Ludlow 6½ miles, Shrewsbury 19 miles.

Two well-equipped modern caravan holiday homes in Area of Outstanding Natural Beauty. Each has three bedrooms, TV, shower room with flush toilet, and kitchen with fridge and microwave. Well behaved pets and children welcome, horses also accommodated. Open Easter to October. THE ANCHORAGE, ANCHOR, NEWCASTLE ON CLUN, CRAVEN ARMS, SHROPSHIRE SY7 8PR (01686 670737). [Pets £10 per week].
e-mail: nancynewcwm@btinternet.com website: www.adamsanchor.co.uk

Ludlow

Lovely and historic town on Rivers Teme and Corve with numerous old half-timbered houses and inns. Worcester 29 miles, Shrewsbury 27, Hereford 24, Bridgnorth 19, Church Stretton 16.

SIR HENRY SIDNEY APARTMENT, LUDLOW CASTLE. Superbly renovated apartment, full of charm and character. Sitting/dining room, two twin bedrooms with en suite bathrooms. Parking space in the heart of Ludlow. A unique opportunity to reside within the walls of Ludlow Castle. Open all year. 01584 87446 for full colour brochure. EnjoyEngland ★★★★★ *SELF CATERING*. [Pets £4 per night].
e-mail: info@ludlowcastle.com website: www.castle-accommodation.com

CLIVE & CYNTHIA PRIOR, MOCKTREE BARNS, LEINTWARDINE, LUDLOW SY7 0LY (01547 540441). Gold Award winning self-catering cottages around a sunny courtyard. Sleep 2-6. Comfortable, well-equipped. Friendly owners. Dogs and children welcome. Non-smoking. Lovely country walks. Ludlow, seven miles. Brochure. NAS Level 1 Accessibility. VB ★★★ [🐾] See also colour advertisement page 252.
e-mail: mocktreebarns@care4free.net website: www.mocktreeholidays.co.uk

THE MOOR HALL, NEAR LUDLOW SY8 3EG (01584 823209; Fax: 01584 824216). Built in 1789, a splendid example of the Georgian Palladian style. Breathtaking views, 5 acre garden. B&B from £30 pppn. AA ★★★★ [🐾]
e-mail: info@moorhall.co.uk website: www.moorhall.co.uk

HENWICK HOUSE, GRAVEL HILL, LUDLOW SY8 1QU (01584 873338). Warm, comfortable Georgian coach house, good traditional English Breakfast. Easy walking distance from town centre and local inns. Lots of nice local walks. TV, tea/coffee making facilities. One double, two twin, and one single room, all en suite. B&B from £28 pppn. ETC ★★★ [🐾]

SALLY AND TIM LOFT, GOOSEFOOT BARN, PINSTONES, DIDDLEBURY, CRAVEN ARMS, SHROPSHIRE SY7 9LB (01584 861326). Four delightful cottages thoughtfully converted and equipped to the highest standard. All with en suite facilities and garden or seating area. One cottage with disabled access. Situated in a secluded valley and ideally located to explore the beautiful South Shropshire countryside. Sleep 2-6. ETC ★★★★ [🐾]
e-mail: info@goosefootbarn.co.uk website: www.goosefootbarn.co.uk

Oswestry

Borderland market town. Many old castles and fortifications. Shrewsbury 16, Vyrnwy 18.

TOP FARM HOUSE, KNOCKIN, NEAR OSWESTRY SY10 8HN (01691 682582). Grade 1 Listed black and white house set in flower-filled gardens. En suite bedrooms. Hearty breakfast. Convenient for the Welsh Border, Shrewsbury, Chester and Oswestry. ETC/AA ★★★★ Guesthouse.
e-mail: p.a.m@knockin.freeserve.co.uk website: www.topfarmknockin.co.uk

PEN-Y-DYFFRYN COUNTRY HOTEL, NEAR RHYDYCROESAU, OSWESTRY SY10 7JD (01691 653700). Picturesque Georgian Rectory quietly set in Shropshire/ Welsh Hills. 12 en suite bedrooms, four with private patios. 5-acre grounds. No passing traffic. Johansens recommended. Dinner, Bed and Breakfast from £85.00 per person per day. AA ★★★. [🐾 pw!]
e-mail: stay@peny.co.uk website: www.peny.co.uk

Staffordshire

Leek, Stafford

Situated in Staffordshire Moorlands, cosy 3 bedroomed cottage with four-poster (sleeps 6), overlooking picturesque countryside. Fully equipped, comfortably furnished and carpeted throughout. An ideal base for visits to Alton Towers, the Potteries and Peak District. Patio, play area. Cot and high chair available. Laundry room with auto washer and dryer. Electricity and fresh linen inclusive. Terms from £230 to £375.

EDITH & ALWYN MYCOCK
'ROSEWOOD COTTAGE'
LOWER BERKHAMSYTCH FARM, BOTTOM HOUSE, NEAR LEEK ST13 7QP
Tel & Fax: 01538 308213
www.rosewoodcottage.co.uk

WYNDALE GUEST HOUSE 199 Corporation St, Stafford ST16 3LQ
01785 223069 • wyndale@aol.com • www.wyndaleguesthouse.co.uk

Comfortable Victorian Guest House situated quarter mile from Stafford town centre and 3 miles from County Showground. Small nature reserve across the road ideal for dog walking.

Leek

Village 10 miles from Stoke-on-Trent.

EDITH & ALWYN MYCOCK, ROSEWOOD COTTAGE, LOWER BERKHAMSYTCH FARM, BOTTOM HOUSE, NEAR LEEK ST13 7QP (Tel & Fax: 01538 308213). Cosy three bedroomed cottage with four-poster, sleeps six. Fully equipped and carpeted. Electricity and linen inclusive, laundry room. Ideal base for Alton Towers, Potteries and Peak District. Terms £230 to £375. [Pets £7.50 per week] website: www.rosewoodcottage.co.uk

Stafford

Town on River Sow, 14 miles south of Stoke-on-Trent.

MRS N. ROBINSON, WYNDALE GUEST HOUSE, 199 CORPORATION STREET, STAFFORD ST16 3LQ (01785 223069). Comfortable Victorian Guest House situated quarter mile from Stafford town centre and 3 miles from County Showground. Small nature reserve across the road ideal for dog walking. ETC ★★★ [🐾]
e-mail: wyndale@aol.com   website: www.wyndaleguesthouse.co.uk

---

Visit the FHG website
www.holidayguides.com
for details of the wide choice of accommodation featured in the full range of FHG titles

Warwickshire

THE MIDLANDS

Leamington Spa, Stratford-Upon-Avon, Warwick

Bubbenhall House
www.bubbenhallhouse.com

A charming country house offering superior bed and breakfast accommodation, located in the heart of Warwickshire, between Royal Leamington Spa and Coventry.
Paget's Lane, Bubbenhall, Warwickshire CV8 3BJ
Tel/Fax: 02476 302409 • e-mail: wharrison@bubbenhallhouse.freeserve.co.uk

This year let your dog enjoy the holiday fun!

Stratford-upon-Avon

BOOK NOW AND THE DOG GOES FREE!
For your dog to go FREE, quote reference PW/09 when booking your stay

Prices start from **£9.00** per person, per night. Based on 6 persons sharing

Only one mile from the centre of Stratford-upon-Avon.

Call Now For A Holiday Hire Brochure
Tel: 01789 293438

Avon Estates Ltd
Holiday & Home Parks

Riverside Caravan Park, Tiddington Road,
Stratford-upon-Avon, Warwickshire CV37 7AB
Tel: 01789 292312 Email: riverside@stratfordcaravans.co.uk
www.stratfordcaravans.co.uk
Family owned and run parks, for that personal touch.

THE CROFT
ETC/AA ★★★★

Haseley Knob, Warwick CV35 7NL • Tel & Fax: 01926 484 447
• Friendly family country guesthouse • non-smoking
• All rooms en suite or private bathroom, TV, hairdryer, tea/coffee
• Central location for Warwick, Stratford, Coventry and NEC.

e-mail: david@croftguesthouse.co.uk   www.croftguesthouse.co.uk

---

Free or reduced rate entry to
Holiday Visits and Attractions - see our
READERS' OFFER VOUCHERS on pages 445-454

Publisher's note

While every effort is made to ensure accuracy, we regret that FHG Guides cannot accept responsibility for errors, misrepresentations or omissions in our entries or any consequences thereof. Prices in particular should be checked.
We will follow up complaints but cannot act as arbiters or agents for either party.

CLIFTON CRUISERS, CLIFTON WHARF, VICARAGE HILL, CLIFTON, RUGBY, WARWICKSHIRE CV23 0DG (01788 543570; Fax: 01788 579799). Varied choice of boat layouts and accommodation to satisfy the requirements of most family and holiday groups (sleeping 2-8). Starting base centrally situated on the waterway network. [🐕]
e-mail: info@cliftoncruisers.com   website: www.cliftoncruisers.com

Leamington Spa

Spa town on River Leam, 8 miles South of Coventry.

MRS HARRISON, BUBBENHALL HOUSE, PAGET'S LANE, BUBBENHALL CV8 3BJ. (Tel/Fax: 02476 302409). A charming country house offering superior bed and breakfast accommodation, located in the heart of Warwickshire, between Royal Leamington Spa and Coventry. Pet friendly. AA ★★★★ [🐕]
e-mail: wharrison@bubbenhallhouse.freeserve.co.uk   website: www.bubbenhallhouse.com

Stratford-Upon-Avon

Historic town famous as Shakespeare's birth place and home. Birmingham 24, Warwick 8 miles.

RIVERSIDE CARAVAN PARK, TIDDINGTON ROAD, STRATFORD-UPON-AVON CV37 7BE (01789 292312). Luxury Caravans, sleep 6. Fully equipped kitchens, bathroom/ shower/WC. Also two riverside Cottages, all modern facilities to first-class standards. Private fishing. On banks of River Avon. [Pets £15 weekly.]
e-mail: riverside@stratfordcaravans.co.uk   website: www.stratfordcaravans.co.uk

Warwick

Town on the River Avon, 9 miles south-west of Coventry, with medieval castle and many fine old buildings.

DAVID & PATRICIA CLAPP, CROFT GUESTHOUSE, HASELEY KNOB, WARWICK CV35 7NL (Tel & Fax: 01926 484 447). All bedrooms en suite or with private bathroom, some ground floor. Non-smoking. Picturesque rural setting. Central for NEC, Warwick, Stratford, Stoneleigh and Coventry. B&B single £40, double/twin £60. ETC/AA ★★★★ [Dogs £3 per night]
e-mail: david@croftguesthouse.co.uk   website: www.croftguesthouse.co.uk

---

Other specialised holiday guides from FHG

PUBS & INNS OF BRITAIN • **COUNTRY HOTELS** OF BRITAIN
WEEKEND & SHORT BREAK HOLIDAYS IN BRITAIN
THE GOLF GUIDE WHERE TO PLAY, WHERE TO STAY
500 GREAT PLACES TO STAY • **SELF-CATERING HOLIDAYS** IN BRITAIN
BED & BREAKFAST STOPS • **CARAVAN & CAMPING HOLIDAYS**
FAMILY BREAKS IN BRITAIN

Published annually: available in all good bookshops or direct from the publisher:
FHG Guides, Abbey Mill Business Centre, Seedhill, Paisley PA1 1TJ
Tel: 0141 887 0428 • Fax: 0141 889 7204
e-mail: admin@fhguides.co.uk • www.holidayguides.com

Worcestershire
Bishop's Frome, Great Malvern

Five Bridges Cottages
Nestled in the heart of the Herefordshire cider apple and hop growing regions, the cottages are set within the owner's 4-acre garden and smallholding.

Five Bridges Cottages
Near Bishop's Frome,
Worcester WR6 5BX
e-mail: info@fivebridgescottages.co.uk
www.fivebridgescottages.co.uk
Tel: 01531 640340

Whitewells Farm Cottages
Ridgeway Cross, Near Malvern, Worcs WR13 5JR
Tel: 01886 880607 • Fax: 01886 880360
info@whitewellsfarm.co.uk • www.whitewellsfarm.co.uk

Seven well-established cottages converted from old farm buildings and a hop kiln, full of charm and character with original exposed timbering. The cottages are exceptionally clean and comfortable and equipped to the highest standards. One cottage suitable for the disabled with full wheelchair access. Idyllically set around a duckpond with two and a half acres of the property being a fully-fenced woodland plantation, ideal for exercising dogs, on or off the lead.

Set in unspoilt countryside with outstanding views of the **Malvern Hills** on the **Herefordshire/Worcestershire border. Ideal base for touring Worcestershire, Herefordshire, the Malverns, Gloucestershire, Welsh mountains, Cotswolds and Shakespeare country**.

Electricity and linen included in price.
Short breaks and long lets, suitable for relocation.
Children and pets welcome. Open all year.

**Colour brochure available from:
Denis Kavanagh.**

Silver Award Winners 'Heart of England Excellence in Tourism Awards' Self-Catering Holiday of the Year

CROFT GUEST HOUSE • *Bransford, Worcester WR6 5JD* • AA ★★
16th-18thC country house in Teme Valley, 4 miles from Worcester and Malvern. Comfortable, non-smoking house. Three en suite guest rooms (two double, one family) and two with washbasins are available. Colour TV, radio alarm and courtesy tray. TV lounge, residential licence. Dogs welcome by arrangement. *Full English breakfast and evening meals from home-grown/made or locally sourced produce.* B&B £28-£38 single, £47-£65 double. *Ann & Brian Porter*
Tel: 01886 832227 • e-mail: dogs@brianporter.orangehome.co.uk • www.croftguesthouse.com

Harmony House - B&B Accommodation with a difference
Perched on the western side of the Malvern Hills, Harmony House welcomes all who come to stay. Enjoy one of our relaxing therapies, wonderful views, breakfast tailored to your specific desires, and a peaceful night's sleep in one of our three spacious en suite bedrooms. All have tea-making facilities, radio/tape/CD player (but no TV). Non-smoking. Well behaved dogs welcome.
184 West Malvern Road, Malvern, Worcestershire WR14 4AZ • Tel: 01684 891850
e-mail: Catherine@HarmonyHouseMalvern.com • www.HarmonyHouseMalvern.com

Worcestershire

Great Malvern, Malvern, Worcester

Grrrrrrrrreatest views in England!

Dogs greeted with a Bonio, guests with a smile!....
Superbly located high on the Malvern Hills you'll find this 3★ Country House Hotel. Accommodation extends over three buildings, so ideal for late night 'walkies'. Direct access to hills, 2 AA restaurant Rosettes, over 600 wines.

Cottage in the Wood
Holywell Rd, Malvern, Worcestershire, WR14 4LG
01684 58 88 60 www.cottageinthewood.co.uk

MALVERN HILLS HOTEL
AA ★★★ HOTEL

Wynds Point, Malvern WR13 6DW

Enchanting family-owned and run hotel nestling high in the hills. Direct access to superb walking with magnificent views. Oak-panelled lounge, log fire, real ales, fine food and friendly staff. Great animal lovers.

Tel: 01684 540690
www.malvernhillshotel.co.uk

MOSELEY FARM BED AND BREAKFAST
Moseley Road, Hallow, Worcester WR2 6NL
Tel: 01905 641343 • Fax: 01905 641416
e-mail: moseleyfarmbandb@aol.com
www.moseleyfarmbandb.co.uk

17th Century former farmhouse with large enclosed garden. Rural location, 4 miles from Worcester providing reasonably priced, comfortable acccommodation with Full English Breakfast or Room only. Three family (2 en suite) and one single room, all with Freeview TV, radio alarm clocks, tea/coffee making facilities and free WiFi access. use of fridge, toaster and microwave in dining room. Off-road parking for several vehicles, including Transit vans and trailers. 20 minutes drive from M5, J5 or J7. From £25pppn.
Pets welcome FREE. Exercise pets within enclosed garden or via rights of way to local nature reserve.

Visit the FHG website
www.holidayguides.com

for details of the wide choice of accommodation featured in the full range of FHG titles

Worcestershire

Bishop's Frome

Village 4 miles south of Bromyard.

FIVE BRIDGES COTTAGES, NEAR BISHOP'S FROME, WORCESTER WR6 5BX (01531 640340). Nestled in the heart of the Herefordshire cider apple and hop growing regions, the cottages are set within the owner's 4-acre garden and smallholding. [pw! ⚐]
e-mail: info@fivebridgescottages.co.uk   website: www.fivebridgescottages.co.uk

Great Malvern

The historical centre of the town of Malvern, famous for its large priory, dating from the 11thC.

WHITEWELLS FARM COTTAGES, RIDGEWAY CROSS, NEAR MALVERN WR13 5JR (01886 880607; Fax: 01886 880607). Charming converted Cottages, sleep 2–6. Fully equipped with colour TV, microwave, barbecue, fridge, iron, etc. Linen, towels also supplied. One cottage suitable for the disabled with full wheelchair access. Short breaks, long lets, large groups. ETC ★★★★ [pw! Pets £10 per week.] Also see Display Advert. Contact: DENIS KAVANAGH.
e-mail: info@whitewellsfarm.co.uk   website: www.whitewellsfarm.co.uk

ANN AND BRIAN PORTER, CROFT GUEST HOUSE, BRANSFORD, WORCESTER WR6 5JD (01886 832227). 16th-18th century country house. 10 minutes from Worcester, Malvern and M5. Non-smoking house. Family Room. Bedrooms have en suite (3), colour TV, tea and coffee tray, hairdryer, radio alarm. Dinners available. Dogs welcome. AA ★★ [⚐]
e-mail: dogs@brianporter.orangehome.co.uk   website: www.croftguesthouse.com

HARMONY HOUSE, 184 WEST MALVERN ROAD, MALVERN WR14 4AZ (01684 891650). On the western side of the Malvern Hills. Wonderful views, breakfast tailored to your specific desires, and three spacious en suite bedrooms. Non-smoking. Well behaved dogs welcome.
e-mail: Catherine@HarmonyHouseMalvern.com   website: www.HarmonyHouseMalvern.com

THE COTTAGE IN THE WOOD, HOLYWELL ROAD, MALVERN (01684 588860). High on Malvern Hills. Accommodation over three buildings. 2 AA Restaurant Rosettes, over 600 wines. "Best view in England" - The Daily Mail. Call for brochure. ★★★
website: www.cottageinthewood.co.uk

Malvern

Victorian spa town, now a busy shopping centre and home to an annual music festival.

MALVERN HILLS HOTEL, WYNDS POINT, MALVERN WR13 6DW (01684 540690). Enchanting family-owned and run hotel nestling high in the hills. Direct access to superb walking with magnificent views. Oak-panelled lounge, log fire, real ales, fine food and friendly staff. Great animal lovers. AA ★★★ [Pets £5 per night].
website: www.malvernhillshotel.co.uk

Worcester

Cathedral city on River Severn, 24 miles south-west of Birmingham.

MOSELEY FARM BED & BREAKFAST, MOSELEY ROAD, HALLOW, WORCESTER WR2 6NL (01905 641343; Fax: 01905 641416).17th Century former farmhouse with large enclosed garden. Rural location, 4 miles from Worcester. Full English Breakfast or Room only. Three family (2 en suite) and one single room, all with Freeview TV, radio alarm clocks, tea/coffee making facilities and free WiFi access. Off-road parking. 20 minutes drive from M5, J5 or J7. From £25pppn. [⚐]
e-mail: moseleyfarmbandb@aol.com   website: www.moseleyfarmbandb.co.uk

---

Symbols

⚐   Indicates that pets are welcome free of charge.
£   Indicates that a charge is made for pets: nightly or weekly.
pw!   Shows some special provision for pets; exercise facility, feeding or accommodation arrangement.
⌂   Indicates separate pets accommodation.

East Yorkshire

Beverley, Bridlington, Driffield, Flamborough, Grindale

Robeanne House

Family B&B • Country location, 18 miles from historic York • Ideal for coast and Moors, racing, Beverley, Cycle Route 66 and Wolds Way • Beautiful country house and gardens • All rooms en suite • For bookings please contact *Jeanne Wilson*
Robeanne House, Driffield Lane, Shiptonthorpe, York YO43 3PW
AA ★★★ *Awards for Comfort & Hospitality*
e-mail: *enquiries@robeannehouse.co.uk* • *www.robeannehouse.co.uk*
Tel: 01430 873312

THE TENNYSON
19 TENNYSON AVENUE, BRIDLINGTON YO15 2EU
Tel: 01262 604382

Friendly, good quality guest house offering spacious en suite rooms. Ground floor room available. Non-smoking. Evening meals by arrangement. An easy walk to town centre, North Beach and cliff walks. B&B from £25pppn. Dogs £5 per stay. AA ★★★
www.thetennyson-brid.co.uk

The Old Mill Hotel & Restaurant

Friendly country house hotel in tranquil Yorkshire Wolds. Renowned in-house restaurant provides à la carte and bar meal menu. Beautiful walks, Heritage Coastline, golf, clay pigeon shooting and the famous North York Moors all nearby. The hotel is within easy reach of Beverley, York, Scarborough and Bridlington. Why not come and meet our four Labradors?! B&B per room: £58 single, £85 double. Discount on stays 3+ nights **Mill Lane, Langtoft, Near Driffield YO25 3BQ**
01377 267284 • enquiries@old-mill-hotel.co.uk • www.old-mill-hotel.co.uk
AA ★★

Old Cobbler's Cottage
North Dalton

Pretty cottage with garden. Overlooking picturesque village pond with its ducks and fish. Good walking area and easy access to York and coast. Local pub serving real ale and good food within 20 yards.
01377 217662/217523/07801 124264
e-mail: chris.wade@adastra-music.co.uk
www.waterfrontcottages.co.uk

fully equipped kitchen • living room with open fire and TV/DVD • diningroom • toilet/shower • double bedroom • single bedroom (extra Z-bed available) • conservatory • small patio • off-street parking for one car • gas central heating through out

THORNWICK & SEA FARM HOLIDAY CENTRE, Flamborough YO15 1AU
Tel: 01262 850369 • e-mail: enquiries@thornwickbay.co.uk

Set on the spectacular Heritage Coast with unrivalled coastal scenery • Within easy reach of the North East coast holiday resorts • Six-berth extra wide caravans and fully equipped two-bedroom chalets for hire • Tents and tourers welcome • Caravan Holiday Homes available • Bars, entertainment, shop • Coarse fishing lake • Health Suite with pool, sauna, gym and steam room on site. ETC ★★★★ *David Bellamy Silver Award*
www.thornwickbay.co.uk

Smithy Cottage Grindale, East Yorkshire YO16 4XU

Unique & charming 4-star rated detached single storey 200-year-old former Blacksmiths. Ideal for exploring Heritage Coast, Filey and Bridlington. Spacious, period features, 4-poster bed, log fire, restored to high standard. Parking. Sleeps 4.
Tel: 01904 448925 • e-mail: karen.coman@virgin.net • www.thesmithy.info

East Yorkshire

Hornsea, Howden, Kilnwick Percy

Cherry Tree · Hornsea
Cosy well appointed holiday home in Hornsea, on East Yorkshire Coast. In quiet cul-de-sac off town centre. Large conservatory. Open all year.
Cherry Tree, Cowden Parva Farm, Main Road, Cowden, Aldbrough HU11 4UG
Tel 01964 527245 • Fax 01964 527521 • e-mail: leonardritaruth@yahoo.co.uk

Apple Tree Cottages
Two Self Catering Cottages or Farmhouse B&B on a Yorkshire family farm. You're guaranteed a wonderful stay in friendly, well appointed comfortable surroundings.
Vivienne & John Sweeting, Apple Tree Cottages, The Dairy Farm, Saltmarshe, Howden, East Yorkshire DN14 7RX
Tel: 01430 430 677 • Mobile: 07960 300 337
e-mail: vivienne.sweeting@btinternet.com • www.appletree-cottages.co.uk

PAWS-A-WHILE

Small family B&B set in forty acres of parkland twixt York and Beverley. Golf, Walking, Riding. Pets and horses most welcome. Brochure available.
Tel : 01759 301168 • Mobile: 07711 866869
e-mail: paws.a.while@lineone.net
www.pawsawhile.net
Kilnwick Percy, Pocklington YO42 1UF

Beverley

Popular medieval market and county town in the East Riding of Yorkshire, 8 miles from Kingston upon Hull, 10 miles from Market Weighton and 12 from Hornsea.

ROBEANNE HOUSE, DRIFFIELD LANE, SHIPTONTHORPE, YORK YO43 3PW (01430 873312). Family B&B, country location, 18 miles from historic York. Ideal for coast, Moors, racing, Beverley, Cycle Route 66 and Wolds Way. Beautiful country house and gardens. All rooms en suite. Contact: JEANNE WILSON. AA ★★★ [pw! Pets £5 per night]
e-mail: enquiries@robeannehouse.co.uk   website: www.robeannehouse.co.uk

Bridlington

Traditional family resort with picturesque harbour and a wide range of entertainments and leisure facilities. Ideal for exploring the Heritage coastline and the Wolds.

THE TENNYSON, 19 TENNYSON AVENUE, BRIDLINGTON YO15 2EU (01262 604382). Friendly, good quality guest house offering spacious en suite rooms. Ground floor room available. Non-smoking. Evening meals by arrangement. An easy walk to town centre, North Beach and cliff walks. B&B from £25pppn. AA ★★★ [Pets £5 per stay].
website: www.thetennyson-brid.co.uk

Driffield

Town 11 miles south west of Bridlington.

THE OLD MILL HOTEL & RESTAURANT, MILL LANE, LANGTOFT, NEAR DRIFFIELD YO25 3BQ (01377 267284). Friendly country house hotel in Yorkshire Wolds. A la carte and bar meal menu. Beautiful walks, Heritage Coastline, golf, clay pigeon shooting and famous North York Moors all nearby. Why not come and meet our four Labradors?! AA ★★ [pw! Pets £10 per stay]
e-mail: enquiries@old-mill-hotel.co.uk   website: www.old-mill-hotel.co.uk

OLD COBBLER'S COTTAGE, NORTH DALTON. Pretty cottage with garden looking over village mere with its ducks and fish. Good walking area and easy access to York and coast. Open fire. Local pub serving real ale and good food within 20 yards. For details contact (01377 217662/217523/07801 124264). ETC ★★★ [🐾]
e-mail: chris.wade@adastra-music.co.uk				website: www.waterfrontcottages.co.uk

Flamborough

Village 4 miles NE of Bridlington.

THORNWICK & SEA FARM HOLIDAY CENTRE, FLAMBOROUGH YO15 1AU (01262 850369). Set on the spectacular Heritage Coast with unrivalled coastal scenery. Six-berth caravans and chalets for hire. Tents and tourers welcome. Bars, entertainment, shop, pool and gym on site. ETC ★★★★, David Bellamy Silver Award. [Pets £5 per week.]
e-mail: enquiries@thornwickbay.co.uk				website: www.thornwickbay.co.uk

Grindale

Rural hamlet 4 miles from Bridlington. Ideal for touring Wolds, moors and coast.

SMITHY COTTAGE, GRINDALE YO16 4XU (01904 448933). Unique and charming four-star rated detached single storey 200-year-old former Blacksmiths. Ideal for exploring Heritage Coast. Four-poster bed, log fire, restored to high standard. Parking. Sleeps 4.
e-mail karen.coman@virgin.net					website: www.thesmithy.info

Hornsea

Coastal resort 14 miles NE of Hull.

CHERRY TREE, HORNSEA. Cosy well appointed holiday bungalow in quiet cul-de-sac off town centre. Fully equipped. Large conservatory. Open all year. Contact: MRS RITA LEONARD, COWDEN PARVA FARM, MAIN ROAD, COWDEN, ALDBROUGH HU11 4UG (01964 527245; Fax: 01964 527521). Visit Britain ★★★. [Pets £10 per week.]
e-mail: leonardritaruth@yahoo.co.uk

Howden

Small town 3 miles North of Goole.

VIVIENNE & JOHN SWEETING, APPLE TREE COTTAGES, THE DAIRY FARM, SALTMARSHE, HOWDEN DN14 7RX. (01430 430 677; Mobile: 07960 300 337). Two self-catering Cottages or Farmhouse B&B on a Yorkshire family farm. A wonderful stay in friendly, well appointed comfortable surroundings. [Pets £5 per night]
e-mail: vivienne.sweeting@btinternet.com			website: www.appletree-cottages.co.uk

Kilnwick Percy

Located 2 miles east of Pocklington

PAWS-A-WHILE, KILNWICK PERCY, POCKLINGTON YO42 1UF (01759 301168; Mobile: 07711 866869). Small family B & B set in forty acres of parkland twixt York and Beverley. Golf, walking, riding. Pets and horses most welcome. Brochure available. ETC ★★★★ [pw! 🐾]
e-mail: paws.a.while@lineone.net				website: www.pawsawhile.net

Symbols

🐾   Indicates that pets are welcome free of charge.

£   Indicates that a charge is made for pets: nightly or weekly.

pw!   Shows some special provision for pets; exercise facility, feeding or accommodation arrangement.

⌂   Indicates separate pets accommodation.

North Yorkshire

YORKSHIRE 265

Bentham, Carperby, Clapham, Coverdale

HOLMES FARM • Low Bentham, Lancaster LA2 7DE

Attractively converted and well equipped stone cottage adjoining 17th century farm house, sleeping 4. In a secluded position surrounded by 127 acres of beautiful pastureland. Central heating, fridge, TV, washing machine, games room. Ideal base for visiting Dales, Lake District and coast.

Tel: 015242 61198 • www.holmesfarmcottage.co.uk • e-mail: lucy@holmesfarmcottage.co.uk

THE WHEATSHEAF *in Wensleydale*

Excellent en suite accommodation, including four posters, at this comfortable family owned hotel offering the best of local cuisine and comfort.
The Wheatsheaf, Carperby, Near Leyburn DL8 4DF
Tel: 01969 663216; Fax: 01969 663019 • E-mail: info@wheatsheafinwensleydale.co.uk
www.wheatsheafinwensleydale.co.uk

New Inn *Clapham – 'As relaxed as you like'*
Quality Accommodation in the Yorkshire Dales.

A comfortable hotel in the Yorkshire Dales National Park, The New Inn has been lovingly and carefully refurbished, with a fine blend of old and new to retain the characteristics of this fine 18th Century Coaching Inn.

This traditional Village Inn has 19 en suite bedrooms, including ground floor and disabled bedrooms. Residents' lounge, Restaurant, two comfortable bars serving a selection of local ales, fine wines and a large selection of malt whiskies. Our food offers a mix of traditional and modern cooking.

New Inn, Clapham, Near Ingleton, North Yorkshire LA2 8HH
e-mail: info@newinn-clapham.co.uk
www.newinn-clapham.co.uk

Tel: 015242 51203
Fax: 015242 51824

Peacefully situated farmhouse away from the madding crowd. B&B with optional Evening Meal. Home cooking. Pets sleep where you prefer. Ideally positioned for exploring the beautiful Yorkshire Dales.

Mrs Julie Clarke,
Middle Farm, Woodale,
Coverdale, Leyburn,
North Yorkshire DL8 4TY
01969 640271
e-mail: j-a-clarke@hotmail.co.uk

FHG Guides

publish a large range of well-known accommodation guides.
We will be happy to send you details or you can use the order form
at the back of this book.

North Yorkshire

Danby, Goathland, Grassington, Grewelthorpe

The Fox & Hounds Inn

Residential 16th Century Coaching Inn set amidst the beautiful North York Moors. Freshly prepared dishes served every lunchtime and evening. Superb en suite accommodation available, with all rooms having glorious views. Open all year. Special Breaks available November to March. Situated between Castleton and Danby on the Fryup Road.

ETC ★★★★

Ainthorpe, Danby, Yorkshire YO21 2LD
For bookings please Tel: 01287 660218
e-mail: info@foxandhounds-ainthorpe.com
www.foxandhounds–ainthorpe.com

Rose Cottage B&B
Goathland, North Yorkshire YO22 5AN

One of the most beautiful cottages in the North Yorkshire Moors. • Good location for walks and local amenities • Pets allowed • Non smoking • Private parking • Beauty Treatments available. Contact Emma Brice: emmabrice@rosecottage-heartbeat.com
Tel: 01947 896253; Mobile: 07920 474321   www.rosecottage-heartbeat.com

---

Old Hall Inn
Grassington BD23 5HB   (01756 752641) • oldhallinn@fsmail.net

Main Street, Threshfield,

18thC Inn, renowned for fine ales & award-winning cuisine. Large beer garden. Children's outdoor play area. B&B in four en suite bedrooms; quality self-catering available in adjacent cottages. *Well behaved dogs welcome.*
www.oldhallinnandcottages.co.uk

The Foresters Arms
**MAIN STREET, GRASSINGTON, SKIPTON
NORTH YORKSHIRE BD23 5AA**
Tel: 01756 752349
e-mail: theforesters@totalise.co.uk
www.forestersarmsgrassington.co.uk

The Foresters Arms, Grassington, once an old coaching inn, situated in the heart of the Yorkshire Dales. An ideal centre for walking or touring. A family-run business for over 40 years. Serving hand-pulled traditional ales. Home made food served lunchtime and evening. All bedrooms are en suite, having satellite TV and tea/coffee making facilities. Prices £35 single; £70 double. *Proprietor: Rita Richardson*

Fir Tree Farm Holiday Homes - Willow Tree Lodge

Sleeps 4/6. On a privately owned 100-acre farm in beautiful woodland amidst rolling hills, ideal for exploring the Dales. 10 miles from Ripon and 4 miles from Masham. Short breaks available off-peak. Pets welcome.
High Bramley, Grewelthorpe, Ripon HG4 3DL
Tel: 01765 658727 • www.firtree-farm-holidayhomes.co.uk

Publisher's note

While every effort is made to ensure accuracy, we regret that FHG Guides cannot accept responsibility for errors, misrepresentations or omissions in our entries or any consequences thereof. Prices in particular should be checked.

We will follow up complaints but cannot act as arbiters or agents for either party.

North Yorkshire

Harrogate, Hawes

Brimham Rocks Cottages • Self Catering in Yorkshire

Pet-friendly, luxury self-catering cottages in the Yorkshire Dales.
Private hot tubs and heated indoor swimming pool. Disabled access.
High North Farm, Fellbeck, Harrogate HG3 5EY
Tel: 01765 620284 • E-mail: brimhamrc@yahoo.co.uk
www.brimham.co.uk

Southfield Farm Holiday Cottages • Darley, Harrogate HG3 2PR

Two well equipped holiday cottages between Harrogate and Pateley Bridge. Ideal for touring the Dales, with York within easy driving distance. Sleep 3/4 and 6/7. Ample parking. Well behaved pets welcome.

01423 780258 • e-mail: info@southfieldcottages.co.uk • www.southfieldcottages.co.uk

HELME PASTURE, LODGES & COTTAGES
Old Spring Wood

Hartwith Bank, Summerbridge
Harrogate, N. Yorks HG3 4DR
Tel: 01423 780279
e-mail: helmepasture@btinternet.com
www.helmepasture.co.uk

Holidays for Discriminating Dogs
Yorkshire Dales
- Sniffing trails
- Top paw category
- 29 acre woodland walks
- Area of Outstanding Natural Beauty
- David Bellamy Gold Conservation Award
- Watch wildlife from quality accommodation
- Central: Harrogate, York, Skipton, Herriot/Bronte Country

RELAX IN THE HEART OF YORKSHIRE

RUDDING HOLIDAY PARK

LUXURY COTTAGES AND TIMBER LODGES IN BEAUTIFUL SURROUNDINGS

- Deer House family pub
- Children's adventure playground
- Pets welcome • Games room
- Heated outdoor swimming pool and paddling pool
- 18 hole pay & play golf course plus floodlit driving range • 6 hole short course

FOLLIFOOT, HARROGATE HG3 1JH
TEL: 01423 870439 | FAX: 01423 870859
e-mail - holiday-park@ruddingpark.com
www.ruddingpark.co.uk

Cocklake House

MALLERSTANG CA17 4JT • 017683 72080
Charming, High Pennine Country House B&B in unique position above Pendragon Castle in Upper Mallerstang Dale offering good food and exceptional comfort to a small number of guests. Two double rooms with large private bathrooms. Three acres riverside grounds. Dogs welcome.

Please mention **Pets Welcome!**
when making enquiries about accommodation featured in these pages

Hawes

Experience the unique atmosphere and traditional hospitality at...

Simonstone Hall

Hawes, North Yorkshire DL8 3LY

Set in magnificent countryside near the market town of Hawes, Simonstone Hall is a beautifully restored country house hotel with spectacular views over the dale and surrounding fell.
- Outstanding Bar Meals and Sunday Lunches served in the Game Tavern, and Orangery, our Restaurant, provides an elegant setting for our wide selection of fine foods and wines.
- An excellent base for walking and exploring the Dales.
- Pets welcome in selected rooms.

A relaxed, friendly establishment with open fires, four-poster beds and experienced staff to look after all your needs..

Telephone: 01969 667255
Fax: 01969 667741
enquiries@simonstonehall.com
www.simonstonehall.com

AA ★★ HOTEL

STONE HOUSE HOTEL

Licensed Country House Hotel & Restaurant overlooking Magnificent Wensleydale

23 Quality En Suite Bedrooms
(some with private conservatories opening onto Gardens)

Delicious food & Fine Wines

The Perfect Venue for a relaxing break deep in the heart of the Yorkshire Dales.

Dogs genuinely welcome – Short Breaks available now

Sedbusk, Hawes
North Yorkshire DL8 3PT

Tel: 01969 667571
www.stonehousehotel.co.uk

North Yorkshire

Hawes, Helmsley

COUNTRY COTTAGE HOLIDAYS
DRYDEN HOUSE ◆ MARKET PLACE ◆ HAWES ◆ N. YORKS DL8 3RA

80 Cottages in the lovely Yorkshire Dales. Our Cottages feature colour TV, central heating, open fires, superb views, gardens, private parking and many allow pets. Sleep 1-10. Short breaks throughout the year - Rents from £120 per Break. Weekly Rents from £200 per week. Brochure / Booking Line open 9.00am - 6.00pm daily (Answer machine out of hours).

Browse/book our properties on www.countrycottageholidays.co.uk

Telephone **WENSLEYDALE (01969) 667 654**

Valley View Farm

Old Byland, Helmsley, York,
North Yorkshire YO62 5LG
Telephone: 01439 798221

JOHN & SALLY ROBINSON'S
HOLIDAY COTTAGES

Our six cottages, sleeping 2-10 are situated on a working farm within the scenic countryside of the North York Moors National Park, close to Rievaulx Abbey and five miles from the delightful market town of Helmsley. There is good walking with several walks mapped into the surrounding countryside from the farm. Enjoy rural peace and tranquillity in an ideal location for exploring Yorkshire. Dogs welcome by arrangement. Choice of cottages for 2. Short breaks are offered, subject to availability. Optional on-line booking.

e-mail: sally@valleyviewfarm.com
www.valleyviewfarm.com

THE BLACK SWAN HOTEL • YORKSHIRE

The Black Swan Hotel has dominated the market square of Helmsley for centuries, – a local landmark as well as a luxury Yorkshire hotel. Guests come for a variety of reasons – romantic interludes, great food, boutique shopping, walking on the North Yorkshire Moors, weddings and business meetings ... not forgetting our award-winning Tearoom and Patisserie.

The Black Swan Hotel, Market Place, Helmsley, Yorkshire YO62 5BJ
t: 01439 770466 • e: enquiries@blackswan-helmsley.co.uk
www.blackswan-helmsley.co.uk

270 YORKSHIRE — North Yorkshire

Helmsley, High Bentham, Ingleton, Knaresborough, Leyburn, Malham, Northallerton, Pickering

VisitBritain Silver Award ★★★★

Laskill Grange • Near Helmsley
AA ★★★★

Delightful country house is set in a one-acre garden which has a lake with ducks, swans, peacock and a visiting otter. All rooms lovingly cared for and well equipped. Four bedrooms are in beamed outbuildings and open onto a lawn. All rooms en suite. Generous cuisine using local fresh produce, and vegetarians catered for. Open all year. B&B from £28.50-£50. Also 7 luxury self-catering cottages.

Laskill Grange, Hawnby, Near Helmsley YO62 5NB (Contact Sue Smith)
01439 798268 • e-mail: laskillgrange@tiscali.co.uk • www.laskillgrange.co.uk

Lowther Hill Caravan Park

Small licensed site set in the Yorkshire Dales with uninterrupted panoramic views. Easy access to the Dales, coast and Lakes. Rally field and barn for use in wet weather. Tourers and motorhomes welcome.

High Bentham, North Yorkshire LA2 7AN
Contact: Mrs I. Carr • Tel: 01524 261657
www.caravancampingsites.co.uk/northyorkshire/lowtherhill.htm

GALE GREEN COTTAGE

A warm welcome, great food and superb scenery at our friendly B&B ideally located for all types of hill and mountain walking in one of England's natural beauty spots.
Two double and one twin rooms, all en suite. Guest lounge

Jill Howarth, Gale Green Cottage, Ingleton, North Yorkshire LA6 3NJ
Telephone: 015242 41245 • E-mail: jill@galegreen.com • www.galegreen.com

Newton House, Knaresborough

Delightful Georgian Guest Accommodation. Spacious, tastefully decorated, exceptionally well equipped rooms. Ideal base for exploring Yorkshire.
• Genuine warm welcome • Comfortable sitting-room • DAB radios, TVs, WIFI
• Molton Brown toiletries • Licensed • **Tel: 01423 863539**
www.newtonhouseyorkshire.com newtonhouse@btinternet.com
AA 4 Star Highly Commended • AA Breakfast award

THE OLD STAR, WEST WITTON, LEYBURN DL8 4LU

Former 17th century Coaching Inn now run as a guest house. Oak beams, log fire, home cooking. En suite B&B from £27 pppn.
e-mail: enquiries@theoldstar.com   www.theoldstar.com
BARBARA & BARRIE MARTIN   01969 622949

Malham - Miresfield Farm •

In beautiful gardens bordering village green and stream. Well known for excellent food. 11 bedrooms, all with private facilities. Full central heating. Two well furnished lounges and conservatory for guests' use. ETC ★★★. B&B from £24pppn. **Mr C. Sharp,**
Miresfield Farm, Malham, Skipton BD23 4DA • Tel: 01729 830414

These former farm buildings have been converted into four well-equipped cottages (sleep 2/4), cosily heated for year round appeal. Centrally located between Dales and Moors with York, Whitby and Scarborough all within easy driving distance. Weekly rates from £190 inclusive of all linen, towels, heating and electricity. Short breaks available. Pub food 1.5 miles, golf two miles, shops three miles. Pets welcome. *Brochure:*
Julie & Jim Griffith, Hill House Farm, Little Langton, Northallerton DL7 0PZ (01609 770643) • info@hillhousefarmcottages.com • www.hillhousefarmcottages.com

BANAVIE
ETC ★★★★

Mrs Ella Bowes, Banavie, Roxby Road, Thornton-le-Dale, Pickering YO18 7SX Tel: 01751 474616

Large stone-built semi-detached house set in Thornton-le-Dale. Ideal for touring. One family bedroom and two double bedrooms, all en suite. All with TV, shaver points, central heating and tea-making facilities. Open all year. Car park, cycle shed. B&B from £27pppn. Hygiene Certificate held. Your pets are very welcome.
www.banavie.uk.com • e-mail: info@banavie.uk.com

North Yorkshire

YORKSHIRE 271

Pickering, Port Mulgrave, Scalby Nabs (Scarborough), Scarborough, Skipton

The White Swan Inn at Pickering
Market Place, Pickering, North Yorkshire YO18 7AA
Tel: 01751 472288 • Fax: 01751 475554
e-mail: welcome@white-swan.co.uk
www.white-swan.co.uk

AA Rosette since 1996 • ETC ★★★

16th century inn, with a buzz. Relaxed and informal atmosphere with friendly and professional staff. A passion for good food, fine wine and people.

Discover our exclusive meat supply from The Ginger Pig - a top butcher, with fantastic rare breed meat farmed just 7 miles from the inn.

Rooms and Suites beyond expectation but affordably priced. The surrounding countryside offers a thousand and one things to do and places to visit.

NORTH YORKSHIRE MOORS NATIONAL PARK

Stone Cottage with log fire in North York Moors National Park. Sleeps 4. Near Cleveland Coastal Footpath, sea view. Non-smoking. Whitby 9 miles. Brochure available.

Mrs J. Hiley, 3 Valley Gardens, Stockton-On-Tees, Teesside TS19 8BE
Tel: 01642 613888

EAST FARM COUNTRY COTTAGES, Scalby Nabs, Scarborough, North Yorks • 01723 353635

Three single storey, two-bedroom stone cottages (no steps/stairs), set in beautiful countryside within the National Park yet only 5 minutes away from Scarborough. All cottages non-smoking, garden and parking. Ideal base for walking and touring the coastline. Terms £220-£510 per week.

e-mail: joeastfarmcottages@hotmail.com • www.eastfarmcountrycottages.co.uk

The very best of coast and country. Luxurious facilities, adventure playground, site shop, 4 acre floodlit dog walk, bus service from park entrance. Adjoining village with pubs and fish shop. Seasonal pitches, supersites, hardstanding and storage. Open 1st March - 31st October.
½ mile to beach, 3 miles to Scarborough, 4 miles to Filey.

Cayton Village Caravan Park Ltd, Mill Lane, Cayton Bay, SCARBOROUGH YO11 3NN
01723 583171 • info@caytontouring.co.uk • www.caytontouring.co.uk

HARMONY COUNTRY LODGE
Limestone Road, Burniston, Scarborough YO13 0DG (Non-Smoking) ETC ★★★★

Unique octagonal peaceful retreat in own grounds with superb 360º views of National Park and sea. Two miles from Scarborough. Parking facilities and fully licensed. B&B £29 to £37. Five-berth caravan available for self-catering from £130 to £340. Local dog walks. Pets welcome.

Sue & Tony Hewitt • Tel: 0800 2985540 • www.harmonycountrylodge.co.uk

Available for Holiday Letting on a weekly or short break basis. Large Victorian terraced house with 7 bedrooms, sleeps up to 14. Suitable for large groups, extended families or just for the luxury of plenty of space! Dogs welcome by arrangement. Well equipped kitchen with a working Aga, dining room, lounge and cosy basement TV room.

Craven House
56 Keighley Road, Skipton BD23 2NB
Tel & Fax: 01756 794657
info@craven-house.co.uk
www.craven-house.co.uk

BECK HALL, MALHAM BD23 4DJ

18th century B&B on the Pennine Way, log fires and huge breakfasts. Four-poster bedrooms. Midweek and 4-night specials. Ideal for exploring the Yorkshire Dales. Tel: 01729 830332
e-mail: simon@beckhallmalham.com
www.beckhallmalham.com

North Yorkshire

Skipton, Stainforth, Staithes, Thirsk

Enjoy Yorkshire at its best

Situated on the A65 Skipton to the Lakes, The Coniston Hotel provides an ideal base for guests wishing to explore the Yorkshire Dales or just get away from it all. Set in a stunning 1400-acre estate with a 24-acre lake, the pet friendly hotel offers 50 en suite bedrooms, a beautiful restaurant and bar with a variety of on-site activities including Clay Pigeon Shooting, Falconry, Land Rover 4x4 Experience and fishing.

Coniston Cold, Skipton,
N.Yorkshire BD23 4EA

01756 748080

info@theconistonhotel.com
www.theconistonhotel.com

The Coniston Hotel

Over 250 super self-catering cottages
IN THE YORKSHIRE DALES, YORK, COAST, MOORS, LANCASHIRE, PEAK and LAKE DISTRICT
Fully illustrated brochure **01756 700872** www.holidaycotts.co.uk
Holiday Cottages Yorkshire Ltd., *Incorporating Red Rose Cottages*
Water St., Skipton, North Yorkshire BD23 1PB

- **2 Hollies Cottages** • **Pet-friendly Self Catering Holiday Accommodation in North Yorkshire**

Traditional Dales 2-bedroom cottage situated in the Yorkshire Dales National Park. Sleeps 4. Open coal fire. Linen provided.
Townhead Cottage, Stainforth, Near Settle, North Yorkshire BD24 9PJ
Tel: **01729 822255 / 824895** • Fax: **01729 822404**
www.stainforth-holiday-cottage-settle.co.uk

Situated on a quiet terrace in the old part of the picturesque, historic village of Staithes, with its artistic and Captain Cook associations, Brooklyn is a solid, red brick house, built in 1921 by a retired sea captain. It has three letting rooms (two doubles, one twin) which are individually decorated with views across the rooftops to Cowbar cliffs. All have a television and tea/coffee making facilities, and although not en suite, do have washbasins. The dining room doubles as a sitting room for guests, and breakfasts are generous, vegetarians catered for, and special diets by arrangement. Pets and children are most welcome.

BROOKLYN B & B

MS M.J. HEALD, BROOKLYN B&B,
BROWN'S TERRACE, STAITHES,
NORTH YORKSHIRE TS13 5BG
Tel: **01947 841396**
m.heald@tiscali.co.uk
www.brooklynuk.co.uk

Foxhills Hideaways • Felixkirk, Thirsk YO7 2DS

Quiet, no hassle holidays in cosy Scandinavian log cabins. Secluded garden setting. Central for the Moors, Dales, York and the coast. Village pub round the corner.

Fully inclusive prices (£250 to £370 per week). Open all year. Pets welcome.

Out of season short breaks from £120 inclusive. Please write or phone for a brochure
TELEPHONE 01845 537575

North Yorkshire
Thirsk, Whitby

YORKSHIRE 273

POPLARS HOLIDAY COTTAGES AND BED & BREAKFAST • THIRSK

The Poplars stands in two acres of lovely gardens with a field for dog walking. We have old brick cottages and new lodges, with bed and breakfast in the Poplars House. Contact
AMANDA RICHARDS, THE POPLARS, CARLTON MINIOTT, THIRSK YO7 4LX
Tel: 01845 522712 • www.thepoplarsthirsk.com

Clitherbecks Farm • Danby • Whitby

Self catering accommodation for up to seven people in this traditional hill farmhouse. Near Danby and the National Parks Moors Centre. Own entrance. Open all year.
Mrs Catherine Harland, Clitherbecks Farm, Danby YO21 2NT
Tel: 01287 660251 • E-mail: nharland@clitherbecks.freeserve.co.uk
www.clitherbecks.freeserve.co.uk

◆ White Rose Holiday Cottages ◆
Whitby • Sleights • Sneaton

Quality cottages and bungalows offering a warm and friendly welcome. Sleeping 1-9. Private parking. Ideal for coast and country.
June & Ian Roberts, 5 Brook Park, Sleights, Near Whitby, North Yorkshire YO21 1RT
Enquiries: Tel: 01947 810763 • www.whiterosecottages.co.uk

Raven Hall COUNTRY HOUSE HOTEL, LODGES & GOLF COURSE
Ravenscar, Scarborough YO13 0ET • 01723 870353 • Fax: 01723 870072
e-mail: enquiries@ravenhall.co.uk • www.ravenhall.co.uk

High above the cliffs where the North York Moors roll down to the sea, this imposing hotel is full of Georgian splendour, and offers outstanding accommodation, superb, typically Yorkshire cuisine and an impressive range of leisure facilities including a 9-hole golf course. A family holiday paradise. AA ★★★   **NEW LUXURY LODGES**

Self-catering two-bedroom cottages,
all fully equipped. Central heating
Whitby 2k • Close to sea and moors
• Dogs welcome • Parking • Camping Site
For further information phone

Tel: 07545 641943
www.swallowcottages.co.uk
karl@swallowcottages.co.uk
KARL HEYES, 15 BEECHFIELD, HIGH HAWSKER
WHITBY YO22 4LQ

North Yorkshire

Whitby, York

ARCHES GUESTHOUSE
Just as a Bed & Breakfast should be

8 Havelock Place, Hudson Street, Whitby YO21 3ER • B&B £30-£40pppn

A traditional seaside B&B, offering outstanding cleanliness, comfort, and great breakfasts. Centrally located, The Arches is the ideal base for experiencing the old world charms of this historic seaside town, exploring the beautiful North Yorkshire Moors and Coast, or just relaxing. Pets, with well behaved owners, may stay free of charge!
• Ground floor rooms • Pet-friendly • Family-friendly • Bikers & Hikers welcome. • Book on line.

Ruth & Dick Brew (01947 601880 or 0800 9154250)
• e-mail: archeswhitby@freeola.com • www.whitbyguesthouses.co.uk

---

YORK LAKESIDE LODGES
Moor Lane, York YO24 2QU
Tel: 01904 702346
e-mail: neil@yorklakesidelodges.co.uk

Unique in a city! Luxurious Scandinavian lodges, and cottages in mature parkland overlooking large private fishing lake. Nearby superstore with coach to centre every 10 minutes. Easy access to ring road for touring. Open year round.

YORKSHIRE & HUMBERSIDE TOURIST BOARD WHITE ROSE AWARDS FOR TOURISM
WINNER

Award – British Holiday Home Parks Association

ETC 4/5 STARS SELF-CATERING www.yorklakesidelodges.co.uk

HIGH BELTHORPE

Set on an ancient moated site at the foot of the Yorkshire Wolds, this comfortable Victorian farmhouse offers huge breakfasts, private fishing and fabulous walks. With York only 13 miles away, it is a peaceful rural idyll that both dogs and owners will love. Open all year except Christmas. From £25.

Bishop Wilton, York YO42 1SB
Tel: 01759 368238
Mobile: 07786 923330
e-mail: meg@highbelthorpe.co.uk

WOLDS VIEW COTTAGES. Attractive, well equipped accommodation in unspoilt countryside at the foot of the Yorkshire Wolds. Five units, sleeping from three to eight. Themed holidays, with transport provided, exploring the villages and countryside nearby; York only 12 miles. From £145-£540 per week. Short Breaks available. • Pets welcome. • 3 properties suitable for wheelchairs. CAT. 1, 2 AND 3 NATIONAL ACCESSIBLE SCHEME.

For further details contact: **Mrs M.S.A. Woodliffe** Tel: 01759 302172 • Mill Farm, Yapham, Pocklington, York YO42 1PH

ASCOT HOUSE 80 East Parade, York YO31 7YH • Tel: 01904 426826
Fax: 01904 431077 • ETC/AA ★★★★ • ETC SILVER AWARD

An attractive Victorian villa with easy access to the historic city centre by walking or by public transport. Most rooms have four-poster or canopy beds, and family and double rooms are en suite. All rooms have central heating, colour TV and tea/coffee facilities. Singles from £60 to £70, doubles £68 to £80 including Traditional English Breakfast and VAT. Free private enclosed car park.

• e-mail: admin@ascothouseyork.com • www.ascothouseyork.com

ST GEORGE'S
6 ST GEORGE'S PLACE
YORK YO24 1DR

Family-run guest house in quiet cul-de-sac near racecourse. All rooms en suite with colour TV, tea/coffee making facilities. Private parking. Pets welcome by arrangement

ETC/AA ★★★
e-mail: sixstgeorg@aol.com
www.stgeorgesyork.com
01904 625056
From £65 per double or twin room

North Yorkshire

Bentham

Quiet village amidst the fells. Good centre for rambling and fishing. Ingleton 5 miles north-east.

MRS L. J. STORY, HOLMES FARM, LOW BENTHAM, LANCASTER LA2 7DE (015242 61198). Cottage conversion in easy reach of Dales, Lake District and coast. Central heating, fridge, TV, washer, games room. ETC ★★★★. [🐾]
e-mail: lucy@holmesfarmcottage.co.uk website: www.holmesfarmcottage.co.uk

Carperby

Village one mile North of Aysgarth.

THE WHEATSHEAF, CARPERBY, NEAR LEYBURN DL8 4DF (01969 663216; Fax: 01969 663019) Excellent en suite accommodation in 12 bedrooms (including four posters), at this comfortable family-owned hotel offering the best of local cuisine and comfort. [Pets £5 per night].
e-mail: info@wheatsheafinwensleydale.co.uk website: www.wheatsheafinwensleydale.co.uk

Clapham

Village 6 miles NW of Settle.

NEW INN, CLAPHAM, NEAR INGLETON LA2 8HH (015242 51203; Fax: 015242 51824). 'As relaxed as you like'. A comfortable hotel in the Yorkshire Dales National Park. The ideal holiday destination for your pet, be assured of a warm and friendly reception, sit back, close your eyes and soak up the history and atmosphere. ETC ★★. [Pets £5 per night]
e-mail: info@newinn-clapham.co.uk website: www.newinn-clapham.co.uk

Coverdale

Located in the Yorkshire Dales National Park, famous for Middleham Castle, Richard III and the Forbidden Corner..

MRS JULIE CLARKE, MIDDLE FARM, WOODALE, COVERDALE, LEYBURN DL8 4TY (01969 640271). Peacefully situated farmhouse away from the madding crowd. B&B with optional Evening Meal. Home cooking. Pets sleep where you prefer. Ideally positioned for exploring the beautiful Yorkshire Dales. [🐾 pw!]
e-mail: j-a-clarke@hotmail.co.uk

Danby

Village on River Esk 12 miles west of Whitby.

THE FOX & HOUNDS INN, AINTHORPE, DANBY YO21 2LD (01287 660218). Residential 16th Century Coaching Inn. All rooms en suite. Enjoy our real ales or quality selected wines. Freshly prepared food served every day. Winter breaks available Nov-March. Open all year. ETC ★★★★ Inn [Pets £2.75 per night.]
e-mail: info@foxandhounds-ainthorpe.com website: www.foxandhounds-ainthorpe.com

Goathland

Small village high on the North York Moors, famous as the village of Aidensfield in the TV series "Heartbeat".

EMMA BRICE, ROSE COTTAGE B&B, GOATHLAND YO22 5AN (01947 896253; Mobile: 07920 474321). One of the most beautiful cottages in the North Yorkshire Moors. Good location for walks and local amenities. Pets allowed. Non smoking. Private parking. Beauty Treatments available. [🐾]
e-mail: emmabrice@rosecottage-heartbeat.com website: www.rosecottage-heartbeat.com

---

Symbols

- 🐾 Indicates that pets are welcome free of charge.
- £   Indicates that a charge is made for pets: nightly or weekly.
- pw! Shows some special provision for pets; exercise facility, feeding or accommodation arrangement.
- ⌂   Indicates separate pets accommodation.

Grassington

Wharfedale village in attractive moorland setting. Ripon 22 miles, Skipton 9.

OLD HALL INN, MAIN STREET, THRESHFIELD, GRASSINGTON BD23 5HB (01756 752441) 18th Century Inn, renowned for fine ales & award-winning cuisine. Children's outdoor play area. B&B in 4 en suite bedrooms; self-catering available in adjacent cottages. Well behaved dogs welcome.
e-mail: oldhallinn@fsmail.net   website: www.oldhallinncottages.co.uk

FORESTERS ARMS, MAIN STREET, GRASSINGTON, SKIPTON BD23 5AA (01756 752349). The Foresters Arms is situated in the heart of the Yorkshire Dales and provides an ideal centre for walking or touring. Within easy reach of York and Harrogate. ETC ★★★ [🐕]
e-mail: theforesters@totalise.co.uk   website: www.forestersarmsgrassington.co.uk

Grewelthorpe

Village 3 miles south of Masham.

FIR TREE FARM HOLIDAY HOMES - WILLOW TREE LODGE, HIGH BRAMLEY, GREWELTHORPE, RIPON HG4 3DL (01765 658727). Sleeps 4/6. On a privately owned 100-acre farm in beautiful woodland amidst rolling hills, ideal for exploring the Dales. 10 miles from Ripon and 4 miles from Masham. Short breaks available off-peak. ETC ★★★★ . [Pets £20 per week.]
website: www.firtree-farm-holidayhomes.co.uk

Harrogate

Charming and elegant spa town set amid some of Britain's most scenic countryside. Ideal for exploring Herriot Country and the moors and dales. York 22 miles, Bradford 19, Leeds 16.

BRIMHAM ROCKS COTTAGES. Pet-friendly, luxury self-catering cottages in the Yorkshire Dales. Private hot tubs and heated indoor swimming pool. Disabled access. Contact: MRS D. GRAY, HIGH NORTH FARM, FELLBECK, HARROGATE HG3 5EY (01765 620284). EnjoyEngland ★★★★ Self Catering.
e-mail: brimhamrc@yahoo.co.uk   website: www.brimham.co.uk

SOUTHFIELD FARM HOLIDAY COTTAGES, DARLEY, HARROGATE HG3 2PR (01423 780258). Two well equipped holiday cottages between Harrogate and Pateley Bridge. Ideal for touring the Dales, with York within easy driving distance. Ample parking. Well behaved pets welcome.
e-mail: info@southfieldcottages.co.uk   website: www.southfieldcottages.co.uk

ROSEMARY HELME, HELME PASTURE LODGES & COTTAGES, OLD SPRING WOOD, HARTWITH BANK, SUMMERBRIDGE, HARROGATE HG3 4DR (01423 780279). Country accommodation for owners and dogs and numerous walks in unspoilt Nidderdale. Central for Harrogate, York, Herriot and Bronte country. National Trust area. ETC ★★★★, ETC Category 1 for Disabled Access. [pw! Pets £5 per night, £25 per week; some free.]
e-mail: holmepasture@btinternet.com   website: www.helmepasture.co.uk

RUDDING HOLIDAY PARK, FOLLIFOOT, HARROGATE HG3 1JH (01423 870439; Fax: 01423 870859). Luxury cottages and lodges sleeping two to seven people. All equipped to a high standard. Pool, licensed bar, golf and children's playground in the Parkland. Illustrated brochure available. [🐕]
e-mail: holiday-park@ruddingpark.com   website: www.ruddingpark.co.uk

Hawes

Small town in Wensleydale, 14 miles south east of Kirkby Stephen.

COCKLAKE HOUSE, MALLERSTANG CA17 4JT (017683 72080). Charming, High Pennine Country House B&B in unique position above Pendragon Castle in Upper Mallerstang Dale offering good food and exceptional comfort to a small number of guests. Two double rooms with large private bathrooms. Three acres riverside grounds. Dogs welcome. [🐕]

SIMONSTONE HALL, HAWES, WENSLEYDALE DL8 3LY (01969 667255; Fax: 01969 667741). Facing south across picturesque Wensleydale. All rooms en suite with colour TV. Fine cuisine. Extensive wine list. Friendly personal attention. A relaxing break away from it all. AA ★★ [Pets £10 per stay]
e-mail: enquiries@simonstonehall.com   website: www.simonstonehall.com

North Yorkshire

YORKSHIRE 277

STONE HOUSE HOTEL, SEDBUSK, HAWES DL8 3PT (01969 667571). This fine Edwardian country house has spectacular views and serves delicious Yorkshire cooking with fine wines. Comfortable en suite bedrooms, some ground floor. Phone for details. [🐾]
website: www.stonehousehotel.co.uk

COUNTRY COTTAGE HOLIDAYS, DRYDEN HOUSE, MARKET PLACE, HAWES DL8 3RA (01969 667654). 80 cottages in the lovely Yorkshire Dales. Colour TV, central heating, open fires. Gardens, private parking. Many allow pets. Rents from £200 per week. Sleep 1-10. [Pets from £8 per week]
website: www.countrycottageholidays.co.uk

Helmsley

A delightful stone-built town on River Rye with a large cobbled square. Thirsk 12 miles.

JOHN & SALLY ROBINSON'S VALLEY VIEW FARM, OLD BYLAND, HELMSLEY, YORK YO62 5LG (01439 798221). Fully equipped self-catering cottages on working farm in North York Moors. Ideal for touring Yorkshire, or just walking the hills and lanes around. Rural peace and tranquillity. Dogs free. Kennel and run available. ETC ★★★★ [🐾]
e-mail: sally@valleyviewfarm.com   website: www.valleyviewfarm.com

THE BLACK SWAN HOTEL, MARKET PLACE, HELMSLEY YO62 5BJ (01439 770466). Luxury Yorkshire hotel in Helmsley market square. Romantic interludes, great food, boutique shopping, walking on the North Yorkshire Moors, weddings and business meetings. AA ★★★. [Pets £10 per stay]
e-mail: enquiries@blackswan-helmsley.co.uk   website: www.blackswan-helmsley.co.uk

SUE SMITH, LASKILL GRANGE, HAWNBY, NEAR HELMSLEY YO62 5NB (01439 798268). Delightful country house set in one-acre gardens; all rooms en suite. Generous cuisine of a high standard using fresh local produce, vegetarians catered for. Newly installed hot tub. Open all year. Also 7 luxury self-catering cottages. ETC ★★★★ Silver Award, AA ★★★★.[🐾]
e-mail: laskillgrange@tiscali.co.uk   website: www.laskillgrange.co.uk

High Bentham

Small market town situated between the Yorkshire Dales and the Lake District.

MRS I. CARR, LOWTHER HILL CARAVAN PARK, HIGH BENTHAM LA2 7AN, (01524 261657). Small licensed site set in the Yorkshire Dales with uninterrupted panoramic views. Easy access to the Dales, coast and Lakes. Rally field and barn for use in wet weather. [🐾]
website: www.caravancampingsites.co.uk/northyorkshire/lowtherhill.htm

Ingleton

Small village in the heart of Three Peaks Country in the Yorkshire Dales.

JILL HOWARTH, GALE GREEN COTTAGE, INGLETON LA6 3NJ (015242 41245) A warm welcome, great food and superb scenery at our friendly B&B ideally located for all types of hill and mountain walking in one of England's natural beauty spots. Two double and one twin rooms, all en suite. Guest lounge. AA ★★★★. [🐾]
e-mail: jill@galegreen.com   website: www.galegreen.com

Knaresborough

Town on escarpment above the River Nidd, 3 miles NE of Harrogate..

NEWTON HOUSE, KNARESBOROUGH. Winner of the AA Pet Friendly Award – pets genuinely welcomed and lots of great walks nearby. Spacious and comfortable, newly refurbished ensuite accommodation and great breakfasts. AA ★★★★ Highly Commended, AA Breakfast Award. Contact MARK & LISA WILSON, NEWTON HOUSE, 5-7 YORK PLACE, KNARESBOROUGH HG5 OAD (Tel: 01423 863539). [🐾]
e-mail: newtonhouse@btinternet.com   website: www.newtonhouseyorkshire.com

Leyburn

Small market town, 8 miles south-west of Richmond, standing above the River Ure in Wensleydale.

BARBARA & BARRIE MARTIN, THE OLD STAR, WEST WITTON, LEYBURN DL8 4LU (01969 622949). Former 17th century Coaching Inn now run as a guest house. Oak beams, log fire, home cooking. En suite B&B from £27 pppn. ETC ★★★ [🐶]
e-mail: enquiries@theoldstar.com　　　　　website: www.theoldstar.com

Malham

Village in upper Airedale, 5 miles east of Settle, across the moors.

MR C. SHARP, MIRESFIELD FARM, MALHAM, SKIPTON BD23 4DA (01729 830414). In beautiful gardens bordering village green and stream. Excellent food. 11 bedrooms, all with private facilities. Full central heating. Two well-furnished lounges and conservatory. B&B from £24pppn. ETC ★★★ [🐶 pw!]

Northallerton

Town 14 miles South of Darlington.

JULIE & JIM GRIFFITH, HILL HOUSE FARM, LITTLE LANGTON, NORTHALLERTON DL7 0PZ (01609 770643). Sleep 2/4. Four well-equipped cottages, cosily heated for year round appeal. Centrally located between Dales and Moors. Weekly rates from £190 incl. Short breaks available. Golf 2 miles, shops 3 miles, pub food 1.5 miles. Pets welcome. VisitBritain ★★★★ [pw! 🐶]
e-mail: info@hillhousefarmcottages.com　　　　　website: www.hillhousefarmcottages.com

Pickering

Pleasant market town on southern fringe of North Yorkshire Moors National Park with moated Norman Castle. Bridlington 31 miles, Whitby 20, Scarborough 16, Helmsley 13, Malton 3.

MRS ELLA BOWES, BANAVIE, ROXBY ROAD, THORNTON-LE-DALE, PICKERING YO18 7SX (01751 474616). Large stone-built semi-detached house set in Thornton-le-Dale. Ideal for touring. One family bedroom and two double bedrooms, all en suite. All with TV, shaver points, central heating and tea-making facilities. Open all year. Car park, cycle shed. B&B from £27pppn. Welcome Host and Hygiene Certificate held. ETC★★★★[🐶]
e-mail: info@banavie.uk.com　　　　　website: www.banavie.uk.com

THE WHITE SWAN INN AT PICKERING (01751 472288). 16th century inn with a buzz. Dog friendly with excellent: service, rooms, food and wine. "...consistently brilliant.." Please phone or visit our website for a brochure. ETC ★★★, AA Rosette [Pets £12.50 per stay].
e-mail: welcome@white-swan.co.uk　　　　　website: www.white-swan.co.uk

Port Mulgrave

Located 1km north of Hinderwell.

NORTH YORK MOORS NATIONAL PARK. Stone Cottage (sleeps) 4 in North York Moors National Park. Sea view, near Cleveland coastal footpath. Log fire, non-smoking. Whitby 9 miles. Brochure available (01642 613888). [🐶]

Scalby Nabs (Scarborough)

Small town and suburb 2 miles north west of Scarborough.

EAST FARM COUNTRY COTTAGES, SCALBY NABS, SCALBY, SCARBOROUGH (01723 353635). Three single-storey two-bedroom stone cottages (no steps/stairs) in national Park; only 5 minutes from Scarborough. All completely non-smoking. Ideal base for walking or touring. VisitBritain ★★★ [Pets from £10 per week.]
e-mail: joeastfarmcottages@hotmail.co.uk　　　　　website: www.eastfarmcountrycottages.co.uk

North Yorkshire

Scarborough

Very popular family resort with good sands. York 41 miles, Whitby 20, Bridlington 17, Filey 7.

CAYTON VILLAGE CARAVAN PARK LTD, MILL LANE, CAYTON BAY, SCARBOROUGH YO11 3NN (01723 583171). Luxurious facilities, adventure playground, site shop, 4-acre floodlit dog walk. Seasonal pitches, supersites, hardstanding and storage. Open 1st March - 31st October. Half-a-mile to beach adjoining village. ETC ★★★★★, David Bellamy Gold Award. [Pets £1 per night].
e-mail: info@caytontouring.co.uk   website: www.caytontouring.co.uk

SUE AND TONY HEWITT, HARMONY COUNTRY LODGE, LIMESTONE ROAD, BURNISTON, SCARBOROUGH YO13 0DG (0800 2985840). A peaceful retreat set in two acres of private grounds with 360° panoramic views of the National Park and sea. An ideal centre for walking or touring. En suite centrally heated rooms with superb views. Non-smoking, licensed, private parking facilities. B&B from £29 to £37. ETC ★★★★ [Pets £3 per night, £15 per week]
e-mail: mail@harmonylodge.net   website: www.harmonycountrylodge.co.uk

Skipton

Airedale market town, centre for picturesque Craven district. Fine Castle (14th cent). York 43 miles, Manchester 42, Leeds 26, Harrogate 22, Settle 16.

CRAVEN HOUSE, 56 KEIGHLEY ROAD, SKIPTON BD23 2NB (Tel & Fax: 01756 794657). Large terraced house with 7 bedrooms, sleeps up to 14. Suitable for large groups, extended families or just for the luxury of plenty of space! Dogs welcome by arrangement. Well equipped kitchen, dining room, lounge and cosy basement TV room. [🐾]
e-mail: info@craven-house.co.uk   website: www.craven-house.co.uk

BECK HALL, MALHAM BD23 4DJ (01729 830332). 18th century B&B on the Pennine Way, log fires and huge breakfasts. Midweek and 4-night specials. Ideal for exploring the Yorkshire Dales. AA ★★★, WELCOME HOST [🐾]
e-mail: simon@beckhallmalham.com   website: www.beckhallmalham.com

THE CONISTON HOTEL, CONISTON COLD, SKIPTON BD23 4EA (01756 748080). Set in a stunning 1400-acre estate, an ideal base for guests wishing to explore the Yorkshire Dales. 50 en suite bedrooms with full facilities. Special rates for leisure breaks and family rooms. ETC ★★★ Silver Award, AA ★★★. [pw! Pets £10 per stay]
e-mail: info@theconistonhotel.com   website: www.theconistonhotel.com

Over 250 super self-catering Cottages in the Yorkshire Dales, York, Coast, Moors, Lancashire, Peak and Lake District. For our fully illustrated brochure apply: HOLIDAY COTTAGES YORKSHIRE LTD (INCORPORATING RED ROSE COTTAGES), WATER STREET, SKIPTON BD23 1PB (01756 700872). [🐾]
website: www.holidaycotts.co.uk

Stainforth

Picturesque village in the Yorkshire Dales, 2½ miles from Settle.

2 HOLLIES COTTAGES. Traditional Dales 2-bedroom cottage situated in the Yorkshire Dales National Park. Sleeps 4. Open coal fire. Linen provided. Pets welcome. Contact: TOWNHEAD COTTAGES, STAINFORTH, NEAR SETTLE BD24 9PJ (01729 822255 / 824895; Fax: 01729 822404). [🐾]
website: www.stainforth-holiday-cottage-settle.co.uk

Symbols

🐾   Indicates that pets are welcome free of charge.

£   Indicates that a charge is made for pets: nightly or weekly.

pw! Shows some special provision for pets; exercise facility, feeding or accommodation arrangement.

⌂   Indicates separate pets accommodation.

Staithes

Fishing village on North Sea coast 9 miles NW of Whitby.

MS M.J. HEALD, BROOKLYN B&B, BROWN'S TERRACE, STAITHES TS13 5BG (01947 841396). Situated in the old part of picturesque and historic Staithes. Two double and one twin bedrooms available, generous breakfasts, vegetarians catered for. Pets and children most welcome. ETC ★★★ [🐕]
e-mail: m.heald@tiscali.co.uk   πwebsite: www.brooklynuk.co.uk

Thirsk

Market town with attractive square. Excellent touring area. Northallerton 3 miles.

FOXHILLS HIDEAWAYS, FELIXKIRK, THIRSK YO7 2DS (01845 537575). 4 Scandinavian log cabins, heated throughout, linen provided. A supremely relaxed atmosphere on the edge of the North York Moors National Park. Open all year. Village pub round the corner. [🐕]

POPLARS HOLIDAY COTTAGES AND BED & BREAKFAST, THIRSK. The Poplars stands in two acres of lovely gardens with a field for dog walking. We have old brick cottages and new lodges, with bed and breakfast in the Poplars House. Contact AMANDA RICHARDS, THE POPLARS, CARLTON MINIOTT, THIRSK YO7 4LX (01845 522712). ETC ★★★★, Silver Award. [Pets £5 per night B&B, £5 per week SC]
website: www.thepoplarsthirsk.com

Whitby

Charming resort with harbour and sands. Of note is the 13th century ruined Abbey. Stockton-on-Tees 34 miles, Scarborough 20, Saltburn-by-the-Sea 19.

THE SEACLIFFE, 12 NORTH PROMENADE, WHITBY YO21 3JX (Freephone 0808 1682118). Magnificent seafront position overlooking beach and harbour entrance. Lovely scenic walks. Restaurant, bar, lounge, patio garden. Evening meals from £12.95: Lamb Shank to Fillet Steak, Whitby Scampi to Lobster. Private car park (8). Dogs by arrangement. See website for menus and special offers. VB ★★★★ Guest Accommodation [🐕]
e-mail: stay@seacliffehotel.com   website: www.seacliffehotel.com

MRS CATHERINE HARLAND, CLITHERBECKS FARM, DANBY YO21 2NT (01287 660321). Self catering accommodation for up to seven people in this traditional hill farmhouse. Near Danby and the National Parks Moors Centre. Own entrance. Open all year. VisitBritain ★★★. [🐕]
e-mail: nharland@clitherbecks.freeserve.co.uk   website: www.clitherbecks.freeserve.co.uk

WHITE ROSE HOLIDAY COTTAGES, NEAR WHITBY. Quality cottages and bungalows offering a warm and friendly welcome. Sleep 1-9. Private parking. Ideal for coast and country. APPLY: MRS J. ROBERTS (PW), 5 BROOK PARK, SLEIGHTS, NEAR WHITBY YO21 1RT (01947 810763) ETC ★★★-★★★★. [Pets £5 per week, pw!]
website: www.whiterosecottages.co.uk

RAVEN HALL COUNTRY HOUSE HOTEL, LODGES & GOLF COURSE, RAVENSCAR, SCARBOROUGH YO13 0ET (01723 870353; Fax: 01723 870072). This imposing hotel offers oustanding accommodation, superb, typically Yorkshire cuisine and an impressive range of leisure facilities including a 9-hole golf course. A family holiday paradise. AA ★★★. New luxury lodges. [pw! Pets £5 per night.]
e-mail: enquiries@ravenhall.co.uk   website: www.ravenhall.co.uk

SWALLOW HOLIDAY COTTAGES. Discover historic Whitby, pretty fishing villages, way-marked walks. Four cottages, one or two bedrooms. Private parking. Children and dogs welcome. Weekly rates from £195 to £500. Please phone or write for a brochure. KARL HEYES, 15 BEECHFIELD, HIGH HAWSKER, WHITBY YO22 4LQ (07545 641943). [🐕]
e-mail: karl@swallowcottages.co.uk   website: www.swallowcottages.co.uk

ARCHES GUESTHOUSE, 8 HAVELOCK PLACE, HUDSON STREET, WHITBY YO21 3ER. Pet friendly, family-run guesthouse, where a warm welcome and large breakfast is always assured. The ideal base for experiencing the old world charms of this historic seaside town, exploring the beautiful North Yorkshire Moors, or just relaxing. Strictly non-smoking. £30- £40 pppn. RUTH & DICK BREW (01947 601880 or 0800 9154256). [🐕]
e-mail: archeswhitby@freeola.com   website: www.whitbyguesthouses.co.uk

North Yorkshire / West Yorkshire

York

Historic cathedral city and former Roman Station on River Ouse. Magnificent Minster and 3 miles of ancient walls. Facilities for a wide range of sports and entertainments. Horse-racing on Knavesmire. Bridlington 41 miles, Filey 41, Leeds 24, Harrogate 22.

YORK LAKESIDE LODGES, MOOR LANE, YORK YO24 2QU (01904 702346). Self-catering pine lodges. Mature parkland setting. Large fishing lake. Nearby superstore with coach to centre every 10 mins. ETC ★★★★/★★★★★ [pw! Pets £25 per week]
e-mail: neil@yorklakesidelodges.co.uk   website: www.lakesidelodges.co.uk

HIGH BELTHORPE, BISHOP WILTON, YORK YO42 1SB (01759 368238; Mobile: 07786 923330). Set on an ancient moated site at the foot of the Yorkshire Wolds, this comfortable Victorian farmhouse offers huge breakfasts, private fishing and fabulous walks. Dogs and owners will love it! Open all year except Christmas. Prices from £25. ETC ★★★ [pw! 🐾]
e-mail: meg@highbelthorpe.co.uk

WOLDS VIEW COTTAGES. Attractive, well equipped accommodation, sleeping 3-8 (some suitable wheelchairs). Themed holidays, with transport provided. York 12 miles. Pets welcome. MRS M. S. A. WOODLIFFE, MILL FARM, YAPHAM, POCKLINGTON, YORK YO42 1PH (01759 302172).

ASCOT HOUSE, 80 EAST PARADE, YORK YO31 7YH (01904 426826; Fax: 01904 431077). Attractive Victorian villa with easy access to city centre. Family and double rooms en suite. Comfortable residents' lounge, dining room. Single room £60-£70, double room £68-£80. Free private enclosed car park. ETC/AA ★★★★, ETC Silver Award. [🐾]
e-mail: admin@ascothouseyork.com   website: www.ascothouseyork.com

ST GEORGE'S, 6 ST GEORGE'S PLACE, YORK YO24 1DR (01904 625056). Family-run guest house in quiet cul-de-sac near racecourse. All rooms en suite with colour TV, tea/coffee making facilities. Private parking. Pets welcome by arrangement. From £65 double or twin room. ETC/AA ★★★ [🐾]
e-mail: sixstgeorg@aol.com   website: www.stgeorgesyork.com

West Yorkshire

Bingley

THE FIVE RISE LOCKS HOTEL & RESTAURANT, BECK LANE, BINGLEY BD16 4DD
Large Victorian house tucked away in tranquil area, but close main roads, tourist sites, cities. Good views, individual decor, informal style. Comfy sofas, interesting artworks. Antidote to chain hotels. Historic canal locks and excellent walking (dogs and humans) close by.
AA/VisitBritain ★★★★ - Tel: 01274 565296
e-mail: info@five-rise-locks.co.uk • • www.five-rise-locks.co.uk

Bingley

Town on River Aire 5 miles north-west of Bradford.

THE FIVE RISE LOCKS HOTEL & RESTAURANT, BECK LANE, BINGLEY BD16 4DD (01274 565296). Large Victorian house in tranquil area, but close main roads, tourist sites. Good views, individual decor, informal style. Historic canal locks and excellent walking (dogs and humans) close by. AA/VisitBritain ★★★★ [Pets £5 per night]
e-mail: info@five-rise-locks.co.uk   website: www.five-rise-locks.co.uk

Please mention **Pets Welcome!** when making enquiries about accommodation featured in these pages

Durham

Barnard Castle, Bishop Auckland, Castleside, Wolsingham

Laverock Multi-Dog Cottages • Barnard Castle
Two cottages each sleeping up to 5 people. 1st 4 dogs free!! Small charge for 5+. Fantastic views on sheep farm, enclosed gardens, doggy shower room, 10 acre stock free field. 120 foot indoor Agility Building and sheepdog lessons on site.
www.multidogcottages.co.uk   **01833 650695**

Low Lands Farm
Low Lands, Cockfield, Bishop Auckland, Co. Durham DL13 5AW
Tel 01388 718251 • Mobile: 07745 067754
e-mail: info@farmholidaysuk.com • www.farmholidaysuk.com

Two award-winning, beautiful self-catering cottages on a working family farm. If you want peace and quiet in an area of beautiful unspoilt countryside packed with things to see and do, then stay with us. Each cottage sleeps up to four people, plus cot. Beams, log fires, gas BBQ, own gardens and parking. Close to Durham City, the Lake District and Hadrian's Wall. Pets and children most welcome. Terms from £160 to £340, inclusive of linen, towels, electricity and heating. Week-by-week availability/prices on website.

Please contact Alison or Keith Tallentire for a brochure.

Category 3 (one cottage)

Charming farmhouse with stunning views. You will be most welcome. Ideal for Newcastle, Durham, Beamish etc. Bed and Breakfast;dinner available, licensed. Great for pets.
IRENE MORDEY AND DAVID BLACKBURN, BEE COTTAGE FARMHOUSE, CASTLESIDE, CONSETT DH8 9HW (01207 508224)
e-mail: beecottage68@aol.com • www.beecottage.co.uk

Greenwell Hill Farm Cottages

Traditional farm buildings sensitively converted to attractive sandstone cottages offering high standard self-catering accommodation.
TV/DVD • En suite bathrooms
Modern kitchens with fridge/freezer, microwave etc.
Situated in an Area of Outstanding Natural Beauty, within easy reach of many attractions. Ideal for family holidays.
The Stables (sleeps six plus one), The Byre (sleeps two plus two), The Granary (sleeps eight), Barn (sleeps 13), The Gin Gan (sleeps five) and Greenwell Hill Farmhouse (accommodation for ten or more)
Karen Wilson, Greenwell Farm, Tow Law, Co. Durham DL13 4PH • Tel; (01388) 527247
e-mail: enquiries@greenwellhill.co.uk • www.greenwellfarmcottages.co.uk

Visit the FHG website
www.holidayguides.com
for details of the wide choice of accommodation featured in the full range of FHG titles

Durham

Barnard Castle

Named after the castle it was built around, 34 miles south of Newcastle upon Tyne. The Bowes Museum is a popular attraction.

LAVEROCK MULTI-DOG COTTAGES, BARNARD CASTLE (01833 650695). Two cottages each sleeping up to 5 people. Fantastic views on sheep farm, enclosed gardens, doggy shower room, 10 acre stock free field. 120 foot indoor Agility Building and sheepdog lessons on site. [pw! 1st 4 dogs free!! Small charge for 5+].
e-mail: comebyanaway@hotmail.com   website: www.multidogcottages.co.uk

Bishop Auckland

Town on right bank of River Wear, 9 miles south-west of Durham. Castle, of varying dates, residence of the Bishop of Durham.

ALISON & KEITH TALLENTIRE, LOW LANDS FARM, LOW LANDS, COCKFIELD, BISHOP AUCKLAND DL13 5AW (01388 718251; mobile: 07745 067754). Two self-catering cottages on a working livestock farm. Each sleeps up to 4, plus cot. Prices from £160-£340. Call for a brochure. Pets and children most welcome. ETC ★★★★ ETC CATEGORY 3 DISABLED ACCESSIBILITY (one cottage). [Pets £10 per week]
e-mail: info@farmholidaysuk.com   website: www.farmholidaysuk.com

Castleside

A suburb 2 miles south-west of Consett.

DAVID BLACKBURN AND IRENE MORDEY, BEE COTTAGE FARMHOUSE, CASTLESIDE, CONSETT DH8 9HW (01207 508224). Charming farmhouse with stunning views. You will be most welcome. Ideal for Newcastle, Durham, Beamish etc. Bed and Breakfast; dinner available, licensed. Great for pets. VisitBritain ★★★★ [pw! 🐕]
e-mail: beecottage68@aol.com   website: www.beecottage.co.uk

Wolsingham

Town 6 miles NW of Bishop Auckland.

GREENWELL HILL FARM COTTAGES. Superb self-catering accommodation in an Area of Outstanding Natural Beauty overlooking the hills of the North Pennines. Close to leading attractions. Contact: KAREN WILSON, GREENWELL FARM, TOW LAW DL13 4PH (01388 527247)
e-mail: enquiries@greenwellhill.co.uk   website: www.greenwellfarmcottages.co.uk

---

Other specialised holiday guides from FHG

PUBS & INNS OF BRITAIN • **COUNTRY HOTELS** OF BRITAIN
WEEKEND & SHORT BREAK HOLIDAYS IN BRITAIN
THE GOLF GUIDE WHERE TO PLAY, WHERE TO STAY
500 GREAT PLACES TO STAY • **SELF-CATERING HOLIDAYS** IN BRITAIN
BED & BREAKFAST STOPS • **CARAVAN & CAMPING HOLIDAYS**
FAMILY BREAKS IN BRITAIN

Published annually: available in all good bookshops or direct from the publisher:
FHG Guides, Abbey Mill Business Centre, Seedhill, Paisley PA1 1TJ
Tel: 0141 887 0428 • Fax: 0141 889 7204
e-mail: admin@fhguides.co.uk • www.holidayguides.com

NORTHUMBERLAND COTTAGES LTD

A local booking agency, based in the heart of the area between Alnwick and the beautiful sandy beaches of the Heritage Coastline.

Choose from our selection of cottages Telephone 01665 589434 or check availability online at www.northumberlandcottages.com

www.northumberlandcottages.biz Quote FHG

A selection of high quality Holiday Cottages in beautiful coast and country locations throughout Northumberland and the Scottish Borders. All properties have been fully renovated to an excellent standard within the last two years and are fully equipped with everything a holidaymaker needs. Most have wood burning stoves or open fires.

EMAIL holidays@northumberlandcottages.biz   Tel 01289 388938

Acklington, Alnmouth, Alwinton

ACKLINGTON, NORTHUMBERLAND. One, two, three and four-bedroom luxuriously converted stone buildings and farmhouse, set in natural woodland close to the beautiful Northumberland coastline.

BANK HOUSE HOLIDAY COTTAGES

Contact Mr S. Stone • 1 Whalton Park, Morpeth NE61 3TU • Tel: 07525 615411
e-mail: info@bankhouseholidaycottages.co.uk • www.bankhouseholidaycottages.co.uk

Saddle Bed & Breakfast
24/25 Northumberland Street, Alnmouth NE66 2RA • Tel: 01665 830476

Friendly, family-run B&B situated in Alnmouth, on the Northumberland coast, with miles of white sandy beaches and unspoilt countryside; two golf courses. Home-cooked Sunday lunch our speciality. All bedrooms en suite. Children and pets most welcome.

Fellside Cottage • Alwinton • Northumberland National Park

Cosy cottage nestling in beautiful Upper Coquet Valley. Fully furnished to a high standard. Open fire. Lovely garden and patio. Sleeps 3. A walker's paradise. **Contact: Mrs D. Straughan, Bedlington Lane Farm, Bedlington NE22 6AA • Tel: 01670 823042**
e-mail: stay@fellsidecottcheviots.co.uk • www.fellsidecottcheviots.co.uk

Please mention **Pets Welcome!** when making enquiries about accommodation featured in these pages

www.holidayguides.com

Northumberland

Bamburgh, Belford

Waren House Hotel

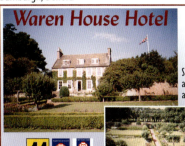

Waren Mill, Belford, Near Bamburgh,
Northumberland NE70 7EE
Tel: 01668 214581 • Fax: 01668 214484
e-mail: enquiries@warenhousehotel.co.uk
www.warenhousehotel.co.uk

Situated majestically above the natural birdlife sanctuary of Budle Bay, this attractive Georgian house offers today's visitors a rare treat for true relaxation along with a central point for venturing through the delights of North Northumberland and the Scottish Borders, including Bamburgh Castle, the Farne Islands, Holy Island and Alnwick Castle and Gardens. The hotel has a reputation for good food which is locally sourced and is accompanied by a substantial wine list.

*Please do "discover" Waren House –
it will be a choice you will never regret.*

The Mizen Head Hotel

Lucker Road, Bamburgh,
Northumberland NE69 7BS

Beautifully refurbished hotel • Locally produced food.
Public bar offers good food and real ales, live music, with an open log fire in winter. Children welcome – family rooms are available with cots if required. Car park. Pets welcome in bedrooms and bar. Local attractions include Bamburgh Castle and Holy Isle. Three-and-a-half mile sandy beach five minutes away. Pets welcome. For golfers discounts can be arranged. Short break details on request.

Tel: 01668 214254 • Fax: 01668 214104
www.mizenheadhotel.co.uk
e-mail: info@mizenheadhotel.co.uk

BLUE BELL FARM

HOLIDAY COTTAGES   BELFORD

www.bluebellfarmbelford.co.uk

Bluebell Farm enjoys a quiet central position in the village of Belford, three miles from the Heritage Coast and within easy walking distance of all village amenities.

Sleep 4-6. Each cottage is equipped with gas cooker, microwave, fridge/freezer or fridge, coffee machine, kettle, toaster and colour television, most with DVD player.

All have gas-fired central heating; living/dining/kitchen areas are open plan.

**Mrs Phyl Carruthers, Bluebell Farm, Belford,
Northumberland NE70 7QE
e-mail: corillas@tiscali.co.uk
or call 01668 213362 for bookings**

286 **NORTH EAST ENGLAND** — Northumberland
Belford, Berwick-Upon-Tweed, Chathill

Etive Cottage
Warenford, Near Belford NE70 7HZ

Etive is a well-equipped two bedroomed stone cottage with double glazing and central heating. Situated on the outskirts of the hamlet of Warenford with open views to the Bamburgh coast. Fenced garden and secure courtyard parking. Pet and owners welcome pack on arrival. Pets welcome to bring along well behaved owners.

Regional Winner - Winalot 'Best Place to Stay'
For brochure contact Jan Thompson

Tel: 01668 213233
e-mail: janet.thompson1@homecall.co.uk

2, THE COURTYARD, BERWICK-UPON-TWEED

Secluded Self Catering Townhouse in heart of old Berwick. Planted courtyard garden and sunny verandah. Historic ramparts 400 yards. Choice of walks. Ideal for exercising pets.
Contact: J Morton, 1, The Courtyard, Church Street, Berwick-Upon-Tweed, TD15 1EE (01289 308737)
e-mail: patmosphere@yahoo.co.uk • www.berwickselfcatering.co.uk

---

Friendly Hound Cottage
Ford Common, Berwick-upon-Tweed TD15 2QD

Set in a quiet rural location, convenient for Holy Island, Berwick, Bamburgh and the Heritage Coastline. Friendly Hound Cottage is a well established, newly refurbished B&B offering top quality accommodation, excellent breakfasts, and a warm welcome. We invite you to arrive as our guests and leave as our friends.

Tel: 01289 388554 • www.friendlyhoundcottage.co.uk

Doxford Farm Cottages • Northumberland

Comfortable self-catering family accommodation on working farm situated amidst unspoilt wooded countryside, five miles from the coast. 8 stone built terrace cottages.
Contact: Sarah Shell, Doxford Farm, Chathill, Alnwick, Northumberland NE67 5DY
Tel: 01665 579348 • mobile: 07734 247277 • e-mail: sarah@doxfordfarmcottages.com
www.doxfordfarmcottages.com   VisitBritain ★★★/★★★★

Northumberland

NORTH EAST ENGLAND

Corbridge, Eals, Haltwhistle, Hexham

The Hayes • Corbridge   www.hayes-corbridge.co.uk

Stable and *Bothy*

Formerly stables, now converted into two cottages, each sleeps up to 5. Each has one double and one twin bedroom, and shower room upstairs; downstairs cloakroom; living and dining areas. Electric cooker, fridge, microwave, washing machine and dishwasher; TV, CD/DVD; central heating throughout. Wifi available. Pets welcome.
Newcastle Road, Corbridge, Northumberland NE45 5LP
Tel: 01434 632010 • e-mail: stay@hayes-corbridge.co.uk

Stay in stunning Northumberland •• Stonecrop

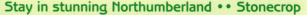

Nestling in the South Tyne Valley in the small hamlet of Eals is this white-washed cottage with its own orchard. Recently renovated, with modern comforts - a new kitchen and bathroom, a cosy log stove and 3 bedrooms. Well behaved pets welcome.
Contact: Richard Parker, Eastgate, Milburn, Penrith, Cumbria CA10 1TN
Tel: 01768 361509 • www.stonecrop.co.uk

Scotchcoulthard • Haltwhistle, Northumberland NE49 9NH
01434 344470 • *Props: A.D. & S.M. Saunders*
e-mail: scotchcoulthard@hotmail.co.uk • www.scotchcoulthard.co.uk

Situated in 178 acres within Northumberland National Park, fully equipped self-catering cottages (sleep 2/7). All bedrooms en suite; open fires. Fridge/freezer, colour TV, microwave; all except one have dishwasher and washing machine. Linen, towels, all fuel incl. Heated indoor pool, games room. Rare breed farm animals. Children and dogs welcome.

KATH AND BRAD DOWLE • SAUGHY RIGG FARM
TWICE BREWED, HALTWHISTLE NE49 9PT • 01434 344120

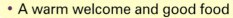

Close to the best parts of Hadrian's Wall
- A warm welcome and good food
- All rooms en suite
- Parking • TV
- Central heating.
- Children and pets welcome
- Open all year
- Prices from £35 pppn.

e-mail: info@saughyrigg.co.uk • www.saughyrigg.co.uk

Struthers Farm ❖ Catton, Allendale, Hexham NE47 9LP

A warm welcome in the heart of England. Splendid local walks, panoramic views.
Double/twin en suite rooms, central heating. Good farmhouse cooking.
Ample safe parking. Near Hadrians Wall. Children welcome, pets by prior arrangement.
Open all year. Bed and Breakfast from £30; Optional Evening Meal from £12.50.

Contact Mrs Ruby Keenleyside • 01434 683580 • www.struthersfarmbandb.com

Northumberland

Hexham, Longhorsley, Wooler

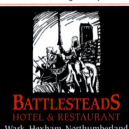

Dating from 1747, this stone-built inn and restaurant features excellent bar meals and à la carte menus, good choice of wines, and cask and conditioned beers.

A friendly, family-run hotel, with 17 en suite bedrooms, including ground floor rooms with disabled access, it is ideally placed for Hadrian's Wall, Kielder and Border Reiver Country.
• Pets by arrangement only.

From £50-£60pppn

SILVER AWARD

BATTLESTEADS
HOTEL & RESTAURANT
Wark, Hexham, Northumberland
NE48 3LS. TEL: (01434) 230 209
Email: info@battlesteads.com
www.battlesteads.com

Northumberland
★★★★ **Self-catering Holiday Cottage**

Sleeps 8. Bring your horses and dogs on holiday and explore our fabulous countryside, beaches and many local equestrian facilities.

For further information and contact details go to:
www.westmoorfarm.co.uk
mob: 0781 624 5678
e-mail: carolyn@westmoorfarm.co.uk

Superior self catering accommodation in a traditional Northumbrian steading, Secluded and tranquil. Sleeps 4-12. Horses and dogs welcome.
Lynney Holden, Crookhouse, Kirknewton, Wooler NE71 6TN
T: 01668 216113 • e-mail: stay@crookhousecottages.co.uk

CROOKHOUSE www.crookhousecottages.co.uk

Other specialised holiday guides from FHG

PUBS & INNS OF BRITAIN • **COUNTRY HOTELS** OF BRITAIN
WEEKEND & SHORT BREAK HOLIDAYS IN BRITAIN
THE GOLF GUIDE WHERE TO PLAY, WHERE TO STAY
500 GREAT PLACES TO STAY • **SELF-CATERING HOLIDAYS** IN BRITAIN
BED & BREAKFAST STOPS • **CARAVAN & CAMPING HOLIDAYS**
FAMILY BREAKS IN BRITAIN

Published annually: available in all good bookshops or direct from the publisher:
FHG Guides, Abbey Mill Business Centre, Seedhill, Paisley PA1 1TJ
Tel: 0141 887 0428 • Fax: 0141 889 7204
e-mail: admin@fhguides.co.uk • www.holidayguides.com

Northumberland

NORTH EAST ENGLAND 289

NORTHUMBERLAND COTTAGES LTD. A local booking agency, based in the heart of the area between Alnwick and the beautiful sandy beaches of the Heritage Coastline. Choose from our selection of inland and coastal cottages. Telephone 01665 589434 or check availability online. [Pets £20 per week]
e-mail: enquiries@northumberlandcottages.com   website: www.northumberlandcottages.com

A selection of high quality Holiday Cottages in beautiful coast and country locations throughout Northumberland and the Scottish Borders. All properties fully renovated and equipped. Most with open fires/wood burning stoves. (01289 388938). Quote FHG. [Pets £10 per week]
e-mail: holidays@northumberlandcottages.biz   website: www.northumberlandcottages.biz

Acklington

Village 3 miles south west of Amble.

MR STEVEN STONE, BANK HOUSE HOLIDAY COTTAGES, 1 WHALTON PARK, MORPETH NE61 3TU (07525 615411). One, two, three and four-bedroom luxuriously converted stone buildings and farmhouse, set in natural woodland close to the beautiful Northumberland coastline. VisitBritain ★★★★ Self Catering. [🐕]
e-mail: info@bankhouseholidaycottages.co.uk   website: www.bankhouseholidaycottages.co.uk

Alnmouth

Seaside village situated at the mouth of the River Aln.

SADDLE B&B, 24/25 NORTHUMBERLAND STREET, ALNMOUTH NE66 2RA (01665 830476). Friendly, family-run B&B on the Northumberland coast. Home-cooked Sunday lunches. Car park. All bedrooms en suite. Children and pets most welcome. [🐕]

Alwinton

Village in Upper Coquetdale, 9 miles from Rothbury.

FELLSIDE COTTAGE, ALWINTON. Cosy cottage nestling in beautiful Upper Coquet Valley. Fully furnished to a high standard. Open fire. Lovely garden and patio. Sleeps 3. A walker's paradise. Walkers and Cyclists Welcome. VisitBritain ★★★★. Contact: MRS D. STRAUGHAN, BEDLINGTON LANE FARM, BEDLINGTON NE22 6AA (01670 823042). [🐕]
e-mail: stay@fellsidecottcheviots.co.uk   website: www.fellsidecottcheviots.co.uk

Bamburgh

Village on North Sea coast with magnificent castle. Grace Darling buried in churchyard.

WAREN HOUSE HOTEL, WAREN MILL, BAMBURGH NE70 7EE (01668 214581). Luxurious Country House Hotel. Excellent accommodation, superb food, moderately priced wine list. Rural setting. No children under 14 please. ETC ★★★ Silver Award, AA ★★★ One Rosette.[🐕]
e-mail: enquiries@warenhousehotel.co.uk   website: www.warenhousehotel.co.uk

THE MIZEN HEAD HOTEL, BAMBURGH NE69 7BS (01668 214254; Fax: 01668 214104). A warm welcome awaits owners and pets alike at the Mizen Head. Close to the beautiful Northumbrian coastline and just a short drive from many lovely walks in the Ingram Valley. The hotel boasts log fires, live music, good food and real ales.
e-mail: info@mizenheadhotel.co.uk   website: www.mizenheadhotel.co.uk

Belford

Village 14 miles SE of Berwick-Upon-Tweed.

MRS PHYL CARRUTHERS, BLUEBELL FARM, BELFORD NE70 7QE (01668 213362). In a quiet central position in the village of Belford, three miles from the Heritage Coast and within easy walking distance of all village amenities. Sleep 4-6. Each cottage is very well equipped, with gas-fired central heating; living/dining/kitchen areas are open plan. [Pets £20 per week]
e-mail: corillas@tiscali.co.uk   website: www.bluebellfarmbelford.co.uk

ETIVE COTTAGE, WARENFORD, NEAR BELFORD NE70 7HZ. Well-equipped two-bedroomed cottage with double glazing, central heating. Open views to coast. Fenced garden; secure parking. Pet and owners welcome pack. Pets welcome to bring along well behaved owners. Regional Winner, Winalot 'Best Place to Stay'. VisitBritain ★★★★★ Self-catering. Brochure: JAN THOMPSON (01668 213333). [🐾]
e-mail: janet.thompson1@homecall.co.uk

Berwick-upon-Tweed

Border town at mouth of River Tweed 58 miles north west of Newcastle and 47 miles south east of Edinburgh. Medieval town walls, remains of a Norman Castle.

2, THE COURTYARD, BERWICK-UPON-TWEED. Secluded Self catering Townhouse in heart of old Berwick. Planted courtyard garden and sunny verandah. Historic ramparts 400 yards. Choice of walks. Ideal for exercising pets. Contact: J. MORTON, 1, THE COURTYARD, CHURCH STREET, BERWICK -UPON-TWEED, TD15 1EE (01289 308737). ETC ★★★ [pw! 🐾]
e-mail: patmosphere@yahoo.co.uk   website: www.berwickselfcatering.co.uk

FRIENDLY HOUND COTTAGE, FORD COMMON, BERWICK-UPON-TWEED TD15 2QD (01289 388554) Set in a quiet rural location, convienient for Holy Island, Berwick, Bamburgh and the Heritage coastline. Come and enjoy our top quality accommodation, excellent breakfasts, and warm welcome. Arrive as our guests and leave as our friends. VB ★★★★ [🐾]
website: www.friendlyhoundcottage.co.uk

Chathill

Hamlet 4 miles SW of Seahouses.

SARAH SHELL, DOXFORD FARM COTTAGES, CHATHILL, ALNWICK NE67 5DY (01665 579348; mobile: 07734 247277). Comfortable self-catering family accommodation on working farm situated amidst unspoilt wooded countryside, five miles from the coast. 8 stone built terrace cottages. VisitBritain ★★★/★★★★ [Pets £20 per week].
e-mail: sarah@doxfordfarmcottages.com   website: www.doxfordfarmcottages.com

Corbridge

Small town on the north bank of the River Tyne, 3 miles west of Hexham. Nearby are remains of Roman military town of Corstopitum.

MR & MRS MATTHEWS, THE HAYES GUEST HOUSE, NEWCASTLE ROAD, CORBRIDGE NE45 5LP (01434 632010). Stone-built stables in grounds of large country house converted into two self-catering cottages, each accommodating 4/5. WiFi available. ETC ★★★ [Pets £12.50 per week]
e-mail: stay@hayes-corbridge.co.uk   website: www.hayes-corbridge.co.uk

Eals

Village 7 miles from Haltwhistle, 8 miles from Alston.

STONECROP. A white-washed cottage with its own orchard; recently renovated, with modern comforts - a new kitchen and bathroom, a cosy log stove and 3 bedrooms. Well behaved pets welcome. Contact: RICHARD PARKER, EASTGATE, MILBURN, PENRITH, CUMBRIA CA10 1TN (01768 361509)
website: www.stonecrop.co.uk

Publisher's note

While every effort is made to ensure accuracy, we regret that FHG Guides cannot accept responsibility for errors, misrepresentations or omissions in our entries or any consequences thereof. Prices in particular should be checked.

We will follow up complaints but cannot act as arbiters or agents for either party.

Northumberland

Haltwhistle

Small market town about one mile South of Hadrian's Wall.

A.D. & S.M. SAUNDERS, SCOTCHCOULTHARD, HALTWHISTLE NE49 9NH (01434 344470). Situated in 178 acres within Northumberland National Park, fully equipped self-catering cottages (sleep 2/7). Linen, towels, all fuel incl. Heated indoor pool, games room. Rare breed farm animals. Children and dogs welcome. [🐾]
e-mail: scotchcoulthard@hotmail.co.uk   website: www.scotchcoulthard.co.uk

KATH AND BRAD DOWLE, SAUGHY RIGG FARM, TWICE BREWED, HALTWHISTLE NE49 9PT (01434 344120). Close to the best parts of Hadrian's Wall. A warm welcome and good food. All rooms en suite. Parking. TV. Central heating. Children and pets welcome. Open all year. Prices from £35 pppn. ETC ★★★★ [Pets £5 per night]
e-mail: info@saughyrigg.co.uk   website: www.saughyrigg.co.uk

Hexham

Market town on south bank of the River Tyne, 20 miles west of Newcastle-upon-Tyne.

MRS RUBY KEENLEYSIDE, STRUTHERS FARM, CATTON, ALLENDALE, HEXHAM NE47 9LP (01434 683580). Panoramic views, splendid walks. Double/twin rooms, en suite bathrooms, central heating. Good farmhouse cooking. Ample safe parking. Children welcome. Pets by prior arrangement. Open all year. ETC ★★★★.
website: www.struthersfarmbandb.com

BATTLESTEADS HOTEL & RESTAURANT, WARK, HEXHAM NE48 3LS (01434 230209). Friendly family-run hotel with 17 en suite bedrooms including ground floor with disabled access. Excellent bar meals and à la carte menus; good choice wines and beers. Pets by arrangement only. VisitBritain ★★★★ Inn. [Pets £5 per night].
e-mail: info@battlesteads.com   website: www.battlesteads.com

Longhorsley

Village 6 miles NW of Morpeth.

★★★★ SELF-CATERING HOLIDAY COTTAGE (Mobile: 0781 624 5678). Sleeps 8. Bring your horses and dogs on holiday and explore our fabulous countryside, beaches and many local equestrian facilities. For further information and contact details visit our website. [🐾].
e-mail: carolyn@westmoorfarm.co.uk   website: www.westmoorfarm.co.uk

Wooler

Small town on Harthope Burn 15 miles NW of Alnwick.

LYNNEY HOLDEN, CROOKHOUSE, KIRKNEWTON, WOOLER NE71 6TN (01668 216113). Superior self catering accommodation in a traditional Northumbrian steading, Secluded and tranquil. Sleeps 4-12. Horses and dogs welcome. VisitBritain ★★★★. [🐾 pw!]
e-mail: stay@crookhousecottages.co.uk   website: www.crookhousecottages.co.uk

---

**Free or reduced rate entry to
Holiday Visits and Attractions - see our
READERS' OFFER VOUCHERS on pages 445-454**

292 NORTH WEST ENGLAND — Cheshire

Balterley, Chester, Macclesfield

Balterley Green Farm — Deans Lane, Balterley, Near Crewe CW2 5QJ
Tel: 01270 820214
Jo and Pete Hollins offer guests a friendly welcome to their home on a 145-acre working farm in quiet and peaceful surroundings. Situated on the Cheshire/Staffordshire border within easy reach of Junction 16 on the M6. Convenient for Chester, Alton Towers and the Potteries. Two family rooms en suite; two double and two twin en suite in converted cottage, also available for self catering. Bed and Breakfast from £25pp. Caravans and tents welcome. Pets £2 per night.

THE EATON HOTEL CITY ROAD, CHESTER CH1 3AE
Tel: 01244 320540 • Fax: 0870 6221691
Ideally located for you and your dog, in the heart of Chester, with parking, and bordering the Shropshire Union Canal towpath.
www.eatonhotelchester.co.uk

Newton Hall — Tattenhall, Chester CH3 9NE • www.newtonhallfarm.co.uk
Enjoy a quiet, relaxing holiday on our family-run farm. Newton Hall is a part 16thC timbered country house with lovely gardens and views of Beeston and Peckforton Castles. We are close to the Canal and Sandstone Trail for enjoyable walks. Chester is only 15 minutes by car; also on good bus route. Breakfast consists of fresh, locally sourced produce, served in our elegant dining room overlooking the gardens. Ample secure parking. B&B £35-£50pppn.
ETC ★★★★ SILVER AWARD
Tel: 01829 770153 • Mobile: 07974 745654 • e-mail: saarden@btinternet.com

Astle Farm East • Chelford, Macclesfield SK10 4TA
A warm and friendly welcome awaits on this picturesque arable farm surrounded by a large garden. We offer you a quiet stay in an idyllic setting. All bedrooms en suite, open all year. Pets & children welcome.
Tel & Fax: 01625 861270 • e-mail: gill.farmhouse@virgin.net
www.astlefarmeast.co.uk

Balterley

Small village two miles west of Audley.

MR & MRS HOLLINS, BALTERLEY GREEN FARM, DEANS LANE, BALTERLEY, NEAR CREWE CW2 5QJ (01270 820214). 145-acre farm in quiet and peaceful surroundings. Within easy reach of Junction 16 on the M6. Bed and Breakfast from £25pp. Also cottage for self-catering. Caravans and tents welcome. [pw! Pets £2 per night]

Chester

Former Roman city on the River Dee, with well-preserved walls and beautiful 14th century Cathedral. Liverpool 25 miles

THE EATON HOTEL, CITY ROAD, CHESTER CH1 3AE (01244 320540; Fax: 0870 6221691). Ideally located for you and your dog, in the heart of Chester, with parking, and bordering the Shropshire Union Canal towpath. [🐕]
website: www.eatonhotelchester.co.uk

MRS ANNE ARDEN, NEWTON HALL, TATTENHALL, CHESTER CH3 9NE (01829 770153; Mobile: 07974 745676). Part 16thC country house on a family-run farm, surrounded by beautiful scenery, with views of Beeston and Peckforton Castles. Ideal for a quiet, relaxing holiday. Chester 15 minutes' drive. ETC ★★★★ Silver Award [🐕]
e-mail: saarden@btinternet.com
website: www.newtonhallfarm.co.uk.

Macclesfield

Town 10 miles south of Stockport.

MRS STUBBS, ASTLE FARM EAST, CHELFORD, MACCLESFIELD SK10 4TA (Tel & Fax: 01625 861270). A warm and friendly welcome awaits on this picturesque arable farm surrounded by a large garden. We offer you a quiet stay in an idyllic setting. All bedrooms en suite, open all year. ETC ★★. [⌂ 🐕]
e-mail: gill.farmhouse@virgin.net
website: www.astlefarmeast.co.uk

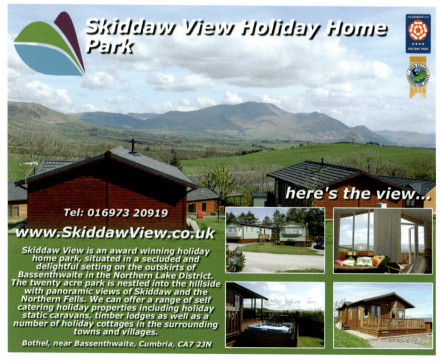

NEWBY BRIDGE HOTEL	RIVERSIDE HOTEL	DAMSON DENE HOTEL
Overlooking Lake Windermere	*Overlooking River Kent*	*Tranquil Rural Location*

Many rooms feature four-poster beds, some with en suite jacuzzi bath
Seasonal Breaks from £118 per person for two nights including Dinner, Bed and Breakfast.

Newby Bridge Hotel	Riverside Hotel	Damson Dene Hotel
Newby Bridge	Beezon Road	Crosthwaite
Cumbria	Kendal	Cumbria
LA12 8NA	Cumbria	LA8 8JE
Tel: 015395 31222	LA9 6EL	Tel: 015395 68676
info@newbybridgehotel.co.uk	Tel: 015397 34861	info@damsondene.co.uk
	info@riversidekendal.co.uk	

Stunning Offers... Stunning Hotels... Stunning Locations....
www.bestlakesbreaks.co.uk

Choose from 300 pet friendly cottages

CUMBRIAN Cottages

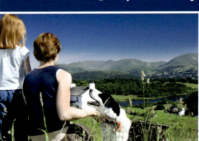

Superb locations throughout the Lake District and Cumbria. All VisitBritain graded.
Contact us for a brochure or visit our website.

www.cumbrian-cottages.co.uk
Tel: 01228 599950
Lines open 7 days 9am - 9pm (5.30pm Sat)

Alston

Cumberland Inn
Tel: 01434 381875
Townfoot, Alston, Cumbria CA9 3HX
A comfy retreat in the secluded North Pennines. Home-made hearty fare available all day. All 5 rooms are en suite. Muddy dogs and boots welcome.
Pets welcome in bedrooms and bar. No charge for pets.
stay@cumberlandinnalston.com • www.cumberlandinnalston.com

Please mention **Pets Welcome!**
when making enquiries about accommodation featured in these pages

Rock House Estate • Valley View, Nenthead, Alston CA9 3NA

DOGS & CATS WELCOME — pet towel, blanket, water bowl, clean-up bags & a ball thrower provided!
Five well equipped cottages sleeping 2, 4, 7, 7, or 14. Undiscovered Cumbria, accessible to the Lakes, Dales and Borders. The 100-acre estate is surrounded by spectacular views. Pets allowed off lead in fields without grazing sheep. Ideal for walking; dog-friendly pub with good food within one mile. All linen, towels and fuel included. Cots and high chairs available. Each cottage has some of the following features:- four-poster bed, corner bath, sauna, flagstone floor, beamed ceiling, real fire. See website for details. Short breaks available. Dogs and cats welcome at £20 each. Open all year.
01434 382 684 • Info@RockHouseEstate.co.uk • www.RockHouseEstate.co.uk ALSTON • Cumbria

Brathay Lodge

Guest accommodation in bright contemporary style
Spacious en suite bedrooms, spa baths with shower over. Some ground floor rooms with own entrance. Double, twin and family rooms. Private off road parking.
From £30 pppn. Pets welcome. Short walk to park/lake.
Brathay Lodge, Rothay Road, Ambleside LA22 0EE
Tel: 015394 32000 • e-mail: info@brathay-lodge.co.uk • www.brathay-lodge.co.uk

•••AMBLESIDE•••
2 LOWFIELD, OLD LAKE ROAD

Ground floor garden flat half a mile from town centre; sleeps 4. Lounge/diningroom, kitchen, bathroom/WC, two bedrooms, one with en suite shower. Linen supplied. Children and pets welcome. Parking for one car. Bookings Saturday to Saturday. Terms from £160 to £300 per week.

Contact: MR P. F. QUARMBY, 3 LOWFIELD, OLD LAKE ROAD, AMBLESIDE LA22 0DH
Tel: 015394 32326 • • • • • e-mail: paul.quarmby@zen.co.uk

Kirkstone Foot

Superior Cottage & Apartment Complex, set in peaceful gardens adjoining the Lakeland Fells & Village centre. Luxury Bathrooms & Fully Fitted Kitchens
ETC FOUR & FIVE STAR RATING AMONGST THE BEST IN BRITAIN
PETS WELCOME IN MANY UNITS
Brochures & Reservations Tel: 015394 32232
Kirkstone Pass Road, Ambleside, Cumbria LA22 9EH

enquiries@kirkstonefoot.co.uk
www.kirkstonefoot.co.uk

SPECIAL VALUE BREAK: commence your midweek break on a Monday and stay Thursday night FREE OF CHARGE.

LATEST NEWS: 2 night short notice bookings at the weekend, subject to availability.

PRICES: our prices include all gas, electricity, bed linen and towels. There is NO booking fee and NO credit card charge.

Greenhowe Caravan Park
Great Langdale, English Lakeland.

Greenhowe is a permanent Caravan Park with Self Contained Holiday Accommodation. Subject to availability Holiday Homes may be rented for short or long periods from 1st March until mid-November. The Park is situated in the heart of the Lake District some half a mile from Dungeon Ghyll at the foot of the Langdale Pikes. It is an ideal centre for Climbing, Fell Walking, Riding, Swimming, or just a lazy holiday.

Please ask about Short Breaks.
NEW LODGES THIS YEAR

Greenhowe Caravan Park

Great Langdale, Ambleside
Cumbria LA22 9JU

For free colour brochure
Telephone: (015394) 37231
Fax: (015394) 37464
www.greenhowe.com

Cumbria — North West England

Ambleside, Appleby-in-Westmorland

'Beyond Bed & Breakfast'
- Quiet location near Ambleside centre • Swimming pool, sauna and hot tub • Conservatory and sun terrace • Private car parking • Traditional and contemporary en suite rooms • Family-run, friendly welcome

www.oldvicarageambleside.co.uk

The Old Vicarage
Vicarage Road, Ambleside LA22 9DH
Tel: 015394 33364 • Contact Ian, Helen or Liana

Lyndale Guest House
Ambleside, The Lake District

Lyndale Guest House offers an individual and relaxed atmosphere where you will receive a warm welcome and outstanding hospitality. Ideally situated just 5 minutes' walk from the picturesque village of Ambleside and a 5 minute walk from Waterhead on the shores of Windermere. Excellent location for ramblers, with many walks starting from the front door; for cyclists with overnight storage; and for those seeking a relaxed getaway. Built of Lakeland stone in Victorian times, Lyndale offers comfortable, spacious bed & breakfast accommodation to suit families, groups, friends, couples, individuals and pets. Alison and Alan look forward to welcoming you to Lyndale Guest House.

Low Fold, Lake Road, Ambleside, Cumbria LA22 0DN
Tel: 015394 34244 • e-mail: alison@lyndale-guesthouse.co.uk
www.lyndale-guesthouse.co.uk

015394 32330
www.smallwoodhotel.co.uk

Smallwood House
Compston Road, Ambleside, Cumbria LA22 9DH

...where quality and the customer come first
En suite rooms • Car parking • Leisure Club Membership

015394 36611
Betty Fold, Hawkshead Hill, Ambleside LA22 0PS
e-mail: claire@bettyfold.co.uk • www.bettyfold.co.uk

Situated near Hawkshead and Tarn Hows, large country house in spacious grounds in the heart of Lake District National Park. Betty Fold offers self-catering accommodation in ground floor apartment with private entrance, sleeps 4. One double en suite and one small twin with bathroom and colour TV. Open-plan kitchen/livingroom with electric cooker, fridge, microwave, dishwasher. Terms inclusive of heat, light, power, bed linen and towels.

Our 3-star cottages and snug apartment are the delight of families, couples, walkers, and those seeking me-time in a stunning rural location. With two National Parks on the doorstep, just open the front door of the 1,2 & 3 bedroom cottages for stress-free days in fresh, hillside air and old fashioned family fun. Dogs very welcome and open all year.

Milburn Grange Holiday Cottages
Knock, Appleby, Cumbria CA16 6DR • Tel: 017683 61867
e-mail: petswelcome@milburngrange.co.uk • www.milburngrange.co.uk

Barrow-in-Furness, Bowness-on-Windermere

Premier hotel accommodation set in 14 acres of private woodland and gardens. Luxurious suites and bedrooms, all individually decorated with en suite facilities; some with four-poster beds.
The Restaurant offers warm, friendly service in sumptuous surroundings, with mouth-watering dishes and a dazzling array of hand picked wines. Stunning Lake District surroundings.

Abbey House Hotel, Abbey Road, Barrow-in-Furness, Cumbria LA13 0PA
Tel: 01229 838244 • e-mail: enquiries@abbeyhousehotel.com • www.abbeyhousehotel.com

Windermere Lake Holidays
Holiday houseboats on the lake shore with stunning views.
Sleep 4. Pets welcome. Open all year round.
For brochure: Tel: 015394 43415
e-mail: email@lakewindermere.net   www.lakewindermere.net

Oakfold House   www.oakfoldhouse.co.uk
Beresford Road, Bowness-on-Windermere, Cumbria LA23 2JG
Award winning Victorian guesthouse. Free WiFi. Close to Lake Windermere, shops, restaurants and Beatrix Potter attraction. Car Park. Gardens.
Tel: 015394 43239 • e-mail: oakfoldhouse@fsmail.net

Farlam Hall Hotel Brampton, Cumbria CA8 2NG
Tel: 016977 46234 • Fax: 016977 46683
Standing in four acres of gardens, with its own lake, Farlam Hall has that indefinable quality that makes a stay here something really special. Fine quality cuisine, individually decorated and well-equipped guest rooms. Ideal touring centre for the Lakes, Borders & Hadrian's Wall.
e-mail: farlam@relaischateaux.com • www.farlamhall.co.uk

AA ★★★
Inspectors' Choice
Relais & Chateaux

Walk your dog straight from the cottages up the hill and on to the fells. 7 cottages on North Pennines farm, sleeping 2-8; excellent base for Hadrian's Wall, Scottish Borders and the Lake District. Local food cooked by Harriet and delivered to your cottage.
Tel: 016977 3435 • e-mail: stay@longbyres.co.uk
www.longbyres.co.uk

Long Byres at Talkin Head

Woodend Cottages between the Eskdale and Duddon Valleys

Woodend, Ulpha, Broughton-in-Furness LA20 6DY
Woodend is remote and surrounded by hills and moorland, with views towards Scafell Pike. The cottages and house offer cosy accommodation for two to six people.
SHORT BREAKS AVAILABLE OUT OF SEASON.
*Visit our website at www.woodendcottage.com
or phone 019467 23277*

www.holidayguides.com

Cumbria
Carlisle, Cartmel, Cockermouth

GRAHAM ARMS HOTEL
Longtown, Near Carlisle, Cumbria CA6 5SE

A warm welcome awaits at this 200-year-old former Coaching Inn. Situated six miles from the M6 (J44) and Gretna Green, The Graham Arms makes an ideal overnight stop or perfect touring base for the Scottish Borders, English Lakes, Hadrian's Wall and much more. 16 comfortable en suite bedrooms, including four-poster and family rooms with TV, radio, free Wi-Fi etc. Meals and snacks served throughout the day. Friendly 'local's bar' and 'Sports bar' serving real ale, extra cold lagers, cocktails and a fine selection of malt whiskies. Secure courtyard parking for cars, cycles and motorcycles. Beautiful woodland and riverside walks. Pets welcome with well behaved owners!

Visit our website on www.grahamarms.com • Tel: 01228 791213 • Fax: 01228 794110
e-mail: office@grahamarms.com • www.grahamarms.com
Bed and full traditional breakfast £34– £39. Special rates for weekend and midweek breaks. ETC ★★

NEW PALLYARDS, HETHERSGILL, CARLISLE CA6 6HZ
Tel: 01228 577308

Serviced and self-catering accommodation, located approximately 12 miles north east of Carlisle, an ideal location for visiting Hadrian's Wall, the Lake District, Kielder Forest, Gretna and the Scottish Borders.
New Pallyards is a small farm of 65 acres, and the accommodation comprises a converted farmhouse and self-catering cottages.

B&B: en suite bedrooms (single, twin, double and family). Some ground floor rooms suitable for disabled guests. Award-winning breakfasts. Dogs/pets by arrangement.

Self-Catering: well appointed, spacious, centrally heated cottages (1-4 bedrooms). Children's play area. **See website specials.**

e-mail: newpallyards@btinternet.com • www.4starsc.co.uk
For details contact Georgina and John Elwen

Seven cottages sleeping 2-6. Set behind a large Georgian house set in parkland on the side of Hamps Fell. Beautiful garden, great walks. Pets and children welcome. Open all year. Please telephone for details.

Contact: MR M. AINSCOUGH, LONGLANDS AT CARTMEL, GRANGE-OVER-SANDS LA11 6HG • 015395 36475 • Fax: 015395 36172
e-mail: longlands@cartmel.com • www.cartmel.com

THE MANOR HOUSE, OUGHTERSIDE, ASPATRIA, CUMBRIA CA7 2PT
e-mail: richardandjudy@themanorhouse.net • www.themanorhouse.net

Our lovely manor farmhouse dates from the 18th century, retaining many original features and several acres of land. Spacious en suite rooms, tea/coffee making facilities, TV and lots of little extras. Peaceful surroundings, easy access to the Western Lakes and Solway Coast. All pets welcome. Bed & Breakfast from £25. Evening meals by arrangement.
Inspection Commended.

016973 22420

THE PHEASANT *Bassenthwaite Lake*

Generations of like-minded customers have enjoyed the unique atmosphere of this traditional Cumbrian hostelry. Tastefully renovated bedrooms, bathrooms and lounges have maintained our long established reputation for exceptional comfort with character. This, combined with customary fine dining and outstanding hospitality, adds the important personal touch.

Bassenthwaite Lake, Near Cockermouth, Cumbria CA13 9YE
Tel: 017687 76234 • Fax: 017687 76002
e-mail: info@the-pheasant.co.uk • www.the-pheasant.co.uk

ETC ★★★ Silver Award
★★★ (83% rating)

Cumbria
Cockermouth, Coniston

ROSE COTTAGE

Family-run guest house on the outskirts of Cockermouth. Warm, friendly atmosphere. Ample off-road parking. All rooms en suite with colour TV, tea/coffee, central heating and all have double glazing.

Pets most welcome in the house (excluding dining room), and there are short walks nearby. Ideal base for visiting both Lakes and coast.

Lorton Road, Cockermouth
Cumbria CA13 9DX
Tel & Fax: 01900 822189
www.rosecottageguest.co.uk

The Derwent Lodge
Embleton, Near Bassenthwaite,
Cockermouth CA13 9YA • Tel: 017687 76606

A warm welcome awaits you and your pet at the Derwent Lodge. Choose from luxury self-catering apartments or our en suite hotel rooms or suites. Light snacks and meals served daily in our cosy lounge bar or licensed restaurant. Ideally located for touring the Western Lake District and coast. Private car park and adjoining field for exercising dogs!
For a full colour brochure or further information please call **017687 76606**

INDOOR POOL AND FITNESS SUITE
www.thederwentlodge.co.uk • email: enquiries@thederwentlodge.co.uk

The Sun in Coniston offers a unique mix of bar, restaurant & four star inn, with the kind of comfortable informality and atmosphere that many attempt but few achieve.

At its heart is a great bar with 8 real ales on hand-pull, 4 draft lagers, 20+ malts and 30+ wines. The food is freshly prepared using locally sourced ingredients and can be enjoyed in the bar, in the conservatory, outside on the front & on the terrace. The 8 recently refurbished ensuite bedrooms overlook the village with superb panoramic views. Extra thick mattresses & quality comforters help ensure a good nights sleep.

bar, restaurant & 4 star inn
www.thesunconiston.com

THE SUN CONISTON LA21 8HQ
t: 015394 41248 f: 015394 41219 e: info@thesunconiston.com

Cumbria

Coniston, Duddon Valley

The Coppermines & Lakes - Cottages

Unique English Lakeland cottages for 2-30 people
Quality and character in stunning mountain scenery. Log fires, exposed beams.
Weekends and Short Breaks.

Book online: www.coppermines.co.uk

Tel: 015394 41765

Pets very welcome!

The Estate Office, The Bridge, Coniston, Cumbria LA21 8HJ

BROCKLEBANK GROUND HOLIDAY COTTAGES
TORVER, CONISTON LA21 8BS

Four luxury cottages in a quiet rural setting, sleeping 2, 4, 7 & 10. Excellent walking from the door. Dog friendly pubs 600 yards. Short breaks available. Prices from £275. ETC ★★★★

info@brocklebankground.com • www.brocklebankground.com

THE YEWDALE HOTEL Yewdale Road, Coniston LA21 8DU
Tel: 015394 41280 • info@yewdalehotel.com • www.yewdalehotel.com

Central for all the scenic delights of the Lake District and activities such as fishing, boating, canoeing, walking and pony trekking. 8 en suite bedrooms with TV and tea-making. Bar and dining room offer varied menus featuring fresh local produce. Excellent Cumbrian breakfasts.

Waterhead Hotel Coniston LA21 8AJ

Situated alongside Coniston Water, The Waterhead Hotel makes a perfect retreat. •23 en suite bedrooms; one Junior Suite • Mountain View Restaurant • Lounge bar with Lake views • Open to non-residents • Non-smoking • Ideal base for outdoor activities, also lake cruises and historic houses (Beatrix Potter, John Ruskin).
Tel: 015394 41244 • Fax: 015394 41193 • www.waterhead-hotel.co.uk

---

In the heart of the Lake District National Park, just 4 miles from the summit of Scafell Pike. Self-contained holiday cottage (sleeps 4). Large open-plan kitchen. Well behaved dogs free of charge. Available all year. Private enclosed garden with patio and parking. *Contact Sandra Swainson.*

**COCKLEY BECK FARM COTTAGE, SEATHWAITE,
BROUGHTON-IN-FURNESS LA20 6EQ • 01229 716480**
www.cockleybeck.co.uk • e-mail: Sandra@cockleybeck.co.uk

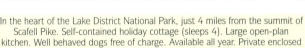

NORTH WEST ENGLAND — Cumbria

Eskdale, Gosforth, Grange-over-Sands, Grasmere

Fisherground Farm, Eskdale, Cumbria

Fisherground is a lovely traditional hill farm, with a stone cottage and three pine lodges, sharing an acre of orchard. Ideal for walkers, nature lovers, dogs and children, we offer space, freedom, peace and tranquillity. We have a games room, a raft pool and a station on the miniature railway! Good pubs nearby serve excellent bar meals.

Ian & Jennifer Hall, Orchard House, Applethwaite, Keswick, Cumbria CA12 4PN

017687 73175 • e-mail: holidays@fisherground.co.uk • www.fisherground.co.uk

---

THE BOOT INN

Boot, Eskdale, Cumbria CA19 1TG • Tel: 019467 23224
e-mail: enquiries@bootinn.co.uk • www.bootinn.co.uk

With walks for all abilities from the front door and a truly warm welcome for you and your dogs, along with good food and clean, comfortable rooms - this is people and doggie heaven! Please call for brochure. B&B from £40ppn. Special breaks available.

(formerly The Burnmoor Inn)

BLENG BARN COTTAGE *Self-catering three bedroom holiday cottage, situated on a family-run mixed working farm in its own secluded valley. Sleeps 6+4. Many traditional features and modern facilities. A perfect base for a leisurely break or a variey of activity holidays. Pets welcome by arrangement.*

Mill House Farm, Wellington, Seascale, Cumbria CA20 1BH
Tel: 07801 862237 & 07775 512918 • Fax: 01946 725 671
e-mail: info@blengfarms.co.uk • www.blengfarms.co.uk

Hampsfell House Hotel

In two acres of private grounds, just a few minutes' walk from the town centre. Eight well appointed en suite bedrooms. Relax in the traditionally decorated lounges and then enjoy the best of fresh Cumbrian produce in the elegant dining room, where fine wines complement the table d'hôte and à la carte menus. Grange-over-Sands makes an ideal base for exploring the Lake District. Pets welcome, excellent dog walking facilities. Short Break option available.

Hampsfell Road, Grange-over-Sands LA11 6BG • Tel: 015395 32567
www.hampsfellhouse.co.uk • enquiries@hampsfellhouse.co.uk

From £30 per person per night. • 3 nights for the price of 2 from £100, 1st April to 31st March, Sunday-Thursday. • November-March, any 3 nights for the price of 2.

LAKE VIEW COUNTRY HOUSE & SELF-CATERING APARTMENTS
GRASMERE LA22 9TD • 015394 35384/35167

4 rooms B&B or 3 Self-Catering apartments in unrivalled, secluuded location in the village with wonderful views and lakeshore access. All B&B rooms en suite, some with whirlpool baths. Ground floor accommodation available. No smoking. Featured in Michelin Guide.

Midweek Breaks available in B&B • Winter Short Breaks available in S/C accommodation.

GRASMERE HOTEL BROADGATE, GRASMERE LA22 9TA • 015394 35277

Charming 13-bedroom Country House Hotel, with ample parking and a licensed lounge. All rooms recently refurbished, with en suite facilities. Award-winning restaurant overlooking gardens, river and surrounding hills. Lovely park right next door for exercising dogs. Special breaks throughout the year.

AA ★★ AA Rosette Restaurant • ETC ★★ Silver Award

e-mail: enquiries@grasmerehotel.co.uk • www.grasmerehotel.co.uk

Cumbria
Hawkshead, Ireby, Kendal

THE KINGS ARMS HOTEL
Hawkshead, Ambleside, Cumbria LA22 0NZ
015394 36372 • www.kingsarmshawkshead.co.uk
Join us for a relaxing stay amidst the green hills and dales of Lakeland, and we will be delighted to offer you good food, homely comfort and warm hospitality in historic surroundings. We hope to see you soon!
- SELF-CATERING COTTAGES ALSO AVAILABLE -

Cottages in and around Hawkshead. Great walks and lakes for swimming, dog-friendly pubs, open fires to lie in front of... owners will enjoy it too!
Tel: 015394 42435
www.lakeland-hideaways.co.uk
Hideaways, The Square, Hawkshead LA22 0NZ

2 Moot Hall, Ireby, Cumbria CA7 1DU
Lovely cottage, part of 16th century Moot Hall in unspoilt village. Delightful walks in Uldale Fells and northern Lake District. Sleeps 4. Linen/fuel/electricity included in weekly charge of £280 to £400. Open all year. Reductions for PAT, Assistance and Rescue Dogs.
Tel: 01423 360759 • e-mail: ruthboyes@virgin.net
www.irebymoothall.co.uk

Two modern caravans, fully double glazed, gas central heating. Double and twin bedrooms, kitchen with fridge and microwave, spacious lounge/dining area with TV and video or DVD, toilet and shower. On traditional working farm set in 140 acres of beautiful countryside.
Short breaks available out of season.

Mrs L. Hodgson, Patton Hall Farm, Kendal LA8 9DT • 01539 721590
stay@pattonhallfarm.co.uk   www.pattonhallfarm.co.uk

RUSSELL FARM Burton-in-Kendal, Carnforth, Lancs LA6 1NN
Tel: 01524 781334 • email: miktaylor@farming.co.uk
Bed and Breakfast • Ideal centre for touring Lakes and Yorkshire Dales, or as a stopover for Scotland or the South • Good food, friendly atmosphere on working dairy farm • Modernised farmhouse • Guests' lounge with woodburning stove. • **Contact Anne Taylor for details.**

Primrose Cottage
Orton Road, Tebay, Cumbria CA10 3TL

Bed & Breakfast and Self-Catering Accommodation

Self-contained ground floor flat and 3 purpose-built self-catering bungalows for disabled guests, with electric bed, jacuzzi and large, wheel-in bathroom. Excellent rural location for North Lakes and Yorkshire Dales. Pets welcome, very friendly. One-acre garden.
Tel: 015396 24791 • e-mail: primrosecottebay@aol.com • www.primrosecottagecumbria.co.uk

Mirefoot Cottages • Self-catering in the Lake District
5 Star, pet friendly, self-catering cottages in a superb rural location in the Lake District National Park. All cottages sleep 2. Fully equipped with TV (Freeview), DVD, WiFi, gas central heating. Tennis court, private parking.
Mirefoot Cottages, Mirefoot, Kendal, Cumbria LA8 9AB
Tel: 01539 720015 • e-mail: booking@mirefoot.co.uk • www.mirefoot.co.uk

NORTH WEST ENGLAND — **Cumbria**

Kendal, Keswick

Stonecross Manor Hotel — Milnthorpe Road, Kendal, Cumbria LA9 5HP

Established in 1857 as an orphanage, Stonecross Manor Hotel offers easy access to town, ample car parking, local cuisine, conference and banquet facilities, indoor swimming pool and fourposter bedrooms.

Tel: 01539 733559   Fax: 01539 736366   Email: info@stonecrossmanor.co.uk   www.stonecrossmanor.co.uk

MARY MOUNT HOTEL

Set in 4½ acres of gardens and woodlands on the shores of Derwentwater. 2½ miles from Keswick in picturesque Borrowdale. Superb walking and touring. All rooms en suite with colour TV and tea/coffee making facilities. Licensed. Brochure on request.

BORROWDALE, NEAR KESWICK CA12 5UU • 017687 77223
• e-mail: mawdsley1@aol.com • www.marymounthotel.co.uk

Overwater Hall

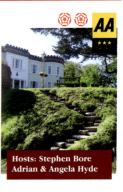

Overwater, Ireby,
Near Keswick, Cumbria CA7 1HH • Tel: 017687 76566
e-mail: welcome@overwaterhall.co.uk
www.overwaterhall.co.uk

Our elegant, family-run Country House Hotel offers you the best in traditional comforts, award-winning food and friendly hospitality. Peacefully secluded yet within only a short drive of the popular centres of the Lake District, this is the ideal place for a real break.

Dogs genuinely welcome in your room, in one of our lounges, the bar, and in our 18 acres of grounds.

Special four-night breaks available all year from £340 per person, inclusive of Dinner and Breakfast.

Please telephone us for a brochure, or refer to our website for further information.

Hosts: Stephen Bore
Adrian & Angela Hyde

DERWENT WATER MARINA, PORTINSCALE, KESWICK CA12 5RF

Lakeside self-catering apartments. Three apartments sleep 2, one apartment sleeps 6. Superb views over the lake and fells. Includes TV, heating and bed linen. Non-smoking. Watersports and boat hire available on site.

Tel: 017687 72912 for brochure • e-mail: info@derwentwatermarina.co.uk • www.derwentwatermarina.co.uk

Traditional Lakeland hotel with friendly atmosphere. Home cooking, cosy bar, comfortable lounge and some riverside rooms.
Winter and Summer discount rates. Brochure and Tariff available.

ROYAL OAK HOTEL, BORROWDALE, KESWICK CA12 5XB
017687 77214 • e-mail: info@royaloakhotel.co.uk
www.royaloakhotel.co.uk

KESWICK COTTAGES   ETC ★★★★   Tel: 017687 78555

8 Beechcroft, Braithwaite, Keswick Cumbria CA12 5TH

Superb selection of cottages and apartments in and around Keswick. All of our properties are well maintained and thoroughly clean. From a one bedroom cottage to a four bedroom house we have something for everyone. Children and pets welcome. Contact us for a free colour brochure.

e-mail: info@keswickcottages.co.uk • www.keswickcottages.co.uk

Cumbria
Keswick

SEYMOUR HOUSE

Tel: 017687 72764
Freephone: 0800 056 6401
Mobile: 07721 957899
e-mail: enquiries@seymour-house.com

Seymour House is set midway between Keswick town and Derwentwater "Queen of the Lakes", offering 7 well appointed en suite rooms. All diets catered for.

36 Lake Road, Keswick, Cumbria CA12 5DQ
www.seymour-house.com

Horse and Farrier Inn
Threlkeld, Keswick CA12 4SQ

Situated beneath Blencathra, in an ideal location for walking or touring the Lake District. All 15 bedrooms en suite, with TV, tea/coffee making and hairdryer. Award-winning food and restaurant. Open all year. Pets welcome.

Tel: 017687 79688 • Fax: 017687 79823
info@horseandfarrier.com
www.horseandfarrier.com

Rickerby Grange

Portinscale, Keswick, Cumbria CA12 5RH
Set within its own garden with private car parking, in the picturesque village of Portinscale near the shores of Lake Derwentwater within walking distance of the market town of Keswick. Ideally situated for exploring all parts of the Lakes. Offering comfort, friendly service, these being the essential qualities provided by the resident proprietor. A well-stocked bar offering local beers; comfortable lounge and elegant dining room where a four course dinner can be enjoyed with a varied selection of wines. All rooms en suite with tea and coffee making facilities, colour TV, telephone.

DB&B from £56. Winter Breaks: 3 nights DB&B £150pp.
Brochure on request, contact Des or Carol Taylorson on 017687 72344
e-mail: stay@rickerbygrange.co.uk • www.rickerbygrange.co.uk

LAKELAND Cottage Holidays

Self-catering cottages for you and your pets in and around Keswick and beautiful Borrowdale

017687 76065
Email: info@lakelandcottages.co.uk
www.lakelandcottages.co.uk

Cumbria

Keswick, Kirkby-in-Furness, Kirkby Lonsdale

Low Briery Riverside Holiday Village • Keswick
A selection of high quality cottages, timber lodges, apartments and caravans, all to ★★★★ standard. Indoor centre with children's pool, sauna, table tennis, pool table and toddlers' play area. Quiet and peaceful riverside location, ideal for exploring Lake District.
Tel: 017687 72044 • www.keswick.uk.com

Woodside
Ideally situated away from the busy town centre yet only a short walk down the C2C bridleway to the town. All rooms are en suite, and we have ample private parking and large gardens. Being a family-run establishment, you are guaranteed a friendly reception. After a good night's sleep you will be ready for a hearty English breakfast together with cereal, fruit and yoghurt. Dogs welcome by arrangement. B&B from £35pp.
Ann & Norman Pretswell, Woodside, Penrith Road, Keswick CA12 4LJ • 017687 73522
www.woodsideguesthouse.co.uk

COLEDALE INN   ETC ★★★
Braithwaite, Near Keswick, Cumbria CA12 5TN Tel: 017687 78272
A friendly, family-run Victorian Inn in a peaceful hillside position above Braithwaite, and ideally situated for touring and walking. All bedrooms are warm and spacious, with en suite shower room and colour television. Children are welcome, as are pets. Home-cooked meals, and real ales. Open all year.   www.coledale-inn.co.uk

Janet and Peter, 1 Friars Ground, Kirkby-in-Furness LA17 7YB

Tel: 01229 889601

"Sunset Cottage" is a spacious self-catering 17th century two or three bedroom former yeoman farmer's cottage with a large south-facing enclosed garden. Patio furniture is provided for your use. Original features include inglenook fireplace with logburning stove, oak beams, flagstone floor in the kitchen and oak panelling. There is a beautiful solid oak and beech fully integrated kitchen with dishwasher and washer/dryer. WiFi broadband is available on request. Tariff includes bed linen, towels, electricity/oil and logs for the fire. Panoramic views over sea/mountains, ideal for walking, birdwatching. Coniston/Windermere 30 minutes. Non-smoking. Terms from £160.00. Open all year. Debit/credit cards accepted."
e-mail: enquiries@southlakes-cottages.com • www.southlakes-cottages.com

Barbon Inn

Barbon, Near Kirkby Lonsdale, Cumbria LA6 2LJ Tel: 015242 76233
Friendly 17th century Coaching Inn • 10 bedrooms.
Country pursuits within the immediate area.
Nestling in Lune Valley between Lake District & Yorkshire Dales.
e-mail: info@barbon-inn.co.uk • www.barbon-inn.co.uk

The Snooty Fox • Kirkby Lonsdale LA6 2AH

The Snooty Fox is a charming Jacobean Inn, with 9 en suite rooms and a restaurant offering the finest local, seasonal produce. Situated in the heart of the market town of Kirkby Lonsdale and boasting a range of fine cask ales and malt whiskies. The Snooty Fox is the perfect base from which to explore both the Lake District and Yorkshire Dales.
Tel: 01524 271254 • www.thesnootyfoxhotel.co.uk

A warm welcome awaits you at ULLATHORNS, a working farm situated in the unspoilt Lune Valley. The farmhouse is dated 1617. One family/twin/double and one double, both en suite, with TV and drink making facilities. Visitors' lounge with log-burning stove. A hearty breakfast is served at individual tables. Ample car parking. An ideal touring base for Lakes and Dales or as a stopover point as situated between M6 junctions. Non-smoking. B&B from £27 (based on two sharing) with reductions for children. Short break offers. VisitBritain ★★★★   Contact: Pauline Bainbridge, Ullathorns Farm, Middleton, Kirkby Lonsdale LA6 2LZ • Tel: 015242 76214
Mobile: 07800 990469 • e-mail: pauline@ullathorns.co.uk • www.ullathorns.co.uk

Cumbria
Kirkoswald

"YOUR PETS & YOUR HOLIDAY"
Combine COMFORT, PEACE AND QUIET, RELAX, FISH, STROLL OR WALK
(SECLUDED COTTAGES with private fishing)

Tranquil, comfortable cottages, set in their own secret valley, overlooking the fishing lakes amidst Lakeland's beautiful Eden Valley countryside, only 30 minutes' drive from Ullswater, North Pennines, Hadrian's Wall and Scottish Borders.

★ Well fenced exercise areas for dogs.
★ Clean, well maintained and equipped.
★ Linen provided. ★ Beds freshly made for you.
★ Exceptional wildlife and walking area.
★ Excellent Coarse Fishing for residents only.
★ Golf courses nearby. ★ You & your pets very welcome.
★ Kennel available if required. ★ Open all year – breaks/weeks.

Flexible Terms
Relax and escape to "YOUR" hideaway in the country.

Tel/Fax 01768 898711 24hr Brochure line

e-mail: info@crossfieldcottages.co.uk
www.crossfieldcottages.co.uk

Booking & Availability
01768 898711, 6-10 p.m. or SAE to:

CROSSFIELD COTTAGES, KIRKOSWALD, PENRITH, CUMBRIA CA10 1EU
RING NOW! It's never too early or too late!

ETC ★★★   **PETS – NO PROBLEM!**   Owned by Vets

NORTH WEST ENGLAND — Cumbria

Kirkby Stephen, Lake District, Lamplugh (near Loweswater), Langdale

Cocklake House
MALLERSTANG CA17 4JT • 017683 72080
Charming, High Pennine Country House B&B in unique position above Pendragon Castle in Upper Mallerstang Dale offering good food and exceptional comfort to a small number of guests. Two double rooms with large private bathrooms. Three acres riverside grounds. Dogs welcome.

"Your own country house in the Lakes"
Two luxury holiday houses available to rent in the Lake District.

Routen House

Routen House is a beautiful old farmhouse set in 4 acres in an outstanding position with fabulous views over Ennerdale Lake. Fully modernised while retaining the character of the old farmhouse, it has been furnished to a very high standard. Sleeps 12 plus cot.

Little Parrock is an elegant Victorian Lakeland stone house a short walk from the centre of Grasmere with large rooms and a wealth of period features. Lovely private garden. Fully modernised to a very high standard; real log fires. Sleeps 10 plus cot.

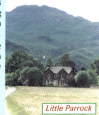
Little Parrock

Both houses are non-smoking but pets are very welcome. Please contact:
Mrs J. Green • Tel: 01604 505115 • e-mail: joanne@routenhouse.co.uk
www.routenhouse.co.uk • www.littleparrock.co.uk

Felldyke Cottage Holidays • "a warm and friendly welcome"
Visiting the Western Lakes? Then why not stay in this lovely 19th century cottage. Sleeps 4, short breaks can be arranged. Pets are welcome. Open all year, for you to enjoy the Lake District in all its guises.
Mrs A. Wilson • 01946 861151 • dockraynook@talk21.com
www.felldykecottageholidays.co.uk   VB ★★★★

Rose Cottage • Cumbria

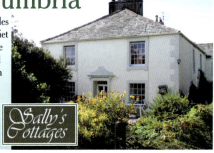

Situated just three miles from Loweswater and four miles from Ennerdale, Rose Cottage is very much on the quiet side of the Lake District yet is within easy reach of the hustle and bustle of Keswick & Cockermouth should you desire it. The cottage is lovely throughout with an open-plan kitchen and sitting room, cosy coal fire, two bedrooms and enclosed garden. Pets are welcome.

Please contact Sally Fielding on 01768 779445 for more details or visit www.millgillhead.co.uk

---

THE BRITANNIA INN

Book with this advert and claim a FREE bottle of French house wine at dinner

Elterwater, Langdale, Cumbria LA22 9HP
Tel: 015394 37210

A 500 year-old quintessential Lakeland Inn nestled in the centre of the picturesque village of Elterwater amidst the imposing fells of the Langdale Valley. Comfortable, high quality en suite double and twin-bedded rooms. Dogs welcome.
Enquire about our Mid-Week Special Offers. Relax in the oak-beamed Bars or Dining Room whilst sampling local real ales and dishes from our extensive menu of fresh, home-cooked food using lots of Cumbrian produce.
Quiz Night most Sundays.

www.britinn.co.uk • e-mail: info@britinn.co.uk

Cumbria
NORTH WEST ENGLAND

Langdale, Lazonby, Little Langdale, Millom, Newby Bridge, Penrith

Some of the loveliest cottages in the Lake District with stunning scenery on their doorsteps are ready to welcome you and your pets. Prices vary. Please visit our website.
ETC ★★★ - ★★★★★
e-mail: enquiries@wheelwrights.com
www.wheelwrights.com

WHEELWRIGHTS HOLIDAY COTTAGES, ELTERWATER, NEAR AMBLESIDE LA22 9HS
Tel: 015394 38305
Fax: 015394 37618

Delightful country cottage for two in Cumbria's Eden Valley

Open fire. Secure garden. Village location. Walks from the door, or take the Settle Carlisle railway to explore this unspoilt area. Lake District and North Pennines a short drive away. A warm welcome awaits pets and their well behaved owners.

Contact Penny on 01768 870558 for more details or e-mail: stayatnumberthree@postmaster.co.uk

HIGHFOLD COTTAGE • LITTLE LANGDALE

Very comfortable Lakeland cottage, ideally situated for walking and touring. Superb mountain views. Sleeps 5. Personally maintained. Pets welcome. Weekly £260–£550. MRS C.E. BLAIR, 8 THE GLEBE, CHAPEL STILE, AMBLESIDE LA22 9JT • 015394 37686 • www.highfoldcottage.co.uk

Holiday Cottage • Lake District • Tel 01229 717174

Some holiday cottages won't have dogs – some tolerate them – we more or less insist on them! We have a 300-year-old two-bedroom cottage on the west coast of Cumbria within the National Park. Traditional cottage, oak beams etc. but with all mod cons, fully centrally heated. Secure garden and an attached 3-acre deer-fenced playground for dogs. Easy access to Eskdale and Wasdale and close to miles of dog-friendly beaches.

A well tended, uncrowded and wooded site set amidst picturesque fells between the Cartmel peninsula and the southern tip of Lake Windermere. On-site facilities: flush toilets • hot showers • laundry facilities • hair dryers • deep freeze • gas on sale Tourers (30 pitches) £16 per night (incl. electricity & VAT). Tents (30 pitches) £14 - £16 per night. Auto Homes £16. All prices for outfit, plus 2 adults and 2 children. Open March 1st to October 31st.

Oak Head Caravan Park, Ayside, Grange-over-Sands LA11 6JA
Contact: Mr A.S.G. Scott • Tel: 015395 31475 • www.oakheadcaravanpark.co.uk

VB ★★★★

Between Keswick and Penrith and close to the shores of lovely Ullswater, this friendly and well-appointed inn enjoys sweeping fell views and is a haven for a variety of outdoor pursuits. Known for its excellent varied food and real ales. Tastefully furnished bedrooms have en suite facilities, colour television and tea and coffee-makers and there are three self-catering cottages (VB ★★★★).

The Troutbeck Inn, Troutbeck, Penrith, Cumbria CA11 0SJ • Tel: 017684 83675
Fax: 017684 87071 • e-mail: info@troutbeckinn.com • www.thetroutbeckinn.com

LYVENNET COTTAGES Five different cottages (including 5-Star Steel's Mill) in and around the small farming village of Kings Meaburn in beautiful unspoilt 'Lyvennet Valley'. Ideal touring centre for the Lakes, Dales, Hadrian's Wall; superb area for dog walks. Attractively furnished, fuel, power and linen inclusive. All have colour TV, microwave, fridge, washing machine, central heating, parking and private fishing. Children, pets and horses welcome, cots and highchairs on request. Open all year. Terms from £130 to £440.

Contact: Janet Addison, Keld Farm, Kings Meaburn, Penrith, Cumbria CA10 3BS
Tel: 01931 714661/714226 • Fax: 01931 714598 • www.lyvennetcottages.co.uk • ETC 4/5 ★

CHURCH COURT COTTAGES, GAMBLESBY, PENRITH CA10 1HR

Four beautiful, well-equipped, sandstone cottages in picturesque village. Excellent traffic-free walks from doorstep. Wonderful views of the hills of the Lake District and North Pennines. Penrith 15 minutes.

Contact: MARK COWELL or PATRICIA CLOWES – 01768 881682
e-mail: cottages@gogamblesby.co.uk   www.gogamblesby.co.uk

Cumbria
Penrith

- Individual AA 3 Star, family owned hotel set in the dramatic Cumbrian fells
- Cosy lounge and bar with log fire, 50 contemporary bedrooms with luxurious bathrooms
- AA Rosette award winning restaurant - 24 hour room/lounge service also available
- Maximum 2 pets per room, small surcharge per pet - please advise on booking
- Located between J.38 & J.39 on the M6, Cumbria • 015396 24351 • westmorlandhotel.com

Your Stepping Stone to the Cumbrian Lake District

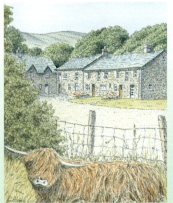

Award-winning Carrock Cottages are four renovated stone built cottages set on the fringe of the Lakeland Fells. A quiet rural location near the lovely villages of Hesket Newmarket with its award-winning brewery, Caldbeck and Greystoke. Explore the beauty of the Lake District National Park or head North to historic Carlisle and on to Hadrian's Wall.

Fell walking & other activities close to hand as well as excellent restaurants.

A warm welcome guaranteed.

Accommodation for 1 to 18 people.

On-site games room, home-cooked meal service.

Carrock House, Hutton Roof, Penrith, Cumbria CA11 0XY
Tel: Malcolm or Gillian on 01768 484 111 or Fax: 017684 888 50
www.carrockcottages.co.uk • info@carrockcottages.co.uk

Cumbria — NORTH WEST ENGLAND
Penrith, Ravenglass, St Bees, Silloth-on-Solway, Ullswater

The BOOT & SHOE
Greystoke, Penrith, Cumbria CA11 0TP
Tel: 01768 483343
e-mail: info@bootandshoegreystoke.co.uk
www.bootandshoegreystoke.co.uk

16th Century Inn in the heart of the legendary village of Greystoke. This popular village pub is full of charm, character and history. Excellent food, en suite accommodation and ambience. Conveniently situated to explore the Lake District, you can always be sure of a warm welcome.

Brown Cow Inn — Waberthwaite,
Near Ravenglass, Cumbria LA19 5YJ   Tel: 01229 717243
Home-cooked food at prices you can afford. Four real ales. Four en suite rooms. Wheelchair access. Food served daily. Beer garden. Pets welcome in bar area and rooms.
e-mail: browncowinn@btconnect.com

★ Seacote Park ★
The Beach, St Bees, Cumbria CA27 0ET
Tel: 01946 822777 • Fax: 01946 824442
reception@seacote.com • www.seacote.com

Adjoining lovely sandy beach on fringe of Lake District, modern luxury holiday caravans for hire, fully equipped to sleep up to 8. Full serviced touring pitches and tent area. Convenient for Ennerdale, Eskdale and Wasdale, plus some of England's finest mountains. Holiday caravans also for sale. Hotel bar for food and drinks.

Tarnside Caravan Park
5 miles from St Bees. Sea and Tarn Fishing. Club.

Seven Acres Caravan Park
Close to Eskdale and Wasdale and some of England's finest mountains

Tanglewood Caravan Park
CAUSEWAY HEAD, SILLOTH-ON-SOLWAY, CUMBRIA CA7 4PE

TANGLEWOOD is a family-run park on the fringes of the Lake District National Park. It is tree-sheltered and situated one mile inland from the small port of Silloth on the Solway Firth, with a beautiful view of the Galloway Hills. Large modern holiday homes are available from March to January, with car parking beside each home. Fully equipped except for bed linen, with end bedroom, panel heaters in bedrooms and bathroom, electric lighting, hot and cold water, toilet, shower, gas fire, fridge and colour TV, all of which are included in the tariff. Touring pitches also available with electric hook-ups and water/drainage facilities, etc. Play area. Licensed lounge with adjoining children's play room. Pets welcome free but must be kept under control at all times. Full colour brochure available. AA THREE PENNANTS ★★★
TEL: 016973 31203 • e-mail: tanglewoodcaravanpark@hotmail.com • www.tanglewoodcaravanpark.co.uk
• DOWNLOADABLE BROCHURE WITH TARIFF AND BOOKING FORM AVAILABLE ON WEBSITE. •

Land Ends Cabins, Watermillock, Near Ullswater CA11 0NB
TEL: 017684 86438 • Only one mile from Ullswater, our four detached log cabins have a peaceful fellside location in 25-acre grounds with two pretty lakes. Ducks, moorhens, red squirrels and wonderful birdlife. Doggy heaven! Sleep 2-5. e-mail: infolandends@btinternet.com • www.landends.co.uk

312 NORTH WEST ENGLAND — Cumbria

Ullswater, Wasdale, Wigton

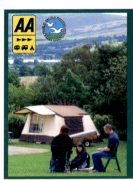

Cove Park is a peaceful caravan & camping park overlooking Lake Ullswater, surrounded by Fells with beautiful views. The park is very well-maintained. We are ideally situated for walking, watersports and all of the Lake District tourist attractions in the North Lakes. Facilities include clean heated showers and washrooms with hand and hair dryers, washing and drying machines, iron & board, and a separate washing up area and a freezer for ice packs. We offer electric hook-ups with hardstandings, and plenty of sheltered grass for campers.

Cove Caravan & Camping Park
Watermillock, Penrith, Cumbria CA11 0LS
- Tel: 017684 86549 • www.cove-park.co.uk

FARRIERS LOFT, FELL VIEW HOLIDAYS, GLENRIDDING CA11 OPJ

1st Floor Apartment Sleeps 4-5.

Lovely, comfortable, well equipped accommodation in an idyllic location between Glenridding and Patterdale.
Magnificent views of the surrounding fells.
Shared use of gardens.
*sitting room • dining room with bed settee
two double bedrooms • bathroom • kitchen*
Short Breaks available out of season.
Please look at the website or call for a brochure.
017684 82795 • enquiries@farriersloft.com
www.farriersloft.com

The Bridge Inn, once a coach halt, is now a fine, comfortable, award-winning country inn, offering hospitality to all travellers and visitors.

The Inn has an excellent reputation for good food, with "real" food served in the Dalesman Bar, or in the Eskdale Room. We serve an excellent selection of Jennings real ales. 16 bedrooms. Weddings and other private and business functions catered for in our function room. Licensed for civil ceremonies, partnerships, naming ceremonies and renewal of vows.

10 minute drive to "Britain's favourite view – Wastwater".
This unspoiled area of the Lake District offers superb walking and climbing.

**Bridge Inn, Santon Bridge, Wasdale CA19 1UX
Tel: 019467 26221 • Fax: 019467 26026
e-mail: info@santonbridgeinn.com**
www.santonbridgeinn.com

A spacious well-equipped, comfortable cottage on a working farm. Superlative setting and views, large kitchen/dining room, Aga, lounge, open fire, TV/video/DVD, three bedrooms, bathroom, separate shower room. Linen, towels, electricity, logs and coal inclusive. Children and pets very welcome. Extensive garden. Storage heaters, washing machine, dishwasher. Easy reach Lake District, Scottish Borders and Roman Wall.
Sleeps 2-8 • Prices from £266–£480
Available all year.
Short breaks by arrangement.

kerr_greenrigg@hotmail.com

FOXGLOVES COTTAGE. Mr & Mrs E. and J. Kerr,
Greenrigg Farm, Westward, Wigton CA7 8AH • 016973 42676

Cumbria

NORTH WEST ENGLAND

Windermere

LANGDALE CHASE HOTEL
Windermere, Cumbria LA23 1LW
Tel: 015394 32201

Magnificent country house hotel with over six acres of beautifully landscaped grounds sloping to the edge of Lake Windermere. Panoramic views of lake and fells, log fires, excellent food, and friendly, professional staff all ensure a memorable stay.

e-mail: sales@langdalechase.co.uk • www.langdalechase.co.uk

Cumbria Tourist Board - Hotel of the Year 2005 Silver Award
Website of the Year Award 2005 • Taste of England Award 2005

Quality Holiday Homes in England's Beautiful Lake District

Hundreds of VisitBritain inspected and graded properties throughout the southern and central Lake District. Lakelovers are sure to have a property to meet your needs. Free Leisure Club membership with every booking
Tel: 015394 88855 • Fax: 015394 88857 • e-mail: bookings@lakelovers.co.uk • www.lakelovers.co.uk
Lakelovers, Belmont House, Lake Road, Bowness-on-Windermere, Cumbria LA23 3BJ

WATERMILL INN & BREWERY, INGS, NEAR WINDERMERE
LA8 9PY • 01539 821309 • Fax: 01539 822309.

Ruby and friends (Dogs) welcome you to the award-winning Inn. 16 real ales. Cosy fires, en suite rooms, excellent bar meals. Doggie water and biscuits served in the bar. Good doorstep dog walking.

e-mail: info@Lakelandpub.co.uk • www.Lakelandpub.co.uk

Other specialised holiday guides from **FHG**

PUBS & INNS OF BRITAIN • **COUNTRY HOTELS** OF BRITAIN
WEEKEND & SHORT BREAK HOLIDAYS IN BRITAIN
THE GOLF GUIDE WHERE TO PLAY, WHERE TO STAY
500 GREAT PLACES TO STAY • **SELF-CATERING HOLIDAYS** IN BRITAIN
BED & BREAKFAST STOPS • **CARAVAN & CAMPING HOLIDAYS**
FAMILY BREAKS IN BRITAIN

Published annually: available in all good bookshops or direct from the publisher:
FHG Guides, Abbey Mill Business Centre, Seedhill, Paisley PA1 1TJ
Tel: 0141 887 0428 • Fax: 0141 889 7204
e-mail: admin@fhguides.co.uk • www.holidayguides.com

CUMBRIAN COTTAGES. Choose from 300 pet-friendly cottages. Superb locations throughout the Lake District and Cumbria. All VisitBritain graded. Contact us for a brochure or visit our website. Tel: 01228 599950 (lines open 7 days 9am-9pm (5.30pm Sat). [Pets £15 per week.]
website: www.cumbrian-cottages.co.uk

STAY LAKELAND. A range of high quality self-catering holiday accommodation in the Lake District and Cumbria, including traditional cottages, houses, timber lodges and holiday static caravans. All ★★★ minimum and inspected annually by VisitBritain (0845 468 0936) [🐕]
website: www.staylakeland.co.uk

Alston

Small market town 16 miles NE of Penrith.

CUMBERLAND INN, TOWNFOOT, ALSTON CA9 3HX (01434 381875). A comfy retreat in the secluded North Pennines. Home-made hearty fare available all day. All 5 bedrooms are en suite. Muddy dogs and boots welcome. Pets welcome in bedrooms and bar. No charge for pets
e-mail: stay@cumberlandinnalston.com   website: www.cumberlandinnalston.com.

PAUL & CAROL HUISH, ROCK HOUSE ESTATE, VALLEY VIEW, NENTHEAD, ALSTON CA9 3NA (01434 382 684). Five luxury cottages sleeping 2, 4, 7, 7, or 14. Undiscovered Cumbria, accessible to the Lakes, Dales and Borders. 100 acre estate is surrounded by spectacular views. Short breaks available. Open all year. VisitBritain ★★★/★★★★. [Pets £20 each].
e-mail: Info@RockHouseEstate.co.uk   website: www.RockHouseEstate.co.uk

Ambleside

Popular centre for exploring Lake District at northern end of Lake Windermere. Picturesque Stock Ghyll waterfall nearby, lovely walks. Associations with Wordsworth. Penrith 30 miles, Keswick 17, Windermere 5.

BRATHAY LODGE, ROTHAY ROAD, AMBLESIDE LA22 0EE (015394 32000) Spacious en suite bedrooms, spa baths with shower over. Ground floor rooms with own entrance. Double, twin and family rooms, rates from £30 pppn. Pets welcome. Private off-road parking. EnjoyEngland ★★★★. [Pets £5 per night]
e-mail: info@brathay-lodge.co.uk   website: www.brathay-lodge.co.uk

2 LOWFIELD, OLD LAKE ROAD, AMBLESIDE. Ground floor garden flat half a mile from town centre; sleeps 4. Lounge/diningroom, kitchen, bathroom/WC, two bedrooms, one with en suite shower. Linen supplied. Children and pets welcome. Parking. Terms from £160 to £300 per week. Contact: MR P. F. QUARMBY, 3 LOWFIELD, OLD LAKE ROAD, AMBLESIDE LA22 0DH (015394 32326) [🐕]
e-mail: paul.quarmby@zen.co.uk

KIRKSTONE FOOT, KIRKSTONE PASS ROAD, AMBLESIDE LA22 9EH (015394 32232; Fax: 015394 32805). Superior cottage and apartment complex, set in peaceful gardens, adjoining the Lakeland fells and village centre. Open all year. ETC ★★★★ [pw! Pets £5.00 per night]
e-mail: enquiries@kirkstonefoot.co.uk   website: www.kirkstonefoot.co.uk

GREENHOWE CARAVAN PARK, GREAT LANGDALE, AMBLESIDE LA22 9JU (015394 37231; Fax: 015394 37464). Permanent Caravan Park with Self Contained Holiday Accommodation. An ideal centre for Climbing, Fell Walking, Riding, Swimming, or just a lazy holiday. ETC ★★★★ [Pets £6 per night, £30 per week]
website: www.greenhowe.com

**THE OLD VICARAGE, VICARAGE ROAD, AMBLESIDE LA22 9DH (015394 33764). 'Rest a while in style'. Quality B&B set in tranquil wooded grounds in the heart of the village. Car park. All rooms en suite. Kettle, clock/radio, TV. Heated indoor pool, sauna, hot tub, sun lounge and rooftop terrace. Special breaks. Friendly service where your pets are welcome. Telephone Ian or Helen Burt. [🐕]
website: www.oldvicarageambleside.co.uk**

LYNDALE GUEST HOUSE LAKE ROAD, AMBLESIDE LA22 0DN (015394 34244) Nestled midway between Lake Windermere and Ambleside village, with superb views of Loughrigg Fell and the Langdales beyond. Excellent base for walking, touring, or just relaxing. [🐕]
e-mail: alison@lyndale-guesthouse.co.uk   website: www.lyndale-guesthouse.co.uk

Cumbria

SMALLWOOD HOUSE, COMPSTON ROAD, AMBLESIDE LA22 9DJ (015394 32330). Where quality and the customer come first. En suite rooms, car parking, leisure club membership. ETC ★★★★ [Pets £3 per night]
website: www.smallwoodhotel.co.uk

BETTY FOLD, HAWKSHEAD HILL, AMBLESIDE LA22 0PS (015394 36611). Ground floor apartment sleeping four. Private entrance. Set in peaceful and spacious grounds, ideal for walkers and families with pets. Open all year. [pw! Pets £2 per night.]
e-mail: claire@bettyfold.com website: www.bettyfold.co.uk

Appleby-in-Westmorland

Located in the Eden Valley, ideal for walking, riding, fishing and cycling. Annual events include The Gypsy Horse Fair and the Jazz Festival.

MILBURN GRANGE HOLIDAY COTTAGES, KNOCK, APPLEBY CA16 6DR (017683 61867) 1,2 & 3 bedroom cottages and a snug apartment in a stunning rural location. Two National Parks on the doorstep. Dogs very welcome and open all year. VisitBritain ★★★ Self Catering. [Pets free if you mention Pets Welcome!]
e-mail: petswelcome@milburngrange.co.uk website: www.milburngrange.co.uk

Barrow-in-Furness

Victorian town with rich industrial heritage, set against the backdrop of Lake District mountains.

ABBEY HOUSE HOTEL, ABBEY ROAD, BARROW IN-FURNESS LA13 0PA (01229 838282). Premier hotel accommodation set in 14 acres of private woodland and gardens. Luxurious suites and bedrooms, all individually decorated with en suite facilities; some with four-poster beds. [Pets £15 per night]
e-mail: enquiries@abbeyhousehotel.com website: www.abbeyhousehotel.com

Bassenthwaite

Village on Bassenthwaite Lake with traces of Norse and Roman settlements.

SKIDDAW VIEW HOLIDAY HOME PARK, BOTHEL, NEAR BASSENTHWAITE CA7 2NJ (016973 20919). Holiday static caravans, timber lodges and a range of traditional holiday cottages. Handy for Keswick, Cockermouth etc. 4-acre pet walking field. ETC ★★★★ [pw!🐾]
website: www.skiddawview.co.uk

Bowness-on-Windermere

Location on East shore of Lake Windermere adjoining Windermere town.

WINDERMERE LAKE HOLIDAYS. Holiday houseboats on the lake shore with stunning views. Sleep 4. Open all year round. Pets welcome. For brochure: 015394 43415. [Pets £10 per week]
e-mail: email@lakewindermere.net website: www.lakewindermere.net

OAKFOLD HOUSE, BERESFORD ROAD, BOWNESS-ON-WINDERMERE LA23 2JG (015394 43239) Award-winning Victorian Guesthouse. Free WiFi. Close to Lake, steamers, shops, restaurants and Beatrix Potter attraction. Car park. Gardens. VisitBritain ★★★★ Gold Award. [🐾]
e-mail: oakfoldhouse@fsmail.net website: www.oakfoldhouse.co.uk

---

Visit the FHG website
www.holidayguides.com
for details of the wide choice of accommodation featured in the full range of FHG titles

Brampton

Market town with cobbled streets. Octagonal Moat Hall with exterior staircases and iron stocks.

FARLAM HALL HOTEL, BRAMPTON CA8 2NG (016977 46234; Fax: 016977 46683). Standing in four acres of gardens, with its own lake, Farlam Hall offers fine quality cuisine and individually decorated guest rooms. Ideal touring centre for the Lakes, Borders and Hadrian's Wall. AA Three Stars Inspectors' Choice, Relais & Chateaux. [🐕]
e-mail: farlam@relaischateaux.com   website: www.farlamhall.co.uk

LONG BYRES AT TALKIN HEAD (016977 3435). Walk your dog straight from the cottages up the hill and on to the fells. 7 cottages on North Pennines farm, sleeping 2-8; excellent base for Hadrian's Wall, Scottish Borders and the Lake District. Local food cooked by Harriet and delivered to your cottage. [🐕]
e-mail: stay@longbyres.co.uk   website: www.longbyres.co.uk

Broughton-in-Furness

Village 8 miles NW of Ulverston.

PAUL SANDFORD, WOODEND COTTAGES, WOODEND, ULPHA, BROUGHTON-IN-FURNESS LA20 6DY (019467 23277). Woodend is remote and surrounded by hills and moorland, with views towards Scafell Pike. The cottages and house offer cosy accommodation for two to six people. Short breaks available out of season.
website: www.woodendcottage.com

Carlisle

Important Border city and former Roman station on River Eden. Castle is of historic interest, also Tullie House Museum and Art Gallery. Good sports facilities inc. football and racecourse. Kendal 45 miles, Dumfries 33, Penrith 18.

GRAHAM ARMS HOTEL, ENGLISH STREET, LONGTOWN, CARLISLE CA6 5SE (01228 791213; Fax: 01228 794110). 16 bedrooms en suite, including four-poster and family rooms, all with tea/coffee facilities, TV and radio. Secure courtyard locked overnight. Pets welcome with well-behaved owners. ETC ★★ [🐕]
e-mail: office@grahamarms.com   website: www.grahamarms.com

GEORGINA & JOHN ELWEN, NEW PALLYARDS, HETHERSGILL, CARLISLE CA6 6HZ (01228 577308). Relax and see beautiful North Cumbria and the Borders. Self-catering cottages; Bed and Breakfast also available in en suite rooms. Dogs/pets by arrangement. See website specials.[Pets from £10 per week]
e-mail: newpallyards@btinternet.com   website: www.4starsc.co.uk

Cartmel

Village 4 miles south of Newby Bridge.

RATHER SPECIAL COTTAGES. Seven cottages sleeping 2-6. Set behind a large Georgian house set in parkland on the side of Hamps Fell. Beautiful garden, great walks. Pets and children welcome. Open all year. Please telephone for details. ETC ★★★★. Contact: MR M. AINSCOUGH, LONGLANDS AT CARTMEL, GRANGE-OVER-SANDS LA11 6HG (015395 36475; Fax: 015395 36712). [🐕]
e-mail: longlands@cartmel.com   website: www.cartmel.com

Cockermouth

Market town and popular touring centre for Lake District and quiet Cumbrian coast. On Rivers Derwent and Cocker. Penrith 30 miles, Carlisle 26, Whitehaven 14, Keswick 12.

THE MANOR HOUSE, OUGHTERSIDE, ASPATRIA CA7 2PT (016973 22420). 18th century manor farmhouse retaining many original features and several acres of land. Spacious en suite rooms, tea/coffee making facilities, TV and lots of little extras. All pets welcome. Inspection Commended. [🐕]
e-mail: richardandjudy@themanorhouse.net   website: www.themanorhouse.net

THE PHEASANT, BASSENTHWAITE LAKE, NEAR COCKERMOUTH CA13 9YE (017687 76234; Fax: 017687 76002). Traditional Cumbrian hostelry with tastefully renovated accommodation, fine dining and outstanding hospitality. ETC ★★★ Silver Award, AA ★★★ and Rosette
e-mail: info@the-pheasant.co.uk   website: www.the-pheasant.co.uk

ROSE COTTAGE GUEST HOUSE, LORTON ROAD, COCKERMOUTH CA13 9DX (Tel & Fax: 01900 822189). Family-run guest house on the outskirts of Cockermouth. Warm, friendly atmosphere. Parking. All rooms en suite with colour TV, tea/coffee, central heating. Pets welcome. Ideal base for visiting both Lakes and coast. ETC/AA ★★★★ [🐾]
website: www.rosecottageguest.co.uk

THE DERWENT LODGE, EMBLETON, NEAR BASSENTHWAITE, COCKERMOUTH CA13 9YA (017687 76606). A warm welcome awaits you and your pet. Choose from luxury self-catering apartments or en suite hotel rooms/suites. Indoor pool and fitness suite. Ideal for touring Western Lakes and coast.
e-mail: enquiries@thederwentlodge.co.uk   website: www.thederwentlodge.co.uk

Coniston

Village 8 miles south-west of Ambleside, dominated by Old Man of Coniston (2635ft).

LAKELAND HOUSE, TILBERTHWAITE AVENUE, CONISTON LA21 8ED (015394 41303). Contemporary guest accommodation, hearty breakfasts, from £27.50 per person. Self-catering cottage also available, sleeping six, with lake views. [Pets £10 per week]
e-mail: info@lakelandhouse.co.uk   website: www.lakelandhouse.co.uk

THE SUN, CONISTON LA21 8HQ (015394 41248; Fax 015394 41219). Unique mix of great bar, restaurant and Four Star inn in extremely comfortable and informal atmosphere. Locally sourced food. Eight refurbished bedrooms with superb views. ETC ★★★★ [Pets £10 per night]
e-mail: info@thesunconiston.com   website: www.thesunconiston.com

THE COPPERMINES AND CONISTON LAKES COTTAGES (015394 41765). Unique Lakeland cottages for 2 – 30 of quality and character in stunning mountain scenery. Log fires, exposed beams. Pets welcome! ★★★ - ★★★★ Book online. [Pets £25 per stay]
website: www.coppermines.co.uk

BROCKLEBANK GROUND HOLIDAY COTTAGES, TORVER, CONISTON LA21 8BS (015394 49588). Four luxury cottages in a quiet rural setting, sleeping 2,4,7 & 10. Excellent walking from the door. Dog-friendly pubs 600 yards. Short breaks available. Prices from £275. ETC ★★★★. [🐾]
e-mail: info@brocklebankground.com   website: www.brocklebankground.com

THE YEWDALE HOTEL, YEWDALE ROAD, CONISTON LA21 8DU (015394 41280). Central for activities such as fishing, boating, canoeing, walking and pony trekking. 8 en suite bedrooms with TV and tea-making. Bar and dining room offer varied menus featuring fresh local produce. Excellent Cumbrian breakfasts. ETC ★★★ [Pets £6 per night]
e-mail: info@yewdalehotel.com   website: www.yewdalehotel.com

WATERHEAD HOTEL, CONISTON LA21 8AJ (015394 41244; Fax: 015394 41193). Situated alongside Coniston Water, The Waterhead Hotel makes a perfect retreat. 23 en suite bedrooms, one junior suite. Mountain View Restaurant, lounge bar with views across the Lake. Non-smoking. Ideal base for outdoor activities, also lake cruises and historic houses. [Pets £5 per night, £35 per week].
website: www.waterhead-hotel.co.uk

Crosthwaite

Hamlet 5 miles west of Kendal.

DAMSON DENE HOTEL, CROSTHWAITE LA8 8JE (015395 68676). Tranquil location only 10 minutes from Lake Windermere. Best Lakes Breaks from £118 per person for 2 nights. [🐾 pw!]
e-mail: info@damsondene.co.uk   website: www.bestlakesbreaks.co.uk

Please mention **Pets Welcome!** when making enquiries about accommodation featured in these pages

Duddon Valley

Majestic valley running between Cockley Beck and Duddon Bridge.

COCKLEY BECK FARM COTTAGE, SEATHWAITE, BROUGHTON-IN-FURNESS LA20 6EQ (01229 716480). In the heart of the Lake District National Park, just 4 miles from the summit of Scafell Pike. Self-contained holiday cottage (sleeps 4). Large open-plan kitchen. Well behaved dogs free of charge. Available all year. Private enclosed garden with patio and parking. [🐾 pw!]
e-mail: Sandra@cockleybeck.co.uk   website: www.cockleybeck.co.uk

Eskdale

Lakeless valley, noted for waterfalls and ascended by a light-gauge railway. Tremendous views. Roman fort. Keswick 35 miles, Broughton-in-Furness 10 miles.

FISHERGROUND FARM, ESKDALE. Traditional hill farm, with a stone cottage and three pine lodges, ideal for walkers, nature lovers, dogs and children. Games room, raft pool and a station on the miniature railway! Good pubs nearby. ETC ★★★. IAN & JENNIFER HALL, ORCHARD HOUSE, APPLETHWAITE, KESWICK CA12 4PN (017687 73175) [🐾]
e-mail: holidays@fisherground.co.uk   website: www.fisherground.co.uk

THE BOOT INN (FORMERLY THE BURNMOOR INN), BOOT, ESKDALE CA19 1TG (019467 23224). Nine en suite bedrooms. Dogs and their owners made very welcome. Special breaks available all year. Call for a brochure. [🐾]
e-mail: enquiries@bootinn.co.uk   website: www.bootinn.co.uk

Gosforth

Small village in Western Lake District, set within the Cumbria National Park, close to the Wasdale and Eskdale Valleys.

BLENG BARN COTTAGE, MILL HOUSE FARM, WELLINGTON, SEASCALE CA20 1BH (07801 862237 & 07775 512918; Fax: 01946 725671. Self-catering 3-bedroom holiday cottage on a large working farm. Sleeps 6+4. Many traditional features and modern facilities. ETC ★★★★ Self Catering.[🐾]
e-mail: info@blengfarms.co.uk   website: www.blengfarms.co.uk

Grange-over-Sands

Edwardian seaside resort on the edge of the Lake District National Park.

HAMPSFELL HOUSE HOTEL, HAMPSFELL ROAD, GRANGE-OVER-SANDS LA11 6BG (015395 32567). In two acres of private grounds, just a few minutes' walk from the town centre. The eight en suite bedrooms are well appointed. Enjoy the best of fresh Cumbrian produce in the elegant dining room. Ideal base for exploring the Lake District. AA ★★ [Pets £5 per night].
e-mail: enquiries@hampsfellhouse.co.uk   website: www.hampsfellhouse.co.uk

Grasmere

Village famous for Wordsworth associations; the poet lived in Dove Cottage (preserved as it was), and is buried in the churchyard. Museum has manuscripts and relics.

LAKE VIEW COUNTRY HOUSE & SELF-CATERING APARTMENTS, GRASMERE LA22 9TD (015394 35384/35167). 4 rooms B&B or 3 Self-Catering apartments in unrivalled, secluded location in the village with wonderful views and lakeshore access. All B&B rooms en suite, some with whirlpool baths. Ground floor accommodation available. No smoking. Featured in Michelin Guide.

GRASMERE HOTEL, BROADGATE, GRASMERE LA22 9TA (015394 35277). Charming 13 bedroom Country House Hotel, with ample parking and a licensed lounge. All rooms recently refurbished with en suite facilities. Award-winning restaurant overlooking gardens, river and surrounding hills. Special breaks throughout the year. AA ★★ and Rosette; ETC ★★ Silver Award.[Pets £5 per stay].
e-mail: enquiries@grasmerehotel.co.uk   website: www.grasmerehotel.co.uk

Cumbria

NORTH WEST ENGLAND

Hawkshead

Quaint village in Lake District between Coniston Water and Windermere. The 16th century Church and Grammar School, which Wordsworth attended, are of interest. Ambleside 5 miles.

THE KINGS ARMS HOTEL, HAWKSHEAD, AMBLESIDE LA22 0NZ (015394 36372). Join us for a relaxing stay amidst the green hills and dales of Lakeland, and we will be delighted to offer you good food, homely comfort and warm hospitality in historic surroundings. We hope to see you soon! Self-catering cottages also available.[🐾, pets £20 per week s/c]
website: www.kingsarmshawkshead.co.uk

LAKELAND HIDEAWAYS, THE SQUARE, HAWKSHEAD LA22 0NZ (015394 42435). Cottages in and around Hawkshead. Great walks and lakes for swimming, dog friendly pubs, open fires to lie in front of... owners will enjoy it too. [Pets £20 per week].
e-mail: bookings@lakeland-hideaways.co.uk   website: www.lakeland-hideaways.co.uk

2 MOOT HALL, IREBY CA7 1DU (01423 360759). Lovely cottage, part of 16th century Moot Hall in unspoilt village; delightful walks in Uldale Fells and northern Lake District. Sleeps 4. Linen/fuel/electricity incl. Open all year. Reductions for PAT, Assistance and Rescue Dogs. [🐾]
e-mail: ruthboyes@virgin.net   website: www.irebymoothall.co.uk

Kendal

Market town and popular centre for touring the Lake District. Of historic interest is the Norman castle, birthplace of Catherine Parr. Penrith 25 miles, Lancaster 22, Ambleside 13.

RIVERSIDE HOTEL, BEEZON ROAD, KENDAL LA9 6EL (015397 34861). Lovely riverside location. Best Lakes Breaks from £118 per person for 2 nights. [🐾 pw!]
e-mail: info@riversidekendal.co.uk   website: www.bestlakesbreaks.co.uk

MRS L. HODGSON, PATTON HALL FARM, KENDAL LA8 9DT (01539 721590). 2 Modern caravans, fully double glazed, gas central heating. Double and twin bedrooms, kitchen, spacious lounge/dining area, toilet and shower. Traditional working farm set in 140 acres of beautiful countryside. [Pets £10/£15 per week].
e-mail: stay@pattonhallfarm.co.uk   website: www.pattonhallfarm.co.uk

ANNE TAYLOR, RUSSELL FARM, BURTON-IN-KENDAL, CARNFORTH, LANCS. LA6 1NN (01524 781334). Bed and Breakfast. Ideal centre for touring Lakes and Yorkshire Dales. Good food, friendly atmosphere on working dairy farm. Modernised farmhouse. Guests' own lounge. [🐾]
e-mail: miktaylor@farming.co.uk

MRS HELEN JONES, PRIMROSE COTTAGE, ORTON ROAD, TEBAY CA10 3TL (015396 24791). Adjacent M6 J38 (10 miles north of Kendal). Excellent rural location for North Lakes and Yorkshire Dales. Superb facilities, jacuzzi bath, king and four-poster beds. One acre garden. Self-contained ground floor flat and 3 purpose-built self-catering bungalows for disabled guests, with electric bed, jacuzzi and large, wheel-in bathroom. Pets welcome, very friendly. VisitBritain★★★★ Guest Accommodation. [🐾]
e-mail: primrosecottebay@aol.com   website: www.primrosecottagecumbria.co.uk

MIREFOOT COTTAGES, MIREFOOT, KENDAL LA8 9AB (Tel: 01539 720015). 5 Star, pet friendly, self-catering cottages in a superb rural location in the Lake District National Park. All cottages sleep 2. Fully equipped with TV (Freeview), DVD, WiFi, gas central heating. Tennis court, private parking. VB ★★★★★ [Pets £10 per week]
e-mail: booking@mirefoot.co.uk   website: www.mirefoot.co.uk

STONECROSS MANOR HOTEL, MILNTHORPE ROAD, KENDAL LA9 5HP (01539 733559; Fax: 01539 736386). Stonecross Manor offers easy access to town, ample parking, local cuisine, conference and banquet facilities, indoor swimming pool, and four-poster bedrooms. [Pets £10 per night].
e-mail: info@stonecrossmanor.co.uk   website: www.stonecrossmanor.co.uk

---

Symbols

🐾 Indicates that pets are welcome free of charge.

£ Indicates that a charge is made for pets: nightly or weekly.

pw! Shows some special provision for pets; exercise facility, feeding or accommodation arrangement.

⌂ Indicates separate pets accommodation.

Keswick

Famous Lake District resort at north end of Derwentwater with Pencil Museum and Cars of the Stars Motor Museum. Carlisle 30 miles.

MARY MOUNT HOTEL, BORROWDALE, NEAR KESWICK CA12 5UU (017687 77223). Set in 4½ acres of gardens and woodlands on the shores of Derwentwater. 2½ miles from Keswick in picturesque Borrowdale. Superb walking and touring. All rooms en suite with colour TV and tea/coffee making facilities. Licensed. Brochure on request. ETC ★★ [pw! Pets £10 per week.]
e-mail: mawdsley1@aol.com   website: www.marymounthotel.co.uk

OVERWATER HALL, OVERWATER, NEAR IREBY, KESWICK CA7 1HH (017687 76566). Elegant Country House Hotel in spacious grounds. Dogs very welcome in your room. 4 night mid-week breaks from £340 per person, inclusive of Dinner and Breakfast. Mini breaks also available all year. Award-winning restaurant. AA ★★★ and Two Rosettes. See also advertisement on page 304 [pw! 🐾]
e-mail: welcome@overwaterhall.co.uk   website: www.overwaterhall.co.uk

DERWENT WATER MARINA, PORTINSCALE, KESWICK CA12 5RF Lakeside self-catering apartments. Three apartments sleep 2, one apartment sleeps 6. Superb views over the lake and fells. Includes TV, heating and bed linen. Non-smoking. Watersports and boat hire available on site. Tel: 017687 72912 for brochure. [🐾]
e-mail: info@derwentwatermarina.co.uk   website: www.derwentwatermarina.co.uk

ROYAL OAK HOTEL, BORROWDALE, KESWICK CA12 5XB (017687 77214). Traditional Lakeland hotel with friendly atmosphere. Home cooking, cosy bar, comfortable lounge and some riverside rooms. Winter and Summer discount rates. Brochure and tariff available. [🐾]
e-mail: info@royaloakhotel.co.uk   website: www.royaloakhotel.co.uk

KESWICK COTTAGES, 8 BEECHCROFT, BRAITHWAITE, KESWICK CA12 5TH (017687 78555). Cottages and apartments in and around Keswick. Properties are well maintained and clean. From a one bedroom cottage to a 4-bedroom house. Children and pets welcome. ETC ★★★★ [Pets £15 per week]
e-mail: info@keswickcottages.co.uk   website: www.keswickcottages.co.uk

ANDY & CHARLOTTE PETERS, SEYMOUR HOUSE, 36 LAKE ROAD, KESWICK CA12 5DQ (01768 772764; Freephone: 0800 0566401; mobile: 07721 957899). Set in quiet cul-de-sac, 3 minutes' walk from town centre, Theatre by the Lake, and Derwentwater (Queen of the Lakes). 7 well appointed rooms, all en suite. Special diets catered for, as well as normal English breakfast. Open all year includiding Christmas. [Pets £5 per night, £15 per week.]
e-mail: enquiries@seymour-house.com   website: www.seymour-house.com

HORSE AND FARRIER INN, THRELKELD, KESWICK CA12 4SQ (017687 79688; Fax: 017687 79823). Ideal location for walking or touring the Lake District. All 15 bedrooms en suite, with TV, tea/coffee making and hairdryer. Award-winning food and restaurant. Open all year. Pets welcome. ETC ★★★★
e-mail: info@horseandfarrier.com   website: www.horseandfarrier.com

RICKERBY GRANGE, PORTINSCALE, KESWICK CA12 5RH (017687 72344). Delightfully situated in quiet village. Licensed. Imaginative home-cooked food, attractively served. Open all year. Private car park. VisitBritain ★★★★ Guest House. [🐾]
e-mail: stay@rickerbygrange.co.uk   website: www.rickerbygrange.co.uk

Warm, comfortable houses and cottages in Keswick and beautiful Borrowdale, welcoming your dog. Inspected and quality graded. LAKELAND COTTAGE HOLIDAYS, KESWICK CA12 4QX (017687 76065; Fax: 017687 76869). [Pets £2 per day, £14 per week.]
e-mail: info@lakelandcottages.co.uk   website: www.lakelandcottages.co.uk

LOW BRIERY HOLIDAYS (017687 72044). A peaceful and scenic riverside location just outside Keswick. A choice of cottages, timber lodges and holiday caravans to suit all budgets. ETC ★★★★ [Pets £20 per week]
website: www.keswick.uk.com

WOODSIDE, PENRITH ROAD, KESWICK CA12 4LJ (017687 73522). Friendly family-run establishment. All our rooms are en suite. We have ample private parking and large gardens. Non-smoking. Dogs welcome. [🐾]
website: www.woodsideguesthouse.co.uk

COLEDALE INN, BRAITHWAITE, NEAR KESWICK CA12 5TN (017687 78272). Friendly, family-run Victorian Inn in peaceful situation. Warm and spacious en suite bedrooms with TV. Children and pets welcome. Open all year. ETC ★★★ [🐾]
website: www.coledale-inn.co.uk

Cumbria

Kirkby-in-Furness

Small coastal village (A595). 10 minutes to Ulverston, Lakes within easy reach. Ideal base for walking and touring.

SUNSET COTTAGE. Self-catering 17th century two/three bedroom character cottage with garden. Original features. Panoramic views over sea/mountains; Coniston/Windermere 30 minutes. Non-smoking. Open all year. VisitBritain ★★★★ Contact: JANET AND PETER, 1 FRIARS GROUND, KIRKBY-IN-FURNESS LA17 7YB (01229 889601). [Pets £20 per pet]
e-mail: enquiries@southlakes-cottages.com   website: www.southlakes-cottages.com

Kirkby Lonsdale

Georgian buildings and quaint cottages. Riverside walks from medieval Devil's Bridge.

BARBON INN, BARBON, NEAR KIRKBY LONSDALE LA6 2LJ (015242 76233). Friendly 17th century Coaching Inn with 10 bedrooms. Country pursuits within the immediate area. Nestling in Lune Valley between Lake District and Yorkshire Dales. [pw! Pets £10 per stay]
e-mail: info@barbon-inn.co.uk   website: www.barbon-inn.co.uk

THE SNOOTY FOX, KIRKBY LONSDALE LA6 2AH (01524 271308). Charming Jacobean Inn, offering 9 en suite rooms, award-winning restaurant and lounge bar, the perfect base from which to explore both the Lake District and Yorkshire Dales. AA ★★★★ [🐾]
e-mail: snootyfoxhotel@talktalk.net   website: www.thesnootyfoxhotel.co.uk

MRS PAULINE BAINBRIDGE, ULLATHORNS FARM, MIDDLETON, KIRKBY LONSDALE LA6 2LZ (015242 76214; Mobile: 07800 990689). 17th Century farmhouse on a working farm situated in the Lune Valley. B&B from £27. Children and well-behaved pets welcome. Non-smoking. VisitBritain ★★★★ [🐾]
e-mail: pauline@ullathorns.co.uk   website: www.ullathorns.co.uk

Kirkby Stephen

Small town on River Eden, 9 miles South of Appleby.

COCKLAKE HOUSE, MALLERSTANG CA17 4JT (017683 72080). Charming, High Pennine Country House B&B in unique position above Pendragon Castle in Upper Mallerstang Dale offering good food and exceptional comfort to a small number of guests. Two double rooms with large private bathrooms. Three acres riverside grounds. Dogs welcome. [🐾]

Kirkoswald

Village in the Cumbrian hills, lying north west of the Lake District. Ideal for touring. Penrith 7 miles.

SECLUDED COTTAGES WITH PRIVATE FISHING, KIRKOSWALD CA10 1EU (24 hour brochure line 01768 898711, manned most Saturdays). Quality cottages, clean, well equipped and maintained. Centrally located for Lakes, Pennines, Hadrian's Wall, Borderland. Enjoy the Good Life in comfort. Pets' paradise. Guests' coarse fishing. Bookings/enquiries 01768 898711. ETC ★★★ [pw! £2 per pet per night, £14 per week].
e-mail: info@crossfieldcottages.co.uk   website: www.crossfieldcottages.co.uk

Lake District

North west corner of England between A6/M6 and the Cumbrian Coast. Fells, valleys and 16 lakes, the largest being Lake Windermere.

LAKE DISTRICT. Two luxury houses available to rent in the Lake District. Routen House, sleeps 12 plus cot. Fully modernised, outstanding position in 4 acres. Little Parrock, sleeps 10 plus cot, short walk from centre of Grasmere with real log fire and private garden. Both houses non-smoking. MRS J. GREEN (01604 505115).
e-mail: joanne@routenhouse.co.uk   www.routenhouse.co.uk / www.littleparrock.co.uk

Lamplugh (near Loweswater)

Hamlet 7 miles south of Cockermouth.

FELLDYKE COTTAGE HOLIDAYS, LAMPLUGH. Visiting the Western Lakes? Then why not stay in this lovely 19th century cottage. Sleeps 4, short breaks can be arranged. Pets are welcome. Open all year. Contact MRS A. WILSON (01946 861151). VB ★★★★ [pw!🐾].
e-mail: dockraynook@talk21.com   website: www.felldykecottageholidays.co.uk

ROSE COTTAGE. Three miles from Loweswater and four miles from Ennerdale, lovely throughout. Open plan kitchen and sitting room, cosy coal fire, two bedrooms and enclosed garden. Pets welcome. Contact SALLY FIELDING (01768 779445). [Pets £15 per week]
website: www.millgillhead.co.uk

Langdale

Dramatic valley area to the west of Ambleside, in the very heart of the National Park.

THE BRITANNIA INN, ELTERWATER, AMBLESIDE LA22 9HP (015394 37210; Fax: 015396 78075). 500-year-old traditional lakeland inn. Extensive, home-cooked menu, real ales, cosy bars, log fires. Comfortable, high quality en suite accommodation. Well-behaved pets welcome. ETC ★★★ [🐾]
e-mail: info@britinn.co.uk   website: www.britinn.co.uk

WHEELWRIGHTS HOLIDAY COTTAGES, ELTERWATER, NEAR AMBLESIDE LA22 9HS (015394 38305; Fax: 015394 37618). Some of the loveliest cottages in the Lake District with stunning scenery on their doorsteps are ready to welcome you and your pets. Prices vary. Please visit our website. ETC ★★★ - ★★★★★ [🐾]
e-mail: enquiries@wheelwrights.com   website: www.wheelwrights.com

Lazonby

Village on River Eden 6 miles North of Penrith.

Delightful country cottage for two in Cumbria's Eden Valley. Open fire. Secure garden. Village location. Lake District and North Pennines a short drive away. A warm welcome awaits pets and their well behaved owners. Contact PENNY CLAY, MILLSTONE COTTAGE, LAZONBY CA10 1AJ (01768 870558).
e-mail: stayatnumberthree@postmaster.co.uk

Little Langdale

Hamlet 2 miles west of Skelwith Bridge. To west is Little Langdale Tarn, a small lake.

HIGHFOLD COTTAGE, LITTLE LANGDALE. Very comfortable Lakeland cottage, ideally situated for walking and touring. Superb mountain views. Sleeps 6. Personally maintained. Pets welcome. Weekly £260–£550. VB ★★★. MRS C.E. BLAIR, 8 THE GLEBE, CHAPEL STILE, AMBLESIDE LA22 9JT (015394 37686). [🐾]
website: www.highfoldcottage.co.uk

Millom

Small coastal town in the South Western Lake District.

HOLIDAY COTTAGE - LAKE DISTRICT (01229 717174). 300-year-old two-bedroom cottage on the west coast of Cumbria within the National Park. Traditional cottage, oak beams etc. Secure garden and an attached 3-acre deer-fenced playground for dogs. Close to miles of dog-friendly beaches. [pw! 🐾]

Please mention **Pets Welcome!**
when making enquiries about accommodation featured in these pages

Cumbria

Newby Bridge

Village 8 miles NE of Ulverston

NEWBY BRIDGE HOTEL, NEWBY BRIDGE LA12 8NA (015395 31222). Overlooking the southern shores of Lake Windermere. Best Lakes Breaks from £118 per person for 2 nights. [🐾 pw!]
e-mail: info@newbybridgehotel.co.uk   website: www.bestlakesbreaks.co.uk

MR A.S.G. SCOTT, OAK HEAD CARAVAN PARK, AYSIDE, GRANGE-OVER-SANDS LA11 6JA (015395 31475). A well tended, uncrowded and wooded site set amidst picturesque fells. Flush toilets, hot showers, laundry facilities, hair dryers, deep freeze, gas on sale. Tourers (30 pitches), Tents (30 pitches), Auto Homes. Open March 1st to October 31st. [🐾]
website: www.oakheadcaravanpark.co.uk

Penrith

Market town and centre for touring Lake District. Of interest are 14th century castle, Gloucester Arms (1477) and Tudor House. Excellent sporting facilities. Windermere 27 miles, Keswick 18.

THE TROUTBECK INN, TROUTBECK, PENRITH CA11 0SJ (017684 83635; Fax: 017684 87071). Close to the shores of lovely Ullswater, this friendly and well-appointed inn enjoys sweeping fell views and is a haven for a variety of outdoor pursuits, Excellent varied food and real ales. Tastefully furnished en suite bedrooms. Three self-catering cottages. VisitBritain ★★★★ Inn/★★★★ S/C [Pets £5-£15 per week].
e-mail: info@troutbeckinn.co.uk   website: www.thetroutbeckinn.co.uk

LYVENNET COTTAGES. Five different cottages in and around the small farming village of Kings Meaburn in beautiful unspoilt 'Lyvennet Valley'. Ideal touring centre for the Lakes and Dales. JANET ADDISON, KELD FARM, KINGS MEABURN, PENRITH CA10 3BS (01931 714661/714226; Fax: 01931 714598). ETC ★★★★/★★★★★
website: www.lyvennetcottages.co.uk

CHURCH COURT COTTAGES, GAMBLESBY, PENRITH CA10 1HR. Four beautiful, well-equipped, sandstone cottages in picturesque village. Excellent traffic-free walks from doorstep. Wonderful views of the hills of the Lake District and North Pennines. Penrith 15 minutes. Contact: MARK COWELL or PATRICIA CLOWES (01768 881682). [🐾]
e-mail: cottages@gogamblesby.co.uk   website: www.gogamblesby.co.uk

WESTMORLAND HOTEL, ORTON, PENRITH, CUMBRIA CA10 3SB (015396 24351). Family-owned hotel in Cumbrian Fells. 50 en suite bedrooms. Cosy lounge. All day lounge menu and bar. Pets welcome at small charge, maximum 2 pets per room. AA ★★★ /Rosette. [Pets £7.50 per night]
website: www.westmorlandhotel.com

CARROCK COTTAGES. Four renovated, award-winning, stone-built cottages set on the fringe of the Lakeland Fells. Games room. Home cooked meals service. Ideal for fell walking. Excellent restaurants nearby. A warm welcome guaranteed. ETC ★★★★★ GOLD AWARD. Contact MALCOLM OR GILLIAN (01768 484111; Fax: 01768 488850). [Pets £25 per week each].
e-mail: info@carrockcottages.co.uk   website: www.carrockcottages.co.uk

BOOT & SHOE INN, GREYSTOKE, PENRITH CA11 0TP (01768 483343). Popular 16thC Inn in the heart of the legendary village of Greystoke. Full of charm, character and history. Excellent food, en suite accommodation and ambience. Conveniently situated to explore the Lake District.
e-mail: info@bootandshoegreystoke.co.uk   website: www.bootandshoegreystoke.co.uk

Ravenglass

Coastal hamlet, with a restored steam railway known as "La'al Ratty".

BROWN COW INN, WABERTHWAITE, NEAR RAVENGLASS LA19 5YJ (01229 717243). Home-cooked food at prices you can afford. Four real ales. Four en suite rooms. Wheelchair access. Food served daily. Beer garden. Pets welcome in bar area and rooms.
e-mail: browncowinn@btconnect.com

St Bees

Village 4 miles south of Whitehaven.

SEACOTE PARK, THE BEACH, ST BEES CA27 0ET(01946 822777; Fax: 01946 824442). Adjoining lovely sandy beach on fringe of Lake District, modern luxury holiday caravans for hire. Full serviced touring pitches and tent area. St Bees is convenient for touring. We also have two other Caravan Parks close by, Tarnside and Seven Acres. ETC ★★★★. Rose Award Park. [Pets £3 per night, £20 per week in hire caravans; free of charge in tourers and tents]
e-mail: reception@seacote.com   website: www.seacote.com

Silloth-on-Solway

Solway Firth resort with harbour and fine sandy beach. Mountain views. Golf, fishing. Penrith 33 miles, Carlisle 23, Cockermouth 17.

MR AND MRS M.C. BOWMAN, TANGLEWOOD CARAVAN PARK, CAUSEWAY HEAD, SILLOTH CA7 4PE (016973 31253). Friendly country site, excellent toilet and laundry facilities. Tourers welcome or hire a luxury caravan. Open 1st March to January 31st. Telephone or e-mail for a brochure. AA THREE PENNANTS. [🐕]
e-mail: tanglewoodcaravanpark@hotmail.com   website: www.tanglewoodcaravanpark.co.uk

Ullswater

Lake stretching for 7 miles with attractive Lakeside walks.

LAND ENDS CABINS, WATERMILLOCK, NEAR ULLSWATER CA11 0NB (017684 86438). Only 1.5 miles from Ullswater, our four detached log cabins have a peaceful fellside location in 25-acre grounds with two pretty lakes. Doggy heaven! Sleep 2-5. ETC ★★★ [🐕]
e-mail: infolandends@btinternet.com   website: www.landends.co.uk

COVE CARAVAN & CAMPING PARK, WATERMILLOCK, PENRITH CA11 0LS (017684 86549). Well-maintained and peaceful park overlooking Lake Ullswater surrounded by Fells. Ideally situated for walking, watersports and all Lake District attractions. Electric hook-ups with hardstandings, sheltered grass for campers. AA 3 PENNANTS. [Pets £1 per night]
website: www.cove-park.co.uk

FARRIERS LOFT, FELL VIEW, GLENRIDDING, PENRITH CA11 0PJ (017684 82795). Sleep 2-5. Lovely, comfortable, well equipped accommodation in an idyllic location between Glenridding and Patterdale. Magnificent views of the surrounding fells. Short Breaks available out of season.
e-mail: enquiries@farriersloft.com   website: www.farriersloft.com

Wasdale

Hamlet 1 mile north east of Wast Water

THE BRIDGE INN, SANTON BRIDGE, HOLMROOK CA19 1UX (019467 26221; Fax: 019467 26026). Award-winning country inn providing good food and accommodation. 16 en suite bedrooms. Ideal for exploring the Western Lakes and fells. Well behaved dogs welcome. [Pets £6 per stay].
e-mail: info@santonbridgeinn.com   website: www.santonbridgeinn.com

Wigton

Market town 11 miles SW of Carlisle.

FOXGLOVES COTTAGE, WIGTON. Sleeps 2-8. Spacious, well-equipped comfortable cottage on working farm. Children and pets very welcome. Easy reach Lake District, Scottish Borders and Roman Wall. Available all year. Short breaks by arrangement. MR & MRS E. & J. KERR, GREENRIGG FARM, WESTWARD, WIGTON CA7 8AH (016973 42676). [pw! First pet free, second or more £10 per week]
e-mail: kerr_greenrigg@hotmail.com

Cumbria

NORTH WEST ENGLAND

Windermere

Famous resort on lake of same name, the largest in England. Magnificent scenery. Car ferry from Bowness, one mile distant. Kendal 9 miles.

LOW SPRINGWOOD HOTEL, THORNBARROW ROAD, WINDERMERE LA23 2DF (015394 46383). Millie and Lottie (Boxers) would like to welcome you to their peaceful Hotel in its own secluded gardens. Lovely views of Lakes and Fells. All rooms en suite with colour TV etc. Some four-posters. Brochure available. [🐾 pw!]

LANGDALE CHASE HOTEL, WINDERMERE LA23 1LW (015394 32201). Magnificent country house hotel with grounds sloping to the edge of Lake Windermere. Panoramic views, log fires, excellent food and friendly professional staff ensure a memorable stay. [Pets £3 per night]
e-mail: sales@langdalechase.co.uk   website: www.langdalechase.co.uk

Hundreds of self-catering holiday homes in a variety of wonderful locations, all well equipped and managed by our caring staff. Pets welcome. Free leisure club membership. For brochure, contact: LAKELOVERS, BELMONT HOUSE, LAKE ROAD, BOWNESS-ON-WINDERMERE LA23 3BJ. (015394 88855; Fax: 015394 88857). ETC ★★★ - ★★★★★ [Pets £20 per week.]
e-mail: bookings@lakelovers.co.uk   website: www.lakelovers.co.uk

WATERMILL INN & BREWERY, INGS, NEAR WINDERMERE LA8 9PY (01539 821309; Fax: 01539 822309). Ruby and friends (Dogs) welcome you to the award-winning Inn. 16 real ales. Cosy fires, en suite rooms, excellent bar meals. Doggie water and biscuits served in the bar. Good doorstep dog walking. ETC ★★★★ [Pets £4 per night (includes donation to Dogs' Trust).]
e-mail: info@Lakelandpub.co.uk   website: www.Lakelandpub.co.uk

326 NORTH WEST ENGLAND — Lancashire

Blackburn, Blackpool, Carnforth, Thornley

THE BROWN LEAVES COUNTRY HOTEL, LONGSIGHT ROAD, COPSTER GREEN, NEAR BLACKBURN BB1 9EU • 01254 249523 • Fax: 0845 557 0608
Situated on the A59 halfway between Preston and Clitheroe, five miles from Junction 31 on M6 in beautiful Ribble Valley. All rooms ground floor, en suite facilities, satellite TV, tea-making and hairdryer. Guests' lounge and bar lounge. Car parking. Pets by arrangement. All credit cards welcome. **www.brownleavescountryhotel.co.uk**

The Brayton Hotel
7-8 Finchley Road, Gynn Square,
BLACKPOOL FY1 2LP
info2@the-brayton-hotel.com
www.the-brayton-hotel.com

- Quiet and pleasantly located licensed hotel.
- Overlooking Gynn Gardens and the promenade.
- Short drive or tram ride to all the attractions.
- Full 'Restaurant Style' menu served every day.
- Dogs most welcome and free. Open all year.

Phone: 01253 351645

Locka Old Hall Cottage Arkholme, near Kirkby Lonsdale LA6 1BD
Small cottage with open fire in easy reach of Lake District, Yorkshire Dales and Lancashire coast. Lawned garden with views over fells and Ingleborough. Quiet location. Sleeps 2 (+2 on sofa bed).
Tel: 015242 21561 • e-mail: cottage@locka.co.uk • www.locka.co.uk

Loudview Barn • Thornley • Near Preston
Self-catering stone barn conversion in peaceful location in Forest of Bowland. Exceptional views across unspoilt countryside.
Unit 1: one double, one twin and bunk beds • Unit 2: one double and one twin
Contact: **Mr & Mrs Starkey, Loudview Barn, Rams Clough Farm, Thornley, Preston PR3 2TN**
Tel: **01995 61476** • e-mail: **loudview@ic24.net** • **www.loudview.co.uk**

Blackburn

Former mill town with a rich industrial heritage, set in the heart of Lancashire's Hill Country.

THE BROWN LEAVES COUNTRY HOTEL, LONGSIGHT ROAD, COPSTER GREEN, NEAR BLACKBURN BB1 9EU (01254 249523; Fax: 0845 557 0608). Situated on the A59 halfway between Preston and Clitheroe, five miles from Junction 31 on M6 in beautiful Ribble Valley. All rooms ground floor, en suite facilities, satellite TV, tea-making and hairdryer. Guests' lounge and bar lounge. Car parking. Pets by arrangement. All credit cards welcome. [🐾]
website: www.brownleavescountryhotel.co.uk

Blackpool

Famous resort with fine sands and many attractions and vast variety of entertainments. Blackpool Tower (500ft). Three piers. Manchester 47 miles, Lancaster 26, Preston 17, Fleetwood 8.

THE BRAYTON, 7-8 FINCHLEY ROAD, GYNN SQUARE, BLACKPOOL FY1 2LP (01253 351645). Quiet licensed hotel overlooking Gynn Gardens and the promenade. Full 'restaurant style' menu served daily. Dogs most welcome. Open all year. [🐾]
e-mail: info2@the-brayton-hotel.com   website: www.the-brayton-hotel.com

Symbols

🐾	Indicates that pets are welcome free of charge.
£	Indicates that a charge is made for pets: nightly or weekly.
pw!	Shows some special provision for pets; exercise facility, feeding or accommodation arrangement.
⌂	Indicates separate pets accommodation.

Carnforth

Town 6 miles North of Lancaster.

LOCKA OLD HALL COTTAGE, ARKHOLME, NEAR KIRKBY LONSDALE LA6 1BD (015242 21561). Small cottage with open fire in easy reach of Lake District, Yorkshire Dales and Lancashire coast. Lawned garden with views over fells and Ingleborough. Quiet location. Sleeps 2 (+2 on sofa bed). [🐕]
e-mail: cottage@locka.co.uk　　　　　　　　　website: www.locka.co.uk

Thornley

Town 7 miles West of Clitheroe, 4 miles from Longridge.

LOUDVIEW BARN. Self-catering stone barn conversion in peaceful location in Forest of Bowland. Exceptional views across unspoilt countryside. Unit 1: one double, one twin and bunk beds; Unit 2: one double and one twin. ETC ★★★★ Contact: MR & MRS STARKEY, LOUDVIEW BARN, RAMS CLOUGH FARM, THORNLEY, PRESTON PR3 2TN (01995 61476). [🐕]
e-mail: loudview@ic24.net　　　　　　　　　website: www.loudview.co.uk

---

Free or reduced rate entry to
Holiday Visits and Attractions - see our
READERS' OFFER VOUCHERS on pages 445-454

Other specialised holiday guides from **FHG**

PUBS & INNS OF BRITAIN • **COUNTRY HOTELS** OF BRITAIN
WEEKEND & SHORT BREAK HOLIDAYS IN BRITAIN
THE GOLF GUIDE WHERE TO PLAY, WHERE TO STAY
500 GREAT PLACES TO STAY • **SELF-CATERING HOLIDAYS** IN BRITAIN
BED & BREAKFAST STOPS • **CARAVAN & CAMPING HOLIDAYS**
FAMILY BREAKS IN BRITAIN

Published annually: available in all good bookshops or direct from the publisher:
FHG Guides, Abbey Mill Business Centre, Seedhill, Paisley PA1 1TJ
Tel: 0141 887 0428 • Fax: 0141 889 7204
e-mail: admin@fhguides.co.uk • www.holidayguides.com

Ratings & Awards

For the first time ever the AA, VisitBritain, VisitScotland, and the Wales Tourist Board will use a single method of assessing and rating serviced accommodation. Irrespective of which organisation inspects an establishment the rating awarded will be the same, using a common set of standards, giving a clear guide of what to expect. The RAC is no longer operating an Hotel inspection and accreditation business.

Accommodation Standards: Star Grading Scheme

Using a scale of 1-5 stars the objective quality ratings give a clear indication of accommodation standard, cleanliness, ambience, hospitality, service and food, This shows the full range of standards suitable for every budget and preference, and allows visitors to distinguish between the quality of accommodation and facilities on offer in different establishments. All types of board and self-catering accommodation are covered, including hotels,
B&Bs, holiday parks, campus accommodation, hostels, caravans and camping, and boats.

VisitBritain and the regional tourist boards, enjoyEngland.com, VisitScotland and VisitWales, and the AA have full details of the grading system on their websites

The more stars, the higher level of quality

★★★★★
exceptional quality, with a degree of luxury

★★★★
excellent standard throughout

★★★
very good level of quality and comfort

★★
good quality, well presented and well run

★
acceptable quality; simple, practical, no frills

National Accessible Scheme

If you have particular mobility, visual or hearing needs, look out for the National Accessible Scheme. You can be confident of finding accommodation or attractions that meet your needs by looking for the following symbols.

 Typically suitable for a person with sufficient mobility to climb a flight of steps but would benefit from fixtures and fittings to aid balance

 Typically suitable for a person with restricted walking ability and for those that may need to use a wheelchair some of the time and can negotiate a maximum of three steps

 Typically suitable for a person who depends on the use of a wheelchair and transfers unaided to and from the wheelchair in a seated position. This person may be an independent traveller

 Typically suitable for a person who depends on the use of a wheelchair in a seated position. This person also requires personal or mechanical assistance (eg carer, hoist).

SCOTLAND

Inverawe Holiday Cottages, Taynuilt, Argyll, page 339

Scotland

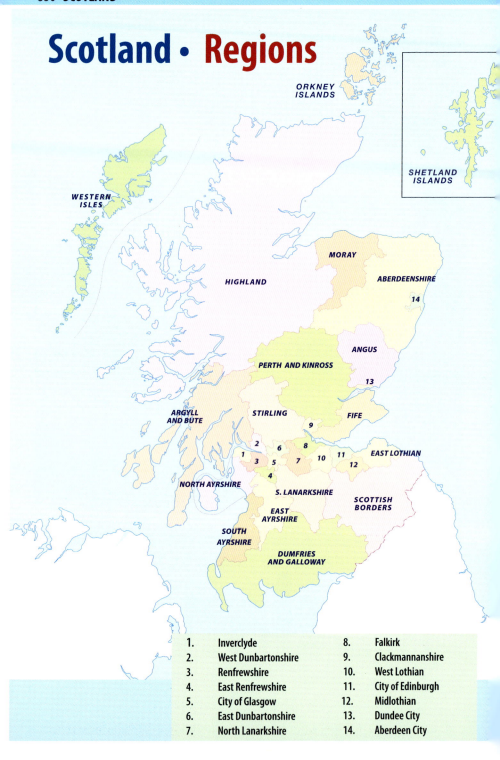

Aberdeen, Banff & Moray

Ballater, Glenlivet, Stonehaven, Turriff

This friendly, family-run hotel is set in 2 acres of woodlands with magnificent views across the golf course to the mountains. Pets are welcome in our Pine Terrace rooms which are all comfortable twin rooms. Come to the Glen Lui for a great Scottish experience. Fantastic food and wines. Short breaks available throughout the year.

Glen Lui Hotel, 14 Invercauld Road, Ballater AB35 5PP
013397 55402 • e-mail: infos@glen-lui-hotel.co.uk • www.glen-lui-hotel.co.uk

CAMBUS O'MAY HOTEL

This family-run country house hotel is situated four miles east of Ballater overlooking the River Dee and its environs. The hotel prides itself on the old-fashioned standards of comfort and service it offers to its guests. Excellent food is available from the table d'hôte menu which changes daily and can be complemented by fine wines from the cellar. The 12 bedrooms have en suite facilities and the hotel is centrally heated throughout.

The area affords a wealth of interests such as hill walking, golf, fishing, and shooting, and there are many historic sites including Balmoral Castle.

**Ballater
Aberdeenshire AB35 5SE
Tel & Fax: 013397 55428
www.cambusomayhotel.co.uk**

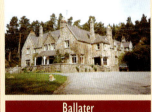

Beechgrove Cottages — Glenlivet

Traditional stone cottages set amidst beautiful surroundings near rivers Avon and Livet. All modernised and very comfortable. Fishing available. Ideal for exploring Highlands, Castle & Whisky Trails, walking, skiing, golf. Contact: The Post Office, Tomnavoulin, Ballindalloch AB37 9JA
Tel: 01807 590220 • www.beechgrovecottages.co.uk

Woodside of Glasslaw

Modern bungalow with six centrally heated en suite bedrooms with colour TV and hospitality trays. Accessible for disabled guests. Wifi available. Stonehaven two miles. STB/AA ★★★★
MRS AILEEN PATON, 'WOODSIDE OF GLASSLAW', STONEHAVEN AB39 3XQ
Tel: 01569 763799 • aileen@woodsideofglasslaw.co.uk
www.woodsideofglasslaw.co.uk

Forglen Cottages......escape to the country

This country estate lies along the beautiful Deveron River and our comfortable secluded cottages all have private gardens, with six miles of our own walks on their doorsteps. Unspoilt sandy beaches only nine miles away, and the market town of Turriff is only two miles. Enjoy Cairngorms, Royal Deeside, picturesque fishing villages and castles. Ideal for top golf courses, free brown trout fishing. Well behaved pets are very welcome to stay free of charge.
*Terms: from £209 weekly. Open year round.
5 cottages sleeping 4-9 people.*

*For a brochure contact: Simon Pearse, Holiday Cottages,
Forglen Estate, Turriff, Aberdeenshire AB53 4JP
Tel: 01888 562918 • www.forglen.co.uk
e-mail: reservations@forglen.co.uk*

Please mention **Pets Welcome!**
when making enquiries about accommodation featured in these pages

Ballater

Village and resort 14 miles east of Braemar.

GLEN LUI HOTEL, 14 INVERCAULD ROAD, BALLATER AB35 5PP (013397 55402). Friendly, family-run hotel set in 2 acres of woodlands. Pets are welcome in our comfortable Pine Terrace twin rooms. Come to the Glen Lui for a great Scottish experience. Fantastic food and wines. Short breaks.
e-mail: infos@glen-lui-hotel.co.uk   website: www.glen-lui-hotel.co.uk

CAMBUS O'MAY HOTEL, BALLATER AB35 5SE (Tel & Fax: 013397 55428). Family-run country house hotel 4 miles east of Ballater. Excellent food; 12 en suite bedrooms. Ideal area for hill walking, golf, fishing and visiting Balmoral Castle etc.
website: www.cambusomayhotel.co.uk

Glenlivet

Located 8 miles north of Tomintoul. Distilleries and State forest.

BEECHGROVE COTTAGES, GLENLIVET. Traditional stone cottages set amidst beautiful surroundings near rivers Avon and Livet. All modernised and very comfortable. Fishing available. Ideal for exploring Highlands, Castle and Whisky Trails, walking, skiing, golf. Contact: THE POST OFFICE, TOMNAVOULIN, BALLINDALLOCH AB37 9JA (01807 590520) [🐕]
website: www.beechgrovecottages.co.uk

Stonehaven

Fishing port on East Coast, 13 miles south of Aberdeen.

MRS AILEEN PATON, 'WOODSIDE OF GLASSLAW', STONEHAVEN AB39 3XQ (01569 763799). Modern bungalow with six centrally heated en suite bedrooms with colour TV and hospitality trays. Stonehaven two miles. Accessible for disabled guests. STB/AA ★★★★
e-mail: aileen@woodsideofglasslaw.co.uk   website: www.woodsideofglasslaw.co.uk

Turriff

Small town in agricultural area, 9 miles south of Banff.

SIMON PEARSE, COUNTRY COTTAGES, FORGLEN ESTATE, TURRIFF AB53 4JP (01888 562918). Estate on the beautiful Deveron River. Sandy beaches only nine miles away, Turriff two miles. 5 cottages sleeping 4–9. From £209 weekly. Open all year. Ideal for top golf courses, free brown trout fishing. Well-behaved dogs welcome. [🐕]
e-mail: reservations@forglen.co.uk   website: www.forglen.co.uk

Angus & Dundee
Finavon

Braehead B&B - The Dog-friendly B&B!!
Here at Braehead we offer a very warm welcome to our guests and their four-legged friends. We have 3 guest rooms, all with en suite shower rooms. There is an outside enclosed area and ample car parking. Our Golden Retriever and Newfoundland love making new friends, so come and stay with us in the lovely Angus countryside.
Braehead Cottage, Finavon, By Forfar, Angus DD8 3PX   Tel: 01307 850715
e-mail: dogsbandb@btinternet.com   www.braeheadbandb.co.uk

BRAEHEAD COTTAGE, FINAVON, BY FORFAR DD8 3PX (01307 850715). The Dog-friendly B&B!! We offer a very warm welcome to our guests and their four-legged friends. Three guest rooms, all with en suite shower rooms. Outside enclosed area and ample car parking. Our Golden Retriever and Newfoundland love making new friends. [pw! 🐕]
e-mail: dogsbandb@btinternet.com   website: www.braeheadbandb.co.uk

Argyll & Bute

SCOTLAND

Appin, Ardfern, Ardnamurchan

ARDTUR COTTAGES

Two adjacent cottages in secluded surroundings. Ideal for hill walking, climbing, pony trekking, boating and fly fishing. Shop one mile; sea 200 yards; car essential; pets allowed.

MRS J PERY, ARDTUR, APPIN PA38 4DD (01631 730223 or 01626 834172)
e-mail: pery@btinternet.com • www.ardturcottages.com

The Galley of Lorne Inn
Ardfern, Argyll • Tel: 01852 500 284

Escape with your pet to the wilds of Argyll

- 17th Century Drovers Inn
- Loch-side Location in Ardfern, near Oban & Lochgilphead
- Cosy En-suite Bedrooms
- Mouthwatering Menu with Local Seafood, Meats & Game
- Friendly, Welcoming Staff
- Log fires, Real Ales & Malts
- Beach, Forest & Hill Walks
- Golf, Horseriding & Fishing
- Easy Access to Hebridean Islands

www.galleyoflorne.co.uk Rated Excellent on Tripadvisor!

GO WEST! ESCAPE TO ARDNAMURCHAN & MULL

Steading Holidays is a family-run business located in Ardnamurchan, Britain's most westerly point. All with superb views, our quality cottages are located throughout Ardnamurchan and Mull and provide a peaceful and unhurried retreat amongst sandy beaches with spectacular sea views to the Western Isles. The area is a true haven for fishermen, birdwatchers, divers, yachtsmen, photographers and hill walkers – or for simply enjoying the tranquillity. Dogs welcome with miles of woodland, coastal and hill walks.

For details call Steading Holidays
01972 510 262

www.steading.co.uk

FHG Guides

publish a large range of well-known accommodation guides.
We will be happy to send you details or you can use the order form
at the back of this book.

Argyll & Bute

Cairndow, Campbeltown, Dunoon, Inveraray

CAIRNDOW, ARGYLL.
AT THE HEAD OF LOCH FYNE

A comfortable holiday cottage at the head of the longest sea loch in Scotland. **INVERFYNE** (pictured left), a very spacious cottage with 3 twin bedded and one double rooms. The cottage overlooks the estuary and old bridge. There is a piano in the 32' living room and a large utility/drying room makes this an excellent choice for country lovers and dog owners. Linen and electricity are included. Achadunan Estate is set amidst lovely walking country. Golden eagles and deer are your neighbours. Achadunan is home to Fyne Ales micro brewery. Details available from:

Mrs A. Delap, Achadunan, Cairndow, Argyll PA26 8BJ
Tel & Fax: 01499 600 238
www.argyllholidaycottages.com

Cairndow Stagecoach Inn

A Warm Scottish Welcome on the Shores of Loch Fyne

Cairndow, Argyll PA26 8BN
Tel: 01499 600286 • Fax: 01499 600220
www.cairndowinn.com

Discounted rates for golfers at Inveraray Golf Club. Tee times available at Loch Lomond.

★ Historic Coaching Inn on Loch Fyne
★ 18 well-appointed en suite bedrooms
★ 7 de luxe bedrooms; 5 new Lochside rooms
★ Excellent cuisine in Stables Restaurant and lounge meals all day
★ Amenities include lochside beer garden, sauna, and solarium.

Rhoin Holidays — *A Brand New Holiday Experience!*

Enjoy a holiday on a working farm. Self-catering conversion, sleeps 5. Stabling and paddocks adjacent. Ideal for walking, golf, surfing, riding. Well behaved dogs welcome.

Rhoin Holidays, Rhoin Farm, Kilmenzie, by Campbeltown, Argyll PA28 6NT
Tel: 01586 820220 • e-mail: info@rhoinholidays.co.uk • www.rhoinholidays.co.uk

ABBOT'S BRAE HOTEL

West Bay, Dunoon, Argyll PA23 7QJ
Tel: 01369 705021 • Fax: 01369 701191
e-mail: info@abbotsbrae.co.uk • www.abbotsbrae.co.uk

Award-winning, small Country House Hotel set in its own secluded woodland garden with breathtaking views of the sea and hills. Very spacious en suite bedrooms including four-poster, king-size and twin rooms. The welcoming, homely atmosphere, peaceful surroundings and appetising menus will ensure a memorable stay. Special offers in spring and autumn. Pets stay free. Ideal base to explore the Western Highlands, situated at the Gateway to Scotland's first National Park.

For further details contact either Colin or Christine.

Halftown Cottages • St Catherine's, Argyll

Heart of the West Highlands. 55 miles from Glasgow and across Loch Fyne from Inveraray. Two radically modernised 18thC farm cottages. Wholly secluded woodland site just above the loch. A real 'chill out' place for humans and animals. Extensive woodland, lochside and hillside walking. Nearby top class restaurants. Extensive day touring.
Tel: 01369 860750 or book direct on www.argyllcottages.com

Rockhill Waterside Country House

Est 1960

Tel: 01866 833218

Ardbrecknish, By Dalmally, Argyll PA33 1BH
www.rockhillfarmguesthouse.co.uk

17th century guest house in spectacular waterside setting on Loch Awe with breathtaking views to Ben Cruachan, where comfort, peace and tranquillity reign supreme.

Small private Highland estate breeding Hanoverian competition horses. 1200 metres free trout fishing. Three delightful rooms with all modern facilities. First-class highly acclaimed home cooking. Wonderful area for touring the Western Highlands, Glencoe, the Trossachs and Kintyre.
Ideal for climbing, walking, bird and animal watching. Boat trips locally and from Oban (30 miles) to Mull, Iona, Fingal's Cave and other islands.

Dogs' Paradise!   *Also Self-Catering Cottages*

Argyll & Bute

Isle of Gigha, Kilchattan Bay, Loch Goil, Oban

The community-owned Isle of Gigha (Gaelic: God's Island) is known as The Jewel of the Inner Hebrides. The Atlantic's crystal clear waters surround this six-mile long magical isle, and lap gently on to its white sandy beaches - creating an aura of peace and tranquillity.

The Gigha Hotel caters admirably for the discerning holidaymaker with comfortable accommodation and first class cuisine, including fresh local seafood. There are also holiday cottages available.

A must for any visitor is a wander around the famous sub-tropical Achamore Gardens, where palm trees and many other exotic plants flourish in Gigha's mild climatic conditions.

The Isle of Gigha Heritage Trust retails quality island-related craft products, some of which have utilised the Trust's own tartan. Other activities on offer include organised walks, bird watching, sea fishing, a nine-hole golf course and alternative therapies.

Call us on **01583 505254** Fax: **01583 505244**
www.gigha.org.uk

St Blane's Hotel Kilchattan Bay, Isle of Bute PA20 9NW

In one of the most serene and breathtaking locations on Bute, this traditional, family-run, pet-friendly, licensed Hotel offers superior en suite accommodation. It is a perfect base for walking, golf, windsurfing and other water sports. Open to non-residents, and with free moorings for visiting yachts, you can drop by for a meal or drink in the largest beer garden on the island!

01700 831224 • e-mail: info@stblaneshotel.com • www.stblaneshotel.com

Darroch Mhor Chalets
Carrick Castle, Loch Goil, Argyll PA24 8AF

Chill out in Scotland's first national park. Five self catering chalets nestling on the shores of Loch Goil, each with superb lochside views and offering a peaceful and relaxing holiday in the heart of Argyll Forest Park. Each chalet has two bedrooms, living room with colour TV, fitted kitchen with fridge, freezer, microwave, toaster etc. and bathroom with bath and overhead shower. Car parking by each chalet. Great hill walking.

Ideal for pets, genuinely pet-friendly • Open all year – weekly rates £140-£295. Weekend & short breaks available all year, reductions for 2 persons. One pet free.
Tel: **01301 703249** • E-mail: mail@argyllchalets.com • www.argyllchalets.com

Small, family-run guest house where we aim to make your stay as comfortable as possible. All rooms have central heating, colour TV and hospitality trays; some en suite. Full Scottish breakfast or Continental if preferred. Ample private parking. Situated 10 minutes' walk from the town centre, train, boat and bus terminals. Oban boasts regular sailings to the Islands, and an excellent golf course, as well as walking, cycling, fishing.

A warm welcome awaits you all year round. Tel: **01631 562267**
MRS STEWART, GLENVIEW, SOROBA ROAD, OBAN PA34 4JF

Publisher's note

While every effort is made to ensure accuracy, we regret that FHG Guides cannot accept responsibility for errors, misrepresentations or omissions in our entries or any consequences thereof. Prices in particular should be checked.
We will follow up complaints but cannot act as arbiters or agents for either party.

Argyll & Bute
Oban

SCOTLAND

TRALEE BAY HOLIDAYS

Self-catering holidays in luxury lodges and new caravans. This immaculate 5-Star park is located on the West Coast of Scotland, near Oban. The wooded surroundings, sandy beach and stunning sea views make Tralee Bay the perfect place for a holiday at any time of year. With a play area, mini golf, fly fishing, woodland walks, boat slipway, and endless supply of RABBITS, the park offers something for everyone. Pets welcome at £15.

Tralee Bay Holidays, Benderloch, by Oban, Argyll PA37 1QR
e-mail: tralee@easynet.co.uk
www.tralee.com

Tel: 01631 720255/217

Lagnakeil

Highland lodges

Our timber lodges and four cottages are set in a tranquil, scenic wooded glen overlooking Loch Feochan, only 3 miles from Oban, 'Gateway to the Isles'. Equipped to a high standard, including linen & towels. Country pub only a short walk up the Glen. OAP discount. Free loch fishing. Special breaks from £55 per lodge per night, weekly from £250–£1450. Lodges/cottages sleep 1–12 comfortably in 1–5 bedrooms.

Contact: **Colin & Jo Mossman**
Lagnakeil Highland Lodges, Lerags, Oban PA34 4SE
Tel: 01631 562746 • e-mail: info@lagnakeil.co.uk
www.lagnakeil.co.uk

COLOGIN
COUNTRY CHALETS
Oban

All Scottish Glens have their secrets: let us share ours with you – and your pets

Tranquil country glen less than 3 miles from Oban • Free fishing for wild brown trout on our hill loch • Waymarked forest trails for you and your pet • The Barn Country Inn serves food and drink all year round, so you don't have to self-cater if you don't want to • Family-run complex with excellent facilities. Our cosy chalets, lodges, cottages and private houses are set around an old farm and can sleep from 2-14. Pets are very welcome (2 maximum). Sky TV, wi-fi access and much more. *Call now for our colour brochure or check our website for live availability and secure online booking.*

MRS LINDA BATTISON, COLOGIN FARMHOUSE, LERAGS GLEN, BY OBAN, ARGYLL PA34 4SE
Tel: 01631 564501 • Fax: 01631 566925
e-mail: info@cologin.co.uk • www.cologin.co.uk

A DOG'S LIFE IN LUXURY AT MELFORT PIER & HARBOUR

Sixteen Luxury Houses, scattered along the shores of tranquil Loch Melfort in Argyll.

Each house has a sauna/spa bath, Digital TV and Wifi. Private beaches and plenty of hill walking. Excellent base for touring the Highlands. Family restaurant and bar on site. Prices start from £95 to £235 per night. Sleep 2-6. Start any day of the week – open all year.

2 Pets very welcome. mention this advert and get one pet for free!
 Tel: 01852 200 333 • www.mellowmelfort.com

LOCH MELFORT HOTEL & RESTAURANT
Arduaine, By Oban, Argyll PA34 4XG
Tel: 01852 200233 • Fax: 01852 200214
e-mail: reception@lochmelfort.co.uk
website: www.lochmelfort.co.uk
STB ★★★ and 3 Medallions for Food • AA ★★★ and 2 Rosettes

Set in 17 acres of pasture and woodland with wonderful views across the bay, this splendid hotel offers everything one could wish for, whether for a short break or a more extended holiday. The attractively decorated en suite bedrooms boast a comprehensive range of facilities; those in the Cedar Wing have their own balcony or patio, while the main building houses the traditional-style luxury of the superior rooms. Diners can enjoy superb views across the loch while contemplating the mouth-watering menus which make full use of the excellent local produce. Meals can also be taken in the bistro bar, a favourite with passing yachtsmen making use of the mooring facilities. There is so much to see and do in this unspoilt area, and nearby Oban has frequent ferry services to Mull and the Inner Hebrides.

Argyll & Bute

Tarbert, Taynuilt

Four cottages in architect designed conversion of home farm. Spacious accommodation for 2-7 persons. Stone fireplaces for log fires. Wonderful walks and scenery, peace and quiet. Winter breaks available. Easy access to island ferries. Pets welcome. Open all year. Colour brochure • From £250-£760 • ASSC • STB ★★
Dunmore Court, Near Tarbert, Argyll PA29 6XZ • Tel: 01880 820654
e-mail: bookings@dunmorecourt.com • www.dunmorecourt.com

SKIPNESS ESTATE, By Tarbert, Argyll PA29 6XU
Tel: 01880 760207 • Fax: 01880 760208 • e-mail: sophie@skipness.freeserve.co.uk

This unspoilt, peaceful, West Highland estate with its own historic castle, medieval chapel and way-marked walks has traditional cottages to let all year round. Each cottage has an open fire and television. Properties sleep 4-10. All cottages have magnificent views and beautiful surrounding countryside and coastline. Safe, sandy beaches can be enjoyed on the estate, with fishing, pony trekking and golf nearby. Skipness village facilities include a shop/post office and the seasonal licensed Seafood Cabin. Local ferries to Arran, Gigha, Islay and Jura.
PETS WELCOME. Apply for rates and further details: Sophie James.
FARM HOLIDAY GUIDE DIPLOMA • STB ★★/★★★ SELF-CATERING

West Loch Hotel

By Tarbert, Loch Fyne, Argyll PA29 6YF
Tel: 01880 820283 • Fax: 01880 820930
www.westlochhotel.co.uk
e-mail: westlochhotel@btinternet.com

Family-run, 18th century coaching inn of character, well situated for a relaxing holiday. It is renowned for outstanding food. Excellent for hill-walking and enjoying the wide variety of wildlife. Attractions include castles, distilleries, gardens and sandy beaches.

Inverawe Cottages
Taynuilt, Argyll PA35 1HU

Inverawe Holiday Cottages

Three self-catering cottages offer a wonderful haven to relax. Comfortable, cosy and welcoming. Cottages sleep 2, 4/5, 6/7. Inverawe is a paradise for dogs, children and adults alike.
Phone: 01866 822777 • e-mail: cottages@inverawe.co.uk • www.inverawe-cottages.co.uk

---

Free or reduced rate entry to
Holiday Visits and Attractions - see our
READERS' OFFER VOUCHERS on pages 445-454

FHG Guides

publish a large range of well-known accommodation guides.
We will be happy to send you details or you can use the order form
at the back of this book.

Appin

Mountainous area bounded by Loch Linnhe, Glen Creran and Glencoe.

MRS J PERY, ARDTUR, APPIN PA38 4DD (01631 730223 or 01626 834172). Two adjacent cottages in secluded surroundings. Ideal for hill walking, climbing, pony trekking, boating and fly fishing. Shop one mile; sea 200 yards; car essential; pets allowed.[🐕]
e-mail: pery@btinternet.com   website: www.ardturcottages.com

Ardfern

On west side of Loch Craignish, 4 miles west of Kilmartin.

THE GALLEY OF LORNE INN, ARDFERN PA31 8QN (01852 500284). 17thC drovers' inn in lochside location near Oban and Lochgilphead. Cosy en suite bedrooms, mouthwatering menu, friendly staff. Log fires, real ales and malts. Pets welcome, with miles of beach, forest and hill walks. [Pets £7.50 per night]
website: www.galleyoflorne.co.uk

Ardnamurchan

Peninsula on West Coast running from Salen to Ardnamurchan Point.

STEADING HOLIDAYS, ARDNAMURCHAN & MULL. A family-run business located in Britain's most westerly point. All with superb views, our quality cottages provide a peaceful and unhurried retreat amongst sandy beaches with spectacular sea views. Contact MRS JACQUI CHAPPLE, THE STEADING, KILCHOAN, ARCHARACLE PH 36 4LH (01972 510 262).
website: www.steading.co.uk

Cairndow

Village at mouth of Kinglas Water on Loch Fyne in Argyll, near head of Loch.

Comfortable holiday cottage at the head of the longest sea loch in Scotland, in lovely walking country. Sleeps up to eight people. Linen and electricity included. STB ★★★ Self Catering. MRS DELAP, ACHADUNAN, CAIRNDOW, ARGYLL PA26 8BJ (Tel & Fax: 01499 600238).
website: www.argyllholidaycottages.com

CAIRNDOW STAGECOACH INN, CAIRNDOW PA26 8BN (01499 600286; Fax: 01499 600220). Well-appointed en suite bedrooms. Excellent cuisine in Stables Restaurant and lounge meals all day. Amenities include lochside beer garden, sauna and solarium. AA ★★★ Inn.
website: www.cairndowinn.com

Campbeltown

Fishing port at head of loch, 30 miles south of Tarbert.

RHOIN HOLIDAYS, RHOIN FARM, KILKENZIE, BY CAMPBELTOWN PA28 6NT (01586 820220). Enjoy a holiday on a working farm. Self-catering conversion, sleeps 5. Stabling and paddocks adjacent. Ideal for walking, golf, surfing, riding. STB ★★★★ [🐕]
e-mail: info@rhoinholidays.com   website: www.rhoinholidays.com

Dalmally

Small town in Glen Orchy to the south-west of Loch Awe, with romantic Kilchurn Castle (14th century). Edinburgh 98 miles, Glasgow 69, Ardrishaig 42, Oban 25, Inveraray 16.

ROCKHILL WATERSIDE COUNTRY HOUSE, ARDBRECKNISH, BY DALMALLY PA33 1BH (01866 833218). 17th century guest house on waterside with spectacular views over Loch Awe. Three delightful rooms with all modern facilities. First-class home cooking.
website: www.rockhillfarmguesthouse.com

Please mention **Pets Welcome!**
when making enquiries about accommodation featured in these pages

Argyll & Bute

Dunoon

Town and resort in Argyll, 4 miles west of Gourock across Firth of Clyde.

ABBOTS BRAE HOTEL, WEST BAY, DUNOON PA23 7QJ (01369 705021; Fax: 01369 701191). Small welcoming hotel at the gateway to the Western Highlands with breathtaking views. Comfortable, spacious, en suite bedrooms, quality home cooking and select wines. [🐕]
e-mail: info@abbotsbrae.co.uk   website: www.abbotsbrae.co.uk

Inveraray

18thC Royal burgh on the shores of Loch Fyne, 35 miles south of Oban.

HALFTOWN COTTAGES, ST CATHERINE'S (01369 860750). Heart of the West Highlands. 55 miles from Glasgow and across Loch Fyne from Inveraray. Two radically modernised 18thC farm cottages. Wholly secluded woodland site just above the loch. A real 'chill out' place for humans and animals.
website: www.argyllcottages.com

Isle of Gigha

A tranquil island, one of the Inner Hebrides just of the west coast of Scotland. A haven for birds and wildlife.

GIGHA HOTEL, ISLE OF GIGHA PA41 7AA (01583 505254; Fax: 01583 505244). Beautiful, tranquil island. Explore the white sandy bays and lochs; famous Achamore Gardens. Easy walking, bike hire, birds, wildlife and wild flowers. Dog-friendly. Holiday cottages also available. [🐕]
website: www.gigha.org.uk

Kilchattan Bay

Quiet seaside village with wide bay on the East coast of Bute.

ST BLANE'S HOTEL, KILCHATTAN BAY, ISLE OF BUTE PA20 9NW (01700 831224). Traditional, family-run, pet-friendly, licensed Hotel offering superior en suite accommodation. Perfect base for walking, golf, windsurfing and other water sports. Open to non-residents. [🐕]
e-mail: info@stblaneshotel.com   website: www.stblaneshotel.com

Loch Goil

Six mile long loch stretching from Lochgoilhead to Loch Long.

DARROCH MHOR, CARRICK CASTLE, LOCH GOIL PA24 8AF (01301 703249; Fax: 01301 703348). Five self-catering Chalets on the shores of Loch Goil in the heart of Argyll Forest Park. Fully equipped except linen. Colour TV, fitted kitchen, carpeted. Pets very welcome. Open all year. [🐕]
e-mail: mail@argyllchalets.com   website: www.argyllchalets.com

Oban

Popular Highland resort and port, yachting centre, ferry services to Inner and Outer Hebrides. Sandy bathing beach at Ganavan Bay. McCaig's Tower above town is Colosseum replica built in 1890s.

MRS STEWART, GLENVIEW, SOROBA ROAD, OBAN PA34 4JF (01631 562267). Small family-run guest house, 10 minutes' walk from train, boat and bus terminal. A warm welcome awaits you all year round. [🐕]

TRALEE BAY HOLIDAYS, BENDERLOCH, BY OBAN PA37 1QR (01631 720255/217). Overlooking Ardmucknish Bay. The wooded surroundings and sandy beaches make Tralee the ideal destination for a self-catering lodge or caravan holiday anytime of the year. STB ★★★★★ [Pets £3 per night]
e-mail: tralee@easynet.co.uk   website: www.tralee.com

COLIN & JO MOSSMAN, LAGNAKEIL HIGHLAND LODGES, LERAGS, OBAN PA34 4SE (01631 562746). Our Timber Lodges and four cottages are set in a tranquil, scenic wooded glen overlooking Loch Feochan, only 3 miles from the picturesque harbour town of Oban: "Gateway to the Isles". Lodges equipped to a high standard, including linen and towels, country pub a short walk. OAP discount. Free loch fishing. Special Breaks from £55 per lodge per night, weekly from £250-£1450. Sleep 1-12 comfortably. VisitScotland ★★★/★★★★ Self-Catering. [Pets £20 per week].
e-mail: info@lagnakeil.co.uk   website: www.lagnakeil.co.uk

SCOTLAND — Argyll & Bute

MRS LINDA BATTISON, COLOGIN COUNTRY CHALETS, LERAGS GLEN, BY OBAN PA34 4SE (01631 564501; Fax: 01631 566925). Cosy chalets, lodges, cottages and houses, all conveniences. Situated on farm, wildlife abundant. Launderette, licensed bar serving home-cooked food. Free fishing. Playpark. STB ★★★/★★★★ Self-Catering [pw! Pets £20 per week.]
e-mail: info@cologin.co.uk
website: www.cologin.co.uk

MELFORT PIER AND HARBOUR, KILMELFORD, BY OBAN PA34 4XD (01852 200333; Fax: 01852 200329). Superb Lochside houses each with Sauna, Spa bath, Digital TV, Telephone, Wifi, on the shores of Loch Melfort. Excellent base for touring Argyll and the Isles. From £95 to £235 per night. Sleeps 2-6. 2 pets very welcome. Service with a smile. [Pets £15 each per stay]
website: www.mellowmelfort.com

LOCH MELFORT HOTEL & RESTAURANT, ARDUAINE, BY OBAN PA34 4XG (01852 200233; Fax: 01852 200214). Stunning views down the Sound of Jura to the Islands. Located between Inveraray and Oban, beside the famous Arduaine Gardens. Excellent award-winning cuisine, comfortable accommodation, and friendly and attentive service. [🐾]
e-mail: reception@lochmelfort.co.uk
website: www.lochmelfort.co.uk

Tarbert

Fishing port on isthmus connecting Kintyre to the mainland.

DUNMORE COURT, KILBERRY ROAD, NEAR TARBERT PA29 6XZ (01880 820654). Four cottages sleeping 2-7. Wonderful walks and scenery, peace and quiet. Winter breaks available. Easy access to island ferries. Terms from £250-£600. Open all year. ASSC member. STB ★★ SELF CATERING. [🐾]
e-mail: bookings@dunmorecourt.com
website: www.dunmorecourt.com

Peaceful, unspoilt West Highland estate. Traditional cottages, with open fires. Sleep 4–10. Pets welcome. Walks, pony trekking, golf nearby. APPLY SOPHIE JAMES, SKIPNESS CASTLE, BY TARBERT PA29 6XU (01880 760207; Fax: 01880 760208). STB ★★/★★★ [🐾]
e-mail: sophie@skipness.freeserve.co.uk

WEST LOCH HOTEL, BY TARBERT, LOCH FYNE PA29 6YF (01880 820283; Fax: 01880 820930). Family-run, 18th century coaching inn, well situated for a relaxing holiday. It is renowned for outstanding food. Excellent for hill-walking and enjoying the wide variety of wildlife. Attractions include castles, distilleries, gardens and sandy beaches. STB ★★ Inn. [🐾]
e-mail: westlochhotel@btinternet.com
website: www.westlochhotel.co.uk

Taynuilt

Village in Argyll 1km south west of Bonawe.

INVERAWE COTTAGES, TAYNUILT PA35 1HU (01866 822777). Three self-catering cottages offer a wonderful haven to relax. Comfortable, cosy and welcoming. Sleep 2, 4/5, 6/7. Inverawe is a paradise for dogs, children and adults alike.
e-mail: cottages@inverawe.co.uk
website: www.inverawe-cottages.co.uk

Symbols

- 🐾 Indicates that pets are welcome free of charge.
- £   Indicates that a charge is made for pets: nightly or weekly.
- pw! Shows some special provision for pets; exercise facility, feeding or accommodation arrangement.
- ⌂   Indicates separate pets accommodation.

Ayrshire & Arran

Ayr, Brodick, Lamlash, Whiting Bay

Esplanade, Ayr KA7 1DT
Ayr's only seafront hotel, just five minutes' walk from town centre.
Lunches, dinners and bar suppers served.

A welcome guest. In all my years of experience of this business, I have never received a complaint about a dog slamming bedroom doors late at night, talking loudly in the corridors or driving away noisily from the car park when other guests are trying to sleep. Never has a dog made cigarette burns on the carpets, furniture or in the bath. No dog has ever stolen my towels, sheets or ashtrays. No cheque written by a dog has ever bounced and no dog has ever tried to pay with a stolen credit card. Never has a dog insulted my waitress or complained about food or wine. Neither have we ever had a dog who was drunk. In short you are welcome whenever you wish to come to this hotel and if you can vouch for your master, you are welcome to bring him along too!!

Phone now for free colour brochure. Under the personal supervision of Mr & Mrs A.H. Meikle.

Tel: 01292 264384 • Fax: 01292 264011
e-mail: reception@horizonhotel.com
www.horizonhotel.com

The Isle of Arran
AA "Inspectors' Choice" Hotel
VisitScotland "Gold Award" Hotel
& 5-Star Self-catering Cottages
www.kilmichael.com • 01770 302219

Dyemill Lodges · Isle of Arran

Six Scandinavian designed pinewood lodges and two holiday homes offer comfortable accommodation in surroundings full of natural beauty and interest, yet close to all the amenities of Lamlash village.
Contact: Dyemill House, Monamhor Glen, Lamlash, Isle of Arran KA27 8NT
Tel: 01770 600419 • e-mail: enquiries@dyemill.co.uk • www.dyemill.co.uk

Strathconon Cottage · *Self Catering Accommodation* · Isle of Arran

Luxury self catering holiday accommodation in a beautiful secluded location. 300 yards from the seafront and within easy reach of shops and restaurants. Ideal base for up to 10 people. Category 3 Disabled Access. Well behaved pets are welcome by prior arrangement.

Jim and Moira Finlayson,
"Suilven", Southend, Argyll PA28 6RF
Phone: 01586 830323
Email: enquiries@arranselfcatering.com
www.arranselfcatering.com

Please mention **Pets Welcome!**
when making enquiries about accommodation featured in these pages

Ayr

Popular family holiday resort with sandy beaches. Excellent shopping, theatre, racecourse.

HORIZON HOTEL, ESPLANADE, AYR KA7 1DT (01292 264384; Fax: 01292 264011). Highly recommended for golf breaks; special midweek rates. Coach parties welcome. Lunches, dinners and bar suppers served. Phone now for free colour brochure. [🐕]
e-mail: reception@horizonhotel.com   website: www.horizonhotel.com

Brodick

Resort on east coast of Isle of Arran, Ferry connection to mainland.

KILMICHAEL HOTEL (01770 302219). AA "Inspectors' Choice" Hotel. VisitScotland "Gold Award" Hotel and 5-Star Self-catering Cottages
website: www.kilmichael.com

Lamlash

Village on east coast of Isle of Arran, 3 miles south of Brodick.

DYEMILL LODGES, ISLE OF ARRAN. Six Scandinavian designed pinewood lodges and two holiday homes offer comfortable accommodation in surroundings full of natural beauty and interest, yet close to all the amenities of Lamlash village. Contact: PAUL & SUE ARCHER, DYEMILL HOUSE, MONAMHOR GLEN, LAMLASH, ISLE OF ARRAN KA27 8NT (01770 600419). STB ★★★.
e-mail: enquiries@dyemill.co.uk   website: www.dyemill.co.uk

Whiting Bay

Village on east coast of Isle of Arran.

STRATHCONON COTTAGE, ISLE OF ARRAN. Luxury self catering holiday accommodation in a beautiful secluded location, 300 yards from the seafront. For up to 10 people. Category 3 Disabled Access. Well behaved pets welcome by prior arrangement. Contact: JIM AND MOIRA FINLAYSON, "SUILVEN", SOUTHEND, ARGYLL PA28 6RF (01586 830523). STB ★★★★.
e-mail: enquiries@arranselfcatering.com   website: www.arranselfcatering.com

---

Other specialised holiday guides from FHG

PUBS & INNS OF BRITAIN • **COUNTRY HOTELS** OF BRITAIN
WEEKEND & SHORT BREAK HOLIDAYS IN BRITAIN
THE GOLF GUIDE WHERE TO PLAY, WHERE TO STAY
500 GREAT PLACES TO STAY • **SELF-CATERING HOLIDAYS** IN BRITAIN
BED & BREAKFAST STOPS • **CARAVAN & CAMPING HOLIDAYS**
FAMILY BREAKS IN BRITAIN

Published annually: available in all good bookshops or direct from the publisher:
FHG Guides, Abbey Mill Business Centre, Seedhill, Paisley PA1 1TJ
Tel: 0141 887 0428 • Fax: 0141 889 7204
e-mail: admin@fhguides.co.uk • www.holidayguides.com

Borders

Bonchester Bridge, Cockburnspath, Duns, Eyemouth

WAUCHOPE COTTAGES Four single storey detached timber cottages sleeping 2-4, all with enclosed large gardens. Quiet location with stunning scenery and forest walks direct from the door.
Dogs most welcome. Self-catering.
BONCHESTER BRIDGE, HAWICK TD9 9TG • 01450 860630
e-mail: wauchope@btinternet.com • www.wauchopecottages.co.uk

Tower Farm Holidays

Near the village of Cockburnspath on the stunning east coast of the Scottish Borders. There are two houses at Tower Farm available to rent for holidays and short breaks.

Perfect for small or large groups wanting to get away for a break or mark a special occasion. A huge range of activities and many places to visit, an abundance of local beauty spots, historic sites, visitor attractions, castles and stately homes.

Tower Farm Holidays • Tel: 01368 864 782
e-mail: info@tower-farm.co.uk • www.tower-farm.co.uk

CLOVERKNOWE COTTAGES
COCKBURNSPATH, BERWICKSHIRE

Grading 3* 4* self catering Accommodates 2-8 adults

Marion Lauder, Cloverknowe Cottages, Pathhead Farm,
Cockburnspath, Berwickshire, TD13 5XB,
tel **0136 883 0318** email **mlauder@supanet.com**

Situated on the border of Berwickshire and East Lothian. Our two detached sandstone cottages are located near the coast on working mixed arable farm. Modernised and equipped to high standards, the cottages have large enclosed gardens with ample parking. En suite and ground floor bedrooms are available. Ideal for: Touring the Scottish Borders, East Lothian, Northumberland and Edinburgh (45 mins by car). Walking (direct access to links to the John Muir Way and Southern Upland Way), beaches, birdwatching and relaxing.

Edinburgh 36 miles, Dunbar 8 miles, Berwick upon Tweed 20 miles.

Give yourself and your dogs a quality holiday break in beautiful Duns, Berwickshire
The Barniken House Hotel
Dogs most welcome and sleep with you in your bedroom • Satellite TV, tea/coffee making in all bedrooms • Sun lounge • Luxurious Lounge Bar and Dining Room • Large garden with 9-hole putting green and patio • 18 hole course • Near spectacular scenery, beaches and walks for dogs
The Barniken House Hotel, 18 Murray Street, Duns, Berwickshire TD11 3DE
Tel: 01361 882466 • www.barnikenhousehotel.com

The Herring Queen Waterfront Listed Georgian apartment sleeping 4+4 with glorious views of Eyemouth harbour from every room. Carefully upgraded to maintain its lovely original features while including modern day essentials. Also, **Antonine Wall Cottages,** 2 very well equipped ★★★★ self -catering cottages in Bonnybridge, Stirlingshire
Contact: Fiona Briggs, Bonnyside Road, Bonnybridge, Stirlingshire FK4 2AA
Tel: 01324 811875 • www.theherringqueen.co.uk • www.antoninewallcottages.co.uk

Kingsknowes Hotel Selkirk Road, Galashiels TD1 3HY

A Baronial mansion set in attractive gardens and close to the River Tweed. Elegant public areas and spacious bedrooms. Restaurant and bar. Ideal base for touring.
e-mail: enq@kingsknowes.co.uk • www.kingsknowes.co.uk
Telephone: 01896 758375 • Fax: 01896 750377

Borders

Jedburgh, Kelso

Crailing Old School Crailing, By Jedburgh TD8 6TL
Peacefully situated B&B close to the River Teviot. Ideal area for walking, fishing, golf and horse riding. Self contained lodge with wheelchair/disabled friendly access. Self catering possible. Evening meals by arrangement..
Tel: 01835 850382 • e-mail: info@crailingoldschool.co.uk • www.crailingoldschool.co.uk

Ferniehirst Mill Lodge A chalet-style guest house set in grounds of 25 acres. All rooms en suite with tea/coffee making facilities. Well behaved pets (including horses) welcome by arrangement.
AA ★★ ALAN & CHRISTINE SWANSTON, FERNIEHIRST MILL LODGE, JEDBURGH TD8 6PQ • 01835 863279
e-mail: ferniehirstmill@aol.com • www.ferniehirstmill.co.uk

SMAILHOLM MAINS FARM COTTAGES • BY KELSO TD5 7RT

Two cosy farm cottages, each sleeping 5, in a peaceful setting 6 miles from Kelso. Both with open fires, central heating, Sky TV. Close to golf, fishing, walking or a day at the races. Open Jan-Dec. Short Breaks available £150-£250.
Tel: 01573 460285 • e-mail: info@smailholm-mains.co.uk
www.smailholm-mains.co.uk
ASSC   STB ★★★★

Mrs Sarah Fraser-Ballantyne • Tel: 07971 522040 • Fax: 01896 870664
e-mail: enquiries@holidayhomesscotland.co.uk • www.holidayhomesscotland.co.uk
Sleeps 10 + 2 + cots. Tiny Cheviot village. Large handsomely furnished rooms. Close to Tweed & Teviot fishing beats and 25 Golf courses. Wildlife, hill walking, mountain biking, cycling, local produce. Easy driving distance to all amenities. Dogs welcome. Let by week or short break.
GLEBE HOUSE SELF CATERING by Kelso & Jedburgh   STB ★★★★

Westwood House – Kelso
Overlooking Scotland's famous River Tweed

TOTAL "OFF LEAD" FREEDOM FOR DOGS IN ENCLOSED AND SECLUDED GROUNDS

Renovated riverside cottage with 12 acres of paths, through walled gardens and on own private island. 4 bedrooms sleeping 2-8 (+ child), 2 bathrooms, period features, cosy log fire and centrally heated. • Half mile Kelso town • One hour Edinburgh/Newcastle • Half hour Berwick (station) and Northumberland coast.

2-person discounts available • Trout fishing also included
ACHIEVING GOLD IN GREEN TOURISM AND 'HIGHLY COMMENDED' IN SCOTTISH THISTLE AWARDS

For brochure and tariff, from £385 per week fully inclusive of all linen and towels, electricity and heating,
contact:

**Debbie Crawford,
Pippin Heath Farm, Holt,
Norfolk NR25 6SS
Tel: 07788 134 832**

DOGS WELCOME FREE

Welcome Host

Borders

Lauder, Newcastleton, Peebles, Selkirk, West Linton

The Black Bull, Lauder

18th Century Coachng Inn with 8 en suite bedrooms in period character with all modern amenities. Cosy bar, four dining areas. Just 20 minutes from Edinburgh, ideal for exploring Scottish Borders.

The Black Bull Hotel, Market Place, Lauder TD2 6SR • Tel: 01578 722208
e-mail: enquiries@blackbull-lauder.com • www.blackbull-lauder.com

BAILEY MILL COURTYARD
Bailey Mill, Newcastleton, Roxburghshire TD9 0TR
Tel: 016977 48617 • Fax: 016977 48074

Self-catering apartments nestling on the Roxburghshire / Cumbrian border. Also riding holidays with B&B or Full Board. Licensed bar. Colour brochure available.
pam@baileymill.fsnet.co.uk • www.holidaycottagescumbria.co.uk

Cringletie House Hotel, Peebles EH45 8PL   Tel: 01721 725750

Our idyllic rural setting allows our guests to escape the stress and noise of everyday life. We are open all year round, including Christmas and New Year. We welcome well-behaved children and dogs, and we have two rooms where dogs can be accommodated.
enquiries@cringletie.com • www.cringletie.com

Warm, modern farmhouse B&B set in delightful walled garden in the heart of the Scottish Borders. Spacious bedrooms with private bathrooms. Good home cooking using local produce. Loch fishing; grazing for horses; ideal for walking, cycling and horse riding. Well behaved pets welcome. Open all year.
Whitmuir, Selkirk TD7 4PZ • Tel: 01750 721728 • Mobile: 07768 707700
e-mail: whitmuir@btconnect.com • www.whitmuirfarm.co.uk

Two lovely Self-Catering Cottages near Edinburgh

Two well-equipped cottages a mile from West Linton. Set within a beautiful lakeside hideaway country estate at the foot of the Pentland Hills and an easy drive to Edinburgh. Well placed for touring Peeblesshire, The Lothians and Fife. The cottages sleep 4/6, with open fires, digital TV and central heating. Linen and towels can also be supplied. Lovely walks for dogs which are welcome free of charge (max. 2 per cottage). Many people return year after year.
Golf, walking, mountain biking, horse riding and fishing all nearby.

A warm welcome awaits you
"...arrived in the dark, woke up in heaven"

- Dogs welcome, (two per cottage) • Ample parking • Car essential
- Central Edinburgh 19 miles • Park and Ride facilities nearby
- Available all year.

Details from Mrs C.M. Kilpatrick, Slipperfield House,
West Linton EH46 7AA • Tel: 01968 660401
e-mail: cottages@slipperfield.com • www.slipperfield.com

Bonchester Bridge

Village on Rule Water, 6 miles east of Hawick. To east is Bonchester Hill surmounted by ancient earthworks.

WAUCHOPE COTTAGES, BONCHESTER BRIDGE, HAWICK TD9 9TG (01450 860630). Four single storey detached timber cottages sleeping 2-4, each with enclosed large garden. Quiet location with stunning scenery and forest walks direct from the door. Dogs most welcome. Self-catering. [🐕]
e-mail: wauchope@btinternet.com   website: www.wauchopecottages.co.uk

Cockburnspath

Attractive village in the Scottish Borders 8 miles south east of Dunbar.

TOWER FARM HOLIDAYS (01368 864782)   Near village of Cockburnspath on East Coast. Two houses available to rent for holidays and short breaks. Perfect for small or large groups. STB ★★★★ SELF-CATERING. [pw! 🐕]
e-mail: info@tower-farm.co.uk   website: www.tower-farm.co.uk

MARION LAUDER, CLOVERKNOWE COTTAGES, PATHHEAD FARM, COCKBURNSPATH TD13 5XB (01368 830318). Two detached sandstone cottages on the border of Berwickshire and East Lothian. Modernised and equipped to high standards. Large enclosed gardens . Ample parking. En suite and ground floor bedrooms available. [🐕]
e-mail: mlauder@supanet.com

Duns

Picturesque Borders town with nearby ancient fort, castle and Covenanters' stone to commemorate the army's encampment here in 1639. Excellent touring centre. Berwick-upon-Tweed 13 miles.

BARNIKEN HOUSE HOTEL, MURRAY STREET, DUNS TD11 3DE (01361 882466). Dogs most welcome, colour TV and tea coffee facilities in all rooms. Luxurious bar, sun lounge, large garden and car park. Central heating. Near spectacular scenery and ideal walks for dogs. [🐕]
website: www.barnikenhousehotel.com

Eyemouth

Small town on coast, 8 miles north-west of Berwick-upon-Tweed.

THE HERRING QUEEN. Water-front listed Georgian apartment sleeping 4+4 with glorious views of Eyemouth harbour from every room. Carefully upgraded, with modern day essentials. Also, ANTONINE WALL COTTAGES (STB ★★★★), two very well equipped self-catering cottages in Bonnybridge, Stirlingshire. Contact: FIONA BRIGGS, BONNYSIDE ROAD, BONNYBRIDGE FK4 2AA (01324 811875).
websites: www.theherringqueen.co.uk   www.antoninewallcottages.co.uk

Galashiels

Picturesque town on the A7 Carlisle to Edinburgh, with a good choice of shops and leisure activities.

KINGSKNOWES HOTEL, SELKIRK ROAD, GALASHIELS TD1 3HY (01896 758375; Fax: 01896 750377). A Baronial mansion set in attractive gardens and close to the River Tweed. Elegant public areas, spacious bedrooms. Ideal base for touring. AA ★★★
e-mail: enq@kingsknowes.co.uk   website: www.kingsknowes.co.uk

Jedburgh

Small town on Jed water, 10 miles north-east of Hawick. Ruins of abbey founded in 1138.

CRAILING OLD SCHOOL, CRAILING, BY JEDBURGH TD8 6TL (01835 850382). Peacefully situated B&B close to the River Teviot. Ideal area for walking, fishing, golf and horse riding. Self contained lodge with wheelchair/disabled friendly access. Self catering possible. Evening meals by arrangement. AA ★★★★ [pw! Pets £2 per night, £10 per week]
e-mail: info@crailingoldschool.co.uk   website: www.crailingoldschool.co.uk

ALAN & CHRISTINE SWANSTON, FERNIEHIRST MILL LODGE, JEDBURGH TD8 6PQ (01835 863279). A chalet style guest house set in grounds of 25 acres. All rooms en suite with tea/coffee making facilities. Well behaved pets (including horses) welcome by arrangement. AA ★★ [🐕]
e-mail: ferniehirstmill@aol.com   website: www.ferniehirstmill.co.uk

Borders   SCOTLAND 349

Kelso

Market town 18 miles north-west of Hawick and 20 miles south-west of Berwick-upon-Tweed.

MRS KIRSTY B. SHAW, SMAILHOLM MAINS FARM COTTAGES, BY KELSO TD5 7RT   (01573 460318). Two cosy farm cottages, each sleeping 5, in a peaceful setting 6 miles from Kelso. Both with open fires, central heating, Sky TV. Close to golf, fishing, walking or a day at the races. Short breaks available. STB ★★★★[🐕]
e-mail: info@smailholm-mains.co.uk   website: www.smailholm-mains.co.uk

GLEBE HOUSE SELF-CATERING (07971 522 040; Fax: 01896 870 664). By Kelso and Jedburgh. Sleeps 10+2+cots. Large handsomely furnished rooms. Easy driving distance pubs, shops etc. Dogs welcome. STB ★★★★ SELF-CATERING. [🐕]
e-mail: enquiries@holidayhomescotland.co.uk   website: www.holidayhomescotland.co.uk

WESTWOOD HOUSE, OVERLOOKING SCOTLAND'S FAMOUS RIVER TWEED. Enclosed and secluded riverside cottage with walled gardens and own private island. Sleeps 2-8 persons plus child, from £385 per week. 2 person discounts. For brochure contact: DEBBIE CRAWFORD, PIPPIN HEATH FARM, HOLT, NORFOLK NR25 6SS (07788 134832). [🐕]

Lauder

Former Royal Burgh on A68 between Edinburgh and Scottish Borders, close to Lammermuir Hills.

THE BLACK BULL HOTEL, MARKET PLACE, LAUDER TD2 6SR   (01578 722208). 18th Century Coachng Inn with 8 en suite bedrooms in period character with all modern amenities. Cosy bar, four dining areas. Just 20 minutes from Edinburgh, ideal for exploring Borders. AA ★★★★.
e-mail: enquiries@blackbull-lauder.com   website: www.blackbull-lauder.com

Newcastleton

Small village nestling in the valley of Liddesdale, ideal base for touring.

BAILEY MILL COURTYARD, BAILEY MILL, NEWCASTLETON TD9 0TR (016977 48617; Fax: 016977 48074). Self-catering apartments nestling on the Roxburghshire / Cumbrian border. Also riding holidays with B&B or Full Board. Licensed bar. Colour brochure available. ETC★★/★★★
e-mail: pam@baileymill.fsnet.co.uk   website: www.holidaycottagescumbria.co.uk

Peebles

Royal Burgh 23 miles south of Edinburgh with a good choice of shops and outdoor activities.

CRINGLETIE HOUSE HOTEL, PEEBLES EH45 8PL (01721 725750). Our idyllic rural setting allows our guests to escape the stress and noise of everyday life. We welcome well-behaved children and dogs, and we have two rooms where dogs can be accommodated. Open all year. AA/STB ★★★★
e-mail: enquiries@cringletie.com   website: www.cringletie.com

Selkirk

Town on hill above Ettrick Water, 9 miles north of Hawick

THE GARDEN HOUSE, WHITMUIR, SELKIRK TD7 4PZ (01750 721728; Mobile: 07768 707700). Comfortable, warm modern farm house B&B. Spacious bedrooms, private bathrooms. Good home cooking. Fishing, walking, cycling and horse riding nearby. Grazing available. Open all year. [🐕]
e-mail: whitmuir@btconnect.com   website: www.whitmuirfarm.co.uk.

West Linton

Village on east side of Pentland hills, 7 miles south-west of Penicuik. Edinburgh 18 miles.

MRS C. M. KILPATRICK, SLIPPERFIELD HOUSE, WEST LINTON EH46 7AA (01968 660401). Two lovely cottages on hideaway country estate near Edinburgh. Sleep 4/6. Available all year. Perfect dog-friendly location. STB ★★★/★★★★ [🐕]
e-mail: cottages@slipperfield.com   website: www.slipperfield.com

SCOTLAND — **Dumfries & Galloway**

Auchencairn, Auldgirth, Canonbie, Castle Douglas, Crossmichael

BALCARY BAY
Country House Hotel
Auchencairn, Near Castle Douglas DG7 1QZ

The hotel offers well appointed bedrooms, all with en suite facilities. Imaginative cuisine is based on local delicacies including seafood. This is an ideal location for exploring the gardens and National Trust properties of South-West Scotland and enjoying walking, birdwatching and golf.

www.balcary-bay-hotel.co.uk
reservations@balcary-bay-hotel.co.uk

Tel: 01556 640217
Fax: 01556 640272
AA ★★★ 2 Rosettes

FRIARS CARSE *COUNTRY HOUSE HOTEL*
Auldgirth, Dumfries DG2 0SA
Tel: 01387 740388 Fax: 01387 740550

Set in 45 acres of woodland. 21 en suite bedrooms. Restaurant serving excellent local cuisine. Private fishing. Putting Green. Golf & Cycling nearby.

www.friarscarse.co.uk

17th Century Coaching Inn.
10 en suite bedrooms, Bar and à la carte Restaurant. Weekend Carvery. Ideal for fishing, walking, touring.
Brian & Yvonne MacAskill
Cross Keys Hotel. Canonbie, Dumfriesshire DG14 0SY
Tel: 013873 71205 • Fax: 013873 71878
enquiries@crosskeys.net • www.crosskeyshotelscotland.co.uk

CROSSKEYS HOTEL CANONBIE

Glenlee Holiday Houses • New Galloway

Five charming holiday cottages in quiet secluded woodland set around a central courtyard. Each cottage is well equipped and comfortably furnished. Woodland walks and spectacular waterfalls. Open fires. An excellent base for exploring Galloway. Pets welcome. Open March-December.
Call Cathy and Richard Agnew on 01644 430212
Glenlee Holiday Homes, New Galloway, Castle Douglas, Kirkcudbrightshire DG7 3SF
e-mail: agnew@glenlee-holidays.co.uk • www.glenlee-holidays.co.uk

---

Craigadam

Working organic sheep farm. Family-run 18th century farmhouse. All bedrooms en suite. Billiard room/honesty bar. Lovely oak-panelled dining room offering Cordon Bleu cooking using local produce such as venison, pheasant and salmon. Trout fishing, walking, and golfing available. STB/AA ★★★★
Tel & Fax: 01556 650233 • Mrs C. Pickup, Craigadam, Castle Douglas DG7 3HU
e-mail: inquiry@craigadam.com • www.craigadam.com

Winner Macallan Taste of Scotland

A natural, unspoilt place for a family holiday. Ideal for fishing, sailing, walking and golfing. Boats, bikes & canoes for hire, touring and camping, lochside caravans to let.

Loch Ken Holiday Park, Parton, Castle Douglas, Dumfries & Galloway DG7 3NE
Tel: 01644 470282 • www.lochkenholidaypark.co.uk

LOCH KEN HOLIDAY PARK

Deeside Bed & Breakfast

Small, family-run accommodation, surrounded by the unspoiled beauty of the Galloway countryside. One double en suite, twin/double with private facilities.
42 Main Street, Crossmichael, Castle Douglas DG7 3AU
Tel: 01556 670239 • Email: info@deesidebandb.co.uk • www.deesidebandb.co.uk

Dumfries & Galloway

SCOTLAND 351

Dalbeattie, Drummore, Dumfries, Ecclefechan, Gatehouse of Fleet

BAREND HOLIDAY VILLAGE — SANDYHILLS, DALBEATTIE DG5 4NU

Situated on the beautiful South West Colvend coast in Dumfries & Galloway. Our chalets are well equipped and centrally heated for all year comfort. On-site boules courts, bar, restaurant, sauna and indoor pool. Wifi internet access available.

Tel: 01387 780663   www.barendholidayvillage.co.uk

Harbour Row Cottages

Mull of Galloway • Drummore

A few short steps from the beach. STB 3/4-Star cottages. Tranquil and unspoiled village. Logan Botanical Gardens, golf, fishing, birdwatching nearby. Unrestricted beaches.

Contact SALLY COLMAN:

• Non-smoking properties available •

01776 840631

www.harbourrow.co.uk

ASSC

AE FARM COTTAGES

Modern accommodation in old stone buildings on a traditional farm, overlooking a peaceful valley, surrounded by hills and forests. Beautiful views, plentiful wildlife and endless paths on the doorstep.

A great country retreat between Dumfries, Moffat and Thornhill.

David & Gill Stewart, GUBHILL FARM, Dumfries DG1 1RL (01387 860648)
e-mail: gill@gubhill.co.uk • www.aefarmcottages.co.uk CATEGORY ONE DISABILITY

Ecclefechan Carlyle House, Ecclefechan, Lockerbie, Dumfriesshire DG11 3DG

Family-run B&B in the heart of the village of Ecclefechan opposite the birthplace of the Victorian historian and essayist Thomas Carlyle. 2 double rooms and a twin room, all with private bathrooms. Television, tea and coffee making facilities in each room. Pets welcome.

Tel: 01576 300322 • e-mail: CarlyleHouse@Ecclefechan.com • www.ecclefechan.com

Carrick Holiday Cottages • Gatehouse of Fleet • Kirkcudbrightshire

Range of self-catering cottages and chalets in beautiful Carrick Bay, sleeping 4-8. Safe sandy beaches, sailing, cycling, walking, birdwatching, golf. Pets welcome.

Owl Cote Byre, Carrick Shore, Gatehouse-of-Fleet, Kirkcudbrightshire DG7 2DT
Tel: 01557 814130; Mob: 07719 263098 • e-mail: cathie@carrick-cottages.co.uk
www.carrickcottages.com • www.carrickcottagesscotland.com

Publisher's note

While every effort is made to ensure accuracy, we regret that FHG Guides cannot accept responsibility for errors, misrepresentations or omissions in our entries or any consequences thereof. Prices in particular should be checked.

We will follow up complaints but cannot act as arbiters or agents for either party.

Dumfries & Galloway

Gatehouse of Fleet, Kirkcudbright, Moffat

RUSKO HOLIDAYS
Secluded Self-Catering House and Cottages in beautiful South-West Scotland

Rusko Holidays offers secluded, quality-assured, traditional self-catering cottages set amid magnificent Scottish scenery in the heart of one of Scotland's National Scenic Areas. Lovely safe sandy beaches, lochs, hills, sub-tropical gardens, golf courses and many places of historic interest.

Accommodation comprises a beautiful large holiday house and 3 charming, cosy, comfortable cottages (one of which is accessible for wheelchairs for disabled holidays), on a lovely private estate on the edge of the Galloway Forest Park. There is an all-weather tennis court, loch and river fishing. Stabling and grazing is available for your own horses and well-behaved pets are very welcome too.

Gatehouse of Fleet,
Castle Douglas DG7 2BS
Tel: 01557 814215
e-mail: info@ruskoholidays.co.uk
www.ruskoholidays.co.uk

GHh GORDON HOUSE HOTEL

The warmest of Scottish welcomes to this family-run hotel with an informal and relaxed atmosphere. Finest Scottish food, excellent accommodation and real value for money.
Well behaved pets, by arrangement, are very welcome.
Gordon House Hotel, 116 High Street, Kirkcudbright DG6 4JQ
Phone: 01557 330670 • Fax: 01557 331040
E-mail: mail@gordon-house-hotel.co.uk
www.gordon-house-hotel.co.uk

A warm welcome is offered at the award-winning **ANNANDALE ARMS HOTEL** to dogs with well-mannered and house-trained owners. There are all the comforts and facilities that owners enjoy such as an excellent restaurant and a relaxing panelled bar. The Hotel has a large private parking area at the rear full of the most exquisite sniffs. £98 per room for dogs travelling with two owners; £60 per room for dogs travelling with one owner. STB ★★★ Hotel
High Street, Moffat DG10 9HF • Tel: 01683 220013 • Fax: 01683 221395
www.annandalearmshotel.com • reception@annandalearmshotel.com

---

BARNHILL SPRINGS Country Guest House, Moffat DG10 9QS

Early Victorian country house overlooking some of the finest views of Upper Annandale. Comfortable accommodation, residents' lounge with open fire. Ideal centre for touring South-West Scotland and the Borders, or for an overnight stop. Situated on the Southern Upland Way half-a-mile from A74/M74 Moffat Junction. Pets free of charge. Bed & Breakfast from £30; Evening Meal by arrangement.
Tel: 01683 220580
AA ★★

Please mention **Pets Welcome!**
when making enquiries about accommodation featured in these pages

Dumfries & Galloway

Newton Stewart, Sanquhar, Stranraer, Thornhill

Bargaly Estate Cottages

Three cottages in the grounds of this historic Scottish estate. 'Bargaly' was once the home of the noted horticulturalist, Andrew Heron, and dates back to 1675.

GATEHOUSE COTTAGE, SQUIRREL COTTAGE and THE GARDENER'S COTTAGE available for holiday lets. Situated in the Bargaly Glen 1½ miles down a scenic country lane, yet only 4 miles from the town of Newton Stewart, 'Gateway to the Galloway Hills', with all facilities. Gentle walks can be taken locally, or a more challenging ramble to the top of Cairnsmore. Cycle hire locally, and the nearby Forest Park Visitor Centre in the Glen has a programme of activities throughout the season. An excellent location for walking, birdwatching, cycling, golf, watersports at Loch Ken, fishing (private 5½ miles stretch for salmon and trout), astronomy (take advantage of our dark skies), horse riding, a plethora of gardens to visit, some fun on the beach, or simply just relaxing. **Pets welcome.**

Visit our website **www.bargaly.com** for more information or call us for a brochure - **01671 401048**
e-mail: **bargalyestate@callnetuk.com**

Galloway's Hidden Retreat

Newark Farm

We offer three different types of quality accommodation and a wide range of facilities.
• Bed and Breakfast • Self-catering • Caravan Club Certified caravan location •
Whether you want to go fishing, walking, mountain biking or simply enjoy the view –
Newark Farm is the ideal location.
Newark Farm, Sanquhar, Dumfriesshire DG4 6HN
Tel: **01659 50263** • Fax: **01659 50795**
e-mail: **info@newarkfarm.com** • **www.newarkfarm.com**

Cross Haven Guesthouse

Family-run Guest House close to ferry, offering quality service and value for money. En suite bedrooms. Ideal for couples, ferry passengers and visitors to Ireland. Pets welcome.
Cross Haven Guest House, Lewis Street, Stranraer, Dumfries & Galloway DG9 7AL • Tel: **01776 700598**
e-mail: **crosshavengh@yahoo.co.uk** • **www.crosshaven.co.uk**

Trigony House Hotel • Thornhill DG3 5EZ

Standing in over 4 acres of woodland and gardens, Trigony is a luxury Country House Hotel with a combination of relaxed style and excellent rustic cuisine. Bess our black Lab will welcome you and should you have a dog of your own they will be more than welcome at our pet-friendly hotel.
e-mail: **info@trigonyhotel.co.uk** • **www.countryhousehotelscotland.com**
Telephone: **01848 331211**

Self-Catering in Thornhill, Dumfriesshire • Sleeps 7 • STB ★★★

One mile from Drumlanrig Castle estate, offering fishing, mountain biking, walking, and 4x4 tours. One twin, one family and one double room, bathroom and shower room, plus enclosed garden. Sky TV, DVD; fully fitted kitchen with washer and dishwasher. Short Breaks available all year; two night break from £152. £292-£462 per week incl. heating, towels and linen. Discounts available for under occupancy - please call to discuss. Tel: **01848 331557** • **www.thornhillselfcatering.co.uk**

Hillcrest Barn

TEMPLAND COTTAGES • **Templand Mains, Thornhill DG3 5AB**
Enjoy the friendly welcome and peaceful tranquillity of Templand, set in the heart of the Nith Valley, only half a mile from Thornhill, with shops, hotels and restaurants. The 6 tastefully converted cottages sleep from 2-6, and have own patio with BBQ, and there is an indoor heated swimming pool and sauna for guests to enjoy.
E-mail: **jacqui@templandcottages.co.uk** • **www.templandcottages.co.uk**
Telephone: **01848 330775** • Fax: **01848 330206**

Hope Cottage, Thornhill, Dumfriesshire DG3 5BJ

Pretty stone cottage in the peaceful conservation village of Durisdeer. Well-equipped self-catering cottage with large secluded garden. Sleeps 5. Towels, linen, heating and electricity included. Pets Welcome.
**For brochure telephone: Mrs S Stannett • 01848 331510
Fax: 01848 331810 • e-mail: a.stann@btinternet.com
www.hopecottage.co.uk**

Dumfries & Galloway

Whithorn, Wigton

Chapel Outon Farmhouse B&B

Old-fashioned B&B hospitality in comfortable and informal surroundings. Non-smoking, spacious yet cosy accommodation and wholesome home cooked food. Let us spoil you and your family and pamper your pet.
Kath & Tim Annison. Whithorn, Dumfries & Galloway DG8 8DH
Tel: 01988 500136 • e-mail: kath@chapelouton.co.uk
www.chapelouton.co.uk

CRAIGLEMINE COTTAGE B&B

With a rural location and peaceful atmosphere it's a wonderful place to unwind for a short break or a longer holiday. We have one double/family room, one single/twin room and dining room/lounge. Prices from £22. Evening meals available on request, including vegetarian or other dietary needs. Non-smoking. Off-road parking. Children welcome (under six years free). Pets welcome. An ideal base for walkers, cyclists, golf or touring. We also cater for amateur astronomers - call for details. Whether exploring the history, countryside or unspoilt beaches there is something for everyone, you can be sure of a friendly welcome all year round. Contact us for more details, or visit our website.

Glasserton, Near Whithorn, Dumfries DG8 8NE
Tel: 01988 500594
e-mail: cottage@fireflyuk.net
www.startravel.fireflyinternet.co.uk

HILLCREST HOUSE Maidland Place, Wigtown DG8 9EU
Tel: 01988 402018

Beautiful Victorian character villa set on edge of national book town. Fabulous views over nature reserve. Six bedrooms, residents' lounge. Evening meals using fresh local produce.
e-mail: info@hillcrest-wigtown.co.uk • www.hillcrest-wigtown.co.uk

Auchencairn

Village 7 miles south of Dalbeattie.

BALCARY BAY COUNTRY HOUSE HOTEL, AUCHENCAIRN, NEAR CASTLE DOUGLAS DG7 1QZ (01556 640217; Fax: 01556 640272). Ideal location for exploring South West Scotland. Well appointed bedrooms, all en suite. Imaginative cuisine based on local produce. STB ★★★, AA ★★★, 2 Rosettes. [🐾]
e-mail: reservations@balcary-bay-hotel.co.uk   website: www.balcary-bay-hotel.co.uk

Auldgirth

Small village on A76.

FRIARS CARSE COUNTRY HOUSE HOTEL, AULDGIRTH DG2 0SA (01387 740388; Fax: 01387 740550). 21 en suite bedrooms. Restaurant serving excellent local cuisine. Private fishing. Snooker room. Putting Green. Golf & Cycling nearby. STB★★★.
website: www.friarscarse.co.uk

Canonbie

Village on River Esk, two miles north of Scottish Border.

CROSS KEYS HOTEL. CANONBIE DG14 0SY (013873 71205; Fax: 013873 71878). 17th Century Coaching Inn. 10 en suite bedrooms. Bar and à la carte Restaurant. Weekend Carvery. STB ★★★. [🐾]
e-mail: enquiries@crosskeys.net   website: www.crosskeyshotelscotland.co.uk

Dumfries & Galloway   SCOTLAND 355

Castle Douglas

Old market town at the northern end of Carlingwalk Loch, good touring centre for Galloway

CATHY AND RICHARD AGNEW, GLENLEE HOLIDAY HOMES, NEW GALLOWAY, CASTLE DOUGLAS DG7 3SF (01644 430212). Five charming holiday cottages in quiet secluded woodland set around a central courtyard. Each cottage is well equipped and comfortably furnished. An excellent base for exploring Galloway. STB ★★★. [🐾]
e-mail: agnew@glenlee-holidays.co.uk   website: www.glenlee-holidays.co.uk

MRS CELIA PICKUP, "CRAIGADAM", CASTLE DOUGLAS DG7 3HU (Tel & Fax: 01556 650233). Family-run 18th century famhouse. All bedrooms en suite. Billiard room/honesty bar. Lovely oak-panelled dining room offering Cordon Bleu cooking using local produce such as venison, pheasant and salmon. Trout fishing, walking and golfing available. STB ★★★★; AA ★★★★ and Breakfast & Dinner Awards. [🐾]
e-mail: inquiry@craigadam.com   website: www.craigadam.com

LOCH KEN HOLIDAY PARK, PARTON, CASTLE DOUGLAS DG7 3NE (01644 470282). A natural, unspoilt place for a family holiday. Ideal for fishing, sailing, walking and golfing. Boats, bikes & canoes for hire, touring and camping, lochside caravans to let. STB ★★★★. AA Three Pennants. David Bellamy Gold Award. [Pets £2 per night, £10 per week]
website: www.lochkenholidaypark.co.uk

Crossmichael

Small village on east side of Loch Ken, 4 miles north of Castle Douglas.

Deeside Bed & Breakfast 42 Main Street, Crossmichael, Castle Douglas DG7 3AU (01556 670239) Small, family-run accommodation, surrounded by the unspoiled beauty of the Galloway countryside. One double en suite, twin/double with private facilities. STB ★★★. [Pets £3 per night].
e-mail: info@deesidebandb.co.uk   website: www.deesidebandb.co.uk

Dalbeattie

Small town in wooded valley on Urr Water, 12 miles form Dumfries.

BAREND HOLIDAY VILLAGE, SANDYHILLS, DALBEATTIE DG5 4NU (01387 780663). On the beautiful South West Colvend coast. Our chalets are well equipped and centrally heated for all year comfort. On-site boules courts, bar, restaurant, sauna and indoor pool. Wifi internet access available. [Pets £3 per night].
website: www.barendholidayvillage.co.uk

Drummore

Coastal location, 4 miles north of Mull of Galloway.

Mull of Galloway, drummore. A few short steps from the beach. STB 3/4-Star cottages; non-smoking cottages available. Tranquil and unspoiled village. Logan Botanical Gardens, golf, fishing, birdwatching nearby. Unrestricted beaches. ASSC. Contact Sally Colman (01776 840631). [£5 per pet].
website: www.harbourrow.co.uk

Dumfries

County town of Dumfries-shire and a former seaport. Dumfries contains many interesting buildings including an 18th century windmill containing a camera obscura. Robert Burns lived in the town before his death in 1796.

DAVID & GILL STEWART, AE FARM COTTAGES, GUBHILL FARM, DUMFRIES DG1 1RL (01387 860648). Modern accommodation in old stone buildings on a traditional farm, overlooking a peaceful valley. Beautiful views, plentiful wildlife and endless paths on the doorstep. Between Dumfries, Moffat and Thornhill. STB ★★★ SELF CATERING, CATEGORY ONE DISABILITY. [🐾]
e-mail: gill@gubhill.co.uk   website: www.aefarmcottages.co.uk

Ecclefechan

Small village 5 miles north of Annan, famous as birthplace of Thomas Carlyle.

CARLYLE HOUSE, ECCLEFECHAN, LOCKERBIE DG11 3DG (01576 300322). Family-run B&B opposite the birthplace of Thomas Carlyle. Easy access from M74. 2 double rooms and a twin room, all with private bathrooms. No smoking. Pets welcome. STB ★★★
e-mail: CarlyleHouse@Ecclefechan.com   website: www.ecclefechan.com

Gatehouse of Fleet

Small town near mouth of Water of Fleet, 6 miles north-west of Kirkcudbright

CARRICK HOLIDAY COTTAGES. Range of self-catering cottages and chalets in beautiful Carrick Bay. Safe sandy beaches, sailing, cycling, walking, birdwatching, golf. Pets welcome. Contact CATHIE TENNANT, OWL COTE BYRE, CARRICK SHORE, GATEHOUSE OF FLEET DG7 2DT (01557 814130; Mob: 07719 263098).
e-mail: cathie@carrick-cottages.co.uk   website: www.carrickcottages.com
www.carrickcottagesscotland.com

RUSKO HOLIDAYS, GATEHOUSE OF FLEET, CASTLE DOUGLAS DG7 2BS (01557 814215). Spacious farmhouse and three charming, cosy cottages near beaches, hills, gardens, castles and golf course. Walking, fishing, tennis. Pets, including horses, welcome. Sleep 2-12. Rates £234-£1382. STB ★★ to ★★★★ Self-Catering. Disabled Awards. [Pets £20 each]
e-mail: info@ruskoholidays.co.uk   website: www.ruskoholidays.co.uk

Kirkcudbright

Town in a sheltered position on north Solway shore, 25 miles from Dumfries.

GORDON HOUSE HOTEL, 116 HIGH STREET, KIRKCUDBRIGHT DG6 4JQ (01557 330670; Fax: 01557 331040). Family-run hotel with an informal and relaxed atmosphere. Finest Scottish food, excellent accommodation and real value for money. Well behaved pets welcome by arrangement.
e-mail: mail@gordon-house-hotel.co.uk   website: www.gordon-house-hotel.co.uk

Moffat

At head of lovely Annandale, grand mountain scenery. Good centre for rambling, climbing, angling and golf. The 'Devil's Beef Tub' is 5 miles, Edinburgh 52, Peebles 33, Dumfries 21.

ANNANDALE ARMS HOTEL, HIGH STREET, MOFFAT DG10 9HF (01683 220013; Fax: 01683 221395). A warm welcome is offered at the Annandale Arms to dogs with well-mannered and house-trained owners. Excellent restaurant and a relaxing panelled bar. STB ★★★ [pw!] 🐾
e-mail: reception@annandalearmshotel.co.uk   website: www.annandalearmshotel.co.uk

BARNHILL SPRINGS COUNTRY GUEST HOUSE, MOFFAT DG10 9QS (01683 220580). Early Victorian country house overlooking some of the finest views of Upper Annandale. Comfortable accommodation, residents' lounge with open fire. Situated on the Southern Upland Way half-a-mile from A74/M74 Moffat Junction. Pets free of charge. Bed & Breakfast from £30; Evening Meal by arrangement. AA ★★ [pw!] 🐾

Newton Stewart

Small town on River Cree 7 miles north of Wigtown.

BARGALY ESTATE COTTAGES, PALNURE, NEWTON STEWART DG8 7BH (01671 401048). Three cottages. The Gatehouse Cottage to the historic Bargaly Estate stands proudly looking over the countryside beyond. Gardener's Cottage was once the home fo the head gardener and lies adjacent to the walled garden. Nestling in a woodland setting lies Squirrel Cottage. Salmon and trout fishing. [Pets £20 per week.].
e-mail: bargalyestate@callnetuk.com   website: www.bargaly.com

Dumfries & Galloway

Sanquhar

Small town on the Southern Upland Way.

NEWARK FARM, SANQUHAR DG4 6HN (01659 50263; Fax: 01659 50975). Three different types of quality accommodation and a wide range of facilities. Bed and Breakfast; Self-catering; Caravan Club Certified caravan location. Ideal location for fishing, walking, mountain biking. STB ★★★ B&B
e-mail: info@newarkfarm.com   website: www.newarkfarm.com

Stranraer

Scotland's gateway to Ireland, only 90 minutes away by fast ferry. Ideal base for outdoor activities.

CROSS HAVEN GUEST HOUSE, LEWIS STREET, STRANRAER DG9 7AL (01776 700598). Family-run Guest House close to ferry, offering quality service and value for money. En suite bedrooms. Ideal for couples, ferry passengers and visitors to Ireland. Pets welcome. STB ★★★.[🐾]
e-mail: crosshavengh@yahoo.co.uk   website: www.crosshaven.co.uk

Thornhill

Small town on River Nith 13 miles north-west of Dumfries. Site of Roman signal station lies to the south.

TRIGONY HOUSE HOTEL, THORNHILL DG3 5EZ (01848 331211). Standing in over 4 acres of woodland and gardens, Trigony is a luxury Country House Hotel with a combination of relaxed style and excellent rustic cuisine. Should you have a dog they will be more than welcome at our pet-friendly hotel.
e-mail: info@trigonyhotel.co.uk   website: www.countryhousehotelscotland.com

HILLCREST BARN. One mile from Drumlanrig Castle estate, offering fishing, mountain biking, walking, and 4x4 tours. One twin, one family and one double room, bathroom and shower room, enclosed garden. Sky TV, DVD; fully fitted kitchen. Short Breaks available all year; terms incl. heating, towels and linen. For details contact: 01848 331557. STB ★★★ [🐾]
website: www.thornhillselfcatering.co.uk

TEMPLAND COTTAGES, TEMPLAND MAINS, THORNHILL DG3 5AB (01848 330775). Set in the heart of the Nith Valley near Thornhill, with shops, hotels and restaurants. Tastefully converted cottages sleep from 2-6. Own patio with BBQ, heated indoor pool and sauna.
e-mail: jacqui@templandcottages.co.uk   website: www.templandcottages.co.uk

HOPE COTTAGE, THORNHILL DG3 5BJ (01848 331510; Fax: 01848 331810). Pretty stone cottage in the peaceful conservation village of Durisdeer. Well-equipped self-catering cottage with large secluded garden. Sleeps 5. Towels, linen, heating and electricity included. Phone MRS S. STANNETT for brochure. STB ★★★★ [🐾]
e-mail: a.stann@btinternet.com   website: www.hopecottage.co.uk

Whithorn

Small town 9 miles south of Wigtown.

KATH & TIM ANNISON, CHAPEL OUTON FARMHOUSE B&B, WHITHORN DG8 8DH (01988 500136) Old-fashioned hospitality in comfortable and informal surroundings. Non-smoking, spacious yet cosy accommodation and wholesome home cooked food. Let us spoil you and your family and pamper your pet. [pw! 🐾]
e-mail: kath@chapelouton.co.uk   website: www.chapelouton.co.uk

MIKE AND HELEN ALEXANDER, CRAIGLEMINE COTTAGE B&B, GLASSERTON, NEAR WHITHORN DG8 8NE (01988 500594). Our rural location makes this a wonderful place to unwind. Ideal for touring, your dog will love the nearby beaches. Evening meal available. STB ★★ [🐾]
e-mail: cottage@fireflyuk.net   website: www.startravel.fireflyinternet.co.uk

Wigtown

Small town on hill above River Cree.

HILLCREST HOUSE, MAIDLAND PLACE, WIGTOWN DG8 9EU (01988 402018). Beautiful character Victorian villa set on edge of national book town. Fabulous views over nature reserve. Six bedrooms, residents' lounge. Evening meals using fresh local produce. [Pets free in kennels, £1 per night indoors]
e-mail: info@hillcrest-wigtown.co.uk   website: www.hillcrest-wigtown.co.uk

358 SCOTLAND — **Edinburgh & Lothians**

North Berwick, Rosewell, West Calder

TANTALLON CARAVAN & CAMPING PARK on Scotland's Famous Golfing Coast
- Disabled facilities (level 2) • Quaint harbour town • Positioned in the heart of East Lothian
- Close to the beach & swimming pool • Good transport links to Edinburgh • Free centrally heated WC facilities • Laundry, food preparation area and dishwashing facilities • Games and television room

Dunbar Road, North Berwick, East Lothian EH39 5NJ • Tel: 01620 893348
e-mail: tantallon@meadowhead.co.uk • www.meadowhead.co.uk

WEST FENTON Court — www.westfenton.co.uk
Luxury self-catering holiday cottages near North Berwick

perfect for families, golf, walking, beaches and relaxation

Kitchen & dining areas for enjoying long, relaxed meals.
Lounge rooms with hardwood floors and sumptuous sofas for relaxing after a day's golf or sightseeing.
Bathrooms - beautifully tiled and equipped.
Bedrooms - tastefully furnished for a comfortable sleep in the quiet of the country.
Patio gardens - lawned and fenced, ideal for barbecues, alfresco dining or an evening drink.

West Fenton Court is located in a conservation area, adjacent to a nature reserve, just one mile south of Gullane and close to North Berwick, ideal for golf, beaches and coastal walks. Edinburgh is just 35 minutes by car or train.
West Fenton, North Berwick, East Lothian EH39 5AL • 01620 842154 • e-mail: info@westfenton.co.uk

Hunter Holiday Cottages Thornton Farm, Rosewell, Edinburgh EH24 9EF
Hunter Holiday Cottages have 2 x two-bedroom and 1 x 3-bedroom cottages situated on our working farm just 20 minutes' drive south of Edinburgh city centre. Pets welcome, great walks on tracks and through woods. For more information visit our website.
Contact Margot Crichton. Telephone for availability for Short Breaks
Tel: 0131-448 0888 • Fax: 0131-440 2082 • e-mail: info@edinburghcottages.com • www.edinburghcottages.com

CROSSWOODHILL FARM HOLIDAY COTTAGES near Edinburgh

Award-winning? Well-equipped? Spacious? Family, pet and disabled friendly? Yes to all these questions. And so much more.... explore our livestock farm, relax in front of a blazing fire with a book, let the kids loose on the toy and games cupboards once home from a wealth of exciting days out. Or play outside. Spoilt for choice with both the area and with 3 very different properties. Each sleeps up to 6.
Winner of 2008 VisitScotland Thistle Award for Accommodation: Customer Care.

Explore: **www.crosswoodhill.co.uk** or **www.fivestarholidaycottage.co.uk**
Contact: Geraldine Hamilton, Crosswoodhill,
West Calder, West Lothian, EH55 8LP
Tel. 01501 785205 • e-mail: cottages@crosswoodhill.co.uk

North Berwick

Town and resort 19 miles east of Edinburgh.

TANTALLON CARAVAN & CAMPING PARK, DUNBAR ROAD, NORTH BERWICK EH39 5NJ (01620 893348). Idyllic location, direct path to beach. Centrally heated WC facilities. Laundry, food preparation area and dishwashing facilities. Disabled facilities (Level 2). STB ★★★★. David Bellamy Gold Award.
e-mail: tantallon@meadowhead.co.uk   website: www.meadowhead.co.uk

WEST FENTON COURT, WEST FENTON, NORTH BERWICK EH39 5AL(01620 842154). Luxury self-catering holiday cottages near North Berwick, perfect for families, golf, walking, beaches and relaxation. Just 35 minutes from Edinburgh. Superbly equipped. STB ★★★★ [Pets £10 per week].
e-mail: info@westfenton.co.uk   website: www.westfenton.co.uk

Edinburgh & Lothians / Fife   SCOTLAND 359

Rosewell

Village 4 miles south west of Dalkeith.

HUNTER HOLIDAY COTTAGES, THORNTON FARM, ROSEWELL, EDINBURGH EH24 9EF (0131 448 0888; Fax: 0131 440 2082). 2 x two-bedroom cottages and 1 x 3-bedroom cottage on working farm 20 minutes' drive Edinburgh. Great walks on tracks and through woods. Contact MARGOT CRICHTON. [Pets £10 per night/week].
e-mail: info@edinburghcottages.com   website: www.edinburghcottages.com

West Calder

Village in West Lothian 4 miles west of Livingston.

CROSSWOODHILL FARM HOLIDAY COTTAGES, NEAR EDINBURGH. Well equipped and spacious properties, family, pet and disabled friendly. Ideal base for exploring this scenic area and for visiting Edinburgh. STB 3/5 Stars. Contact: GERALDINE HAMILTON, CROSSWOODHILL, WEST CALDER, WEST LOTHIAN EH55 8LP (01501 785205).[Pets £20 per week]
e-mail: cottages@crosswoodhill.co.uk   website: www.crosswoodhill.co.uk
                                              www.fivestarholidaycottage.co.uk

Fife
Lower Largo, St Andrews

Main Street, Lower Largo, Fife KY8 6BT
Tel: 01333 320759 • Fax: 01333 320865
email: relax@crusoehotel.co.uk
www.crusoehotel.co.uk

Old-world ambience with fine harbour views. En suite accommodation, outstanding cuisine, free house. Excellent centre for sailing, golf, birdwatching, wind surfing, coastal walks.

COBWEBS in the HEART OF ST ANDREWS

Self catering for five people, opposite the University, at the heart of the Auld Toon.

www.heartofstandrews.co.uk

Just three minutes from the Castle Sands and ten from the famous links and West Sands, our secluded, secure walled garden is perfect for you and your pets.

Telephone us on 01887 822819 or email Frances from the web page.

KINGASK COUNTRY COTTAGES
A selection of luxury self-catering holiday homes and large houses, situated along the beautiful Fife coastline in St Andrews, Kingsbarns and Crail. Pets welcome by arrangement.
All are within easy reach of attractions and are the perfect base for a golfing holiday.
KINGASK HOUSE, ST ANDREWS, FIFE KY16 8PN • TEL: 01334 472011
e-mail: info@kingask-cottages.co.uk • www.kingask-cottages.co.uk

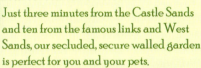

Lower Largo

Village on the bay, 2 miles NE of Leven. Birth place of Alexander Selkirk of Robinson Crusoe fame.

THE CRUSOE HOTEL, MAIN STREET, LOWER LARGO, NEAR ST ANDREWS KY8 6BT. (01333 320759; Fax: 01333 320865). Old-world ambience with fine harbour views. En suite accommodation, outstanding cuisine, free house. Excellent centre for sailing, golf, birdwatching, wind surfing, coastal walks. STB ★★★ Hotel. [🐾]
email: relax@crusoehotel.co.uk   website: www.crusoehotel.co.uk

St Andrews

Home of golf - British Golf Museum has memorabilia dating back to the origins of the game. Remains of castle and cathedral. Sealife Centre and beach Leisure Centre. Excellent sands. Ideal base for exploring the picturesque East Neuk.

COBWEBS. Self-catering for five people, situated opposite the University, just 3 minutes from the Castle Sands and 10 from the famous links. Our secluded, secure walled garden is perfect for you and your pets. Telephone 01887 822819 or e-mail Frances from the web page. STB ★★★★ Self-catering [Pets £25 per pet per week].
website: www.heartofstandrews.co.uk

KINGASK COUNTRY COTTAGES. A selection of luxury self-catering holiday homes and large houses, situated along the beautiful Fife coastline. All are within easy reach of attractions and golf courses. KINGASK HOUSE, ST ANDREWS, FIFE KY16 8PN (01334 472011).
e-mail: info@kingask-cottages.co.uk   website: www.kingask-cottages.co.uk

Highlands

Aviemore, Beauly

Cairngorm Highland Bungalows

Glen Einich, 29 Grampian View,
Aviemore, Inverness-shire PH22 1TF
Tel: 01479 810653 • Fax: 01479 810262
e-mail: linda.murray@virgin.net
www.cairngorm-bungalows.co.uk

Beautifully furnished and well-equipped bungalows ranging from one to four bedrooms. All have colour TV, video, DVD, microwave, cooker, washer-dryer, fridge and patio furniture. Some have log fires. Leisure facilities nearby include golf, fishing on the River Spey, swimming, sauna, jacuzzi, tennis, skating and skiing. Within walking distance of Aviemore. Ideal touring base. Children and pets welcome. Phone for colour brochure. Open all year.

For the very best in Highland Holidays

ASSC

AVIEMORE PINE BANK CHALETS

Enjoy the stunning beauty of the Highlands and the Cairngorm Mountains from our choice of superbly appointed log cabins and chalets. Great location – close to Spey River. Peaceful and relaxing setting. Friendly service staff, selected Sky TV, video, barbecue, mountain bikes. Many activities available. Leisure pool and restaurants nearby. Large choice of style and price.

5 log cabins, 8 chalets, 2 Flats, sleeping up to 6
Open all year £350-£725 per week • Pets Welcome

Dalfaber Road, Aviemore, Inverness-shire PH22 1PX
Tel: 01479 810000
e-mail: pinebankchalets@btopenworld.com
website: www.pinebankchalets.co.uk

CULLIGRAN COTTAGES • GLEN STRATHFARRAR

Pure magic! Come for a spell in a chalet or cottage and this glen will cast one over you!

Nature Reserve with native woodlands and wildlife. 15 miles of private road. Bikes for hire. Fly fishing (salmon and trout) on the rivers Farrar and Glass. Watch the wild deer from your window. Feed the farm deer.

Brochure • Open March-November • Prices from £199-£529

FRANK & JULIET SPENCER-NAIRN, STRUY, NEAR BEAULY, INVERNESS-SHIRE IV4 7JX • Tel/Fax: 01463 761285
e-mail: info@culligrancottages.co.uk
www.culligrancottages.co.uk

Kerrow House
Glen Affric
Cannich, by Beauly
Inverness-shire IV4 7NA

A selection of self-catering accommodation situated in 12 acres of wooded grounds, from Scandinavian-style chalets to a traditional riverside lodge. Sleep 2-8.
B&B also available in Kerrow Guesthouse (no pets).
Tel: 01456 415243 • Mobile: 07944 726489
email : info@kerrow-house.co.uk
www.kerrow-house.co.uk

FHG Guides

publish a large range of well-known accommodation guides.
We will be happy to send you details or you can use the order form at the back of this book.

SCOTLAND — Highlands

Carrbridge, Contin, Dingwall, Drumnadrochit, Fort William

The Pines COUNTRY GUESTHOUSE
DUTHIL, CARRBRIDGE PH23 3ND • 01479 841220

Relax and enjoy our Highland hospitality, woodland setting; all rooms en suite. Traditional or vegetarian home cooking.

B&B from £30 daily; DB&B from £268 weekly. Children and pets welcome.

www.thepines-duthil.co.uk

Privately owned and operated 20-bedroom Country House Hotel with miles of forest walks, many log fires, and great food. Both you and your dog are made to feel most welcome.

Coul House Hotel, Contin, By Strathpeffer, Ross-shire IV14 9ES
Tel: 01997 421487 • Fax: 01997 421945
e-mail: stay@coulhousehotel.com • www.coulhousehotel.com

Cornfield Cottage B&B, Balblair, Near Dingwall IV7 8LT
01381 610766 • stay@blackislebnb.com • www.blackislebnb.co.uk
In a peaceful corner of the Black Isle, this rather special B&B offers one twin bedroom and sitting room with open fire and private bathroom. No charge for dogs; daily doggy creche at small charge. Excellent value. DB&B also available.

Dog-friendly accommodation in the heart of the beautiful Scottish Highlands! B&B in guest wing, sleeps 5. Dogs and owners can roam for miles.

Torran House
Upper Drumbuie, Drumnadrochit, Inverness-shire IV63 6UX
Tel: 01456 459 353
e-mail: enquiries@torranbandb.net
www.torranbandb.net

GLENURQUHART LODGES Situated between Loch Ness and Glen Affric in a spectacular setting ideal for walking, touring or just relaxing in this tranquil location. Four spacious chalets all fully equipped for six people, set in wooded grounds. Owner's hotel adjacent where guests are most welcome in the restaurant and bar. **Near Drumnadrochit, Inverness IV63 6TJ** • Tel: 01456 476234 • Fax: 01456 476286
www.glenurquhart-lodges.co.uk • e-mail: carol@glenurquhartlodges.co.uk

---

Linnhe LOCHSIDE HOLIDAYS — **Corpach, Fort William, Inverness-shire PH33 7NL** • Almost a botanical garden, Linnhe is unique and one of the most beautiful Lochside parks in Britain. Close to Ben Nevis and Fort William. Excellent facilities including licensed shop, bakery, playgrounds, private beach and free fishing. Pets welcome. Luxury Holiday Caravans (from £220 per week) • Short Breaks from £135 • Tent & Touring Pitches also available • Open mid Dec-end Oct. • Tel: 01397 772376 • Fax: 01397 772007
www.linnhe-lochside-holidays.co.uk • e-mail: relax@linnhe-lochside-holidays.co.uk

---

Great Glen Holidays
Torlundy, Fort William PH33 6SW
Tel/Fax: 01397 703015

Eight spacious, 2-bedroom, timber chalets situated in woodland with spectacular mountain scenery. On working Highland farm. Riding, fishing and walking on farm. Ideal for family holidays, excellent base for touring; four miles from town. Sleep 4-5. Prices from £320 to £550 per week.
e-mail: chris.carver@btconnect.com • www.fortwilliam-chalets.co.uk

Highlands

Fort William, Glen Shiel

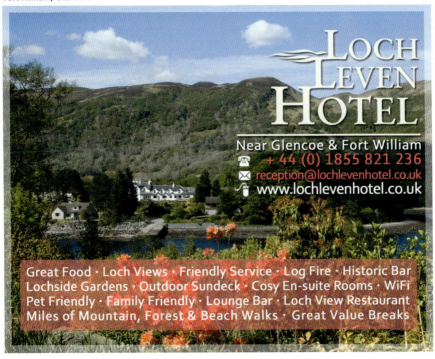

The Clan MacDuff Hotel
Fort William, Inverness-shire PH33 6RW
Tel: (01397) 702341 • Fax: (01397) 706174

This family-run hotel overlooks Loch Linnhe, two miles south of Fort William. Situated in its own grounds in a quiet and peaceful location with a large car park, the hotel is in an excellent location for touring and experiencing the rugged mountains and enchanting coastline of the West Highlands. All bedrooms are en suite, have colour TV, telephone, hairdryer, hospitality tray, radio and alarm clock. This family-managed hotel with its friendly welcoming staff is dedicated to providing good quality and value hospitality.

Bed and breakfast in an en suite room from £27.50pppn.
Spring and Autumn Special Offer - 3 nights Dinner,
Bed & Breakfast from £129pp.
Contact us for a colour brochure or visit our website.

reception@clanmacduff.co.uk • www.clanmacduff.co.uk

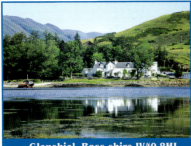

Kintail Lodge Hotel – Shiel Bridge

Beautifully situated on the shores of Loch Duich
6 miles south of Eilean Donan Castle

Spring, Autumn and Winter Short Breaks
Special Offer for 3, 4, or 5 Days – Dogs Welcome

Candlelit Dinners, Log Fires, Big Sofas
and fabulous views, whatever the weather!
We guarantee your comfort and we promise
you the best of Highland food and hospitality.

Glenshiel, Ross shire IV40 8HL
Tel: 01599 511275

e-mail: kintaillodgehotel@btinternet.com
www.kintaillodgehotel.co.uk

Highlands

Grantown-on-Spey, Inverness, Kincraig, Kingussie

TIGH NA SGIATH COUNTRY HOUSE HOTEL,
Dulnain Bridge, Near Grantown-on-Spey PH26 3PA

Former home of the Lipton Tea Family, this elegant mansion house is set in its own fabulous grounds near Grantown-on-Spey. Romantic open log fires, excellent Scottish cuisine using local and organic produce. Seafood and Highland Game feature daily. Vegetarian/gluten free diets catered for. Pets Welcome.

01479 851345 • e-mail: iain@tigh-na-sgiath.co.uk • www.tigh-na-sgiath.co.uk

Rowan Cottage

Charming 2 bedroom timber cottage set in wild heather garden. Fully equipped. Ideal for dog lovers.
Tel/Fax 01456 486711
Mrs Janet Sutherland, Aultnagoire, Errogie,
By Inverness IV2 6UH, Scotland
e-mail: janet@lochnesshideaways.co.uk
www.lochnesshideaways.co.uk

Let us spoil you...

Stunning Georgian Country House surrounded by 6 acres of parkland just outside Inverness. Warm welcome, discreet and attentive service. Outstanding menu of seasonal dishes using the finest local produce. Two charming Garden Cottages in which pets are warmly welcomed.

Dunain Park Hotel, Loch Ness Road, Inverness, IV3 8JN
Tel: 01463 230512 • Fax: 01463 224752
E-mail: info@dunainparkhotel.co.uk • www.dunainparkhotel.co.uk

DUNAIN PARK
HOTEL & RESTAURANT

Only a few minutes' stroll to the village, park and hills; gateway to the Loch Lomond and Trossachs National Park. One double and one twin with private bathroom or shower room, tea/coffee makers, central heating. Varied Scottish Breakfast. Your dogs can sleep in your room and are welcome in the sitting room and garden.

B&B from £25pppn; single by arrangement
REDUCED RATES for 3+ days
DOGS ESPECIALLY WELCOME (and stay free) IN GREAT WALKIES AREA

Lynne & Alistair Ferguson, 'Brochanach', 43 Fingal Road, Killin, Perthshire FK21 8XA
Tel: 01567 820028 • e-mail: alifer@msn.com

Insh House Guesthouse & Self Catering Cottages
Kincraig, By Kingussie PH21 1NU • 01540 651377

Insh House has 5 en suite bedrooms: 1 family, 1 double, 1 twin, 2 singles. B&B from £28pppn. * Fraser & Telford Cottages sleep 4 in a double room and a bunk-bedded room. Open plan living dining area. Weekly from £250. Totally non-smoking. Children and dogs welcome.
e-mail: inshhouse@btinternet.com • www.kincraig.com/inshhouse

STB ★★★

Allt Gynack Guest House
Tel: **01540 661081**

Gynack Villa, 1 High Street, Kingussie, Near Aviemore PH21 1HS
Family owned Victorian guest house in a beautiful part of the Highlands. In its own grounds with private car park. Open all year. Huge range of activities. Excellent restaurants nearby.
e-mail: alltgynack@tiscali.co.uk • www.alltgynack.com

Highlands

SCOTLAND 365

Kingussie, Kinlochbervie, Lairg, Loch Ness

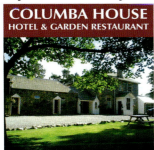

COLUMBA HOUSE
HOTEL & GARDEN RESTAURANT

In an area of oustanding natural beauty. An oasis amidst the magnificent scenery, stunning landscapes and tranquillity, in the foothills of snow-capped peaks of the Cairngorm and Monadhliath mountains. Quiet Highland retreat, nestling in a secluded, landscaped, walled garden with patio for summer time dining. Offering the highest standards of welcoming hospitality, accommodation and customer care, friendly atmosphere. Rooms with their own front doors, perfect for doggie holidays. Candlelit Garden Restaurant, renowned for excellent cuisine and attentive service. Homely, enchanting lounge and cosy bar, offering modern facilities while retaining their original charm. Wireless internet. Nearby Leisure Club free. Wheelchair friendly; wet room. Suberb Penthouse Suite. **B&B from £35.**

Manse Road, Kingussie PH21 1JF • Tel: 01540 661402
e-mail: myra@columbahousehotel.com • www.columbahousehotel.com

The Kinlochbervie Hotel

Pet-friendly, family-run hotel in a most stunning location on the north west coast of Scotland. Superb sea and hill views, beautiful beaches and an abundance of wildlife. Very comfortable en suite rooms, restaurant, bars, coffee shop. From £35 B&B.
Kinlochbervie, by Lairg, Sutherland IV27 4RP
Tel: 01971 521275 • Fax: 01971 521438
e-mail: klbhotel@btconnect.com
www.kinlochberviehotel.com

Lairg Highland Hotel

Lying in the centre of the village, Lairg Highland Hotel is an ideal base from which to tour the North of Scotland. Superb, home-cooked food is served in the restaurant and lounge bar. All bedrooms are furnished to a high standard, with en suite facilities, colour TV and tea/coffee.
Main Street, Lairg, Sutherland IV27 4DB • 01549 402243 • Fax: 01549 402593
www.highland-hotel.co.uk • e-mail: info@highland-hotel.co.uk

WILDERNESS COTTAGES
LOCH NESS/WEST COAST – SELF-CATERING

Escape to the country with Wilderness Cottages and leave behind the hectic lifestyle you lead today. We have a selection of quality self-catering cottages, from rustic appeal to 5-star luxury, from countryside to seashore. Whatever your pastime, be it walking, Munro bagging, cycling, sailing, fishing, birdwatching, or just chilling, we have a cottage for you. Pets with responsible owners are very welcome. Visit our website or phone for our brochure.

Open all year
Sleep 2-16
Pets welcome

CONTACT: Gordon & Corinne Roberts, Roebuck Cottage, Errogie,
Stratherrick, Inverness-shire IV2 6UH • 01456 486358
e-mail: corinne@wildernesscottages.co.uk • www.wildernesscottages.co.uk

Highlands

Loch Ness, Loch Torridon, Muir of Ord, Nethy Bridge,

• **LOCH NESS** • Wildside, Whitebridge, Inverness IV2 6UN

Exceptional riverside lodges close to the spectacular Loch Ness. Mountains, lochs, waterfalls and wildlife abound.

Charming riverside lodges with private lawns, log fires and mountain views. Lodges range from 1, 2 & 3 bedrooms, sleeping from 2 to 8 people. All lodges are non-smoking and enjoy magnificent views. Quiet location with excellent walks from your lodge. Pets welcome. Free fishing.

Tel: 01456 486 373 • Fax: 01456 486 371
e-mail: info@wildsidelodges.com • www.wildsidelodges.co.uk

Tigh an Eilean Hotel
& Shieldaig Bar and Coastal Kitchen

Tigh an Eilean (*"House of the Island"*) is in the picturesque 200-year-old fishing village of Shieldaig in Wester Ross, one of Scotland's last great wildernesses. Here the magnificent Torridon Mountains meet the Western Seas: spectacular walking, deserted beaches, home for seals, otters and sea eagles. Our award-winning hotel restaurant and the Coastal Kitchen next door both look across the sea to the sunset, and serve seafood delivered from the jetty to the kitchen door each day, together with other local specialities.

Good Hotel Guide ★ AA Britain's Best Hotels ★ Good Food Guide.
Shieldaig on Loch Torridon, Ross-shire, IV54 8XN • Tel: 01520 755251 • Fax: 01520 755321
e-mail: tighaneilean@keme.co.uk

Ord House Hotel, Muir of Ord, Ross-shire IV6 7UH

17th Century country house. Extensive gardens and woodlands for dogs to run around in. Large, airy bedrooms.
Log fires. Restaurant with AA Rosette.
Telephone: 01463 870492
e-mail: admin@ord-house.co.uk • www.ord-house.co.uk

01309 672505 **Speyside Cottages** Nethy Bridge, Inverness-shire **in Cairngorm National Park**
Relax in 4 comfortable cottages (sleep 2-7) with fenced gardens, on riverbank with wonderful forest walks. Pets welcome. £200-£595 per week, includes full linen and towels.
Brian and Moira Patrick, 1 Chapelton Place, Forres, Moray IV36 2NL
brian@speysidecottages.co.uk • www.speysidecottages.co.uk

MONDHUIE
CHALETS & B&B
NETHY BRIDGE, INVERNESS-SHIRE PH25 3DF
Tel: 01479 821062

Situated in the country between Aviemore and Grantown-on-Spey, two comfortable, self-catering chalets, or you can have Dinner, B&B in the house. A warm welcome awaits you. Pets welcome. Red squirrels seen daily. Free internet access.

e-mail: david@mondhuie.com • www.mondhuie.com

Highlands

SCOTLAND 367

Nethy Bridge, Poolewe, Rhiconich

Nethy Bridge • Highlands
Balnagowan Mill and Woodlark

Comfortable, modern 3 bedroom cottages in secluded locations in the Cairngorms National Park with an extensive network of woodland and riverside walks on the doorstep, which is ideal for pets. Furnished to a high standard with full central heating. £260 - £590 per week inclusive of electricity, bed linen and towels.
Contact Paula Fraser, 33 Argyle Grove, Dunblane, Perthshire FK15 9DT (01786 824957)
email: paulajfraser@aol.com

VisitScotland ★★★★
ASSC

Poolewe • Wester Ross

Dogs welcome in N/S Bed & Breakfast.
Convenient for local beaches and Torridon Mountains
e-mail: dgeorge@globalnet.co.uk
Tel: 01445 781765 • www.davidgeorge.co.uk

Scottish Tourist Board ★★★ B&B

Crofter's Cottages

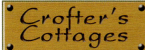

Mr Alexander Urquhart

15 Croft, Poolewe, Ross-shire IV22 2JY
Tel: 01445 781268

Two traditional cottages sleeping 4 and 5 persons. Situated in a scenic and tranquil area, ideal for a "get away from it all" holiday. Crofters Cottages are comfortably furnished, some with antiques and all the essential modern gadgets of today, such as auto-washer/dryer, microwave, fridge, bath and shower. Poolewe is a good base to tour the North West Highlands or for those who enjoy walking, fishing, climbing, golf or maybe just a stroll along one of the many sandy beaches. There are also indoor activities to be enjoyed such as the heated pool and leisure and fitness areas. Close by lie the famous Inverewe Gardens. Pets made welcome.
Low season from £120 – £230 • High season from £250 – £490
Midweek and short breaks available from November – March
e-mail: croftcottages@btopenworld.com
www.crofterscottages.co.uk

RHICONICH HOTEL

Rhiconich, Sutherland,
N.W. Highlands IV27 4RN • Tel: 01971 521224 • Fax: 01971 521732
e-mail: info@rhiconichhotel.co.uk • www.rhiconichhotel.co.uk

STB ★★★

SHE'S YOUR BEST FRIEND, so why leave her at home, bring her to **RHICONICH HOTEL**, she'll be made equally as welcome as you will. A place where we put service, hospitality and really fresh food as a priority, but why don't you come and see for yourself?

Gull Cottage • The Barn •
Rhiconich, Sutherland

Scottish Tourist Board ★★★ SELF CATERING

Situated on the wild and unspoilt west coast of Scotland overlooking Loch Inchard, the last sea loch on the north west coast. Superb scenery with excellent walks on mountains, moors, and the many beaches in the area. High quality accommodation with full central heating. Gull Cottage sleeps 4, both bedrooms en suite. The Barn sleeps 2.
Pets welcome; secure dog run accessed from cottage.
All enquiries to: **Lynn and Graham,**
Gull Cottage, Achriesgill, Rhiconich, Lairg,
Sutherland IV27 4RJ • Tel: 01971 521717
e-mail: grahamandlynn@theuphouse.co.uk
www.theuphouse.co.uk

SCOTLAND — Highlands

Spean Bridge, Tongue, Whitebridge

Achnabobane Farmhouse B&B

Excellent accommodation and comfort. An ideal central base for exploring the Highlands. Comfortable bedrooms, large guest lounge. Evening meals available.

Neil & Elizabeth Ockenden, Achnabobane Farmhouse
Achnabobane, Spean Bridge, Inverness-shire PH34 4EX
Tel: 01397 712919 • e-mail: enquiries@achnabobane.co.uk
www.achnabobane.net

RIVERSIDE LODGES Invergloy, Spean Bridge PH34 4DY
Tel: 01397 712684

The ultimate Highland location, set in 12 acres of woodland gardens, just three uniquely designed lodges sleeping six comfortably. With spectacular views across the loch to the mountains beyond. Each lodge has secure fenced deck areas, ideal for dogs or small children. Private beach with free fishing, stocked lochan, spectacular river gorge. Specimen trees and plants. Centrally located, ideal for all outdoor pursuits or just relaxing!

Tariff from £450-£760 per week with discounts for small parties/long stay. *Proprietors: Steve & Marilyn Dennis.*

Open all year • Linen included
enquiries@riversidelodge.org.uk • www.riversidelodge.org.uk

ASSC

Borgie Lodge Hotel

Skerray, Tongue, Sutherland KW14 7TH

Set in a secluded Highland glen by the stunning River Borgie lies Borgie Lodge, where mouthwatering food, fine wine, roaring log fires and a very warm welcome awaits after a day's fishing, hill walking, pony trekking or walking on the beach. Relax after dinner with a good malt and tales of salmon, trout and deer.

Tel: 01641 521 332
www.borgielodgehotel.co.uk
e-mail: info@borgielodgehotel.co.uk

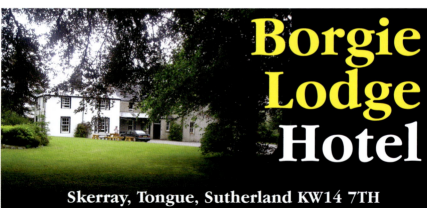

AA ★★

WHITEBRIDGE HOTEL WHITEBRIDGE,
SOUTH LOCH NESS IV2 6UN • 01456 486226 • Fax: 01456 486413

Peaceful location with magnificent mountain views and excellent walks. Friendly locals' bar with home-cooked food.
12 en suite rooms. B&B from £35pppn.
e-mail: info@whitebridgehotel.co.uk • www.whitebridgehotel.co.uk

Highlands   SCOTLAND 369

Aviemore (Inverness-shire)

Scotland's leading ski resort in Spey valley with superb sport and entertainment facilities. All-weather holiday centre.

CAIRNGORM HIGHLAND BUNGALOWS, GLEN EINICH, 29 GRAMPIAN VIEW, AVIEMORE PH22 1TF (01479 810653, Fax: 01479 810262). Well equipped bungalows ranging from one to four bedrooms. Open all year. Leisure facilities nearby. Children and pets welcome. Phone for brochure. STB ★★★-★★★★★ [🐾]
e-mail: linda.murray@virgin.net   website: www.cairngorm-bungalows.co.uk

PINE BANK CHALETS, DALFABER ROAD, AVIEMORE PH22 1PX (01479 810000). Cosy Log Cabins and 8 Quality Chalets, situated near the River Spey. Superb Family/Activity Holidays by mountains. Ideal skiing, walking, fishing and golf. Sky TV. Short breaks available. Pets welcome. Open all year. ASSC Member. Brochure. STB ★★★/★★★★ [Pets £10 per week.]
e-mail: pinebankchallets@btopenworld.com   website: www.pinebankchalets.co.uk

Beauly (Inverness-shire)

Town at head of Beauly Firth, 11 miles west of inverness.

FRANK & JULIET SPENCER-NAIRN, CULLIGRAN COTTAGES, GLEN STRATHFARRAR, STRUY, NEAR BEAULY IV4 7JX (Tel & Fax: 01463 761285). Pure magic! Come for a spell in a chalet or cottage and this glen will cast one over you! Nature Reserve with native woodlands and wildlife. Open March - November. Brochure. Terms from £199-£529. [🐾]
e-mail: info@culligrancottages.co.uk   website: www.culligrancottages.co.uk

KERROW HOUSE, GLEN AFFRIC, CANNICH, BY BEAULY IV4 7NA (01456 415243; Mobile: 07944 726489). A selection of self-catering accommodation situated in 12 acres of wooded grounds, from Scandinavian-style chalets to a traditional riverside lodge. Sleep 2-8. Free fishing; rod hire available. B&B also available (no pets). STB ★★★ [Pets £20 per week - SC only].
email : info@kerrow-house.co.uk   website: www.kerrow-house.co.uk

Carrbridge (Inverness-shire)

Village on River Dulnain, 7 miles north of Aviemore. Landmark Visitor Centre has exhibition explaining history of local environment.

THE PINES COUNTRY GUESTHOUSE, DUTHIL, CARRBRIDGE PH23 3ND (01479 841220). Relax and enjoy our Highland hospitality, woodland setting; all rooms en suite. Traditional or vegetarian home cooking. B&B from £30 daily; DB&B from £268 weekly. Children and pets welcome. AA ★★★ [🐾]
website: www.thepines-duthil.co.uk

Contin (Ross-shire)

Village 2 miles south west of Strathpeffer.

COUL HOUSE HOTEL, CONTIN, BY STRATHPEFFER IV14 9ES (01997 421487; Fax: 01997 421945). Privately owned and operated 20-bedroom Country House Hotel with miles of forest walks, many log fires, and great food. Both you and your dog are made to feel most welcome.
e-mail: stay@coulhousehotel.com   website: www.coulhousehotel.com

Dingwall (Ross-shire)

Town 11 miles north west of Inverness.

CORNFIELD COTTAGE B&B, BALBLAIR, NEAR DINGWALL IV7 8LT (01381 610766). In a peaceful corner of the Black Isle, this rather special B&B offers one twin bedroom and sitting room with open fire and private bathroom. Daily doggy creche at small charge. Excellent value. DB&B also available. [🐾]
e-mail: stay@blackislebnb.co.uk   website: www.blackislebnb.co.uk

---

Symbols

🐾	Indicates that pets are welcome free of charge.
£	Indicates that a charge is made for pets: nightly or weekly.
pw!	Shows some special provision for pets; exercise facility, feeding or accommodation arrangement.
⌂	Indicates separate pets accommodation.

Drumnadrochit (Inverness-shire)

Village on the shores of Loch Ness with "Monster" visitor centre. Sonar scanning cruises.

TORRAN HOUSE, UPPER DRUMBUIE, DRUMNADROCHIT IV63 6UX (01456 459 3530). Dog-friendly accommodation in the heart of the beautiful Scottish Highlands! B&B in guest wing, sleeps 5. Dogs and owners can roam for miles. [🐕]
e-mail: enquiries@torranbandb.net   website: www.torranbandb.net

GLENURQUHART LODGES, BY DRUMNADROCHIT IV63 6TJ (01456 476234; Fax: 01456 476286). Situated between Loch Ness and Glen Affric in a spectacular setting ideal for walking, touring or just relaxing in this tranquil location. Four spacious chalets all fully equipped for six people, set in wooded grounds. Owner's hotel adjacent where guests are most welcome in the restaurant and bar. [Pets £10 per week.]
e-mail: carol@glenurquhartlodges.co.uk   website: www.glenurquhart-lodges.co.uk

Fort William (Inverness-shire)

Small town at foot of Ben Nevis, ideal base for climbers and hillwalkers.

LINNHE LOCHSIDE HOLIDAYS, CORPACH, FORT WILLIAM PH33 7NL (01397 772376; Fax: 01397 772007). Linnhe is unique and one of the most beautiful lochside parks in Britain. Close to Ben Nevis and Fort William. Excellent facilities. Pets welcome. Open mid December-end October. Colour brochure. (Pets £5 per night, £25 per week).
e-mail: relax@linnhe-lochside-holidays.co.uk   website: www.linnhe-lochside-holidays.co.uk

GREAT GLEN HOLIDAYS, TORLUNDY, FORT WILLIAM PH33 6SW (Tel/Fax: 01397 703015). Sleep 4-6. Eight spacious, two-bedroom timber chalets on working Highland farm. Riding, fishing and walking on farm. Ideal for family holidays, excellent touring base. [Pets £15 per week]
e-mail: chris.carver@btconnect.com   website: www.fortwilliam-chalets.co.uk

LOCH LEVEN HOTEL, OLD FERRY ROAD, NORTH BALLACHULISH, NEAR FORT WILLIAM PH33 6SA (01855 821236). En suite rooms with lovely views. Meals using freshly prepared Scottish produce. Secluded garden down to shore. Safe, private parking. Extensive grounds. Great walks. [pw! 🐕]
e-mail: reception@lochlevenhotel.co.uk   website: www.lochlevenhotel.co.uk

THE CLAN MACDUFF HOTEL, FORT WILLIAM PH33 6RW (01397 702341; Fax: 01397 706174). This family-run hotel overlooks Loch Linnhe, two miles south of Fort William, excellent for touring the West Highlands. All rooms have TV, hairdryer, hospitality tray and private facilities. B&B from £27.50pppn. Three nights DB&B from £129pp (Spring/Autumn). STB ★★★ Hotel. Phone or write for colour brochure and tariff. [🐕]
e-mail: reception@clanmacduff.co.uk   website: www.clanmacduff.co.uk

Glen Shiel (Inverness-shire)

Valley on River Shiel in Skye & Lochalsh district.

KINTAIL LODGE HOTEL, SHIEL BRIDGE, GLENSHIEL IV40 8HL (01599 511275). Beautifully situated on the shores of Loch Duich 6 miles south of Eilean Donan Castle. We guarantee your comfort and we promise you the best of Highland food and hospitality. Dogs welcome.
e-mail: kintaillodgehotel@btinternet.com   website: www.kintaillodgehotel.co.uk

Grantown-on-Spey (Inverness-shire)

Market town and resort 19 miles south of Forres.

TIGH NA SGIATH COUNTRY HOUSE HOTEL, DULNAIN BRIDGE, NEAR GRANTOWN-ON-SPEY PH26 3PA (01479 851345). Former home of the Lipton Tea Family, this elegant mansion house is set in its own fabulous grounds. Romantic open log fires, excellent Scottish cuisine using local and organic produce. [Pets £5.50 per night]
e-mail: iain@tigh-na-sgiath.co.uk   website: www.tigh-na-sgiath.co.uk

Highlands SCOTLAND 371

Inverness (Inverness-shire)

Known as "The Capital of the Highlands". Airport, excellent shopping. Ideal touring base.

ROWAN COTTAGE. Charming 2-bedroom timber cottage set in wild heather garden. Fully equipped. Ideal for dog lovers. Contact: MRS JANET SUTHERLAND, LOCH NESS HIDEAWAYS, AULTNAGOIRE, ERROGIE, BY INVERNESS IV2 6UH (Tel/Fax 01456 486711).
e-mail: janet@lochnesshideaways.co.uk   website: www.lochnesshideaways.co.uk

DUNAIN PARK HOTEL & RESTAURANT, LOCH NESS ROAD, INVERNESS IV3 8JN (01463 230512; Fax: 01463 224 532. Stunning Georgian Country House surrounded by 6 acres of parkland. Warm welcome, discreet and attentive service. Two garden cottages welcome pets.
e-mail: info@dunainparkhotel.co.uk   website: www.dunainparkhotel.co.uk

Killin (Perthshire)

Picturesque village at Western head of Loch Tay.

LYNNE AND ALISTAIR FERGUSON, 'BROCHANACH' 43 FINGAL ROAD, KILLIN FK21 8XA (01567 820028). Bed and varied Scottish Breakfast in small, tranquil village in the heart of Highland Perthshire. Ideal touring base. "Good walkies area" – dogs are especially welcome and stay free. [🐾 pw!]
e-mail: alifer@msn.com

Kincraig (Inverness-shire)

Attractive Highland village close to Loch Insh and Glenfeshie, midway between Aviemore and Kingussie.

NICK & PATSY THOMPSON, INSH HOUSE GUESTHOUSE AND SELF-CATERING COTTAGES, KINCRAIG, NEAR KINGUSSIE PH21 1NU (01540 651377). Insh House has 5 en suite bedrooms; 2 self-catering cottages each sleep 4. Ideal for many outdoor activities and good touring base. Dogs and children welcome. Totally non-smoking. STB ★★★ [🐾]
e-mail: inshhouse@btinternet.com   website: www.kincraig.com/inshhouse

Kingussie (Inverness-shire)

Small town on River Spey 28 miles south of Inverness.

ALLT GYNACK GUEST HOUSE, GYNACK VILLA, 1 HIGH STREET, KINGUSSIE, NEAR AVIEMORE PH21 1HS. Family-owned Victorian guest house in a beautiful part of the Highlands. In its own grounds with private car park. Open all year. Huge range of activities. Excellent restaurants nearby. STB ★★★. [🐾]
e-mail: alltgynack@tiscali.co.uk   website: www.alltgynack.com

COLUMBA HOUSE HOTEL AND GARDEN RESTAURANT, MANSE ROAD, KINGUSSIE PH21 1JF (01540 661402). Quiet Highland retreat offering highest standards of hospitality, care and accommodation. Candlelit Garden Restaurant. Ground-floor rooms with own front doors, perfect for doggie holidays. STB ★★★ [pw! Pets £3 per night, £10 per week]
e-mail: myra@columbahousehotel.com   website: www.columbahousehotel.com

Kinlochbervie (Sutherland)

Village on north side of Loch Inchard.

THE KINLOCHBERVIE HOTEL, KINLOCHBERVIE, SUTHERLAND IV27 4RP (01971 521 275; Fax: 01971 521 438). Pet-friendly, family-run hotel in stunning location. Superb sea and hill views, beautiful beaches and an abundance of wildlife. Very comfortable en suite rooms, restaurant, bars, coffee shop. From £35 B&B.
e-mail: klbhotel@btconnect.com   website: www.kinlochberviehotel.com

Lairg (Sutherland)

Village 17 miles west of Golspie..

LAIRG HIGHLAND HOTEL, MAIN STREET, LAIRG IV27 4DB (01549 402243; Fax: 01549 402593). An ideal base from which to tour the North of Scotland. Superb, home-cooked food is served in the restaurant and lounge bar. All bedrooms are furnished to a high standard, with en suite facilities, colour TV and tea/coffee. STB ★★★ [🐾]
e-mail: info@highland-hotel.co.uk   website: www.highland-hotel.co.uk

Loch Carron (Wester Ross)

Scenic area on West Coast of Scotland, 63 miles from Inverness.

THE COTTAGE, STROMECARRONACH, LOCHCARRON WEST, STRATHCARRON. Small, stone-built Highland cottage, double bedroom, shower room, open plan kitchen/living room, fully equipped. Panoramic views over Loch Carron and the mountains. For further details please phone. MRS A.G. MACKENZIE, STROMECARRONACH, LOCHCARRON WEST, STRATHCARRON IV54 8YH (01520 722284) [🐾]
website: www.lochcarron.org

Loch Ness (Inverness-shire)

Home of 'Nessie', extending for 23 miles from Fort Augustus to south of Inverness.

WILDERNESS COTTAGES. Self-catering cottages all around Loch Ness plus small selection of West coast properties. Pets welcome. Please see website for details or for a brochure contact: GORDON & CORINNE ROBERTS, ROEBUCK COTTAGE, ERROGIE IV2 6UH (01456 486358). [1 dog free, extra dogs £10 each per week] STB★★★/★★★★/★★★★★ SELF CATERING
e-mail: corinne@wildernesscottages.co.uk   website: www.wildernesscottages.co.uk

JUSTINE HUDSON, WILDSIDE HIGHLAND LODGES, WILDSIDE, WHITEBRIDGE, INVERNESS IV2 6UN. (01456 486373; Fax: 01456 486371). Charming riverside lodges. Log fires and mountain views. Sleep 2 to 8 people. Pets welcome. Free fishing. STB ★★★★ Self-catering. [Pets £15 per booking].
e-mail: info@wildsidelodges.com   website: www.wildsidelodges.com

Loch Torridon (Wester Ross)

Sea loch in an area of dramatic mountain scenery.

TIGH AN EILEAN HOTEL & SHIELDAIG BAR AND COASTAL KITCHEN, SHIELDAIG ON LOCH TORRIDON IV54 8XN (01520 755251; Fax: 01520 755321). In the picturesque 200-year-old fishing village of Shieldaig. Spectacular walking, deserted beaches. Award-winning restaurant. Fresh seafood delivered daily. Good Hotel Guide, AA Britain's Best Hotels, Good Food Guide.
e-mail: tighaneilean@keme.co.uk

Muir of Ord (Inverness-shire)

Village 20km west of Inverness.

ORD HOUSE HOTEL, MUIR OF ORD IV6 7UH (01463 870492). 17th Century country house. Extensive gardens and woodlands for dogs to run around in. Large, airy bedrooms. Log fires. Restaurant. AA ★★ and Rosette. [pw! 🐾]
e-mail: admin@ord-house.co.uk   website: www.ord-house.co.uk

Nethy Bridge (Inverness-shire)

Popular Strathspey resort on River Nethy with extensive Abernethy Forest to the south. Impressive mountain scenery. Grantown-on-Spey 5 miles.

SPEYSIDE COTTAGES, NETHY BRIDGE. Relax in 4 comfortable cottages (sleep 2-7) with fenced gardens, on riverbank with wonderful forest walks. Pets welcome. £200-£595 per week, includes full linen and towels. Contact BRIAN AND MOIRA PATRICK, 1 CHAPELTON PLACE, FORRES, MORAY IV36 2NL (01309 672505).
e-mail: brian@speysidecottages.co.uk   website: www.speysidecottages.co.uk

MONDHUIE CHALETS & B&B, NETHY BRIDGE PH25 3DF (01479 821062). Situated in the country between Aviemore and Grantown-on-Spey, two comfortable, self-catering chalets, or you can have Dinner, B&B in the house. A warm welcome awaits you. Pets welcome. Red squirrels seen daily. Free internet access. [🐾]
e-mail: david@mondhuie.com   website: www.mondhuie.com

BALNAGOWAN MILL AND WOODLARK, NETHY BRIDGE. Comfortable, modern 3 bedroom cottages in secluded locations in the Cairngorms National Park. Woodland and riverside walks on the doorstep. Ideal for pets. Furnished to a high standard with full central heating. £260-£590 per week incl. of electricity, bed linen and towels. VisitScotland ★★★★. ASSC MEMBER. Contact PAULA FRASER, 33 ARGYLE GROVE, DUNBLANE FK15 9DT (01786 824957) [🐾]
e-mail: paulajfraser@aol.com

Highlands

SCOTLAND 373

Poolewe (Ross-shire)

Village lying between Lochs Ewe and Maree with the River Ewe flowing through.

POOLEWE, WESTER ROSS. (01445 781765) Dogs welcome in non-smoking Bed & Breakfast. Convenient for local beaches and Torridon Mountains. Please phone or e-mail for further information. STB ★★★ B&B [🐕]
e-mail: dgeorge@globalnet.co.uk   website: www.davidgeorge.co.uk

MR A. URQUHART, CROFTERS COTTAGES, 15 CROFT, POOLEWE IV22 2JY (01445 781 268). Two traditional cottages situated in a scenic and tranquil area, ideal for a "get away from it all" holiday. Comfortably furnished with all mod cons. [🐕]
e-mail: croftcottages@btopenworld.com   website: www.crofterscottages.co.uk

Rhiconich (Sutherland)

Locality at the head of Loch Inchard on west coast of Sutherland District.

RHICONICH HOTEL, SUTHERLAND, N. W. HIGHLANDS IV27 4RN (01971 521224; Fax: 01971 521732). She's your best friend so why leave her at home, bring her to Rhiconich Hotel, she'll be made equally as welcome as you will. A place where we put service, hospitality and really fresh food as a priority, but why don't you come and see for yourself? STB ★★★ [🐕]
e-mail: info@rhiconichhotel.co.uk   website: www.rhiconichhotel.co.uk

LYNN & GRAHAM, GULL COTTAGE, ACHRIESGILL, RHICONICH, SUTHERLAND IV27 4RJ (01971 521717). High quality accommodation on the wild and unspoilt west coast. Superb scenery and excellent walks on mountains, moors and beaches. Pets welcome; secure dog run. STB ★★★ Self-Catering. [🐕]
e-mail: grahamandlynn@theuphouse.co.uk   website: www.theuphouse.co.uk

Spean Bridge (Inverness-shire)

Village on River Spean at foot of Loch Lochy. Site of WWII Commando Memorial.

NEIL & ELIZABETH OCKENDEN, ACHNABOBANE FARMHOUSE, ACHNABOBANE, SPEAN BRIDGE PH34 4EX (01397 712919). Excellent accommodation and comfort. An ideal central base for exploring the Highlands. Local area has wide variety of outdoor pursuits, wildlife and attractions. STB ★★★.
e-mail: enquiries@achnabobane.co.uk   website: www.achnabobane.net

RIVERSIDE LODGES, INVERGLOY, SPEAN BRIDGE PH34 4DY (01397 712684). The ultimate Highland location. Three lodges, each sleep 6, in 12 acres of woodland garden on Loch Lochy. Free fishing. Open all year. Pets welcome. Brochure on request. STB ★★★★ [🐕]
e-mail: enquiries@riversidelodge.org.uk   website: www.riversidelodge.org.uk

Tongue (Sutherland)

Village near north coast of Caithness District on east side of Kyle of Tongue.

BORGIE LODGE HOTEL, SKERRAY, TONGUE KW14 7TH (Tel & Fax: 01641 521332). Set in a secluded Highland glen lies Borgie Lodge. Try pony trekking, fishing and forest walks. Open fires and fine dining. AA ★★ and Rosette, STB ★★★★ [🐕]
e-mail: info@borgielodgehotel.co.uk   website: www.borgielodgehotel.co.uk

Whitebridge (Inverness-shire)

Hamlet in the heart of the Scottish Highlands, 4 miles from Loch Ness and 9 miles from Fort Augustus.

WHITEBRIDGE HOTEL, WHITEBRIDGE, SOUTH LOCH NESS IV2 6UN (01456 486226; Fax: 01456 486413). Peaceful location with magnificent mountain views and excellent walks. Friendly locals' bar with home-cooked food. 12 en suite rooms. B&B from £35pppn. AA ★★[🐕]
e-mail: info@whitebridgehotel.co.uk   website: www.whitebridgehotel.co.uk

SCOTLAND — Lanarkshire

Biggar, Harthill

WALSTON MANSION FARMHOUSE

Well known for its real home-from-home atmosphere, hearty breakfast menu and delicious evening meals. Pets by arrangement. Ideal touring base.
Margaret Kirby, Walston, Carnwath, By Biggar ML11 8NF
Tel: 01899 810338 • Fax: 01899 810334
e-mail: margaret.kirby@walstonmansion.co.uk • www.walstonmansion.co.uk

CARMICHAEL COUNTRY COTTAGES

Westmains, Carmichael, Biggar ML12 6PG • Tel: 01899 308336 • Fax: 01899 308481

200 year old stone cottages in this 700 year old family estate. We guarantee comfort, warmth and a friendly welcome in an accessible, unique, rural and historic time capsule. We farm deer, cattle and sheep and sell meats and tartan - Carmichael of course. Open all year. Terms from £225 to £595. 15 cottages with a total of 32 bedrooms. Private tennis court and fishing loch, cafe, farm shop and visitor centre

ASSC   e-mail: chiefcarm@aol.com • www.carmichael.co.uk/cottages   STB 2-4 Stars

Blairmains Farm, Harthill ML7 5TJ   Tel: 01501 751278

Attractive farmhouse on small farm of 72 acres. Immediately adjacent to Junction 5 of M8 motorway. Ideal centre for touring, with Edinburgh, Glasgow, Stirling 30 minutes' drive. One double, three twin, one single (three en suite); bathroom; sittingroom, diningroom; sun porch. Central heating. Children welcome. Pets welcome. Ample grounds for walking. Car essential – parking. Bed and Breakfast from £20; weekly rates available. Reduced rates for children. Open all year.   e-mail: heather@blairmains.freeserve.co.uk • www.blairmains.co.uk

Biggar

Small town set round broad main street. Gasworks museum, puppet theatre seating 100, street museum displaying old shop fronts and interiors. Peebles 13 miles.

WALSTON MANSION FARMHOUSE, WALSTON, CARNWATH, BY BIGGAR ML11 8NF (01899 810338; Fax: 01899 810334). Well known for its real home-from-home atmosphere, hearty breakfast menu and delicious evening meals. Pets by arrangement. Ideal touring base.
e-mail: margaret.kirby@walstonmansion.co.uk   website: www.walstonmansion.co.uk

CARMICHAEL COUNTRY COTTAGES, CARMICHAEL ESTATE, BY BIGGAR ML12 6PG (01899 308336; Fax: 01899 308481). Our stone cottages nestle in the woods and fields of our historic family-run estate. Ideal homes for families, pets and dogs. 15 cottages, 32 bedrooms. STB ★★/★★★★ Self catering. Open all year. £225 to £595 per week. [pw! 🐾]
e-mail: chiefcarm@aol.com   website: www.carmichael.co.uk/cottages

Harthill

Village 5 miles south-west of Bathgate

MRS STEPHENS, BLAIRMAINS FARM, HARTHILL ML7 5TJ (01501 751278; Fax: 01501 753383). Attractive farmhouse on small farm. Ideal for touring. Children welcome. Bed and Breakfast from £20; weekly rates available. Reduced rates for children. Open all year. [🐾]
e-mail: heather@blairmains.freeserve.co.uk   website: www.blairmains.co.uk

Pet-Friendly
Pubs, Inns & Hotels
on pages 438-443
Please note that these establishments may not feature in the main section of this book

Perth & Kinross

Aberfeldy, Crieff, Glenshee, Huntingtower (Perth), Killiekrankie

Acharn, By Aberfeldy

Escape the rat race in comfort, peace and tranquillity.
Loch, woodlands and mountains.
Ideal for walking around farmland in majestic scenery.
Each lodge has own enclosed garden.
Self-catering. £230-£615.

Tel: 01887 830209

Fax: 01887 830802

e-mail: remony@btinternet.com
www.lochtaylodges.co.uk

LOCH TAY LODGES

DULL FARM HOLIDAY LODGES

Luxury accommodation with panoramic views in two pine lodges on small farm near Aberfeldy, in the heart of Perthshire.
Fully equipped, well maintained; completely fenced.
Touring, walking, fishing, golf or simply enjoy the peace and tranquillity.
Prices from £170 per week.
Short Breaks available.

Aberfeldy, Perthshire PH15 2JQ
Tel: 01887 820270
info@dullfarm.freeserve.co.uk
www.self-cateringperthshire.com

ABERTURRET COTTAGE, CRIEFF, PERTHSHIRE

Beautiful traditional cottage with enormous private garden by the river. Three bedrooms (sleeps 4 or 5). Rural situation but just one mile outside the town of Crieff. Excellent base for walking, cycling and exploring Perthshire. Heating, bedlinen and towels included in price.

Contact: JUDY WATT on 01764 650064 or judywatt@aberturret.com • www.aberturret.com

Dalnoid Holiday Cottages, Glenshee, Perthshire

2 cottages each sleeping 4, including king-size with en suite. Large open-plan living area. Underfloor heating throughout and wood-burning stoves. Private enclosed gardens and access to 6 acres. Ideal base for walking.
Prices £315 - £550 per week. Short breaks available.

Contact details: Sue Smith • Tel: 01250 882200
e-mail: info@dalnoid.co.uk • www.dalnoid.co.uk

HUNTINGTOWER PERTH

ORCHARD COTTAGE, modern 2-bedroom cottage, with large garden room and log fire, STB Disablity Award 3. Also available STABLE COTTAGE, one bedroom with bed settee. Central heating and power included in our prices. Secluded private grounds with ample walking areas and large pond.

Mrs G. Mackintosh, The Plantation, Huntingtowerfield, Perth PH1 3JL
Tel & Fax: 01738 620783
e-mail: sales@perthcottage.com • www.perthcottage.co.uk

Atholl Cottage • Killiecrankie • Perthshire

Delightful stone cottage offers high quality accommodation for 5 people.
Log Fire. Private grounds. Ideal for exploring historic countryside.
For further details contact: **Joan Troup, Dalnasgadh, Killiecrankie, Pitlochry, Perthshire PH16 5LN • Tel: 01796 470017 • Fax: 01796 472183**
e-mail: info@athollcottage.co.uk • www.athollcottage.co.uk

Perth & Kinross
Killin, Lochearnhead, Pitlochry

Only a few minutes' stroll to the village, park and hills; gateway to the Loch Lomond and Trossachs National Park. Your dogs can sleep in your room and are welcome in the sitting room and garden.

DOGS ESPECIALLY WELCOME (and stay free) IN GREAT WALKIES AREA

'Brochanach', 43 Fingal Road, Killin Perthshire FK21 8XA
Tel: 01567 820028 • e-mail: alifer@msn.com

WESTER LIX

At Wester Lix we offer two self contained properties both with their own unique character and style for that real "home from home" comfort. Wester Lix is set in a peaceful rural location surrounded by hills and overlooking our own private lochan.

We are three miles from Killin. Wester Lix is an excellent base for all outdoor activities including water sports, whilst also being ideally central for sightseeing.

Both Jonna's Cottage and The Farm House offer stylish accommodation for groups or families of 4 (5 by arrangement) with oil fired central heating and double glazing, wood burning stove/open fire and TV with Sky Digital. Jonna's has the addition of both bedrooms being en suite – plus it also offers a sauna as well as a private decking area with dining furniture. Well behaved pet, or pets are welcome by arrangement.

Gill and Dave Hunt, The Steading, Wester Lix, Perthshire FK21 8RD
Tel: 01567 820990 or 07747862641
e-mail: gill@westerlix.net • www.westerlix.net

CLACHAN COTTAGE HOTEL
Lochearnhead, Perthshire FK19 8PU

• Family hotel on shores of Loch Earn in a spectacular lochside setting. • Within Loch Lomond & Trossachs National Park, 29 miles from Stirling.
• 30 Munros within 30 minutes

AWARD-WINNING TASTE OF SCOTLAND RESTAURANT
GROUP/SOCIETY RATES • **PETS WELCOME** •
Tel: 01567 830247 • Fax: 01567 830300
www.clachancottagehotel.com

Four attractive, comfortable and spacious pine lodges (one assisted disabled facilities) and two modern caravan holiday homes set in a secluded woodland garden just south of Pitlochry. Well behaved pets welcome in all units. Great walks in surrounding area.
01796 473080 • www.dalshian-chalets.co.uk
e-mail: info@dalshian-chalets.co.uk

Perth & Kinross

Pitlochry, St Fillans, Strathyre

The White House • Moulin, Pitlochry, Perthshire PH16 5EL

A mid 17th Century cottage on quiet village side street. Sleeps 6. Fully equipped. Central Highland location means many historical attractions and golf courses nearby.
Contact: Mr Guy James, The Yellow House, Springhill, Eastington, Stonehouse, Gloucestershire GL10 3AT • Tel: 01453 823992/755552 • Mob: 07767 330986
e-mail: jamesth9@aol.com • www.thewhitehousemoulin.com

The finest lochside setting in the Southern Highlands

Fine dining in award winning two AA Red Rosette Restaurant or more informal Bistro both offering imaginative modern Scottish cuisine using only the best fresh local produce

Centrally placed in Scotland to enjoy many scenic day trips. For the energetic there is a wide variety of walks, or as an alternative how about a Munro?

Individually decorated hotel bedrooms, and four poster rooms, many with loch views, or secluded hillside chalets.

Hi there fellow four-leggers, you are all very welcome here free, as long as you bring your charges. We have great walking and of course an excellent chef. We can also now offer the Pet Concierge Service, please check the website. Pleas call for Best Deals. **Sham** *and* **Pagne** *(Resident Canine Reservations Managers).*

The Four Seasons Hotel
St Fillans, Perthshire PH6 2NF
Tel: 01764 685333   e-mail: sham@thefourseasonshotel.co.uk

THE MUNRO INN Strathyre, Perthshire FK18 8NA
Tel: 01877 384333 • www.munro-inn.com

Chilled out Robbie warmly welcomes doggy friends to the Munro Inn in beautiful Highland Perthshire. Perfect base for walking, cycling, climbing, water sports, fishing or relaxing! Great home cooking, lively bar, luxurious en suite bedrooms, drying room, broadband internet.

Visit the FHG website
www.holidayguides.com
for details of the wide choice of accommodation featured in the full range of FHG titles

Perth & Kinross
Strathyre

ARDOCH LODGE

12 acres of grounds surrounded by spectacular mountain scenery, a peaceful and tranquil setting for our two log cabins and cottage. Whatever the weather there is much to see and do with plenty of walking straight from the door. Up to four dogs allowed in each property.

Telephone 01877 384666 or email ardoch@btinternet.com for a brochure

Ardoch Lodge, Strathyre,
near Callander FK18 8NF
www.ardochlodge.co.uk

Aberfeldy

Small town standing on both sides of Uriar Burn near its confluence with the River Tay. Pitlochry 8 miles.

LOCH TAY LODGES, REMONY, ACHARN, ABERFELDY PH15 2HR (01887 830209). Enjoy hill walking, golf, sailing or touring. Salmon and trout fishing available. Log fires. Pets welcome. Walks along loch shore from house. STB ★★★ SELF CATERING in village close to Loch. For brochure, contact MRS P. W. DUNCAN MILLAR at above address. [🐾]
e-mail: remony@btinternet.com   website: www.lochtaylodges.co.uk

SHEILA AND PETER CAMPBELL, DULL FARM HOLIDAY LODGES, ABERFELDY PH15 2JQ (01887 820270). Luxury accommodation in 2 pine lodges on small farm. Fully equipped, well maintained; completely fenced. Panoramic views. Touring, walking, fishing, golf. Short Breaks available. [Pets £10 per week].
e-mail: info@dullfarm.freeserve.co.uk   website: www.self-cateringperthshire.com

Crieff

Town and resort 16 miles west of Perth.

ABERTURRET COTTAGE, CRIEFF. Beautiful traditional cottage with enormous private garden by the river. Three bedrooms (sleeps 4 or 5). Excellent base for walking, cycling and exploring Perthshire. Heating, bedlinen and towels incl. in price. Contact JUDY WATT (01764 650064). [Pets £15 per week]
e-mail: judywatt@aberturret.com   website: www.aberturret.com

Glenshee

Very popular winter sports area, good base for touring.

DALNOID HOLIDAY COTTAGES, GLENSHEE. Two cottages each sleeping 4, including king-size with en suite. Underfloor heating throughout and wood-burning stoves. Private enclosed gardens. Ideal base for walking. Prices £315 - £550 per week. Short breaks available. SUE SMITH (01250 882320). [🐾]
e-mail: info@dalnoid.co.uk   website: www.dalnoid.co.uk

Perth & Kinross

Huntingtower

Village 3 miles north west of Perth.

ORCHARD COTTAGE, modern 2-bedroom cottage, with large garden room and log fire, £350 - £700 per week. STABLE COTTAGE, one bedroom with bed settee, £250 - £450 per week. Central heating and power included. Secluded private grounds with ample walking areas and large pond. Open all year. Short Breaks available. STB ★★★★. STB Disablity Award 3. Contact: MRS G. MACKINTOSH, THE PLANTATION, HUNTINGTOWERFIELD, PERTH PH1 3JL (Tel & Fax: 01738 620783). [Dogs £20 per week, small animals free of charge].
e-mail: sales@perthcottage.co.uk   website: www.perthcottage.co.uk

Killiecrankie

Village on River Garry 3 miles south east of Blair Atholl.

ATHOLL COTTAGE, KILLIECRANKIE. Delightful stone cottage offers high quality accommodation for 5 people. Log fire. Private grounds. Ideal for exploring historic countryside. For further details contact: JOAN TROUP, DALNASGADH, KILLIECRANKIE, PITLOCHRY PH16 5LN (01796 470017; Fax: 01796 472183). [🐕]
e-mail: info@athollcottage.co.uk   website: www.athollcottage.co.uk

Killin

Village at confluence of Rivers Dochart and Lochay at head of Loch Tay.

LYNNE AND ALISTAIR FERGUSON, 'BROCHANACH' 43 FINGAL ROAD, KILLIN FK21 8XA (01567 820028). Bed and varied Scottish Breakfast in small, tranquil village in the heart of Highland Perthshire. Ideal touring base. "Good walkies area" – dogs are especially welcome and stay free. [🐕 pw!]
e-mail: alifer@msn.com

GILL & DAVE HUNT, THE STEADING, WESTER LIX, KILLIN FK21 8RD (01567 820990 & 07747 862641). Two fully equipped self contained properties with Sky TV, wood-burning stove/open fire. One with sauna and private decking. Well behaved pet, or pets by arrangement. [Pets £15 per week for first pet, then £5 per pet]
e-mail: gill@westerlix.net   website: www.westerlix.net

Kinloch Rannoch

Village at foot of Loch Rannoch.

KILVRECHT CAMP SITE, KINLOCH RANNOCH, PERTHSHIRE (01350 727284; Fax: 01350 727811). Secluded campsite on a level open area in quiet, secluded woodland setting. Fishing available for brown trout on Loch Rannoch. Several trails begin from campsite. Please write, fax or telephone for further information. [🐕]

Lochearnhead

Village at head of Loch Earn 6 miles South of Killin.

CLACHAN COTTAGE HOTEL, LOCHEARNHEAD FK19 8PU (01567 830247; Fax: 01567 830300). Well placed in central Scotland for touring. Excellent walking, mountain biking and fishing. Watersports available from the hotel. Award-winning "Taste of Scotland" restaurant. [🐕]
website: www.clachancottagehotel.com

Pitlochry

Popular resort on River Tummel in beautiful Perthshire Highlands. Excellent golf, loch and river fishing. Famous for summer Festival Theatre; distillery, Highland Games.

DALSHIAN CHALETS, OLD PERTH ROAD, PITLOCHRY PH16 5TD (01796 473 080). Four lovely pine lodges and two modern caravan holiday homes set in woodland garden. Five minutes from Pitlochry. Well behaved pets welcome in all units. ASSC. STB ★★★★ [Pets £15 per week]
e-mail: info@dalshian-chalets.co.uk   website: www.dalshian-chalets.co.uk

THE WHITE HOUSE, MOULIN, PITLOCHRY PH16 5EL. A mid 17th Century cottage on quiet village side street. Sleeps 6. Fully equipped. Many historical attractions and golf courses nearby. STB ★★. Contact: GUY JAMES, THE YELLOW HOUSE, SPRINGHILL, EASTINGTON, STONEHOUSE, GLOUCESTERSHIRE GL10 3AT (01453 823992/755552; Mob:07767 330986). [Pets £15 per week]
e-mail: jamesth9@aol.com   website: www.thewhitehousemoulin.com

St Fillans

Village at foot of Loch Earn, 5 miles west of Comrie.

THE FOUR SEASONS HOTEL, ST FILLANS PH6 2NF (01764 685333). Ideal holiday venue for pets and their owners. Spectacular Highland scenery, walking, fishing, watersports. Wonderful food. Full details on request. STB ★★★ Hotel, AA ★★★ and 2 Red Rosettes, Signpost, Best Loved Hotels. [🐾]
e-mail: sham@thefourseasonshotel.co.uk   website: www.thefourseasonshotel.co.uk

Strathyre

Village set in the centre of Strathyre State Forest.

THE MUNRO INN, STRATHYRE FK18 8NA (01877 384333). Chilled out Robbie warmly welcomes doggy friends to the Munro Inn in beautiful Highland Perthshire. Perfect base for walking, cycling, climbing, water sports, fishing or relaxing! Great home cooking, lively bar, luxurious en suite bedrooms, drying room, broadband internet.
website: www.munro-inn.com

YVONNE & JOHN HOWES, ARDOCH LODGE, STRATHYRE FK18 8NF (01877 384666). Two log cabins and cottage in wonderful mountain scenery, excellent touring base. Comfortably furnished and well equipped. Pets most welcome. STB ★★★/★★★★ SELF CATERING. [pw! 🐾]
e-mail: ardoch@btinternet.com   website: www.ardochlodge.co.uk

Stirling & The Trossachs
Aberfoyle

TROSSACHS HOLIDAY PARK by Aberfoyle, Stirlingshire

- 40 acre landscaped park with oak and bluebell wood
- 45 exclusive touring pitches - mostly fully serviced with water, drainage, 16 amp electricity and TV hook up • Sheltered camping area
- Shop • Games/TV lounge • Launderette • Children's play area
- Toilets, free showers and hair dryers
- Woodland walk • Enclosed dog walk
- Seasonal and Mini Season enquiries welcomed

The perfect base to explore the Trossachs National Park.
Our holiday caravans offer peace and quiet with views to the hills.

Trossachs Holiday Park, by Aberfoyle, Stirlingshire FK8 3SA
Tel: 01877 382 614 • Fax: 01877 382 732 • Freephone: 0800 1971971
e-mail: info@trossachsholidays.co.uk • www.trossachsholidays.co.uk

Aberfoyle

Small town at heart of Loch Lomond and Trossachs National Park.

TROSSACHS HOLIDAY PARK, BY ABERFOYLE FK8 3SA (01877 382 614; Fax: 01877 382 732; Freephone: 0800 1971292). 40 acre landscaped park with 45 exclusive touring pitches - mostly fully serviced. The perfect base to explore the Trossachs National Park. Enclosed dog walk. STB ★★★★★. David Bellamy Gold Award.
e-mail: info@trossachsholidays.co.uk   website: www.trossachsholidays.co.uk

Scottish Islands - Isle of Harris / Isle of Lewis SCOTLAND 381

Isle of Harris
Leverburgh

Carminish House Bed and Breakfast

Secluded, spacious, traditionally built B&B, with three twin/double en suite rooms, lounge with panoramic views over the Sound of Harris. Payphone, satellite TV, Wi-Fi. Ideal place to explore the Western Isles. Garden and parking. Full Scottish breakfast. Excellent local places to eat. Non-smoking. Children and pets welcome.
Contact Howard and Sallie Lomas, 1A Strond, Leverburgh, Isle of Harris HS5 3UD
Tel: 01859 520400 • E-mail: info@carminish.com • www.carminish.com

Leverburgh

Village on S.W. Coast of Harris 4 miles N.W. of Rennish Point.

HOWARD AND SALLIE LOMAS, CARMINISH HOUSE, 1A STROND, LEVERBURGH HS5 3UD (01859 520400) Secluded, spacious, traditionally built B&B, with three twin/double en suite rooms. Panoramic views. Payphone, satellite TV, Wi-Fi. Garden and parking. Non-smoking. Children and pets welcome. STB ★★★★.[🐾]
e-mail: info@carminish.com   website: www.carminish.com

Isle of Lewis
Stornoway

Excellent Stornoway-based Bed & Breakfast in light, modern and spacious 7-bedroomed family home.
Jannel Bed & Breakfast, 5 Stewart Drive,
Stornoway, Isle of Lewis HS1 2TU
T: 0800 634 3270
E: stay@jannel-stornoway.co.uk
www.jannel-stornoway.co.uk

Stornoway

Chief town of Lewis, with large natural harbour.

Jannel Bed & Breakfast, 5 Stewart Drive, Stornoway, Isle of Lewis HS1 2TU (0800 634 3270). Excellent Stornoway-based Bed & Breakfast in light, modern and spacious 7-bedroomed family home. Enclosed garden. Off-street parking. Children and pets welcome. STB ★★★★.[🐾]
e-mail: stay@jannel-stornoway.co.uk   website: www.jannel-stornoway.co.uk

Symbols

🐾	Indicates that pets are welcome free of charge.
£	Indicates that a charge is made for pets: nightly or weekly.
pw	Shows some special provision for pets; exercise facility, feeding or accommodation arrangement.
⌂	Indicates separate pets accommodation.

"Torlochan" • Isle of Mull

Torlochan is a small croft situated in the centre of the Isle of Mull, with views over Loch na Keal. It is an ideal base from which to explore all of Mull.

We have two comfortable spacious log cabins, which have been completely refurbished in 2009 with new kitchens, bathrooms, lighting and wooden flooring. They can sleep 4 people and cost from £350 per week; short winter breaks from £60 per night, minimum 3 nights.

The Farmhouse has a lounge, kitchen/dining room, two sitting rooms with open fire and log stove. It sleeps 6 people from £595 per week and can sleep 8 when using a separate log cabin with twin bedroom for an additional £200 per week.

More information from:
**Hylda Marsh,
Baliscate House,
Tobermory, Isle of Mull PA75 6QA
Tel: 01688 302048 • Fax: 01688 302251
e-mail: info@islandholidaycottages.com
www.torlochan.com
www.islandholidaycottages.com**

Torlochan

Situated in the centre of Mull, 20 minutes from Tobermory and 25 minutes from Craignure.

TORLOCHAN, GRULINE, ISLE OF MULL. Situated in centre of Mull with views over Loch na Keal, two log cabins and a farmhouse for self-catering. [£10 per dog per week; other pets free]
e-mail: info@islandholidaycottages.com   www.torlochan.com/www.islandholidaycottages.com

---

Other specialised holiday guides from FHG

PUBS & INNS OF BRITAIN • **COUNTRY HOTELS** OF BRITAIN
WEEKEND & SHORT BREAK HOLIDAYS IN BRITAIN
THE GOLF GUIDE WHERE TO PLAY, WHERE TO STAY
500 GREAT PLACES TO STAY • **SELF-CATERING HOLIDAYS** IN BRITAIN
BED & BREAKFAST STOPS • **CARAVAN & CAMPING HOLIDAYS**
FAMILY BREAKS IN BRITAIN

Published annually: available in all good bookshops or direct from the publisher:
FHG Guides, Abbey Mill Business Centre, Seedhill, Paisley PA1 1TJ
Tel: 0141 887 0428 • Fax: 0141 889 7204
e-mail: admin@fhguides.co.uk • www.holidayguides.com

Scottish Islands - Orkney Islands

SCOTLAND

Kirkwall, Orphir, South Ronaldsay, Stenness

The Pickaquoy Centre Caravan & Camping Park • Kirkwall, Orkney
Tel: 01856 879900 • www.pickaquoy.co.uk • e-mail: enquiries@pickaquoy.com

The St Magnus Cathedral is the central feature of Kirkwall, Orkney's main town, a relaxing and interesting centre from which to explore the surrounding areas. The site is situated within The Pickaquoy Centre complex, an impressive modern leisure facility offering a range of activities for all the family.

Birsay Outdoor Centre/ Caravan & Camping Site
A new site located in the picturesque north west of Orkney

Point of Ness Caravan & Camping Site • Stromness, Orkney
Stromness is a small, picturesque town with impressive views of the hills of Hoy. The site is one mile from the harbour in a quiet, shoreline location. Many leisure activities are available close by, including fishing, sea angling, golf and a swimming & fitness centre.

For Birsay and Point of Ness contact: Department of Education & Recreation Services, Orkney Islands Council, Kirkwall, Orkney KW15 1NY • Tel: 01856 873535 ext. 2404

LITTLE BU · ORPHIR · ORKNEY

Little Bu is a self-catering chalet-bungalow maintained to a very high standard and sleeping six. Open-plan livingroom/dining area and newly fitted kitchen, verandah, patio/decking area, large garden and garden furniture. Close to the sea.
Contact: Mrs Shephard, Windbreck, Butchers Lane, Boughton, Northampton NN2 8SL
Tel: 01604 843275 • jshephard@northamptonshire.gov.uk • www.littlebu.com

Banks of Orkney Self-catering and B&B

Two cottages (STB ★★★) and converted barn (STB ★★★★). Located close to ferries, with stunning views over the Pentland Firth. Each cottage sleeps up to 2, and the barn sleeps 5/7. Licensed restaurant on site. For details contact:
**Carole Fletcher, Banks of Orkney, South Ronaldsay KW17 2RW
Tel: 01856 831605 • www.banksoforkney.co.uk**

Outbrecks in Orkney offer exceptional and unique self-catering cottages. Open all year – dogs welcome

Within an outstanding National Scenic Area, unwind and relax in comfort, explore the spectacular surrounding countryside and view incredible skies and sunsets. All our non-smoking accommodation is situated within its own private acres of dog-walking fields, in fabulous sea and loch locations by the archaeological World Heritage Site in Stenness.
Each cottage is within 200 metres of the shore, except for Harefields (which nestles in its own land). Please check our website for availability.

Harefields (sleeping up to 8) **Raingoose** (sleeping up to 5) and **Pine Trees** (sleeping 2) are all superbly finished, individually designed and spacious. Each, with its own garden, commands fabulous views and has plenty of space to exercise your dog.
£220 - £600 per week inclusive of electricity and linen.

**Contact: Adrian and Lesley Francis, Outbrecks, Stenness, Orkney KW16 3EY
Tel: 01856 851 223 • e-mail: accommodation@outbreckscottages-orkney.co.uk
www.outbreckscottages-orkney.co.uk**

Visit the FHG website
www.holidayguides.com

for details of the wide choice of accommodation featured in the full range of FHG titles

Kirkwall

Largest town in Orkney, ideal base for exploring the many historic attractions in the islands.

ORKNEY ISLANDS COUNCIL, KIRKWALL KW15 1NY (01856 873535 ext. 2404). The Pickaquoy Centre Caravan & Camping Park, Kirkwall; Birsay Outdoor Centre / Caravan & Camping Site, North West of Orkney; Point of Ness Caravan & Camping Site, Stromness.

Orphir

Located on the mainland 7 miles south west of Kirkwall.

LITTLE BU, ORPHIR, ORKNEY. Little Bu is a self-catering chalet-bungalow maintained to a very high standard and sleeping six. Open-plan livingroom/dining area and newly fitted kitchen, verandah, patio/decking area, large garden and garden furniture. Close to the sea. STB ★★★ Self Catering. Contact: Mrs Shephard, Windbreck, Butchers Lane, Boughton, Northampton NN2 8SL (01604 843275) [🐕]
e-mail: jshephard@northamptonshire.gov.uk   website: www.littlebu.com

South Ronaldsay

Most southerly of the main islands of Orkney .

BANKS OF ORKNEY SELF-CATERING AND B&B. Two cottages (STB ★★★) and converted barn (STB ★★★★). Located close to ferries, with stunning views over the Pentland Firth. Each cottage sleeps up to 2, and the barn sleeps 5/7. Licensed restaurant on site. For details contact: CAROLE FLETCHER, BANKS OF ORKNEY, SOUTH RONALDSAY KW17 2RW (01856 831605).
website: www.banksoforkney.co.uk

Stenness

Locality on mainland at SE of Loch Stenness 4 miles west of Finstown.

ADRIAN AND LESLEY FRANCIS, OUTBRECKS, STENNESS KW16 3EY (01856 851 223) Exceptional self-catering cottages in fabulous sea and loch locations in outstanding National Scenic Area. Sleep 2-8. Open all year. Non-smoking. Dogs welcome. STB ★★★★.
e-mail: accommodation@outbreckscottages-orkney.co.uk
website: www.outbreckscottages-orkney.co.uk

North Uist
Locheport

Tigh Alasdair • North Uist Set on the family croft at Sidinish, Locheport, this beautiful self catering cottage is surrounded by moorland, sheep and water all at once. It enjoys unhindered views of Locheport, the hills of Bureaval, Eaval and Lees, not to mention spectacular sunsets. It offers all modern comforts in a traditional island setting, situated between the south shore of Loch Euphort (sea water) and Loch an Ghoil (fresh water). Sleeps 4. *For details contact:*
Janet MacDonald, Two Island Cottages, 285 Hillpark Drive, Glasgow G43 2SD
Tel: 0141 585 3155 / 0778 0937 577 • www.tighalasdair.co.uk

Locheport

Location on shore of sea loch, 5 miles south west of Lochmaddy.

TIGH ALASDAIR, NORTH UIST. Set on the family croft at Sidinish, Locheport, this beautiful self catering cottage enjoys unhindered views of Locheport, the hills of Bureaval, Eaval and Lees, not to mention spectacular sunsets. It offers all modern comforts in a traditional island setting. Sleeps 4. For details contact: JANET MACDONALD, TWO ISLAND COTTAGES, 285 HILLPARK DRIVE, GLASGOW G43 2SD (0141 585 3155 / 0778 0937 278). [pw! 🐕]
website: www.tighalasdair.co.uk

Carreg-Ddu, Elan Valley, see Oak Wood Lodges, Rhayader, Powys, page 424

Wales

Anglesey & Gwynedd

Bala, Barmouth, Bodorgan, Caernarfon

❖ Ty Gwyn ❖

Tel: 01678 521267 or 520234

• **TY GWYN** • Static six-berth luxury caravan with two bedrooms, shower, bathroom, colour TV, microwave, etc. on private grounds.

Situated two miles from Bala in beautiful country area. Ideal for walking, sailing, fishing and canoeing. 30 miles from nearest beach. Pets welcome

Contact: **MRS A. SKINNER, TY GWYN, RHYDUCHAF, BALA LL23 7SD**

LAWRENNY LODGE
BARMOUTH, ANGLESEY & GWYNEDD LL42 1SU • Tel: 01341 280466

Seven bedroom guest accommodation (all en suite) overlooking the harbour and estuary and only five minutes from beach. Perfect area for long walkies. Evening meal available. Varied restaurant menu, residential licence and private car park.
• e-mail: enquiries@lawrennylodge.co.uk • www.lawrennylodge.co.uk

Llwyndu Farmhouse

Llanaber, Barmouth, Gwynedd LL42 1RR

16th century farmhouse hotel. Stunning location with views over Cardigan Bay and its huge sandy beaches. All bedroom en suite and very individual, some in converted granary. Super food, local beers and good wine list. Cosy, informal atmosphere amidst oak beams, inglenooks and history.

Tel: 01341 280144
e-mail: intouch@llwyndu-farmhouse.co.uk
www.llwyndu-farmhouse.co.uk

Islawrffordd Caravan Park • Tal-y-Bont, Gwynedd LL43 2BQ

Situated on the Snowdonia coastline, just north of Barmouth, our park offers a limited number of caravans for hire. Our touring caravan field has been modernised to super pitch quality including hard standing with each plot being reservable. Camping field with new state-of-the-art toilet block. Park facilities include: • shop • laundry • indoor heated pool • jacuzzi • sauna • bar • amusements • food bars • **Tel: 01341 247469** • **Fax: 01341 242639**
e-mail: info@islawrffordd.co.uk • www.islawrffordd.co.uk

Croeso

• Comfortable three-bedroomed house
• Enclosed garden • Near beaches, common, forest
• Fully equipped; bedding and electricity inclusive
• Colour TV/DVD player, microwave • Dogs and children welcome. WTB ★★★

£235 to £435 per week

MRS J. GUNDRY, FARMYARD LODGE, BODORGAN, ANGLESEY LL62 5LW • Tel: 01407 840977

9 unique self-catering holiday cottages overlooking Caernarfon Bay with a backdrop of Snowdonia. Cottages sleep between 2 and 8 people. Private beach and glade. All cottages centrally heated and have private gardens. Pets welcome free. Village of Clynnog Fawr within walking distance. Short Breaks out of season.

Bach Wen Farm, Clynnog Fawr, Caernarfon, Gwynedd LL54 5NH

Tel: 01286 660336
www.bachwen.co.uk

Bach Wen Farm & Cottages

Plas-Y-Bryn Chalet Park

Bontnewydd,
Near Caernarfon LL54 7YE
Tel: 01286 672811

Our small park is situated two miles from the historic town of Caernarfon.

Set into a walled garden it offers safety, seclusion and beautiful views of Snowdonia. It is ideally positioned for touring the area. Shop and village pub nearby.

A selection of chalets and caravans available at prices from £205 (low season) to £465 (high season) per week for the caravans and £150 (low season) to £610 (high season) per week for the chalets. Well behaved pets always welcome.

e-mail: philplasybryn@aol.com
www.plasybryn.co.uk

 Three fully modernised cottages, sited three miles outside Caernarfon. Ample parking, ground level access. Spacious kitchen/diner. Large lounge. Digital TV, DVD, all mod. cons. Oil central heating. Short drive to Snowdonia Mountains and one mile from sandy beaches.

Cae Berllan Holiday Cottages North Wales

MRS A.M. OWENS, CAE BERLLAN, TYN LON, LLANDWROG, CAERNARFON LL54 5SN • 01286 830818

Caernarfon Bay Caravan Park and Holiday Bungalows

A quiet, peaceful static Caravan Park with Holiday Bungalows in beautiful North Wales. 50 yards from an award winning Dinas Dinlle beach. Picturesque views from the foothills of Snowdonia's National Park. Caernarfon 7 miles.
Dinas Dinlle, Caernarfon, Gwynedd LL54 5TW • Tel 01286 830492
e-mail: info@caernarfonbaycaravanpark.com • www.caernarfonbaycaravanpark.com

---

❖ Rhos Country Cottages ❖

A superb collection of secluded country cottages with private gardens, surrounded by wildflower meadows. Chill out, relax and listen to birdsong; walk the Lleyn Coastal Path from the garden gate or explore the Snowdonia National Park. Private fishing and rough shooting by arrangement. The cottages are heated and really warm in winter.

Open all year. VisitWales ★★★★★ Quality Award

Rhos Country Cottages, Criccieth, Porthmadog LL52 0PB
Telephone: 0776 986 4642 or 01758 720047
e-mail: cottages@rhos.freeserve.co.uk   www.rhos-cottages.co.uk

PARC WERNOL PARK
Chwilog, Pwllheli LL53 6SW
01766 810506 • e-mail: catherine@wernol.co.uk

- Panoramic views • Peaceful and quiet
- Ideal for touring Lleyn and Snowdonia
- 4 miles Criccieth and Pwllheli • 3 miles beach • Cycle route
- Free coarse fishing lake • Safe children's play area
- Games room • Footpaths • Dog exercise field
- Self-catering holidays
- 1, 2 & 3 bedroom cottages
- 2 and 3 bedroom caravans and chalets • Colour brochure
- Personal attention at all times
- A truly Welsh welcome.

www.wernol.co.uk

TYDDYN HEILYN
CHWILOG, CRICCIETH LL53 6SW

Comfortably renovated Welsh stone cottage with character. Cosy, double-glazed, centrally heated and enjoying mild Gulf Stream climate with holiday letting anytime. Two bedrooms with sea views. Ample grounds with enclosed garden with doggy walk.

Positioned on Llyn Peninsula, 3 miles Criccieth, on edge Snowdonia, with 1½ mile tree-lined walk to beach. Very central for touring.

Tel: 01766 810441 • e-mail: tyddyn.heilyn@tiscali.co.uk

Anglesey & Gwynedd

Criccieth, Dulas Bay, Dyffryn Ardudwy, Ffestiniog, Holyhead, Llanbedr

A warm welcome awaits you in comfortable self-catering cottages. Easily accessible to numerous attractions, or enjoy tranquillity of countryside.
From £140-£420. Short breaks (min 2 nights) from £80. Pets welcome.

**MRS M. WILLIAMS,
GAERWEN FARM, YNYS,
CRICCIETH, GWYNEDD LL52 0NU
Tel: 01766 810324
e-mail: gaerwen@btopenworld.com
www.gaerwenfarmcottages.co.uk**

Award winning Country House standing in 20 acres of woodland, gardens and fields. High standard of accommodation in family, twin and double rooms, all en suite. Pets welcome. Stabling/grazing available.
MRS G. McCREADIE, DERI ISAF, DULAS BAY, ANGLESEY LL70 9DX
Tel: 01248 410536 • Mobile: 07721 374471
e-mail: mccreadie@deriisaf.freeserve.co.uk • www.angleseyfarms.com/deri.htm

WINNER ENILLYDD 2010

Pentre Mawr Farm ❖

Relax in the peace and quiet of this working farm situated between Barmouth and Harlech. Inglenook fireplaces, spacious en suite bedrooms, and a homely atmosphere. Village shops, pubs, Cambrian Coast station and beach all within walking distance. Ample parking. Pets welcome. No children under 12.
Phone Sue Owen for a colour brochure.

**Dyffryn Ardudwy, Gwynedd LL44 2ES
Tel: 01341 247 413   www.pentre-mawr.co.uk**

★★★★ Farmhouse

Relax or be active at Plas Blaenddol
Tel: 01766 762406

Luxury self-catering on this private estate. Set in 9 acres of lawns, woodland, streams and lake, Old Bell House (sleeps up to 10) is very suitable for pets, with its original slate and tiled ground floor. Central location for relaxing or walking, mountain biking, rafting etc.   VisitWales ★★★★
D. Lea & Z. Richardson, Plas Blaenddol, Llan Ffestiniog, Gwynedd LL41 4PH
e-mail: snowhols@SnowdoniaSolutions.co.uk • www.plasblaenddol.co.uk

Boathouse Hotel
Tranquil setting overlooking the harbour
• Ferry terminal 4 minutes
On the edge of country park and marina
• Luxury en suite bedrooms at affordable prices • Quality meals and chef's specials
• Lunches and afternoon teas
• Ample free parking

**BOATHOUSE HOTEL • NEWRY BEACH • HOLYHEAD • ANGLESEY LL65 1YF
Tel: 01407 762094 • e-mail: boathousehotel@supanet.com
www.boathouse-hotel.co.uk**

Tan-y-Rhiw Holiday Cottage • Llanbedr
A detatched secluded stone cottage set in its own grounds, offering a comfortable holiday whilst retaining its 18th century character. Sleeps up to eight people comfortably plus cot. Harlech 3 miles.
Carol & Paul Richardson 15 Cheswardine Lane, Norton, Nr Shifnal, Shropshire TF11 9EQ
Tel/Fax 01952 730212 • E-mail: tan.y.rhiw@btinternet.com • www.tan-y-rhiw.co.uk
★★★★

Anglesey & Gwynedd
WALES 391
Pentraeth, Pwllheli, Trearddur Bay

Pen-y-Garnedd Farm Cottage
Near Pentraeth, Isle of Anglesey. Telephone bookings: 01248 450580
Fully refurbished detached cottage on a working smallholding. Electric heating and logburner in lounge. One double bedroom; second bedroom with bunk beds and single bed. Fully equipped kitchen. Bathroom with power shower. Enclosed garden. Close to beaches and coastal walks.
Low Season Short Breaks. **Caravan Club Approved Site (CCL5)**
Well behaved children and pets welcome. Open all Year.

WTB ★★★

Tel: 01758 730 375 • e-mail: post@crugeran.com
www.crugeran.com

Crugeran
Gwyliau fferm – Farm holidays

Self-catering holiday accommodation in comfortable large farmhouse (sleeps 12). Lovingly furnished and decorated throughout, with quality reproduction pieces and welcoming colours on a neutral background. Pets welcome. Beautiful sandy beaches, walking, golf, sea fishing trips and plenty of water sport facilities are available. Mrs R. Parry, Crugeran, Sarn Mellteyrn, Pwllheli, Gwynedd LL53 8DT

Cefn Coed Holiday Cottages are situated on the south coast of the Lleyn Peninsula with sweeping panoramic views of Snowdonia, Cardigan Bay and the Meirionnydd Mountains. Three holiday cottages to let, all of which are of a very high standard and have enclosed gardens. Sleep 4/6.

Cefn Coed, Chwilog, Pwllheli, Gwynedd LL53 6NX
Telephone: 01766 810259
E-mail: enquiries@cefncoedholidays.co.uk • www.cefncoedholidays.co.uk

Wales Cymru ★★★   Wales Cymru ★★★★

Comfortable self-catering holiday bungalows sleeping 2-7 near Trearddur's lovely beaches. Indoor heated swiming pool, licensed club, tennis court. Local, beautiful headland walks, fishing, golf and horse riding. Ideal location to explore Anglesey and the North Wales coast; near Holyhead.

TREARDDUR HOLIDAY BUNGALOWS
LON ISALLT TREARDDUR BAY ANGLESEY LL65 2UP
Tel: 01407 860294 • e-mail: trearholiday@btconnect.com • www.holiday-bungalows.co.uk

Blackthorn Farm is a family-run Bed and Breakfast, Camping and Touring site. Situated in an idyllic spot on Holy Island in North Wales. Set in 18 acres of outstanding unspoilt beauty with panoramic views.
Blackthorn Farm, Penrhos Feilw, Trearddur Bay, Anglesey, North Wales LL65 2LT
01407 765262 • enquiries@blackthornfarm.co.uk • www.blackthornleisure.co.uk
WINNER: Best Caravan/Camping Site of the Year 2009   Wales Cymru ★★★★

Bala

Natural touring centre for Snowdonia. Narrow gauge railway runs along side of Bala lake, the largest natural lake in Wales. Golf, sailing, fishing, canoeing.

TY GWYN - two-bedroomed luxury caravan in private grounds. Situated just two miles from Bala in beautiful country area, ideal for walking, sailing, fishing and canoeing. Only 30 miles from seaside. Contact: MRS A. SKINNER, TY GWYN, RHYDUCHAF, BALA LL23 7SD (01678 521327). [🐾]

Barmouth

Modern seaside resort with two miles of sandy beaches. Surrounding hills full of interesting archaeological remains.

LAWRENNY LODGE, BARMOUTH LL42 1SU (01341 280466). Seven bedroom guest accommodation overlooking the harbour and estuary. Perfect area for long walkies. Evening meal available. Residential licence and private car park. [🐾]
e-mail: enquiries@lawrennylodge.co.uk   website: www.lawrennylodge.co.uk

MRS PAULA THOMPSON, LLWYNDU FARMHOUSE, LLANABER, BARMOUTH LL42 1RR (01341 280144). Converted 16th century farmhouse retaining many original features. Cosy lounge and character dining room. Bedrooms are modern and well equipped, some with four-poster beds. WTB ★★★★ [🐾]
e-mail: intouch@llwyndu-farmhouse.co.uk   website: www.llwyndu-farmhouse.co.uk

ISLAWRFFORDD CARAVAN PARK, TAL-Y-BONT, GWYNEDD LL43 2BQ (01341 247269; Fax: 01341 242639). On the Snowdonia coastline, just north of Barmouth, our park offers a limited number of caravans for hire; touring caravan field and camping also available. Facilities include: shop, laundry, indoor heated pool, jacuzzi, sauna, bar, amusements, food bars. [Pets £2 per night].
e-mail: info@islawrffordd.co.uk   website: www.islawrffordd.co.uk

Beaumaris

Elegant little town dominated by castle built by Edward I in 13th century. Museum of Childhood has Victorian toys and music boxes.

"QUALITY COTTAGES', CERBID, SOLVA, HAVERFORDWEST, PEMBROKESHIRE SA62 6YE (01348 837871). Cottages set in all coastal areas, enjoy unashamed luxury, highest residential standards. Log fires. Linen supplied. Pets welcome, free. [pw! 🐾]
website: www.qualitycottages.co.uk

Bodorgan

A rural area in South West Anglesey.

CROESO. Comfortable three-bedroomed house. Enclosed garden. Near beaches, common, forest. Fully equipped, bedding and electricity inclusive. Colour TV/DVD player, microwave. Dogs and children welcome. £235-£435 per week. WTB ★★★ [🐾] Contact: MRS J. GUNDRY, FARMYARD LODGE, BODORGAN, ANGLESEY LL62 5LW (01407 840977).

Caernarfon

Historic walled town and resort, ideal for touring Snowdonia. Museums, Segontium Roman Fort, magnificent 13th century castle. Old harbour, sailing trips.

BACH WEN FARM & COTTAGES, CLYNNOG FAWR, CAERNARFON LL54 5NH (01286 660336). 9 unique high quality self-catering Holiday Cottages overlooking Caernarfon Bay. Sleep 2-8. All have private gardens. Village within walking distance. Short Breaks out of season. [🐾]
e-mail: bachwen@aol.com   website: www.bachwen.co.uk

PLAS-Y-BRYN CHALET PARK, BONTNEWYDD, NEAR CAERNARFON LL54 7YE (01286 672811). Two miles from Caernarfon. It offers safety, seclusion and beautiful views of Snowdonia. Ideally positioned for touring. Well behaved pets always welcome. WTB ★★★★ [Pets £20 per week].
e-mail: philplasybryn@aol.com   website: www.plasybryn.co.uk

MRS A.M. OWENS, CAE BERLLAN, TYN LON, LLANDWROG, CAERNARFON LL54 5SN (01286 830818). Three fully modernised cottages, sited three miles outside Caernarfon. Ample parking, ground level access. Spacious kitchen/diner. Large lounge. Digital TV, DVD, all mod. cons. Oil central heating. Short drive to Snowdonia Mountains and one mile from sandy beaches.

CAERNARFON BAY CARAVAN PARK AND HOLIDAY BUNGALOWS, DINAS DINLLE, CAERNARFON LL54 5TW (01286 830492). Quiet, peaceful static Caravan Park with Holiday Bungalows in beautiful North Wales. 50 yards from an award-winning beach. Picturesque views from the foothills of Snowdonia's National Park. Caernarfon 7 miles. WTB★★★★.
e-mail: info@caernarfonbaycaravanpark.com   website: www.caernarfonbaycaravanpark.com

Criccieth

Popular family resort with safe beaches divided by ruins of 13th century castle. Salmon and sea trout fishing. Festival of Music and Arts in the summer.

"QUALITY COTTAGES', CERBID, SOLVA, HAVERFORDWEST, PEMBROKESHIRE SA62 6YE (01348 837871). Cottages set in all coastal areas, enjoy unashamed luxury, highest residential standards. Log fires. Linen supplied. Pets welcome, free. [pw! 🐾]
website: www.qualitycottages.co.uk

S A. M. JONES, RHOS COUNTRY COTTAGES, CRICCIETH, PORTHMADOG LL52 0PB (01758 720047 or 0776 986 4642). Superb collection of secluded country cottages with private gardens. Private fishing and rough shooting by arrangement. Open all year. VisitWales ★★★★★ [🐾]
e-mail: cottages@rhos.freeserve.co.uk   website: www.rhos-cottages.co.uk

Anglesey & Gwynedd WALES

PARC WERNOL PARK, CHWILOG, PWLLHELI LL53 6SW (01766 810506). Peaceful and quiet, ideal for touring. Self-catering holidays – 1,2 & 3 bedroom cottages, 2 and 3 bedroom caravans and chalets. Colour brochure. [Pets £15 per dog per week.]
e-mail: catherine@wernol.co.uk   website: www.wernol.co.uk

MRS ANN WILLIAMS, TYDDYN HEILYN, CHWILOG, CRICCIETH LL53 6SW (01766 810441). Comfortably renovated Welsh stone cottage. Double-glazed, centrally heated and enjoying mild Gulf Stream climate. Ample grounds with enclosed garden with doggy walk. 1½ mile tree-lined walk to beach. [🐕]
e-mail: tyddyn.heilyn@tiscali.co.uk

A warm welcome awaits you in comfortable self-catering cottages. Easily accessible to numerous attractions, or enjoy tranquillity of countryside. Short breaks available. Pets welcome. MRS M. WILLIAMS, GAERWEN FARM, YNYS, CRICCIETH LL52 0NU (01766 810324).[🐕]
e-mail: gaerwen@btopenworld.com   website: www.gaerwenfarmcottages.co.uk

Dulas Bay

On north-east coast of Anglesey, between Amlwch and Moelfre.

MRS G. McCREADIE, DERI ISAF, DULAS BAY, ANGLESEY LL70 9DX (01248 410536; Mobile: 07721 374471). Award winning Country House in 20 acres of woodland, gardens and fields. Family, twin and double rooms, all en suite. Pets welcome. Stabling/grazing available. WTB ★★★★ Country House [Dogs £3.00 per night]
e-mail: mccreadie@deriisaf.freeserve.co.uk   website: www.angleseyfarms.com/deri.htm

Dyffryn Ardudwy

Village 5 miles north of Barmouth.

SUE OWEN, PENTRE MAWR FARM, DYFFRYN ARDUDWY LL44 2ES. (01341 247413). Working farm between Barmouth and Harlech. Inglenook fireplaces, spacious en suite bedrooms, and a homely atmosphere.Village shops, pubs, beach all within walking distance. Ample parking. No children under 12. WTB ★★★★ Farmhouse [Pets £10 per stay].
website: www.pentre-mawr.co.uk

Ffestiniog

A small village in Gwynedd, North Wales, lying south of Blaenau Ffestiniog, 9 miles east of Porthmadoc.

PLAS BLAENDDOL, LLAN FFESTINIOG LL41 4PH (01766 762406). Luxury self-catering on private estate in the heart of Snowdonia. Old Bell House sleeps up to 10 and is very suitable for pets. Central location for walking, mountain biking, rafting etc. VisitWales ★★★★ [Pets £15 per week]
e-mail: snowhols@SnowdoniaSolutions.co.uk   website: www.plasblaenddol.co.uk

Harlech

Small stone-built town dominated by remains of 13th century castle. Golf, theatre, swimming pool, fine stretch of sands

"QUALITY COTTAGES", CERBID, SOLVA, HAVERFORDWEST, PEMBROKESHIRE SA62 6YE (01348 837871). Cottages set in all coastal areas, enjoy unashamed luxury, highest residential standards. Log fires. Linen supplied. Pets welcome, free. [pw! 🐕]
website: www.qualitycottages.co.uk

Holyhead

Port & industrial town on Holy Island, Anglesey.

BOATHOUSE HOTEL, NEWRY BEACH, HOLYHEAD, ANGLESEY LL65 1YF (01407 762094). Tranquil setting overlooking the harbour; on edge of country park and marina. Luxury en suite. Quality meals. Ample free parking. [Pets £5 per night].
e-mail: boathousehotel@supanet.com   website: www.boathouse-hotel.co.uk

WALES
Anglesey & Gwynedd

Llanbedr

Ideal base for exploring mountains and coast of Snowdonia, just 3 miles from Harlech.

TAN-Y-RHIW HOLIDAY COTTAGE. A detatched secluded stone cottage set in its own grounds, offering a comfortable holiday whilst retaining its 18th century character. Sleeps up to eight people comfortably plus cot. Contact: CAROL & PAUL RICHARDSON,15 CHESWARDINE LANE, NORTON, NEAR SHIFNAL TF11 9EQ (Tel/Fax 01952 730212). WTB ★★★★.[🐕]
e-mail: tan.y.rhiw@btinternet.com   website: www.tan-y-rhiw.co.uk

Llanddona

Village on Anglesey 3 miles north west of Beaumaris

"QUALITY COTTAGES', CERBID, SOLVA, HAVERFORDWEST, PEMBROKESHIRE SA62 6YE (01348 837871). Cottages set in all coastal areas, enjoy unashamed luxury, highest residential standards. Log fires. Linen supplied. Pets welcome, free. [pw] 🐕]
website: www.qualitycottages.co.uk

Morfa Nefyn

Picturesque village 2 miles west of Nefyn.

"QUALITY COTTAGES', CERBID, SOLVA, HAVERFORDWEST, PEMBROKESHIRE SA62 6YE (01348 837871). Cottages set in all coastal areas, enjoy unashamed luxury, highest residential standards. Log fires. Linen supplied. Pets welcome, free. [pw] 🐕]
website: www.qualitycottages.co.uk

Pentraeth

Village on Anglesey, near Red Wharf Bay.

PEN-Y-GARNEDD FARM COTTAGE, PENTRAETH (01248 450580). Cosy cottage on friendly working smallholding. Sleeps 5, log burner and heating. Well behaved children and pets welcome. Close to beaches and coastal Wales. Low Season Short Breaks. Caravan Club Approved Site. WTB ★★★ [🐕].

Porthmadog

Harbour town with mile-long Cob embankment, along which runs Ffestiniog Narrow Gauge Steam Railway to Blaenau Ffestiniog. Pottery, maritime museum, car museum. Good beaches nearby.

"QUALITY COTTAGES', CERBID, SOLVA, HAVERFORDWEST, PEMBROKESHIRE SA62 6YE (01348 837871). Cottages set in all coastal areas, enjoy unashamed luxury, highest residential standards. Log fires. Linen supplied. Pets welcome, free. [pw] 🐕]
website: www.qualitycottages.co.uk

Pwllheli

Market town with harbour, 8 miles west of Criccieth

MRS RHIAN PARRY, CRUGERAN, SARN MELLTEYRN, PWLLHELI LL53 8DT (01758 730 375). Self catering holiday accommodation in large farmhouse (sleeps 12). Beaches, walking, golf, sea fishing trips and plenty of water sport facilities are available.
e-mail: post@crugeran.com   website: www.crugeran.com

CEFN COED HOLIDAY COTTAGES, CEFN COED, CHWILOG, PWLLHELI LL53 6NX. (01766 810259) Three holiday cottages to let, sleep 4/6. On the south coast of the Lleyn Peninsula with sweeping panoramic views of Snowdonia, Cardigan Bay and the Meirionnydd Mountains. WTB ★★★/★★★★. [Pets £20 per week]
e-mail: enquiries@cefncoedholidays.co.uk   website: www.cefncoedholidays.co.uk

Anglesey & Gwynedd

Red Wharf Bay

Deep curving bay with vast expanse of sand, very popular for sailing and swimming.

"QUALITY COTTAGES', CERBID, SOLVA, HAVERFORDWEST, PEMBROKESHIRE SA62 6YE (01348 837871). Cottages set in all coastal areas, enjoy unashamed luxury, highest residential standards. Log fires. Linen supplied. Pets welcome, free. [pw! 🐕]
website: www.qualitycottages.co.uk

Trearddur Bay

Attractive holiday spot set amongst low cliffs on Holy Island, near Holyhead. Golf, sailing, fishing and swimming.

TREARDDUR HOLIDAY BUNGALOWS, LON ISALLT, TREARDDUR BAY, ANGLESEY LL65 2UP (01407 860494). Comfortable self-catering holiday bungalows sleeping 2-7 near Trearddur's lovely beaches. Locally, beautiful headland walks, fishing, golf and horse riding. Ideal location to explore Anglesey and the North Wales coast. Terms from £100-£580 per week.
e-mail: trearholiday@btconnect.com   website: www.holiday-bungalows.co.uk

BLACKTHORN FARM, PENRHOS FEILW, TREARDDUR BAY LL65 2LT (01407 765262). Family-run Bed and Breakfast, Camping and Touring site in an idyllic spot on Holy Island in North Wales. Set in 18 acres of outstanding unspoilt beauty with panoramic views. VisitWales ★★★★, Winner: Best Caravan/Camping Site of the year 2009. [Pets £5 per night B&B, £2 per night in caravan/campsite.]
e-mail: enquiries@blackthornfarm.co.uk   website: www.blackthornleisure.co.uk

Tywyn

Pleasant seaside resort, start of Talyllyn Narrow Gauge Railway. Sea and river fishing, golf.

"QUALITY COTTAGES', CERBID, SOLVA, HAVERFORDWEST, PEMBROKESHIRE SA62 6YE (01348 837871). Cottages set in all coastal areas, enjoy unashamed luxury, highest residential standards. Log fires. Linen supplied. Pets welcome, free. [pw! 🐕]
website: www.qualitycottages.co.uk

Other specialised holiday guides from FHG

PUBS & INNS OF BRITAIN • **COUNTRY HOTELS** OF BRITAIN

WEEKEND & SHORT BREAK HOLIDAYS IN BRITAIN

THE GOLF GUIDE WHERE TO PLAY, WHERE TO STAY

500 GREAT PLACES TO STAY • **SELF-CATERING HOLIDAYS** IN BRITAIN

BED & BREAKFAST STOPS • **CARAVAN & CAMPING HOLIDAYS**

FAMILY BREAKS IN BRITAIN

Published annually: available in all good bookshops or direct from the publisher:
FHG Guides, Abbey Mill Business Centre, Seedhill, Paisley PA1 1TJ
Tel: 0141 887 0428 • Fax: 0141 889 7204
e-mail: admin@fhguides.co.uk • www.holidayguides.com

Around the magnificent coast of Wales
Pembrokeshire, Cardigan Bay, Snowdonia, Anglesey, Lleyn Peninsula, Borders

Choose from over 300 Quality Cottages

Pets Welcome Free

A small specialist agency with over 40 years experience letting quality cottages.

Enjoy unashamed luxury in traditional Welsh Cottages. Situated near safe sandy beaches and in the heart of Wales — famed for scenery, walks, wild flowers, birds, badgers and foxes.

Pets welcome FREE at most of our properties

Leonard Rees, Quality Cottages, Cerbid, Solva, Haverfordwest, Pembrokeshire. SA62 6YE

Telephone: (01348) 837871 for our FREE Colour Brochure

www.qualitycottages.co.uk

100s of pictures of quality cottages and beautiful Wales

Seaside Cottages

In Idyllic North Wales
www.waleshols.com

We have a large selection of self-catering seaside and country cottages, bungalows, farmhouses, caravans etc. offering superb, reasonably priced accommodation for owners and their pets. Our brochures contain details of all you need for a wonderful holiday – please telephone for your FREE copies now.

Manns Holidays, Shaw's Holidays & Snowdonia Tourist Services

www.mannsholidays.com
www.shawsholidays.com
www.snowdoniatourist.com

01758 701 702 (24 hrs)

Betys-y-Coed

Glan-y-Borth HOLIDAY VILLAGE

WELCOME TO Glan-y-Borth Holiday Village, family-run and situated in the Conwy Valley on the edge of the famous Snowdonia National Park.

It has all the facilities you expect - and more - for an ideal "get away from it all" weekend or for a family holiday. We have something to offer visitors of all ages with our gardens, safe playing area, floodlit covered barbecue area, and disabled accommodation.

Glan-y-Borth Holiday village comprises 20 Holiday Cottages / flats, accommodating from between 2 to 8 people. 6 are specially designed and created for the disabled, where you will find every detail designed for your comfort. They are all on one level, with doorways 33 inches wide. Bathrooms have full access for wheelchairs into the shower, and all kitchen units are at a comfortable level. The landscaped gardens are ramped for ease of movement around the site, to ensure that all our guests enjoy their stay with us.

We cannot guarantee the weather but we do promise you a very warm welcome!

Betws Road, Llanrwst, Gwynedd
North Wales LL26 0HE
Tel: 01492 641543   Fax: 01492 641369
email:admin@glanyborth.co.uk
www.glanyborth.co.uk

WALES

North Wales
Betws-y-Coed, Colwyn Bay, Conwy

Hill farm in Wales. TV, teamaking, en suite. Set in National Park/Snowdonia. Very quiet and well off the beaten track. A great welcome and good food. Many return visits. £25 B&B.

MISS MORRIS, TY COCH FARM-TREKKING CENTRE, PENMACHNO, BETWS-Y-COED LL25 0HJ
01690 760248 • e-mail: cindymorris@tiscali.co.uk

NORTH WALES HOLIDAYS
Cedarwood Chalets • Cottages • Coach House

High quality cottages, cosy chalets and large coach house for 2-9, overlooking sea at Bron-Y-Wendon or in picturesque valley at Nant-Y-Glyn. 16 units in total. Wide range of facilities with many leisure activities nearby. Short breaks all year. Pets welcome. VisitWales 2-5 Stars.

**Bron-Y-Wendon & Nant-Y-Glyn Holiday Parks,
Wern Road, Llanddulas, Colwyn Bay LL22 8HG**
e-mail: stay@northwales-holidays.co.uk
www.northwales-holidays.co.uk

For colour brochures telephone: **01492 512903/ 512282** or visit our website

Tal-y-Fan Cottage and Alltwen Cottage

We have two luxurious self-catering country cottages for rental. Newly developed and well appointed, these properties can accommodate up to four people comfortably. They are located nearby the sleepy village of Dwygyfylchi, with spectacular views. Ideal touring centre for Snowdonia, two and a half miles to Conwy, five to Llandudno and Colwyn Bay; three minutes' walk to the village. Pony trekking, golf and fishing locally.

*Terms from £395. Suitable for disabled access.
Pets and children welcome. Short Breaks available.
Non-smoking.*

**Mr John Baxter, Glyn Uchaf,
Conwy Old Road, Dwygyfylchi,
Penmaenmawr, Conwy LL34 6YS
Tel & Fax: 01492 623737/622053**

www.glyn-uchaf.co.uk

Tyn-y-Groes, Near Conwy

Homely Victorian stone cottage in picturesque Conwy valley. Mountain views. Enjoy walking, mountains, beaches, bird watching. Bodnant Gardens, RSPB reserve and Conwy castle, harbour and marina close by. Victorian Llandudno, Betws-y-Coed, Anglesey, Caernarfon and Snowdon easy distance. Good local food and pubs. Enclosed garden, patio furniture. Parking. Gas fired central heating. Lounge with gas fire, dining room, kitchen, utility. Two double bedded rooms, one small single; blankets/duvet provided. Bathroom with bath, shower, toilet and basin. Colour TV, electric cooker, fridge, microwave, washing machine and tumbler dryer. Terms £240-£330; heating, electricity included. Linen extra. Pets welcome. Open all year. No children under five years..

**Mrs G. Simpole, 105 Hay Green Road, Terrington-St-Clement, King's Lynn, Norfolk PE34 4PU
Tel: 01553 828897
Mobile: 0798 9080665**

Brongain

Please mention **Pets Welcome!**
when making enquiries about accommodation featured in these pages

TREFRIW • CONWY VALLEY SNOWDONIA

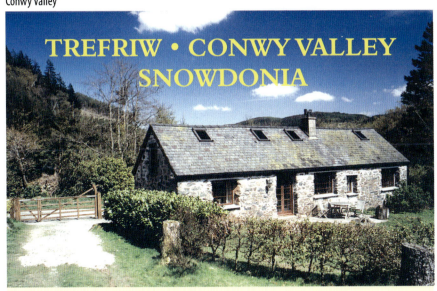

Secluded cottages, log fire and beams
Dogs will love it – a place of their dreams
Plenty of walks around mountains and lakes
Cosy and tranquil – it's got what it takes.
It's really a perfect holiday let
For up to 2-7 people, plus their pet(s).

Apply: Mrs Williams
Tel: 01724 733990 or 07711 217 448 (week lets only)

WALES

North Wales

Conwy, Conwy Valley, Llandudno

Sychnant Pass House
Sychnant Pass Road, Conwy LL32 8BJ
Tel: 01492 596868 • Fax: 01492 585486
e-mail: bre@sychnant-pass-house.co.uk
www.sychnant-pass-house.co.uk

Millie and Maisie, our lovely collies, would love to welcome your four-legged friends to their home in the hills above Conwy. Sychnant Pass House is a lovely Victorian House set in two acres with a little pond and stream running through it. Step out of our garden and straight onto Snowdonia National Park land where you can walk for miles with your dogs. Just over two miles from the beach and one-and-a-half miles from Conwy, it is an ideal base from which to tour Wales. All our rooms are en suite, our garden rooms have French windows opening into the garden which are ideal for pets. We have a lovely sitting room that you can share with your best friends after dinner which is served in our informal, friendly restaurant, doggie bags are always available. Your four-legged friends and their folk are most welcome here. **Bed & Breakfast from £50 per person**

Yr Hafod Country House

Quality Country House Hotel Accommodation and Restaurant in Trefriw, near Betws-y-Coed in Snowdonia, North Wales

Trefriw, Llanrwst — *Conwy Valley LL27 0RQ*

Relax in this centuries-old farmhouse. Exceptional food (top grade in the last three WTB inspections), warm hospitality, and a strong sense of style, combine to create a special stay for guests. As well as some 2½ acres of grounds, there are walks in the woods, beside waterfalls, or along the banks of the River Conwy, where you can exercise your dog.

Tel: 01492 640029 • e-mail: stay@hafod-house.co.uk • www.hafod-house.co.uk

Vine House Bed & Breakfast
23 Church Walks, Llandudno LL30 2HG
Tel: 01492 876493 • www.vinehouse-llandudno.co.uk

Molly (our Cocker Spaniel) will welcome you with a happy bark to our comfortable family-run guest house.

We are situated opposite the Great Orme Tramway, as well as being close to the town centre, Promenade and beach. There are views to the Great Orme or the sea from all rooms.

North Wales

Llandudno, Llandyrnog, Llangollen

The Moorings • *Ideal Holiday Apartments*

The Moorings offers you a range of accommodation to suit all, with great parking facilities and easy access to beautiful beaches, coastline and an assortment of attractions. Available all year round with a choice from 8 different apartments to suit your needs.

The Moorings, 3 Abbey Road, Llandudno, Conwy LL30 2EA
Tel: 01492 876175 • E-mail: stay@themooringsholidays.co.uk • www.themooringsholidays.co.uk

The Warwick Hotel • Llandudno

www.thewarwickhotel.net

"All the family are welcome at the Warwick Hotel in Llandudno – including Pets!"

Comfortable, relaxing and family friendly hotel. 14 tastefully decorated en suite bedrooms with colour TV and tea and coffee making facilities. Hairdryers, clock radios, cots and ironing facilities available.

The Warwick Hotel, 56 Church Walks, Llandudno, North Wales LL30 2HL
Tel: 01492 876423 • Fax: 01492 877908 • e-mail info@thewarwickhotel.com

Pentre Mawr House

Llandyrnog, Denbigh, North Wales LL16 4LA
Tel: 01824 790732
e-mail: info@pentremawrcountryhouse.co.uk
www.pentremawrcountryhouse.co.uk

Molly and Millie, our lovely collies, would love to welcome your four-legged friends to their family's ancestral home of 400 years with woodland, park and riverside meadows, all within easy reach of Chester and the coast.

The en suite bedrooms have all the little extras to make your stay special. Two new suites have hot tubs. There is a heated swimming pool in the walled garden and lovely sittingrooms where you can sit with your best friends after dinner. Furry folk and their families are most welcome here. B&B from £50.00

The Hand at Llanarmon

Standing in the glorious and hidden Ceiriog Valley, The Hand at Llanarmon radiates charm and character. With 13 comfortable en suite bedrooms, roaring log fires, and fabulous food served with flair and generosity, this is a wonderful base for most country pursuits, or just relaxing in good company.

Llanarmon D.C., Ceiriog Valley, Near Llangollen, North Wales LL20 7LD
reception@thehandhotel.co.uk • www.TheHandHotel.co.uk • Tel: 01691 600666

Ted, Fred and Megan are waiting to greet new friends!

The Golden Pheasant is an 18th Century Hotel & Inn ideally situated for pets, especially dogs. The old world charm bar has an open range fire, pews and slate floor and real ale; comfortable lounges and two restaurants which have extensive and imaginative menus, all freshly prepared by our chef.

Accommodation ranges from cosy Inn rooms located in the older part of the building to superior larger bedrooms and four-poster rooms with whirlpool baths, which have wonderful views of the valley.

Situated in the beautiful Ceiriog Valley, which is a heaven for walking, with its unspoilt country lanes, paths with wild flower banks and verges, all with panoramic views of the valley.

2 nights D,B&B from £135 pp. B&B from £90, two sharing. Pets from £5 per night.

Llwynmawr, Glyn Ceiriog, Near Llangollen LL20 7BB
Tel: 01691 718281 • Fax: 01691 718479
e-mail: info@goldenpheasanthotel.co.uk   website: www.goldenpheasanthotel.co.uk

THE GOLDEN PHEASANT
Country Hotel & Inn

Please mention **Pets Welcome!**
when making enquiries about accommodation featured in these pages

The Northwood

The Northwood is a family-run guesthouse in the heart of Rhos-on-Sea 175 yards from high class shops, promenade & sea. The en suite single, double, twin and family bedrooms are tastefully furnished. All have colour television and hospitality tray with tea/coffee/drinking chocolate, and biscuits. Dinners are available from May to October, vegetarian meals and special dietary needs are available. The menu is changed daily. Dogs get a Welsh sausage for breakfast.

47 Rhos Road, Rhos-on-Sea, Colwyn Bay LL28 4RS
Telephone: 08450 533105
e-mail: welcome@thenorthwood.co.uk
www.thenorthwood.co.uk

AA ★★★ Guest House

Sunnydowns Hotel

★★★ Quality Hotel

66 Abbey Road, Rhos-on-Sea, Colwyn Bay, Conwy, North Wales LL28 4NU
Tel: 01492 544256 Fax: 01492 543223
(Proprietor: Mike Willington)
A Non-Smoking Hotel

A 3 star family-run hotel situated in a quiet area and just a two minute level walk to the beach & shops. High standard of comfort and cleanliness, car park, bar, games room with pool table, Nordic sauna, restaurant, TV lounge.

Our restaurant is non-smoking, serving freshly prepared good home cooking. The towns of Llandudno, Colwyn Bay & Conwy are only five minutes' drive away and just ten minutes to the mountains and castles of Snowdonia and the Isle of Anglesey.

OAP discounts, large family rooms & family suites available. All en suite bedrooms have digital TV with approximately 40 channels, clock radio, tea/coffee making facilities, hairdyer, mini-bar, refrigerator, telephone and central heating. Available on request are irons, trouser press, room service and laundry service. Broadband internet access available throughout the hotel.

All rooms fitted with personal digital room safe. Microwave available for guests' use.
Also a fitness/exercise machine in games room; all available free of charge for all our guests.

Dogs are very welcome and can stay at a small charge. They are allowed in your bedroom with you and in the hotel except the restaurant. Meals also served in the bar where dogs are allowed.

For further information, please phone or write for our colour brochure
e-mail: sunnydowns-hotel@tinyworld.co.uk • www.sunnydownshotel.co.uk

North Wales

NORTH WALES HOLIDAY COTTAGES. Self-catering cottages and farmhouses in the beautiful regions of the Conwy Valley, coastal resorts, Vale of Clwyd, Northern and Southern Snowdonia, Lleyn Peninsula and Anglesey. Phone 01492 582 492. [🐾]
e-mail: info@nwhc.co.uk   website: www.pw.nwhc.co.uk

'QUALITY COTTAGES', CERBID, SOLVA, HAVERFORDWEST, PEMBROKESHIRE SA62 6YE (01348 837871). Cottages set in all coastal areas, enjoy unashamed luxury, highest residential standards. Log fires. Linen supplied. Pets welcome, free. [pw! 🐾]
website: www.qualitycottages.co.uk

SEASIDE COTTAGES. MANN'S, SHAW'S AND SNOWDONIA TOURIST SERVICES (01758 701 702). Large selection of self-catering seaside and country cottages, bungalows, farmhouses, caravans etc. offering superb, reasonably priced accommodation for owners and their pets. Please telephone for brochure.
websites: www.mannsholidays.com   www.shawsholidays.com   www.snowdoniatourist.com

Betws-y-Coed

Popular mountain resort in picturesque setting where three rivers meet. Trout fishing, craft shops, golf, railway and motor museums, Snowdonia National Park Visitor Centre. Nearby Swallow Falls are famous beauty spot.

GLAN-Y-BORTH HOLIDAY VILLAGE, BETWS ROAD, LLANRWST, GWYNEDD LL26 0HE (01492 641543; Fax: 01492 641369). Situated in the Conwy vally. Panoramic views. 20 Holiday cottages/flats. 6 specially designed for the disabled. Ideal for family holiday or weekend break.
e-mail: admin@glanyborth.co.uk   www.glanyborth.co.uk

MISS MORRIS, TY COCH FARM-TREKKING CENTRE, PENMACHNO, BETWS-Y-COED LL25 0HJ (01690 760248). Hill farm in Wales. TV, teamaking, en suite. Set in National Park/Snowdonia. Very quiet and well off the beaten track. A great welcome and good food. Many return visits. £25 B&B. [🐾]
e-mail: cindymorris@tiscali.co.uk

Colwyn Bay

Lively seaside resort with promenade amusements. Attractions include Mountain Zoo, Eirias Park; golf, tennis, riding and other sports. Good touring centre for Snowdonia. The quieter resort of Rhos-on-Sea lies at the western end of the bay.

NORTH WALES HOLIDAYS, BRON-Y-WENDON AND NANT-Y-GLYN HOLIDAY PARKS, WERN ROAD, LLANDDULAS, COLWYN BAY LL22 8HG (01492 512903/512282). Cottages with sea views at Bron-Y-Wendon or chalets, cottages and coach house in picturesque valley at Nant-Y-Glyn. 16 units in total. VisitWales 2-5 Stars [Pets £10 per week].
e-mail: stay@northwales-holidays.co.uk   website: www.northwales-holidays.co.uk

Conwy

One of the best preserved medieval fortified towns in Britain on dramatic estuary setting. Telford Suspension Bridge, many historic buildings, lively quayside (site of smallest house in Britain). Golf, pony trekking, pleasure cruises.

TAL-Y-FAN COTTAGE AND ALLTWEN COTTAGE. Two luxurious self-catering country cottages accommodating up to four people. Spectacular views. Ideal touring centre for Snowdonia. Pony trekking, golf and fishing locally. Pets and children welcome. Short Breaks available. Non-smoking. Contact: MR JOHN BAXTER, GLYN UCHAF, CONWY OLD ROAD, DWYGYFYLCHI, PENMAENMAWR, CONWY LL34 6YS (Tel & Fax: 01492 623737/622053) WTB ★★★★★. [🐾]
website: www.glyn-uchaf.co.uk

BRONGAIN, TYN-Y-GROES, CONWY. Homely Victorian stone cottage, picturesque Conwy Valley. Snowdonia Mountain views. Enjoy lakes, mountains, walking, bird watching, beaches, Bodnant, RSPB, Conwy Castle. £240-£330. Contact: MRS G. M. SIMPOLE, 105 HAYGREEN ROAD, TERRINGTON ST CLEMENT, KINGS LYNN, NORFOLK PE34 4PU (01553 828897; Mobile: 0798 9080 665) [pw! 🐾]

SYCHNANT PASS HOUSE, SYCHNANT PASS ROAD, CONWY LL32 8BJ (01492 596868; Fax: 01492 585486). A lovely Victorian House set in two acres with a little pond and stream. Step out of our garden and straight onto Snowdonia National Park land. Walk for miles with your dogs. All rooms en suite. B&B from £50. AA ★★★★★ and Rosette. [🐾]
e-mail: bre@sychnant-pass-house.co.uk   website: www.sychnant-pass-house.co.uk

Conwy Valley

Fertile valley with wood and moor rising on both sides. Many places of interest in the area.

Secluded cottages with log fire and beams. Dogs will love it. Plenty of walks around mountains and lakes. For 2 - 7 people plus their pet(s). MRS WILLIAMS (01724 733990 or 07711 217 448) week lets only. [🐕]

HAFOD COUNTRY HOUSE, TREFRIW, CONWY VALLEY LL27 0RQ (01492 640029; Fax: 01492 641351). Historic, centuries-old house. Over two acres of grounds. Excellent food in restaurant. Short breaks available. Well behaved dogs welcome. Non-smoking. WTB ★★★★, AA ★★★★ [Pets £5 per night, £30 per week]
e-mail: stay@hafod-house.co.uk   website: www.hafod-house.co.uk

Llandudno

Coastal resort at base of Peninsula running out to Great Ormes Head.

VINE HOUSE BED & BREAKFAST, 23 CHURCH WALKS, LLANDUDNO LL30 2HG (01492 876493). Molly (our Cocker Spaniel) will welcome you with a happy bark to our comfortable family-run guest house. Opposite the Great Orme Tramway, and close to the town centre, Promenade and beach. VisitWales ★★★ Guest Accomodation. [Pets £5 per night]
website: www.vinehouse-llandudno.co.uk

THE MOORINGS, 3 ABBEY ROAD, LLANDUDNO LL30 2EA (01492 8767750) Offering you a range of accommodation to suit all, with great parking facilities and easy access to beautiful beaches, coastline and an assortment of attractions. Available all year round with a choice from 8 different Apartments to suit your needs. VisitWales ★★★ [🐕]
e-mail: stay@themooringsholidays.co.uk   website: www.themooringsholidays.co.uk

THE WARWICK HOTEL, 56 CHURCH WALKS, LLANDUDNO LL30 2HL (01492 876823; Fax: 01492 877908). Comfortable, relaxing and family friendly hotel. 14 tastefully decorated en suite bedrooms with colour TV and tea and coffee making facilities. Hairdryers, clock radios, cots and ironing facilities available. WTB ★★.
e-mail info@thewarwickhotel.net   website: www.thewarwickhotel.net

Llandyrnog

Village 4 miles east of Denbigh.

PENTRE MAWR COUNTRY HOUSE, LLANDYRNOG LL16 4LA (01824 790732) Ancestral home of 400 years with woodland, park and riverside meadows, within easy reach of Chester and coast. Heated swimming pool. All rooms en suite. Pets most welcome. AA ★★★★★ and Dinner Award [🐕]
e-mail: info@pentremawrcountryhouse.co.uk   www.pentremawrcountryhouse.co.uk

---

Symbols

- 🐕 Indicates that pets are welcome free of charge.
- £ Indicates that a charge is made for pets: nightly or weekly.
- pw! Shows some special provision for pets; exercise facility, feeding or accommodation arrangement.
- ⌂ Indicates separate pets accommodation.

Free or reduced rate entry to Holiday Visits and Attractions - see our
READERS' OFFER VOUCHERS on pages 445-454

North Wales

Llangollen

Famous for International Music Eisteddfod held in July. Plas Newydd, Valle Crucis Abbey nearby. Standard gauge steam railway; canal cruises; ideal for golf and walking.

THE HAND AT LLANARMON, LLANARMON D.C., CEIRIOG VALLEY, NEAR LLANGOLLEN LL20 7LD (01691 600666). Standing in the glorious Ceiriog Valley, The Hand at Llanarmon radiates charm and character. 13 comfortable en suite bedrooms, log fires, and fabulous food, a wonderful base for most country pursuits. [🐕]
e-mail: reception@thehandhotel.co.uk   website: www.TheHandHotel.co.uk

GOLDEN PHEASANT COUNTRY HOTEL, GLYN CEIRIOG, NEAR LLANGOLLEN LL20 7BB (01691 718281; Fax: 01691 718479). Situated in the beautiful Ceiriog Valley. All 19 rooms en suite, colour TV and tea/coffee making facilities. Pets welcome in all rooms (except restaurant and lounge). WTB/AA ★★★ [pw! £5 per night per pet, £35 per week]
e-mail: info@goldenpheasanthotel.co.uk   website: www.goldenpheasanthotel.co.uk

Rhos-on-Sea (Conwy)

Popular resort at east end of Penrhyn Bay, adjoining Colwyn Bay to the north-west.

THE NORTHWOOD, 47 RHOS ROAD, RHOS-ON-SEA, COLWYN BAY LL28 4RS (08450 533105). Family-run guesthouse in the heart of Rhos-on-Sea 175 yards from high class shops, promenade and sea. Tastefully furnished bedrooms. Vegetarian meals and special dietary needs are available. AA ★★★. [🐕]
e-mail: welcome@thenorthwood.co.uk   website: www.thenorthwood.co.uk

SUNNYDOWNS HOTEL, 66 ABBEY ROAD, RHOS-ON-SEA, CONWY LL28 4NU (01492 544256; Fax: 01492 543223). A 3 star luxury family hotel just two minutes' walk to beach and shops. All rooms en suite with digital TV with approximately 40 channels, tea/coffee facilities and central heating. Hotel has bar, pool room and car park. A non-smoking hotel. [Pets £3 per night]
e-mail: sunnydowns-hotel@tinyworld.co.uk   website: www.sunnydownshotel.co.uk

WALES — Carmarthenshire

Bronwydd Arms, Laugharne, Llandeilo, Llandovery, Llanelli, Llansteffan

CWMDWYFRAN FARM HOLIDAY COTTAGES

Swallow View and Nuthatch Cottage have recently been refurbished to a high standard. Open-plan kitchen/dining/living areas; fully equipped kitchen; lounge with digital Freeview TV. Each sleeps 4. Centrally located for exploring coast and countryside.

Cwmdwyfran Farm Holiday Cottages,
Cwmdwyfran, Bronwydd Arms, Carmarthenshire, SA33 6JF
Tel: 01267 281419 • e-mail: info@cwmdwyfran.co.uk • www.cwmdwyfran.co.uk

SIR JOHN'S HILL FARM HOLIDAY COTTAGES
Laugharne, Carmarthenshire SA33 4TD
Stables Cottage • Tel: 01994 427001

In one of the finest locations in West Wales with spectacular views of coast and countryside, Stables Cottage is the perfect place for a relaxing break. Here at Sir Johns Hill Farm we specialise in dog-friendly holidays and aim to make their holiday just as good as yours. They will have a great time at the farm which is well away from the main road, and there are lots of great country walks and long sandy beaches nearby too.

www.sirjohnshillfarm.co.uk

Relax at The Maerdy in one of six traditional cottages set within two acres of secure gardens at **MAERDY COTTAGES**. From this idyllic centre enjoy local walks and famous gardens and discover the beautiful coast and countryside of Carmarthenshire. Each cottage is equipped to give maximum comfort...two cottages are fully wheelchair accessible, and all are ideal for families of all ages. Home cooked evening meals available. Open all year.

Maerdy Cottages, Taliaris, Llandeilo, Carmarthenshire SA19 7DA • Tel: 01550 777448
e-mail: enquiries@maerdyholidaycottages.co.uk • www.maerdyholidaycottages.co.uk

WTB ★★★★

Llanerchindda Farm Guest House & Self Catering Cottages
Cynghordy, Llandovery, Carmarthenshire SA20 0NB

Family-run 3 star guest house with 9 bedrooms & 2 self-catering cottages sleeping up to 6 and 10 people. Situated near Llandovery, Mid Wales with spectacular views of the Brecon Beacons. Pets welcome. Walking, bird watching & many other activities available near by.
B&B from £34.50 per night, self-catering from £70.00 per night.

www.cambrianway.com • Tel: 01550 750274 • e-mail: info@cambrianway.com

WTB ★★★

Best Western Diplomat Hotel
Felinfoel, Llanelli SA15 3PJ
Tel: 01554 756156 • Fax: 01554 751649
AA/WTB ★★★

The Diplomat Hotel offers a rare combination of charm and character, with excellent well appointed facilities to ensure your comfort. Explore the Gower Peninsula and the breathtaking West Wales coastline. Salmon & trout fishing, horse riding, golf, and motor racing at Pembrey are all within reach.

**e-mail: reservations@diplomat-hotel-wales.com
www.bw-diplomathotel.co.uk**

Brig y Don Holiday Apartment • Llansteffan • Carmarthenshire

escape to our quality 4-star apartment beside a sandy beach • sleeps 2
dog friendly • estuary views • glorious coastal and woodland walks
friendly village • truly, a dog's paradise!
Tel: Liz on 01267 241585
e-mail: enquiries@brigydon-holidays.co.uk • www.brigydon-holidays.co.uk

Carmarthenshire

Bronwydd Arms

Village 2 miles north of Carmarthen.

CWMDWYFRAN FARM HOLIDAY COTTAGES, CWMDWYFRAN, BRONWYDD ARMS SA33 6JF (01267 281419) Two beautiful semi detached holiday cottages in a secluded and peaceful location. Refurbished to a high standard. Each sleeps 4. Ideal for exploring coast and countryside. WTB ★★★★. [Pets £15 per week].
e-mail: info@cwmdwyfran.co.uk website: www.cwmdwyfran.co.uk

Laugharne

Village on the River Taf estuary, 4 miles south of St Clears, burial place of Dylan Thomas.

SIR JOHN'S HILL FARM HOLIDAY COTTAGES, LAUGHARNE SA33 4TD. STABLES COTTAGE 01994 427001. Specialising in dog-friendly holidays, a very comfortable cottage in one of the finest locations in West Wales, with spectacular views, lots of great country walks, and long sandy beaches nearby. [pw! £15 per week.]
website: www.sirjohnshillfarm.co.uk

Llandeilo

Town on River Towy, 14 miles east of Carmarthen.

MAERDY COTTAGES, TALIARIS, LLANDEILO SA19 7DA (01550 777448). Six traditional cottages set within two acres of secure gardens. Each cottage is equipped to give maximum comfort, two cottages are fully wheelchair accessible, and all are ideal for families of all ages. Home cooked evening meals available. Open all year. WTB ★★★★. [First pet free, others £5 per night, £20 per week].
e-mail: enquiries@maerdyholidaycottages.co.uk website: www.maerdyholidaycottages.co.uk

Llandovery

Small town 17 miles west of Brecon; remains of Norman castle.

LLANERCHINDDA FARM GUEST HOUSE & SELF CATERING COTTAGES, CYNGHORDY, LLANDOVERY SA20 0NB (01550 750274). Family run guest house with 9 bedrooms & 2 self catering cottages sleeping up to 6 and 10 people. Situated near Llandovery. Pets welcome. B&B from £34.50 per night, self-catering from £70.00 per night. WTB ★★★ [Pets £4 per night]
e-mail: info@cambrianway.com website: www.cambrianway.com

Llanelli

Village on the River Taf estuary, 10 mile north-west of Swansea.

THE DIPLOMAT HOTEL, FELINFOEL ROAD, AELYBRYN, LLANELLI SA15 3PJ (01554 756156; Fax: 01554 751649). Privately owned and operated with warmth and generous hospitality. The Diplomat Hotel offers a rare combination of charm and character with excellent well appointed facilities to ensure your comfort and convenience. WTB/AA ★★★ [Pets £5 per night]
e-mail: reservations@diplomat-hotel-wales.com website: www.bw-diplomathotel.co.uk

Llansteffan

Picturesque village overlooked by Norman castle on the headland.

MRS LIZ DUTCH, BRIG Y DON HOLIDAYS, LLANSTEFFAN SA33 5LW (01267 241585). Escape to our quality apartment beside a sandy beach. Sleeps 2, dog friendly. Estuary views, glorious coastal and woodland walks. Friendly village. Truly, a dog's paradise! WTB ★★★★. [pw! 🐾]
e-mail: enquiries@brigydon-holidays.co.uk website: www.brigydon-holidays.co.uk

408 WALES
Ceredigion
Aberaeron, Cardigan, Pontrhyfendigaid

Prices start from £9.00 per person, per night
Based on 4 persons sharing

Enjoy the beautiful scenery & coastal walks...
...and why not bring the dog!

BOOK NOW AND THE DOG GOES FREE!
For your dog to go FREE, quote reference PW/09 when booking your stay

- Self-catering accommodation
- 36 acres of spectacular coastal scenery
- Countryside and coastal walks
- Follow the Dylan Thomas Trail
- Horse riding • Tennis court
- A secluded pebble beach • Pets welcome
- Play area and games room
- BBQ and licensed bar
- Weekend breaks and weekday specials also available!

Gilfach Holiday Village, West Coast Wales

Gilfach Holiday Village, Llwyncelyn, Aberaeron, Ceredigion SA46 OHN. Telephone: **01545 580 288**
or visit our website **www.selfcateringinwales.com**

Gilfach Holiday Village

Penwern fach holiday cottages

Character stone cottages.
Peaceful setting with lovely views. Beautiful coastline.
Indoor swimming pool nearby. Log fires.
Penwern Fach Cottages
Ponthirwaun, near Cenarth, Cardigan, Ceredigion SA43 2RL
Tel: 01239 710694 • e-mail: info@penwernfach.co.uk
www.penwernfach.co.uk

Wales Cymru ★★★★

Ty Gwyn Lodge

Wales Cymru ★★★★

In the Teifi valley between Cardigan Bay and the Cambrian Mountains
Ty Gwyn Lodge is a traditionally built, converted stone barn that can sleep up to 5/6, self catering. Exposed beams and wooden floorboards give a cosy, comfortable feel together with all the modern appliances expected.
Lisburne Road, Pontrhydfendigaid, Ceredigion SY25 6EJ
Tel: 01974 831408 • Fax: 01974 831567
email: enquiry@tygwynlodge.co.uk • www.tygwynlodge.co.uk

Pet-Friendly
Pubs, Inns & Hotels
on pages 438-443

Please note that these establishments may not feature in the main section of this book

Ceredigion
WALES 409

Aberaeron

Attractive little town on Cardigan Bay, good touring centre for coast and inland. The Aeron Express Aerial ferry offers an exciting trip across the harbour. Marine aquarium; Aberarth Leisure Park nearby.

GILFACH HOLIDAY VILLAGE, LLWYNCELYN, NEAR ABERAERON SA46 OHN (01545 580288). Choice of modern Bungalows (up to 6 persons) or luxury 2/3 person apartments. Fully equipped, linen available, colour TV. Horse and pony riding. Tennis. Write or phone for brochure pack to the Manager. [Pets £15 per week.]
e-mail: info@stratfordcaravans.co.uk   website: www.selfcateringinwales.com
or www.stratfordcaravans.co.uk

Aberporth

Popular seaside village offering safe swimming and good sea fishing. Good base for exploring Cardigan Bay coastline.

"QUALITY COTTAGES', CERBID, SOLVA, HAVERFORDWEST, PEMBROKESHIRE SA62 6YE (01348 837871). Cottages set in all coastal areas, enjoy unashamed luxury, highest residential standards. Log fires. Linen supplied. Pets welcome, free. [pw! 🐕]
website: www.qualitycottages.co.uk

Cardigan

Historic town on the banks of the Teifi estuary, with excellent leisure facilities.

PENWERN FACH COTTAGES, PONTHIRWAUN, NEAR CENARTH, CARDIGAN SA43 2RL (01239 710694). Character stone cottages. Peaceful setting with lovely views. Beautiful coastline. Indoor swimming pool nearby. Log fires. WTB ★★★★.[Pets £20 per week]
e-mail: info@penwernfach.co.uk   website: www.penwernfach.co.uk

Ciliau Aeron

Village in undulating country just inland from the charming Cardigan Bay resorts of New Quay and Aberaeron. New Quay 12 miles, Aberaeron 6

"QUALITY COTTAGES', CERBID, SOLVA, HAVERFORDWEST, PEMBROKESHIRE SA62 6YE (01348 837871). Cottages set in all coastal areas, enjoy unashamed luxury, highest residential standards. Log fires. Linen supplied. Pets welcome, free. [pw! 🐕]
website: www.qualitycottages.co.uk.

Llangrannog

Pretty little seaside village overlooking a sandy beach. Superb cliff walk to NT Ynys Lochtyn, a secluded promontory.

"QUALITY COTTAGES', CERBID, SOLVA, HAVERFORDWEST, PEMBROKESHIRE SA62 6YE (01348 837871). Cottages set in all coastal areas, enjoy unashamed luxury, highest residential standards. Log fires. Linen supplied. Pets welcome, free. [pw! 🐕]
website: www.qualitycottages.co.uk

Pontrhydfendigaid

Village on River Teifi, home to an annual eisteddfod.

TY GWYN LODGE, LISBURNE ROAD, PONTRHYDFENDIGAID SY25 6EJ (01974 831408; Fax: 01974 831567). Traditionally built, converted stone barn that can sleep up to 5/6, self catering. In the Teifi valley between Cardigan Bay and the Cambrian Mountains. Cosy, comfortable with all modern appliances.
email: enquiry@tygwynlodge.co.uk   website: www.tygwynlodge.co.uk

Symbols

🐕   Indicates that pets are welcome free of charge.
£   Indicates that a charge is made for pets: nightly or weekly.
pw! Shows some special provision for pets; exercise facility, feeding or accommodation arrangement.
⌂   Indicates separate pets accommodation.

Around the magnificent coast of Wales
Pembrokeshire, Cardigan Bay, Snowdonia, Anglesey, Lleyn Peninsula, Borders

Choose from over 300 Quality Cottages

Pets Welcome Free

A small specialist agency with over 40 years experience letting quality cottages.

Enjoy unashamed luxury in traditional Welsh Cottages. Situated near safe sandy beaches and in the heart of Wales — famed for scenery, walks, wild flowers, birds, badgers and foxes.

Pets welcome FREE at most of our properties

Leonard Rees, Quality Cottages, Cerbid, Solva, Haverfordwest, Pembrokeshire. SA62 6YE

Telephone: (01348) 837871 for our FREE Colour Brochure

www.qualitycottages.co.uk

100s of pictures of quality cottages and beautiful Wales

Pembrokeshire

Boncath, Broad Haven, Croft, Crymych, Fishguard

Cottages at Fron Fawr

Four PET FRIENDLY cottages, converted from Welsh slate and stone barns offering modern holiday living with a contemporary design and feel.
* 3 and 4 bedrooms * Private enclosed gardens * 48 acres of fields and woodlands.
* Children's play area, boules court and outdoor hot-tub.
Coast and beaches 5 miles; use of leisure facilities at owner's other site 5 miles way.

• CLYDEY COTTAGES PEMBROKESHIRE •
www.clydeycottages.co.uk • info@clydeycottages.co.uk • Tel.: 01239 698619

Valley View Cottages

Newchapel, Boncath, Pembrokeshire SA37 0HH Tel: 01239 841850
Newly renovated luxury cottages with superb country views. Sleep 1-6.
Fully equipped for all year comfort. Children and pets welcome.
Prices from £245 per week; heating, electricity, linen and towels included.
Ideally located for walking, birdwatching, beaches, outdoor pursuits and lots more.
e-mail: info@valleyviewcottages.co.uk • www.valleyviewcottages.co.uk

PEMBROKESHIRE NATIONAL PARK.

Three-bedroom fully furnished holiday lodge, within easy walking distance of sandy beaches and the Coastal Footpath. Ideal centre for family holidays, walking, birdwatching. Sleeps 6 + cot. From £140 to £375 per week.
MRS L.P. ASHTON, 10 ST LEONARDS ROAD, THAMES DITTON, SURREY KT7 0RJ
020-8398 6349 • e-mail: lejash@aol.com • www.33timberhill.com

Croft Farm & Celtic Cottages
• Pembrokeshire •

Croft makes the ideal place for a main holiday or short break. Delightful barn conversions provide superbly comfortable accommodation. Enjoy the luxury indoor heated pool, sauna, spa pool and gym facilities. Close to sandy beaches, bays and coastal National Park. Good walking country. Indoor and outdoor play areas. Colourful gardens. Friendly farm animals. Pets welcome.

For a brochure please contact Andrew and Sylvie Gow,
Croft Farm & Celtic Cottages, Croft, Near Cardigan, Pembrokeshire SA43 3NT
Tel: 01239 615179 • www.croft-holiday-cottages.co.uk
e-mail: info@croft-holiday-cottages.co.uk

Three extremely comfortable, well equipped self-catering cottages (WTB ★★★★★). One is particularly suitable for wheelchair users. Each cottage has its own enclosed garden; other amenities include safe indoor and outdoor play areas and a summer house. Ideally located for outdoor pursuits; many safe and accessible beaches close by; daily hire of ocean kayaks available.
Julie & Adrian Charlton • Tel:01239 891394 • e-mail: info@ploughcottages.co.uk
The Plough, Eglwyswrw, Crymych, Pembs SA41 3UJ • www.ploughcottages.co.uk

Welcome to Ivybridge
where your pet is as welcome as you are!

Situated in a quiet part of Goodwick, Ivybridge is a family-run modern guest house, all rooms are en suite and have Freeview TV and hot drinks tray. Try our small heated indoor pool.
Evening meals served, licensed bar open daily. Private car park.
Close by are walks to the sea which you and your pet will enjoy.

Ivybridge Guest House, Drim Mill, Dyffryn, Goodwick SA64 0JT
Tel: 01348 875366
e-mail: ivybridge5366@aol.com • www.ivybridgeleisure.co.uk

Pembrokeshire

Fishguard, Haverfordwest, Llanteg

Fishguard Holiday Park
Sunny West Wales
Superb holiday park near town,
Shops & sandy beaches. Club
Free nightly entertainment. Swimming pool
And much more...
TEL: 01348 872462 • www.howellsleisure.co.uk

Haven Cottages
Sycamore Lodge, Nolton Haven SA62 3NH
Tel: 01437 710200
e-mail: info@havencottages.co.uk
www.havencottages.co.uk

Cottages sleeping 2-8 persons. All fully equipped. Children and pets welcome.
Sympathetically converted cottages occupying beach front.

NOLTON HAVEN QUALITY COTTAGES
Tel: 01437 710263
WTB ★★★ – ★★★★★

Ideal for out of season breaks. Most with sea views, some 30 yards from safe, sandy beach. Central heating, open fires. Sleep 2 to 20. 8-bedroom farmhouse sleeps 20.

Contact: Jim & Joyce Canton, Nolton Haven Farmhouse, Nolton Haven, Haverfordwest SA62 6NH
e-mail: PW8@noltonhaven.com
www.noltonhaven.com

Scamford Caravan Park • Peaceful family-run park
Close to the Coastal Path and lovely sandy beaches. 25 luxurious caravans with Four Star Tourist Board grading. Playground. Pets welcome.
Richard & Christine White Tel/Fax: 01437 710304
www.scamford.com • e-mail: holidays@scamford.com
SCAMFORD CARAVAN PARK, KEESTON, HAVERFORDWEST SA62 6HN

garnisaf.com
HOLIDAY COTTAGE, B&B AND CAMPING

Within the Pembrokeshire National Park, minutes' walk from the coastal path, surrounded by stunning scenery and wildlife habitats. We offer 4★ B&B, evening meals, 5★ self-catering accommodation and a small secluded campsite with campfires and picnic benches.
Garn Isaf, Abercastle, Haverfordwest, Pembrokeshire SA62 5HJ
Tel & Fax: 01348 831838 • Mobile: 07969 529929
www.garnisaf.com

Keeston Hill Cottage
KEESTON, HAVERFORDWEST SA62 6EJ   Tel: 01437 710440
Two fully equipped comfortable apartments sleeping 4/5 each, in a beautifully converted cottage with garden. 2½ miles from fabulous beaches. A short walk to our family-run restaurant/bar. Open all year. Prices from £220 to £435 per week; heating, electricity and linen incl.
e-mail: enquiries@keestonhillcottage.co.uk • www.keestonhillcottage.co.uk

LLANTEGLOS ESTATE   01834 831677/831371   VisitWales 3/4 Stars
Charming self-contained Woodland Lodges in quiet estate. Wonderful views of coast and country. Safe children's play area. Fully licensed clubhouse. Miles of sandy beaches. Attractions for all ages and interests. For further details/colour brochure: **TONY & JANE BARON, LLANTEGLOS ESTATE, LLANTEG, NEAR AMROTH, PEMBROKESHIRE SA67 8PU**
e-mail: llanteglosestate@supanet.com • www.llanteglos-estate.com
WTB ★★★★

Pembrokeshire
Newport

WALES 413

Hotel Cottages & Restaurant

Gellifawr is located in the beautiful Gwaun Valley in the Pembrokeshire Coast National Park, about four miles from the coast and beaches at Newport Sands. The area in which they are situated is designated a Site of Special Scientific Interest. Perfect for walking, bird watching, hiking, cycling, nature watching, beaches, sightseeing or just relaxing in the friendly and comfortable welcoming environment.

This is Bluestone country where the famous stones at Stonehenge originated. The area has many fascinating historical features. It lies in an unspoiled rural area, surrounded by farms, with many footpaths and bridleways and an abundance of wildlife.

This 19th century stone farmhouse has been lovingly restored, ensuring a warm welcome to this family-run hotel. The seven en suite bedrooms are spacious, and have tea/coffee making facilities and colour TV. The non-smoking restaurant offers varied à la carte and bistro menus, and is open to non-residents. There is also a well-stocked bar, where a log-burning fire and friendly staff will ensure an enjoyable visit.

Self-catering accommodation is available in double glazed, centrally heated cottages (one to three bedrooms), set around a landscaped courtyard, with modern kitchens and all the comforts of home. This scenic area is ideal for walking, birdwatching, cycling, or just relaxing.

Pontfaen, Near Fishguard SA65 9TX
Tel: 01239 820343
e-mail: info@gellifawr.co.uk
www.gellifawr.co.uk

Wales Cymru ★★★

Wales Cymru ★★★★

Lochmeyler Farm Guesthouse

Tel: 01348 837724
Fax: 01348 837622
e-mail: stay@lochmeyler.co.uk
www.lochmeyler.co.uk

Mrs Morfydd Jones
Llandeloy,
Pen-y-Cwm,
Near Solva,
St Davids,
Pembrokeshire
SA62 6LL

A warm welcome awaits you at Lochmeyler, a 220 acre dairy farm in the centre of the St Davids Peninsula. It is an ideal location for exploring the beauty of the coast and countryside.
There are 12 bedrooms, four of them in the adjacent cottage suites. All are en suite, non-smoking, luxury rooms with colour TV, video and refreshment facilities. Rooms serviced daily. Children 10 years and over are welcome. Well behaved dogs are welcome in some of our rooms. Dogs are not permitted to be left unattended in the rooms. There are kennel facilities for owners wishing to leave their dogs during the day. We do not charge for dogs or the kennel facilities.

Open all year round.
Credit cards accepted.
Colour brochure on request.

DAILY RATES
Bed & Breakfast per person per night £35.00 - £40.00
Optional Dinner every night @ £20.00 per person

Pembrokeshire

Llechryd, Moylegrove, Rosemarket, St Davids

Castell Malgwyn Country House Hotel
Llechryd, Cardigan, Pembrokeshire SA43 2QA
Well behaved dogs welcome. Set on the banks of the River Teifi in large grounds. Excellent food in Lily's Restaurant.
Tel: 01239 682382 • www.castellmalgwyn.co.uk
e-mail: reception@malgwyn.co.uk

ENJOY THE BEAUTY OF THE NORTH PEMBROKESHIRE COAST WITH YOUR DOGS

3 WELSH COTTAGES with enclosed gardens. Pets free of charge. Paddock for exercise. Dog-friendly bay and beaches within walking distance, with spectacular views. Bed linen included. **Tel: 01239 881 280**

Four luxury cottages set around landscaped courtyard. Fenced pond, child play and recreational areas to rear. Ideal for walkers, cyclists, watersports. Sandy beaches and historic sites. Central location.

Church View Holiday Cottages
Church View, Rosemarket, Pembrokeshire SA73 1JG
Tel: 07850 954781 • e-mail: info@churchviewcottages.co.uk
www.churchviewcottages.co.uk

www.ffynnonddofn.co.uk — Delightful cottage in quiet lane between St Davids and Fishguard, with panoramic views over spectacular coastline. Ideal for walking; rocky coves and safe, sandy beaches nearby. The cottage is fully carpeted, warm, comfortable and very well-equipped, sleeping six in three bedrooms, plus cot. Washing machine, tumble dryer, freezer, microwave, DVD/video. Large games room, children's toys, pleasant secure garden. Perfect for early or late holidays, with central heating and double glazing. Parking. Shop one mile. Footpath to beach. Open all year.

FFYNNON DDOFN

Terms from £350, including heating and electricity. Brochure on request.

Mrs B. Rees White, Brickhouse Farm, Burnham Road, Woodham Mortimer, Maldon, Essex CM9 6SR (01245 224611)

St Davids Holiday Cottages

Superbly appointed self-catering cottages (sleep 2-6) situated on the spectacular North Pembrokeshire coast

Spectacular scenery • Beautiful beaches
Wonderful walking • Peace and quiet

• All cottages appointed to the highest standards and available all year round

• Dogs welcome in most properties

For details contact:
Peter Davies, No 6 Hamilton Street,
Fishguard, Pembrokeshire SA65 9HL
Tel: 01348 872266

e-mail: peter@stdavidsholidays.co.uk
www.stdavidsholidays.co.uk

WALES — Pembrokeshire

St Davids, Saundersfoot, Whitland

FELINDRE COTTAGES • www.felindrecottages.co.uk
Porthgain, St Davids, Pembrokeshire SA62 5BH
Self-catering cottages with panoramic sea and country views. Five minutes' walk from Coastal Path, picturesque fishing village of Porthgain and a great pub! Peaceful location. Short breaks available. One well-behaved dog welcome, except school holidays. WTB graded.
Tel: 01348 831220 • e-mail: steve@felindrecottages.co.uk

PEMBROKESHIRE SHEEPDOGS, TREMYNYDD FACH, ST DAVIDS SA62 6DB
A working sheep farm, whose fields extend down to the sea. Farm B&B (in cosy cottages) and Self-catering (in farmhouse and chalet) available. Spectacular and unspoilt stretch of coastal path abounding with rare species of plants and wildlife.
Tel: 01437 721677 • Fax: 01437 720308
e-mail: info@sheepdogtraining.co.uk • www.sheepdogtraining.co.uk

Vine Cottage GUEST HOUSE

The Ridgeway,
Saundersfoot SA69 9LA
(Non-smoking)
Coastal village outskirts.
Sandy beaches and coast path nearby.
Award-winning garden for guests' and dogs' relaxation and exercise.
Tel: 01834 814422 • www.vinecottageguesthouse.co.uk

A country estate of over 450 acres, including 2 miles of riverbank. See a real farm in action, the hustle and bustle of harvest, newborn calves and lambs. Choose from 6 character stone cottages, lovingly converted traditional farm buildings, some over 200 years old.

www.davidsfarm.com

Each cottage is fully furnished and equipped, electricity and linen included, with all year round heating. Children welcome. Brochure available. Contact: **Mrs Angela Colledge,**
Gwarmacwydd, Llanfallteg, Whitland, Pembrokeshire SA34 0XH
Self Catering ★★★★ Cottages   t 0800 321 3699

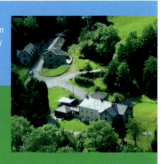

'QUALITY COTTAGES', CERBID, SOLVA, HAVERFORDWEST, PEMBROKESHIRE SA62 6YE (01348 837871). Cottages set in all coastal areas, enjoy unashamed luxury, highest residential standards. Log fires. Linen supplied. Pets welcome, free. [pw! 🐕]
website: www.qualitycottages.co.uk

Boncath

Small hamlet 5 miles south of Cardigan.

CLYDEY COTTAGES PEMBROKESHIRE – COTTAGES AT FRON FAWR. Four pet-friendly cottages, 3/4 bedrooms. Enclosed gardens. 48 acres of fields and woodlands. Children's play area. Coast 5 miles. Tel: 01239 698619. [Pets £25 per week]
e-mail: info@clydeycottages.co.uk   website: www.clydeycottages.co.uk

Pembrokeshire   WALES 417

VALLEY VIEW COTTAGES, NEWCHAPEL, BONCATH SA37 0HH (01239 841850). Newly renovated luxury cottages with superb country views. Sleep 1-6. Fully equipped. Children and pets welcome. Prices from £245 per week. Heating, electricity, linen and towels included. WTB★★★★. [Pets £20 per week]
e-mail: info@valleyviewcottages.co.uk   website: www.valleyviewcottages.co.uk

Bosherton

Village 4 miles south of Pembroke, bordered by 3 man-made lakes, a haven for wildlife and covered in water lilies in early summer.

"QUALITY COTTAGES', CERBID, SOLVA, HAVERFORDWEST, PEMBROKESHIRE SA62 6YE (01348 837871). Cottages set in all coastal areas, enjoy unashamed luxury, highest residential standards. Log fires. Linen supplied. Pets welcome, free. [pw! 🐾]
website: www.qualitycottages.co.uk

Broad Haven

Village on St Bride's Bay, 6 miles west of Haverfordwest.

PEMBROKESHIRE NATIONAL PARK. Sleeps 6 + cot. Three-bedroom fully furnished Holiday Lodge. Walking distance sandy beaches and coastal footpath. £140 to £375 per week. MRS L.P. ASHTON, 10 ST LEONARDS ROAD, THAMES DITTON, SURREY KT7 0RJ (020-8398 6349). [🐾]
e-mail: lejash@aol.com   website: www.33timberhill.com

Croes Goch

Hamlet 6 miles north east of St Davids

"QUALITY COTTAGES', CERBID, SOLVA, HAVERFORDWEST, PEMBROKESHIRE SA62 6YE (01348 837871). Cottages set in all coastal areas, enjoy unashamed luxury, highest residential standards. Log fires. Linen supplied. Pets welcome, free. [pw! 🐾]
website: www.qualitycottages.co.uk

Croft

Located 2 miles SW of Cardigan.

CROFT FARM & CELTIC COTTAGES, CROFT, NEAR CARDIGAN SA43 3NT (01239 615179). Featured in Daily Mail. Stone barn conversions with luxury indoor heated pool, sauna, spa pool and gym. Colourful gardens, indoor and outdoor play areas. VisitWales ★★★★★/★★★★ *SELF CATERING*. Pets welcome. [Pets £4 per night, £28 per week, pw!]
e-mail: info@croft-holiday-cottages.co.uk   website: www.croft-holiday-cottages.co.uk

Crymych

Village 8 miles south of Cardigan.

PLOUGH COTTAGES. Three extremely comfortable cottages; one suitable for wheelchair users. Each cottage has its own enclosed garden. Ideally located for outdoor pursuits; many safe and accessible beaches close by. WTB ★★★★★ Contact: JULIE & ADRIAN CHARLTON, THE PLOUGH, EGLWYSWRW, CRYMYCH SA41 3UJ (01239 891394)
e-mail: info@ploughcottages.co.uk   website: www.ploughcottages.co.uk

Fishguard

Small town at end of Fishguard Bay

IVYBRIDGE GUEST HOUSE, DRIM MILL, DYFFRYN, GOODWICK SA64 0JT (01348 875366). Stay at Ivybridge, all rooms en suite. Evening meals served. Small heated indoor pool. Private car park. Pets welcome! [Pets £7 per stay].
e-mail: ivybridge5366@aol.com   website: www.ivybridgeleisure.co.uk

FISHGUARD HOLIDAY PARK, PEMBROKESHIRE (01348 872462). Superb holiday park near town, shops and sandy beach. Club. Free nightly entertainment. Swimming pool.
website: www.howellsleisure.co.uk

Haverfordwest

Administrative and shopping centre for the area; ideal base for exploring National Park. Historic town of narrow streets; museum in castle grounds; many fine buildings.

HAVEN COTTAGES. Quality beachfront cottages, sleep 2-8, adjacent sandy beach. Well equipped. Open all year. Winter breaks. Contact: SYCAMORE LODGE, NOLTON HAVEN SA62 3NH (01437 710200). [Pets £10 per week].
e-mail: info@havencottages.co.uk   website: www.havencottages.co.uk

NOLTON HAVEN QUALITY COTTAGES. Ideal for out of season breaks. Most with sea view. 30 yards from safe, sandy beach. Sleep 2-20. 8-bedroom farmhouse sleeps 20. WTB ★★★/★★★★/★★★★★ Self-Catering. Contact: JIM & JOYCE CANTON, NOLTON HAVEN FARMHOUSE, NOLTON HAVEN, HAVERFORDWEST SA62 6NH (01437 710263).
e-mail: PW8@noltonhaven.com   website: www.noltonhaven.com

SCAMFORD CARAVAN PARK, KEESTON, HAVERFORDWEST SA62 6HN (Tel & Fax: 01437 710304). 25 luxurious caravans (shower, fridge, microwave, colour TV). Peaceful park near lovely sandy beaches. Playground. Launderette. Pets welcome. WTB ★★★★ Holiday Park.
e-mail: holidays@scamford.com   website: www.scamford.com

GARN ISAF, ABERCASTLE, HAVERFORDWEST SA62 5HJ (Tel & Fax: 01348 831838; Mobile: 07969 529929). Within the Pembrokeshire National Park, surrounded by stunning scenery. 4★ B&B and 5★ self catering accommodation. Secluded campsite, picnic benches. [One pet free s/c, in B&B £5 per night].
website: www.garnisaf.com

CLARE HALLETT, KEESTON HILL COTTAGE, KEESTON, HAVERFORDWEST SA62 6EJ (01437 710440). Two apartments sleeping 4/5 each in cottage with garden. A short walk to our family-run restaurant/bar. Open all year. From £220 to £435 per week. Heating, electricity and linen included. [🐾]
e-mail: enquiries@keestonhillcottage.co.uk   website: www.keestonhillcottage.co.uk

Llanteg

Hamlet 4 miles south of Whitland.

TONY & JANE BARON, LLANTEGLOS ESTATE, LLANTEG, NEAR AMROTH SA67 8PU (01834 831677 /831371). Self-contained Woodland Lodges. Sleep 6. Children's play area. Licensed bar. Visitor attractions. Open all year. Call for brochure. VisitWales ★★★/★★★★ Self Catering [Pets £6 per night, £35 per week.]
e-mail: llanteglosestate@supanet.com   website: www.llanteglos-estate.com

Llechryd

Village on the A484 3 miles from Cardigan.

CASTELL MALGWYN COUNTRY HOUSE HOTEL, LLECHRYD, CARDIGAN SA43 2QA (01239 682382) Well behaved dogs welcome. Set on the banks of the River Teifi in large grounds. Excellent food in Lily's Restaurant. [Pets f10 per night]
e-mail: reception@malgwyn.co.uk   website: www.castellmalgwyn.co.uk

Lydstep

Small hamlet 3 miles south west of Tenby.

CELTIC HAVEN, LYDSTEP, NEAR TENBY SA70 7SG (01834 870000). Escape, relax, unwind, explore at Wales most complete resort. Exhilarating cliff-top walks, stunning scenery and several dog-friendly beaches. Luxury cottages; superb leisure facilities; spa and restaurant. [Pets £20 per stay].
e-mail: welcome@celtichaven.com   website: www.celtichaven.co.uk

Symbols

🐾 Indicates that pets are welcome free of charge.

£   Indicates that a charge is made for pets: nightly or weekly.

pw! Shows some special provision for pets; exercise facility, feeding or accommodation arrangement.

▢   Indicates separate pets accommodation.

Pembrokeshire

Moylegrove

Village 4 miles west of Cardigan.

NORTH PEMBROKESHIRE COAST. 3 WELSH COTTAGES with enclosed gardens. Paddock for exercise. Dog-friendly bay and beaches within walking distance, with spectacular views. Bed linen included. (01239 881 280). [🐾]

Newgale

On St Bride's Bay 3 miles east of Solva. Long beach where at exceptionally low tide the stumps of a submerged forest may be seen.

"QUALITY COTTAGES', CERBID, SOLVA, HAVERFORDWEST, PEMBROKESHIRE SA62 6YE (01348 837871). Cottages set in all coastal areas, enjoy unashamed luxury, highest residential standards. Log fires. Linen supplied. Pets welcome, free. [pw! 🐾]
website: www.qualitycottages.co.uk

Newport

Small town at mouth of the River Nyfer, 9 miles south west of Cardigan. Remains of 13th-century castle.

"QUALITY COTTAGES', CERBID, SOLVA, HAVERFORDWEST, PEMBROKESHIRE SA62 6YE (01348 837871). Cottages set in all coastal areas, enjoy unashamed luxury, highest residential standards. Log fires. Linen supplied. Pets welcome, free. [pw! 🐾]
website: www.qualitycottages.co.uk

GELLIFAWR HOTEL & COTTAGES, PONTFAEN, NEWPORT SA65 9TX (01239 820343). Family-run hotel with seven en suite bedrooms; restaurant offers à la carte and bistro menus. Also self-catering cottages (1-3 bedrooms) set around landscaped courtyard. Scenic area, ideal for walking or just relaxing. WTB ★★★/★★★★
e-mail: info@gellifawr.co.uk   website: www.gellifawr.co.uk

Rosemarket

Peaceful village just off A477 in the heart of Pembrokeshire countryside.

CHURCH VIEW HOLIDAY COTTAGES, CHURCH VIEW, ROSEMARKET SA73 1JG (07850 954877). Four luxury cottages set around landscaped courtyard. Fenced pond, child play and recreational areas. Ideal for walkers, cyclists, watersports. Sandy beaches. WTB ★★★★. [Pets £10 per week]
e-mail: info@churchviewcottages.co.uk   website: www.churchviewcottages.co.uk

St Davids

Smallest cathedral city in Britain, shrine of Wales' patron saint. Magnificent ruins of Bishop's Palace. Craft shops, farm parks and museums; boat trips to Ramsey Island.

"QUALITY COTTAGES', CERBID, SOLVA, HAVERFORDWEST, PEMBROKESHIRE SA62 6YE (01348 837871). Cottages set in all coastal areas, enjoy unashamed luxury, highest residential standards. Log fires. Linen supplied. Pets welcome, free. [pw! 🐾]
website: www.qualitycottages.co.uk

MRS M. JONES, LOCHMEYLER FARM GUEST HOUSE, LLANDELOY, PEN-Y-CWM, NEAR SOLVA, ST DAVIDS, PEMBROKESHIRE SA62 6LL (01348 837724; Fax: 01348 837622). Welcome Host Gold Award. 12 en suite luxury bedrooms, four in the cottage suites adjacent to the house. All bedrooms non-smoking, with TV, video and refreshment facilities. Children 10 years and over welcome. WTB ★★★★★ *FARM*, AA★★★★★★ [pw! 🐾]
e-mail: stay@lochmeyler.co.uk   website: www.lochmeyler.co.uk

FFYNNON DDOFN, LLANON, LLANRHIAN, NEAR ST DAVIDS. Comfortable, well-equipped cottage with panoramic coastal views. Sleeps 6. Fully carpeted with central heating. Large games room. Open all year. Pets welcome free of charge. Brochure on request from: MRS B. REES WHITE, BRICKHOUSE FARM, BURNHAM RD, WOODHAM MORTIMER, MALDON, ESSEX CM9 6SR (01245 224611). [🐾]
website: www.ffynnonddofn.co.uk

WALES — Pembrokeshire

ST DAVIDS HOLIDAY COTTAGES. Superbly appointed self-catering cottages (sleep 2-6) situated on the spectacular North Pembrokeshire coast. Available all year round. Dogs welcome in most. For details contact: PETER DAVIES, 6 HAMILTON STREET, FISHGUARD SA65 9HL (01348 872266). [🐕]
e-mail: peter@stdavidsholidays.co.uk   website: www.stdavidsholidays.co.uk

FELINDRE COTTAGES, PORTHGAIN, ST DAVIDS SA62 5BH (01348 831220). Self-catering cottages with panoramic sea and country views. Five minutes' walk from Coastal Path, picturesque fishing village of Porthgain and a great pub! Peaceful location. Short breaks available. One well-behaved dog welcome, except school holidays. WTB graded. [pw! £10 per week]
e-mail: steve@felindrecottages.co.uk   website: www.felindrecottages.co.uk

PEMBROKESHIRE SHEEPDOGS, TREMYNYDD FACH, ST DAVIDS SA62 6DB (01437 721677; Fax: 01437 720308). B&B (in cosy cottages) and Self-catering (in farmhouse and chalet) on working sheep farm. Spectacular and unspoilt stretch of coastal path with plants and wildlife. Peaceful location.
e-mail: info@sheepdogtraining.co.uk   website: www.sheepdogtraining.co.uk

Saundersfoot

Popular resort and sailing centre with picturesque harbour and sandy beach. Tenby 3 miles

VINE COTTAGE GUEST HOUSE, THE RIDGEWAY, SAUNDERSFOOT SA69 9LA (01834 814422). Coastal village outskirts. Sandy beaches and coast path nearby. Award-winning garden for guests' and dogs' relaxation and exercise. Non-smoking throughout. AA ★★★★ [pw! Pets £5 per stay.]
e-mail: enquiries@vinecottageguesthouse.co.uk   website: www.vinecottageguesthouse.co.uk

Solva

Picturesque coastal village with sheltered harbour and excellent craft shops. Sailing and watersports; sea fishing, long sandy beach.

'QUALITY COTTAGES', CERBID, SOLVA, HAVERFORDWEST, PEMBROKESHIRE SA62 6YE (01348 837871). Cottages set in all coastal areas, enjoy unashamed luxury, highest residential standards. Log fires. Linen supplied. Pets welcome, free. [pw! 🐕]
website: www.qualitycottages.co.uk

Tenby

Popular resort with two wide beaches. Fishing trips, craft shops, museum. Medieval castle ruins, 13th-century church. Golf, fishing and watersports; boat trips to nearby Caldy Island with monastery and medieval church.

"QUALITY COTTAGES', CERBID, SOLVA, HAVERFORDWEST, PEMBROKESHIRE SA62 6YE (01348 837871). Cottages set in all coastal areas, enjoy unashamed luxury, highest residential standards. Log fires. Linen supplied. Pets welcome, free. [pw! 🐕]
website: www.qualitycottages.co.uk

Whitland

Village 6 miles east of Narberth. Whitland Abbey 2 km.

MRS ANGELA COLLEDGE, GWARMACWYDD FARM, LLANFALLTEG, WHITLAND SA34 0XH (0800 321 3699). Country estate with six character stone cottages, fully furnished and equipped. All linen and electricity included; heated for year-round use. WTB ★★★★ [pw! Pets £10 per pet per week]
website: www.davidsfarm.com

Publisher's note

While every effort is made to ensure accuracy, we regret that FHG Guides cannot accept responsibility for errors, misrepresentations or omissions in our entries or any consequences thereof. Prices in particular should be checked.
We will follow up complaints but cannot act as arbiters or agents for either party.

Powys

Builth Wells, Cilmery, Hay-on-Wye

OLD VICARAGE

• ERWOOD, BUILTH WELLS LD2 3SZ • Tel: 01982 560680 •

Superior views from elevated position in Wye Valley. Pleasant rooms with imaginative furnishings/decor. Drinks tray, TV, washbasin. Comfortable ornate beds with original Welsh blankets. One en suite, two sharing guests' own bathroom. Bacon and sausage from our own pigs, farm eggs, home baked bread and preserves all make a true Welsh farm experience.

e-mail: linda@oldvicwyevalley.co.uk • www.oldvicwyevalley.co.uk   WTB ★★★ Farm

★★★

Caer Beris Manor

GWESTY ★★★ HOTEL

Family-owned three star Country House Hotel set in 27 acres of parkland.
Free salmon and trout fishing on River Wye (two rods) and on River Irfon.
Superb walking and touring. 18 hole Golf Course nearby. Excellent cuisine.
All rooms en suite with telephone, TV and tea making.

DOGS WELCOME!

DB&B from £72.95pppn, from £437.70 weekly
B&B from £59.95pppn. Terms based on 2 sharing

Mrs Katharine Smith, Caer Beris Manor, Builth Wells
Powys LD2 3NP • Tel: 01982 552601 • Fax: 01982 552586
e-mail: caerberis@btconnect.com • www.caerberis.com

Wales Cymru ★★★★

Pwllgwilym
Holiday Cottages

Pwllgwilym, Llanafan Road,
Cilmery, Builth Wells, Powys LD2 3NY
Phone: 01982-552740 • 07909-681881
E-mail: bookings@pwllgwilym-cottages.co.uk
www.pwllgwilym-cottages.co.uk

Pwllgwilym Holiday Cottages are situated two miles from Builth Wells in the lovely village of Cilmery, in Mid Wales. A large barn has been tastefully converted into 3 spacious 4-star cottages with hardwood stairs, flagstone floors, surrounded by a 60 acre farm with lovely views.
• Cottage 'DAN-Y-COED' - Sleeps 4 with disabled facilities. Shared laundry.
• Cottage 'TYCANOL' - Sleeps up to 8 with pull-out settee in the lounge.
• Cottage 'PWLLYN' - Sleeps up to 7 with pull-out settee in the lounge.
All three cottages can be opened out into one large cottage sleeping up to 19. Ideal for large families. Two 6-seater hot tubs.

17th century farm in rural Radnorshire, five miles Hay-on-Wye.
Wonderful walking country. Self-catering apartments sleeping 2-14.
A warm welcome for you and your pet(s). WTB ★★★

MRS E. BALLY, LANE FARM, PAINSCASTLE, BUILTH WELLS LD2 3JS
Tel & Fax: 01497 851605 • e-mail: lanefarm@onetel.com

Powys

Hay-on-Wye, Llandrindod Wells, Llansilin, Machynlleth, Newtown

BASKERVILLE ARMS HOTEL

Delightfully placed in the upper reaches of the Wye Valley with the Black Mountains and Brecon Beacons on the doorstep, this comfortable retreat could not be better placed for lovers of both lush and wild unspoilt scenery. Hay-on-Wye, the 'town of books' is only 1.2 miles away with its narrow streets, antique shops and over 30 bookshops. Run by resident proprietors, June and David, the hotel provides tasty, home-cooked food in bar and restaurant, using the best local produce. With so many pursuits to enjoy in the area, this little hotel is a fine holiday base and well-appointed en suite bedrooms serve the purpose excellently. Totally non-smoking. Single from £45, Double/Twin from £42.

Clyro, Near Hay-on-Wye, Herefordshire HR3 5RZ
Tel: 01497 820670 • *See website for Special Rate Breaks*
e-mail: info@baskervillearms.co.uk • www.baskervillearms.co.uk

The Park House Motel

Crossgates, Llandrindod Wells, Powys LD1 6RF

Set in 3 acres of beautiful Welsh countryside and close to the famous Elan Valley. Accommodation includes static caravans, touring pitches and fully equipped chalets which have a twin or double bedroom, shower room, and kitchen with lounge. Sleeping up to 6, they can be booked for either self-catering or B&B.
Well behaved pets are very welcome.

Tel: 01597 851201 • www.parkhousemotel.net

Self-Catering Accommodation near Offa's Dyke Path

Ingleside • Self-catering Bungalow on working farm. 3 bedrooms – sleeps 5. Living room with colour TV. Kitchen/dining room. Fully equipped. Well behaved dog allowed. 4 miles from Offa's Dyke Path. **5 Star B&B also available.**

Glenice Jones, Lloran Ganol Farm, Llansilin, Oswestry, Shropshire SY10 7QX
Tel: 01691 791296/791287 • Mob: 07779 935009 • Fax: 791296

PETS WELCOME at
The Wynnstay Hotel

Maengwyn Street, Machynlleth, Powys SY20 8AE
Tel: 01654 702941

Award-winning food, wine and beer.
Glorious countryside and miles of sandy beaches.
Masses to do and see.
Good Food Guide & Good Beer Guide Recommended,
Les Routiers "Best Wine List in Britain".
Pets free in kennels, £5 one-off charge in rooms.

e-mail: info@wynnstay-hotel.com • www.wynnstay-hotel.com

The Forest Country Cottages

Hidden in the beautiful Vale of Kerry are 4 pretty self-catering cottages and a B&B in secluded setting, sleeping 2 to 5. Period features, wood-burning stoves, games room, tennis court, play area. Owner is a veterinarian. Perfect to explore the many attractions of Mid Wales.
Paul & Michelle Martin, Forest Cottage, Gilfach Lane, Kerry, Newtown, Powys SY16 4DW
Tel: 01686 621 821 • E-mail: info@forestcottageskerry.co.uk • www.holidaycottagesmidwales.co.uk

Powys
Pen-y-Cae

Craig-y-Nos Castle
Pen-y-Cae, Powys SA9 1GL
Tel: 01639 731167 / 730205 • Fax: 01639 731077
bookings_craigynos@hotmail.com
www.craigynoscastle.com

Craig-y-Nos Castle nestles in the lovely Upper Swansea Valley next to the River Tawe. The castle was the former home of opera diva, Adelina Patti and is now a beautiful hotel with a very haunted history...

Craig-y-nos Castle is situated in an area of outstanding natural beauty. With its wonderful location and the authentic ambience of a Welsh Castle, Craig-y-Nos has plenty to offer. Whether you want a relaxing break, an over night stay, or if you are joining us as part of a function, you can be sure of a totally unique experience.

The Castle benefits from a number of bars and restaurants and is fully equipped to cater for conferences and wedding parties.

Craig-y-nos Castle has a wide variety of accommodation ranging from budget rooms to en-suite and luxury guest rooms overlooking the gardens. Each room is unique in design and is furnished in a traditional fashion in keeping with the Castle's history.

The castle also benefits from Spa facilities, gymnasium and spa that enjoy unsurpassed panoramic views of the Brecon Beacons.

HOTEL FEATURES
- Fantastic Location • Character Bedrooms • Ghost Tours
- Beacons Spa Facilities • Wonderful Public Rooms • En suite Facilities

Pet friendly Accommodation
Good dogs stay at no extra cost
FREE can of dog food (per dog)
for each night of stay when taking a
Mid-Week Break offer

Powys

Presteigne, Rhayader

Whitehall Cottage

Cosy cottage in lovely Border countryside, two miles from Offa's Dyke • Central heating, washing machine, dishwasher, microwave, colour TV, inglenook, woodburner, linen included • Power shower over bath • Sleeps 4 plus cot • Ample parking • Sun-trap garden • On working farm in peaceful hamlet • Children and pets welcome

MRS R. L. JONES, UPPER HOUSE, KINNERTON, NEAR PRESTEIGNE LD8 2PE
Tel: 01547 560207

Oak Wood Lodges

01597 811422

Carreg-Ddu in the spectacular Elan Valley, just a 10 minute drive from Oak Wood Lodges

Llwynbaedd, Rhayader, Powys LD6 5NT
Luxurious Self Catering Log Cabins

situated at approximately 1000 ft above sea level with spectacular views of the Elan Valley and Cambrian Mountains. Enjoy pursuits such as walking, pony trekking, mountain biking, fishing and bird watching in the most idyllic of surroundings. Excellent touring centre.
Dogs welcome. Short Breaks as well as full weeks. Open all year round.

www.oakwoodlodges.co.uk

The Elan Valley - Tyn-y-Castell Self-catering Chalet

Spectacular scenery and magical walks; around the lakes, through the woods, up on the hills. A doggy paradise and the folks will love it too! Our delightful chalet is warm and comfortable and in a lovely rural location. Enclosed garden. No charge for pets.

Joan Morgan (01982 560402)
e-mail: oldbedw@lineone.net • www.rhayader.net/tynycastell

Powys

Rhayader

DOLWEN • Wye Valley • Radnor • Powys
Warm, spacious holiday bungalow, in the heart of Wales.
Sleeps 6. Wonderful views. Enclosed garden.
Suitable for guests with pets. **Tel: 07877 661838**
http://www.holiday-rentals.co.uk/p97483

Builth Wells

Old country town in lovely setting on River Wye amid beautiful hills. Lively markets; host to Royal Welsh Agricultural Show

MRS LINDA WILLIAMS, OLD VICARAGE, ERWOOD, BUILTH WELLS LD2 3SZ (01982 560680). Superior views from elevated position in Wye Valley. Comfortable ornate beds, one en suite room, two sharing guests' own bathroom. Drinks tray, TV, washbasin. Bacon and sausage from our own pigs, farm eggs, home baked bread and preserves. WTB ★★★ Farm, FHG Diploma Winner 2004.[🐾]
e-mail: linda@oldvicwyevalley.co.uk   website: www.oldvicwyevalley.co.uk

MRS KATHARINE SMITH, CAER BERIS MANOR, BUILTH WELLS LD2 3NP (01982 552601; Fax: 01982 552586). Family-owned country house hotel set in 27 acres of parkland. Free salmon and trout fishing; golf nearby, superb walking and touring. All rooms en suite. WTB/AA ★★★ [Pets £5 per night, £30 per week].
e-mail: caerberis@btconnect.com   website: www.caerberis.com

Cilmery

Village 2½ miles west of Builth Wells.

PWLLGWILYM HOLIDAY COTTAGES, PWLLGWILYM, LLANAFAN ROAD, CILMERY, BUILTH WELLS LD2 3NY (01982-552140/ 07909-681881). A large barn tastefully converted into 3 spacious 4-star cottages with hardwood stairs, flagstone floors. Surrounded by a 60 acre farm with lovely views, two miles from Builth Wells. Sleep 4-8. WTB ★★★★ [Pets £12 per week].
e-mail: bookings@pwllgwilym-cottages.co.uk   website: www.pwllgwilym-cottages.co.uk

Hay-on-Wye

Small market town at north end of Black Mountains, 15 miles north-east of Brecon.

MRS E. BALLY, LANE FARM, PAINSCASTLE, BUILTH WELLS LD2 3JS (Tel & Fax: 01497 851605). 17th century farm in rural Radnorshire, five miles Hay-on-Wye. Wonderful walking country. Self-catering apartments sleeping 2-14. A warm welcome for you and your pet(s). WTB ★★★ [🐾]
e-mail: lanefarm@onetel.com

BASKERVILLE ARMS HOTEL, CLYRO, NEAR HAY-ON-WYE HR3 5RZ (01497 820670). Delightfully placed comfortable retreat with well appointed en suite bedrooms. Tasty, home-cooked food in bar and restaurant, using the best local produce. Special break rates. WTB ★★★.
e-mail: info@baskervillearms.co.uk   website: www.baskervillearms.co.uk

Llandrindod Wells

Popular inland resort, Victorian spa town, excellent touring centre. Golf, fishing, bowling, boating and tennis. Visitors can still take the waters at Rock Park Gardens.

THE PARK HOUSE MOTEL, CROSSGATES, LLANDRINDOD WELLS LD1 6RF (01597 851201). In three acres, amidst beautiful countryside near Elan Valley. Static caravans, touring pitches and fully equipped chalets. Restaurant. Pets welcome. [Pets £3 per night, £20 per week. Guide dogs free].
website: www.parkhousemotel.net

Llangurig

Village on River Wye, 4 miles south-west of Llanidloes. Ideal walking countryside.

MRS J. BAILEY, GLANGWY, LLANGURIG, LLANIDLOES SY18 6RS (01686 440697). Bed, breakfast and evening meals in the countryside. Plenty of walking locally. Also caravan and campsite. Prices on request. [🐾]

Llansilin

Village 6 miles west of Oswestry.

Self catering bungalow on working farm. 3 bedrooms, sleeps 5. Living room with colour TV; kitchen/dining room. Fully equipped. 4 miles from Offa's Dyke Path. Well behaved dog allowed. 5 Star B&B also available. GLENICE JONES, LLORAN GANOL FARM, LLANSILIN, OSWESTRY, SHROPSHIRE SY10 7QX (01691 791296/791287; Mob: 07779 935009). Visit Wales ★★★★.

Machynlleth

Attractive old town with half-timbered houses. Ideal for hillside rambles.

THE WYNNSTAY HOTEL, MAENGWYN STREET, MACHYNLLETH SY20 8AE (01654 702941). Award-winning food, wine and beer. Glorious countryside and miles of sandy beaches. Masses to do and see. WTB ★★★. Good Food Guide & Good Beer Guide Recommended, Les Routiers "Best Wine List in Britain". [Pets free in kennels, £5 one-off charge in rooms]
e-mail: info@wynnstay-hotel.com   website: www.wynnstay-hotel.com

Newtown

Situated on the banks of the River Severn. Birthplace of Robert Owen.

PAUL & MICHELLE MARTIN, FOREST COTTAGE, KERRY, NEWTOWN SY16 4DW (01686 621821). Four pretty self-catering cottages and a B&B in secluded setting. Sleep 2-5. Period features, tennis court, games room, play area. Owner is a veterinarian. WTB ★★★★.
e-mail: info@forestcottageskerry.co.uk   website: www.holidaycottagesmidwales.co.uk

Pen-y-Cae

Village 6 miles north east of Ystalyfera.

CRAIG-Y-NOS CASTLE, PEN-Y-CAE SA9 1GL (01639 731167 / 730205; Fax: 01639 731077) Fantastic location in the lovely Upper Swansea Valley. Character en suite bedrooms. Ghost Tours. Beacons Spa Facilities. Mid-week breaks. Dog-friendly accommodation.
e-mail: bookings_craigynos@hotmail.com   website: www.craigynoscastle.com

Presteigne

Attractive old town with half timbered houses. Ideal for hillside rambles and pony trekking.

MRS R. L. JONES, UPPER HOUSE, KINNERTON, NEAR PRESTEIGNE LD8 2PE (01547 560207). Cosy cottage two miles from Offa's Dyke. Central heating, washing machine, dishwasher, microwave, colour TV, inglenook, woodburner, linen included. Power shower over bath. Sleeps 4 plus cot. Children and pets welcome. [🐕].

Rhayader

Small market town on River Wye north of Builth Wells. Popular for angling and pony trekking.

OAK WOOD LODGES, LLWYNBAEDD, RHAYADER LD6 5NT (01597 811422). Luxurious self-catering log cabins with spectacular views of the Elan Valley and Cambrian Mountains. Walking, pony trekking, mountain biking, fishing and bird watching in idyllic surroundings. Phone for brochure. [Dog £20 per week, £13 per short break; additional dogs half price].
website: www.oakwoodlodges.co.uk

DOLWEN, WYE VALLEY. Warm, spacious holiday bungalow, 4 miles from the market town of Rhayader. 3 bedrooms, 2 bathrooms, sun lounge and large sitting room. Private, enclosed garden. Suitable for guests with pets. Tel: 07877 661818. [🏠 🐕]
website: http://www.holiday-rentals.co.uk/p97483

TYN-Y-CASTELL SELF-CATERING CHALET. Spectacular scenery and magical walks; around the lakes, through the woods, up on the hills. A doggy paradise and the folks will love it too! Our delightful chalet is warm and comfortable and in a lovely rural location. JOAN MORGAN (01982 560402) [🐕]
e-mail: oldbedw@lineone.net   website: www.rhayader.net/tynycastell

South Wales

WALES 427

Abergavenny, Gower Peninsula, Kenfig Hill, Monmouth, Neath, Swansea

HALF MOON INN — Llanthony, Abergavenny NP7 7NN
Set amidst the beautiful scenery of the Vale of Ewyas and dominated by the slopes of the Black Mountains, this attractive inn is a welcome sight, serving traditional ales, cider and good food. The Offa's Dyke and Beacons Way footpaths are only half a mile away. Bed and Breakfast accommodation is available. Dogs welcome. **Tel: 01873 890611**
e-mail: halfmoon@llanthony.wanadoo.co.uk • www.halfmoon-llanthony.co.uk

01792 360624
www.homefromhome.com
e-mail: enquiries@homefromhome.com

Home from Home is proud to offer a wide variety of pet friendly holiday accommodation in the seaside village of Mumbles and on the beautiful Gower Peninsula. The Gower Peninsula and Swansea Bay area is an excellent place to be outdoors breathing in the fresh sea air, particularly if you are with your four-legged friend. Whether you prefer a countryside walk or a stroll on one of the many stunning beaches, the area offers something for everyone.

homefromhome.com — relax unwind enjoy...

OLDWALLS LEISURE — Gower Peninsula
Luxury 5-star dog-friendly B&B and cottages in Area of Outstanding Natural Beauty. 50 acres of land with private lakes and streams. Dog-friendly pub and restaurant. Tennis court and trout fishing on-site. Numerous unspoilt beaches welcome dogs AND horses.
Tel: 01792 391 468   www.oldwallsleisure.com

Wales Cymru ★★★★

Margam Row, Kenfig Hill, Mid Glamorgan CF33 6DP
ruth@minerscottage.com • www.minerscottage.com
open all year round • tel: +44(0) 797 195 0772
Spacious, 3 bedrooms (sleeps 5) with high standards and quietly located with beautiful views over Margam Valley and Swansea Bay. A real home from home, with maple and slate floors and enclosed back garden. One well behaved dog welcome. Linen, towel and fuel included.

Miners Cottage

A spacious and homely 16th century (Grade II Listed) former farmhouse with oak beams and inglenook fireplaces, set in large garden with stream. Easy access to A40. All nine bedrooms are en suite or have private facilities. B&B from £31 to £33 per person. Evening meals by arrangement • Non-smoking • AA ★★★
**ROSEMARY AND DEREK RINGER, CHURCH FARM GUEST HOUSE,
MITCHEL TROY, MONMOUTH NP25 4HZ • 01600 712176**
e-mail: info@churchfarmguesthouse.eclipse.co.uk • www.churchfarmmitcheltroy.co.uk

18th Century luxury Guest House where our aim is to ensure a peaceful, comfortable and relaxing stay. Guest rooms are all en suite and spacious, with views over the Vale of Neath. Licensed bar and restaurant • Vegetarian & other diets catered for • Children welcome • Parking • Non-smoking rooms • Pets welcome by arrangement
Mrs C. Jones, Green Lanterns Guest House, Hawdref Ganol Farm, Cimla, Neath SA12 9SL • 01639 631884 • www.greenlanterns.co.uk
WTB ★★★★

BEST WESTERN ABERAVON BEACH HOTEL
Neath Port Talbot, Swansea Bay SA12 6QP • Tel: 01639 884949
Modern seafront hotel. A warm Welsh welcome awaits you and your pets. miles of flat promenade and a pet-friendly beach. Pets Paradise!! And for you... newly refurbished rooms, fine cuisine, leisure centre and many local attractions. **www.aberavonbeachhotel.com**

South Wales
Wye Valley

Cwrt-y-Gaer
www.cwrt-y-gaer.co.uk
Relaxation ✦ Beautiful Scenery ✦ Comfort

Enjoy the tranquillity of Cwrt-y-Gaer, site of an ancient hilltop fort with 22 acres of peaceful woods and meadows, plus pure soft air to smooth you. Three well equipped self-catering units in converted old stone buildings of Welsh Longhouse, including Byre Cottage, which is specially designed for the wheelchair user.
Quiet area with good access to many places of interest in the Vale of Usk, the Wye Valley and the Forest of Dean. Good walking.
One, four or more dogs welcome FREE.
Open all year. Brochure from:

**Sue & John Llewellyn, Crwt-y-Gaer, Wolvesnewton.
Chepstow, Monmouthshire NP16 6PR
Tel: (01291) 650700
e-mail: john.llewellyn11@btinternet.com**

All units are WTB ★★★. Welcome Host Gold award
One unit is Grade 1 access for the disabled.

CASTLE NARROWBOATS CHURCH ROAD WHARF, GILWERN NP7 0EP (01873 830001). The Monmouthshire & Brecon Canal in South Wales. Discover the beauty of Wales onboard one of our excellent narrowboats. 2-8 berth boats, short breaks available. Pets welcome. For a free colour brochure call Castle Narrowboats:
website: www.castlenarrowboats.co.uk

Abergavenny

Historic market town at south-eastern gateway to Brecon Beacons National Park. Pony trekking, leisure centre; excellent touring base for Vale of Usk.

HALF MOON INN, LLANTHONY, NEAR ABERGAVENNY NP7 7NN (01873 890711). B&B, good food and real ale in 17thC inn. Wonderful scenery of Black Mountains. Good base for walking, pony trekking, birdwatching. Dogs welcome.[Pets £1.50 per night]
e-mail: halfmoon@llanthony.wanadoo.co.uk   website: www.halfmoon-llanthony.co.uk

Gower Peninsula

Britain's first designated Area of Outstanding Natural Beauty with numerous sandy beaches and lovely countryside to explore.

HOME FROM HOME offers a wide variety of pet friendly holiday accommodation in the seaside village of Mumbles and on the beautiful Gower Peninsula. Whether you prefer a countryside walk or a stroll on one of the many stunning beaches, the area offers something for everyone. Contact: 01792 360624. [Pets £15 per week]
e-mail: enquiries@homefromhome.com   website: www.homefromhome.com

South Wales

WALES 429

CULVER HOUSE HOTEL, PORT EYNON, GOWER SA3 1NN (01792 390755). One and two bedroom apartments offer modern fully equipped accommodation, stunning accessible Blue Flag beach location. Continental breakfast included. Prices from £90 per night.
website: www.culverhousehotel.co.uk

OLDWALLS LEISURE (01792 391468). Luxury 5-star dog-friendly B&B and cottages in Area of Outstanding Natural Beauty. 50 acres of land with private lakes and streams. Dog-friendly pub and restaurant. Tennis court and trout fishing on site. Numerous unspoilt beaches welcome dogs AND horses.
website: www.oldwallsleisure.com

Kenfig Hill

Scenic area, ideal for peaceful holiday. Easy access to M4.

MINERS COTTAGE, MARGAM ROW, KENFIG HILL CF33 6DP (07971 950772). Spacious, 3 bedrooms (sleeps 5) with high standards and quietly located with beautiful views over Margam Valley and Swansea Bay. A real home from home, with maple and slate floors and enclosed back garden. One well behaved dog welcome. Linen, towel and fuel included. Open all year. WTB ★★★★
e-mail: ruth@minerscottage.com   website: www.minerscottage.com

Monmouth

Market town at confluence of Rivers Wye and Monnow 20 miles north-east of Newport.

ROSEMARY AND DEREK RINGER, CHURCH FARM GUEST HOUSE, MITCHEL TROY, MONMOUTH NP25 4HZ (01600 712176). A spacious 16th century (Grade II Listed) former farmhouse set in large garden with stream. Easy access to A40. All bedrooms en suite or with private facilities. B&B from £31 to £33 per person. Evening meals by arrangement. Non-smoking. AA ★★★ [🐾].
e-mail: info@churchfarmguesthouse.eclipse.co.uk   website: www.churchfarmmitcheltroy.co.uk

Neath

Town on River Neath 8 miles NE of Swansea.

MRS C. JONES, GREEN LANTERNS GUEST HOUSE, HAWDREF GANOL FARM, CIMLA, NEATH SA12 9SL (01639 631884). 18th Century luxury Guest House with spacious en suite rooms, all with views over the Vale of Neath. Licensed bar and restaurant. Vegetarian & other diets catered for. Pets welcome by arrangement. WTB ★★★★.
website: www.greenlanterns.co.uk

Swansea

Second largest city in Wales with a wide variety of leisure activities and excellent shopping.

BEST WESTERN ABERAVON BEACH HOTEL, NEATH PORT TALBOT, SWANSEA BAY SA12 6QP (01639 884949). Modern seafront hotel. A warm Welsh welcome awaits you and your pets. 2 miles of flat promenade and a pet friendly beach. Pets Paradise!! And for you... newly refurbished rooms, fine cuisine, leisure centre and many local attractions. AA ★★★ [🐾]
website: www.aberavonbeachhotel.com

Wye Valley

Scenic area, ideal for relaxation.

MR & MRS J. LLEWELLYN, CWRT-Y-GAER, WOLVESNEWTON, CHEPSTOW NP16 6PR (01291 650700). 1, 4 or more dogs welcome free. Self-catering, attractively converted stone buildings of Welsh Longhouse. 22 acres, super views of Usk Vale. Brochure. Three units (one suitable for disabled). WTB ★★, Welcome Host Gold Award. [pw! 🐾]
e-mail: john.llewellyn11@btinternet.com   website: www.cwrt-y-gaer.co.uk

430 IRELAND

IMAGINE IRELAND, HOLIDAY COTTAGES (01756 707764). 1500 inspected Holiday Cottages. From £12 per person per night, inc. ferry or car hire. Pets go free. Low car hire and ferry inc. prices. Smaller party prices. Free 100 page brochure.
website: www.imagineireland.co.uk

Co Kerry

Lauragh

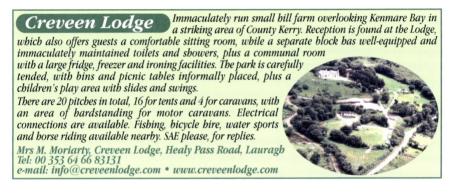

Creveen Lodge Immaculately run small hill farm overlooking Kenmare Bay in a striking area of County Kerry. Reception is found at the Lodge, which also offers guests a comfortable sitting room, while a separate block has well-equipped and immaculately maintained toilets and showers, plus a communal room with a large fridge, freezer and ironing facilities. The park is carefully tended, with bins and picnic tables informally placed, plus a children's play area with slides and swings.
There are 20 pitches in total, 16 for tents and 4 for caravans, with an area of hardstanding for motor caravans. Electrical connections are available. Fishing, bicycle hire, water sports and horse riding available nearby. SAE please, for replies.
Mrs M. Moriarty, Creveen Lodge, Healy Pass Road, Lauragh
Tel: 00 353 64 66 83131
e-mail: info@creveenlodge.com • www.creveenlodge.com

Lauragh

Rural location on Ring of Beara.

MRS M. MORIARTY, CREVEEN LODGE, HEALY PASS ROAD, LAURAGH (00 353 64 66 83131). Small, carefully tended, well equipped park, 16 pitches for tents, 4 for caravans, with hardstanding for motor caravans. Fishing, bicycle hire, water sports and horse riding available nearby. [🐕]
e-mail: info@creveenlodge.com   website: www.creveenlodge.com

Visit the FHG website
www.holidayguides.com
for details of the wide choice of accommodation featured in the full range of FHG titles

NARROWBOATS 431

BOOK ONLINE at www.claymoore.co.uk or Telephone: 01928 717273

Canalboat Holidays from base in Cheshire • Boats sleep 2-10 people • Fully equipped • Car parking • Full Instruction • Fuel included • Day and Short Break Hire • Pets Welcome

Clifton Cruisers — The Holiday Cruising Choice

From short breaks to week-long cruising, we offer a fleet of luxurious narrowboats for holidays in and around the heart of England, from our base in Rugby, on the Oxford canal.

Clifton Wharf, Vicarage Hill, Clifton on Dunsmore, Rugby CV23 0DG
For information and booking please telephone: 01788 543570
email us: info@cliftoncruisers.com
or see our website: www.cliftoncruisers.com

Discover the beauty of Wales
on board one of our excellent narrowboats

Cruising along the Monmouth and Brecon Canal, through the Brecon Beacons National Park, you can take a short break, week or longer.

We have boats for 2-8 people and pets are welcome.
Visit our website for up to date availability.
www.castlenarrowboats.co.uk
or call **01873 830001** for a brochure

Castle Narrowboats, Church Road Wharf, Gilwern, Monmouthshire NP7 0EP

Other specialised holiday guides from FHG

PUBS & INNS OF BRITAIN • **COUNTRY HOTELS** OF BRITAIN
WEEKEND & SHORT BREAK HOLIDAYS IN BRITAIN
THE GOLF GUIDE WHERE TO PLAY, WHERE TO STAY
500 GREAT PLACES TO STAY • **SELF-CATERING HOLIDAYS** IN BRITAIN
BED & BREAKFAST STOPS • **CARAVAN & CAMPING HOLIDAYS**
FAMILY BREAKS IN BRITAIN

Published annually: available in all good bookshops or direct from the publisher:
FHG Guides, Abbey Mill Business Centre, Seedhill, Paisley PA1 1TJ
Tel: 0141 887 0428 • Fax: 0141 889 7204
e-mail: admin@fhguides.co.uk • www.holidayguides.com

Holidays with Horses

A selection of accommodation where horse and owner/rider can be put up at the same address– if not actually under the same roof! We would be grateful if readers making enquiries and/or bookings from this supplement would mention **Pets Welcome!**

ENGLAND

South West/Somerset

**LEONE & BRIAN MARTIN,
RISCOMBE FARM HOLIDAY COTTAGES, EXFORD,
EXMOOR NATIONAL PARK TA24 7NH
(Tel: 01643 831480)
website: www.riscombe.co.uk (with up-to-date vacancy info)**

Four self-catering stone cottages in the centre of Exmoor National Park. Excellent walking and riding country. Dogs and horses welcome. Stabling available. Open all year. VB ★★★★

**WESTERMILL FARM
EXFORD, MINEHEAD TA24 7NJ
(01643 831238; Fax: 01643 831216)
e-mail: pw@westermill.com   website: www.westermill.com**

Cottages (Disabled Catergory 2) in grass paddocks. Ideal for children. Stabling and fields for horses. Wonderful for dogs and owners. Separate campsite by river.

South East/Oxfordshire

**TODDY AND CLIVE HAMILTON-GOULD
TOWER FIELDS, TUSMORE ROAD, NEAR SOULDERN, BICESTER OX27 7HY
(01869 346554)
e-mail: toddyclive@towerfields.com   website: www.towerfields.com**

Ground floor en suite rooms, all with own entrance and ample parking. Breakfast using local produce. Easy reach of Oxford, Stratford-upon-Avon, many National Trust houses. Silverstone, Towcester. Dogs and horses welcome by arrangement.

East of England/Suffolk

MRS JANE BREWER,
LODGE COTTAGE, LAXFIELD ROAD, CRATFIELD, HALESWORTH IP19 0QG
(01986 798830 or 07788 853884)
e-mail: janebrewer@ukonline.co.uk

Pretty 16C thatched cottage retaining some fine period features. Sleeps 4. Pets welcome. Fenced garden. One mile from village. 30 minutes to Southwold and coast. Rural, quiet and relaxing. Brochure.

Midlands/Shropshire

THE ANCHORAGE
ANCHOR, NEWCASTLE on CLUN, CRAVEN ARMS SY7 8PR
(Tel: 01686 670737)
e-mail: nancynewcwm@btinternet.com • website: www.adamsanchor.co.uk

Two well-equipped modern caravan holiday homes in Area of Outstanding Natural Beauty. Perfect for walking, cycling, riding, or just unwinding! Each has three bedrooms, TV, shower room with flush toilet, and kitchen with fridge and microwave. Well behaved pets and children welcome, horses also accommodated. Stabling or grazing; guided rides if required. Open Easter to October.

Yorkshire/East Yorkshire

PAWS-A-WHILE
KILNWICK PERCY, POCKLINGTON YO42 1UF
(01759 301168; Mobile: 07711 866869)
e-mail: paws.a.while@lineone.net • website: www.pawsawhile.net

Small family B & B set in forty acres of parkland twixt York and Beverley. Golf, walking, riding. Pets and horses most welcome. Brochure available. ETC ★★★★

North East / Northumberland

LYNNEY HOLDEN,
CROOKHOUSE, KIRKNEWTON, WOOLER NE71 6TN
(Tel: 01668 216113)
e-mail: stay@crookhousecottages.co.uk • website: www.crookhousecottages.co.uk

Superior self catering accommodation in a traditional Northumbrian steading, Secluded and tranquil. Sleeps 4-12. Horses and dogs welcome. VisitBritain ★★★★.

North West/Cumbria

FARLAM HALL HOTEL
BRAMPTON CA8 2NG.
(016977 46234; Fax: 016977 46683)
e-mail: farlam@relaischateaux.com • website: www.farlamhall.co.uk

Standing in four acres of gardens, with its own lake, Farlam Hall offers fine quality cuisine and individually decorated guest rooms. Ideal touring centre for the Lakes, Borders and Hadrian's Wall. AA Three Stars Inspectors' Choice, Relais & Chateaux.

www.holidayguides.com

SCOTLAND

Dumfries & Galloway

AE FARM COTTAGES
GUBHILL FARM, DUMFRIES DG1 1RL
(01387 860648)
e-mail: gill@gubhill.co.uk • website: www.aefarmcottages.co.uk

Modern accommodation in old stone buildings on a traditional farm, overlooking a peaceful valley. Beautiful views, plentiful wildlife and endless paths on the doorstep. Between Dumfries, Moffat and Thornhill. STB ★★★ SELF CATERING, CATEGORY ONE DISABILITY.

RUSKO HOLIDAYS,
GATEHOUSE OF FLEET, CASTLE DOUGLAS DG7 2BS
(01557 814215)
e-mail: info@ruskoholidays.co.uk • website: www.ruskoholidays.co.uk

Spacious, traditional farmhouse and three charming, cosy cottages near beaches, hills and forest park. Lots of off-road riding amid stunning scenery. Stabling and grazing available for your own horse. Beautiful walking and riding country, fishing and tennis. Rates £234-£1382. BHS Horses Welcome Award, STB ★★ to ★★★★

MR P. JONES
BARGALY ESTATE COTTAGES
PALNURE, NEWTON STEWART,
DUMFRIES & GALLOWAY DG8 7BH
(Tel: 01671 401048)
e-mail: bargalyestate@callnetuk.com   website:www.bargaly.com

Three cottages available all year on Historic Estate. Paddocks available close to cottages. Safe riding, forest trails from the Estate. Local Equestrian centre.

WALES

North Wales

**MISS MORRIS
TY COCH FARM-TREKKING CENTRE
PENMACHNO, BETWS-Y-COED
NORTH WALES LL25 0HJ
(Tel: 01690 760248)
e-mail: cindymorris@tiscali.co.uk**

Hill farm in Wales. TV, teamaking, en suite. Set in National Park/Snowdonia. Very quiet and well off the beaten track. A great welcome and good food. Many return visits. £25 B&B.

Carmarthenshire

**SIR JOHN'S HILL FARM HOLIDAY COTTAGES
LAUGHARNE
CARMARTHENSHIRE SA33 4TD
Stables Cottage (Tel: 01994 427001)
website: www.sirjohnshillfarm.co.uk**

A great place to come if you want to get away from it all with your horse(s) and your dog(s). Beautiful scenery, relaxing rides, including beach rides, and great accommodation.

Powys

**MRS E. BALLY
LANE FARM, PAINSCASTLE, BUILTH WELLS LD2 3JS
(Tel & Fax: 01497 851605)
e-mail: lanefarm@onetel.com**

Self-Catering apartments sleeping 2-14. Nine good stables and ample grazing in the heart of rural Radnorshire with wonderful open riding. Some cross-country jumps. WTB ★★★

Other specialised holiday guides from **FHG**

PUBS & INNS OF BRITAIN • **COUNTRY HOTELS** OF BRITAIN
WEEKEND & SHORT BREAK HOLIDAYS IN BRITAIN
500 GREAT PLACES TO STAY • SELF-CATERING HOLIDAYS IN BRITAIN
BED & BREAKFAST STOPS • CARAVAN & CAMPING HOLIDAYS
FAMILY BREAKS IN BRITAIN • **THE GOLF GUIDE** WHERE TO PLAY, WHERE TO STAY

Published annually: available in all good bookshops or direct from the publisher:
FHG Guides, Abbey Mill Business Centre, Seedhill, Paisley PA1 1TJ
Tel: 0141 887 0428 • Fax: 0141 889 7204
e-mail: admin@fhguides.co.uk • www.holidayguides.com

Visit the Winalot website today!

Winalot knows how important giving your dog a balanced diet and plenty of exercise is for their wellbeing. Our website showcases our great balanced range of foods, and the best walks that Britain can offer for you and your furry friend.

www.winalot-dog.co.uk

Trademark owned by Société des Produits Nestlé S.A., Vevey, Switzerland

Pet-Friendly Pubs

A selection of Pubs and Inns where pets are especially welcome!

The Springer Spaniel

Treburley, near Launceston, Cornwall PL15 9NS
Tel: 01579 370424 • e-mail: enquiries@thespringerspaniel.org.uk
www.thespringerspaniel.org.uk

Country pub providing a warm welcome and specialising in home cooked, fresh, locally sourced food. Emphasis upon game, with beef and lamb from the owner's organic farm. Dogs can snooze by the fire or lounge in the beer garden - water provided

Pet Regulars: some very regular customers and their accompanying owners.

Cumberland Inn   Tel: 01434 381875

Townfoot, Alston, Cumbria CA9 3HX
stay@cumberlandinnalston.com • www.cumberlandinnalston.com

A comfy retreat in the secluded North Pennines. Real beer, real fires and real hospitality await your arrival. Home-made hearty fare available all day to revive flagging spirits. Our 5 recently refurbished rooms are all en suite. Muddy dogs and boots welcome.

Dog bowls filled with water (or even beer).
Pets welcome in bedrooms and bar. No charge for pets.

The Coledale Inn

Braithwaite, Near Keswick, Cumbria CA12 5TN
Tel: 017687 78272
e-mail: info@coledale-inn.co.uk • www.coledale-inn.co.uk

Friendly, family-run Victorian inn in peaceful location. Ideally situated for touring and walking direct from the hotel grounds. Fine selection of wines and local real ales. Families and pets welcome.

Barbon Inn

Barbon, Near Kirkby Lonsdale, Cumbria LA6 2LJ Tel: 015242 76233
Friendly 17th century Coaching Inn with 10 bedrooms.
Country pursuits within the immediate area.
Nestling in Lune Valley between Lake District & Yorkshire Dales.
Large field beyond car park to exercise in.
Pet Regulars: our resident black Lab bitch – TESS

www.barbon-inn.co.uk

PET-FRIENDLY PUBS & INNS 439

Tower Bank Arms
Near Sawrey, Ambleside, Cumbria LA22 0LF • Tel: 015394 36334
enquiries@towerbankarms.com • www.towerbankarms.co.uk

17thC Inn situated in the village of Near Sawrey, next to Hilltop, Beatrix Potter's former home. With many original features, and offering fresh local food and traditional local ales.

Water and treats provided • Dogs allowed in bar and accommodation

Brown Cow Inn   Tel: 01229 717243
Waberthwaite, Near Ravenglass, Cumbria LA19 5YJ
e-mail: browncowinn@btconnect.com

Home-cooked food at prices you can afford. Four real ales. Open fire. Four en suite rooms available. Wheelchair access. Food served daily from 11.30am to 8.30pm. Beer garden.

Pets welcome in bar area and rooms.

THE HOOPS INN & COUNTRY HOTEL
Horns Cross, Near Clovelly, Bideford, Devon EX39 5DL
Tel: 01237 451222 • Fax: 01237 451247
sales@hoopsinn.co.uk   www.hoopsinn.co.uk

Thatched country inn with open log fires. All bedrooms en suite. Splendid base for touring and outdoor pursuits. Dartmoor and Exmoor within easy reach.

PORT LIGHT Hotel, Restaurant & Inn
Bolberry Down, Malborough, Near Salcombe, Devon TQ7 3DY
Tel: (01548) 561384 or (07970) 859992 • Sean & Hazel Hassall
e-mail: info@portlight.co.uk • www.portlight.co.uk

Luxury en suite rooms, easy access onto the gardens. Close to secluded sandy cove (dogs permitted). No charge for pets which are most welcome throughout the hotel. Outstanding food and service. Winner 2004 "Dogs Trust" Best Pet Hotel in England. Self-catering cottages also available.

Pets may dine in bar area • Pet food fridge available

Julie and Shaun invite you to The Trout & Tipple, a quiet pub just a mile outside Tavistock, with a keen following for its real ale, (locally brewed Jail Ale and Teignworthy), real food and real welcome. It is a family-friendly pub – children are welcome – with a games room, patio area, dining room and a large car park. Traditional pub fare is served, with trout from the Tavistock Trout Fishery featuring on the menu; Sunday roasts are very popular.

Dogs welcome, bowls of water and treats available on request.

Parkwood Road, Tavistock Devon PL19 0JS
Tel: 01822 618886
www.troutandtipple.co.uk

The Trout & Tipple

Please mention **Pets Welcome!** when making enquiries about accommodation featured in these pages

The Brewers Arms
Martinstown, Dorchester, Dorset DT2 9LB • 01305 889361
e-mail: jackie_smith54@hotmail.com • www.thebrewersarms.com

Country pub with a lovely garden. Pub food. Amenities include a skittle alley, big car park and a large grassed area (which may be suitable for tents). Chews, water bowls and areas out of the sun
Area in the pub where customers can eat and sit with their dogs.
Pet residents: Jodie and Poppy (both lurchers)

The European Inn   www.european-inn.co.uk
Piddletrenthide, Dorchester, Dorset DT2 7QT
Tel: 01300 348308 • info@european-inn.co.uk

Small country pub with two sumptuous bedrooms.
Taste of the West South West Dining Pub of the Year 2007.
Sister pub to The Gaggle of Geese at Buckland Newton.
Pets welcome throughout • Water/food; fire in winter • Good local walks.
Pet Residents: Summer and her daughters Minnie and Maude (Cocker Spaniels)

The Gaggle of Geese
Buckland Newton, Dorchester, Dorset DT2 7BS
01300 345249 • www.thegaggle.co.uk

Large pub with skittle alley, five acres of land including an orchard. Everything on our menu we make ourselves and as much of it as is locally sourced and seasonal as possible.
Sister pub to The European Inn at Piddletrenthide.
Pets welcome throughout • Water/food; fire in winter

The White Swan
The Square, 31 High Street, Swanage, Dorset BH19 2LJ • 01929 423804
e-mail: info@whiteswanswanage.co.uk • www.whiteswanswanage.co.uk

A pub with a warm and friendly atmosphere, three minutes from the beach. Traditional pub food, Sunday roasts. Large beer garden. En suite accommodation with parking. Free wifi and internet access. TV and pool table. Children and dogs welcome.
Water, treats • Dogs allowed in beer garden, bar area and accommodation.
Pet resident: Bagsy (Sharpei). Regulars: Liddy and Em (Black Labradors), Sally and Sophie (Jack Russells), Patch (Jack Russell), Prince (King Charles Spaniel).

The Silent Woman Inn
Bere Road, Coldharbour, Wareham, Dorset BH20 7PA
Tel: 01929 552909 • www.thesilentwoman.co.uk

Traditional country inn nestling in the heart of Wareham Forest.
Beautiful gardens, log fires in winter. All fresh ingredients, wonderful food.
Real ales, good wines. Adults-only inside.
Water bowls and treats - and affection • Dogs allowed in bar areas and all outside areas except children's play areas.
Pet Residents: Rosie and Ellie (Labs). Regulars: Bruno, Tilly and many others.

The Fisherman's Haunt
Salisbury Road, Winkton, Christchurch, Dorset BH23 7AS
Tel: 01202 477283

Traditional coaching inn with 12 stylishly furnished bedrooms, some adapted for disabled access. Good food, wine and Fuller's cask ales. Close to Bournemouth Airport and many places of interest. Pets welcome.
Pets allowed in main bar and lounge for dining.
Two pet-friendly rooms in accommodation block.

PET-FRIENDLY PUBS & INNS

The Whalebone Freehouse
www.thewhaleboneinn.co.uk

Chapel Road, Fingringhoe, Colchester, Essex CO5 7BG
Tel/Fax: 01206 729307 • vicki@thewhaleboneinn.co.uk

Only minutes from Colchester, the Whalebone offers a wide range of excellent food and real ales. Pets are most welcome inside the pub and in the beer garden. Excellent dog-walking trails in and around Fingringhoe. Water bowls provided on request.

Pet Residents: Rosie and Poppy (Basset Hounds)

The Tunnel House Inn
Coates, Cirencester, Gloucestershire GL7 6PW • 01285 770280
e-mail: bookings@tunnelhouse.com • www.tunnelhouse.com

A traditional Cotswold pub set on the edge of a wood. The perfect haven for pets, families, in fact everyone. Home-cooked pub food, traditional ales and ciders. Endless walks lead off from the pub in all directions.
Pets are welcome in all areas inside and out
Plenty of space; water and occasional treats provided.

The White Buck • 01425 402264
www.fullershotels.com

Bisterne Close, Burley, Ringwood, Hampshire BH24 4AZ

Victorian Inn blending tradition with modern comfort, located in the heart of the New Forest, with 7 stylish bedrooms, excellent restaurant and bar. Play area and log trail available for children. Pets welcome.
Dogs are permitted in the bar area and bedrooms 1, 3 and 8 only.

BLACK HORSE INN
Pilgrims Way, Thurnham, Kent ME14 3LD
Tel: 01622 737185 • info@wellieboot.net • www.wellieboot.net

A homely and welcoming inn with its origins in the 18thC, The Black Horse is adorned with hops and beams, and has an open log fireplace to welcome you in winter. A separate annexe has 30 beautiful en suite bedrooms.

*Pets can stay in B&B rooms • Welcome in bar on lead
Dog bin and poop bags provided • Maps of local walks available.*

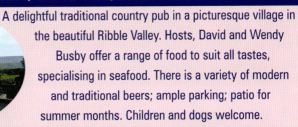

The Assheton Arms, Downham, Near Clitheroe BB7 4BJ

A delightful traditional country pub in a picturesque village in the beautiful Ribble Valley. Hosts, David and Wendy Busby offer a range of food to suit all tastes, specialising in seafood. There is a variety of modern and traditional beers; ample parking; patio for summer months. Children and dogs welcome.

Tel: 01200 441227 • www.assheton-arms.co.uk

www.holidayguides.com

PET-FRIENDLY PUBS & INNS

The Inn at Whitewell • Forest of Bowland
Near Clitheroe, Lancs BB7 3AT • Tel: 01200 448222
reception@innatwhitewell.com • www.innatwhitewell.com

14thC inn in the beautiful Forest of Bowland.
7 miles fishing from our doorstep - trout, sea trout and salmon.
23 glamorous bedrooms, award-winning kitchen.
Voted by *The Independent* "One of the 50 Best UK Hotels"
Pets welcome in all areas except the kitchen!

Stiffkey Red Lion   Tel: 01328 830552
44 Wells Road, Stiffkey, Norfolk NR23 1AJ
e-mail: redlion@stiffkey.com • www.stiffkey.com

5 ground floor en suite bedrooms, 5 on first floor;
all with their own external door.
Pets warmly welcomed

The Dolphin
22 Silver Street, Ilminster, Somerset TA19 0DR • 01460 57904

Cosy, friendly atmosphere. Fully stocked bar, serving a good selection of real ales, lagers, spirits, and fine wines. Excellent home-cooked food served daily. Families welcome. Pool table. Parking nearby. Good walks close by.

Clean water • Dog treats • Pets allowed inside and outside

Old Ship Inn
Uckfield Road, Ringmer, East Sussex BN8 5RP • 01273 814223
e-mail: info@oldshippub.co.uk • www.oldshippub.co.uk

On the A26 between Lewes and Uckfield, this family-run 17thC inn is the perfect place to relax, with food served from 12 to 9.30pm daily. The charming oak-beamed bar and restaurant is set in one acre of well tended, enclosed gardens. Well behaved dogs welcome inside.
Pet Resident: Marley (Bernese Mountain Dog)

The Lamb Inn
High Street, Hindon, Wiltshire SP3 6DP
Tel: 01747 820573 • Fax: 01747 820605
www.lambathindon.co.uk

12th Century historic inn with bedrooms full of character.
Outstanding food and great wine selection.
Pets welcome in the bar and bedrooms. ETC/AA ★★★★

Old Hall Inn   Tel: 01756 752441
Main Street, Threshfield, Grassington, N. Yorks BD23 5HB
oldhallinn@fsmail.net • www.oldhallinnandcottages.co.uk

18thC Inn, renowned for fine ales and award-winning cuisine. Large beer garden. Children's outdoor play area. B&B in four en suite bedrooms; quality self-catering available in adjacent cottages.
Well behaved dogs welcome.

PET-FRIENDLY PUBS & INNS

The Castle Inn
7 Wistowgate, Cawood
Selby, North Yorkshire YO8 3SH   Tel: 01757 268324
info@castleinncawood.co.uk • www.castleinncawood.co.uk

18thC village pub with a 60-seat restaurant and an 18-pitch caravan site. All food is local and fresh.
Water bowls outside.
Pet Resident: Elvis (11-year old Springer Spaniel)

ANNANDALE ARMS HOTEL
HIGH STREET, MOFFAT DG10 9HF
Tel: 01683 220013 • Fax: 01683 221395

A warm welcome is offered to dogs with well-mannered and house-trained owners. There are all the comforts and facilities that owners enjoy such as an excellent restaurant and a relaxing panelled bar. STB ★★★ Hotel.

www.annandalearmshotel.co.uk • pw@annandalearmshotel.co.uk

THE MUNRO INN
Strathyre, Perthshire FK18 8NA• Tel: 01877 384333
www.munro-inn.com

Chilled out Robbie warmly welcomes doggy friends to the Munro Inn in beautiful highland Perthshire. Perfect base for walking, cycling, climbing, water sports, fishing or relaxing! Great home cooking, lively bar, luxurious en suite bedrooms, drying room, broadband internet.

Taking your pet on holiday?
Pets Welcome! now has it own website!

A collection of quality properties where pets will be warmly welcomed. Ranging from self-catering cottages, flats and caravans, to hotels, guest houses and B&Bs. All of the proprietors go out of their way to make the whole family feel at home, and many, being dog owners themselves, have a real understanding and affection for pets.

www.pets-welcome.co.uk

Looking for Holiday Accommodation?

for details of hundreds of properties throughout the UK, visit our website

www.holidayguides.com

445

FHG
·K·U·P·E·R·A·R·D·
**READERS'
OFFER
2010**

LEIGHTON BUZZARD RAILWAY
Page's Park Station, Billington Road,
Leighton Buzzard, Bedfordshire LU7 4TN
Tel: 01525 373888
e-mail: station@lbngrs.org.uk
www.buzzrail.co.uk

*One FREE adult/child with full-fare adult ticket
Valid 14/3/2010 - 31/10/2010*

NOT TO BE USED IN CONJUNCTION WITH ANY OTHER OFFER

FHG
·K·U·P·E·R·A·R·D·
**READERS'
OFFER
2010**

NENE VALLEY RAILWAY
Wansford Station, Stibbington,
Peterborough, Cambs PE8 6LR
Tel: 01780 784444
e-mail: nvrorg@nvr.org.uk
www.nvr.org.uk

*One child FREE with each full paying adult.
Valid Jan. to end Oct. 2010 (excludes galas and pre-ticketed events)*

NOT TO BE USED IN CONJUNCTION WITH ANY OTHER OFFER

FHG
·K·U·P·E·R·A·R·D·
**READERS'
OFFER
2010**

LAPPA VALLEY RAILWAY
Benny Halt, St Newlyn East,
Newquay, Cornwall TR8 5LX
Tel: 01872 510317
e-mail: info@lappavalley.co.uk
www.lappavalley.co.uk

*75p per person OFF up to a maximum of £3
Valid Easter to end October 2010.*

NOT TO BE USED IN CONJUNCTION WITH ANY OTHER OFFER

FHG
·K·U·P·E·R·A·R·D·
**READERS'
OFFER
2010**

NATIONAL SEAL SANCTUARY
Gweek, Helston,
Cornwall TR12 6UG
Tel: 01326 221361
e-mail: seals@sealsanctuary.co.uk
www.sealsanctuary.co.uk

*TWO for ONE - on purchase of another ticket of
equal or greater value. Valid until December 2010.*

NOT TO BE USED IN CONJUNCTION WITH ANY OTHER OFFER

A 70-minute journey into the lost world of the English narrow gauge light railway. Features historic steam locomotives from many countries. **PETS MUST BE KEPT UNDER CONTROL AND NOT ALLOWED ON TRACKS**	**Open:** Sundays and Bank Holiday weekends 14 March to 31 October. Additional days in summer, and school holidays. **Directions:** on south side of Leighton Buzzard. Follow brown signs from town centre or A505/A4146 bypass.

FHG GUIDES, ABBEY MILL BUSINESS CENTRE, PAISLEY PA1 1TJ • www.holidayguides.com

Take a trip back in time on the delightful Nene Valley Railway with its heritage steam and diesel locomotives, There is a 7½ mile ride from Wansford to Peterborough via Yarwell, with shop, museum and excellent cafe at Wansford Station (free parking).	**Open:** please phone or see website for details. **Directions:** situated 4 miles north of Peterborough on the A1

FHG GUIDES, ABBEY MILL BUSINESS CENTRE, PAISLEY PA1 1TJ • www.holidayguides.com

Three miniature railways, plus leisure park with canoes, crazy golf, large children's play area with fort, brickpath maze, wooded walks (all inclusive). Dogs welcome (50p).	**Open:** Easter to end October **Directions:** follow brown tourist signs from A30 and A3075

FHG GUIDES, ABBEY MILL BUSINESS CENTRE, PAISLEY PA1 1TJ • www.holidayguides.com

Set on the beautiful Helford Estuary, the National Seal Sanctuary is Europe's busiest seal rescue centre. Every year the Sanctuary rescues and releases over 30 injured or abandoned seal pups and provides a refuge for those seals/sea lions unable to be returned to the wild.	**Open:** daily (except Christmas Day) from 10am. **Directions:** from A30 follow signs to Helston, then brown tourist signs to Seal Sanctuary.

FHG GUIDES, ABBEY MILL BUSINESS CENTRE, PAISLEY PA1 1TJ • www.holidayguides.com

THE BOND MUSEUM
Southey Hill, Keswick,
Cumbria CA12 5NR
Tel: 017687 74044
e-mail: thebondmuseum@aol.com
www.thebondmuseum.com

One FREE child with two paying adults.
Valid February to October 2010.

NOT TO BE USED IN CONJUNCTION WITH ANY OTHER OFFER

CARS OF THE STARS MOTOR MUSEUM
Standish Street, Keswick
Cumbria CA12 5LS
Tel: 017687 73757
e-mail: cotsmm@aol.com
www.carsofthestars.com

One FREE child with two paying adults
Valid during normal opening times.

NOT TO BE USED IN CONJUNCTION WITH ANY OTHER OFFER

CRICH TRAMWAY VILLAGE
Crich, Matlock
Derbyshire DE4 5DP
Tel: 01773 854321 • Fax: 01773 854320
e-mail: enquiry@tramway.co.uk
www.tramway.co.uk

One child FREE with every full-paying adult
Valid during 2010

NOT TO BE USED IN CONJUNCTION WITH ANY OTHER OFFER

THE MILKY WAY ADVENTURE PARK
The Milky Way, Clovelly,
Bideford, Devon EX39 5RY
Tel: 01237 431255
e-mail: info@themilkyway.co.uk
www.themilkyway.co.uk

10% discount on entrance charge.
Valid Easter to end October (not August).

NOT TO BE USED IN CONJUNCTION WITH ANY OTHER OFFER

For all"Bond" or car fans this is a must! Aston Martins, Lotus, even a T55 Russsian tank from the film "Goldeneye". Also cinema and shop.

Open: 10am to 5pm February to end October; weekends November and December.

Directions: from Penrith (M6) take A66 to Keswick. Free parking.

FHG GUIDES, ABBEY MILL BUSINESS CENTRE, PAISLEY PA1 1TJ • www.holidayguides.com

This world famous motor museum features vehicles from TV and film - Chitty Chitty Bang Bang, Batmobiles, A-Team van, KITT and more. Also souvenir and autograph shop.

Open: 10am to 5pm February half term, and Easter to end November. Weekends only in December.

Directions: M6 to Penrith, A66 to Keswick. Located in centre of town, by Bell Close car park.

FHG GUIDES, ABBEY MILL BUSINESS CENTRE, PAISLEY PA1 1TJ • www.holidayguides.com

A superb family day out in the atmosphere of a bygone era. Explore the recreated period street and fascinating exhibitions. Unlimited tram rides are free with entry. Play areas, woodland walk and sculpture trail, shops, tea rooms, pub, restaurant and lots more.

Open: daily April to end October 10am to 5.30pm.

Directions: eight miles from M1 Junction 28, follow brown and white signs for "Tramway Museum".

FHG GUIDES, ABBEY MILL BUSINESS CENTRE, PAISLEY PA1 1TJ • www.holidayguides.com

The day in the country that's out of this world! With 5 major rides and loads of great live shows. See Merlin from 'Britain's Got Talent' 5 days a week. All rides and shows included in entrance fee.

Open: 10.30am - 6pm. Check for winter opening hours.

Directions: on the main A39 one mile from Clovelly.

FHG GUIDES, ABBEY MILL BUSINESS CENTRE, PAISLEY PA1 1TJ • www.holidayguides.com

449

BARLEYLANDS FARM & CRAFT VILLAGE
Barleylands Road, Billericay,
Essex CM11 2UD
Tel: 01268 290223 • Fax: 01268 290222
e-mail: info@barleylands.co.uk
www.barleylands.co.uk

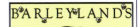

READERS' OFFER 2010

*FREE entry for one child with each full paying adult
Valid during 2010*

NOT TO BE USED IN CONJUNCTION WITH ANY OTHER OFFER

AVON VALLEY RAILWAY
Bitton Station, Bath Road, Bitton,
Bristol BS30 6HD
Tel: 0117 932 5538
e-mail: info@avonvalleyrailway.org
www.avonvalleyrailway.org

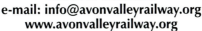
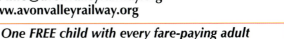

READERS' OFFER 2010

*One FREE child with every fare-paying adult
Valid April-Oct 2010 (not 'Day Out with Thomas' events)*

NOT TO BE USED IN CONJUNCTION WITH ANY OTHER OFFER

CIDER MUSEUM & KING OFFA DISTILLERY
21 Ryelands Street, Hereford,
Herefordshire HR4 0LW
Tel: 01432 354207
e-mail: enquiries@cidermuseum.co.uk
www.cidermuseum.co.uk

READERS' OFFER 2010

*TWO for the price of ONE admission
Valid to end December 2010*

NOT TO BE USED IN CONJUNCTION WITH ANY OTHER OFFER

NATURELAND SEAL SANCTUARY
North Parade, Skegness
Lincolnshire PE25 1DB
Tel: 01754 764345
e-mail: info@skegnessnatureland.co.uk
www.skegnessnatureland.co.uk

READERS' OFFER 2010

*One child admitted FREE when accompanied by full
paying adult on production of voucher. Valid to end 2010.*

NOT TO BE USED IN CONJUNCTION WITH ANY OTHER OFFER

Set in over 700 acres of unspoilt Essex countryside, this former working farm is one of the county's most popular tourist attractions. The spectacular craft village and educational farm provide the perfect setting for a great day out.

Open: 7 days a week. March to October 10am-5pm; November to February 10am-4pm.

Directions: follow brown tourist signs from A127 and A12.

FHG GUIDES, ABBEY MILL BUSINESS CENTRE, PAISLEY PA1 1TJ • www.holidayguides.com

---

The Avon Valley Railway offers a whole new experience for some, and a nostalgic memory for others.

PETS MUST BE KEPT ON LEADS AND OFF TRAIN SEATS

Open: Steam trains operate every Sunday, Easter to October, plus Bank Holidays and Christmas.

Directions: on the A431 midway between Bristol and Bath at Bitton.

FHG GUIDES, ABBEY MILL BUSINESS CENTRE, PAISLEY PA1 1TJ • www.holidayguides.com

---

Learn how traditional cider and perry was made, how the fruit was harvested, milled, pressed and bottled. Walk through original champagne cider cellars, and view 18th century lead crystal cider glasses.

Open: April to October: 10am-5pm Tues-Sat. November to March 11am-3pm Tues-Sat.

Directions: off A438 Hereford to Brecon road, near Sainsbury's supermarket.

FHG GUIDES, ABBEY MILL BUSINESS CENTRE, PAISLEY PA1 1TJ • www.holidayguides.com

---

A specialised collection of animals including seals, penguins, tropical birds and butterflies (April to October), reptiles, aquarium, pets' corner etc. Known worldwide for rescuing orphaned and injured seal pups and returning almost 600 back to the wild.

Open: daily except Christmas Day, Boxing Day and New Year's Day.

Directions: north end of Skegness seafront.

FHG GUIDES, ABBEY MILL BUSINESS CENTRE, PAISLEY PA1 1TJ • www.holidayguides.com

451

NEWARK AIR MUSEUM
The Airfield, Winthorpe, Newark,
Nottinghamshire NG24 2NY
Tel: 01636 707170
e-mail: newarkair@onetel.com
www.newarkairmuseum.org

READERS' OFFER 2010

Party rate discount for every voucher (50p per person off normal admission). Valid during 2010.

NOT TO BE USED IN CONJUNCTION WITH ANY OTHER OFFER

THE HELICOPTER MUSEUM
The Heliport, Locking Moor Road,
Weston-Super-Mare BS24 8PP
Tel: 01934 635227 • Fax: 01934 645230
e-mail: helimuseum@btconnect.com
www.helicoptermuseum.co.uk

READERS' OFFER 2010

*One child FREE with two full-paying adults
Valid from April to October 2010*

NOT TO BE USED IN CONJUNCTION WITH ANY OTHER OFFER

EASTON FARM PARK
Pound Corner, Easton, Woodbridge,
Suffolk IP13 0EQ
Tel: 01728 746475
e-mail: info@eastonfarmpark.co.uk
www.eastonfarmpark.co.uk

READERS' OFFER 2010

*One FREE child entry with a full paying adult
Only one voucher per group. Valid during 2010.*

NOT TO BE USED IN CONJUNCTION WITH ANY OTHER OFFER

MUSEUM OF RAIL TRAVEL
Ingrow Railway Centre, Near Keighley,
West Yorkshire BD21 5AX
Tel: 01535 680425
e-mail: admin@vintagecarriagestrust.org
www.vintagecarriagestrust.org

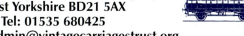

READERS' OFFER 2010

*"ONE for ONE" free admission
Valid during 2010 except during special events (ring to check)*

NOT TO BE USED IN CONJUNCTION WITH ANY OTHER OFFER

A collection of 70 aircraft and cockpit sections from across the history of aviation. Extensive aero engine and artefact displays.	**Open:** daily from 10am (closed Christmas period and New Year's Day). **Directions:** follow brown and white signs from A1, A46, A17 and A1133.

FHG GUIDES, ABBEY MILL BUSINESS CENTRE, PAISLEY PA1 1TJ • www.holidayguides.com

The world's largest helicopter collection - over 70 exhibits, includes two royal helicopters, Russian Gunship and Vietnam veterans plus many award-winning exhibits. Cafe, shop. Flights. **PETS MUST BE KEPT UNDER CONTROL**	**Open:** Wednesday to Sunday 10am to 5.30pm. Daily during school Easter and Summer holidays and Bank Holiday Mondays. November to March: 10am to 4.30pm **Directions:** Junction 21 off M5 then follow the propellor signs.

FHG GUIDES, ABBEY MILL BUSINESS CENTRE, PAISLEY PA1 1TJ • www.holidayguides.com

Family day out down on the farm, with activities for children every half hour (included in entry price). Indoor and outdoor play areas. Riverside cafe, gift shop. For more details visit the website.	**Open:** 10.30am-6pm daily March to September. **Directions:** signposted from A12 in the direction of Framlingham.

FHG GUIDES, ABBEY MILL BUSINESS CENTRE, PAISLEY PA1 1TJ • www.holidayguides.com

A fascinating display of railway carriages and a wide range of railway items telling the story of rail travel over the years. **ALL PETS MUST BE KEPT ON LEADS**	**Open:** daily 11am to 4.30pm **Directions:** approximately one mile from Keighley on A629 Halifax road. Follow brown tourist signs

FHG GUIDES, ABBEY MILL BUSINESS CENTRE, PAISLEY PA1 1TJ • www.holidayguides.com

453

READERS' OFFER 2010

SCOTTISH MARITIME MUSEUM
Harbourside, Irvine,
Ayrshire KA12 8QE
Tel: 01294 278283
Fax: 01294 313211
www.scottishmaritimemuseum.org

TWO for the price of ONE
Valid from April to October 2010

NOT TO BE USED IN CONJUNCTION WITH ANY OTHER OFFER

READERS' OFFER 2010

BO'NESS & KINNEIL RAILWAY
Bo'ness Station, Union Street,
Bo'ness, West Lothian EH51 9AQ
Tel: 01506 822298
e-mail: enquiries.railway@srps.org.uk
www.srps.org.uk

FREE child train fare with one paying adult/concession. Valid March-Oct 2010. Not Days Out with Thomas or Santa Steam trains

NOT TO BE USED IN CONJUNCTION WITH ANY OTHER OFFER

READERS' OFFER 2010

MYRETON MOTOR MUSEUM
Aberlady,
East Lothian EH32 0PZ
Tel: 01875 870288
www.myretonmotormuseum.co.uk

One child FREE with each paying adult
Valid during 2010

NOT TO BE USED IN CONJUNCTION WITH ANY OTHER OFFER

READERS' OFFER 2010

NATIONAL CYCLE COLLECTION
Automobile Palace, Temple Street,
Llandrindod Wells, Powys LD1 5DL
Tel: 01597 825531
e-mail: cycle.museum@powys.org.uk
www.cyclemuseum.org.uk

TWO for the price of ONE
Valid during 2010 except Special Event days

NOT TO BE USED IN CONJUNCTION WITH ANY OTHER OFFER

Scotland's seafaring heritage is among the world's richest and you can relive the heyday of Scottish shipping at the Maritime Museum.

Open: 1st April to 31st October - 10am-5pm

Directions: situated on Irvine harbourside and only a 10 minute walk from Irvine train station.

Steam and heritage diesel passenger trains from Bo'ness to Birkhill for guided tours of Birkhill fireclay mines. Explore the history of Scotland's railways in the Scottish Railway Exhibition. Coffee shop and souvenir shop.

Open: weekends Easter to October, daily July and August.
See website for dates and timetables.

Directions: in the town of Bo'ness. Leave M9 at Junction 3 or 5, then follow brown tourist signs.

On show is a large collection, from 1899, of cars, bicycles, motor cycles and commercials. There is also a large collection of period advertising, posters and enamel signs.

Open: March-Oct: open daily 10.30am to 4.30pm.
Nov-Feb: weekends 11am to 3pm or by special appointment.

Directions: off A198 near Aberlady. Two miles from A1.

Journey through the lanes of cycle history and see bicycles from Boneshakers and Penny Farthings up to modern Raleigh cycles. Over 250 machines on display

PETS MUST BE KEPT ON LEADS

Open: 1st March to 1st November daily 10am onwards.

Directions: brown signs to car park. Town centre attraction.

Index of Towns and Counties

Abbotsbury, Dorset	SOUTH WEST	Bassenthwaite, Cumbria	NORTH WEST
Aberaeron, Ceredigion	WALES	Bath, Somerset	SOUTH WEST
Aberfeldy, Perth & Kinross	SCOTLAND	Beauly, Highlands	SCOTLAND
Aberfoyle, Stirling & The Trossachs	SCOTLAND	Beaumaris, Anglesey & Gwynedd	WALES
Abergavenny, South Wales	WALES	Belford, Northumberland	NORTH EAST
Aberporth, Ceredigion	WALES	Belper, Derbyshire	MIDLANDS
Acklington, Northumberland	NORTH EAST	Bentham, North Yorkshsire	YORKSHIRE
Aldeburgh, Suffolk	EAST	Bere Regis, Dorset	SOUTH WEST
Alfriston, East Sussex	SOUTH EAST	Berrynarbor, Devon	SOUTH WEST
Alnmouth, Northumberland	NORTH EAST	Berwick-Upon-Tweed, Northumberland	
Alston, Cumbria	NORTH WEST		NORTH EAST
Alston, Cumbria	PET FRIENDLY PUBS	Betws-y-Coed, North Wales	WALES
Alwinton, Northumberland	NORTH EAST	Beverley, East Yorkshire	YORKSHIRE
Ambleside, Cumbria	NORTH WEST	Bibury, Gloucestershire	SOUTH WEST
Appin, Argyll & Bute	SCOTLAND	Bicester, Oxfordshire	SOUTH EAST
Appleby-in-Westmorland, Cumbria		Bideford, Devon	SOUTH WEST
	NORTH WEST	Bideford, Devon	PET FRIENDLY PUBS
Appledore, Devon	SOUTH WEST	Bigbury-on-Sea, Devon	SOUTH WEST
Ardfern, Argyll & Bute	SCOTLAND	Biggar, Lanarkshire	SCOTLAND
Ardnamurchan, Argyll & Bute	SCOTLAND	Bingley, West Yorkshire	YORKSHIRE
Arundel, West Sussex	SOUTH EAST	Bishop Auckland, Durham	NORTH EAST
Ashbourne, Derbyshire	MIDLANDS	Bishop's Castle, Shropshire	MIDLANDS
Ashburton, Devon	SOUTH WEST	Bishop's Frome, Worcestershire	MIDLANDS
Ashford, Kent	SOUTH EAST	Blackburn, Lancashire	NORTH WEST
Ashurst, Hampshire	SOUTH EAST	Blackpool, Lancashire	NORTH WEST
Ashwater, Devon	SOUTH WEST	Blandford, Dorset	SOUTH WEST
Auchencairn, Dumfries & Galloway	SCOTLAND	Blue Anchor, Somerset	SOUTH WEST
Auldgirth, Dumfries & Galloway	SCOTLAND	Bodmin Moor, Cornwall	SOUTH WEST
Aviemore, Highlands	SCOTLAND	Bodmin, Cornwall	SOUTH WEST
Axminster, Devon	SOUTH WEST	Bodorgan, Anglesey & Gwynedd	WALES
Ayr, Ayrshire & Arran	SCOTLAND	Boncath, Pembrokeshire	WALES
Bacton-on-Sea, Norfolk	EAST	Bonchester Bridge, Borders	SCOTLAND
Bala, Anglesey & Gwynedd	WALES	Bonchurch, Isle of Wight	SOUTH EAST
Ballater, Aberdeen, Banff & Moray	SCOTLAND	Bosherton, Pembrokeshire	WALES
Balterley, Cheshire	NORTH WEST	Botallack, Cornwall	SOUTH WEST
Bamburgh, Northumberland	NORTH EAST	Boughton Monchelsea, Kent	SOUTH EAST
Bantham, Devon	SOUTH WEST	Bournemouth, Dorset	SOUTH WEST
Barmouth, Anglesey & Gwynedd	WALES	Bourton-on-the-Water, Gloucs	SOUTH WEST
Barnard Castle, Durham	NORTH EAST	Bowness-on-Windermere, Cumbria	
Barnoldby-le-Beck, Lincolnshire	MIDLANDS		NORTH WEST
Barnstaple, Devon	SOUTH WEST	Bradworthy, Devon	SOUTH WEST
Barrow-in-Furness, Cumbria	NORTH WEST	Brampton, Cumbria	NORTH WEST
Barton-upon-Humber, Lincolnshire	MIDLANDS	Braunton, Devon	SOUTH WEST

Index of Towns and Counties

Brean, Somerset	SOUTH WEST		Chittlehamholt, Devon	SOUTH WEST
Bridgnorth, Shropshire	MIDLANDS		Christchurch, Dorset	SOUTH WEST
Bridgwater, Somerset	SOUTH WEST		Christchurch, Dorset	PET FRIENDLY PUBS
Bridlington, East Yorkshire	YORKSHIRE		Chulmleigh, Devon	SOUTH WEST
Bridport, Dorset	SOUTH WEST		Church Stretton, Shropshire	MIDLANDS
Brighton, East Sussex	SOUTH EAST		Ciliau Aeron, Ceredigion	WALES
Brixham, Devon	SOUTH WEST		Cilmery, Powys	WALES
Broad Haven, Pembrokeshire	WALES		Cirencester, Gloucestershire	SOUTH WEST
Broadstairs, Kent	SOUTH EAST		Cirencester, Gloucestershire	PET FRIENDLY PUBS
Broadwoodwidger, Devon	SOUTH WEST		Clapham, North Yorkshire	YORKSHIRE
Brodick, Ayrshire & Arran	SCOTLAND		Clearwell (Forest of Dean), Gloucs.	SOUTH WEST
Bronwydd Arms, Carmarthenshire	WALES		Clevedon, Somerset	SOUTH WEST
Broughton-in-Furness, Cumbria	NORTH WEST		Clitheroe, Lancashire	SCOTLAND
Bude, Cornwall	SOUTH WEST		Clitheroe, Lancashire	PET FRIENDLY PUBS
Builth Wells, Powys	WALES		Cockburnspath, Borders	SCOTLAND
Bungay, Suffolk	EAST		Cockermouth, Cumbria	NORTH WEST
Burford, Oxfordshire	SOUTH EAST		Colchester, Essex	EAST
Burford, Shropshire	MIDLANDS		Colchester, Essex	PET FRIENDLY PUBS
Burnaston, Derbyshire	MIDLANDS		Colebrook, Devon	SOUTH WEST
Burnham Market, Norfolk	EAST		Colwyn Bay, North Wales	WALES
Burton Joyce, Nottinghamshire	MIDLANDS		Combe Martin, Devon	SOUTH WEST
Burwell, Cambridgeshire	EAST		Coniston, Cumbria	NORTH WEST
Bury St Edmunds, Suffolk	EAST		Contin, Highlands	SCOTLAND
Buxton, Derbyshire	MIDLANDS		Conwy Valley, North Wales	WALES
Caernarfon, Anglesey & Gwynedd	WALES		Conwy, North Wales	WALES
Cairndow, Argyll & bute	SCOTLAND		Corbridge, Northumberland	NORTH EAST
Caister-on-Sea, Norfolk	EAST		Coverdale, North Yorkshire	YORKSHIRE
Campbeltown, Argyll & Bute	SCOTLAND		Cowes, Isle of Wight	SOUTH EAST
Canonbie, Dumfries & Galloway	SCOTLAND		Crackington Haven, Cornwall	SOUTH WEST
Canterbury, Kent	SOUTH EAST		Crantock, Cornwall	SOUTH WEST
Cardigan, Ceredigion	WALES		Craven Arms, Shropshire	MIDLANDS
Carlisle, Cumbria	NORTH WEST		Criccieth, Anglesey & Gwynedd	WALES
Carnforth, Lancashire	NORTH WEST		Crieff, Perth & Kinross	SCOTLAND
Carperby, North Yorkshire	YORKSHIRE		Croes Goch, Pembrokeshire	WALES
Carrbridge, Highlands	SCOTLAND		Croft, Pembrokeshire	WALES
Cartmel, Cumbria	NORTH WEST		Cromer, Norfolk	EAST
Castle Douglas, Dumfries & Galloway	SCOTLAND		Crossmichael, Dumfries & Galloway	SCOTLAND
Castleside, Durham	NORTH EAST		Crosthwaite, Cumbria	NORTH WEST
Chalford, Gloucestershire	SOUTH WEST		Crymych, Pembrokeshire	WALES
Charmouth, Dorset	SOUTH WEST		Cullompton, Devon	SOUTH WEST
Chathill, Northumberland	NORTH EAST		Dalbeattie, Dumfries & Galloway	SCOTLAND
Cheddar, Somerset	SOUTH WEST		Dalmally, Argyll & Bute	SCOTLAND
Cheltenham, Gloucestershire	SOUTH WEST		Danby, North Yorkshire	YORKSHIRE
Chesham, Buckinghamshire	SOUTH EAST			
Chester, Cheshire	NORTH WEST			
Chichester, West Sussex	SOUTH EAST			
Chiddingly, East Sussex	SOUTH EAST			

FHG Guides

Index of Towns and Counties

Dartmoor, Devon	SOUTH WEST	Exeter, Devon	SOUTH WEST
Dartmouth, Devon	SOUTH WEST	Exford, Somerset	SOUTH WEST
Deal, Kent	SOUTH EAST	Exmoor, Devon	SOUTH WEST
Dereham, Norfolk	EAST	Exmoor, Somerset	SOUTH WEST
		Eyemouth, Borders	SCOTLAND
Dingwall, Highlands	SCOTLAND	Fairford, Gloucestershire	SOUTH WEST
Diss, Norfolk	EAST	Fairlight, East Sussex	SOUTH EAST
Dorchester, Dorset	SOUTH WEST	Falmouth, Cornwall	SOUTH WEST
Dorchester, Dorset	PET FRIENDLY PUBS	Ffestiniog, Anglesey & Gwynedd	WALES
Driffield, East Yorkshire	YORKSHIRE	Finavon, Angus & Dundee	SCOTLAND
Drummore, Dumfries & Galloway	SCOTLAND	Fishguard, Pembrokeshire	WALES
Drumnadrochit, Highlands	SCOTLAND	Flamborough, East Yorkshire	YORKSHIRE
Duddon Valley, Cumbria	NORTH WEST	Fordingbridge, Hampshire	SOUTH EAST
Dulas Bay, Anglesey & Gwynedd	WALES	Forest of Dean, Gloucestershire	SOUTH WEST
Dumfries, Dumfries & Galloway	SCOTLAND	Fort William, Highlands	SCOTLAND
Dunoon, Argyll & Bute	SCOTLAND	Fowey, Cornwall	SOUTH WEST
Duns, Borders	SCOTLAND	Foxley, Norfolk	EAST
Dunsford, Devon	SOUTH WEST	Freshwater, Isle of Wight	SOUTH EAST
Dunster, Somerset	SOUTH WEST	Gainsborough, Lincolnshire	MIDLANDS
Dyffryn Ardudwy, Anglesey & Gwynedd	WALES	Galashiels, Borders	SCOTLAND
Eals, Northumberland	NORTH EAST	Gatehouse of Fleet, Dumfries & Galloway	
Eastergate, West Sussex	SOUTH EAST		SCOTLAND
Ecclefechan, Dumfries & Galloway	SCOTLAND	Glen Shiel, Highlands	SCOTLAND
Ely, Cambridgeshire	EAST	Glenlivet, Aberdeen, Banff & Moray	SCOTLAND
Eskdale, Cumbria	NORTH WEST	Glenshee, Perth & Kinross	SCOTLAND
Evershot, Dorset	SOUTH WEST	Goathland, North Yorkshire	YORKSHIRE

Bodmin Moor — photo courtesy of Cutkive Wood Holiday Lodges, Liskeard, Cornwall

Index of Towns and Counties

Gosforth, Cumbria	NORTH WEST
Gower, South Wales	WALES
Grange-over-Sands, Cumbria	NORTH WEST
Grantham, Lincolnshire	MIDLANDS
Grantown-on-Spey, Highlands	SCOTLAND
Grasmere, Cumbria	NORTH WEST
Grassington, North Yorkshire	YORKSHIRE
Grassington, North Yorkshire	PET FRIENDLY PUBS
Great Malvern, Herefordshire	MIDLANDS
Great Malvern, Worcestershire	MIDLANDS
Great Yarmouth, Norfolk	EAST
Grewelthorpe, North Yorkshire	YORKSHIRE
Grindale, East Yorkshire	YORKSHIRE
Grittleton, Wiltshire	SOUTH WEST
Hadleigh, Suffolk	EAST
Haltwhistle, Northumberland	NORTH EAST
Happisburgh, Norfolk	EAST
Harlech, Anglesey & Gwynedd	WALES
Harrogate, North Yorkshire	YORKSHIRE
Harthill, Lanarkshire	SCOTLAND
Haverfordwest, Pembrokeshire	WALES
Hawes, North Yorkshire	YORKSHIRE
Hawkshead, Cumbria	NORTH WEST
Hay-on-Wye, Powys	WALES
Helford, Cornwall	SOUTH WEST
Helmsley, North Yorkshire	YORKSHIRE
Helston, Cornwall	SOUTH WEST
Hereford, Herefordshire	MIDLANDS
Hexham, Northumberland	NORTH EAST
Hexwworthy (Dartmoor), Devon	SOUTH WEST
High Bentham, North Yorkshire	YORKSHIRE
Hindon, Wiltshire	SOUTH WEST
Hindon, Wiltshire	PET FRIENDLY PUBS
Holsworthy, Devon	SOUTH WEST
Holyhead, Anglesey & Gwynedd	WALES
Honiton, Devon	SOUTH WEST
Hope Cove, Devon	SOUTH WEST
Hope Valley, Derbyshire	MIDLANDS
Horncastle, Lincolnshire	MIDLANDS
Hornsea, East Yorkshire	YORKSHIRE
Howden, East Yorkshire	YORKSHIRE
Huntingtower, Perth & Kinross	SCOTLAND
Ilfracombe, Devon	SOUTH WEST
Ilminster, Somerset	SOUTH WEST
Ilminster, Somerset	PET FRIENDLY PUBS
Ingleton, North Yorkshire	YORKSHIRE
Inveraray, Argyll & Bute	SCOTLAND
Inverness, Highlands	SCOTLAND
Ipswich, Suffolk	EAST
Ireby, Cumbria	NORTH WEST
Isle of Gigha, Argyll & Bute	SCOTLAND
Jedburgh, Borders	SCOTLAND
Kelso, Borders	SCOTLAND
Kendal, Cumbria	NORTH WEST
Kenfig Hill, South Wales	WALES
Kessingland, Suffolk	EAST
Keswick, Cumbria	NORTH WEST
Keswick, Cumbria	PET FRIENDLY PUBS
Kilchattan Bay, Argyll & Bute	SCOTLAND
Killiecrankie, Perth & Kinross	SCOTLAND
Killin, Highlands	SCOTLAND
Killin, Perth & Kinross	SCOTLAND
Kilnwick Percy, East Yorkshire	YORKSHIRE
Kincraig, Highlands	SCOTLAND
King's Lynn, Norfolk	EAST
King's Nympton, Devon	SOUTH WEST
Kingsbridge, Devon	SOUTH WEST
Kingston -Upon-Thames, Surrey	SOUTH EAST
Kington, Herefordshire	MIDLANDS
Kingussie, Highlands	SCOTLAND
Kinloch Rannoch, Perth & Kinross	SCOTLAND
Kinlochbervie, Highlands	SCOTLAND
Kirkby Lonsdale, Cumbria	NORTH WEST
Kirkby Lonsdale, Cumbria	PET FRIENDLY PUBS
Kirkby Stephen, Cumbria	NORTH WEST
Kirkby-in-Furness, Cumbria	NORTH WEST
Kirkcudbright, Dumfries & Galloway	SCOTLAND
Kirkoswald, Cumbria	NORTH WEST
Kirkwall, Orkney Islands	SCOTLAND
Knaresborough, North Yorkshire	YORKSHIRE
Lairg, Highlands	SCOTLAND
Lake District, Cumbria	NORTH WEST
Lamlash, Ayrshire & Arran	SCOTLAND
Lamplugh, Cumbria	NORTH WEST
Langdale, Cumbria	NORTH WEST
Langton-by-Wragby, Lincolnshire	MIDLANDS
Lapford, Devon	SOUTH WEST
Lauder, Borders	SCOTLAND
Laugharne, Carmarthenshire	WALES
Launceston, Cornwall	SOUTH WEST
Launceston, Cornwall	PET FRIENDLY PUBS
Lauragh, Co. Kerry	IRELAND

Index of Towns and Counties

Houses of Parliament as seen from the London Eye

Laxfield, Suffolk	EAST	Loch Ness, Highlands	SCOTLAND
Lazonby, Cumbria	NORTH WEST	Loch Torridon, Highlands	SCOTLAND
Leamington Spa, Warwickshire	MIDLANDS	Lochcarron, Highlands	SCOTLAND
Ledbury, Herefordshire	MIDLANDS	Lochearnhead, Perth & Kinross	SCOTLAND
Leek, Staffordshire	MIDLANDS	Locheport, North Uist	SCOTLAND
Leominster, Herefordshire	MIDLANDS	Long Melford, Suffolk	EAST
Leverburgh, Isle of Harris	SCOTLAND	Longhorsley, Northumberland	NORTH EAST
Leyburn, North Yorkshire	YORKSHIRE	Longrock, Cornwall	SOUTH WEST
Liskeard, Cornwall	SOUTH WEST	Looe, Cornwall	SOUTH WEST
Little Langdale, Cumbria	NORTH WEST	Lostwithiel, Cornwall	SOUTH WEST
Lizard, Cornwall	SOUTH WEST	Louth, Lincolnshire	MIDLANDS
Llanbedr, Anglesey & Gwynedd	WALES	Lower Largo, Fife	SCOTLAND
Llanddona, Anglesey & Gwynedd	WALES	Lowestoft, Norfolk	EAST
Llandeilo, Carmarthenshire	WALES	Ludlow, Shropshire	MIDLANDS
Llandovery, Carmarthenshire	WALES	Lulworth Cove, Dorset	SOUTH WEST
Llandrindod Wells, Powys	WALES	Lulworth, near (Wareham), Dorset	SOUTH WEST
Llandudno, North Wales	WALES	Lydford, Devon	SOUTH WEST
Llandyrnog, North Wales	WALES	Lyme Regis, Dorset	SOUTH WEST
Llanelli, Carmarthenshire	WALES	Lymington, Hampshire	SOUTH EAST
Llangollen, North Wales	WALES	Lyndhurst, Hampshire	SOUTH EAST
Llangrannog, Ceredigion	WALES	Lynton/Lynmouth, Devon	SOUTH WEST
Llangurig, Powys	WALES	Mablethorpe, Lincolnshire	MIDLANDS
Llansilin, Powys	WALES	Macclesfield, Cheshire	NORTH WEST
Llansteffan, Carmarthenshire	WALES	Machynlleth, Powys	WALES
Llanteg, Pembrokeshire	WALES	Malham, North Yorkshire	YORKSHIRE
Llechryd, Pembrokeshire	WALES	Malvern, Worcestershire	MIDLANDS
Loch Goil, Argyll & Bute	SCOTLAND	Marazion, Cornwall	SOUTH WEST

Index of Towns and Counties

Margate, Kent	SOUTH EAST	Newquay, Cornwall	SOUTH WEST
Market Harborough, Leics & Rutland	MIDLANDS	Newton Stewart, Dumfries & Galloway	SCOTLAND
Matlock, Derbyshire	MIDLANDS		
Mawgan Porth, Cornwall	SOUTH WEST	Newtown, Powys	WALES
Melton Mowbray, Leics & Rutland	MIDLANDS	North Berwick, Edinburgh & Lothians	SCOTLAND
Membury, Berkshire	SOUTH EAST	North Perrott, Dorset	SOUTH WEST
Mevagissey, Cornwall	SOUTH WEST	North Somercotes, Lincolnshire	MIDLANDS
Millom, Cumbria	NORTH WEST	North Walsham., Norfolk	EAST
Milton Keynes, Buckinghamshire	SOUTH EAST	Northallerton, North Yorkshire	YORKSHIRE
Minehead, Somerset	SOUTH WEST	Norwich, Norfolk	EAST
Moffat, Dumfries & Galloway	SCOTLAND	Noss Mayo, Devon	SOUTH WEST
Monmouth, South Wales	WALES	Oban, Argyll & Bute	SCOTLAND
Morfa Nefyn, Anglesey & Gwynedd	WALES	Okehampton, Devon	SOUTH WEST
Mortehoe, Devon	SOUTH WEST	Old Hunstanton, Norfolk	EAST
Mousehole, Cornwall	SOUTH WEST	Orford, Suffolk	EAST
Moylegrove, Pembrokeshire	WALES	Orphir, Orkney Islands	SCOTLAND
Much Cowarne, Herefordshire	MIDLANDS	Oswestry, Shropshire	MIDLANDS
Muir of Ord, Highlands	SCOTLAND	Ottery St Mary, Devon	SOUTH WEST
Mundesley-on-Sea, Norfolk	EAST	Oxford, Oxfordshire	SOUTH EAST
Nailsworth, Gloucestershire	SOUTH WEST	Padstow, Cornwall	SOUTH WEST
Nayland, Suffolk	EAST	Paignton, Devon	SOUTH WEST
Near Sawrey, Cumbria	NORTH WEST	Peak District, Derbyshire	MIDLANDS
Near Sawrey, Cumbria	PET FRIENDLY PUBS	Peebles, Borders	SCOTLAND
Neath, South Wales	WALES	Penrith, Cumbria	NORTH WEST
Nethy Bridge, Highlands	SCOTLAND	Pentraeth, Anglesey & Gwynedd	WALES
New Forest, Hampshire	SOUTH EAST	Pen-y-Cae, Powys	WALES
Newby Bridge, Cumbria	NORTH WEST	Penzance, Cornwall	SOUTH WEST
Newgale, Pembrokeshire	WALES	Perranporth, Cornwall	SOUTH WEST
Newport, Pembrokeshire	WALES	Pickering, North Yorkshire	YORKSHIRE

Cardiff Castle   photo courtesy Cardiff County Council

Index of Towns and Counties

Pitlochry, Perth & Kinross	SCOTLAND
Plymouth, Devon	SOUTH WEST
Polegate, East Sussex	SOUTH EAST
Polperro, Cornwall	SOUTH WEST
Polruan, Cornwall	SOUTH WEST
Pontrhydfendigaid, Ceredigion	WALES
Poole, Dorset	SOUTH WEST
Poolewe, Highlands	SCOTLAND
Port Gaverne, Cornwall	SOUTH WEST
Port Isaac, Cornwall	SOUTH WEST
Port Mulgrave, North Yorkshire	YORKSHIRE
Porthleven, Cornwall	SOUTH WEST
Porthmadog, Anglesey & Gwynedd	WALES
Portland, Dorset	SOUTH WEST
Portreath, Cornwall	SOUTH WEST
Portwrinkle, Cornwall	SOUTH WEST
Presteigne, Powys	WALES
Pulborough, West Sussex	SOUTH EAST
Pwllheli, Anglesey & Gwynedd	WALES
Quantock Hills, Somerset	SOUTH WEST
Ravenglass, Cumbria	NORTH WEST
Ravenglass, Cumbria	PET FRIENDLY PUBS
Red Wharf Bay, Anglesey & Gwynedd	WALES
Rhayader, Powys	WALES
Rhiconich, Highlands	SCOTLAND
Rhos-on-Sea (Conwy), North Wales	WALES
Ringmer, West Sussex	SOUTH EAST
Ringmer, West Sussex	PET FRIENDLY PUBS
Ringwood, Hampshire	SOUTH EAST
Ringwood, Hampshire	PET FRIENDLY PUBS
Rosemarket, Pemrokeshire	WALES
Rosewell, Edinburgh & Lothians	SCOTLAND
Ross-on-Wye, Herefordshire	MIDLANDS
Rye, East Sussex	SOUTH EAST
Saffron Walden, Essex	EAST
Salcombe, Devon	SOUTH WEST
Salcombe, Devon	PET FRIENDLY PUBS
Salisbury, Wiltshire	SOUTH WEST
Sanquhar, Dumfries & Galloway	SCOTLAND
Saundersfoot, Pembrokeshire	WALES
Saxmundham, Suffolk	EAST
Scalby Nabs (Scarborough)	YORKSHIRE
Scarborough, North Yorkshire	YORKSHIRE
Seaford, East Sussex	SOUTH EAST
Seaton, Devon	SOUTH WEST
Selby, North Yorkshire	YORKSHIRE
Selby, North Yorkshire	PET FRIENDLY PUBS
Selkirk, Borders	SCOTLAND
Selsey, West Sussex	SOUTH EAST
Sherborne, Dorset	SOUTH WEST
Sidmouth, Devon	SOUTH WEST
Silloth-on-Solway, Cumbria	NORTH WEST
Skipton, North Yorkshire	YORKSHIRE
Solva, Pembrokeshire	WALES
South Cerney, Gloucestershire	SOUTH WEST
South Ronaldsay, Orkney Islands	SCOTLAND
Southsea, Hampshire	SOUTH EAST
Spean Bridge, Highlands	SCOTLAND
St Agnes, Cornwall	SOUTH WEST
St Andrews, Fife	SCOTLAND
St Austell, Cornwall	SOUTH WEST
St Bees, Cumbria	NORTH WEST
St Davids, Pembrokeshire	WALES
St Fillans, Perth & Kinross	SCOTLAND
St Ives, Cambridgeshire	EAST
St Ives, Cornwall	SOUTH WEST
St Margaret's Bay, Kent	SOUTH EAST
St Mary's, Isles of Scilly	SOUTH WEST
St Mawes, Cornwall	SOUTH WEST
St Mawgan, Cornwall	SOUTH WEST
St Tudy, Cornwall	SOUTH WEST
St Wenn, Cornwall	SOUTH WEST
Stafford, Staffordshire	MIDLANDS
Stainforth, North Yorkshire	YORKSHIRE

Visit the FHG website
www.holidayguides.com
for details of the wide choice of accommodation featured in the full range of FHG titles

Index of Towns and Counties

Staithes, North Yorkshire	YORKSHIRE	Torrington, Devon	SOUTH WEST
Stenness, Orkney Islands	SCOTLAND	Totland Bay, Isle of Wight	SOUTH EAST
Stiffkey, Norfolk	EAST	Trearddur Bay, Anglesey & Gwynedd	WALES
Stiffkey, Norfolk	PET FRIENDLY PUBS	Tregarne, Cornwall	SOUTH WEST
Stonehaven, Aberdeen, Banff & Moray	SCOTLAND	Tresco, Isles of Scilly	SOUTH WEST
Stornoway, Isle of Lewis	SCOTLAND	Truro, Cornwall	SOUTH WEST
Stow-on-the-Wold, Gloucestershire	SOUTH WEST	Turriff, Aberdeen, Banff & Moray	SCOTLAND
Stranraer, Dumfries & Galloway	SCOTLAND	Tywyn, Anglesey & Gwynedd	WALES
Stratford-upon-Avon, Warwickshire	MIDLANDS	Ullswater, Cumbria	NORTH WEST
Strathyre, Perth & Kinross	SCOTLAND	Upper Hasfield, Gloucestershire	SOUTH WEST
Strathyre, Perth & Kinross	PET FRIENDLY PUBS	Ventnor, Isle of Wight	SOUTH EAST
Streatley, Berkshire	SOUTH EAST	Wadebridge, Cornwall	SOUTH WEST
Stroud, Gloucestershire	SOUTH WEST	Wareham, Dorset	SOUTH WEST
Studland Bay, Dorset	SOUTH WEST	Wareham, Dorset	PET FRIENDLY PUBS
Swanage, Dorset	SOUTH WEST	Warwick, Warwickshire	MIDLANDS
Swanage, Dorset	PET FRIENDLY PUBS	Wasdale, Cumbria	NORTH WEST
Swansea, South Wales	WALES	Watchet, Somerset	SOUTH WEST
Symonds Yat, Gloucestershire	SOUTH WEST	Wells, Somerset	SOUTH WEST
Tackley/Kidlington, Oxfordshire	SOUTH EAST	West Bexington, Dorset	SOUTH WEST'
Tarbert, Argyll & Bute	SCOTLAND	West Calder, Edinburgh & Lothians	SCOTLAND
Taunton, Somerset	SOUTH WEST	West Linton, Borders	SCOTLAND
Tavistock, Devon	SOUTH WEST	Westbury, Wiltshire	SOUTH WEST
Tavistock, Devon	PET FRIENDLY PUBS	Weston-super-Mare, Somerset	SOUTH WEST
Taynuilt, Argyll & Bute	SCOTLAND	Weybourne, Norfolk	EAST
Tenby, Pembrokeshire	WALES	Whitby, North Yorkshire	YORKSHIRE
Thame, Oxfordshire	SOUTH EAST	Whitebridge, Highlands	SCOTLAND
Thirsk, North Yorkshire	YORKSHIRE	Whithorn, Dumfries & Galloway	SCOTLAND
Thornbury, Gloucestershire	SOUTH WEST	Whiting Bay, Ayrshire & Arran	SCOTLAND
Thornham, Norfolk	EAST	Whitland, Pembrokeshire	WALES
Thornhill, Dumfries & Galloway	SCOTLAND	Wigton, Cumbria	NORTH WEST
Thornley, Lancashire	NORTH WEST	Wigtown, Dumfries & Galloway	SCOTLAND
Thorpe Market, Norfolk	EAST	Williton, Somerset	SOUTH WEST
Thurlestone, Devon	SOUTH WEST	Windemere, Cumbria	NORTH WEST
Thurne, Norfolk	EAST	Winterton-on-Sea, Norfolk	EAST
Thurnham, Kent	SOUTH EAST	Wolsingham, Durham	NORTH EAST
Thurnham, Kent	PET FRIENDLY PUBS	Woodhall Spa, Lincolnshire	MIDLANDS
Tintagel, Cornwall	SOUTH WEST	Woolacombe, Devon	SOUTH WEST
Tiverton, Devon	SOUTH WEST	Wooler, Northumberland	NORTH EAST
Tongue, Highlands	SCOTLAND	Worcester, Worcestershire	MIDLANDS
Torbay, Devon	SOUTH WEST	Wye Valley, South Wales	WALES
Torlochan, Isle of Mull	SCOTLAND	Yarmouth, Isle of Wight	SOUTH EAST
Torquay, Devon	SOUTH WEST	Yelverton, Devon	SOUTH WEST
		York, North Yorkshire	YORKSHIRE

Please mention **Pets Welcome!**
when making enquiries about accommodation featured in these pages

Other FHG titles for 2010

FHG Guides Ltd have a large range of attractive holiday accommodation guides for all kinds of holiday opportunities throughout Britain. They also make useful gifts at any time of year. Our guides are available in most bookshops and larger newsagents but we will be happy to post you a copy direct if you have any difficulty. POST FREE for addresses in the UK. We will also post abroad but have to charge separately for post or freight.

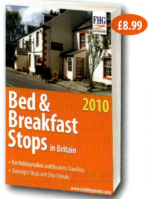
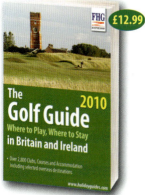

500 Great Places to Stay in Britain
- Coast & Country Holidays
- Full range of family accommodation

Bed & Breakfast Stops in Britain
- For holidaymakers and business travellers
- Overnight stops and Short Breaks

The Golf Guide
Where to play, Where to stay.
- Over 2800 golf courses in Britain with convenient accommodation.
- Holiday Golf in France, Portugal, Spain, USA and Thailand.

Pubs & Inns of Britain
- Including Dog-friendly Pubs
- Accommodation, food and traditional good cheer

Country Hotels of Britain
- Hotels with Conference, Leisure and Wedding Facilities

Caravan & Camping Holidays in Britain
- Campsites and Caravan parks
- Facilities fully listed

 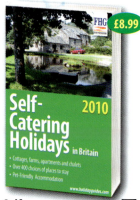 

Family Breaks ☐	**Self-Catering Holidays** ☐	**Weekend & Short Breaks** ☐
in Britain	in Britain	in Britain
• Accommodation, attractions and resorts	• Cottages, farms, apartments and chalets	• Accommodation for holidays and weekends away
• Suitable for those with children and babies	• Over 400 places to stay	
	• Pet-Friendly accommodation	

Tick your choice above and send your order and payment to

FHG Guides Ltd. Abbey Mill Business Centre
Seedhill, Paisley, Scotland PA1 1TJ
TEL: 0141- 887 0428 • FAX: 0141- 889 7204
e-mail: admin@fhguides.co.uk

Deduct 10% for 2/3 titles or copies; 20% for 4 or more.

Send to: NAME ....

ADDRESS ....

....

....

POST CODE ....

I enclose Cheque/Postal Order for £ ....

SIGNATURE ....DATE ....

Please complete the following to help us improve the service we provide.

How did you find out about our guides?:

☐ Press   ☐ Magazines   ☐ TV/Radio   ☐ Family/Friend   ☐ Other